THE BELIEVER AND THE POWERS THAT ARE

THE BELIEVER AND THE POWERS THAT ARE

Cases, History, and Other Data
Bearing on the Relation
of Religion and Government

John T. Noonan, Jr.

MACMILLAN PUBLISHING COMPANY
NEW YORK

Collier Macmillan Publishers
LONDON

Macmillan Publishing Company
A Division of Macmillan, Inc.
866 Third Avenue, New York, NY 10022

Collier Macmillan Canada, Inc.

Library of Congress Catalog Card Number: 86-28440

Printed in the United States of America

printing number
1   2   3   4   5   6   7   8   9   10

Library of Congress Cataloging in Publication Data

Noonan, John Thomas, 1926—
        The believer and the powers that are.

        Includes indexes.
        1. Religious liberty—United States—Cases.
2. Church and state—United States.   I. Title.
KF48783.A7N66   1987   344.73′09   86–28440
ISBN 0–02–923161–1   347.3049

Excerpts in this book have been reprinted by permission of the following:
   The New English Bible. © The Delegates of the Oxford University Press and The Syndics of the
Cambridge University Press 1961, 1970.
   The Papers of Thomas Jefferson. Copyright 1950. © 1978 renewed by Princeton University Press.
   The Complete Writings of Menno Simons. © 1956 Herald Press.
   The Correspondence of Sir Thomas More. Copyright © 1947, © 1975 renewed by Princeton University
Press.
   The Papers of James Madison. Copyright © 1962 University of Chicago Press.
   The Papers of James Madison. Copyright © 1978 University Press of Virginia.
   "Book Review of Robillard," by John T. Noonan, Jr. © 1985 *American Journal of Comparative Law.*

To David Daube

Student of secular and religious law, master of both Testaments,
bridger of continents and worlds.

Contents

PART TWO: THE AMERICAN EXPERIENCE

PART THREE: CONTEMPORARY CONTROVERSIES

Prefatory Note

John T. Noonan, Jr.'s book is one of several publications commissioned by a project on church and state funded by the Lilly Endowment through Princeton University and intended both to interest scholars and students in the church–state issue in American culture and to enlarge general appreciation of this neglected topic. In addition to this casebook, the project has commissioned two volumes of bibliographical essays and listings, nine monographic studies, and a summary volume that will review the issue from the colonial period to the present day. Of the monographic studies, four will analyze important developments in church–state relations in various periods of United States history and five will address the topic in societies whose experience contrasts sharply with that of the United States, including Western Christendom, modern Europe, India, modern Japan, and contemporary Latin America. We are grateful to Judge Noonan for his work.

JOHN F. WILSON
Project Director
STANLEY N. KATZ
ALBERT J. RABOTEAU
ROBERT T. HANDY

Introduction

Prior to 1940 the Supreme Court of the United States had never upheld a claim of free exercise of religion, had never found any governmental practice to be an establishment of religion, and had never applied the religion clauses of the First Amendment to the states. The religion clauses were part of the American vision; they were not at work in the judicial process. They were alive in the sense that the ideals they embodied were regularly, if vaguely and inconsistently, acknowledged. Their force and power were yet to be realized.

Beginning in 1940 the Court changed all that. It applied the religion clauses to the states. It vindicated a claim of free exercise of religion. In due time it found an unconstitutional establishment of religion. With the sonorous simplicity of John Marshall laying out the foundations, the Court set out basic principles in the new area of law it was creating. The course of development for the next two generations, from 1940 to 1986, has been vigorous. No area of modern law, it may be boldly asserted, has been so marked by sectarian struggle, so strained by fundamental fissures, so reflective of deep American doubts and aspirations.

Cases have been chosen for inclusion here because they are controlling precedents—for example, the great trio of the early 1940s, *Cantwell, Barnette,* and *Ballard*—or because they, as it were, continue the conversation, refining, elaborating, and qualifying—for example, the 1985 cases of *Aguilar, Ball,* and *Jaffree*—or because they are representative of a pattern—for example, the decisions of the Supreme Judicial Court of Massachusetts in the first part of the nineteenth century. Being concrete, the cases exemplify principles, challenge principles, qualify principles, generate principles. Issuing from conflict, they reveal the losing as well as the winning arguments. Being brought by litigants, they reflect the play of persons in the process.

"A page of history is worth a volume of logic." "The life of the law has not been logic but experience." These two axioms of Holmes—always given lip service by law schools but rarely taken seriously in academic milieus where the arts of logic flourish—are here, if anywhere, the keys of understanding. It is not only a matter of grasping the intentions of the Founding Fathers (a necessity if our national notion of a written Constitution as bedrock is to have validity). It is also a matter of empathetically appropriating the experience that undergirds the constitutional principles of free exercise and no establishment. The experience that made the law is capturable only through history. To know the price other systems have exacted, to know the prize we have, we must immerse ourselves in history.

In law school everything gets classified. Religion becomes a category, and categories are easy to manipulate. A sense of the hard, living reality of religion for believers—the sense that they believe that they are responding to a living transcendent intelligent Being—is easy to lose. One function of history is to put its student in the perspective of those for whom the overriding reality was that God was making demands of them. Without that awareness of a power higher than the physical power of the state there would have been nothing to keep separate from the state; the law would have been the measure of obligation. Judaism, followed by Christianity, brought an obligation to obey God and established criteria for conscience that surpassed the law. Society was split by this spiritual requirement. In theory at any rate, conscience was made supreme because of each person's higher allegiance. From this higher sphere, too, came the paradigms of justice and mercy and constancy that provided guidance as the law was formed. To sense the reality of religion for the believers is to glimpse how the law was modeled.

Interacting, religion and law have affected each other. The history of that interaction is Jewish, Catholic, Protestant. It is scriptural, patristic, scholastic, Reformation, Enlightenment. It is Near Eastern, Roman, European, North American. It consists in theology, philosophy, political science, jurisprudence. It is exemplified in the earliest great treatise on the common law, *The Laws and Customs of England.* It is illustrated by the assassination of Thomas Becket at Canterbury, the burning of Joan of Arc at Rouen, the martyrdom of Thomas More at Tyburn and of Hugh Latimer at Oxford. It is contained in the writings of the great Welsh defender of religious freedom, Roger Williams, and the writings and acts of the American fathers of religious freedom, Thomas Jefferson and James Madison. It involves the active persecution in America in the eighteenth century of the Baptists, in the nineteenth century of the Mormons, and in the twentieth century of the Jehovah's Witnesses and the strain throughout American history of hostility to the Catholics. It involves the crusades conducted under religious auspices for the abolition of slavery, the end of polygamy, the prohibition of alcohol, the vindication of civil rights, and the elimination of abortion. The history consists in specific speeches, memorable declarations, public and private letters, concrete deeds. It carries the most precious values and most terrible memories of our culture.

Religous liberty exists more fully today in America than in 1770 when Baptists were flogged in Virginia, or in 1790 when Catholics could not hold office in Massachusetts, or in 1870 when neither a Catholic nor a Jew could be a governor or legislator in New Hampshire, or in 1890 when the Church of Latter-Day Saints of Jesus Christ was dissolved by act of Congress, or in 1930 when conscientious pacifists could not become citizens. Absolute religious liberty never existed and still does not exist. It has been approached asymptotically.

Too often the votaries of religion forget the evil that has been done in God's name. Too often the critics of religion forget that the cultural concepts on which they depend are owed to religion. Impartial history—impartial at least in so far as "the lot of humanity allows"— presents the bad and the good that religion has bestowed on our civilization. The religious impulse, like the sexual, is powerful, not easily trammeled and not easily eliminated from any phase of life. A history of mankind might be written in terms of the foolishness and wickedness that sexual desire or religious aspiration has caused. But it would be incomparably foolish to think humankind could get along without either impulse.

No believer in God need deny that religion has often been the excuse for cruelty and wickedness. In Scripture itself the hypocrites who cry "Lord, Lord" are assured of their condemnation, and our religious traditions from Isaiah onward have rung with denunciations of the folly and the lethargy and the corruption of official leaders of God's flock. No enemy of the exploitation of human beings by religion should deny that the very terms he invokes in judgment—justice and truth and judgment itself—come from religious roots.

Religion is the realm of the spirit. But the good and the bad effected by religion have very often been achieved through the impact of religion on the organs of government. Recurrent problems are these:

1. *Limits.* What is the limit to the logic that the truth is to be brought to everyone? What is the limit to the logic that everyone is entitled to the full free exercise of religion? The first question was once the problem of believers. Underlying the question is the assumption

that you have to doubt either your power or your premises if you do not use force in support of the truth. The second question is the more modern problem. The question is faced not only by those who are skeptical about religious truth and by those pragmatically committed to tolerance to secure peace but also by those who from their view of religion or the requirements of human dignity are constrained not to coerce conscience. The problem is most severe when recognition for the rights of conscience endangers the ability of the nation to defend itself by arms. Dependence on nuclear arms has made the dilemma acute.

Separation of sex and state is a popular idea today—to get the government out of the bedroom is axiomatic. It is urged that if we can accept religious pluralism, we can live with a variety of sexual styles, none specially favored or disfavored by the government. The approach converges with religious pluralism as it is seen that the foundation of the laws on sexual conduct is religious. If we proclaim liberty of choice as to the foundations, why not as to the derivative propositions? This extension of religious freedom has yet to be fully tested. The present compromise, not wholly stable, sees marriage as a secular enterprise that can survive separated from religion. The problem of limits recurs.

2. *Neutrality.* Is it possible for a government to govern without taking positions affecting religion? For example, every government must tax. The tax will fall on religious bodies or it will not; there is no third option. Are there neutral rules of law to decide intrachurch disputes and are there neutral state agencies to adjudicate between believers and nonbelievers? Are the judges marvelously above doctrinal prejudice so that they among all Americans are truly neutral or are they self-deluded in their claim to be enforcing impartial principle?

3. *The Definition and Special Place of Religion.* Is religion one of many expressions of the human mind so that it is best understood and treated legally as a subdivision of speech? What religion does not largely consist in the communication of words? Can religion be defined to differentiate it from nonreligious verbal systems? Is religion indeed susceptible of a single definition? Religion was once defined in terms of duty to God. In a society where Buddhism is commonly viewed as a religion this definition no longer works. Is secular humanism, as the Supreme Court has suggested, a religion? Is Marxist communism a religion by metaphor or in reality?

Because of the magnitude of its claims or the intensity of the devotion it inspires, are believers in religion (a) to be peculiarly favored by the law in relation to fraud, medical malpractice, and the use of hallucinogens? (b) to be specially helped or handicapped in relation to the education of their children? (c) to be permitted to participate in the political system only if their ideas meet with the approval of the elite or only if they do not win too often or too much?

This book sets out documents by which these recurrent questions may be explored. But why speak of such abstractions as "religion" and "government?" The existent realities are persons—persons who are religious or not religious, who wield power or do not, but who invariably and necessarily incorporate in their own beings a mixture of beliefs and functions that can be separated only at the level of abstraction. Very few Justices of the United States Supreme Court, for example, have been irreligious men. Justice Holmes is the best known counterinstance, and he had little impact on the law in this area. The Justices who have shaped the law here have been predominantly Christian, mostly Protestant, sometimes the descendants of Protestant ministers—for example, Stephen J. Field, Charles Evans Hughes, and William O. Douglas. The strength of their religious commitment has varied, but no one could fairly charge them with antireligious opinions. They have embodied the state in its most concentrated form—judicial power. They have embodied Christian faith in ways well within the bounds of accepted Christian belief.

Litigants have been identified and lawyers named in many of the cases here collected. The identification of names functions as a reminder that "the law" set out in cases does not fall from heaven and would not be set out at all unless litigants sued and lawyers had experience, skill, persistence. Where would modern case law in this area be without Hayden Covington, Leo Pfeffer, and William Ball? Legal development has been affected by their beliefs.

"Church and State"—the title under which the subject of this book is conventionally classified—is a profoundly misleading rubric. The title triply misleads. It suggests that there is a single church. But in America there are myriad ways in which religious belief is organized. It suggests that there is a single state. But in America there is the federal government, fifty state governments, myriad municipalities, and a division of power among executive, legislative, administrative, and judicial entities, each of whom embodies state power. Worst of all, "Church and State" suggests that there are two distinct bodies set apart from each other in contrast if not in conflict. But everywhere neither churches nor states exist except as they are incorporated in actual individuals. These individuals are believers and unbelievers, citizens and officials. In one aspect of their activities, if they are religious, they usually form churches. In another aspect they form governments. Religious and governmental bodies not only coexist but overlap. The same persons, much of the time, are both believers and wielders of power.

"The power"—often translated as "the powers that be"—is St. Paul's phrase for the force that resides in governments. It is stunningly impersonal. French employs a similar expression, *le pouvoir,* to designate the locus of authority. "The power" conveys the reality, that the force at the state's disposition is greater than that of any individual. The phrase also misleads if it dehumanizes this force so that one forgets that it is human beings who embody it.

Those human beings wielding power are linked by law, and it is the linkages of law as affected by and affecting religious belief that are the subject of this book. American law, dominated by case law climaxing in decisions of the Supreme Court, is a complex and comprehensive process. By "law" I mean constitutional provisions, statutes, and judicial decisions, but I also include a variety of other phenomena that are part of the legal process—legislative debates, presidential proclamations and addresses, the commentary of legal scholars, and the arguments of lawyers. Too truncated a vision of American law is conveyed if these other lawmaking, law-asserting activities are not noticed.

To capture the legal process relating to religion in time, to push back to the experience at its roots and carry it forward to the present, is the purpose of this book as it sets out salient moments in the articulation of the relationship between religious beliefs and legal power. The presentation is generally chronological (how else is history to be understood?). But there is a large exception. When one goes from Part I, "Roots," and Part II, "The American Experience," to Part III, "Current Controversies," one enters an area where decisions of the Supreme Court shape the problematic. If one is not to be completely a captive of the Court's categories, there is need to create one's own. I contend that the six divisions proposed here— Sacred Duties; Belief and Its Organization; Double Effect; Education; Political Participation; and Sexual Morals—produce more intelligibility than does a tracking of the Court's analysis.

Berkeley
August 15, 1986

Acknowledgments

I am grateful to the Oxford University Press, the University of Chicago Press, the University Press of Virginia, the Princeton University Press, Herald Press, and the *American Journal of Comparative Law* for permission to use excerpts from works to which they hold the copyright.

I am greatly indebted to Julie Oseid and Christine Huang for checking citations and authorities, to my daughter Becky for general editorial assistance, and to Pat Boyd for her typing of the manuscript.

Part One
ROOTS

ONE

"You Shall Have No Other God to Set Against Me": Scripture

1. THE TEN COMMANDMENTS

GOD HIMSELF is the lawgiver in the first books of the Bible. The law is shown in Exodus as being revealed to Moses on Mount Sinai three months after the Israelites had come out of Egypt. God promises Israel that it will be God's "very own" if it obeys His will and holds fast to His covenant (Ex. 19:1-18). The Ten Commandments follow, spoken by God (Ex. 20:1-17) and then inscribed by God or Moses on two stone tablets (Ex. 34:28).

Biblically presented, the law is not from the beginning or set in a timeless past. It has a date, a place where it was issued, and a direct sanction: God's favor. From biblical times to the seventeenth century most Jews and Christians read the Bible to state that in these concrete historical circumstances God gave the commandments to Moses. Many Jews and Christians so read the Bible today.

Other readings are also common now. Some writers, for example, see "the original form" of the commandments coming from the Mosaic age but the presentation of them in Exodus as later (*The Jerome Biblical Commentary,* ed. Raymond E. Brown, Joseph A. Fitzmyer, and Roland E. Murphy, 1962, p. 106). The second presentation of the commandments in Deuteronomy is variously seen (ibid., p. 123) as postexilic (480 B.C.), late exilic (540 B.C.1), seventh century (644-609 B.C.), as early as Samuel (1050 B.C.), or as early as Judges (1150 B.C.).

Differences exist between some of the commandments as given in Exodus and Deuteronomy, raising problems for those who would insist that each description of them is meant literally. It recently been argued that the presentation in Deuteronomy has been inspired by reflection on Genesis, with major sins already narrated in Genesis such as Adam's disobedience and Cain's murder now being formally condemned (Calum Carmichael, *Law and Narrative in the Bible,* 1985).

Popularly known as "The Ten Commandments," these prescriptions are described by the Bible itself as "Ten Words" (Deut. 4:13): so God uses words in Genesis to create order. Different numbering systems are used to reach ten. Jews begin with Deut. 5:6 (I brought you out of slavery). Greek Orthodox and most Protestants treat Deut. 5:7 (no other gods) as the first and Deut. 5:8-10 (no images) as the second, so that they then agree with Jews in treating Deut. 5:11 (no misuse of name) as the third, Deut. 5:12 (the Sabbath) as the fourth, Deut.

3

5:16 (honor parents) as the fifth, etcetera. Catholics and Lutherans, following St. Augustine, treat Deut. 5:7-10 (no other gods, no images) as the first, Deut. 5:11 (no misuse of name) as the second, Deut. 5:12 (the Sabbath) as the third, Deut. 5:16 (parents) as the fourth, Deut. 5:17 (murder) as the fifth, and so forth, then separating into the ninth and tenth commandments the prescriptions against coveting a neighbor's wife and a neighbor's goods. Opinion also divides as to whether the commandment is "You shall not murder" or "You shall not kill"—a difference with consequences for pacifism and other moral questions related to killing.

Little doubt exists that, despite the great variety of views on the dating, numbering, and exact meaning of the Ten Commandments, they have been the most influential law code in history. Near the beginning of the religious traditions that were most to influence America, the commandments recognized a Lawgiver above the nation, law based on God's will, and a sanction that depended on obedience to Him. Life, property, truth, marriage, and worship of God were given special status by the Ten. Permanent criteria for judging human enterprises, including governments, came into written existence.

The commandments as preserved in Deuteronomy 5:1-23 follow:

The Lord our God made a covenant with us at Horeb. It was not with our forefathers that the Lord made this covenant, but with us, all of us who are alive and are here this day. The Lord spoke with you face to face on the mountain out of the fire. I stood between the Lord and you at that time to report the words of the Lord; for you were afraid of the fire and did not go up the mountain. The Lord said:

I am the Lord your God who brought you out of Egypt, out of the land of slavery. You shall have no other god to set against me.

You shall not make a carved image for yourself nor the likeness of anything in the heavens above, or on the earth below, or in the waters under the earth.

You shall not bow down to them or worship them; for I, the Lord your God, am a jealous god. I punish the children for the sins of the fathers to the third and fourth generations of those who hate me. But I keep faith with thousands, with those who love me and keep my commandments.

You shall not make wrong use of the name of the Lord your God; the Lord will not leave unpunished the man who misuses his name.

Keep the sabbath day holy as the Lord your God commanded you. You have six days to labour and do all your work. But the seventh day is a sabbath of the Lord your God; that day you shall not do any work, neither you, your son or your daughter, your slave or your slave-girl, your ox, your ass, or any of your cattle, nor the alien within your gates, so that your slaves and slave-girls may rest as you do. Remember that you were slaves in Egypt and the Lord your God brought you out with a strong hand and an outstretched arm, and for that reason the Lord your God commanded you to keep the sabbath day.

Honour your father and your mother, as the Lord your God commanded you, so that you may live long, and that it may be well with you in the land which the Lord your God is giving you.

You shall not commit murder.

You shall not commit adultery.

You shall not steal.

You shall not give false evidence against your neighbour.

You shall not covet your neighbour's wife; you shall not set your heart on your neighbour's house, his land, his slave, his slave-girl, his ox, his ass, or on anything that belongs to him.

These Commandments the Lord spoke in a great voice to your whole assembly on the mountain out of the fire, the cloud, and the thick mist; then he said no more. He wrote them on two tablets of stone and gave them to me.

2. THE CIRCUMCISED HEART

The biblical narrative describes how Moses destroyed the original two tablets of the law because of Israel's behavior at Horeb, worshipping a metal calf (Deut. 9:15-21). God then gives Moses a second chance and inscribes the Ten Words on two new tablets (Deut. 10:1-11). This scene is the prelude to the summary of the law attributed to Moses in Deut. 10:12-11:32. In the excerpt that follows, three things are especially notable: (1) The bold use of symbolic language—"circumcise your heart"—which cannot be meant or understood in any literal way; by act and example this text points from letter to spirit. (2) The image of God as an impartial judge who "does not lift up faces and does not take offerings." "To lift up faces" is related to an Akkadian expression meaning "to stand surety," a legal action accomplished by extending one's hand to the other's face in token of identification. God, this text teaches, will not identify in this way with those He judges; He will not be partial (J. Noonan, *Bribes*, 1984, p. 16) Similarly He will not as Judge receive offerings (*shohadh*), the usual placatory tribute brought a superior by an inferior (*ibid.*, 25). The model of God as non-*shohadh*-taking judge breaks the regular pattern of reciprocity with a powerful, potentially hostile stranger (*ibid.*, pp. 3-4). God as impartial Judge becomes the paradigm for judges in Israel (Deut. 16:18-20). (3) The command to remember the powerless—"the orphan and the widow," traditional figures of the poor since at least 2000 B.C., and the alien. Implicit in the command is that God is the owner of the land. Israel's ownership is not so absolute that the alien can be treated as a thing or as a nothing.

Deuteronomy 10:12-19

What then, O Israel, does the Lord your God ask of you? Only to fear the Lord your God, to comform to all his ways, to love him and to serve him with all your heart and soul. This you will do by keeping the commandments of the Lord and his statutes which I give you this day for your good. To the Lord your God belong heaven itself, the highest heaven, the earth and everything in it; yet the Lord cared for your forefathers in his love for them and chose their descendants after them. Out of all nations you were his chosen people as you are this day. So now you must circumcise the foreskin of your hearts and not be stubborn any more, for the Lord your God is God of gods and Lord of lords, the great, mighty, and terrible God. He does not take up faces and does not take offerings. He secures justice for widows and orphans, and loves the alien who lives among you, giving him food and clothing. You too must love the alien, for you once lived as aliens in Egypt.

The Vision of Isaiah, Prophet and Poet

Isaiah is dated to the eighth century B.C. according to his own account of his prophesying beginning at the end of the reign of King Uzziah of Jerusalem (Is. 6:1). He is a critic of existing religious practices in Israel and by the same token a critic of those in power. The existence of a Ruler above the rulers, of Law above current conventions are the predicates of his preaching. The dualism of governmental power and a Higher Power is at the foundation of his fierce message. "Whatever is is right" is not a norm Isaiah can accept.

Note that his attack on a religion based on sacrifices to God appears to be absolute; that it is paralleled by his attack on *shohadh* offered to human judges (Is. 1:23); and that it makes moral conduct, not ritual, the measure of piety.

Isaiah 1:1–23

The vision received by Isaiah son of Amoz concerning Judah and Jerusalem during the reigns of Uzziah, Jotham, Ahaz, and Hezekiah, kings of Judah.

Hark you heavens, and earth give ear,
   for the Lord has spoken:
 I have sons whom I reared and brought up,
 but they have rebelled against me.
The ox knows its owner
   and the ass its master's stall;
 but Israel, my own people,
 has no knowledge, no discernment.
O sinful nation, people loaded with iniquity,
race of evildoers, wanton destructive children
     who have deserted the LORD,
     spurned the Holy One of Israel
     and turned your backs on him.
 Where can you still be struck
   if you will be disloyal still?
   Your head is covered with sores,
   your body diseased;
from head to foot there is not a sound spot in you—
nothing but bruises and weals and raw wounds
  which have not felt compress or bandage
   or soothing oil.
Your country is desolate, your cities lie in ashes.
Strangers devour your land before your eyes;
 it is desolate as Sodom in its overthrow.
   Only Zion is left,
 like a watchman's shelter in a vineyard,
 a shed in a field of cucumbers,
  a city well guarded.
If the LORD of Hosts had not left us a remnant,
 we should soon have been like Sodom,
  no better than Gomorrah.
Hear the word of the LORD, you rulers of Sodom;
attend, you people of Gomorrah, to the instruction of our God:
  Your countless sacrifices, what are they to me?
  says the Lord.
 I am sated with whole-offerings of rams
  and the fat of buffaloes;
 I have no desire for the blood of bulls,
  of sheep and of he-goats.
 Whenever you come to enter my presence—
who asked you for this?
 No more shall you trample my courts.
  The offer of your gifts is useless,
 the reek of sacrifice is abhorrent to me.

New moons and sabbaths and assemblies,
    sacred seasons and ceremonies, I cannot endure.
I cannot tolerate your new moons and your festivals;
    they have become a burden to me,
        and I can put up with them no longer.
    When you lift your hands outspread in prayer,
I will hide my eyes from you.
Though you offer countless prayers,
    I will not listen.
There is blood on your hands;
    wash yourselves and be clean.
Put away the evil of your deeds,
    away out of my sight.
Cease to do evil and learn to do right,
pursue justice and champion the oppressed;
give the orphan his rights, plead the widow's cause.

Come now, let us argue it out,
    says the LORD
Though your sins are scarlet,
    they may become white as snow;
    though they are dyed crimson,
    they may yet be like wool.
    Obey with a will,
and you shall eat the best that earth yields;
    but, if you refuse and rebel,
    locust-beans shall be your only food.
The LORD himself has spoken.
How the faithful city has played the whore,
once the home of justice where righteousness dwelt—
    but now murderers!
    Your silver has turned into base metal
and your liquor is diluted with water.
Your very rulers are rebels, confederate with thieves;
    every man of them loves an offering
        and itches for a gift;
        they do not give the orphan his rights,
    and the widow's cause never comes before them.

3. MARTYRDOM FOR GOD'S LAW

The teaching of the Hebrew Bible on the supremacy of God was reflected upon and absorbed by Jews in the Middle East as Israel came under foreign domination. In the Second Book of Maccabees, a Greek composition addressed to the Jews of Alexandria after 124 B.C., the persecution of Antiochus Epiphanes earlier in the century is the occasion for celebrating obedience to God unto death. The text describes how Eleazar, a leading teacher of the law, refused the ruler's order to eat pork and so was flogged to death (2 Mac. 6:18–30). Seven brothers were then tortured to turn them into porkeaters. After six have died, the story continues:

2 Maccabees 7:20–31

The mother was the most remarkable of all and deserves to be remembered with special honour. She watched her seven sons all die in the space of a single day, yet she bore it bravely because she put her trust in the Lord. She encouraged each in turn in her native language. Filled with noble resolution, her woman's thoughts fired by a manly spirit, she said to them: "You appeared in my womb, I know not how; it was not I who gave you life and breath and set in order your bodily frames. It is the Creator of the universe who moulds man at his birth and plans the origin of all things. Therefore he, in his mercy, will give you back life and breath again, since now you put his laws above all thought of self."

Antiochus felt that he was being treated with contempt and suspected an insult in her words. The youngest brother was still left, and the king, not content with appealing to him, even assured him on oath that the moment he abandoned his ancestral customs he would make him rich and prosperous, by enrolling him as a King's Friend and entrusting him with high office. Since the young man paid no attention to him, the king summoned the mother and urged her to advise the lad to save his life. After much urging from the king, she agreed to persuade her son. She leaned towards him, and flouting the cruel tyrant, said in their native language: "My son, take pity on me. I carried you nine months in the womb, suckled you three years, reared you and brought you up to your present age. I beg you, child, look at the sky and the earth; see all that is in them and realize that God made them out of nothing, and that man comes into being in the same way. Do not be afraid of this butcher; accept death and prove yourself worthy of your brothers, so that by God's mercy I may receive you back again along with them."

She had barely finished when the young man spoke out: "What are you all waiting for? I will not submit to the king's command; I obey the command of the law given by Moses to our ancestors."

4. EARLY CHRISTIANS AND THE ROMAN EMPIRE

The probable date of the letter that follows is A.D. 57–58; the place of composition, Corinth; the author certainly the man who called himself Paul, converted about twenty years earlier from Judaism to being a follower of Jesus Christ (Joseph A. Fitzmyer, "A Life of Paul" and "The Letter to the Romans," *Jerome Biblical Commentary* 2:218, 291–292). The ruling caesar was Nero who had been emperor since A.D. 54; the famous fire in the Circus Maximus which he blamed on the Christians did not occur until A.D. 64. Paul was confidently to "appeal to Caesar" (Acts 25:11) as late as A.D. 60. His advice on the proper attitude to the authorities immediately follows exhortations to bless one's persecutors, to forgo vengeance, and to live in peace (Rom. 12:14–21); it immediately precedes a summary of the commandments culminating in the repetition of the thought, "Love is therefore the fullness of the law" (Rom. 13:10).

Paul refers to the government as the *"exousia,"* "the powers," not "the authorities" or "the state," as some translations put it. He personifies the power as God's agent but does not, it seems, cease to think of it as an "it" rather than individual men. No criteria of this agency of the divine are suggested, but one probably would be mistaken to read these lines as contrary to the long prophetic tradition of criticizing "the power."

Letter to the Romans 13:1-8

Let every soul be subject to the higher powers, for there is no power except by God, and those that are have been ordained by God. Hence he who resists the power has opposed the ordinance of God. Those who oppose will receive judgment for themselves.

Rulers are not a terror for good work but for evil. Do you want not to fear the power? Do good, and you will have praise from it. It is God's minister to you for the good. But if you do evil, fear. It does not carry the sword in vain. God's minister, it is an avenger for wrath to the one practicing evil. Therefore it is necessary to be subject, not only because of wrath but also because of conscience.

So pay taxes. For they are servants of God who attend to this very thing. Pay each what you owe him—the tax to whom you owe the tax, the tribute to whom you owe the tribute, fear to whom you owe fear, honor to whom you owe honor. Owe nothing to anyone except to love one another, for he who loves the other has fulfilled the law.

5. JESUS IN MARK

Like many other teachings of Paul, the teaching about rulers put in Greek abstractions ideas that can be found in, or in harmony with, the sayings of Jesus. (See Harald Riesenfeld, *The Gospel Traditions,* 1970.) That more concrete teaching, as preserved in the Gospel of Mark, commonly dated as written between A.D. 65 and 70, occurs in a dialogue set by Mark in Jerusalem not long before Jesus' death. The "they" referred to are "the chief priests and scribes and elders."

Mark 12:13-17

And they sent him some of the Pharisees and Herodians to catch him in a word. And coming they said to him: "Teacher, we know that you are true and that no one matters to you, for you do not look at men's faces but at truth; you teach the way of God. Is it lawful to give tribute to Caesar, or not? May we give or may we not give?"

But he, knowing their hypocrisy, said to them: "Why do you tempt me? Bring me a denarius that I may see." And they brought it. And he said to them: "Whose image is this and whose inscription?" And they said to him: "Caesar's." Jesus therefore said to them: "What are Caesar's give back to Caesar and what are God's to God."

The question of financial tribute by believers to the state (the exact reverse of the American question of financial support by the state for believers) is crucial. Jesus' answer is on the surface neutral but structured so that the emphasis is on giving what is God's to God. According to Luke 23:2, his enemies twist his teaching into a flat command not to "pay taxes to Caesar" and make this a principal charge against him before Pilate. Reminiscence of this incident colors Paul's teaching to the Romans where the injunction to pay taxes is clearer than in Jesus' saying and where the duty to pay taxes is the final and climactic obligation. See on this, D. Daube in *New Testament Studies* 19, 13, who draws attention to the analogous treatment by Jesus of the obligation to pay a tax to the temple in Jerusalem (Matt. 17:24–27). Both answers are examples of another teaching of Jesus: "Be wise as serpents and harmless as doves" (Matt. 10:16), a verse with perennial attraction to believers pressed by duties imposed by the ruling authorities and conflicting duties to God.

6. PETER BEFORE THE AUTHORITIES

Although far from being the laws of a pagan emperor, the law of the Old Testament was felt as a constraint by the new Christians. For Paul the Law is holy but "now we are rid of the Law" (Rom. 7:6). The author of the Gospel of Luke and Acts of the Apostles, sharing Paul's perspective and writing about A.D. 80, shows Peter and the apostles in confrontation with the council of Jewish authorities in Jerusalem. Peter gives a reason for his defiance, which was to afford an analogy applicable to later conflicts between Caesar and Christ.

Acts of the Apostles 5:27–29

But bringing them they stood before the Sanhedrin. And the chief priest interrogated them, saying: "We gave express orders not to teach in this name, and look, Jerusalem is filled with your teaching, and you seek to charge us with the blood of this man."
    Peter and the apostles answered: "We must obey God rather than man."

7. JESUS BEFORE PILATE

The starkest confrontation with "the power" for a Christian was that of his Lord, Jesus, with the Roman governor of Judea. Chronologically this confrontation and accounts of it preceded Paul's letter to the Romans. The written form preserved in the Gospel of John is as late as A.D. 90. (Bruce Vawter, "The Gospel According to John," *Jerome Biblical Commentary* 2, 416). The contrast between Jesus' kingdom and the Roman empire is sharper than in any exchange related in the Synoptic Gospels. The relation of religious truth to civil power is suggested with Pilate's secular skepticism noted to his discredit. Readers of John know that earlier Jesus had identified himself as the Truth (John 14:6). Pilate is about to order capital punishment for Jesus. Acceptance of the secular penalty is seen as the fulfillment of a mission higher than any secular duty. A stark dualism is set out between "this world" and the world over which Jesus exercises his royalty.

John 18:33–38

Pilate therefore again entered into the praetorium and called Jesus and said to him: "You are the king of the Jews." Jesus answered, "Do you say this by yourself or did others tell you about me?" Pilate answered, "Am I a Jew? Your people and chief priests have delivered you to me. What have you done?"
    Jesus answered, "My kingdom is not of this world. If my kingdom were of this world, my servants would have fought that I not be delivered to the Jews. But now my kingdom is not from here." Pilate accordingly said to him, "Therefore you are a king." Jesus answered, "You say that I am a king. For this I have been born and for this I have come into the world in order to witness to the truth. Everyone who is of the truth hears my voice." Pilate said to him, "What is the truth?"

TWO

Christian Bishop and Imperial Official, A.D. 413–417

BEGINNING WITH PERSECUTION by Nero in the city of Rome in A.D. 64 (Tacitus, *Annals* 15.44) Christians were subject to sporadic persecution in Rome or in Roman provinces up to the year 249 when under the Emperor Decius they were generally persecuted throughout the empire. Christians could clear themselves by sacrificing at a pagan altar (Cyprian, *The Lapsed, Patrologia latina* 4, 486–487). Tolerance for Christians was first officially proclaimed by the Emperor Gallienus (260–268) (see Eusebius, *Ecclesiastical History* 7, 13, 1). By now, Christians were present in the civil service, the army, and the imperial household. But a general persecution was again launched by the Emperor Diocletian who in 295 attempted to purge the army of Christians and in 303 ordered the destruction of all Christian churches and books; in 304 he prescribed death for Christians refusing to offer pagan sacrifice. His successor, Galerius, in 311 issued an Edict of Toleration for Christians (Eusebius 8, 16, 9). On October 28, 312, Constantine won supreme power in the West by his victory at the Milvian bridge on the Tiber. He was convinced that his victory was due to divine inspiration and achieved under the sign of Christ (Lactantius, *The Deaths of the Persecutors* 44; *Patrologia latina* 7, 261; cf. Eusebius, *The Life of Constantine* 1, 27–32). From this date onward, Christians confronted a new phenomenon: an empire whose head was actively pro-Christian.

Constantine almost at once used his office to promote the end of the Donatist schism in Africa (Eusebius, *Ecclesiastical History* 10, 5, 11–20). He used bishops such as Eusebius as counselors of state. He gave legal force to the bishops' decisions in civil cases *(Theodosian Code* 1, 27, 1). He recognized full liberty of leaving legacies to the Church (*ibid.* 16, 2, 4). He declared Sunday a holiday in the courts (*ibid.* 2, 8, 1). He presided in person over the first General Council of the Church, the Council of Nicaea in 325.

Although the short rule of the Emperor Julian, 361–363, interrupted imperial support for the Catholic Church, the fourth century as a whole saw the Christians move from a persecuted minority to an entrenched position within the ruling class. In 380 an imperial decree announced that it was the emperors' will that all the people they ruled should "practice that religion which the divine Apostle Peter transmitted to the Romans" (*Theodosian Code* 16, 1, 2). Bishops and other clerics were granted exemption from public service (*ibid.* 16, 2, 1–3) and a variety of tax exemptions (*ibid.* 16, 2, 8, 10 and 36). As of 355, it was provided that a bishop could be sued only before a bishop (*ibid.* 16, 2, 12) and as of 412, that any cleric could be accused only before a bishop (*ibid.* 16, 2, 41). Illegal entry into a Catholic church was to be capitally punished (*ibid.* 16, 2, 31).

11

The government actively intervened in doctrinal disputes with decrees favoring those who confessed that the Father, Son, and Holy Spirit are "of the same glory" (*ibid.* 16, 1, 3); and the government intervened in the internal discipline of the church, prohibiting priests to have unrelated women in their homes (16, 2, 44). All privileges were denied "heretics and schismatics" (16, 5, 1). Indeed, imperial law forbade "all heresies" (16, 5, 5). Extensive legislation was enacted against the Manichees, depriving them of the right to bequeath or to inherit (16, 5, 7). Apollinarians, Arians, Donatists, Eunomians, Macedonians, Montanists, Phrygians, and Priscillianists were all subjected to penalties as heretics (16, 5, 12 and 25 and 34 and 38 and 39). Governmental coercion drew one line: it did not attempt to punish pure pagans, and pagans still held high office under the Christian emperors. But no one could doubt that Christians played the major part in governing the empire. "God does not reject the powerful, because He is powerful," Jerome mistranslated Job 36:5—a significant mistranslation that, as part of the Latin Vulgate, was to assure Christian officeholders, and reflect their belief, that God was with them in the exercise of governmental power.

Augustine, who came to reflect and write upon these things after almost a century of open Christian influence at the center of power, was born in Tagaste, Numidia, in 354. "An African," as his enemies taunted him, he was familiar with the imperial court but was basically a man from the provinces. He had been a pagan, then a Manichee; he became a Catholic in 387. He was elected bishop of Hippo in Africa in 395. The preeminence of his theological insights and rhetorical skills, his energetic delight in argument and mental combat, his encyclopedic range, his personality, his personal experience, and his willingness to speak personally made him the most influential writer on morals for the Christian West. The problems of government could not escape his attention.

The givens of the situation when he wrote were these: The government was deeply involved with religion. Christians were deeply involved with the government. Christian rulers listened to but did not always follow Catholic bishops. The recent disasters of the empire (for example, Alaric's capture of Rome in 410) made pagans wonder if Christianity was not at the root of their empire's problems.

The letters that follow were addressed by Bishop Augustine to three Roman rulers in Africa. Marcellinus, imperial state secretary and tribune, had been picked by the imperial administrators as a Catholic official with an interest in theology and was sent to represent the emperor at Carthage in 411 in a conference between Catholic and Donatist bishops planned by the government to abolish "the pestilence" of Donatism (*Theodosian Code* 16, 5, 44).

Marcellinus had presided and then gone on to judge the cases of certain Donatist extremists, the Circumcellions, who were charged with actual violence. The first letter to him here was written after these trials; the second addresses the kind of problem a conscientious Christian using power had to face at every moment.

Marcellinus was himself the victim of imperial power. In 413 he was executed on nonreligious grounds as a rebel, but he entered the Roman Martyrology as a saint. Augustine thought enough of him to address *The City of God* to him in 413 (Book 1, Chapter 1). He did not remove his name after his disgrace and execution.

The letters to Marcellinus are conventionally numbered 133 and 138.

1. THE DUTY OF MERCY

Augustine to Marcellinus (Letter 133)

To the Excellent and Deservedly Distinguished Lord, his Very Dear Son, Marcellinus, health in the Lord from Augustine.

Several of the Circumcellions and clerics of the Donatist party whom care of public discipline had removed from Hippo for trial of their actions have, I learn from Your Nobility, confessed what they committed against the Catholic priest, Restitutus, and that as to the mutilation of another Catholic priest, Innocent, they dug out an eye and cut off a finger. I have been filled with the greatest worry that Your Highness judge that they be struck with such severity of law that they suffer the kind of things that they have done. By this letter I beg the faith which you have in Christ that, through the mercy of Christ the Lord, you do not do this nor permit it to be done under any circumstances.

We can distance ourselves from their death when they are seen to be presented for trial, not at our accusation, but at that of those to whom vigilance belongs for the safeguarding of public peace. Nonetheless we do not want the sufferings of the servants of God to be vindicated with equal punishments as if by the law of the talion. Not that we forbid taking from wicked men license to do crimes, but we want this to suffice, so that alive and mutilated in no part of their bodies they may be directed from their mad restlessness to healthful rest by the coercion of the law or assigned from their evil works to some useful work. This is also called condemnation, but who does not understand that it should be called a benefit rather than a punishment where neither bold savagery is given rein nor the medicine of penance is withheld?

Christian judge, fulfill the office of a father. Be angry at wickedness in such a way that you take care to remember humanity. Do not let yourself exercise the lust of revenge against the atrocities of sinners. Apply your will to care for the sinners' wounds. Do not lose that fatherly diligence which you kept in your investigation when you extracted the confession of such great crimes, not by stretching on the rack, not by tearing on hooks, not by burning in fire, but by the blows of rods. This form of coercion is used by teachers of the liberal arts, by parents themselves, and often by bishops in public trials.

Do not, then, punish severely what you found out gently. There is a greater need to investigate than to punish. For this reason even the mildest men diligently and pressingly investigate a hidden crime to find those they then spare. It is generally necessary that an investigation be carried out sharply, so that, when the crime is clear, mildness may appear. All good things assuredly love to be set in the light, not on account of human glory, but, as the Lord says, that "they may see your good works and glorify your Father who art in heaven." And so it is not enough for the Apostle to advise us to be mild but to make it known to all. "Let your mildness," he says, "be known to all"; and elsewhere "showing mildness to all men." Hence that most celebrated clemency of Saint David when he mercifully spared the enemy delivered into his hands would not have shone unless his power had equally appeared. Do not, then, let your power of punishment make you harsh, when the necessity of inquiry did not shake your spirit of mildness. You have found out the crime, do not seek the executioner when you refused to use the torturer in discovering it.

Finally, you have been sent for the welfare of the Church. This, I contend, is expedient for the Catholic Church or—that I may not appear to surpass the limit of my concern—this benefits the Church belonging to the diocese of Royal Hippo. If you do not hear a friend asking, hear a bishop advising. Since I speak to a Christian, especially on such a matter, I shall say without arrogance: it is appropriate for you to hear a bishop commanding, Excellent and Deservedly Distinguished Lord and Very Dear Son.

I know the ecclesiastical cases have been mostly referred to Your Excellency, but because I believe responsibility for them belongs to that very illustrious and distinguished man, the proconsul, I have also sent a letter for him. I ask you not to mind giving it to him yourself and if necessary citing it to him. I beg you both not to judge inopportune our intercession or suggestion or solicitude, and not to cheapen, by reciprocal punishments of the enemies by whom they suffered, the sufferings of the Catholic servants of God which ought to be useful for the spiritual building up of the weak. Rather, break judicial severity. You are sons of the Church. Do not fail to commend your faith and the mildness of your Mother.

May almighty God increase all good things for Your Nobility, Excellent and Deservedly Distinguished Lord and Very Dear Son.

2. CHRISTIAN AS RULER

Augustine to Marcellinus (Letter 138)

Now let us see what that is which follows in your letter. You added that they say that "Christ's preaching and teaching are in no part fit for the morals of the commonwealth: it is clear that his commandment is that we must return evil for evil to no one, and that to him who strikes us we must offer the other cheek and give our coat to him who takes our shirt and walk twice as far with him who makes us go." All these they assert to be contrary to the morals of the commonwealth. "Who," they say, "would suffer something to be taken from him by the enemy? Who would not wish by the law of war to return evil to the ravagers of a Roman province?"

Words of this kind from objectors or from those who are not objecting but inquiring, I could perhaps only refute with labor, but these discussions are held with men who have been liberally educated. What need then for me to work longer and not ask them how they who made the commonwealth large and rich when it was small and poor could have governed and enlarged it when "they preferred to pardon rather than pursue the injuries they received?" How could Cicero, extolling the morals of Caesar the ruler of the commonwealth, say, "He was accustomed to forget nothing, except injuries." He said this either as a great admirer or as a great flatterer. If he spoke as an admirer, he had known such a Caesar. If he spoke as a flatterer, he showed that the prince of the city ought to be as he inaccurately proclaimed him to be.

But what is it not to return evil for evil except to abhor the lust of revenge? What is it to prefer to pardon rather than pursue injuries received except to forget them? When they read these things in their authors, they exclaim over them and applaud them. Morals appear to be described and proclaimed by which a city which would rule over so many people was worthy to rise, because "they preferred to pardon rather than pursue injuries received." But when they read that divine authority commands that evil is not to be returned for evil and when this healthy advice sounds from a higher place to congregations of the people, in public schools for both sexes and for every age and rank, religion is accused as if it were the enemy of the commonwealth. . . .

How many great commandments of harmony, not worked out by human arguments but written by divine authority, are read in the churches of Christ! Who so foreign to that religion or so deaf that he does not know? To this belong these things which pertain to action more than learning. "Offer your other cheek to the one striking you. Give your shirt to one wanting to take your coat. Walk twice the way with one forcing you to go." Assuredly these things are done to overcome evil with good or rather that, in the evil man, the evil be conquered by the good and the man be freed not from an exterior and alien evil but from his own interior evil by which he is more seriously and ruinously wasted than by the inhumanity of any exterior enemy.

Therefore he who overcomes evil by good patiently loses temporal advantages in order to teach how for the sake of faith and justice those things are to be despised by which the other loving them too much became evil. So the wrongdoer learns from him to whom he did the injury what sort of things they are on account of which he did the injury; and repentant, he is won to harmony, than which nothing is more useful to the city—conquered not by the strength of savagery but by the benevolence of patience. This is rightly done when it appears that it will benefit him for whose sake it is done, working amendment and harmony in him. It is certainly to be done with this intention, even if another result follows and he refuses to be corrected or pacified. This medicine must be applied for the sake of the one to be corrected and pacified as if he were to be cured and healed.

Otherwise if we attend to the words and think they are to be kept literally, the right cheek is not to be offered if the left is struck; for He says, "If anyone strikes you on the right cheek, offer him the left." But the left is struck more often because the blow is easier for the right hand of the striker. But it is usually understood as if it said, "If anyone pursues your better goods, offer him your worse; lest being zealous for vengeance rather than patience, you despise eternal things for temporal, when temporal are to be despised for eternal as the left is for the right."

This intention has always been that of the holy martyrs: they justly demand an ultimate judgment when no place of amendment longer remains—the final and supreme Judgment. Now we must beware that out of desire for vengeance we lose (to say nothing more) patience itself which is to be held above all that an enemy can take from us against our will.

Another Gospel-writer of the same opinion made no mention of the right cheek but named only "one cheek" and "the other" and that "the other" may be somewhat more understood, he simply commands the same patience. Therefore a just and devout man ought to bear patiently the malice of those whom he seeks to become good; so that the number of the good will increase rather than that he add himself by equal malice to the number of the evil.

Finally, these commandments relate more to the preparation of the heart, which is within, than to the deed which is done openly. Patience with benevolence is to be held in the secret place of the spirit and to be made manifest when it appears it will benefit those to whom we ought to wish well. This is clearly shown because the Lord Jesus himself, a singular example of patience, replied when He was struck on the face: "If I have spoken wrongly, prove the wrong; if well, why strike me"? He did not—if we look at the words—fulfill his own commandment; for He did not offer the other side to the one striking him but instead prohibited the one who did the injury from increasing it. But He came prepared not only to be struck on the face but even to be killed, crucified, for the sake of those by whom He suffered these things. For them He said as He hung on the cross: "Father, pardon them because they know not what they do."

The Apostle Paul did not seem to have fulfilled the commandment of his Lord and Teacher. When he himself was struck on the face, he said to the chief priest: "God shall strike you, whitewashed wall. You sit judging me according to the law and you order me to be struck contrary to the law." And when the bystanders said, "You do injury to the chief priest," he wanted to warn them by his mockery so that those who were wise would understand that now at the coming of Christ the whitewashed wall was to be destroyed—that is, the hypocrisy of the priesthood of the Jews. Indeed he said: "I did not know, brother, that he is the chief, for it is written, 'You shall not curse the chief of your people.'" Beyond doubt he had grown up in this people and had there learned the law and could not not know that this man was the chief priest nor could he have deceived in any way those to whom he was known into believing that he did not know.

These commandments of patience are therefore always to be kept in the heart, and benevolence is to be fulfilled in the will, so that evil is not returned for evil. But many things must be done with those who are unwilling, beating them with a certain kindly severity and taking into account not their will but what is useful for them. Their literature had lavishly praised such acts at the start of the commonwealth. In correcting a son, however severely, paternal love is surely never lost. Yet what he who is to be cured by pain against his will does not want and is pained by, happens.

In the same way if this earthly commonwealth keeps the Christian commandments, wars themselves will be waged not without benevolence so that thought is more readily taken for the conquered in a fellowship pacified in piety and justice. He whose license to do iniquity is snatched away is beneficially conquered, for nothing is less happy than the happiness of sinners. Impunity from punishment nourishes this happiness while an evil will like an internal enemy is strengthened. Depraved and distorted mortal hearts think human affairs are happy when they notice the splendor of the coverings and do not notice the fall of the souls; when a mass of theaters are thrown up while the foundations of the virtues are dug away; when there is a glorious madness of expenditure while the works of mercy are laughed at; when actors luxuriate in the midst of riches, while the poor scarcely have necessities; when God, who cries out against this public evil with the public voice of his teaching, is blasphemed by impious peoples; and such gods are sought in whose honor these theatrical decorations of bodies and souls are celebrated.

If God permits these things to go on, He is the more gravely angered. If He lets them go unpunished, He punishes more terribly. But when He overturns what supports vices, and turns rich lusts into poverty, He opposes them mercifully. Mercifully, if it can be done, let even wars be waged by the good so that those dominated by licentious desires will lose these vices which ought to be extirpated or suppressed by just rule.

If Christian discipline faulted all wars, when the soldiers in the Gospel asked for advice as to salvation it should have been said: "Throw away your arms. Separate yourself entirely from the soldiery." But what was said to them was: "Shake down no one. Blackmail no one. Let your wages suffice for you." He who commands that their own wages should suffice surely does not forbid them to fight. Hence, let those who say that the teaching of Christ is against the commonwealth grant the kind of army with such soldiers as the teaching of Christ orders that these should be; let them grant such provincial administrators, such husbands, such spouses, such parents, such sons, such masters, such slaves, such kings, such judges, even such tax collectors and agents for debts due the Treasury as Christian teaching commands, and let them dare to say that it is against the commonwealth. Let them not hesitate to acknowledge that, if it is observed, it is the great salvation of the commonwealth.

3. THE DUTY TO INTERCEDE

Macedonius, governor of Africa, was written to in 414, the year after Marcellinus' death. Roman law recognized the right of a Catholic bishop to intervene where a judge's "negligence or favoritism" threatened the safety of a defendant. (*Theodosian Code* 9, 40, 16). Augustine apparently understood this concession broadly, and Macedonius had challenged his practice. The letter that follows not only defended the bishop's right to plead for mercy but, in a later passage not quoted here, referred to the obligation of a judge not to take money for his judgment. Delicately and by allusion only, Augustine indicated that a bribed judge was under obligation like other criminals to make restitution. He does not say that Macedonius is in this posture but in this letter so eloquently stressing the need for mercy, Augustine discreetly reminds Macedonius that he may need it too.

Augustine to Macedonius (Letter 153)

Augustine, bishop, the servant of Christ and his household, to his beloved son, Macedonius, greetings in the Lord.

A man so very busy as you are in human affairs with matters of state and so very attentive not to his own interest but others'—as to which I congratulate you—I ought not to deprive of conversation or detain with a preamble. Receive then what you either wanted to know through me or to find out if I knew. If you judged the matter trivial or excessive, you would have thought that among so many and great necessary cares there was no need to take care for it.

You ask me why I say that it belongs to the office of the priesthood to intervene for the guilty and why I am offended if I fail, as if I had not been discharging what was my duty. You say that you seriously doubt whether this arises from religion. Then you add why are you so aroused. You say, "If sins are so prohibited by the Lord that indeed no opportunity of repenting is granted after the first sin, how can I argue from religion that whatever the crime was, it is to be forgiven"? More passionately, you further urge, "What I want to be unpunished, I approve. If it is clear that he who approves an act, no less than its author, is bound in any matter of sin, it is certain that I am bound in fellowship of fault as often as I want a guilty man to be unpunished."

Whom would you not frighten by these words if one did not know your kindness and humanity? I who know you do not doubt that you wrote these things in order to inquire and not to give a decision. I answer the more quickly with other words of yours. As though you did not want me to delay with this question or foresaw what I would say or advised me what I should say, you said: "Besides, here is what is more serious. All sins seem forgivable when the guilty promise amendment."

Therefore, before I discuss that more serious point which follows in your letter, I shall take what you have given and use it to remove that barrier by which our intercessions seem repressible. Assuredly we intercede for all sins as much as opportunity is granted, because "all sins seem forgivable when the guilty promise amendment." This is your judgment; and it is mine.

In no way, then, do I approve the fault which I want corrected; nor what is done wrongly do I want to be unpunished because it pleases me. But I pity the man and I detest his crime or outrage. The more his vice displeases me, the less I want the vicious man to die without being corrected. Common and easy it is to hate evil men because they are evil. Rare and dutiful it is to love the same men because they are men, so that in one man you simultaneously disapprove his fault and approve his nature and more justly hate the fault because it befouls the nature you love. He who is the foe of crime in order to be the liberator of the man is, therefore, not bound in a partnership of iniquity but in that of humanity.

Moreover, there is no other place to correct morals except in this life. After it, one will have whatever he found pleasure in. Therefore, I am compelled by charity for humankind to intercede for the guilty, so that they do not so finish this life by punishment that when it is finished they cannot finish the punishment.

Do not doubt that this my duty arises from religion. God "with whom there is no iniquity," whose power is supreme, who sees not only how each one is but also how each one will be, who alone cannot slip in judging because He cannot be deceived in judging, nevertheless as the Gospel says, "makes his sun rise upon the good and the bad, and rains upon the just and the unjust." Of His wonderful goodness I am an imitator, the Lord Christ exhorting, "Love your enemies. Do good to those who hate you and pray for those who persecute you so that you may be sons of your Father who is in heaven, who makes his sun rise upon the good and the bad, and rains upon the just and unjust." That many abuse this divine pardon and mildness to their own destruction, who does not know? Rebuking such and seriously reproving them, the Apostle says, "But do you think, man, you who judge those who do such things, and do them yourself, that you will escape the judgment of God? Do you despise the riches of his kindness and patience and long-suffering? Are you unaware that the kindness of God leads you to penitence? But according to your hardness and impertinent heart, you heap up wrath for yourself on the day of wrath and of the just revelations of the judgment of God, who returns to each one according to his work." These persevere in their weakness: should God therefore not persevere in his patience, punishing by means of a few things in this world lest divine providence not be believed to be, and keeping many things for the final examination, so that his future judgment will be justified?

That heavenly Teacher does not, I think, command us to love iniquity when He commands us to love our enemies, to do good to those who hate us, to pray for those who persecute us, although beyond doubt if we devoutly worship God we cannot have any enemies or any aroused against us with bitter hatreds and persecutors except the godless. Are the godless therefore to be loved? Are we to do good to the godless? Are the godless even to be prayed for? Assuredly, yes. For He who commands this is God. Yet He does not by this compact add us to the fellowship of the godless, just as by sparing them and granting them life and safety He does not become their fellow. His intention, so far as it is given a devout man to know it, is what the Apostle sets out, saying, "Are you unaware that the patience of God leads you to penitence?" To this I want to add that the sins of those for whom I intervene I do not spare or favor.

Certain men whose crimes are evident, when they have been freed by your severity, I still keep from the fellowship of the altar, so that by doing penance and punishing themselves they can please Him whom by sinning they despised. For he who truly repents does nothing less than this: the evil he did he does not permit to be unpunished. God—whose high and just judgment so despises evil—spares him who in this way does not spare himself. He spares the unjust and the wicked and grants them life and safety, even the many whom He knows will not do penance, and shows his patience. How much more should I be merciful to those who promise amendment when I am uncertain whether they will do what they promise, so that I bend your rigor by interceding for them. For them I pray to the Lord from whom nothing about their future morals is hidden; and I do so without rashness, because He himself commands this.

Iniquity sometimes so makes progress among men that even after they have done penance, even after they have been reconciled to the altar, they commit similar or more serious things. Yet God makes his sun also rise on such; nor less than before does He bestow on them the very ample gifts of life and health. Although in the Church the humble place of penance is not granted them, still God does not forget his patience upon them. Suppose one of this number were to say, "Either give me again the place of doing penance or allow me in despair to do whatever shall please so far as I can with my own resources and am not prohibited by human laws, in fornication and every lust condemned by God but praiseworthy among most men; or if you call me back from this wickedness, say whether it benefits me at all for my future life if in this life I despise the enticements of the most seductive pleasure, if I resist the enticements of lust, if I withdraw my body even from many lawful and conceded things in order to chastise it, if I punish myself by doing penance more fiercely than before, if I groan more miserably, weep more fully, live better, support the poor more generously, burn more ardently with the charity that covers a multitude of sins"—which of us would be so mad as to say to this man, "None of these things will help you later. Go, at least savor the sweetness of this life." God avert such monstrous sacrilegious madness! Cautiously and salubriously it is provided that place for most humble penance is granted only once in the Church, lest, for the sick, cheap medicine be less useful which is the more salubrious the less it is held in contempt. Nonetheless who would dare to say to God, "Why do you again spare this man who has bound himself in the toils of iniquity after his first repentance?" Who would dare to say that what the Apostle says, "Are you unaware that the patience of God leads you to repentance?" does not work as to them; or that these are excepted from the saying, "Blessed are all who trust in Him," or that "Act manfully and let your heart be comforted, all you who hope in the Lord" does not apply to them.

Upon sinners, so great is the patience, so great is the mercy of God that those who amend their souls in this temporal life are not condemned in eternity. He looks to no one to furnish Him mercy for no one is more blessed than He, no one more powerful, no one more just. Is it necessary therefore for men to be like this toward men? Whatever praise we pile up in this life, we say it is not without sin—if we said otherwise, as it is written, "We deceive ourselves and the truth is not in us."

One role is the accuser's; another the defender's; another the intercessor's; another the judge's (it would be too long and it is unnecessary in this speech to discourse upon the duties proper to each). But the avengers of crimes—in this office moved not by their own anger but ministers of the laws and vindicators not of their own injuries but of those done to others, and so necessarily like judges—are themselves terrified by the divine judgment, so that they think God's mercy is needed on account of their own sins. They do not think it a fault in their duty if they act mercifully toward those over whose life or death they have lawful power.

4. THE DUTY TO COERCE

Three years later Augustine addressed another governor of Africa, Boniface, sending him a small treatise, *The Correction of the Donatists*, setting out the difference between the heretical Arians and the Donatists who are described as "rebels against the unity of Christ," and going on to describe the imperial laws intended to increase peace and unity. The letter reflects a distinct evolution in Augustine's thought. The Donatists are to be driven into the Church by force. He still retains the notion of mild force expressed in the letter of 412 to Marcellinus. He still harbors the view, also expressed to Marcellinus, that the infliction of moderate punishment can be paternal and medicinal. Scourging is not execution. But embracing in principle the use of coercion against schismatics and heretics, he lays a general foundation for religious persecution. True, the death penalty would run counter to his rationale as well as to his repeated pleas for mercy; but it was to prove impossible to draw his nice line between the severe and lenient infliction of pain. From one perspective, Augustine merely rationalizes a century of religious persecution by Christian emperors and sets limits. From another perspective he provides the charter of the Inquisition.

Augustine, *The Correction of the Donatists* (Letter 185)

Those who refuse to have just laws enacted against their own impieties say that the Apostles did not seek such from the kings of the earth. They do not consider that the time then was something else and that all things are done at their own times. Then there was no emperor who had believed in Christ, no emperor who would serve Him by passing laws in favor of religion and against impiety. . . . not yet was the time as to which the psalm says, "And now, kings, understand: learn you who judge the earth, serve the Lord in fear and rejoice in Him with fear." In what way, then, do kings serve the Lord in fear except by prohibiting and punishing with religious severity those things that are done against the commandments of the Lord? For he serves in one way because he is a man and in another way because he is king. Because he is man he serves by living faithfully; but because he is also king he serves by prescribing just laws and prohibiting the contrary, providing sanction with due vigor, just as Ezechias served by destroying the groves and temples of idols in those high places which had been set up against the commandments of God. . . .

Why, since free will has been divinely given to man, are adulteries punished by the laws and sacrileges permitted? Is it a lighter matter for a soul not to keep faith in God than for a woman not to keep it with her husband?

Or if these things which are committed not in contempt but in ignorance of religion are to be punished more mildly, are they therefore to be neglected?

Will anyone doubt that it is better for men to be led by teaching, rather than forced by fear of punishment or suffering, to worship God? But that one way is better is not a reason that the other should be neglected. It has benefited many, as we have proved by experience and do prove, that they first be compelled by fear of suffering so that afterward they can be taught or carry out in act what they have learned in words. . . . Many as it were bad slaves and in a way wicked runaways are called back to the Lord by the lash of temporal scourges.

Who can love us more than Christ who laid down his life for his Church? Yet while He had called Peter and the other Apostles by word alone, He not only compelled Paul (formerly Saul, afterward a great builder of His Church but first a ferocious destroyer) by word but He also prostrated him with power, and in order to lead him from the savagery of his dark unbeliefs to the desire of the light of the heart, he first struck him with bodily blindness. . . . They are accustomed to cry, "To believe or not believe is free. On whom would Christ use force? Whom would He compel?" Look, they have the Apostle Paul. Let them recognize in him that Christ first compelled and then taught, first struck and then compelled. It is wonderful how he who, compelled by bodily pain, entered into the gospel, labored more in the gospel than all those who were called by word alone and that in him whom greater fear drove to charity, "perfect charity drove out fear."

Why, then, should the Church not compel her lost sons to return if the lost sons have compelled others to be lost? . . .

Hence the Lord Himself first commands the guests to be brought to his great wedding feast but afterward has them compelled; for when the slaves cried, "Lord it is done as you command," he said, "Go out into the highways and hedges and whomever you find compel them to enter." In those, therefore, who were first brought in gently obedience was fulfilled, but in those who were compelled disobedience was coerced. . . . Therefore if the power which the Church has received by divine gift through religion and faith in the time of kings is exercised as it should be, those who are found in the highways and hedges—that is, in heresies and schisms—are compelled to come in. Let them not blame her because they are compelled but let them pay attention when they are compelled.

But before those laws by which they are compelled to enter the sacred banquet were sent to Africa, it seemed to some of our brothers, and to me as well, that although the madness of the Donatists raged everywhere, we should not ask the emperors to have a punishment set against this heresy. . . .

But the greater mercy of God, who knew the terror of these laws and a certain medicinal harassment to be necessary for the wicked and cold minds of many and for the hardness which could not be changed by words but could by some degree of severity of discipline, then so acted that our representatives could not obtain what they sought. Very heavy complaints of some bishops from other districts came ahead of us—bishops who had suffered many evil things and had been thrown out of their sees, especially the horrible and unbelievable maltreatment of Maximian, Catholic Bishop of Bagai. The result was that our mission had nothing to do, for a law had already been promulgated that the heresy of the Donatists was of such monstrousness that it seemed crueler to spare it.

Augustine's interpretation of the compulsion used on Paul would have justified the use of force to make Jews and pagans convert. Neither he nor the Church nor the empire went so far. The thrust of Augustine's exegesis was restrained by the practice of the empire.

THREE

The Freedom of the Church: The English Experience, 1160–1260

IN ENGLAND, only seven centuries after Augustine, secular princes were as selectively attentive to bishops as Roman governors had been. But bishops now enjoyed such secular possessions and popular influence that princes paid great attention to their selection and often arranged that their own candidate be chosen. Apart from local bishops, the pope himself was an international figure with whom princes had to reckon. Beginning in the eleventh century, reformers of the Church had placed their hopes on a strong papacy; Gregory VII, building on the ideals of his predecessor Gregory I, had challenged the empire in the name of reform. By the mid-twelfth century the organization the reformers had desired was in place. The pope had his own bureaucracy, the Curia, and he sat as the acknowledged head of related judicial and administrative systems whose reach extended to every corner of Europe from Ireland in the West to Hungary in the East.

A new kind of law book was in circulation in the courts of the Church—the *Concordia discordantium canonum (Harmony of the Unharmonious Canons)* of Gratian. The *Harmony* (also known as the *Decretum*) had been put together in the 1130s and 1140s at the center of European legal studies, Bologna. It was a law professor's case book; a resolution of conflicting texts; and a giant compendium of canons (excerpts from Scripture and the Fathers, especially Augustine; decrees of church councils; case decisions and legislation by popes). The book exhibited the complex and developed legal system the Church now possessed to decide such questions as when a marriage existed and when an heir was legitimate; who had title to a see or a parish or a tithe; what heresy was and how it was to be adjudicated. Its completion also assured more complexity and development. Its existence was a challenge to a more embryonic legal system such as England's.

Nearly everyone in England was in name a Christian. A small, sporadically persecuted Jewish population existed. Heresy was rare and unorganized. No one disputed that the pope was the head of the Church, although sometimes there were two popes claiming election, between whom a choice had to be made. The real problems lay in the interaction of the overlapping legal systems of pope and prince, problems mostly handled ad hoc by mutual accommodation. "Interpenetration" is the term used by a great historian to describe the relationship, and he finds it "thoroughgoing" (David Knowles, *Becket,* 1970, p. 59). The prince did not think it alien to his duties to be involved with both the personnel and the property of the Church. The Church could not not be involved with issues that affected public policy and public peace. The murder of Thomas Becket dramatized the difficulties when accommodation failed.

1. THE BECKET CONTROVERSY

Thomas Becket was born about 1118 in London, the son of Norman gentry. He studied the liberal arts in Paris from 1136 to 1138, served as private secretary to a baron, and at age twenty-five set out on an ecclesiastical career as a member of the staff of Theobald, archbishop of Canterbury. A decade later, Theobald recommended him to Henry II as his chancellor; the easy movement of clerical personnel into royal service was normal (Knowles, 6–9, 27).

Henry was twenty-one, fifteen years Thomas's junior, and just beginning his reign. Thomas became his "heart and wisdom," without whose will "nothing happened" (*Foliot to Thomas*, 1166, Rolls Series 67, 522). Thomas was not the king's lustful boon companion as depicted in Anouilh's play (Knowles, 41), but he was devoted to his political interests, for example, plotting the conquest of Ireland, an excursion for which the pope's blessing was thought desirable and was secured (John of Salisbury, *Metalogion* 4, 4). As John's letter to Bartholomew of June 1166, *infra,* indicates, he also encroached on the Church's domain to get revenue for the crown. In those days, Thomas was "a great gamesman" (*John of Salisbury to Bartholomew of Exeter* (Letter 187), in John of Salisbury, *Letters* 2, 244).

In 1162, at the king's urging, the monks of Christ Church, Canterbury, chose Thomas to succeed Theobald as archbishop. Thomas not only accepted but to the king's chagrin resigned as chancellor. He was now his own master and the steward, as he saw it, of Christ. Within the year he was at odds with Henry over whether clerics could be punished by the royal courts after conviction of a crime and punishment by a church court. Beyond any political disagreement, Henry felt the bitterness of a patron who sees his protégé thwart his will.

In 1164 Thomas and the other bishops swore to observe the Constitutions of Clarendon, which let the Church try clerics, the royal judges punish them, and in other ways limited the immunity and freedom of action of the bishops. Thomas almost instantly repented his surrender, suspended himself from saying mass for forty days, and wrote the pope asking to be absolved from his oath to the king (Knowles, 92–93). Henry retaliated by summoning Thomas to answer a charge against him by one of his tenants. When Thomas failed to appear, he was fined all his movable goods for contempt, and the king went on to have his barons try Thomas for not accounting for all the funds he had received as chancellor. In October 1164 he was found guilty (Knowles, 94, 98). By these maneuvers within his own legal system, the king, as he thought, challenged Thomas on turf where the king set the rules. But in Thomas's view the king was violating the ancient tradition of a bishop's immunity from civil suit. Thomas appealed to the pope, Alexander III, to quash the verdicts. The other bishops of England—some of them hostile to Thomas, some of them pressured by the king—filed a separate appeal with the pope. The bishops eventually asked the pope to condemn the archbishop or at least let the case be tried by a papal legate in England (Knowles, 97–98, 104).

For the next six years the only litigation that went on was in the canonical system with the pope as Supreme Judge acting in person or by legates. Thomas issued excommunications against various bishops, clerics, and royal officials. As John's letter to Bartholomew, July 1166, *infra,* indicates, Thomas was hesitant to anathematize Henry in person, but a canon adopted in 1139 excommunicated a person who laid violent hands on a cleric; the king appeared to fall within this class (Gratian, 17, 4, 29).

Thomas was a Marcellinus teaching by example more than by word. The intellectual through whose eyes the controversy is captured was John of Salisbury, the greatest literary genius of the twelfth century. John was also the author of the *Policraticus (The Ruler of the City)*, a treatise on government enriched by classical allusions and many concrete examples, a work on politics unequaled in Western Europe up to the sixteenth century. In the course of it John advanced the doctrine that the sword of the king is given by the Church, so that "the prince is a certain kind of deputy of the priesthood." (*Policraticus* 4.3, ed. C. I. Webb, 1909).

Thomas inherited John from Theobald's staff, and John stayed with him in exile, returned with him to England, and was present when he was killed. His letters from exile, which follow, describe how Thomas's party scorned the bishops on the king's side, doubted the pope's constancy, and saw the fight as one for the freedom of the Church against evil incarnate.

The translation is based on the Latin text of W. J. Millor and C. N. L. Brooke, *The Letters of John of Salisbury* (1979), vol. 2, Letters 168 and 174.

John to Bartholomew, Bishop of Exeter, June 1166

. . . All things are said to be full of snares so that it is not safe for good men to have oral or written commerce with each other. I know not what game wickedness is plotting against innocence. The prick of conscience stings and burns continually, so that all men and all things are felt suspect. . . .

Someone will say that this imposition of tax and the harassment of the churches is to be wholly turned back on his [the king's] chancellor [Thomas] who now rules as archbishop, as I believe (or, as his rivals lie, *claims* to rule as archbishop)—at that time the king was directed by him as he chose in everything, and he [Thomas] led him to this as he did to many other evils. I know this to be false, since I know that at that time he [Thomas] did not obey the authority of lust but the dictate of necessity. Nonetheless, I do not doubt that he [Thomas] was the servant of wickedness, and so I judge him punishable by the highest law. . . .

Recently, he [the king] gathered in conference at Chinon his nobles and staff, who are known to have energy and practice in evil pursuits and to be wise in suggesting and doing evil. He zealously inquired, using promises, threats, and much protestation, what plan he should use against the Church. Most bitterly he complained about the Archbishop of Canterbury. . . . He wept and said this Canterbury would take away both his body and his soul. Finally he said they were all traitors who refused to apply work and care to save him from the trouble of one man.

[Meanwhile Archbishop Thomas has excommunicated various clerics and royal officials and summoned the king to give satisfaction.] Now the archbishop has made the summons public and has invited him [the king] to the fruit of penance. He has threatened shortly to pass a judgment of anathema against him unless he has a good flavor and makes satisfaction for his audacities against the Church. But yet he will not do that willingly, nor do I know any of his household who is inclined to this judgment.

That document [the Constitutions of Clarendon] which contains the wickedness of the malignant against the Church (which they call grandfatherly customs) he [Thomas] publicly condemned, binding with the chain of the anathema all who rely on its authority. With the advice of the Roman Church he especially condemned these chapters by name:

> That it is not lawful for a bishop to excommunicate a tenant of the king without the king's permission.
> That it is not lawful for a bishop to try any members of his diocese for perjury or breach of faith.
> That clerics may be brought to secular courts.
> That the king or other laymen may try cases concerning churches and tithes.
> That except after seeking the pardon of the king and his officials, no case may be appealed to the Apostolic See.

That it is not lawful for an archbishop or bishop or any other person to respond
to the summons of the Lord Pope apart from the king's permission.
Also other things in this fashion which are found contrary to divine laws and the
constitutions of the Holy Fathers.

But he [Thomas] has absolved all the bishops from the promise they made of observing
this document contrary to ecclesiastical rule. He also proclaimed this by letter to the
archbishops and bishops, just as he had been advised by the Roman Church.

John to Bartholomew, Bishop of Exeter, July 1166

. . . Whatever the bishops wrote in haste in their appeal, whatever they proclaimed of
his [the king's] piety and kindness, justice and lovability and respect for the priesthood,
the French and the Latins would more readily believe anything about him that was
impious toward God and inhuman toward humans. Hence all who hear greatly wonder
and are amazed at the conscience, the impudence, the chutzpah with which you bishops
dared to assert, commit to writing and confirm with evidences of episcopal authority
the innocence of a man whose injustices are a legend to all, whose deceits and acts of
violence the whole world has known. In what fashion did a venerable body composed
of so many and so great Fathers give false testimony in subversion of justice and for
the benefit of malice? For these are the words of your document on behalf of the king,
whose cause your notary is trying to justify: "The king promises all justice and is ready
to do it with deeds. He thinks it a sweet service to be warned to correct any offense
he has committed against God. He is not only ready to make satisfaction in general
but to make satisfaction in this matter if the law demands it." . . .

People say, "How sound, how saintly is the preaching of the bishops of England!
How sincere and uncorrupted is their witness for the liberty of the Church! How true
is the declaration of the priests! They proclaim what a jester or actor would not speak
without suffering shame".

. . . The bishops say (perhaps more truly the bishop) that it is peace. But all cry
out that it is not peace but bitterness most bitter. But if indeed he [the king] demands
only due customs, as your Demosthenes asserts, he surely ought to be content with
those that are not the enemies of divine laws, that are not against good morals, that
do not dishonor the priesthood, that do not offer danger to souls, that do not subvert
the liberty of Mother Church, from whose hand he received the sword to guard her
and beat off her wrongs. But in his desire, all things are contrary just as that writing
of his condemned by the authority of the Holy Fathers and by the mouth of the
Supreme Pontiff bears witness, as do the daily complaints of the clergy and the people.
I fear that the bishops themselves will be compelled to act against their own document
and to unpreach what they preach and to justify the cause they now condemn and to
condemn the cause they justify.

The signed attestation is indeed drafted in the name of all of them, but it is confirmed
only by the seals of three bishops, to wit, the chief of the London synagogue; my lord
and friend, the bishop of Winchester, whom I now spare; and Hereford, indeed an old
scholastic but a novice bishop, equally powerful in learning and in eloquence. Their
authority would be high if their good reputation was not prejudiced by their consent
to wickedness and attestation of manifest falsehood; of this both the letter and attachment
of their seal convicts them. . . .

But I hear that all [of the bishops] have given authority to the document. If they
saw it first, it was most impious to offer witness to such wickedness. If they did not
see it, it was most stupid to give authority to another's wickedness by placing on it
their characters. . . .

Since God disposed otherwise, your scribe [Gilbert] could not be what he ambitioned
to be, archbishop of Canterbury. Hence with the consent, counsel, and authority of

those in the English Church who persecute Christ, he became chief of the synagogue. Recently the king wrote him by his archdeacon Ralph de Diceto that he commits to his judgment as to that of a father and most faithful friend his whole kingdom and the case which is between him and the Church. . . .

Christ, I issue a summons for you. I call you to judgment, you who are unfailing truth. On the Last Day of Judgment, I shall, if reason allows, prove your lie, unless each one is judged by the judgment by which he has judged and receives reciprocal measure for measure.

. . . [The archbishop] does not believe the appeal which the bishops have made against him to be of any moment. But for those who do think it to have some force, such as the king, the bishops, and the nobles, making the prudence of the flesh their aim, it was necessary to allow everything belonging to the archbishop to stay in the same state, because nothing should be changed while an appeal is pending. But later, by the king's command, the Chaplain William and other clerics were taken prisoner (I say nothing of the laymen); the property of the Church was removed; and they were abominably treated. Therefore the archbishop has reported to the Lord Pope that the king himself has fallen under the canon and by his own deed is excommunicate, unless perhaps the Apostolic See believes ecclesiastical laws are to be compared to those civil laws which, as Anacharsis the Scythian said, are like spiders' webs catching flies but letting larger flying things through. . . .

Know this for certain that unless the king surrenders William the Chaplain, his head shall carry the judgment of anathema, and he will not now be spared in anything if he dares to try such things.

Appeals from Thomas's excommunications were lodged with the pope, who sometimes but not always restrained the archbishop. At no point were the issues treated from only a legal viewpoint. Alexander III was seriously threatened by a rival pope, who had the backing of the German emperor; Alexander was not anxious to make a permanent enemy of Henry. Realistically he was also aware of how hard it would be to make Henry act against his will within his kingdom. Yet he did not desire to desert Thomas or the legal principles Thomas was defending. For Alexander the obvious solution was compromise, not a clearcut judicial verdict.

Thomas, an exile in France, thought Henry was untrustworthy and knew him to be cruel; he had exiled all of Thomas's relations including "babes in the cradle and those still clinging to the breasts of their mothers" and told them to go to Thomas as the one responsible (Knowles, 109). Thomas found the pope's diplomacy disheartening, and he became convinced the king's money played a corrupt part in producing policy shifts at the Curia. Under the principle of restitution set out by Augustine to Macedonius and now established in the canon law (Gratian, C.14, q.6, c.l), the king should have restored the profits he illegally derived from the estates of Canterbury; instead, Thomas thought he was using the profits to pay off certain cardinals (Noonan, *Bribes*, 165–169). Disgusted and worn down, Thomas went through a pro forma reconciliation with Henry with all the real problems left to be worked out later.

The following, Letter 303, was written after Thomas had gone through the formal reconciliation with Henry. The last sentence of the second paragraph can be read as unconscious prophecy.

John to William Brito, subprior; to Robert, the sacristan; and to the magistrates of the Canterbury Church, Mid-October 1170

Your prayers and the desires of the faithful, the merciful and mercy-hearted Lord has heard to his own honor as many and sure signs show. He restores peace to the English

Church and recalls from exile your father. Would that your ears had been near the mouth of the Lord King when at the conference of the kings recently held between Blois and Amboise [Fréteval] he sent away the archbishop to receive permission swiftly from the French, to whom he was bound, and to return with all speed to him, then to cross over to England.

Therefore, as it has been arranged, God willing, he will depart here on the feast of All Saints and will purposely and by agreement return to his own. As quickly as he can, he will make the city of the saints shine by his return to Canterbury.

You, then, as you wish there to be provision in the future for the honor and welfare of your church, run to meet your father. Do not delay to send across the sea something of faith, of friendship, of devotion or counsel by which he can lessen his burden and be perpetually bound harmlessly to you. Now redeem your delay. . . .

Thomas returned to England, renewed an excommunication of three disobedient bishops, and in so doing roused again the wrath of Henry. On the afternoon of December 29, 1170, four knights of Henry's entourage burst into his cathedral.

John had once advised Thomas to stand on principle at the risk of martyrdom but when the armed knights were on the premises he told Thomas that he was not anxious for death. He accompanied Thomas into the cathedral but dove into a recess before the assault began (Knowles 114, 144, 147). In Letter 305 he writes, then, not necessarily as an eyewitness but as one who was very close to the scene, which he survived to become, six years later, bishop of Chartres:

John to John, Bishop of Poitiers, Early 1171

But he was ready to suffer, as I said, in the church before the altar of Christ—a martyr before he was struck. When he heard that he was asked for—when the knights who had come for this shouted out in the crowd of clerics and monks, "Where is the archbishop?"—he met them on the steps which he had mostly climbed. With an intrepid countenance he said, "Here I am. What do you want?" One of the deadly knights, in a spirit of fury, flung at him, "That now you die. For it is impossible that you live longer." But the archbishop replied with as much steadiness of speech as of spirit (in my opinion, with respect to all the martyrs, I confidently say that none of them was steadier in his passion): "And I for my God am ready to die, and for the declaration of justice and the liberty of the Church. But if you seek my head, I forbid on the part of Almighty God and under anathema that you harm any other, whether monk or cleric or layman, of high or low degree. They are immune from punishment as they have stood apart from the case. Not to them but to me is it to be imputed if any of them undertook the cause of the Church in her labor. I embrace death freely, as long as the Church obtains peace and liberty in the shedding of my blood."

Who has seemed more fervent in love? He was offering himself to his persecutors for the law of God. He took care only that his neighbors be harmed in nothing. Did not his words seem to express Christ who in his passion said, "If you seek me, let these go" [John 18:8].

After he said these things, he saw that the butchers had drawn their swords. He lowered his head in the fashion of one who prays and uttered these last words, "To God and Blessed Mary and to the holy patrons of this Church and to Blessed Denis I commend myself and the Church's cause."

Who will tell what followed without sighs, sorrow, tears? Piety does not permit one to relate each individual thing which the most cruel butchers did. They held the fear of God in contempt. They were forgetful of faith and of all humanity.

It was not enough for them to profane the church and stain a most sacred day with the blood of a priest and his killing. The crown of his head which the anointing of the sacred chrism had dedicated to God they—it is terrible even to say it—cut off and with their deadly swords drew out the brain of the dead man and most cruelly scattered it over the pavement with his blood and bones. More inhuman were they than those who crucified Christ who judged that his legs should not be broken as had been the legs of those who were alive, when they saw that he had died.

In all these tortures the martyr, with unconquered spirit and wonderful steadiness, spoke not a word nor let out a cry nor emitted a groan. He opposed neither his arm nor a garment to the one striking him, but he held his bowed head immobile, which he had exposed to the swords with wonderful virtue until it was consummated, and at length falling on the ground he did not move foot or hand, and his body lay straight.

To see this controversy as Church versus State is an anachronism. The Church was divided; the king was not a modern bureaucracy ideologically hostile to the Church's claims. Henry was a man at least in part reponding as a man to what he saw as pride and disloyalty and acting with personal meanness to reach Thomas in his relatives. That the bishops were divided was important to him not only politically but personally. In good conscience he could say that he was not attacking the Church when learned churchmen were on his side. The pattern is familiar. But from the viewpoint of the universal Church, Thomas died for his defense of its claims. Two years and two months after his death, he was proclaimed a saint, canonized by Alexander III himself. His cult was celebrated from a mosaic in his honor in the Norman cathedral in Monreale, Sicily, to stories about his integrity told in the schools of Paris (Noonan, *Bribes*, 176). During the next 600 years the Church was often to be in conflict with Christian monarchs who had their own ideas as to how to limit the jurisdiction of the Church. For popes or bishops involved in any of these encounters Thomas was an exemplar of adherence to principle and resistance to royal pretensions. By his life and by his death he had an impact on European views of the relation of bishop to prince.

2. THE GREAT CHARTER

A favorite stumper in English history classes is: Who signed Magna Carta? The answer is: No one, the document having been agreed to but not signed by King John. A comparable conundrum is: How long was Magna Carta the law of England? The answer is: About two months. The grant was then formally invalidated by John's legal overlord. Only Magna Carta as reissued by Henry III had the long life into the mid-nineteenth century that is popularly credited to the famous document. This history, and the origins of Magna Carta, both arise from the interaction of the Church with the English crown.

The see of Canterbury became vacant in 1205. The monks of Christ Church, the normal electors, were challenged by the suffragan bishops as to who would choose the new archbishop. King John, the talented Henry II's untalented youngest son, backed the bishops. The monks appealed to the pope, at the time Innocent III, the most energetic of all the medieval popes.

Innocent, as a student at Paris, had made a pilgrimage to the shrine of St. Thomas. From his perspective, St. Thomas had "laid down his life for the Church's liberty" and yet "his blood" had borne no fruit. The English king continued to dominate the Church. The pope now saw his opportunity. The king's agents intimated that they were ready to pay over 11,000 silver marks for the right result, but Innocent detested such bribes and stayed on "the royal road" of impartiality (*Gesta Innocentii III*, c. 131, Migne, *Patrologia latina*, vol. 214). He quashed the election that had already been held and called the electors of Christ Church to

Rome. Voting in his presence, they chose his candidate, Cardinal Stephen Langton (*Gesta*, c. 131).

Langton was an admirable choice—an honest, highly intelligent Englishman who had made a great reputation as a scholar in Paris and had been called to Rome from Paris by Innocent, who may already have had him in mind as the ideal man for Canterbury. It was, however, intolerable to the king that a man so unknown to him should hold the premier see of his realm. He asked the pope to reconsider and put papal relatives on his payroll to influence the reconsideration (Noonan, *Bribes*, 195). "Strong and steady," as he saw himself, Innocent consecrated Langton with his own hands (*Gesta*, c. 131).

John reacted as his father would have reacted. He expelled from their monastery the monks whose representatives had elected Langton. He put Langton's own father to flight in fear of his life and confiscated his estate. He announced that the new archbishop could not land in England. Innocent replied with the threat of a general interdict of England. After months of fruitless negotiations, the interdict took effect in March 1208. While it lasted, the only sacraments that could lawfully be administered in the country were those to the dying. To restrain their ruler the English as a whole were subjected to sacramental starvation (Christopher R. Cheney, *Pope Innocent III and England*, 1976, 298–302).

War between pope and prince went on for five years. John confiscated clerical properties of various kinds. Innocent insisted on the interdict. In 1213 John faced invasion by France. Unrest among his own subjects and the desire for papal support impelled him to abject surrender. On May 13, 1213, he submitted to the papal legates and offered to make restitution for the damages the Church had suffered. On May 15, 1213, he made restitution by a remarkable gesture—the conveyance of England and Ireland to the pope and his successors in office. "We have offended God and Our Mother Holy Church in many things," he declared. "We will to humble ourselves" (John to All Christ's Faithful, May 15, 1213, *Patrologia latina*, 216, 878–880). After conveyance, the pope gave the countries back to John as fiefs. John became the vassal of the pope. He continued to hold the kingdoms in consideration of doing homage as a liegeman to his overlord, the pope, vowing henceforth to defend "the Patrimony of Blessed Peter and in particular the kingdom of England and the kingdom of Ireland," and agreeing to pay an annual cash tribute—700 silver marks for England, 300 for Ireland, the whole 1,000 to be paid in two semiannual installments (*ibid.*).

Cardinal Stephen Langton then set off for England and within a year had drafted reforms which the king must carry out. Among them was the proposition, "King John grants that he will not take men without judgment nor accept anything for doing justice, nor perform injustice" (W. L. Warren, *King John*, 1978, pp. 215–247). Clause 40 of Magna Carta existed in embryo.

In early 1215 mutinous barons were in revolt against the king. The pope was now on John's side. As overlord, it was his duty to protect his vassal. Moreover, the pope was planning a crusade, the king had taken the crusader's cross, and the barons could not be allowed to disrupt the crusade. Langton was rebuked for stirring up the barons (Cheney 368–379).

On June 15, 1215, the bishops of England led by Langton, a party of barons, and the papal legate Pandulph secured John's consent at Runnymede to the document that was to be celebrated as "The Great Charter." A remarkably heterogeneous set of reforms was outlined within its limits, from provisions on the dowry of widows to provisions pledging the king not to sell justice and to respect the freedom of the Church. A month later John duplicitously appealed to Rome to annul his agreement.

The case was put to Innocent, not in terms of the substantive provisions of the document but in terms of how it had been secured. A familiar legal doctrine was that a promise was voidable if the promisor had been subjected to the kind of fear that would cow "a steady man." John, Innocent held, had been subjected to fear that would have cowed "the steadiest man." In a decretal letter issued on August 24, 1215, not long after Magna Carta had reached Rome, Innocent annulled it. Only after Innocent's and John's death was it reissued without challenge in the reign of Henry III.

There follow a portion of Magna Carta, based on the Latin text in James C. Holt, *Magna Carta* (1965), and Innocent III's annulment of it, the letter *Etsi karissimus,* based on the Latin text in Christopher R. Cheney and W. H. Semple, eds., *Selected Letters of Pope Innocent III concerning England, 1198–1216* (1953).

Magna Carta

The Preamble

John, by the grace of God King of England, Lord of Ireland, Duke of Normandy and Aquitaine and Count of Anjou, to his archbishops, bishops, abbots, earls, barons, justices, foresters, sheriffs, stewards, servants, and to all his officials and loyal subjects, Greetings.

Know that before God, for the health of our soul and the souls of our ancestors and heirs, to the honour of God, the exaltation of the holy Church, and amendments of our kingdom by the advice of our reverend Fathers, Stephen, Archbishop of Canterbury, Primate of all England, and Cardinal of the holy Roman Church; Henry, Archbishop of Dublin; William of London, Peter of Winchester, Jocelin of Bath and Glastonbury, Hugh of Lincoln, Walter of Worcester, William of Coventry, Benedict of Rochester [the seven bishops of England], Master Pandulf subdeacon and member of the Pope's household, Aymeric, Master of the Knights Templar in England; William Marshal, Earl of Pembroke; William, Earl of Salisbury; William, Earl of Warren; William, Earl of Arundel; Alan de Galloway, Constable of Scotland, Warin Fitz Gerald, Hubert de Burgh, Seneschal of Poitou, Peter Fitz Herbert, Hugh de Neville, Matthew Fitz Herbert, Thomas Basset, Alan Basset, Philip Daubeny, Robert de Roppeley, John Marshal, John Fitz Hugh, and other our loyal subjects:

Clause 1

In the first place we have granted to God, and by this present charter have confirmed for us and our heirs in perpetuity, that the English Church shall be free, and shall have her rights entire, and her liberties inviolate. That we wish this to be observed is evident that of our own free will, before the outbreak of the disputes before us and our barons, we granted and confirmed by charter the freedom of the elections, which is considered to be of the greatest necessity and importance to the English Church. . . .

Preamble to Clauses 2–63

To all free men of our kingdom, we have also granted, for us and for our heirs for ever, all the underwritten liberties, to be had and held by them and their heirs . . . forever.

. . .

Clause 62

All the ill will, hatreds, and bitterness, that have arisen between us and our subjects, clergy and laity, from the date of the quarrel, we have completely remitted and pardoned to every one. . . . We have caused letters patent to be made to the barons, as a testimony to this security and to the concessions set out above, over the seals of the lord Stephen, Archbishop of Canterbury, of the lord Henry, Archbishop of Dublin, the other bishops named above and Master Pandulf.

Clause 63

Wherefore it is our will and command that the English church shall be free, and that men in our kingdom shall have and keep all these liberties, rights and concessions, freely and quietly, fully and wholly, for themselves and their heirs, of us and our heirs, for ever.

Given under our hand in the meadow that is called Runnymede, between Windsor and Staines, on the fifteenth day of June, in the seventeenth year of our reign.

Innocent III to all Christ's Faithful, *Etsi Karissimus,* August 24, 1215

Innocent, bishop, servant of the servants of God, to all the faithful of Christ who will see this document, health and apostolic blessing.

Although our most well-beloved son in Christ, John, illustrious king of the English, violently offended God and the Church, in consequence of which we bound him with the knot of excommunication and subjected his kingdom to ecclesiastical interdict, nonetheless he himself, by the merciful inspiration of Him who does not will the death of the sinner but that he be converted and live, at length returned to his heart. Humbly he made satisfaction to God and the Church so that he not only gave recompense for losses and restitution of what had been taken but also granted plenary liberty to the English Church. Further when we lifted both our sentences, he granted his own kingdom of England and of Ireland to Blessed Peter and the Roman Church, receiving it from us as a fief under an annual return of 1,000 marks after he had sworn an oath of fidelity to us, as appears in his privilege furnished with a gold seal. Desiring to please Almighty God still further, he reverently put on the sign of the lifegiving cross, intending to go to the relief of the Holy Land and splendidly prepared to go.

But the enemy of the human race, who is always accustomed to envy good deeds, by his cunning arts stirred up against him the barons of England, so that those who helped him when he was offending the Church, now when he had converted and made satisfaction to the Church, perversely rose against him.

Matters of dispute had arisen between them, and several days had been fixed to treat of peace between them. Meanwhile, formal envoys had been sent to us. With them we had careful conversation and after full deliberation we wrote by them to the English archbishop and bishops, charging and commanding them to apply diligent zeal and effective effort to reformation, so that there would be true and full harmony between them. By apostolic authority they were to declare void all leagues and agreements which perchance had been formed from the time discord arose between the kingdom and the priesthood. By sentence of excommunication they were to forbid anyone to form such things in the future. They were prudently to warn and effectively to enjoin the magnates and nobles of England to strive to please the king himself by manifest proofs of devotion and humility; and then if they did decide to ask anything of him to implore him not arrogantly but humbly, maintaining the royal honor and rendering the customary services which they and their predecessors gave to him and his predecessors; for the king should not be despoiled of these without judgment. In this way they could more easily obtain what they sought. We by our letters asked the king, and warned him for the remission of his sins to treat the aforesaid magnates and nobles benignly and to attend mercifully to their just petitions, so that they, rejoicing with us, might recognize how he was changed to a better state by divine grace, and so that by this they and their heirs might serve him more readily and more loyally. We also asked him to grant them full security in coming, staying, and returning, so that if perchance they could not come to harmony, the dispute might be decided by their peers in his court according to the laws and customs of the kingdom.

But, before the envoys had returned with this provident and just command, the barons treated their oath of fidelity with utter contempt. If the king had unjustly injured them, they nonetheless should not have acted against him as if in their own case they were the judges and executors of judgment. Vassals, they publicly conspired against their lord; and knights, they conspired against the king. They not only presumed to make war against him; they joined with his most open enemies; and they occupied and devastated his lands and even invaded the city of London, which is the seat of the kingdom and was treacherously surrendered to them.

Meanwhile, the aforesaid envoys returned to England, and the king offered them the fullness of justice according to the form of our mandate. The barons spurned this completely and began to stretch out their hands to worse things. Hence the king himself appealed to our tribunal and offered to show them justice before us, to whom judgment of this case belonged by reason of our lordship. This they wholly rejected. Then he offered that four prudent men chosen by him and by them should, together with us, end the dispute which had arisen with them. He promised that before anything else he would repeal all abuses whatever which had been introduced into England in his time. But they did not deign to accept this. Finally, the king declared to them that since the lordship of the kingdom belonged to the Roman Church, he himself could not and ought not to change anything affecting it to our prejudice without our special mandate. Hence he again appealed to our tribunal and put himself and his kingdom with all his honor and right under Apostolic protection. When he made no progress in this way, he demanded that the archbishop and bishops execute our mandate, defend the rights of the Roman Church, and safeguard him according to the form of the privilege conceded to those signed with the cross. When they wished to do nothing of the sort, he saw himself almost bereft of all advice and aid, and he did not dare deny what they dared to ask. Hence, compelled by the force and fear which could fall on even the steadiest man, he accepted a settlement with them which is not only vile and shameful but also illegal and unjust in undue diminution and derogation of both his right and his honor.

But the Lord has spoken to us in the Prophet: "I have set you over peoples and kingdoms to root out and to destroy, to build and to plant"; and by another Prophet: "Loose the bonds of wickedness, undo the oppressive bundles." Therefore we refuse to ignore audacity of such great malignity in contempt of the Apostolic See, to the loss of royal rights, the shame of the English people, and the serious endangering of the whole enterprise of the Crucified, which would surely be imminent unless we by our authority entirely revoked things extorted in this way from such a just prince, signed with the cross, even if he wanted to observe them. On behalf of Almighty God, Father and Son and Holy Spirit, and by the authority also of the blessed Apostles Peter and Paul, and by our own authority, with the common advice of our brethren, we utterly reject and condemn this sort of settlement. Under threat of anathema we forbid that the aforesaid king dare to observe it and that the barons with their accomplices ask him to observe it. We completely annul and hold void both the Charter and the obligations and guarantees made on its account or flowing from it, so that never shall they have any force.

Let it be lawful for no man to infringe this document of annulment and prohibition or temerariously dare to oppose it. If anyone should presume to attempt this, let him know he will incur the wrath of Almighty God and His Blessed Apostles Peter and Paul.

Given at Anagni, August 24, in the eighteenth year of our pontificate.

3. THE LAWS AND CUSTOMS OF ENGLAND

In the same generation in which Magna Carta was reissued, work was begun on what was to be for the next 500 years the most remarkable treatise on English law—*De legibus et consuetudinibus Angliae (The Laws and Customs of England).* Its "prime mover" was William de Ralegh (Samuel E. Thorne, Introduction, *The Laws and Customs of England,* 1970, 3, xxxvi). Ralegh in the 1220s was the law clerk of the royal judge Martin de Pateshull, and in 1229 he became a royal judge himself. In 1234 Henry III made him Chief Justice. At this time he possessed "the talent of friendship with the king" (Robert Grosseteste to William de Ralegh, 1236, Rolls Series 25, 94). He represented the king in a request to magnates of the realm for a contribution of property. He was not afraid in 1234 to hold null an outlawry passed by the king (*Bracton's Notebook,* ed. F. W. Maitland, Case 857).

Ralegh's career changed dramatically in 1239 when he was elected bishop of Norwich and left judicial office. In 1240 the monks of Winchester chose him as bishop of Winchester. Henry had his own candidate for the see, and there ensued a battle between king and former counselor which, while it never reached the depths of Henry II's quarrel with Becket, showed that Henry III could be rough. In the end Ralegh was vindicated by litigation before the pope and took possession of his see in 1244; the king let himself be reconciled.

The treatise that Ralegh presumably began as a law clerk and continued as a judge (the great bulk of the cases are from the 1220s and 1230s) passed into the hands of Ralegh's protégé, Henri de Bratton, who became a royal judge in 1245. Bratton added to the manuscript, revised it a little, and left it unpublished on his death in 1268. Nine years later his heirs circulated copies, and it began its career as a legal authority attributed to Bratton. In 1569 the first printed edition erroneously fixed the spelling of the author's name as Bracton.

The treatise for our purposes is of great interest in its bland fusion of canon law, Roman law, cases, and customs as together constituting the common law of England. "Interpenetration" was still going on. The authors did not care what the sources of the rules were if they believed the rules were current in England. In this way, for example, the canon law on cooperation in homicide—set out by decretal letters of Alexander III to cover the accomplices in Thomas Becket's death—became here the common law of England.

Divine sanctions, as will be seen below, are used as the chief deterrent to bribery. Their description in Book I is taken bodily from a popular tract written by Innocent III as a young cardinal, *The Misery of the Human Condition,* Book III, chapter 20. For Ralegh-Bratton the terrors of the Last Judgment are as integral to the English legal system as a writ for appointing justices. The heavenly sanction is the only effective insurer of the integrity of the judge. God's punishments are also a chief, though not the only, sanction against a lawless king.

Faith in a future accounting to the Lord and papal case law were no strangers to Ralegh and Bratton, both clerics, both holding ecclesiastical appointments that gave them independent incomes. They incorporated their beliefs into English law as easily as the king used them to provide royal justice. But there were also tensions of which they were acutely aware. They made express acknowledgment of the two different jurisdictions of the crown and the priesthood. They tacitly ignored areas where canon law clashed with English custom.

Three examples will suffice:

1. Canon law provided an elaborate system for determining the existence of a marriage, of which the Church was taken to be the only judge. Ralegh-Bratton, in some cases involving the existence of marriage, cut off all appeal to the pope (*Laws and Customs* 3, 372–373; 4, 302–305).

2. Canon law expressly held that if a child was born from intercourse outside of marriage to parents otherwise free to marry, their subsequent marriage legitimated the child (Alexander III to Bartholomew, bishop of Exeter, *Decretals of Gregory IX* 4, 17, 6, *Tanta est vis matrimonii*). English law expressly held such a child to be a bastard, incapable of inheriting as a lawful heir (*Laws and Customs* 4, 294). Robert Grosseteste, the outspoken bishop of Lincoln, wrote Ralegh reminding him of his duty to follow canon law on this point. Grosseteste thought the divine law also acknowledged the child's legitimacy. He threatened Ralegh with

damnation at the Last Judgment if he did not conform (Grosseteste to Ralegh, 1236, Rolls Series 25, 94). But Ralegh stuck to the hard laws and customs of his country.

3. Canon law forbade a cleric to participate in any way in a judgment of blood. Innocent III's Fourth Lateran Council in 1215 had legislated this prohibition for the universal church (*Conciliorum oecumenicorum decreta*, ed. J. Alberigo, 1973, c. 18). Ralegh, like many other bishops, enacted the prohibition in legislation for his own diocese of Norwich (F. W. Powicke and Christopher R. Cheney, *Councils and Synods with Other Documents Relating to the English Church*, 1964, I, 348). Nonetheless, when *Laws and Customs* (2, 340) treated of the death penalty, nothing was said as to the disqualification of clerics to pronounce it. Both Ralegh and Bratton as royal judges must have had to pronounce it many times (James B. Given, *Society and Homicide in Thirteenth-Century England*, 1977, p. 101). Their obligation to the crown was silently permitted to override their obligation to the Church.

No ideological formula, no neat allotment of the roles of the prince and the pope, no clear logic govern the way Ralegh-Bratton handle the two spheres of the secular and the spiritual. They did not use Magna Carta, fresh and comprehensive though it was, to determine what was "the liberty of the Church." Their one true guide was experience, largely their own experience which had been molded by custom. The spiritual and secular interpenetrated. Experienced ecclesiastics who were also royal judges were able to decide what the relation should be.

Ralegh-Bratton, *The Laws and Customs of England,* Introduction

. . . The purpose of this undertaking is that quarrels may be quieted and vices repressed and peace and justice kept in the kingdom. But it must be set under ethics as if it were moral science, because it treats of morals. . . .

Let no fool or ignoramus presume to ascend the judgment seat which is as if the throne of God, lest for light be put darkness and for darkness light, and in the manner of a madman with ignorant hand he strike the innocent with the sword and free the injurious; lest he fall from on high as from the throne of God—he who began to fly before he had wings. And if one should judge and be made a judge, let him take care for himself lest by judging perversely and against the laws for prayer or price, for the stipend of a small temporal gain, he presume to purchase for himself the sorrow of eternal lamentation.

What the Punishment Is for Him Who Judges Evilly

And let him not on the day of the Lord's wrath feel Him avenging, Him who said, "Vengeance is mine, and I shall reciprocate"—on that day when the kings and princes of the earth shall weep and moan when they see the Son of Man because of terror of his tortures where gold and silver will not free them. Who may not fear that trial in which the Lord will be accuser, advocate, and judge? From his judgment there cannot be appeal, because the Father has given all judgment to the Son. He closes and no one opens. He opens and no one closes. Strict judgment! There men shall render account not only as to deeds but even of every idle word they have spoken.

Who therefore will be able to flee the anger that is to come? For the Son of Man shall send his angels who will gather from the kingdom of God all scandals and those who do wickedness and make of them bundles to be burnt. They shall send them into the furnace of fire. There, there will be weeping and gnashing of teeth, groans and moans, outcries, lamentations and agonies, shrieking and screeching, fear and trembling, suffering and travail, fire and stink, darkness and dread, bitterness and boisterousness, calamity and craving, distress and dejection, oblivion and orderlessness, torturings and tearings, torments and terrors, hunger and thirst, frigidity and heat, brimstone and fire burning forever and ever.

Let each one beware of that judgment where the Judge is frighteningly strict, unbearably severe, immeasurably offended, violently angered; His judgment not commutable; the prison inescapable; the tortures without end, without intermission; the torturers, who never tire and never pity, horrible. Fear unsettles; conscience condemns; thoughts reproach; it is not permitted to flee. Hence Blessed Augustine, "My great sins are too many! When anyone has God as just Judge and his own conscience as the witness, he need fear nothing except his own case." . . .

Persons

. . . The king in his kingdom has no peer because otherwise he would lose command; for a peer has no power over a peer. Much less ought he to have a superior or one more powerful than he, because then he would be inferior to those subject to him, and inferiors cannot be peers with superiors. But the king himself ought to be under no man but under God and under the law; for the law makes the king.

Let the king therefore render to the law what the law renders to him, to wit, domination and power. For there is no king where will and not law dominates. And because he ought to be under the law since he is the vicar of God, he is clearly close to the likeness of Jesus Christ, whose vice-regent he is on earth. The true mercifulness of God chose this most powerful way to destroy the work of the devil, although for the ineffable recovery of the human race many ways were open to Him; and so He used not the power of force but the reason of justice. And so He willed to be under the law that He might buy back those who were under the law. He did not will to use strength but judgment. So also the Blessed Procreator of God, the Virgin Mary, Mother of the Lord, who by a singular privilege was above the law, nonetheless in order to give an example of humility did not refuse to be subjected to established laws. So then the king—lest his power stay unbridled.

Therefore there ought not to be anyone in his kingdom greater in attention to the law. But he ought to be the last or as if the last in receiving judgment if he seeks it. If it is sought from him, although a writ does not run against him, there will be place for a petition to correct and amend his act. If he will not do it, it is sufficient penalty for him that he wait for God the Avenger. . . .

Actions

What Judgment Is, and In What the Duty of a Judge Consists, Namely Three Things

We must see, therefore, what a judgment is. And it must be known that in any action whatsoever a judgment is the act of three persons—the judge, the plaintiff, and the defendant. Persons of this sort are to be understood broadly, to wit, that there be at least two persons between whom the dispute lies and at least a third who judges.

It is said: "Look at what you do, for you do not exercise the judgment of man but of God, and that which you judge shall redound upon you. Let the fear of the Lord be with you and do everything with care. For with our Lord God there is no wickedness nor taking up of persons nor desire for offerings which blind the eyes of the wise and twist the words of the just," as is read in Ecclesiasticus, Chapter 20: "Courtesy-presents and gifts blind the eyes of judges."

He who said gifts or offerings meant every kind of offering: (1) an offering from the hand—that sort of thing is something corporeal that is offered; (2) an offering from the tongue, which is a flattering and fawning petition, a public proclamation of praise, a symphony celebrating vain glory; (3) an offering from obedience, which is service bestowed and received in return for which the straightness of judgment is twisted. Nor does an offering from blood kinship merit being called anything less when for the blood line the line of straight judgment is made crooked; for, in this, blood responds to blood.

Offerings of these kinds are assuredly described by the name of "defilements," and human law inflicts a serious punishment on the judge corrupted by defilements, that is, by dirty offerings: if a judge or justice contracts with a litigant for a certain part of the lawsuit, the *Codex* at the Julian law, *Repetundae,* says, "Let all triers of cases and judges keep their hands from money, and let them not think another's lawsuit to be booty for them. The final judge in even private litigation who is the same as a merchant shall be compelled to undergo the loss established by law." The loss or penalty shall be that he shall restore what he receives fourfold, as the *Codex* says at the very end of the same law; for there they are bound to repay the fourfold whether they received something during their administration or afterward, whatever the title or veil when they pretend that a title of gift or sale has intervened. In truth, he is defiled whom the truth of judgment does not adorn. Where favoritism or hatred, fear, envy or reward induce its contrary, the truth of judgment falls into the courtyard. As to this it can be said, "Woe to that defiled man through whom truth became defiled in the swamps of the courtyards." He shall not be numbered among the blessed of whom it is said, "Blessed is he who shakes his hands free from every offering."

Nonetheless, one must not abstain from every offering. It is most avaricious and most vile to receive from everyone and everywhere. But to receive from no one will be inhuman. A friend may receive from a friend at the sole prompting of friendship and love.

The Power of the Judge

It is necessary that he who judges have jurisdiction, ordinary or delegated, if his judgments are to be valid. And it does not suffice that he have jurisdiction unless he have the power of coercion. If he could not require execution of his judgments, they would be illusory. An ordinary judge does not have jurisdiction and execution in every case, for laws are separate and limited.

The Division of the Jurisdictions of the Priesthood and the Kingdom

There are spiritual cases in which a secular judge has neither power to try them nor (since he lacks power of coercion) execution. In these cases the judgment belongs to the ecclesiastical judges who rule and defend the priesthood.

There are also secular cases whose judgment belongs to the kings and princes who defend the kingdom. Ecclesiastical judges must not meddle with them, for their laws or jurisdictions are limited and separate, except when sword ought to help sword. For there is a great difference between the priesthood and the kingdom.

The Regulation of the Jurisdictions of the Kingdom . . . (Nothing for the Present as to the Priest)

Since nothing as to the regulation of the priesthood belongs to this treatise, we must see about those things that belong to the kingdom. Who, primarily and powerfully, can and ought to judge? And it must be known that it is the king himself, and no other, if he alone is sufficient. To this he is bound by power of an oath; for at his coronation he must in an oath offered in the name of Jesus Christ promise the people subject to him these three things:

The Oath Which the King must Make at his Coronation

First, that he will command, and as his strength allows work, that for the Church of God and for the whole Christian people true peace be observed in all his time. Second, that he will prevent rapacity and all wickedness to men of every degree. Third, that in all judgments he will command equity and mercy, so that a clement and merciful God may grant him His mercy and by his justice all may enjoy a firm peace.

FOUR

"Bound That I Should Not Obey My Prince": The Contested Supremacy of Conscience, 1250–1560

1. THOMAS AQUINAS ON FORCE AND FAITH

FIDES—FAITH—IS THE CENTRAL VALUE Thomas is defending here. Modern translators translate *fides* in a feudal relation as "fealty." They translate *fides* in marriage as "fidelity." They translate *fides* in religion as "belief." They lose the triple tie that binds the analogues of the concept together. Thomas is for keeping faith to an overlord, faith to a spouse, faith in God. The same principle that justifies the Church in making the married or members of a religious order keep their vows justifies making those who have accepted the faith keep it. The *infidelis*—the infidel, the unfaithful—is to be forced back into the fold.

Thomas Aquinas has the title "the Angelic Doctor," and he writes like an angel—that is, with a clarity, sobriety, and dispassionateness that suggest a being outside this world. Nonetheless, what he has to teach on religion and governmental power is far from angelic, and it is possible to see in his position the convergence of various earthly currents. First, he came from a family of seven children, of whom he was the youngest boy; he always felt secure, he never felt persecuted. Second, he came from a family of feudal lords who ruled Roccasecca under the emperor; fealty was a high value. Third, he had spent years in the neighborhood of the papal court and was the friend of Pope Clement IV and Pope Urban IV: he had a strong regard for the papal government and the canon law. Fourth, intellectually speaking most important, he had become an admirer of Aristotle and at the very time that he was writing the Second Part of the *Summa Theologiae (S.T.)* quoted below, he was also commenting on Aristotle's *Nicomachean Ethics*.

From Aristotle came Thomas's language of whole and part. Human beings are parts, the community is a whole. The parts are, naturally, subordinated to the whole. The parts can be sacrificed to the whole. With this vocabulary, Thomas defends the death penalty in general, arguing that the community has the right to lop off a putrid member (*S.T.* 2–2, 64, 2). The Christian view that human destiny transcends the state is somehow lost from his account.

Aristotle helps to explain his intellectual stance, but Aristotle had nothing to say on heresy. Important here was what was accepted by other authorities he acknowledged: Augustine above all, and the canon law found in Gratian and Gregory IX's *Decretals.* Authority as such was not, however, decisive. As will be seen in the argument below, there were venerable teachers— the Gospel itself, never a small authority—that pointed to more merciful and more magnanimous conclusions. Practice was decisive. In the world Thomas knew, heretics were sent to the flames. The most chilling statement, perhaps, in what follows—startling in a religion built on the imitation of God—is that where forgiveness of heretics is concerned, the Church "cannot imitate God."

Another reflection of the accepted environment is the statement that "the Jews are the slaves of the Church," made as part of a legal justification for the canon that directs the gratuitous manumission of a slave who becomes a Christian, whose owners are Jewish. The Church, Thomas argues, can dispose of Jewish property this way because the Jews themselves are her slaves. The argument is legal, but Thomas provides no legal citations, and no canon embodied this precise teaching. Nonetheless, the statement reflected a common belief of medieval Christendom and can be found in decretal letters of such thirteenth-century popes as Innocent III and Gregory IX (see Edward A. Synan, *The Popes and the Jews in the Middle Ages,* 1965, 108 and 226; for the two relevant decretals of Innocent III, translated by Synan, 221–229, see Innocent III, *Epistolae, PL* 215, 501, and 1291). The idea was never taken to its logical legal conclusion with Christians or ecclesiastics feeling free to sell Jews as chattels, but it undoubtedly contributed to the oppressive social conditions in which Jews were often subjected to extortion and pillage.

Thomas, aged about forty-five, and a master of the University of Paris, wrote what follows at Paris between 1270 and 1272. What he had to say on any topic proved to be extraordinarily influential. Canonized in 1323, he was named a Doctor of the Church in 1567. Pope Clement VIII declared that "no error is to be found in his works." As recently as the *Code of Canon Law* (1917), canon 1366.2 prescribed that all priests were to be educated "according to the method, doctrine and principles of the Angelic Doctor."

The following text is a translation of the Latin of the Leonine edition of the *Summa Theologiae.* For further reading in English, the Blackfriars translation of the 1970s is recommended.

Summa Theologiae 2–2

Q. 10 Infidelity in General

Article 8. Are infidels to be forced to the Faith? I proceed to the eighth article:

1. It appears that infidels are in no way to be forced to the faith. For it is said in Matthew [13:28] that the slaves asked the householder in whose field the tares were sown, "Shall we go and gather them?" and he replied, "No, lest in gathering up the tares, you eradicate the wheat with them" On this Chrysostom says [*PG* 58:477]: "The Lord says these things to forbid killings. For it is necessary not to kill the heretics, because if you kill them you must kill many of the saints at the same time." Therefore it seems by a parallel reason that other infidels are not to be forced to the faith.

2. Moreover, the *Decretum* [Gratian, 45, 5] reads as follows: "The holy synod commands as to the Jews that force is henceforth not to be inflicted on any of them to make them believe." Therefore by parallel reason other infidels are not to be compelled to the faith.

3. Further, Augustine says [*On John,* Tract 26, c.2, *PL* 35, 1607]: A man can do other things unwillingly, but "he cannot believe except willingly." But the will cannot be forced. Therefore it appears that infidels are not to be forced to the faith.

4. Further, Ezekiel in the person of God says [18:23]: "I do not will the death of sinners." But we ought to conform our will to the divine will, as said above. Therefore we too should not will that infidels be killed.

But to the contrary is what is said in Luke [14:23]: "Go out into the highways and hedges and force them to enter that my house may be filled." But men enter by faith into the house of God, that is, into Holy Church. Therefore, some are to be forced to the faith.

Reply: It must be said that some infidels have not received the faith, such as the gentiles and the Jews; and such are in no way to be forced to the faith so that they believe, because to believe depends on the will. They are nonetheless to be forced by the faithful, if they can, not to impede the faith by blasphemies or evil persuasions or open persecutions. And on this account the faithful of Christ frequently wage war against infidels, not to force them to believe (because even if they conquered them and held them captive they should leave them in their liberty as to whether they wish to believe), but on this account, to force them not to impede the faith of Christ.

But there are other infidels who once received the faith and professed it, such as heretics and every apostate; and such are to be forced even physically to fulfill what they promised and to hold to what they once received.

1. To the first objection, it must be said that by that text some have understood that not the excommunication but the killing of heretics is forbidden, as is clear from the cited text of Chrysostom. And so Augustine to Vincentius says in regard to himself [PL 33, 330]: "This was my first opinion, that no one should be forced to the unity of Christ, but we should act by words and fight by argument. . . . But my opinion was overcome not by the words of those contradicting it but by the example of facts. . . . [For terror of the law was so advantageous that many say], "Thank the Lord, who has broken our chains." Therefore when the Lord says, "Let them both grow until the harvest," how it is to be understood appears from what follows: "lest perchance in gathering up the tares you eradicate the wheat with them." This sufficiently shows, as Augustine says, "when that danger is not present—that is, when the crime of anyone is known to everyone and appears hateful so that he has no defenders or none such by whom a schism could occur, let severe discipline not sleep."

2. To the second objection, it must be said that Jews, if in no way they accept the faith, are in no way to be forced to the faith. But if they have received the faith, they must by necessity be forced to retain the faith, as is said in the same chapter.

3. To the third objection, it must be said that to vow depends on the will, to fulfill the vow is a matter of necessity. In this way to accept the faith depends on the will, but to keep it, once accepted, is a matter of necessity. And therefore heretics are to be forced to keep the faith. For Augustine says to Count Boniface [*The Correction of the Donatists, supra,* I]: "What is that these men are accustomed to cry, 'to believe or not to believe is free? On whom does Christ inflict force?' Let them recognize in Paul Christ first forcing and then teaching. . . ."

4. To the fourth objection, it must be said as Augustine says in the same epistle [PL 33:807]: "None of us wants any heretic to perish. . . . But the house of David did not deserve to have peace until Absalom, David's son, was extinguished in the war he waged against his father. . . ." Thus too the Catholic Church, if by the loss of some she gathers up others, cures the sorrow of her motherly heart by the liberation of so many peoples.

. . .

Article 10. Can infidels have authority or dominion over the faithful?

[He holds that if the faithful are not subject to infidels, the Church will not permit them to become subject to them. But if the infidels already possess such authority it continues unless the Church determines to the contrary.]

But this the Church sometimes does and sometimes does not. As to those infidels who are subjected in temporal subjection to the Church and her members, the Church has decreed this law, that a slave of Jews, when he becomes a Christian, shall be at once liberated from slavery without any price being paid, if he had been a slave from birth. But if he were purchased for commerce, then within three months he should be offered for sale [Gregory IX, *Decretals* 5, 6, 1]. Nor does the Church do any injury by this law, for the Jews themselves are the slaves of the Church, so she can dispose of their property, just as secular princes issue many laws about their subjects in favor of liberty. But as to infidels who are temporally not subject to the Church or her members, the Church has not decreed the said law, although legally she could establish it; and she acts in this way to avoid scandal, just as the Lord showed He could excuse himself from the tax because the sons are free, but yet He ordered the tax to be paid to avoid scandal. . . .

Article 11. Are the rites of infidels to be tolerated?
3. Further, the sin of infidelity is the gravest, as was said above. But other sins such as adultery, theft, and things of this sort are not tolerated but punished by law. Therefore the rites of infidels should not be tolerated.

But to the contrary is what Gregory says in the *Decretum* concerning the Jews [of Naples] [Gratian, D. 45,3]: "Let them have free permission to observe and celebrate all their festivals, just as they themselves till now and their forefathers for ages past have held them."

Reply: It must be said that human rule is derived from divine rule and ought to imitate it. But although God is almighty and supremely good, yet He permits some evils to happen in the universe which He could forbid, because if they were removed greater goods would be taken away or even worse evils would follow. Therefore those who preside in human government in the same way rightly tolerate some evils lest some goods be taken away or even some worse things be incurred.
[Thomas goes on to argue that Jewish ceremonies are related to Christian ones as a kind of foreshadowing and so should be tolerated. He continues:]

But the rites of other infidels, which bear nothing true or useful, are not to be tolerated in the same way except perhaps to avoid some evil, to wit, scandal or a division that could arise from this or an obstacle to the salvation of those who would gradually be converted to the faith if they were tolerated. On this account the Church has sometimes tolerated the rites of even heretics and pagans when there was a great multitude of infidels.

Q. 11   Heresy

Article 3. Should Heretics Be Tolerated?
1. It seems that heretics should be tolerated. For the Apostle says [2 Tim 2:24]: "The servant of God must be mild, correcting with modesty those who resist the truth so that God may grant them repentance and they will know the truth and escape from the snares of the devil." But if heretics are not tolerated but handed over to death, the opportunity of repenting will be taken from them. Therefore this seems to be contrary to the commandment of the Apostle.

2. Moreover, what is necessary to the Church is to be tolerated. But heresies are necessary in the Church. For the Apostle says [1 Cor 11:19]: "It is necessary that there be heresies in order that those who are approved may be manifest among you." Therefore it seems that heretics should be tolerated.

3. Further, the Lord commanded his servants to let the tares grow until the harvest [Matt 13:30], that is, until the end of the world, as it is explained there. But by tares are meant heretics, according to the exposition of the saints. These heretics are to be tolerated.

But to the contrary is what the Apostle says: "After the first and second correction, avoid the heretical man. You know that one of this sort is perverted [Titus 3:10]."

Reply: It must be said that two things about heretics are to be considered: one on their part, the other on the part of the Church. On their part there is sin for which they deserve not only to be separated by excommunication from the Church but even by death to be excluded from the world. For it is much more serious to corrupt the faith through which the soul lives than to counterfeit money through which temporal life is supported. Hence, if counterfeiters of money or other malefactors are justly handed over at once to death by secular princes, so much more heretics, once they are convicted by heresy, cannot only be excommunicated but justly killed.

But on the part of the Church there is mercy for the conversion of the errant. And therefore she does not condemn at once but "after the first and second correction," as the Apostle says. Then, if he is still found pertinacious, the Church, no longer hoping for his conversion, provides for the welfare of others, separating him from the Church by sentence of excommunication; and she further leaves him to secular judgment to be eliminated from the world by death. For Jerome says, and the *Decretum* has it [Gratian, C. 24, 3, 16]: "Putrid flesh is to be cut off, and the scabby sheep is to be driven off from the fold, lest the whole house, mass, body, and flock burn, become corrupt, putrify, and die. Arius was one spark in Alexandria, but when he was not at once crushed, his flame devastated the whole world."

1. To the first objection, it must therefore be said that it is modesty to correct the first and second times. But if he refuses to return, he is then held as one perverted, as is clear in the text of the Apostle that was cited.

2. To the second objection, it must be said that the usefulness arising from heresy happens beyond the heretics' intention, that is, the steadiness of the faithful is proved, as the Apostle says, and we shake off sluggishness, more attentively searching the divine Scriptures, as Augustine says [*About Genesis, Against the Manichees, PL* 34, 173]. But their intention is to corrupt the faith, and this is the maximum harm. And therefore we must look at that which is per se from their intention, so that they are excluded; rather than at that which is beyond their intention, that they may be borne with.

3. To the third objection, it must be said as it is put in the *Decretum* [Gratian, C. 24, 3, 37]: "Excommunication is one thing, eradication is another." For someone is excommunicated for this purpose, as the Apostle says, that his spirit may become saved on the day of the Lord. If nonetheless heretics are totally eradicated by death, it is not contrary to the commandment of the Lord, which is to be understood of that case where the tares cannot be extirpated without extirpation of the wheat, as was said above about unbelievers in general.

Article 4. Shall those returning from heresy be received by the Church? . . .

2. Further, the Lord commands Peter to forgive his sinning brother not only seven times but up to seventy times seven [Matt. 18:22]. . . .

But to the contrary, the decretal *Ad Abolendam, Heretics,* c. 9, [Gregory IX, *Decretals* 5, 7, 9]: If any, after abjuring error, shall be found to have relapsed into the heresy they have abjured, they shall be left to secular judgment.

Reply: . . . If returning heretics were always received so as to be preserved in their lives and other temporal goods, this could be to the prejudice of the salvation of others: both because if they relapsed again they would infect others, and because if they escaped without punishment, others would more securely lapse again into heresy. . . .

1. To the first objection, it must therefore be said that in the judgment of God those who return are always received: for God is the searcher of hearts and He knows who are truly returning. But the Church cannot imitate this. She presumes that they did not truly return who after they had been received again relapsed. Therefore she does not deny them a way of salvation but she does not safeguard them from the peril of death.

2. To the second objection, it must be said that the Lord is speaking to Peter about forgiving a sin committed against oneself, which must always be forgiven so that the returning brother is spared. But it is not to be understood as to a sin against a neighbor

or against God, which, as Jerome says [*Glossa ordinaria* on Matthew 18:15], "is not in our discretion to forgive." In this matter a measure is set by law according to what fits the honor of God and the advantage of our neighbors.

3. To the third objection, it must be said that other infidels who have never received the faith, when they are converted to the faith, have not yet shown any sign of unsteadiness about the faith as do relapsed heretics. And so there is no similarity in the character of the two cases.

Q. 12 Apostasy

Article 1. Does apostasy belong to infidelity?
[Among kinds of infidelity, Thomas distinguished heresy, a sin committed by those "professing the faith of Christ" (q. 11, art. 1) and "apostasy," a sin committed by one "withdrawing from the faith" (q. 12, art. 1). As to the latter he concluded that in an absolute sense, apostasy is a species of infidelity; it is called "the apostasy of treachery."]

Article 2. Because of apostasy, does a prince lose rule over his subjects so that they are not bound to obey him?

1. I proceed in this way to the second article:
It appears that on account of apostasy a prince does not lose rule over his subjects so that they are not bound to obey him, for Ambrose says, and the *Decretum* has it [Gratian, C. 11, q. 3, c. 94]: "The Emperor Julian, although he was an apostate, still had under him Christian soldiers, who, when he told them, 'Fight for the defense of the commonwealth,' obeyed him." Therefore, on account of the apostasy of a prince, subjects are not absolved from his rule. . . .

But to the contrary is what Gregory VII says [Gratian, C. 11, q. 6, c. 4]:"We, holding to the statutes of our holy predecessors, by Apostolic authority absolve from their oath those who are bound by fidelity or oath to the excommunicated, and we forbid them in every way to observe fidelity until the latter make satisfaction." But as a decretal says, apostates such as heretics are excommunicated. Therefore, princes apostasizing from the faith are not to be obeyed.

Reply: . . . But it does not belong to the Church to punish infidelity in those who have never received the faith, according to the Apostle's dictum, "What is it to me to judge those who are outside?" [1 Cor. 5:12]. But she can punish by a sentence the infidelity of those who have received the faith. And they are conveniently punished by providing that they cannot rule over believing subjects, for this could tend to great corruption of the faith: as has been said [Prov 6:14], "An apostate man plots evil with his heart and sows discord," intending to separate men from the faith. And so as soon as anyone is declared by a sentence to be excommunicate on account of apostasy from the faith, his subjects are *ipso facto* absolved from his rule and the oath of fidelity by which they were bound to him. . . .

3. To the third objection, it must be said that apostasy from the faith totally separates a man from God, as has been said; which does not happen in any other sin.

Thomas scarcely emerges as a liberal, but on one important point his commitment to reason and the primacy of reason in moral conduct leads to what was liberal in comparison to the dominant opinion of the day. Alexander of Hales—a teacher at Paris who might justly be regarded as the first English jurisprudent—taught that an erring conscience did not oblige. An erring conscience was contrary to the law of God; it could not be right to follow it (Alexander, *"De conscientia,"* in Odon Lottin, *Psychologie et morale aux XIIe et XIIIe siècles,* 1948, 2, 356–357. Thomas, as will be seen, teaches to the contrary that a man must follow his conscience.

Taken seriously, this doctrine carried the seed of religious liberty. Thomas took away nearly all that he had established by arguing in the next article, below, that an erring conscience, although it must be followed, did not always excuse from sin: the error could be voluntary or negligent and therefore sinful. He nonetheless left open the possibility that the error, whatever it was, could be without fault. His illustrations suggest that he thinks a mistake of fact will excuse, a mistake of law will not.

But nothing in his analysis confines an excusable mistake to a mistake of fact. A mistake of law, even a mistake of faith, would seem in some cases to be as involuntary as the hypothetical case he supposes of a man mistaking another woman for his wife. If mistake can be involuntary, and if error is excusable, and if a man must follow his conscience, however mistaken, with what justice can he be punished if he is conscientiously a heretic or apostate?

Thomas did not engage in that kind of reasoning. But contemporaries saw where his thought led. The Franciscan Matthaeus of Aquasparta objected that if Thomas were right, "the heretics would act correctly in doing what they think they ought to do" (Joseph Lecler, *Toleration and the Reformation,* English trans. 1960, 1, 99–100). Lecler, a historian of the idea of tolerance, concludes that Thomas's position was of real importance for the future (ibid. 1, 99).

Summa Theologiae 1–2

Q. 19   The Goodness and the Malice of the Interior Act of the Will

Article 5. Whether Erring Reason is Binding

1. It appears that will differing from erring reason is not bad. For, as has been said, reason is the rule of the human will inasmuch as reason is derived from the eternal law. But erring reason is not derived from the eternal law. Therefore, erring reason is not the rule of a human will; therefore, the will is not bad if it differs from erring reason.

2. Further, according to Augustine [Sermon 62, c. 8, *PL* 38, 421] the commandment of an inferior power does not bind if it is contrary to the commandment of a superior power, as if the proconsul ordered something which the emperor prohibits. But erring reason sometimes proposes something that is against the commandment of a superior, namely God, Whose power is supreme. Therefore, the dictate of erring reason does not bind; therefore, the will is not bad if it differs from erring reason.

3. Further, every bad will is reduced to some species of malice. But the will differing from erring reason cannot be reduced to some species of malice—for example, if erring reason errs in this, that it dictates that one is to commit fornication, the will of him who did not will to fornicate could not be reduced to any malice. Therefore, will differing from erring reason is not bad.

But, to the contrary, as was said in the First Part, conscience is nothing else but the application of knowledge to some action. But knowledge is in the reason. Therefore, will differing from erring reason is against conscience. But also the will is bad; for it is said by the Apostle in Romans [14:3], "All which is not from faith is sin," that is, all that is against conscience. Therefore, will differing from erring reason is bad.

Reply: It must be said that since conscience is in a certain way the dictate of reason—for, as has been said, it is a certain application of knowledge to action—it is the same thing to ask, "Whether will differing from erring reason is bad" as to ask, "Whether erring conscience binds."

About this some [*e.g.,* Alexander of Hales] have distinguished three kinds of acts—some are generically good, some are indifferent, some are generically bad. They say, therefore, that if reason or conscience dictates something to be done that is generically good, there is no error there; similarly, if it dictates something not to be done that is generically bad, by the same reason the good is commanded and the bad prohibited. But if reason or conscience dictates to someone that he is bound to do from command those things that are in themselves bad, or that those things that are in themselves good are prohibited, it will be an erring reason or conscience. Similarly, if reason or conscience dictates to someone that what is in itself indifferent (for instance, to pick up a stalk from the earth) is prohibited or commanded, it will be an erring reason or conscience. They say, therefore, that reason or conscience erring about indifferent things, whether commanding or prohibiting, is binding, so that will differing from such erring reason will be bad and a sin. But erring reason or conscience commanding those things that are not themselves bad or prohibiting those that are not themselves good and necessary to salvation does not bind; hence, in such matters the will differing from erring reason or conscience is not bad.

But this is said irrationally, for in indifferent things the will differing from erring reason or conscience is bad in some way because of the object on which the goodness or badness of the will depends—not because of the object according to its own nature but according to what by accident is apprehended by the reason as good to be done or bad to be avoided. And because the object of the will is that which is proposed by the reason, as has been said, in that something is proposed by the reason as bad, the will, as long as it is borne toward that, takes on the character of the bad.

This happens not only in indifferent things but even in those good or bad in themselves. For not only that which is indifferent can accidentally take on the character of good or bad, but that which is good can take on the character of bad, or that which is bad can take on the character of good because of the apprehension of the reason.

For example, to abstain from fornication is a certain good, yet the will is not borne to this good except as it is proposed by reason. If, therefore, it is proposed as bad by erring reason the will is borne toward this under the character of bad. Hence, the will will be bad because it wills the bad, not indeed what is bad in itself, but what is accidentally bad because of the apprehension of the reason.

Similarly, to believe in Christ is good in itself and necessary for salvation, but the will is not borne toward this except according to what is proposed by reason. Hence, if it is proposed by reason as bad, the will will be borne to this as bad, not because it is bad in itself, but because it is accidently bad from the apprehension of reason. That is why the Philosopher [Aristotle] says in the *Ethics* [7, 1 and 2] that strictly speaking one is lacking in self-control who does not follow right reason, but accidentally he is lacking in self-control who does not follow false reason.

Hence it must be said absolutely that every will differing from reason, whether right or erring, is always bad.

1. To the first objection, it must be said that the judgment of erring reason, although it is not derived from God, yet is proposed by erring reason as true. Consequently it is derived from God, from Whom is every truth.

2. To the second objection, it must be said that the statement of Augustine has place when it is recognized that an inferior power is commanding something against the commandment of a superior power. But if someone should believe that the commandment of the proconsul was the commandment of the emperor, he would flout the commandment of the emperor in flouting the commandment of the proconsul. Similarly, if any man should recognize that human reason is dictating something against the commandment of God, he would not be obliged to follow reason; but then reason would not be totally erring. But when erring reason proposes something as the commandment of God, then it is the same thing to flout the dictate of reason and the commandment of God.

To the third objection it must be said that when reason apprehends something as bad it always apprehends it under some character of badness, for example, because it is contrary to a divine commandment or because it is a scandal or something of this kind; and then such bad will is reduced to such a species of malice.

Article 6. Is Will Agreeing with Erring Reason Good?

1. It seems that will agreeing with erring reason is good. For, just as will disagreeing with reason tends toward that which the reason judges bad, so will agreeing with reason tends toward that which reason judges good. But will disagreeing with even an erring reason is bad. Therefore will agreeing with even an erring reason is good.

2. Further, will agreeing with a commandment of God and the eternal law is always good. But the eternal law and the commandment of God is proposed to us by the apprehension of even an erring reason. Therefore the will agreeing with even erring reason is good.

3. Further, the will disagreeing with erring reason is bad. If, therefore, will agreeing with erring reason is also bad, it seems that every will of one who has an erring reason is bad, and so such a man will be entangled and will sin from necessity—which is awkward. Therefore will agreeing with erring reason is good.

But, to the contrary, the will of the killers of the apostles was bad, but yet it agreed with their erring reason, according to John [16:7]: "The hour comes when everyone who kills you will think he is offering service to God." Therefore the will agreeing with erring reason can be bad.

Reply: It must be said that just as the previous question was the same as the question. "Whether an erroneous conscience obliges," so this question is the same as "Whether an erroneous conscience excuses."

But this question depends on what was said above [q. 6, Art. 8] about ignorance. It was said above that ignorance sometimes causes something involuntary but sometimes does not. And because moral good and evil consist in an act insofar as it is voluntary, as is evident from what has gone before, it is clear that that ignorance which causes something involuntary takes away the character of moral good and evil, but not that ignorance which does not cause something involuntary. I speak of ignorance directly willed as that on which the act of the will bears, and indirectly, when because of negligence someone does not wish to know what he is bound to know, as said above.

If, therefore, reason or conscience errs by an error that is voluntary either directly or indirectly because of negligence, because it is in error about that which one is bound to know, then such an error of reason or conscience does not excuse the will agreeing with the reason of conscience erring in such a way. But if the error which causes the involuntary comes from ignorance of some circumstance apart from any negligence, then such error of reason or conscience excuses so that the will agreeing with the erring reason is not bad—for example, if the erring reason dictates that a man is bound to approach another's wife, the will agreeing with this reason is bad in that this error arises from ignorance of the law of God, which he is bound to know; but if reason errs in this, that one believes some woman is his wife and when she seeks the marital debt he wishes to know her, his will is excused so that it was not bad because this error arises from ignorance of a circumstance that excuses and causes the involuntary.

1. To the first objection, it must be said therefore as Dionysius says [*PG* 3, 729], "Good is caused from the wholeness but evil from any particular defect," and, therefore, that to which the will is borne should be called bad, it suffices either that it be in its nature bad or that it be apprehended as bad; but that to be good it is required that it be good in both ways.

2. To the second objection, it must be said that the eternal law cannot err, but human reason can err; and therefore will agreeing with human reason is not always right and is not always agreeing with the eternal law.

3. To the third objection, it must be said that just as in logic when one thing is inappropriately given, others necessarily follow, so in morals when one inappropriate thing is posited, others necessarily follow. Suppose that someone seeks empty glory, whether he does what he is bound to do because of the empty glory or fails to do it, he will always sin. Yet he is not entangled because he can always set aside his bad intention. Similarly, supposing there is an error of reason or conscience which proceeds from a nonexcusable ignorance, it is necessary that evil always follow in the will. Yet

the man is not entangled because he can withdraw from his error since his ignorance is conquerable and voluntary.

2. JOAN AT THE STAKE

The system for punishing heretics, enacted into canon law and endorsed by Thomas Aquinas and the rest of the theologians, assumed and assured maximum cooperation between the ecclesiastical courts, which tried the suspected heretic, and the secular authorities, which put him or her to death if he or she were found to have relapsed. Such cooperation was a thin legal fiction protecting the position taken at the Fourth Lateran Council that clerics were forbidden to participate in blood judgments (*supra*, III, 3). Sometimes, as in the case of Joan of Arc, the fiction was so thin when the death penalty was imposed by the prince that it was abandoned altogether; the only judgment was the Church's. But even where the form was maintained, ecclesiastics permitted themselves to take this Pilate-like posture at the cost of enabling the secular authorities to manipulate the canonical system to produce verdicts desired by the secular power. The trial of Joan of Arc is a spectacular example of such manipulation.

Joan was born in Domrémy, Lorraine, in 1412. At the age of thirteen she heard voices telling her it was her mission to save France. At seventeen, a peasant girl, she acted on her voices, left home and presented herself at the French court. King Charles VII, harried by the English who claimed a large part of his domain, agreed to see her, had her examined by theologians, and was convinced enough to give her a try. Four months after leaving home Joan was put at the head of a French army and sent to relieve besieged Orléans. She raised the siege, then led the troops to a second spectacular victory that opened the way to Reims and Charles's coronation. The following year, 1430, Joan was taken prisoner by the Burgundians, who for a price delivered her to their English allies.

The English could scarcely have been expected to believe that it was God's will that they be driven from France and that Joan was His agent. In all good faith, they thought she must be aided by diabolical powers. They were certain that an ecclesiastical court would penetrate her sophistries and uncover her true character. They were aware that not only she but her patron Charles VII would be disgraced by a trial in which she was shown not to be a true Christian.

Henry VI of England directed Pierre Cauchon, bishop of Beauvais, the diocese where Joan had been taken captive, to proceed against her as a heretic. Such royal directives to begin an inquisitional process were standard procedure in both England and France (see P. Doncoeur, S.J., and Y. Lanhers, *La Réhabilitation de Jeanne La Pucelle. L'enquête ordonnée par Charles VII,* 1956, 9).

The trial began on February 21, 1431. At a decisive moment in the process, on May 19, 1434, a group of consultants to the court from the faculty of theology of the University of Paris subscribed to the statement that they found her "a liar, inspired by the devil, erring in the Faith, a sorcerer, an idolator, a blasphemer of God and the saints, a schismatic, a heretic, and an apostate" (*ibid.* at 15). On May 24 she was found guilty of heresy. She abjured all her errors and, as was common where the heretic's sin was great, was not released but committed to prison. Five days later she was found to have relapsed, for the reason that appears in the testimony below. She was burned the next day.

Moving with unaccountable sluggishness, Charles VII ordered a royal inquiry eighteen years later into the validity of the trial of the girl to whom he owed his crown. The close relation of the secular powers with the Church is again excellently illustrated by this procedure, which had no warrant in canon law. The king's extralegal investigations, whose results were communicated to the pope, resulted in a papal commission being set up by Calixtus III. After further inquiries, this commission in 1456 quashed the original verdict. In May 1920, in the aftermath of the French victory in World War I, Joan was canonized.

The record of the royal inquiry gives a remarkable picture of the collaboration of churchmen with their rulers and a picture of the kind of persons whose cooperation was needed to produce the conviction. Cauchon, the presiding bishop, was not quite sixty, an accomplished diplomat, whose patron in promotion to office had been the duke of Burgundy and whose services had been used before by Henry VI of England (C. Laplatte, "Cauchon," *Dictionnaire d'histoire et de géographie ecclésiastiques*, 1953 12, 4–6). He was a political bishop, who knew who his masters were. Defenders still assert that he was no worse than others of his time (*ibid.*). The defense is an indictment of the institutional arrangements that put such men in the dress of pastors. It is hard to read the testimony that follows without applauding Paul Claudel's pun on his name in the script for Poulenc's oratorio where "Cochon, Cochon, Cochon" mocks the murderous judge. It is certainly "Peter Pig" who plays a game of Gotcha with Joan and on the flimsiest of pretexts finds that she has relapsed. The legal fiction the bishop so cynically exploits is brushed aside by Joan who exclaims, "It is by you I die." Peter Pig advises her at this moment to be patient.

Cauchon himself had once been the rector of the University of Paris, and the theology faculty of the University was "the soul of the trial" (*ibid.* at 6). Beaupère is an example. The willingness of such learned men to put their skills at the service of the prosecution is an instance of that misplaced *machismo* all too frequently found in academics dabbling in practical affairs. In Beaupère's case it is accompanied by a decided whiff of antifeminism; and no one can doubt that the fact that Joan was an extraordinary woman was a goad to some of those who condemned her.

Two members of religious orders, Ladvenu and Ysambart, in their testimony, *infra*, recall the kindnesses they did for Joan and celebrate her heroism. They are having it both ways. They signed the declaration that she was a lying, devil-inspired heretic. Ysambart was one of those who found she had relapsed (Doncoeur and Lanhers, 15).

Lohier, the distinguished canon lawyer whose behavior is described by Manchon, is another type. He pointed out all that was illegal about the trial with a fine eye for procedural irregularities. He then left town. He did not want to die. Few do. Manchon himself is the most interesting witness of all—Mr. Average Man, the honest notary, who tries to keep the record he makes free from error, who genuinely regrets Joan's death, but whose willingness to work at the trial makes it possible for the trial to go on. "If I don't do it then someone else will," he surely thought. The gesture he makes at the end, using some of his fee to buy a missal to pray for Joan, reflects a wonderful mixture of piety and guilt.

Peter Pigs, chauvinists, lawyers who went somewhere else like Lohier, pious priests whom fear could bend, honest men like Manchon—these were the kind of men that made the system work by which governmental force was used to maintain religion and, as had been long before predicted, ended by killing saints.

Inquiry Before a Royal Commission, March 4 and 5, 1450

1. Brother Ysambart de la Pierre of the Augustinians of the convent of Rouen, a priest, being sworn and examined the fifth day of March, A.D. 1449, declares:

Once, in my presence and that of many others, Joan, exhorted and solicited to submit to the Church, replied that she willingly would submit to the Roman Pontiff and asked that she be taken to him, but that in no way would she submit to those present who were conducting her trial, because—as she often said—they were her enemies. I counseled her to submit to the Council of Basel then in session. She asked what a General Council was. I replied that it was a universal assembly of the whole Church and of Christianity itself, and that in this Council there were many men on her side as well as on the side of the English. When she heard that, she declared, "Oh, are there people there on our side?" I said, "Yes." She at once replied that she indeed wanted to submit to that Council. But the Bishop of Beauvais, full of fury and contempt, shouted at me, "In the devil's name, shut up!" And he immediately ordered the notary not to record the submission which she had made to the General Council. Because of this and many other things, I suffered grave threats from the English and their officials that unless I was silent in the future, I would be tied and tossed in the Seine. . . .

I went in person to Monseigneur the bishop of Avranches, a very old and wise man, who like others had been requested to give his opinion on this case. He asked me what Saint Thomas taught as to the submission that ought to be made to the Church. I gave him in writing my view, to wit, that in matters of doubt bearing on the faith, recourse is always to be had to the Supreme Pontiff or a General Council. And the good bishop was of the same opinion. And the other bishop appeared to be unhappy with this reply. This opinion was not transcribed in the record, which seems to have been composed maliciously.

After her confession and partaking of the Eucharist, the judgment against her was promulgated, and she was declared a heretic and excommunicate. I saw well and perceived very clearly—because I was always near her during the whole business and at her end—that she was in no way condemned by the secular judge to death or to burning, even though the secular judge was present and seated on the platform or scaffolding where she was preached to and finally abandoned to secular judgment. But without sentence or judgment she was delivered to the executioner and to burning. They said to the executioner without further sentence, "Do your duty." . . .

The executioner came to me and my associate, Brother Martin Ladvenu, immediately after the burning, impelled by a wonderful and terrible penitence. It was as if he despaired of receiving pardon from God after what he had done to her, who, as he said, was such a holy woman. He also affirmed that although he had several times put the wood and coals upon her entrails and heart, he could in no way consume her heart or reduce it to cinders; and at this he was amazed, as if it were an evident miracle.

2. The venerable and religious man, Brother Jean Toutmouille of the Order of Preachers, distinguished professor of sacred theology, of the convent of St. Jacques of Rouen belonging to the said order, aged forty-two or thereabouts, having been sworn and examined on the fifth day of March, declares:

. . .

On that day on which Joan was abandoned to secular judgment and delivered to the fire, I was in the morning in the jail with Brother Martin Ladvenu, who was sent to her by the bishop of Beauvais to announce to her her approaching death and to lead her to true patience and to hear her confession. All these things Martin very carefully and charitably did. And he told Joan that it was necessary because of her relapse that she die that day by fire and burning and so her judges had ordained. When she heard the terrible death that awaited her, she began to cry out very sorrowfully, loudly, and tearfully, with every gesture of intense pain, "Alas, how cruelly they treat me. My body, which is whole and uncorrupted, will be burned by fire. I would choose rather, if it could be done, to have my head cut off seven times than be burnt by fire."

She wept and said, "If I had been in the custody of the Church, to whom I had submitted, and been guarded by men of the Church and not by armed men and enemies, it would never have happened to me. And as to this as from so many injuries I appeal to God the Supreme Judge." She then complained in a remarkable way about the harassment and violence which had been offered her or attempted against her by her guards and others brought into her from the time of her abjuration.

Afterwards the bishop of Beauvais, the judge, arrived and she at once said to him, "Bishop, I die by you." He replied, "Joan, you will not have patience. You are in this case because you did not keep what you promised and you relapsed." She replied, "Alas, if you had put me in your jail with fit church guards, this would not have happened to me. That is why I appeal from you to God."

3. The religious and respectable man, Brother Martin Ladvenu, of the Order of Preachers and of the said convent of St. Jacques in Rouen, the special confessor and director of Joan at the end of her life, was questioned on the same day, on certain points as above, and declares:

. . .

Joan revealed to me that in that prison, after her abjuration, she was very violently attacked with violence and seduction by a certain English lord; and she said publicly that this was the reason why she was moved to resume male dress. Hence near the end of her life Joan said to the bishop, "Look, by you I am dying. If you had put me in Church jails and I had been kept by men of the Church and not by my English enemies, it would not have happened to me this way."

4. A venerable and discreet man, Monsieur Guillaume Manchon, a priest fifty years old or thereabouts, canon of the collegial church of Notre Dame d'Andeley, curé of the parish church St. Nicholas of Rouen, notary of the archiepiscopal court of Rouen, sworn and examined March 4, 1449, deposes:

I was a notary at the trial of Joan from the beginning to the end, and with me was Monsieur Guillaume Colles, called Boscguillaume.

In my opinion, on the part of those who had charge of conducting and managing the trial—to wit, Monseigneur of Beauvais and the masters sent from Paris to investigate the cases, and the English too, at whose instigation the trial was had—the proceeding was rather with hatred and contempt for the cause of the king of France than for anything she had done. My reasons follow.

First, one Nicolas Loyseleur, who was of the household of Monseigneur of Beauvais and was totally on the side of the English (for, another time, when the king was before Chartres, he went to get the king of England to raise the siege) pretended that he was from the land of the Maid and by this means found a way of having access, speech and familiarity with her, telling her news of the land that pleased her; and he asked to be her confessor; and what she told him in secret he found a way of getting to the ears of the notaries. Indeed at the beginning of the trial I and Boscguillaume, with witnesses, were secretly placed in an adjoining room where there was a hole through which we listened, so that we could report what she said or confessed to Loyseleur. And it seems to me that what the Maid said or related familiarly to Loyseleur, he reported to the notaries, and from these things a memorandum was made up for interrogatories at the trial, so a way could be found of catching her.

Again, after the trial had begun, Master Jean Lohier, a grave Norman cleric, came to the city of Rouen, and it was communicated to him what the bishop of Beauvais had written hereon; and Lohier asked a delay of two or three days to look at it. To this it was replied that he give his opinion at the next session, and he was forced to do so. And Master Jean Lohier, having looked at the trial, said that it was worth nothing, for several reasons. First, it did not have the form of an ordinary trial. Then, it was being carried on in an enclosed and shut-up place where those in attendance did not have plain and pure freedom to speak their pure and plain will. Then, it treated in this way the honor of the king of France, on whose side she was, without calling him or anyone who was on that side. Then, an indictment had not been framed, nor any charges, and so this woman, who was a simple girl, did not have any guide to reply to these numerous masters and doctors on the great matters, especially those which, as she said, touched upon revelations. For these reasons it seemed to him that the trial was worthless.

At this Monseigneur of Beauvais was indignant at Lohier, and although Monseigneur of Beauvais told him that he might remain to see the trial, Lohier replied that he would not stay longer. And Monseigneur of Beauvais, who was staying at the house where Master Jean Bidault now lives near St. Nicholas the Painter, left at once and went to the masters—to wit, Master Jean Beaupère, Jacques de Touraine, Nicolas Midi, Pierre Morice, Thomas de Courcelles, and Loyseleur—and said to them, "Look at Lohier who wants us to frame beautiful interrogatories for our trial. He discredits everything and says it's worth nothing. To believe him we would have to begin everything again, and all we have done would be worth nothing." After reciting the reasons why Lohier wanted to discredit it, Monseigneur of Beauvais exclaimed, "I see on what foot he limps. By Saint John we will do nothing about it. We will continue our trial as we have begun."

And this was a Saturday afternoon in Lent; and the next morning I spoke to Lohier at Notre Dame and asked him what he thought of the trial and of Joan. He answered me, "You see how they are proceeding. They will catch her in words, if they can—as in assertions where she says, 'I know for certain as regards the apparitions.' If she said, 'It seems to me' instead of 'I am certain,' it is my opinion that no one could condemn her. They seem to me to proceed more out of hatred than otherwise. And for that reason I'll no longer stay here. I do not want to be in it." And indeed the rest of his days he stayed in Rome, where he died the dean of the Rota.

At the beginning of the trial, for five or six days I put in writing the answers and excuses of the Maid; and sometimes the judges, speaking in Latin, wanted to force me to change the sense of her words and to say what I had not heard. By command of Monseigneur of Beauvais, two men sat in a window near the judges with a curtain drawn so that they could not be seen. These men wrote and reported what there was in the charges against Joan, leaving out her excuses. And I think they were Loyseleur and the cleric Beaupère, who were not notaries. After the session was over, in the afternoon, when I compared what had been written, these two had reported differently and had not put in any excuses; at which Monseigneur of Beauvais got very angry at me. And in those parts of the record where "Note" is written, there was a controversy, and new interrogations had to be made about it; and it was found that what I had written was true.

In writing the record I was asked several times by Monseigneur of Beauvais and these masters to write what they imagined and contrary to the sense of the Maid. And several times where there were things that did not please them they would say, "Don't write it down. It doesn't serve the trial." Nonetheless I never wrote anything except according to my understanding and conscience. . . .

I saw Joan led to the scaffold. There were 700 or 800 soldiers around her carrying swords; and there was no man so bold to speak to her to advise her, except Brother Martin Ladvenu and Monsieur Jean Massieu. Patiently she heard the sermon straight through. Afterwards she made thanksgiving and prayed and lamented most notably and devoutly, so that the judge-prelates and everyone else in attendance, hearing it, were moved to great weeping. And I never wept so much for anything that happened to me. And one month later I could not put myself at peace, and with part of the money I had from the trial I bought a small missal which I still have so that I could pray for her. As for her final penitence, I never saw greater signs of a Christian.

5. Monsieur Jean Massieu, priest, *curé* of one of the sections of the parish church of St. Candre of Rouen, formerly dean of the clergy of Rouen, fifty years old or thereabouts, sworn and examined the fifth day of March, declares:

I was present at the trial of Joan every time she was present before judges and clerics; and because of my office I was appointed clerk to Monsieur Jean Benedicite, the Promoter in the case, to cite Joan and all the others who were summoned in this case. And it seems to me from what I saw that the proceedings were taken out of hatred and with favoritism, in order to disparage the honor of the king of France whom she served, and for vengeance, in order to make her die; and not according to reason and the honor of God and the Catholic faith. . . .

I mean also by this that when I was leading her back to prison from being before the judges on the fourth or fifth day, a priest named Monsieur Eustace Turquetil asked me, "What do you think of her answers? Will she burn? What will happen?" To which I replied, "Up to now I have only seen goodness and honor in her, but as to the end I don't know what it will be, God knows!" The priest reported my reply to the king's people; and it was said that I was not friendly to the king. And on this occasion I was sent for in the afternoon by Monseigneur of Beauvais, the judge, and he spoke to me of these things and told me to take care not to be misunderstood or they would make me drink one more time than I should. And I think that if it had not been for Notary Manchon, who excused me, I would never have escaped. . . .

That day, after dinner, in the presence of the counselors of the Church, she took off her men's clothes and put on women's dress as she had been directed. That was Thursday or Friday after Pentecost; and the men's clothes were put in a bag in the same room where she was held prisoner. She stayed guarded there by five Englishmen, three of whom stayed during the night in the room and two outside, at the door of the room. I know for certain that at night she slept chained by the legs with two pairs of iron chains and tightly tied by a chain crossing the feet of her bed, held to a great piece of wood, five or six feet long, that locked with a key. And when Sunday morning came, the day of the Trinity, and she had to rise, as she reported and said to me, she asked her English guards, "Unchain me so I may get up." Then one of the Englishmen took away from her the women's garments she had on her, and they emptied the bag that held the men's clothes; and they threw the clothes at her saying, "Get up." And they threw the women's garments in the bag. At this, she reported, they told her to dress in the men's clothes which they had given her, and she replied, "Sirs, you know it is forbidden me. Without fail I will not take it again." And still they refused to give her the other, so the contention lasted until noon. And finally, out of bodily necessity, she was forced to go outside and to wear the men's clothes. When she returned, they refused to give her the other, whatever prayer or request she made.

This she told me the following Tuesday after dinner. On this day the Promoter had taken me with him to the prison. And the Promoter left to go with Monseigneur of Warwick; and I stayed with her. Immediately I asked her why she had resumed the men's clothing; and she declared what I just said. . . .

When she was released by the Church, I was still with her; and with great devotion she asked to have a cross. Hearing this, one of the English who was there made a little one of wood with the ends of a stick, which he gave her; and devoutly she received it and kissed it, making piteous lamentations and acknowledgements to God our Redeemer who had suffered on the cross for our redemption, of which cross she had the sign and image. And she put the cross in her breast, between her flesh and her clothes. And besides, she humbly asked me to have the cross brought from the church so that she could constantly see it up to death. And I had the cleric from the parish of St. Sauveur bring it. When it was brought, she embraced it very tightly for a long time, and she held it until she was tied to the stake.

While she was making these devotions and piteous lamentations, I was much hurried by Englishmen, even by some of their leaders, to leave her in their hands, so they could make her die sooner. They said to me who as best I could was comforting her on the scaffold, "What, priest, will you make us dine here?" And immediately, without any form or indication of judgment, they sent her to the fire, saying to the master of the business, "Do your duty." And so she was led out and tied; and she continued her praises and devout lamentations toward God and his saints. With her last words, as she passed, she loudly cried, "Jesus."

6. The venerable and careful man, Master Jean Beaupère, master of theology, canon of Rouen, seventy years old or thereabouts, declares:

With regard to the apparitions mentioned in the trial of Joan, I was and still am very much of the opinion that the apparitions were rather from natural causes and human invention than from a supernatural cause; but I always refer to the trial.

Before she was taken to St. Ouen to be preached to in the morning, I by myself with permission entered into Joan's prison and warned Joan that she would soon be led to the scaffold to be preached to; and I said to her that if she was a good Christian, she would say on the scaffold that she put all her deeds and sayings in the ordering of our Holy Mother Church and especially of the ecclesiastical judges. She answered that she would do so. And so she did on the scaffold, on being asked by Master Nicholas Midi. This being observed and considered this time, she was sent back after her abjuration, although some of the Englishmen accused the Bishop of Beauvais and the men from Paris of favoring Joan's errors.

After this abjuration and after she had put on her women's dress which she had received in the prison, it was reported to the judges the next Friday or Saturday that Joan had repented of having put aside men's clothing and had taken up women's clothing. For that reason, Monseigneur of Beauvais, the judge, sent me and Master Nicholas Midi to the castle in the hope of speaking to Joan and inducing and admonishing her to persevere and take care not to relapse. But we could not find the one who had the key of the prison; and while we were waiting for the prison guard, several Englishmen in the courtyard of the castle spoke threatening words, as Midi told me—to wit, any one who would throw us both in the river would be well employed. Because of these words we returned; and on the castle bridge, Midi, as he told me, heard similar words, or something like them, pronounced by other Englishmen; at which we were frightened and came away without speaking to Joan.

In my opinion, if Joan had had wise and frank directors, she would have spoken many words useful for her justification and not spoken several which made for her condemnation.

As to Joan's innocence, she was very subtle, with the subtlety that belongs to a woman, as it seems to me. And I did not know from any words of hers that she had been corrupted in her body.

In regard to her final penitence, I do not know what to say, for the Monday after the abjuration I left Rouen to go to Basle on behalf of the University of Paris, and she was condemned the following Tuesday, and I had no news of her condemnation until I heard it spoken of at Lisle in Flanders.

3. THE FOUR THOMASES
"There was Thomas Wolsey, and Thomas Cromwell,
And Thomas Cranmer and me,"

Thomas More might have written. The four, whose baptismal name testifies to the continued popularity in England of the martyred defender of the freedom of the Church, were the four principal actors as constitutional change occurred in the position of the Church in England. Their master was the king himself, Henry VIII, a figure with a will, an ego, and a theological temper of his own (see J. J. Scarisbrick, *Henry VIII*, 1968); but without the four Thomases the scenario of change would not have been the same.

Thomas Wolsey (1475–1530) was "the great cardinal," who in person unified ecclesiastical interests and the power of the state, enjoying the special privileges of a papal legate as well as the almost unlimited confidence of young Henry VIII, and ruling as chief minister from 1515 until his abrupt fall in October 1529. Wolsey's pursuit of personal profit, his failure to reform recognized abuses in the Church, his cynical and unrealistic attempt to have Henry's marriage to Catherine of Aragon annulled set the stage on which the constitutional change occurred.

When Wolsey was removed from office for his failure to get the annulment, he was at once indicted for having violated the Statute of Praemunire, a fourteenth-century enactment making it a "contempt," with unspecified but awful penalties, to take "out of the realm" a case that should have been tried in the king's court or suing "in any other court, to defeat or impeach the judgments given in the King's Court" (27 Edw. III, Stat. 1, c.1 [2 Pickering Stat. 72], 1353). The statute was a typical medieval check on papal claims and had been successfully enforced against papal appointees to benefices contested by Englishmen (Robert E. Rodes, Jr., *Lay Authority and Reformation in the English Church*, 1982, 28, 47, 63). Its application to Wolsey was another matter. He had exercised his legatine powers with the enthusiastic support of the king; the first hearings of the great annulment case had been before him as co-legate. Nonetheless he pleaded guilty and forfeited all his property, (G. R. Elton, *Reform and Reformation*, 1977, 112). His case is instructive: the king already had in medieval legislation a supple tool for controlling his clergy's relations with Rome.

The recognized jurisdiction of the clergy was very wide. Marriages and their annulment; wills and their probate; tithes, ecclesiastical dues (*e.g.*, mortuaries), and their collection; and a variety of moral offenses—sexual misbehavior, breach of any promise, usury, defamation— all fell within the jurisdiction of ecclesiastical courts (Rodes, 12–21). Clerical immunity and sanctuary had provided oases of mercy and a constant irritant to anyone seriously interested in law enforcement (*ibid.*, 29–33, 70–71). The Parliament that met in 1529 was to be "the Reformation Parliament" and was to stay in session until 1536. Its concerns were not merely anticlerical. For example, it enacted a statute making a homosexual act punishable by death (the Buggery Act, 25 Hen. VIII, c. 6 [4 Pick. Stat. 267], 1533). But in this first session it showed its sensitivity to old grievances about the clergy. It limited benefices and made it a crime to seek a dispensation to hold several, 21 Hen. VIII, c. 3 [4 Pick. Stat. 180], 1529). It limited what could be charged for probate (c, 5). It limited what could be charged as mortuaries (c. 6). These laws trenched on the spiritual jurisdiction and arguably invaded it. They would not have been enacted if reform had not been in the air, but they were not radical. When Henry VIII encouraged such legislation, he was already in the anticlerical camp (Scarisbrick 245).

Thomas More (1477–1535) succeeded Wolsey as chancellor, the first layman ever to hold the office. Ironically, as it was to seem, the very appointment of a layman was a signal by Henry VIII of the king's new turn of mind. More was fifty-two, a London lawyer's son, who had gone from a successful legal practice to service as a royal counselor in 1518. In his *Utopia*, published before he held high office, he had imagined a Nowhere where no one was molested for his religious opinion, although disbelievers in God or a future life were barred from office. In the 1520s he had become a polemicist against the new heretics, and as chancellor he encouraged enforcement of the statute against heresy. The king knew from the start that More did not believe in his case for an annulment and for a time tolerated his noncooperation here while other agents continued to press the case in Rome.

The matter of the marriage, an accident on which so much was to turn, was constitutionally within the jurisdiction of the Church; and at the apex of that jurisdiction was the pope, who had awarded Henry for his anti-Lutheran writing the title of "Defender of the Faith." Exasperated by delay, seeing clearly that whatever the legal merits of his case (they were little) the pope would never decide in his favor because the pope was politically under the thumb of the Emperor Charles, Henry soured on his propapal attitude and listened to the counsels of those who proposed a new and daring course. The chief counselors were Thomas Cromwell (1485–1540) and Thomas Cranmer (1489–1556).

Cromwell, who had gained his administrative experience serving Wolsey, was a layman who turned out to believe in such reforms as the Bible in English. He had convictions, energy, organizing ability, and legal skill. By 1530 he was a member of the royal Council (Elton 137, 168–173). Thomas Cranmer was an academic and cleric from Cambridge who in the same year was enlisted to win academic support for Henry's annulment. As yet there was no break with Rome. But early in 1531 fresh charges of praemunire were brought against selected English bishops for having recognized Wolsey as legate. Yielding to this legal blackmail the Convocation of southern bishops voted 100,000 pounds to the king. In the same year, the payment of annates to the pope was in effect suspended; the pope was put on notice not only of the king's displeasure but of the king's ability to hurt him. (23 Hen. VIII c. 20, 1531).

In May 1532, the Convocation asked the king to protect the liberties of the Church: Magna Carta was invoked. Henry, steeled by his more radical counselors, replied by demanding subservience, and the cowed clerics surrendered, the Convocation passing a declaration entitled "The Submission of the Clergy," granting the king power to approve or disapprove their canons (Elton 154–155). This concession can be interpreted as small, as Rodes, 84–85, does, an acknowledgement that canons could not be the law of the land without the royal assent; or major, as Elton does, an abandonment of the pope as legislator for the Church. Thomas More resigned the day after it was passed; it may reasonably be inferred that he read the concession as fatal and foresaw the course the king would now follow. Parliament passed a statute whose preamble referred to England as an empire "governed by one supreme head and king," beneath whom there was a "spirituality [sic] and temporalty [sic]" (24 Hen. VIII c. 12 [4 Pick. Stat. 257], 1532). The germ of revolution was planted.

In August 1532 the old archbishop of Canterbury died and Henry seized the opportunity to ask the pope that Cranmer, a mere archdeacon, succeed him. Cranmer had secretly gone through a marriage ceremony with the niece of a leading Lutheran in Germany (Scarisbrick, 401). According to the law of the Church and of England, he was living with a concubine. He had to choose between keeping this woman in sin and abandoning Rome. Pope Clement VII, although warned that there was something unsuitable about Cranmer, was eager to oblige Henry and sent the bull of nomination (ibid. 310). In March 1533 Cranmer was consecrated, taking the usual oath of obedience to the pope (Elton, 175). In the same month Parliament enacted The Submission of the Clergy and Restraint of Appeals Act, confirming the clergy's subordination as to legislation (25 Hen. VIII c. 19, 1533). The act also made a broad expansion of praemunire, cutting off appeals to Rome in cases such as annulment suits where appeals traditionally had been taken.

In late May Cranmer annulled Henry's marriage to Catherine on the ground of affinity (her previous marriage to his brother Arthur, allegedly consummated and invalidly dispensed; for the details, *see* Henry Ansgar Kelly, *The Matrimonial Trials of Henry VIII*, 1976, 210). Anne Boleyn was crowned queen on June 1, 1533. In July the pope excommunicated Henry.

Parliament then passed the Act of Succession declaring Henry and Catherine's marriage void and Henry and Anne's marriage "perfect," and requiring from every adult male an oath of allegiance to Anne and her issue; to refuse was to be guilty of "misprision of high treason" (25 Hen. VIII c. 22 [4 Pick. Stat. 305], 1533). Commissioners to enact the oath were appointed, and on April 17, 1534, Thomas More, two years in retirement, was summoned to take the oath. The remarkable letter that follows was written soon afterward, addressed to Margaret, his oldest daughter, aged 29. It is, of course, not an unqualified defense of the supremacy of conscience; but it is a defense of even a doubtful conscience against coercion by the secular power.

More's silence sealed his fate. In November 1534, under Cromwell's management, a special bill of attainder was passed condemning him to death for his failure (Elton, 188). In the same session two general laws were passed—the Act of Supremacy, declaring the king to be "the only supreme head in earth of the church of England," without any qualifying reference to the law of Christ (26 Hen. VIII c. 1 [4 Pick. 312], 1534); and the Treason Act, making it treason maliciously to say in writing or by mouth that the king was a schismatic or heretic or to deny him any of his titles (26 Hen. VIII c. 13 [4 Pick. 337], 1534).

Elton describes what happened as a "revolution" (Elton, 196). Rodes, on the other hand, stresses the continuity with the medieval church and, a Catholic, emphasizes the reformers' view that what they were achieving was only an "updating" (Rodes, 93). Was it revolution or only *aggiornamento?*

There was a great deal of continuity. Ecclesiastical jurisdiction of marriages and wills, for example, was not touched. No new regime, however revolutionary, writes on a *tabula rasa.* But destruction of the monasteries and dissolution of the religious orders liquidated two main institutions of the old church with revolutionary thoroughness. The coercive means used were not extraconstitutional but their purpose was: to compel consent to a religious proposition whose truth depended upon a statute. Even more significant from the perspective of this book, the elimination of papal government of the Church tilted the balance in favor of greater governmental control of the Church. "The freedom of the Church," as proclaimed in Magna Carta, (supra, III, 2), was a formula weighted toward the preeminence of the Church. The king as "supreme head" was a formula weighted toward preeminence of the state. Paradoxically, in the long run, the formula was to make for greater freedom of conscience for everyone. Secular governments did not have a jealous interest in doctrinal purity. But the argument here is not whether the results were good or ill (I should say both), but whether constitutional revolution was effected: I should say that it was.

More himself was not disposed of by the bill of attainder, but was proceeded against under the Treason Act. Convicted in June 1535 of denying the king's supremacy over the church, he was executed on July 6, 1535; he was canonized as a martyr in 1933.

The following letter is from the *Correspondence of Thomas More,* edited by Elizabeth Frances Rogers (Princeton, 1947).

Thomas More to His Daughter Margaret
(Tower of London)
(C. 17 April 1534)

When I was before the Lords at Lambeth, I was the first that was called in, although Master Doctor the Vicar of Croydon had come before me, and several others. After the cause of my being sent for was declared to me (whereof I somewhat marveled in my mind, considering that they sent for no more temporal men but me) I desired the sight of the oath, which they showed me under the great seal. Then I desired the sight of the Act of Succession, which was delivered to me in a printed roll. After which I read separately by myself and considered the oath with the act, and I showed them that my purpose was not to put any fault either on the act or any man that made it, upon the oath or any man that swore it, nor to condemn the conscience of any other man. But as for myself in good faith my conscience so moved me in the matter that though I would not refuse to swear to the succession, yet unto the oath that there was offered me I could not swear without the risking of my soul to perpetual damnation. And that if they doubted whether I would refuse the oath only for the grudge of my conscience, or for any other fantasy, I was ready therein to satisfy them by my oath. Which if they trusted not, what should they be the better to give me any oath? And if they trusted that I would therein swear true, then trusted I that of their goodness they would not move me to swear the oath that they offered me, perceiving that the swearing was against my conscience.

Unto this my Lord Chancellor said that they all were sorry to see me say this and see me thus refuse the oath. And they all said that on their faith I was the very first that ever refused it; which would cause the King's Highness to conceive great suspicion of me and great indignation toward me. And therewith they showed me the roll and let me see the names of the lords and the commons who had sworn and subscribed their names already. Which notwithstanding, when they saw that I refused to swear the same myself, not blaming any other man that had sworn, I was in conclusion commanded to go down into the garden and thereupon I tarried in the old burned chamber that looks into the garden and would not go down because of the heat. During that time I saw Master Doctor Latimer come into the garden, and there he walked with various other doctors and chaplains of my Lord of Canterbury, and very merry I saw him, for he laughed and took one or two about the neck so handsomely that if they had been women I would have believed that he had become wanton. After that came Master Doctor Wilson from the lords and was with two gentlemen brought past me and in a gentlemanly way sent straight to the Tower. What time my Lord of Rochester was called in before them, that I cannot tell. But at night I heard that he had been before them, but where he remained that night and so forth until he was sent hither, I never heard. I heard also that Master Vicar of Croydon and all the remnant of the priests of London that were sent for were sworn, and that they had such favor at the Council's hand that they were not made to linger nor to dance any long attendance to their travail and cost as suitors are sometimes wont to be, but were sped apace to their great comfort, so far forth that Master Vicar of Croydon, either for gladness or for dryness, or else that it might be seen *(quod ille notus erat pontifici)* went to my lords buttery bar and called for drinks, and drank *(valde familiariter)*.

When they had played their pageant and were gone out of the place, then was I called in again. And then was it declared to me what a number had sworn, even since I went aside, and gladly without any sticking. Wherein I laid no blame on any man but for my own self answered as before. Now as well then as before, they somewhat laid into me for obstinacy that, whereas before since I refused to swear, I would not declare any special part of that oath that grudged my conscience and open the causes why. For thereunto I had said to them that I feared lest the King's Highness would, as they said, take displeasure enough toward me for the mere refusal of the oath. And that if I should open and disclose the causes why, I should therewith but further exasperate his Highness, which I would in no wise do, but rather would I abide all the danger and harm that might come towards me than to give his Highness any occasion for further displeasure more than the offering of the oath to me of pure necessity constrained me. However, when they various times imputed this to me as stubborness and obstinacy, that I would neither swear the oath nor yet declare the causes why, I inclined thus far toward them, that, rather than be accounted obstinate, upon the King's gracious license, or rather his commandment—as might be my sufficient warrant—that my delcaration should not offend his Highness nor put me in danger of any of his statutes, I would be content to declare the causes in writing and beyond that to give an oath at the beginning that if I might find those causes by any man answered in such a way as I might think my own conscience satisfied, I would after that with all my heart swear the principal oath too.

To this I was answered that although the King would give me license under his letters patent, yet it would not serve against the statute, to which I said that if I had them I would stand to the trust of his honor at my peril for the rest. But yet I thought that if I might not declare the causes without peril, then to leave them undeclared is no obstinacy.

My Lord of Canterbury taking hold upon that which I had said, that I condemned not the conscience of them that swore, said to me that it appeared well that I did not take it for a very sure and certain thing that I might not lawfully swear, but rather as a thing uncertain and doubtful. But then, said my Lord, you know for a certainty and a thing without doubt that you are bound to obey your sovereign lord, your King, and therefore you are bound to leave the doubt of your unsure conscience in refusing the oath and take the sure way in obeying your prince, and swear it. Now it was all so in my own mind I thought myself not defeated, yet this argument seemed suddenly so subtle and with such authority coming out from so noble a prelate's mouth that I could answer nothing thereto but only that I thought myself I might not well do so, because in my conscience this was one of the cases in which I was bound that I should not obey my prince, since whatever other folk thought in the matter (whose conscience and learning I would not condemn nor take upon myself to judge), yet in my conscience the truth seemed on the other side. Wherein I had not informed my conscience suddenly nor slightly but at long leisure and with diligent search in the matter. And of truth if that reason is conclusive, then have we a ready way to avoid all perplexities. For in whatsoever matters the doctors stand in great doubt the King's commandment given upon whatever side he chooses, resolves all the doubts.

Then said my Lord of Westminster to me that howsoever the matter seemed to my mind, I had cause to fear that my own mind was erroneous when I saw the Great Council of the Realm determine the contrary of my mind, and that, therefore, I ought to change my conscience. To that I answered that if there were no men but myself upon my side, and the whole Parliament upon the other, I would be sore afraid to lean to my own mind alone against so many. But on the other side, if it so be that in some things for which I refuse the oath, I have (as I think I have) upon my part as great a Council and a greater too, I am not then bound to change my conscience and would confirm it to the Council of one realm against the General Council of Christendom. Upon this, Master Secretary (as one that tenderly favors me) said and swore a great oath that he would rather that his only son (who is in truth a goodly young gentleman and shall I trust come to much worship) had lost his head than that I should thus have refused the oath. For surely the King's Highness would now conceive a great suspicion against me and think of the matter of the nun of Canterbury was all contrived by my drift. To which I said that the contrary was true and well known and whatsoever should mishap me, it lay not in my power to help it without peril of my soul. Then did my Lord Chancellor repeat before me my refusal to Mister Secretary, as to him that was going unto the King's Grace. And in the rehearsing, this Lordship repeated again that I denied not but was content to swear to the succession. Whereunto I said that as for that point I would be content so that I might see my oath in that point so framed in such a manner as might stand with my conscience.

Then said my Lord: "Mary! Master Secretary mark that too that he will not swear that either only in some certain manner." "Verily no, my Lord," quote I, "but that I will see it made in such wise first as I shall myself see that I shall neither be foresworn nor swear against my conscience." Surely as to swear to the succession I see no peril, but I thought and think it reason, that to my own oath I myself look well and be of counsel in the fashion, and never intend to swear for a piece and set my hand to the whole oath. How be it (as help me God) as touching the whole oath, I never withdrew any man from it nor never advised any to refuse it nor never put, nor will, any scruple in any man's head, but leave every man to his own conscience. And me thinks in good faith that so were it good reason that every man should leave me to mine.

4. A CANDLE NEVER EXTINGUISHED

Hugh Latimer (1492–1555) was "the most popular, as he was the most influential, preacher of the English Reformation." To his admirers, he was "the Apostle to the English" (Allan G. Chester, *Selected Sermons of Hugh Latimer,* (1968, xiii). That he died at the stake showed that Catholics had not yet learned anything from More's martyrdom.

Ordained a Catholic priest in 1515, a bachelor of divinity from Cambridge in 1524, Latimer at Cambridge came to reject scholasticism and to appeal to the Bible alone for his theology. By 1528 he was demanding that a Bible in English be authorized. By 1530 he was known at Cambridge as one working for a favorable opinion from the university on the invalidity of Henry's marriage to Catherine. A little later he was asked to preach before the king and given a royal preferment (*ibid.* at xiii–xx).

Latimer then rose as Cranmer, his friend, rose. In 1534 he was made chaplain of the king. In the same year, in More's letter to Margaret, *supra*, we glimpse him in the garden with Cranmer as More watches critically. In the summer of 1535 he was chosen to open Convocation as it met to draw up articles of faith for the English Church; he rebuked the corruption in the Court of Arches and the inactivity of Convocation in the past (Latimer, "The Sermon Before Convocation," *ibid.* at 15, 22).

In 1539, at Henry VIII's urging, Parliament passed "An Act Abolishing Diversity of Opinions" (31 Hen. VIII c. 14), making it a crime of heresy, punishable by death by burning, to write or "hold opinion" that after the consecration the bread and wine did not become "the natural body and blood of the Saviour Jesus Christ conceived of the Virgin Mary." This Article and five others, collectively called "the six whips," repudiated the Protestant wing of the Anglican Church. Latimer resigned his bishopric and was put under house arrest. Released in 1540, he was forbidden to preach and was banished from London. He spent six years in obscurity and was then imprisoned for doubting the statute's teaching on transubstantiation. He was related in 1547 under the new king, Edward VI, and in 1548 was invited to preach at Paul's Cross and before the king. He boldly denounced bribery in high places (Noonan, *Bribes,* 313–315). When the Protector Somerset fell, he retired to Lincolnshire and kept on preaching.

In July 1533 Mary Tudor, a Catholic, became queen. Parliament enacted a statute declaring Henry and Catherine's marriage good, Cranmer's judgment on it corrupt, and Mary legitimate, 1 Mary, c. 1, 6 Pick. Stat. 3. Two months later, Latimer and Cranmer were summoned before the Privy Council for examination. They were imprisoned in the Tower, then moved to Oxford and examined before thirty-three doctors of divinity and found to be heretical. Under Edward the statute on the burning of heretics had been repealed. Legality was observed, and nothing was done to the distinguished prisoners before the law was reenacted in December 1554, 1 Philip and Mary, c. 6, 6 P. Stat. 32. Further delays put a final trial off until September 30, 1555.

John Foxe's work, commonly known as *The Book of Martyrs,* is a martyrology culminating in an account of Protestants killed by those the author describes as "the Persecutors of God's Truth, commonly called Papists." It has the perspective of a polemic by a Protestant who himself had lived through the Marian persecution; it was to count in English history "as much as Drake's drum." The work was first published in 1559 in Basel, four years after Latimer's death, under the title *Rerum in Ecclesia gestarum, quae postremis et periculosis his temporibus evenerunt;* it was put in English in 1563 (D. M. Loades, *The Oxford Martyrs,* 264–266). As the emphasis of the title on "these latter days" suggests, Foxe was a millenarium with an interest in the apocalyptic significance of the martyrdoms. Recent historical scholarship such as Loades's still relies on his account of Latimer's end.

What follows is from Foxe's *Acts and Monuments of These Latter and Perilous Days* (1968 reprint of 1870 edition).

The Behavior of Dr. Ridley and Master Latimer, at the Time of Their Death, Which Was the 16th of October, 1555.

Upon the north-side of the town, in the ditch over against Balliol-college, the place of execution was appointed: and for fear of any tumult that might arise, to let the burning of them, the lord Williams was commanded, by the queen's letters, and the householders of the city, to be there assistant, sufficiently appointed. And when every thing was in a readiness, the prisoners were brought forth by the mayor and the bailiffs.

Master Ridley had a fair black gown furred, and faced with foins, such as he was wont to wear being bishop, and a tippet of velvet furred likewise about his neck, a velvet night-cap upon his head, and a corner cap upon the same, going in a pair of slippers to the stake, and going between the mayor and an alderman, etc.

After him came master Latimer in a poor Bristol frieze frock all worn, with his buttoned cap, and a kerchief on his head, all ready to the fire, a new long shroud hanging over his hose, down to the feet: which at the first sight stirred men's hearts to rue upon them, beholding on the one side, the honour they sometime had, and on the other, the calamity whereunto they were fallen.

Master doctor Ridley, as he passed toward Bocardo, looked up where master Cranmer did lie, hoping belike to have seen him at the glass-window, and to have spoken unto him. But then master Cranmer was busy with friar Soto and his fellows, disputing together, so that he could not see him, through that occasion. Then master Ridley, looking back, espied master Latimer coming after, unto whom he said, "Oh, be ye there?" "Yea," said master Latimer, "have after as fast as I can follow." So he, following a pretty way off, at length they came both to the stake, the one after the other, where first Dr. Ridley entering the place, marvellous earnestly holding up both his hands, looked towards heaven. Then shortly after espying master Latimer, with a wonderous cheerful look he ran to him, embraced, and kissed him; and, as they that stood near reported, comforted him, saying, "Be of good heart, brother, for God will either assuage the fury of the flame, or else strengthen us to abide it."

With that went he to the stake, kneeled down by it, kissed it, and most effectuously prayed, and behind him master Latimer kneeled, as earnestly calling upon God as he. After they arose, the one talked with the other a little while, till they which were appointed to see the execution, removed themselves out of the sun. What they said I can learn of no man.

Then Dr. Smith, of whose recantation in king Edward's time ye heard before, began his sermon to them upon this text of St. Paul, "If I yield my body to the fire to be burnt, and have not charity, I shall gain nothing thereby." Wherein he alleged that the goodness of the cause, and not the order of death, maketh the holiness of the person; which he confirmed by the examples of Judas, and of a woman in Oxford that of late hanged herself, for that they, and such like as he recited, might then be adjudged righteous, which desperately sundered their lives from their bodies, as he feared that those men that stood before him would do. But he cried still to the people to beware of them, for they were heretics, and died out of the church. And on the other side, he declared their diversity in opinions, as Lutherans, (Œcolampadians, Zuinglians, of which sect they were, he said, and that was the worst: but the old church of Christ, and the catholic faith believed far otherwise. At which place they lifted up both their hands and eyes to heaven, as it were calling God to witness of the truth: the which countenance they made in many other places of his sermon, where as they thought he spake amiss. He ended with a very short exhortation to them to recant, and come home again to the church, and save their lives and souls, which else were condemned. His sermon was scant; in all, a quarter of an hour.

Dr. Ridley said to master Latimer, "Will you begin to answer the sermon, or shall I?" Master Latimer said, "Begin you first, I pray you." "I will," said master Ridley.

Then, the wicked sermon being ended, Dr. Ridley and master Latimer kneeled down upon their knees towards my lord Williams of Thame, the vice-chancellor of Oxford, and divers other commissioners appointed for that purpose, who sat upon a form thereby; unto whom master Ridley said, "I beseech you, my lord, even for Christ's sake, that I may speak but two or three words." And whilst my lord bent his head to the mayor and vice-chancellor, to know (as it appeared) whether he might give him leave to speak, the bailiffs and Dr. Marshall, vice-chancellor, ran hastily unto him, and with their hands stopped his mouth, and said, "Master Ridley, if you will revoke your erroneous opinions, and recant the same, you shall not only have liberty so to do, but also the benefit of a subject; that is, have your life." "Not otherwise?" said master Ridley. "No," quoth Dr. Marshal. "Therefore if you will not so do, then there is no remedy but you must suffer for your deserts." "Well," quoth master Ridley, "so long as the breath is in my body, I will never deny my Lord Christ, and his known truth: God's will be done in me!" And with that he rose up, and said with a loud voice, "Well then, I commit our cause to Almighty God, which shall indifferently judge all." To whose saying, master Latimer added his old posy, "Well! there is nothing hid but it shall be opened." And he said, he could answer Smith well enough, if he might be suffered.

Incontinently they were commanded to make them ready, which they with all meekness obeyed. Master Ridley took his gown and his tippet, and gave it to his brother-in-law master Shipside, who all his time of imprisonment, although he might not be suffered to come to him, lay there at his own charges to provide him necessaries, which from time to time he sent him by the serjeant that kept him. Some other of his apparel that was little worth, he gave away; other the bailiffs took.

He gave away besides, divers other small things to gentlemen standing by, and divers of them pitifully weeping, as to sir Henry Lea he gave a new groat; and to divers of my lord Williams's gentlemen some napkins, some nutmegs, and rases of ginger; his dial, and such other things as he had about him, to every one that stood next him. Some plucked the points off his hose. Happy was he that might get any rag of him.

Master Latimer gave nothing, but very quietly suffered his keeper to pull off his hose, and his other array, which to look unto was very simple: and being stripped into his shroud, he seemd as comely a person to them that were there present, as one should lightly see; and whereas in his clothes he appeared a withered and crooked silly old man, he now stood bolt upright, as comely a father as one might lightly behold.

Then master Ridley, standing as yet in his truss, said to his brother, "It were best for me to go in my truss still." "No," quoth his brother, "it will put you to more pain: and the truss will do a poor man good." Whereunto master Ridley said, "Be it, in the name of God;" and so unlaced himself. Then, being in his shirt, he stood upon the foresaid stone, and held up his hand and said, "O heavenly Father, I give unto thee most hearty thanks, for that thou hast called me to be a professor of thee, even unto death. I beseech thee, Lord God, take mercy upon this realm of England, and deliver the same from all her enemies."

Then the smith took a chain of iron, and brought the same about both Dr. Ridley's and master Latimer's middles: and, as he was knocking in a staple, Dr. Ridley took the chain in his hand, and shaked the same, for it did gird in his belly, and looking aside to the smith, said, "Good fellow, knock it in hard, for the flesh will have his course." Then his brother did bring him gunpowder in a bag, and would have tied the same about his neck. Master Ridley asked, what it was. His brother said, "Gunpowder." "Then," said he, "I take it to be sent of God; therefore I will receive it as sent of him. And have you any," said he, "for my brother;" meaning master Latimer. "Yea sir, that I have" quoth his brother. "Then give it unto him," said he, "betime; lest ye come too late." So his brother went, and carried of the same gunpowder unto master Latimer.

In the mean time Dr. Ridley spake unto my lord Williams, and said, "My lord, I must be a suitor unto your lordship in the behalf of divers poor men, and especially in the cause of my poor sister: I have made a supplication to the queen's majesty in their behalfs. I beseech your lordship for Christ's sake, to be a mean to her grace for them. My brother here hath the supplication, and will resort to your lordship to certify you hereof. There is nothing in all the world that troubleth my conscience, I praise God, this only excepted. Whilst I was in the see of London, divers poor men took leases of me, and agreed with me for the same. Now I hear say the bishop that now occupieth the same room, will not allow my grants unto them made, but, contrary unto all law and conscience, hath taken from them their livings, and will not suffer them to enjoy the same. I beseech you, my lord, be a mean for them: you shall do a good deed, and God will reward you."

Then they brought a faggot, kindled with fire, and laid the same down at Dr. Ridley's feet. To whom master Latimer spake in this manner: "Be of good comfort, master Ridley, and play the man. We shall this day light such a candle, by God's grace, in England, as I trust shall never be put out."

And so the fire being given unto them, when Dr. Ridley saw the fire flaming up towards him, he cried with a wonderful loud voice, "In manus tuas, Domine, commendo spiritum meum: Domine receipe spiritum meum." And after, repeated this latter part often in English, "Lord, Lord, receive my spirit;" master Latimer crying as vehemently on the other side, "O Father of heaven, receive my soul!" who received the flame as it were embracing of it. After that he had stroked his face with his hands, and as it were bathed them a little in the fire, he soon died (as it appeareth) with very little pain or none. And thus much concerning the end of this old and blessed servant of God, master Latimer, for whose laborious travails, fruitful life, and constant death, the whole realm hath cause to give great thanks to Almighty God.

FIVE

The Critics of Persecution, 1554–1674

1. "IF THOSE IN GOVERNMENT TRULY KNEW CHRIST . . . ."

The Reformation did not bring religious toleration but increased religious persecution. There were more heretics to be persecuted; moreover, the heretics themselves also persecuted for religion's sake. Martin Luther, Henry VIII, John Calvin, Huldrych Zwingli all endorsed the principle that the secular sword should suppress Christian dissenters; all approved of actual persecutions (Lecler, *Toleration* 1, 162 [Luther authorizes the death penalty for Anabaptists], 328 [Calvin agrees that Michael Servetus, a Unitarian, shall be burned], 200 [Zwingli persecutes the Anabaptists]). The Reformation, however, did smash the old system of Christianity sufficiently so that advocates of toleration appeared. In the first place it stimulated the spread of small sects that were doomed to be minorities and, if persecution was permissible, to be persecuted. Such splinter groups had far more practical incentive to embrace toleration as a principle than had the membership of a dominant church. In the second place, as Protestant churches spread, it became impracticable if not impossible to wipe out all the heretics. Stalemate was the practical situation. Acceptance of the stalemate began to look reasonable. In the third place, the Reformation freed some theological minds to think of the Christian Church as a wholly spiritual body or even a purely spiritual force, spurning worldly assistance. The Catholic Christian tradition was full of acknowledgments of the spiritual nature of the Church. Thomas Aquinas, for example, had defined the New Law as the life of the Spirit in the believer's heart (*Summa Theologiae* 1–2, q. 106, art. 1). But the close involvement of the pope and bishops with terrestrial goods and power had weighed down the spiritual. Now emphasis on the spiritual could predominate and with it a deliberate rejection of unspiritual means for the protection of the spiritual kingdom.

Erasmus (1466–1536) was a Catholic who in 1526 extended Thomas Aquinas's reason for tolerating pagans to the toleration of Lutherans in Germany (Lecler, 1, 119). His more general criticism of unnecessary dogma, his intellectual openness, and his love of peace also inclined him and those who followed him to toleration. The Erasmians encouraged the idea of religious reconciliation within Germany (ibid. 261). In line with Erasmian thought, Emperor Maximilian II in 1568 granted legal toleration to the Lutheran lords within his realm and practical toleration to other Lutherans (*ibid.* 268). In this *modus vivendi* the impossibility of the Catholic emperor ruling without good relations with his Lutheran subjects was acknowledged.

In 1573 at the Warsaw Confederation the nobles and gentry of Poland agreed to an even broader recognition of religious difference. "To preserve the common peace between separated and differing people in faith and worship" and "because in our commonwealth there is significant disagreement in the matter of the Christian religion. . . . we mutually pledge . . . that those of us who disagree about religion shall keep peace among ourselves, refrain from bloodshed over differences of faith or changes of church, nor punish by imprisonment or confiscation. . . ." The king was to swear to uphold this pact (A. Brückner, "The Polish Reformation in the Sixteenth Century," in *Polish Civilization*, ed. M. Giergielwic, 1979, 81). This tolerance extended not only to Catholics, Lutherans, and Calvinists but also to groups denying the divinity of Christ such as the Socinians, Unitarians, and Antitritarians (ibid. 83). For a period, Poland was the most tolerant Christian country in the world. The basis of tolerance was the pragmatic one of securing peace for the state.

Believers in a spiritual Church tended also to be minorities who experienced the pain of persecution. Sebastian Franck (1499–1542) was a minority of one. A Dominican priest who became a Lutheran, he ultimately took the position that "the spiritual, invisible Church" was to be ruled "without exterior means." For him a list of heretics of old became a list of martyrs; and the use of persecution became itself a mark of heresy. Marvelously, the tables were turned on the heresy-hunter, who by his very action proclaimed himself guilty of the sin he hunted. His brothers, Franck declared, were any who wished him well, "Papist, Zwinglian, Anabaptist, or even Turk . . . even if he is a Jew or Samaritan I want to love him and do him as much good as in me lies." The great phrase from Deuteronomy on God as a judge was once more evoked: God is not an *acceptor personarum*, that is, God does not discriminate. Neither, then, should we (Lecler, 1, 166–175).

Other theologians denying that the material sword should be used to defend the spiritual church began to write, for example, Caspar Schwenckfeld (1489–1561), a layman from Silesia (Lecler, 1, 176–185; and Valentine Weigel (1537–1588), outwardly a Lutheran minister, in his heart a believer in a purely invisible Church that eschewed force (Lecler, 1, 186–188). A theologian who had greater impact than Franck or Weigel, because he gathered about him a community, was Menno Simons (1493–1559).

Menno Simons was the Catholic parish priest in his home parish of Witmarsum in Friesland when in 1534 he wrote his first book rebuking the Anabaptists who had resorted to force in ruling the town of Münster. In 1535 he announced that he was himself an Anabaptist, that is, one who believed in the necessity of "again baptizing" because infant baptism was ineffective, and a year later he became the leader of the scattered Anabaptist brethren in Holland. For the remainder of his life he labored as a bishop among the Anabaptists in Holland, Cologne, Holstein, and Baltic Germany. In 1542 the empire put a price of 100 guilders on his head and only sporadically was he safe from betrayal or capture, prosecution and death for heresy. He is recognized not as the founder of the church that bears his name—the church had been founded in Zurich in 1525—but as its inspiring spirit when the faith was threatened by "dungeon, fire, and sword" (Harold S. Bender, "A Brief Biography of Menno Simons," *The Complete Writings of Menno Simons*, 1956, 4–28).

Appealing solely to Scripture, Menno developed a strong concept of the doctrine and moral conduct required of true believers. While the Church he had known as a young man had been tolerant of many sinners, he was clear that the ungodly should be excommunicated and shunned. The "obstinate schismatic . . . and those who do not abide in the doctrine of Christ, who lead an offensive life, or greedy people who lead a soft and easy life at the expense of others shall not be allowed a place in the holy house" (Menno, *Instruction on Excommunication*, *Works* 1, 968). Parents must shun excommunicated children; children, excommunicated parents; a spouse, an excommunicated spouse (ibid. 971). Strict spiritual discipline compensated for civil toleration.

Menno's main doctrinal work, *Fondamentboek*, was published in Dutch in 1539. (His followers were not called by his last name because that would have made them "Simonians," a term already established as a disparaging epithet for those who bought or sold the Spirit like Simon Magus.) Menno's reply to a Reformed minister in Emden, East Friesland, Gellius Faber, *Een klare beantwoordinge over eene schrift Gellii Fabri,* was composed in Northern Germany. The excerpt that follows is from the translation from the Dutch by Leonard Verduin, edited by John Christian Wenger, *The Complete Writings of Menno Simons* 1, 623.

Reply to Gellius Faber (1554)

In the last place he writes of us, saying, "Experience has taught that their teachers and prophets are not such teachers and prophets of God. And that they are not the people of God, I have, perhaps, already proved too powerfully. From which, then, it is clear that our magistrates do right by not letting them proceed in their wicked course but obstructing them diligently. And we might, in pastoral and paternal faithfulness or solicitude for the church of Christ, lest the church be quite destroyed, speak and conclude a bit more sternly concerning them. But then we would be called persecutors and bloodhounds by them."

Reply. Jeremiah, Micah, Elijah, Christ Jesus, and Paul could not pass for the true prophets and servants of God with the perverse; neither can we. But the great Lord shall in due time make it manifest who are the faithful prophets and servants of God and who are not.

Again, to this saying that we are not the people of God, we answer with holy Paul that it is a very small thing that we should be judged with the judgment of men, and especially by men who are so flatly opposed to the ordinance, will, and Word of God as may be seen in the case of Gellius from his writing. Yes, kind reader, if he and similar preachers acknowledged us to be the people of God, they would thereby acknowledge that they are not of that group, a thing which an ambitious carnal person who seeks reputation and fame never will do.

To his assertion that the magistracy does well in obstructing our course which he calls wicked, I reply, that the longer he writes, the more clumsy and offensive he becomes and the more he manifests his blindness. If he is a preacher called by the Spirit of God, then let him show a single letter in all the New Testament that Christ or the apostles have ever called on the magistrates to defend and protect the true church against the attack of the wicked, as, alas, he calls us. No, no, Christ Jesus and His powerful Word and the Holy Spirit are the protectors and defenders of the church, and not, eternally not, the emperor, king, or any worldly potentate! The kingdom of the Spirit must be protected and defended by the sword of the Spirit, and not by the sword of the world. This, in the light of the doctrine and example of Christ and His apostles, is too plain to be denied.

I would say further, if the magistracy rightly understood Christ and His kingdom, they would in my opinion rather choose death than to meddle with their worldly power and sword in spiritual matters which are reserved not to the judgment of man but to the judgment of the great and Almighty God alone. But they are taught by those who have the care of their souls that they may proscribe, imprison, torture, and slay those who are not obedient to their doctrine, as may, alas, be seen in many different cities and countries.

In short, kind reader, if the merciful Lord did not, in His great love, temper the hearts of some of the magistrates, but if they should proceed according to the partisan instigation and blood-preaching of the learned ones, no pious person could endure. But as it is, some are found who, notwithstanding the railing and writing of the learned ones, suffer and bear with the miserable, and for a time show them mercy, a thing for which we will forever give praise to God, the most High, and express our gratitude to such kind and fair governors.

But to his writing that in paternal and pastoral solicitude and faithfulness they might speak and decide a bit more sternly against us, I reply, if he had entered in at the right door of Christ, who is the Prince and Head of all true pastors, and if he had tasted in his heart the friendly and amiable Spirit, nature, and disposition of Christ, then he would not, by any means, think of such a resolution against the blood of others, much less write and mention it. This I know of a certainty, that the Spirit of Christ is not so inclined.

Reader, observe, the reason that he does not write boldly that the magistracy may very well plunge its sword in us, is that he does not want to be called a bloodhound or persecutor; nevertheless he does make it plain that if they should do so, he would call it a praiseworthy thing. Whoever is not quite destitute of understanding, understands very well what his position is in the matter. Oh, doctrine of blood!

2. THE CITY UPON A HILL; THE COVENANT; THE NEW ISRAEL AND THE SEPARATED GARDEN

In 1630 John Winthrop, leader of the Massachusetts Bay Colony, preached to his followers aboard the *Arabella* en route to the new land a sermon he called "Christian Charitee: Modell Hereof" (Winthrop, *Papers* 2, 294–295):

When God giues a speciall Commission he lookes to haue it stricktly obserued in every Article, when hee gaue Saule a Commission to destroy Amaleck hee indented with him vpon certaine Articles and because hee failed in one of the least, and that vpon a faire pretence, it lost him the kingdome, which should haue been his reward, if hee had obserued his Commission: Thus stands the cause betweene God and vs, wee are entered into Covenant with him for this worke, wee haue taken out a Commission, the Lord hath giuen vs leaue to drawe our owne Articles wee haue professed to enterprise these Accions vpon these and these ends, wee haue herevpon besought him of favour and blessing: Now if the Lord shall please to hear vs, and bring vs in peace to the place wee desire, then hath hee ratified this Covenant and sealed our Commission, [and] will expect a strickt performance of the Articles contained in it, but if wee shall neglect the observacion of these Articles which are the ends wee haue propounded, and dissembling with our God, shall fall to embrace this present world and prosecute our carnall intencions, seekeing great things for our selues and our posterity, the Lord will surely breake out in wrathe against vs be revenged of such a periured people and make vs knowe the price of the breache of such a Covenant.

Now the onely way to avoyde this shipwracke and to provide for our posterity·is to followe the Counsell of Micah, to doe Justly, to loue mercy, to walke humbly with our God, for this end, wee must be knitt together in this worke as one man, wee must entertaine each other in brotherly Affeccion, wee must be willing to abridge our selues of our superfluities, for the supply of others necessities, wee must vphold a familiar Commerce together in all meekenes, gentlenes, patience and liberallity, wee must delight in eache other, make others Condicions our owne reioyce together, mourne together, labour, and suffer together, allwayes haueing before our eyes our Commission and Community in the worke, our Community as members of the same body, soe shall wee keepe the vnitie of the spirit in the bond of peace, the Lord will be our God and delight to dwell among vs, as his owne people and will commaund a blessing vpon vs in all our wayes, soe that wee shall see much more of his wisdome power goodnes and truthe then formerly wee haue been acquainted with, wee shall finde that the God of Israell is among vs, when tenn of vs shall be able to resist a thousand of our enemies, when hee shall make vs a prayse and glory, that men shall say of succeeding plantacions: the lord make it like that of New England: for wee must Consider that wee shall be as a Citty vpon a Hill [Mt.5.14] the eies of all people are vppon vs; soe that if wee shall deale falsely with our god in this worke wee haue vndertaken and soe cause him to withdrawe his present help from vs, wee shall be made a story and a by-word through the world, wee shall open the mouthes of enemies to speake euill of the wayes of god and all professours for Gods sake; wee shall shame the faces of many of gods worthy seruants, and cause theire prayers to be turned into Cursses vpon vs till wee be consumed out of the good land whether wee are goeing: And to shutt vpp this discourse with that exhortacion of Moses that faithfull seruant of the Lord in his last farewell to Israell Deut. 30. Beloued there is now sett before vs life, and good, deathe and euill in that wee are Commaunded this day to loue the Lord our God, and to loue one another to walke in his wayes and to keepe his Commaundements and his Ordinance, and his lawes, and the Articles of our Covenant with him that wee may liue and be multiplyed, and that the Lord our God may blesse vs in the land whether wee goe to possesse it: But if our heartes shall turne away soe that wee will not obey, but shall be seduced and worshipp [Serue *cancelled*] other Gods our pleasures, and proffitts, and serue them; it is propounded vnto vs this day, wee shall surely perishe out of the good Land whether wee passe over this vast Sea to possesse it;

Therefore lett vs choose life,
that wee, and our Seede,
may liue; by obeying his
voyce, and cleaueing to him
for hee is our life, and
our prosperity.

Of this sermon a leading authority on contemporary America has written that "In relation to the principal theme of the American mind, the necessity laid upon it for decisions, Winthrop stands at the beginning of our consciousness," Perry Miller, *Nature's Nation* (1967) 6, and a contemporary sociologist sees the sermon as paradigmatic of the way biblical themes were adopted to define the enterprise of the settlers and their implications and obligations, Robert N. Bellah, *The Broken Covenant: American Civil Religion in Time of Trial* (1967) 13.

Imagery and sermon were biblical: the city on a hill from the Gospel, the covenant from Genesis, the whole metaphor from Exodus' story of Moses leading the people of Israel from Egypt to the promised land. Winthrop urged love, and he emphasized community. He did not stress liberty.

The Puritan colony of New Haven, founded in the late 1630s, was even stricter than Massachusetts, Thomas J. Curry, *The First Freedoms: Church and State in America to the Passage of the First Amendment* (1986) 3. The colony provided: "The laws of God as delivered to Moses . . . shall be accounted of moral equity and generally binding on all offenders and be the rule of all courts . . . ," *ibid.* at 224.

When in 1644 Roger Williams published his *Bloudy Tenent of Persecution*, he had had personal experience of what he wrote. Fourteen years earlier, aged about twenty-six, of Welsh antecedents, a graduate of Cambridge University, he had come to the year-old Massachusetts Bay Colony, had been invited to be minister of the church in Boston and had refused. The Puritan leaders of the colony, spiritual elect who had been born again—who were therfore "regenerate"—were dissatisfied with the Anglican Church that embraced the unregenerate, but they had refused to renounce her, "our dear Mother," Edmund S. Morgan, *The Puritan Dilemma* (1958) 53. Williams, a Separatist, not only renounced her but any church that held communion with her, *ibid.* at 117. In the new colony, where each church was a congregation of the reborn—where no bishops existed to enforce uniformity of doctrine—Williams's view had a chance of being accepted by some congregation. In 1635 he was chosen by the church in Salem to be its minister.

The choice was a challenge to the colony. Williams was hailed before the General Court, the civil authority, and charged with teaching four doctrines: that the true owners of "our land," conferred by the king's charter, were the Indians; that one should not pray with the unregenerate or even accept an oath, an act of worship, from the unregenerate; that communion could not be had with the ministers of the Church of England; and that civil power could not be used to enforce religious opinions. Williams cheerfully acknowledged the truth of these charges, Williams, *Mr. Cottons Letter Lately Printed, Examined and Answered* (1644), *The Complete Writings of Roger Williams* (1963) 1, 325. As with Menno, rigidity of spiritual standard accompanied, or compensated for, latitude of civil freedom. On October 9, 1635, the Court ordered him to leave the colony.

Williams believed that the other churches of the colony had forfeited their purity by calling on the civil magistracy to act against him, so Salem should break with them. In the vernacular of modern politics, the General Court played hardball. It notified Salem that it would not have Marblehead Neck if it stayed with Williams. Many other considerations also tied Salem to the rest of the colony. Williams was deserted by the majority of his congregation. Acting on a suggestion by Governor Winthrop, he decided to start a new settlement to the south at Narragansett Bay, and, to avoid being deported to England, he departed abruptly in January 1636 for the southern wilderness.

As Williams saw it, he had voluntarily left "churches resolved to continue in those evils," but because the colony treated church and civil community as coterminous, he had been involuntarily banished from the civil state "in so sharp a time of New England's cold," *ibid.* He had not been put to death, he had been driven to extremities. Punished in part for his religious condemnation of religious persecution, he now conceived a passionate horror of such use of secular force.

Eight years after his flight from Massachusetts, Williams was in London to seek a charter for his new colony, Rhode Island. The English Civil War was in progress. Parliament was largely divided between Presbyterians, favoring control of local churches by a hierachy of governing bodies, and Independents sympathetic to the Congregational model of New England. Neither side believed in religious tolerance. To the theologians of the Independents, Williams addressed *Queries of Highest Consideration,* warning them against "spiritual rape" by using force to compel conscience, Perry Miller, *Roger Williams* (1953) 79, 83. Almost simultaneously he answered his chief critic from Massachusetts, John Cotton, "Teacher of the Church in Boston," attacking the unity of ecclesiastical and civil power that characterized the Bay Colony, *ibid.* at 106–107.

The Christian church, Williams wrote, is "separate from the world." He continued,

and when they opened a gap in the hedge or wall of separation between the garden of the church and the wilderness of the world, God hath ever broke down the wall itself, removed the candlestick, and made his garden a wilderness as at this day" [Williams, *Mr. Cotton's Letter, Writings* 1, 392].

The image of the garden was scriptural, beginning with the description of the Garden of Eden in Genesis. To describe the church as God's garden was commonplace, e.g., Thomas Aquinas, *In sententias Petri Lombardi,* Bk. 1, 140. The wilderness was also scriptural—Moses had led Israel in the wilderness, Christ had prayed in the wilderness, *cf.* George H. Williams, *Wilderness and Paradise in Christian Thought* (1962). What was different in Roger Williams was, first, his lively sense of what a physical wilderness was. It was "an howling wilderness, in frost and snow" that he reminded Cotton he had been forced to enter. Second, "the wall of separation" between garden and wilderness was an unusual metaphor. (On the general use of the metaphor of law as well or bulwark, *see also* Milner S. Ball, *Lying Down Together: Law, Metaphor and Theology* [1985] 23–27.) The wall or hedge, which God himself would break down if a gap was allowed in it, was thought of as a structure protecting the holiness of the church, keeping it from contamination by the world. Third, as important as "wall"— probably more important to Williams—was "separation." Separateness for the holy was the great cause for which he had entered the wilderness. The "wall of separation" was a metaphor destined to have an extraordinary future in American political thought.

In March 1644 Parliament gave Rhode Island a charter. Williams's mission was accomplished. He stayed on to complete *The Bloudy Tenent, of Persecution, for cause of Conscience, discussed, in A Conference betweene Truth and Peace.* The preface addresses Parliament, dominated by Presbyterians, and then "every courteous reader." Saturated in Scripture, he pointedly appealed to the popularity of the English Bible in asking how England with the Bible was better than Spain without it, if the civil power was to determine doctrine. He equally appealed to experience—the experience of killing generated by religious disagreement. In the midst of war, Williams prophetically pointed the way to peace. But peace in his view was not achieved by sacrificing truth. His dialogists, Peace and Truth, are not adversaries.

For over 1300 years Christians had persecuted because they believed it was their duty to uphold the truth. No doubt in individual cases they had been cruel as well as intolerant. But always they had thought that because they were right in their doctrine, they were right in their persecution. Williams told them that they could not be right in doctrine if they believed that persecution was right. Like Sebastian Franck, he made persecution a sign of Christian heresy not faith. A persecuting Christian was a self-canceling phrase. On the foundation of the teaching of Jesus Christ, Williams proclaimed a gospel of liberty of religious belief.

Roger Williams, The Blovdy Tenent, Of PERSECUTION, For Cause Of CONSCIENCE, Discussed, In *A* Conference *Betweene* Trvth And Peace. WHO, In All Tender Affection, Present To The High Court Of PARLIAMENT, (As The *Result* Of Their *Discourse*) These, (Amongst Other *Passages*) Of *Highest Consideration* (1644)

First, that the blood of so many hundred thousand souls of Protestants and Papists, spilt in the wars of present and former ages, for their respective consciences, is not required nor accepted by Jesus Christ the Prince of Peace.

Secondly, pregnant Scriptures and arguments are throughout the work proposed against the doctrine of persecution for the cause of conscience.

Thirdly, satisfactory answers are given to Scriptures, and objections produced by Mr. Calvin, Beza, Mr. Cotton, and the ministers of the New English Churches and others former and later, tending to prove the doctrine of persecution for cause of conscience.

Fourthly, the doctrine of persecution for cause of conscience is proved guilty of all the blood of the souls crying for vengeance under the altar.

Fifthly, all civil states with their officers of justice in their respective constitutions and administrations are proved essentially civil, and therefore not judges, governors, or defenders of the spiritual or Christian state and worship.

Sixthly, it is the will and command of God, that (since the coming of his son the Lord Jesus) a permission of the most paganish, Jewish, Turkish, or antichristian consciences and worships, be granted to all men in all nations and countries: and they are only to be fought against with that sword which is only (in soul matters) able to conquer, to wit, the sword of God's spirit, the word of God.

Seventhly, the state of the land of Israel, the kings and people thereof in peace and war, is proved figurative and ceremonial, and no pattern nor precedent for any kingdom or civil state in the world to follow.

Eighthly, God requireth not an uniformity of religion to be enacted and enforced in any civil state; which enforced uniformity (sooner or later) is the greatest occasion of civil war, ravishing of conscience, persecution of Christ Jesus in his servants, and of all hypocrisy and destruction of millions of souls.

Ninthly, in holding an enforced uniformity of religion in a civil state, we must necessarily disclaim our desires and hopes of the Jews' conversion to Christ.

Tenthly, an enforced uniformity of religion throughout a nation or civil state, confounds the civil and religious, denies the principles of Christianity and civility, and that Jesus Christ is come in the flesh.

Eleventhly, the permission of other consciences and worships than a state professeth, only can (according to God) procure a firm and lasting peace (good assurance being taken according to the wisdom of the civil state for uniformity of civil obedience from all sorts).

Twelfthly, lastly, true civility and Christianity may both flourish in a state or kingdom, not withstanding the permission of divers and contrary consciences, either of Jew or Gentile [Preface, *Writings,* 3, 3–4].

. . .

In vain have English Parliaments permitted English Bibles in the poorest English houses, and the simplest man or woman to search the Scriptures, if yet against their souls' persuasion from the Scripture, they should be forced (as if they lived in Spain or Rome itself without the sight of a Bible) to believe as the Church believes.

Fourthly, having tried, we must hold faith, 1 Thess. 5. upon the loss of a Crown, Revel. 3. We must not let go for all the flea-bitings of the present afflictions, etc. Having bought Truth dear, we must not sell it cheap, not the least grain of it for the whole World, no not for the saving of souls, though our own most precious; least of all the bitter sweetening of a little vanishing pleasure.

For a little puff of credit and reputation from the changeable breath of uncertain sons of men.

For the broken bags of Riches on Eagles' wings: For a dream of these, any or all of these which on our death-bed vanish and leave tormenting stings behind them: Oh how much better is it from the love of Truth, from the love of the Father of lights, from whence it comes, from the love of the Son of God, who is the Way and the Truth, to say as he, John 18.37. For this end was I born, and for this end came I into the World that I might bear witness to the Truth . . . [To Every Courteous Reader, *ibid.* 3, 13].

Lastly, I ask, whether (as men deal with wolves) these wolves at Ephesus were intended by Paul to be killed, their brains dashed out with stones, staves, halberts, guns, etc. in the hands of the Elders of Ephesus, etc.?

TRUTH. Doubtless (comparing spiritual things with spiritual) all such mystical wolves must spiritually and mystically be slain. And the Witnesses of Truth, Revel. II. speak fire, and kill all that hurt them, by that fiery word of God, and that two edged sword in their hand, Psal. 149.

But oh what streams of blood of saints have been and must be shed (until the Lamb have obtained the victory, Rev. 17) by this unmerciful (and in the state of the New Testament, when the Church is spread all the world over) most bloody doctrine, viz. The wolves (heretics) are to be driven away, their brains knocked out and killed, the poor sheep to be preserved for whom Christ died, etc.

Is not this to take Christ Jesus, and make him a temporal king by force? John 6.15. Is not this to make his kingdom of this world, to set up a civil and temporal Israel? [ch. 43, *ibid.* 3, 145]. . . . First, it will appear that in spiritual things they make the garden and the wilderness (as often I have intimated) I say the garden and the wilderness, the church and the world are all one: for thus,

If the powers of the world of civil state, are bound to propose external peace in all godliness for their end, and the end of the church be to preserve internal peace in all godliness, I demand if their end (godliness) be the same, is not their power and state the same also, unless they make the church subordinate to the commonwealth's end, or the commonweal subordinate to the church's end, which (being the governor and setter up of it, and so consequently the judge of it) it cannot be? [c. 86, *ibid.* 3, 233].

PEACE. Yea but they say that "such laws as are conversant about religion, may still be accounted civil laws, as on the contrary an oath doth still remain religious, though conservant about civil matters."

TRUTH. Laws respecting religion are two-fold:

First, such as concern the acts of worship and the worship itself, the ministers of it, their fitness or unfitness, to be suppressed or established: and for such laws we find no footing in the New Testament of Jesus Christ.

Secondly, laws respecting religion may be such as merely concern the civil state, bodies and goods of such and such persons, processing these and these religions, viz. that such and such persons, notorious for mutinies, treasons, rebellions, massacres, be disarmed: again, that no persons Papists, Jews, Turks, or Indians be disturbed at their worship (a thing which the very Indians abhor to practice towards any.) Also that immunity and freedom from tax and toll may be granted unto the people of such or such a religion, as the magistrate pleaseth. Ezra 7.

These and such as are of this nature, concerning only the bodies and goods of such and such religious persons, I confess are merely civil [c. 92, *ibid.* 3, 252].

With less sin ten thousand fold may a natural father force his daughter, or the father of the commonweal force all the maidens in a country to the marriage beds of such and such men whom they cannot love, than the souls of these and other subjects to such worship or ministry, which is either a true or false bed . . . [c. 94, *ibid.* 3, 259].

PEACE. Their third reason is, it will dissolve the continuity of the state, especially theirs, where the walls are made of the stones of the churches.

TRUTH. I answer briefly to this bare affirmation thus, that the true church is a wall spiritual and mystical, Cant. 8.9.

Then consequently a false church or company is a false or pretended wall, and none of Christ's.

The civil state, power and government is a civil wall, etc. and

Lastly, the walls of earth or stone about a city are the natural or artificial wall or defense of it.

Now in consideration of these four walls I desire it may be proved from the Scriptures of truth, how the false spiritual wall or company of false worshipers suffered in a city can be able to destroy the true Christian wall or company of believers.

Again, how this false spiritual wall or false church permitted, can destroy the civil wall, the state and government of the city and citizens, any more than it can destroy the natural or artificial wall of earth or stone.

Spiritual may destroy spiritual, if a stronger and victorious, but spiritual cannot reach to artificial or civil.

PEACE. Yea, but they fear the false spiritual wall may destroy their civil, because it is made of the stones of churches.

TRUTH. If this has reference to that practice amongst them, viz. that none but members of churches enjoy civil freedom amongst them (ordinarily) in imitation of that national church or state of the Jews, then I answer, they that follow Moses' church constitution (which the New English by such a practice implicitly do) must cease to pretend to the Lord Jesus Christ and his institutions.

Secondly, we shall find lawful civil states both before and since Christ Jesus, in which we find not any tidings of the true God or Christ.

Lastly, their civil New English state framed out of their churches may yet stand, subsist and flourish, although they did (as by the word of the Lord they ought) permit either Jews or Turks or antichristians to live amongst them subject unto their civil government [c. 102, *ibid.* 3, 286].

In 1651 John Clark, the leader of the Baptists in Newport, Rhode Island, and his colleague Obadiah Holmes, secretly visited a dying coreligionist in Lynn, Massachusetts. They were detected and tried; Clark was fined, Holmes was whipped. Williams addressed John Endecott, governor of Massachusetts, denouncing these punishments. He published the letter the following year in London where the English government, headed by Oliver Cromwell, was sure to take a hostile view of a colony that persecuted Protestants. To the extent that he could count on that reaction, Williams evened a score. But Cromwell's view of Catholics was less generous; Williams risked defending Catholics, too. An excerpt from the letter follows:

Roger Williams to John Endecott, August, 1651

Be pleased then (honored Sir) to remember that, that thing which we call Conscience is of such a nature, (especially in Englishmen) as once a Pope of Rome at the suffering of an Englishman in Rome, himself observed that although it be groundless, false, and deluded, yet it is not by any arguments or torments easily removed.

I speak not of the stream of the multitude of all nations, which have their ebbings and flowings in religion, (as the longest sword, and strongest arm of flesh carries it). But I speak of Conscience, a persuasion fixed in the mind and heart of a man, which enforceth him to judge (as Paul said of himself a persecutor) and to do so and so, with respect to God, His worship, &c.

This Conscience is found in all mankind, more or less, in Jews, Turks, Papists, Protestants, Pagans, &c. And to this purpose let me freely without offence remember you (as I did Mr. Clarke newly come up from his sufferings amongst you) I say, remember you of the same story I did him, 'twas that of William Hartley, in Queen Elizabeth her days, who receiving the sentence of hanging &c., drawing, spake confidently (as afterwards he suffered), what tell you me of hanging, &c. If I had ten thousand millions of lives, I would spend them all for the Faith of Rome," &c.

I confess, that for confidence no Romish Priest hath ever exceeded the martyrs or witnesses of Jesus: Witness (amongst so many) that holy English woman, who cried out, that if every hair of her head were a life or man, they should burn for the name of the Lord Jesus: But Sir, your principles and conscience bind you not to respect Romish or English, saints or sinners: William Hartley, and that Woman, with all their lives, you are bound by your Conscience to punish (and it may be) to hang or burn, if they transgress against your Conscience, and that because according to Mr. Cotton's monstrous distinction (as some of his chief brethren to my knowledge hath called it) not because they sin in matters of Conscience, (which he denies the magistrate to deal in) but because they sin against their Conscience [*Writings*, 6, 219–221].

Roger Williams deplored in particular the "horrible *oppressions* and horrible *slaughters*" that the Jews had suffered from English kings and people and ventured the thought that to remove guilt and pacify God "a great and weighty Duty" lay upon the state to provide the Jews "some gracious *Expedients.*" Roger Williams, "A *Testimony* to the 4th *Paper* presented by *Major* Butler to the Honorable *Committee* for propagating the *Gospel*," *Writings* 7, 137.

Williams was not a champion of disestablishment or of pacifism. In the *Bloudy Tenet, supra,* he had acknowledged that immunity from taxation could be granted by the civil magistrate on a religious basis. When in 1655 the town of Providence organized a militia, a number of Baptists objected, in the name of religious liberty, to bearing arms. Williams, the President of the Colony, wrote (Williams, *Writings* VI, 278–279):

To the Town of Providence

Providence, January, 1654–5

That ever I should speak or write a tittle, that tends to such an infinite liberty of conscience, is a mistake, and which I have ever disclaimed and abhorred. To prevent such mistakes, I shall at present only propose this case: There goes many a ship to sea, with many hundred souls in one ship, whose weal and woe is common, and is a true picture of a commonwealth, or a human combination or society. It hath fallen out sometimes that both papists and protestants, Jews and Turks, may be embarked in one ship; upon which supposal I affirm, that all the liberty of conscience, that ever I pleaded for, turns upon these two hinges—that none of the papists, protestants, Jews, or Turks be forced to come to the ship's prayers or worship, nor compelled from their own particular prayers or worship, if they practice any. I further add, that I never denied that, notwithstanding this liberty, the commander of this ship ought to command the ship's course, yea, and also command that justice, peace, and sobriety, be kept and practiced, both among the seamen and all the passengers. If any of the seamen refuse to perform their services, or passengers to pay their freight; if any refuse to help, in person or purse, towards the common charges or defence; if any refuse to obey the common laws and orders of the ship, concerning their common peace or preservation; if any shall mutiny and rise up against their commanders and officers; if any should preach or write that there ought to be no commanders or officers, because all are equal in Christ, therefore no masters nor officers, no laws nor orders, nor corrections nor punishments;—I say, I never denied, but in such cases, whatever is pretended, the commander or commanders may judge, resist, compel and punish such transgressors, according to their deserts and merits. This, if seriously and honestly minded, may, if it so please the Father of lights, let in some light to such as willingly shut not their eyes.

I remain studious of your common peace and liberty.

Roger Williams

3. THE LIMITS OF POWER

Menno and Roger Williams were pastors and pioneers. Among the erudite of Europe only Erasmus had ever been a moderate champion of tolerance; even he had not stood for religious liberty. On the whole, intellectuals well into the seventeenth century stood with the old doctrine that some forms of religious dissent were literally intolerable. A new note is sounded in 1670 when a major philosopher used his pen to attack all, or nearly all, forms of civil intolerance. The writer is Baruch Spinoza, and his work *Tractatus theologico-politicus*.

The note is new in another way. It is sounded by one writing against the background of Jewish experience. Spinoza's grandfather Abraham had moved from Portugal to Holland, valuing its tolerance. Spinoza's father Michael was the head of the Jewish community in Amsterdam, and Baruch Spinoza himself was brought up on the Bible and the Talmud. But in 1656, at the age of twenty-four, he was excommunicated by the congregation of which he had been a member. He was thereafter a minority of one, religiously neither Jew nor Christian.

What Spinoza proceeded to do was to develop his own view of the world, retaining the vocabulary of earlier theology but redefining key terms such as "God" and pouring his own content into the redefinition. God, for example, is not for him an intelligent, omnipotent Lawmaker and Judge. In the *Tractatus,* Chapter 19, he specifically denies that God has given any laws. In the *Ethics* God is seen as an impersonal force. As Wolfson has expressed it, Spinoza's "work of rationalization" of religious dogma was to say in effect to the orthodox,

"I see no reason why I should not use your own formulae, but I must give them an interpretation of my own," Harry Wolfson, *The Philosophy of Spinoza* (1969) 1, 22. Spinoza examines religious toleration from the angle of a disbeliever in any religious creed.

Spinoza's friends had included Mennonites, and it is reasonable to see their benign influence in his interest in toleration. But while Menno had used Scripture to prove the rightness of toleration, Spinoza put his views forward in a book that was largely a critique of Scripture. Moreover, he had derived from Descartes a desire for demonstration in philosophy. He wanted to show not merely that religious freedom was desirable but that it was necessary.

The sequel showed how confined he was. The Synod of Delft, a body of the Reformed Church, condemned his book. The Supreme Powers, the States-General, condemned his book. It had been published anonymously—another caution—and he was not pursued in person. But his views were intolerable in tolerant Holland. Spinoza's reputation after his death was that of a dangerous atheist. Neither civil authorities nor Christian moralists were willing to be taught by him. The immediate impact of the *Tractatus* on the thought of Europe was therefore not tangible. The overwhelming fact of history is that a European philosopher for the first time treated liberty of thought and speech as a major good.

The centerpiece of Spinoza's presentation is his treatment of *fides,* that marvelous Latin word meaning religious belief, marital fidelity, feudal fealty, commercial rectitude, and civic faithfulness. Shame on the translators of Spinoza who translate *fides* as "honesty"! Heresy in the Middle Ages had been suppressed in the name of faith. It was the breach of faith that was punished. Spinoza turns the tables. In the name of faith, heresy is *not* to be punished. Faithfulness is corrupted by persecution. As firmly as Franck or Williams, Spinoza inverts the old position and now, on philosophical grounds, makes persecution the enemy of *fides.*

A paradox: a champion of natural law, the Holy Spirit as law within the human heart and the strict limits of secular authority, such as Thomas Aquinas, is a defender of the suppression of heresy by force; an analyst who identifies power with right, like Spinoza, insists that opinion and its expression must be free. Perhaps the paradox proves no more than the inability of even very great philosophers to reason consistently, or no more than that in Thomas's case an institutional context dominated his conclusions, and he did not dwell on history. Spinoza's appeal is ultimately not to philosophical reasoning about power or to observations about irrepressible opinions, but to the history of religious strife. Experience spoke with an authority stronger than any syllogism.

Spinoza, *Theological-Political Treatise,* Chapter 20

If it were equally easy to command minds and tongues, everyone would reign in safety and no rule would be oppressive: for everyone would live according to the wish of the rulers and by their decree alone would judge what is true and false, good or bad, just or unjust. But this, as I have already noted at the start of Chapter 18, cannot be—that is, that a mind be absolutely under the right [*ius*] of another, because no one can transfer to another his own natural right or his faculty of reasoning freely and judging about everything whatsoever; nor can he be compelled to do so. Hence it happens that that rule is regarded as oppressive which is over minds, and that supreme majesty appears to do injury to its subjects and usurp their right when it wants to prescribe to each one what is to be embraced as true and to be rejected as false and what opinions ought to move each mind with devotion to God. These things are the right of each one. No one, even if he wanted to, could yield them.

I grant that judgment can be prejudiced in many and almost incredible ways, so that although it be not directly under the rule of another, yet it so depends on the word of another that it could deservedly be said to be under his right. But whatever art can afford in this matter, it has never happened that human beings have not experienced that each one is full of his own meanings, and that there are as many differences between heads as between palates.

Moses, who not by deceit but by divine virtue had captivated the judgment of his people, was nevertheless not able to avoid their rumors and malignant misinterpretations. Much less any of the other monarchs. But if this could in any way be conceived of, it would be conceivable only in a monarchy, not at all in a democracy where all or a great part of the populace partake collegially in ruling. I think the reason for this is plain to everyone.

Although, then, the Supreme Powers are believed to have a right to everything as the interpreters of the law and of religion, they nevertheless can never achieve a condition where human beings do not judge about everything by their own judgment and are not affected by this or that affection. The Supreme Powers can indeed rightly hold as enemies all who do not absolutely agree with them in all things. But now I do not argue about what they can do with right but about what is useful.

I conceded that they can rightly rule most opressively and send citizens to death for the most trivial reasons. But, because they cannot do such things without great risk to their rule as a whole, I can also deny that they have an absolute capability to do these and similar things, and I can consequently deny that they have an absolute right to do so. For, as I have shown, the rights of the Supreme Powers are determined by their capability.

If, therefore, no one can yield his freedom of judging and feeling what he wishes and if everyone by the greatest law of nature is master of his own thoughts, it follows that never in a commonwealth, except with unhappy results, can it be attempted to have human beings, who think diverse and contrary things, speak only what is prescribed for them by the Supreme Powers. Not even the most expert—I say nothing of the populace—know how to be silent. It is a common human vice to entrust one's plans, when one should be silent, to others.

Therefore, that rule will be most oppressive where each one is denied freedom to say and to teach what he thinks. On the contrary, that rule will be moderate where the same liberty is granted to each. But I also cannot deny that majesty can be injured by words as well as by deed; and so if it is impossible to take away this liberty from subjects entirely, it will be, on the other hand, most pernicious to concede it completely. Therefore I must here inquire how far this liberty can and should be granted, preserving the peace of the commonwealth and preserving the rights of the Supreme Powers. This, as I said at the start of Chapter 16, is my particular object.

It follows most plainly from the foundations of the commonwealth set out above that its ultimate end is not to dominate or to hold human beings with fear and make them under another's right but on the contrary to free each one from fear to live as safely as possible—that is, to let each best keep his own natural right to exist and to work without loss to himself or to others. No, I say, the end of the commonwealth is not to make beasts or automatons out of rational human beings, but rather to let them enjoy their minds and bodies safely in their functions and to let them use reason freely and not to fight with hatred, anger, or deceit nor regard each other in an unjust spirit. The end of the commonwealth, therefore, is, in truth, liberty.

Further, to form a commonwealth we saw that this one thing was necessary: that all power to make decrees be in all, or some, or one; for the free judgment of human beings is so various, and everyone thinks he knows everything, that it cannot happen that all think the same things and speak with one mouth. They could not live peacefully unless each one gave up the right of acting only on the decree of his own mind. Therefore everyone has given up only the right of acting from his own decree, but not the right of reasoning and judging. Hence, preserving the right of the Supreme Powers, no one can act against their decree, but anyone can think and judge, and consequently also speak, against it, provided he merely speaks or teaches and defends what he says with reason, not with deceit, anger, hatred or intent of introducing something into the commonwealth on the authority of his own decree. For example, if anyone shows some statute to be repugnant to sound reason and judges that it should be repealed and submits his opinion to the Supreme Power (which alone can make or repeal statutes), and meanwhile does not act contrary to the statute, he deserves very well of the commonwealth as the best of citizens. But if he acts against the statute to accuse the magistrate of injustice and make him odious to the crowd or in a seditious way tries to abrogate a statute against the magistrate's will, he is simply an agitator and a rebel.

We see, then, how, preserving the rights and authority of the Supreme Powers (that is, preserving the peace of the commonwealth), each one can speak and teach the things he thinks—assuredly if he leaves to the Supreme Powers the decrees for doing everything and does nothing against their decree, even if he often judges it to be contrary to what he judges good and openly thinks ought to be done. He can do this preserving justice and religion; rather, he must do this if he wants to show himself as just and religious. For, as I have already shown, justice depends on the decree of the Supreme Powers. Hence no one can be just unless he lives according to their received decrees. Piety, as I have shown in the preceding chapters, is supreme when it is exercised by serving the peace and tranquility of the commonwealth, and these cannot be kept if each one lives according to his own decision. Hence it is impious to do something by one's own decision against a decree of the Supreme Power to whom one is subject, since if this was permitted to everyone, the ruin of their rule would necessarily follow. He cannot do anything against the decree and dictate of his own reason as long as he acts according to the decrees of the Supreme Power; for at the persuasion of his own reason he has decided to transfer his right of living according to his own judgment to the Supreme Power.

And I can confirm these things from practice. At meetings either of the Supreme Powers or lesser powers, anything is rarely done with the unanimous vote of all the members; yet everything is done by the common decree of all—that is, of those who voted against it as much as of those who voted for it. However, I return to my subject.

We have then seen that on the basis of the fundamentals of the commonwealth each one can use liberty of justice preserving the right of the Supreme Powers. It is not less determined by the fundamentals what opinions in the commonwealth are seditious. Assuredly they are those which as soon as they are proposed remove the compact by which everyone has yielded the right of acting by his own judgment. For example, if anyone thinks that the Supreme Power ought not to have its right, or that no one ought to keep his promises, or that it is necessary for everyone to live according to his own judgment, and other things of this sort directly repugnant to the compact, such a one is seditious—not so much indeed on account of his judgment and opinion as because of the action which such judgments involve, i.e., because by the very fact that he thinks such a thing he dissolves the faith he has tacitly or expressly pledged to the Supreme Power.

Hence other opinions which do not involve an act—that is, the breaking of the compact, vengeance, wrath, etc.—are not seditious; except perhaps in a commonwealth corrupted in some way, where the superstitious and the ambitious, who cannot stand liberal men, have gained such a reputation they have more authority with the populace than the Supreme Powers. I cannot deny that there are also opinions which, although they appear to concern only what is true or false, are proposed and circulated in an unjust spirit; but I have already dealt with these in Chapter 15 in such a way that reason remained free. In short, if we attend to this, that the faith of anyone towards the commonwealth, as towards God, can only be known from his works, i.e., from charity towards his neighbor, we can never doubt that the best commonwealth concedes to each the same liberty of philosophizing as we have shown that faith concedes to each one. I admit that some inconveniences sometimes arise from such liberty, but what was ever so wisely established that no inconvenience could arise from it? He who wants to settle everything by laws will aggravate vices, not correct them. What cannot be prevented must necessarily be conceded, although loss often follows. How many evils arise from lust, envy, avarice, drunkenness and similar things? But these things are put up with because they cannot be prohibited by the command of laws, although in truth they are vices. So much the more should liberty of judgment be granted, which undoubtedly is a virtue and which cannot be suppressed. Add that no inconveniences arise from it which cannot be avoided (as I shall at once show) by the authority of the magistrates. I say nothing as to how this liberty is especially necessary to promote the arts and sciences, for these are cultivated with happy results by those who have free and unprejudiced judgment.

But suppose that this liberty can be suppressed and that human beings can be so restricted that they dare murmur nothing except what is prescribed by the Supreme Powers. It will never happen that they will think nothing except what the Supreme Powers want. Hence it will necessarily follow that human beings will think one thing and say another; and consequently, faith, which is especially necessary in a commonwealth, will be corrupted and an abominable flattery and faithlessness fostered, from which will come frauds and the corruption of every good act. But it is far from being possible that all should speak to order. On the contrary, the more care is taken to deprive human beings of liberty of speech, the more contumaciously they will resist— not indeed the avaricious, the flatterers and other powerless minds whose supreme salvation is to contemplate cash in a chest and to have their stomachs stretched, but those whom good education, integrity of morals, and virtue have made more free. Such human beings are generally so constituted that they bear nothing less patiently than having opinions which they believe to be true held to be criminal and to have held against them as wickedness what moves them to piety towards God and humans. On this account they detest such laws and think that whatever is attempted against the magistrate is not disgraceful but highly honest. For this reason they cause revolts and try every kind of crime.

Since, then, it is established that human nature can be so compared, it follows that laws about opinions do not affect the wicked but the good and are issued not to coerce the malignant but to harass the decent and cannot be defended without great danger to the government. Add that such laws are entirely useless, for those who believe that the opinions condemned by the laws are sound cannot obey the laws, while those who reject the opinions as false receive the laws by which they are condemned as privileges and so triumph in them that a magistrate could not, if he wished, repeal them. Then there are the matters we laid out in Chapter 18 from the history of the Hebrews. Finally, how many schisms have arisen in the Church because magistrates wanted to resolve controversies by laws? For if human beings were not bound by the hope of dragging the laws and the magistrates to their side, and triumphing over their adversaries with the applause of the crowd, and acquiring official honor, they would never fight in an unjust spirit in such a way, nor would such frenzy agitate their minds.

Not only reason but daily experience teaches these things. Laws by which it is commanded what each one should believe and by which it is forbidden to speak or write against this or that opinion are often established to gratify or, rather, to appease the anger of those who cannot stand free talent; such men by certain crooked authority can easily convert the devotion of a rebellious populace to madness and rouse it against whomever they want. How much better it would be to restrain the anger and frenzy of the crowd than to enact useless statutes that cannot be violated except by those who love the virtues and the arts and to reduce the commonwealth to such straits that it cannot support liberal men!

. . . If no servility but faithfulness be of value, and the Supreme Powers are to retain their rule in the best way and not be compelled to yield to the seditious, liberty of judgment must necessarily be granted and human beings must be ruled in such a way that although they openly think different and contrary things, yet they live in concord.

4. "THE TRUE BUSINESS OF RELIGION"

John Locke (1632–1704) is commonly thought of today as a philosopher or political theorist; but that is only because modern interests have been less theological than his. The author of *Infalliblis Interpres Scripturae Non Necessarius* ("An Infallible Interpreter of Scripture Not Necessary," a very early work), of *An Essay for Understanding St. Paul's Epistles by Consulting St. Paul Himself*, of *The Reasonableness of Christianity as Delivered in the Scriptures*, of *Vindication of the Reasonableness of Christianity*, and of *Second Vindication of the Reasonableness of Christianity*, Locke was not merely a religious man. He was a master theologian with his own view of revelation and its exposition, with his own very clear, very moderate, very persuasive vision of the essentials of Christianity free from the dogma and the controversies, the elaborations, and, as he thought, the quibbles that had marred that exposition up to his time. That he constantly appeals to reason and makes reasonableness his criterion should lead no one to suppose that he is a rationalist in the sense of a critic of Christianity superior to its influences. As Christopher Hill has pointed out, "reason" is a social construct, Hill, *Change and Continuity in Seventeenth Century England* (1974) 120. Locke's "reason" is that of a man brought up in the mild Anglicanism of mid-seventeenth-century Oxford, exposed to Latitudinarian influence, and throughly convinced that the moral teachings of Christ are binding norms. It is from the perspective of this theology—tolerant of much doctrinal squabbling, moralistic, firmly antipapal—that Locke wrote his famous *Letter on Toleration*.

Note in particular the opening sentence setting out "the chief characteristic mark of the true church." In the opening paragraphs he then quotes twice from the Gospel of Luke, and once each from Galatians, Romans, and Second Timothy. He proceeds to state what "the business of true religion is." He goes on to elucidate what is the purpose of a church. It is "the public worship of God and by means thereof acquisition of eternal life." A corollary for him is that a church has rules only relating to spiritual matters. As much as for Menno or Roger Williams, for Locke a church is conceived of as a purely spiritual society.

The *Letter* was written to another theologian, Philip van Limborch, professor of divinity at the Arminian or Remonstrant Church at Amsterdam. When the letter first appeared anonymously in Latin, it was plausibly attributed to Limborch himself or to another Arminian divine, Jean LeClerc, *see* Raymond Klibansky, Preface to John Locke, *Epistola de Tolerantia* (1968) xx. The Arminians, who were strongly opposed to the dominant Dutch Calvinists, were already attached to the ideas Locke celebrated: that the essence of Christianity consisted in a few "fundamental articles" and that all who accepted them should treat their other institutional, ritual, and doctrinal differences as unimportant, Jean LeClerc quoted, *ibid.* xvii. Locke, as it were, restated for the Arminians their own convictions. They were precariously perched within the Calvinist commonwealth; Locke was an exile from an England ruled once more by a Catholic king. Sharply different from Spinoza in belief, the religious minority and the exile saw with the same sharpness as Spinoza that religious toleration was a great good.

Locke had one advantage over Spinoza: experience in political affairs. He had in fact been in the service of one of the most active politicians of the age, Anthony Ashley Cooper. Cooper—Lord Ashley when Locke joined his household in 1667—was on his way up. A Roundhead under Oliver Cromwell, he had made a smooth transition when General Monk brought King Charles II back. We see him in Samuel Pepys's *Diary,* ed. Robert Latham and William Matthews (1970), for May 20, 1666, and September 23, 1667, taking bribes for procurement contracts with imperturbable aplomb. By 1672 he was earl of Shaftesbury. Of him is told a famous story that when a lady asked his religion, he replied, "Wise men, madam, are of but one religion," and when she persisted with, "What is that?" he answered, "Wise men never tell," George Macaulay Trevelyan, *England under the Stuarts* (1914) 347. It is hard to read that answer except cynically. Shaftesbury's cynicism and his other vices are not to be attributed to his secretary; but it is clear that Shaftesbury thought of Locke as knowledgeable on religious matters. When Shaftesbury was Lord Chancellor in 1672 he made Locke his secretary for "ecclesiastical preferments"—that is, he put him in charge of patronage in the church, J. W. Gough, Introduction to Locke's *The Second Treatise of Government* viii. And on one religious issue on which Locke was his adviser, Shaftesbury was to stake his political career—the exclusion of Catholics from English political life.

In 1667 when Locke first joined Shaftesbury's staff, Locke wrote *An Essay on Toleration*, many of whose ideas are very similar to the *Letter* of 1686. In early drafts, the greatest difference was the view that if dissenters were organized as a distinct party so as to be "visibly" a danger to the state, the magistrate should suppress them, J. W. Gough, Introduction to Locke's *Epistola de Tolerantia* 18. This hostility was toned down in the final form of the essay; but Locke maintained a persistent intolerance toward "Papists." On the basis of Locke's reasoning, Shaftesbury presented a memorial to the king, urging toleration for all Protestants but not for Catholics, *ibid.* at 21.

In 1672, Shaftesbury pushed the enactment of the Tests Act, providing that all persons holding any civil or military office or receiving any pay or grant of the king should take an oath in court acknowledging the king's supremacy over the Church and a second oath denying that there is "any transubstantiation in the sacrament of the Lord's supper," and should obtain a certificate from the parish minister and churchwarden that they had received "the sacrament of the Lord's supper, according to the usage of the church of England." The statute was entitled "An act for preventing dangers which may happen from popish recusants" and provided that anyone obliged to take the oaths or sacrament who failed to do so would on indictment and conviction lose his office, become incapable of bringing a lawsuit or receiving a legacy, and be subject to a fine of 500 pounds, 25 Charles II, c. 2 (8 Pick. Stat. 389) (1672).

The Tests Act forced out of the Admiralty the king's brother James, a Catholic. In 1679 Shaftesbury, with Locke as one of his lieutenants (*see* Gough, *Introduction to Locke's Second Treatise* ix), began to push the Exclusion Bill that would eliminate James as a Catholic from succession to the throne. In 1681 the bill carried in the Commons. Shaftesbury meanwhile had attempted to have James indicted as a "popish recusant" in criminal violation of the Tests Act. The attempt failed, the king's party engineered a reaction, Shaftesbury himself was tried and acquitted, but in November 1682 he fled the kingdom. In July 1683 leaders of Monmouth's rebellion, for which Shaftesbury was blamed, were executed, Trevelyan 416–423. In September 1683, Locke judged it expedient to follow his master by leaving England for Holland, Gough, *Introduction to the Second Treatise* ix. It is with this deep experience of government, of political intrigue, of the role of religion in politics that Locke wrote the *Letter*.

When Locke wrote in Holland in the winter of 1685–1686, religious tolerance was much debated. It had been vigorously defended in 1682 by Pierre Bayle in an essay in French, Klibansky, x. In October 1685 Louis XIV had revoked the French charter of toleration, the Edict of Nantes, and the barbarous persecution of Protestants in France was causing suffering known to everyone. The intellectual and political currents of the day made Lock's topic vital and insured its immediate success. Three years after it was written in Latin—the language of the learned and of the Continent—it was translated into English. It is this translation, ascribed since 1765 to William Popple, that is used here; for it is the form in which Locke's ideas were disseminated to Englishmen.

Locke himself, apparently out of timidity, never acknowledged his authorship. He angrily rebuked Limborch in 1690 when Limborch was divulging it in Holland. Locke was apparently secure in England. A Protestant monarch held the throne. Locke held a royal appointment as commissioner of appeals. But he wrote Limborch, "You do not know what a situation you have landed me in," *Locke to Limborch*, April 22, 1690, quoted in Klibansky, xxiii. What now seems so much to his credit did not seem wholly creditable then.

Locke, *A Letter Concerning Toleration*

Honoured Sir,

Since you are pleased to inquire what are my thoughts about the mutual toleration of Christians in their different professions of religion, I must needs answer you freely that I esteem that toleration to be the chief characteristic mark of the true Church. For whatsoever some people boast of the antiquity of places and names, or of the pomp of their outward worship; others, of the reformation of their discipline; all, of the orthodoxy of their faith—for everyone is orthodox to himself—these things, and all others of this nature, are much rather marks of men striving for power and empire over one another than of the Church of Christ. Let anyone have never so true a claim to all these things, yet if he be destitute of charity, meekness, and good-will in general towards all mankind, even to those that are not Christians, he is certainly yet short of being a true Christian himself. "The kings of the Gentiles exercise lordship over them," said our Saviour to His disciples, "but ye shall not be so." The business of true religion is quite another thing. It is not instituted in order to the erecting of an external pomp, nor to the obtaining of ecclesiastical dominion, nor to the exercising of compulsive force, but to the regulating of men's lives, according to the rules of virtue and piety. Whosoever will list himself under the banner of Christ, must, in the first place and above all things, make war upon his own lusts and vices. It is in vain for any man to usurp the name of Christian, without holiness of life, purity of manners, benignity and meekness of spirit. "Let everyone that nameth the name of Christ, depart from iniquity." "Thou, when thou art converted, strengthen thy brethren," said our Lord to Peter. It would, indeed, be very hard for one that appears careless about his own salvation to persuade me that he were extremely concerned for mine. For it is impossible that those should sincerely and heartily apply themselves to make other people Christians, who have not really embraced the Christian religion in their own hearts. If the Gospel and the apostles may be credited, no man can be a Christian without charity and without that faith which works, not by force, but by love. Now, I appeal to the consciences of those that persecute, torment, destroy, and kill other men upon pretence of religion, whether they do it out of friendship and kindness towards them or no? And I shall then indeed, and not until then, believe they do so, when I shall see those fiery zealots correcting, in the same manner, their friends and familiar acquaintance for the manifest sins they commit against the precepts of the Gospel; when I shall see them persecute with fire and sword the members of their own communion that are tainted with enormous vices and without amendment are in danger of eternal perdition; and when I shall see them thus express their love and desire of the salvation of their souls by the infliction of torments and exercise of all manner of cruelties. For if it be out of a principle of charity, as they pretend, and love to men's souls that they deprive them of their estates, maim them with corporal punishments, starve and torment them in noisome prisons, and in the end even take away their lives—I say, if all this be done merely to make men Christians and procure their salvation, why then do they suffer whoredom, fraud, malice, and such-like enormities, which (according to the apostle) manifestly relish of heathenish corruption, to predominate so much and abound amongst their flocks and people? These, and such-like things, are certainly more contrary to the glory of God, to the purity of the Church, and to the salvation of souls, than any conscientious dissent from ecclesiastical decisions, or separation from public worship, whilst accompanied with innocence of life. Why, then, does this burning zeal for God, for the Church, and for the salvation of souls—burning I say, literally, with fire and faggot—pass by those moral vices and wickednesses, without any chastisement, which are acknowledged by all men to be diametrically opposite to the profession of Christianity, and bend all its nerves either to the introducing of ceremonies, or to the establishment of opinions, which for the most part are about nice and intricate matters, that exceed the capacity of ordinary understandings? Which of the parties contending about these things is in the right, which of them is guilty of schism or heresy, whether those that domineer or those that suffer, will then at last be manifest when the causes of their separation comes to be judged of. He, certainly, that follows Christ, embraces His doctrine, and bears His yoke, though he forsake both father and mother, separate from the public assemblies and cermonies of his country, or whomsoever or whatsoever else he relinquishes, will not then be judged a heretic.

Now, though the divisions that are amongst sects should be allowed to be never so obstructive of the salvation of souls; yet, nevertheless, adultery, fornication, uncleanliness, lasciviousness, idolatry, and such-like things, cannot be denied to be works of the flesh, concerning which the apostle has expressly declared that "they who do them shall not inherit the kingdom of God." Whosoever, therefore, is sincerely solicitous about the kingdom of God and thinks it his duty to endeavour the enlargement of it amongst men, ought to apply himself with no less care and industry to the rooting out of these immoralities than to the extirpation of sects. But if anyone do otherwise, and whilst he is cruel and implacable towards those that differ from him in opinion, he be indulgent to such iniquities and immoralities as are unbecoming the name of a Christian, let such a one talk never so much of the Church, he plainly demonstrates by his actions that it is another kingdom he aims at and not the advancement of the kingdom of God.

That any man should think fit to cause another man—whose salvation he heartily desires—to expire in torments, and that even in an unconverted state, would, I confess, seem very strange to me, and I think, to any other also. But nobody, surely, will ever believe that such a carriage can proceed from charity, love, or goodwill. If anyone maintain that men ought to be compelled by fire and sword to profess certain doctrines, and conform to this or that exterior worship, without any regard had unto their morals; if anyone endeavour to convert those that are erroneous unto the faith, by forcing them to profess things that they do not believe and allowing them to practise things that the Gospel does not permit, it cannot be doubted indeed but such a one is desirous to have a numerous assembly joined in the same profession with himself; but that he principally intends by those means to compose a truly Christian Church is altogether incredible. It is not, therefore, to be wondered at if those who do not really contend for the advancement of the true religion, and of the Church of Christ, make use of arms that do not belong to the Christian warfare. If, like the Captain of our salvation, they sincerely desired the good of souls, they would tread in the steps and follow the perfect example of that Prince of Peace, who sent out His soldiers to the subduing of nations, and gathering them into His Church, not armed with the sword, or other instruments of force, but prepared with the Gospel of peace and with the exemplary holiness of their conversation. This was His method. Though if infidels were to be converted by force, if those that are either blind or obstinate were to be drawn off from their errors by armed soldiers, we know very well that it was much more easy for Him to do it with armies of heavenly legions than for any son of the Church, how potent soever, with all his dragoons.

The toleration of those that differ from others in matters of religion is so agreeable to the Gospel of Jesus Christ, and to the genuine reason of mankind, that it seems monstrous for men to be so blind as not to perceive the neccessity and advantage of it in so clear a light. I will not here tax the pride and ambition of some, the passion and uncharitable zeal of others. These are faults from which human affairs can perhaps scarce ever be perfectly freed; but yet such as nobody will bear the plain imputation of, without covering them with some specious colour; and so pretend to commendation, whilst they are carried away by their own irregular passions. But, however, that some may not colour their spirit of persecution and unchristian cruelty with a pretence of care of the public weal and observation of the laws; and that others, under pretence of religion, may not seek impunity for their libertinism and licentiousness; in a word, that none may impose either upon himself or others, by the pretences of loyalty and obedience to the prince, or of tenderness and sincerity in the worship of God; I esteem it above all things necessary to distinguish exactly the business of civil government from that of religion and to settle the just bounds that lie between the one and the other. If this be not done, there can be no end put to the controversies that will be always arising between those that have, or at least pretend to have, on the one side, a concernment for the interest of men's souls, and, on the other side, a care of the commonwealth.

The commonwealth seems to me to be a society of men constituted only for the procuring, preserving, and advancing their own civil interests.

Civil interests I call life, liberty, health, and indolency of body; and the possession of outward things, such as money, lands, houses, furniture, and the like.

It is the duty of the civil magistrate, by the impartial execution of equal laws, to secure unto all the people in general and to every one of his subjects in particular the just possession of these things belonging to this life. If anyone presume to violate the laws of public justice and equity, established for the preservation of those things, his presumption is to be checked by the fear of punishment, consisting of the deprivation or diminution of those civil interests, or goods, which otherwise he might and ought to enjoy. But seeing no man does willingly suffer himself to be punished by the deprivation of any part of his goods, and much less of his liberty of life, therefore, is the magistrate armed with the force and strength of all his subjects, in order to the punishment of those that violate any other man's rights.

Now that the whole jurisdiction of the magistrate reaches only to these civil concernments, and that all civil power, right and dominion, is bounded and confined to the only care of promoting these things; and that it neither can nor ought in any manner to be extended to the salvation of souls, these following considerations seem unto me abundantly to demonstrate.

First, because the care of souls is not committed to the civil magistrate, any more than to other men. It is not committed unto him, I say, by God; because it appears not that God has ever given any such authority to one man over another as to compel anyone to his religion. Nor can any such power be vested in the magistrate by the consent of the people, because no man can so far abandon the care of his own salvation as blindly to leave to the choice of any other, whether prince or subject, to prescribe to him what faith or worship he shall embrace. For no man can, if he would, conform his faith to the dictates of another. All the life and power of true religion consist in the inward and full persuasion of the mind; and faith is not faith without believing. Whatever profession we make, to whatever outward worship we conform, if we are not fully satisfied in our own mind that the one is true and the other well pleasing unto God, such profession and such practice, far from being any furtherance, are indeed great obstacles to our salvation. For in this manner, instead of expiating other sins by the exercise of religion, I say, in offering thus unto God Almighty such a worship as we esteem to be displeasing unto Him, we add unto the number of our other sins those also of hypocrisy and contempt of His Divine Majesty.

In the second place, the care of souls cannot belong to the civil magistrate, because his power consists only in outward force; but true and saving religion consists in the inward persuasion of the mind, without which nothing can be acceptable to God. And such is the nature of the understanding, that it cannot be compelled to the belief of anything by outward force. Confiscation of estate, imprisonment, torments, nothing of that nature can have any such efficacy as to make men change the inward judgement that they have framed of things.

It may indeed be alleged that the magistrate may make use of arguments, and, thereby; draw the heterodox into the way of truth, and procure their salvation. I grant it; but this is common to him with other men. In teaching, instructing, and redressing the erroneous by reason, he may certainly do what becomes any good man to do. Magistracy does not oblige him to put off either humanity or Christianity; but it is one thing to persuade, another to command; one thing to press with arguments, another with penalties. This civil power alone has a right to do; to the other, goodwill is authority enough. Every man has commission to admonish, exhort, convince another of error, and, by reasoning, to draw him into truth; but to give laws, receive obedience, and compel with the sword, belongs to none but the magistrate. And, upon this ground, I affirm that the magistrate's power extends not to the establishing of any articles of faith, or forms of worship, by the force of his laws. For laws are of no force at all without penalties, and penalties in this case are absolutely impertinent, because they are not proper to convince the mind. Neither the profession of any articles of faith, nor the conformity to any outward form of worship (as has been already said), can be available to the salvation of souls, unless the truth of the one and the acceptableness of the other unto God be thoroughly believed by those that so profess and practise. But penalties are no way capable to produce such belief. It is only light and evidence that can work a change in men's opinions; which light can in no manner proceed from corporal sufferings, or any other outward penalties.

In the third place, the care of the salvation of men's souls cannot belong to the magistrate; because, though the rigour of laws and the force of penalties were capable to convince and change men's minds, yet would not that help at all to the salvation of their souls. For there being but one truth, one way to heaven, what hope is there that more men would be led into it if they had no rule but the religion of the court and were put under the necessity to quit the light of their own reason, and oppose the dictates of their own consciences, and blindly to resign themselves up to the will of their governors and to the religion which either ignorance, ambition, or superstition had chanced to establish in the countries where they were born? In the variety and contradiction of opinions in religion, wherein the princes of the world are as much divided as in their secular interests, the narrow way would be much straitened; one country alone would be in the right, and all the rest of the world put under an obligation of following their princes in the ways that lead to destruction; and that which heightens the absurdity, and very ill suits the notion of a Deity, men would owe their eternal happiness or misery to the places of their nativity.

These considerations, to omit many others that might have been urged to the same purpose, seem unto me sufficient to conclude that all the power of civil government relates only to men's civil interests, is confined to the care of the things of this world, and hath nothing to do with the world to come.

Let us now consider what a church is. A church, then, I take to be a voluntary society of men, joining themselves together of their own accord in order to the public worshipping of God in such manner as they judge acceptable to Him, and effectual to the salvation of their souls.

I say it is a free and voluntary society. Nobody is born a member of any church; otherwise the religion of parents would descend unto children by the same right of inheritance as their temporal estates, and everyone would hold his faith by the same tenure he does his lands, than which nothing can be imagined more absurd. Thus, therefore, that matter stands. No man by nature is bound unto any particular church or sect, but everyone joins himself voluntarily to that society in which he believes he has found that profession and worship which is truly acceptable to God. The hope of salvation, as it was the only cause of his entrance into that communion, so it can be the only reason of his stay there. For if afterwards he discover anything either erroneous in the doctrine or incongruous in the worship of that society to which he has joined himself, why should it not be as free for him to go out as it was to enter? No member of a religious society can be tied with any other bonds but what proceed from the certain expectation of eternal life. A church, then, is a society of members voluntarily uniting to that end.

It follows now that we consider what is the power of this church and unto what laws it is subject.

Forasmuch as no society, how free soever, or upon whatsoever slight occasion instituted, whether of philosophers for learning, or merchants for commerce, or of men of leisure for mutual conversation and discourse, no church or company, I say, can in the least subsist and hold together, but will presently dissolve and break in pieces, unless it be regulated by some laws, and the members all consent to observe some order. Place and time of meeting must be agreed on; rules for admitting and excluding members must be established; distinction of officers, and putting things into a regular course, and suchlike, cannot be omitted. But since the joining together of several members into this church-society, as has already been demonstrated, is absolutely free and spontaneous, it necessarily follows that the right of making its laws can belong to none but the society itself; or, at least (which is the same thing), to those whom the society by common consent has authorised thereunto.

Some, perhaps, may object that no such society can be said to be a true church unless it have in it a bishop or presbyter, with ruling authority derived from the very apostles, and continued down to the present times by an uninterrupted succession.

To these I answer: In the first place, let them show me the edict by which Christ has imposed that law upon His Church. And let not any man think me impertinent, if in a thing of this consequence I require that the terms of that edict be very express and positive; for the promise He has made us, that "wheresoever two or three are gathered together" in His name, He will be in the midst of them (Mt. 18:20), seems to imply the contrary. Whether such an assembly want anything necessary to a true church, pray do you consider. Certain I am that nothing can be there wanting unto the salvation of souls, which is sufficient to our purpose.

Next, pray observe how great have always been the divisions amongst even those who lay so much stress upon the Divine institution and continued succession of a certain order of rulers in the Church. Now, their very dissension unavoidably puts us upon a necessity of deliberating and, consequently, allows a liberty of choosing that which upon consideration we prefer.

And, in the last place, I consent that these men have a rule in their church, established by such a long series of succession as they judge necessary, provided I may have liberty at the same time to join myself to that society in which I am persuaded those things are to be found which are necessary to the salvation of my soul. In this manner ecclesiastical liberty will be preserved on all sides, and no man will have a legislator imposed upon him but whom himself has chosen.

But since men are so solicitous about the true church, I would only ask them here, by the way, if it be not more agreeable to the Church of Christ to make the conditions of her communion consist in such things, and such things only, as the Holy Spirit has in the Holy Scriptures declared, in express words, to be necessary to salvation; I ask, I say, whether this be not more agreeable to the Church of Christ than for men to impose their own inventions and interpretations upon others as if they were of Divine authority, and to establish by ecclesiastical laws, as absolutely necessary to the profession of Christianity, such things as the Holy Scriptures do either not mention, or at least not expressly command? Whosoever requires those things in order to ecclesiastical communion, which Christ does not require in order to life eternal, he may, perhaps, indeed constitute a society accommodated to his own opinion and his own advantage; but how that can be called the Church of Christ which is established upon laws that are not His, and which excludes such persons from its communion as He will one day receive into the Kingdom of Heaven, I understand not. But this being not a proper place to inquire into the marks of the true church, I will only mind those that contend so earnestly for the decrees of their own society, and that cry out continually, "The Church! the Church!" with as much noise, and perhaps upon the same principle, as the Ephesian silversmiths did for their Diana; this, I say, I desire to mind them of, that the Gospel frequently declares that the true disciples of Christ must suffer persecution; but that the Church of Christ should persecute others, and force others by fire and sword to embrace her faith and doctrine, I could never yet find in any of the books of the New Testament.

The end of a religious society (as has already been said) is the public worship of God and, by means thereof, the acquisition of eternal life. All discipline ought, therefore, to tend to that end, and all ecclesiastical laws to be thereunto confined. Nothing ought nor can be transacted in this society relating to the possession of civil and worldly goods. No force is here to be made use of upon any occasion whatsoever. For force belongs wholly to the civil magistrate, and the possession of all outward goods is subject to his jurisdiction.

But, it may be asked, by what means then shall ecclesiastical law be established, if they must be thus destitute of all compulsive power? I answer: They must be established by means suitable to the nature of such things, whereof the external profession and observation—if not proceeding from a thorough conviction and approbation of the mind—is altogether useless and unprofitable. The arms by which the members of this society are to be kept within their duty are exhortations, admonitions, and advices. If by these means the offenders will not be reclaimed, and the erroneous convinced, there remains nothing further to be done but that such stubborn and obstinate persons, who give no ground to hope for their reformation, should be cast out and separated from the society. This is the last and utmost force of ecclesiastical authority. No other punishment can thereby be inflicted than that, the relation ceasing between the body and the member which is cut off. The person so condemned ceases to be a part of that church.

These things being thus determined, let us inquire, in the next place: How far the duty of toleration extends, and what is required from everyone by it?

And, first, I hold that no church is bound, by the duty of toleration, to retain any such person in her bosom as, after admonition, continues obstinately to offend against the laws of the society. For, those being the condition of communion and the bond of the society, if the breach of them were permitted without any animadversion the society would immediately be thereby dissolved. But, nevertheless, in all such cases care is to be taken that the sentence of excommunication, and the execution thereof, carry with it no rough usage of word or action whereby the ejected person may any wise be damnified in body or estate. For all force (as has often been said) belongs only to the magistrate, nor ought any private persons at any time to use force, unless it be in self-defense against unjust violence. Excommunication neither does, nor can, deprive the excommunicated person of any of those civil goods that he formerly possessed. . . .

But, to speak the truth, we must acknowledge that the Church (if a convention of clergymen, making canons, must be called by that name) is for the most part more apt to be influenced by the Court than the Court by the Church. How the Church was under the vicissitude of orthodox and Arian emperors is very well known. Or if those things be too remote, our modern English history affords us fresh examples in the reigns of Henry VIII, Edward VI, Mary, and Elizabeth, how easily and smoothly the clergy changed their decrees, their articles of faith, their form of worship, everything according to the inclination of those kings and queens. Yet were those kings and queens of such different minds in point of religion, and enjoined thereupon such different things, that no man in his wits (I had almost said none but an atheist) will presume to say that any sincere and upright worshipper of God could, with a safe conscience, obey their several decrees. To conclude, it is the same thing whether a king that prescribes laws to another man's religion pretend to do it by his own judgement, or by the ecclesiastical authority and advice of others. The decisions of churchmen, whose differences and disputes are sufficiently known, cannot be any sounder or safer than his; nor can all their suffrages joined together add a new strength to the civil power. Though this also must be taken notice of—that princes seldom have any regard to the suffrages of ecclesiastics that are not favourers of their own faith and way of worship.

But, after all, the principal consideration, and which absolutely determines this controversy, is this: Although the magistrate's opinion in religion be sound, and the way that he appoints be truly Evangelical, yet, if I be not thoroughly persuaded thereof in my own mind, there will be no safety for me in following it. No way whatsoever that I shall walk in against the dictates of my conscience will ever bring me to the mansions of the blessed. I may grow rich by an art that I take not delight in; I may be cured of some disease by remedies that I have not faith in; but I cannot be saved by a religion that I distrust and by a worship that I abhor. It is in vain for an unbeliever to take up the outward show of another man's profession. Faith only and inward sincerity are the things that procure acceptance with God. The most likely and most approved remedy can have no effect upon the patient, if his stomach reject it as soon as taken; and you will in vain cram a medicine down a sick man's throat, which his particular constitution will be sure to turn into poison. In a word, whatsoever may be doubtful in religion, yet this at least is certain, that no religion which I believe not to be true can be either true or profitable unto me. In vain, therefore, do princes compel their subjects to come into their Church communion, under pretence of saving their souls. If they believe, they will come of their own accord, if they believe not, their coming will nothing avail them. How great soever, in fine, may be the pretence of good-will and charity, and concern for the salvation of men's souls, men cannot be forced to be saved whether they will or no. And therefore, when all is done, they must be left to their own consciences.

Having thus at length freed men from all dominion over one another in matters of religion, let us now consider what they are to do. All men know and acknowledge that God ought to be publicly worshipped; why otherwise do they compel one another unto the public assemblies? Men, therefore, constituted in this liberty are to enter into some religious society, that they meet together, not only for mutual edification, but to own to the world that they worship God and offer unto His Divine Majesty such service as they themselves are not ashamed of and such as they think not unworthy of Him, nor unacceptable to Him; and, finally, that by the purity of doctrine, holiness of life, and decent form of worship, they may draw others unto the love of the true religion, and perform such other things in religion as cannot be done by each private man apart.

These religious societies I call *Churches;* and these, I say, the magistrate ought to tolerate, for the business of these assemblies of the people is nothing but what is lawful for every man in particular to take care of—I mean the salvation of their souls; nor in this case is there any difference between the National Church and other separated congregations.

But as in every Church there are two things especially to be considered—the outward form and rites of worship, and the doctrines and articles of faith—these things must be handled each distinctly that so the whole matter of toleration may the more clearly be understood.

Concerning outward worship, I say, in the first place, that the magistrate has no power to enforce by law, either in his own Church, or much less in another, the use of any rites or ceremonies whatsoever in the worship of God. And this, not only because these Churches are free societies, but because whatsoever is practised in the worship of God is only so far justifiable as it is believed by those that practise it to be acceptable unto Him. Whatsoever is not done with that assurance of faith is neither well in itself, nor can it be acceptable to God. To impose such things, therefore, upon any people, contrary to their own judgment, is in effect to command them to offend God, which, considering that the end of all religion is to please Him, and that liberty is essentially necessary to that end, appears to be absurd beyond expression.

But perhaps it may be concluded from hence that I deny unto the magistrate all manner of power about indifferent things, which, if it be not granted, the whole subject-matter of law-making is taken away. No, I readily grant that indifferent things, and perhaps none but such, are subjected to the legislative power. But it does not therefore follow that the magistrate may ordain whatsoever he pleases concerning anything that is indifferent. The public good is the rule and measure of all law-making. If a thing be not useful to the commonwealth, though it be never so indifferent, it may not presently be established by law.

And further, things never so indifferent in their own nature, when they are brought into the Church and worship of God, are removed out of the reach of the magistrate's jurisdiction, because in that use they have no connection at all with civil affairs. The only business of the Church is the salvation of souls, and it no way concerns the commonwealth, or any member of it, that this or the other ceremony be there made use of. Neither the use nor the omission of any ceremonies in those religious assemblies does either advantage or prejudice the life, liberty, or estate of any man. For example, let it be granted that the washing of an infant with water is in itself an indifferent thing, let it be granted also that the magistrate understand such washing to be profitable to the curing or preventing of any disease the children are subject unto, and esteem the matter weighty enough to be taken care of by a law. In that case he may order it to be done. But will any one therefore say that a magistrate has the same right to ordain by law that all children shall be baptised by priests in the sacred font in order to the purification of their souls? The extreme difference of these two cases is visible to every one at first sight. Or let us apply the last case to the child of a Jew, and the thing speaks itself. For what hinders but a Christian magistrate may have subjects that are Jews? Now, if we acknowledge that such an injury may not be done unto a Jew as to compel him, against his own opinion, to practise in his religion a thing that is in its nature indifferent, how can we maintain that anything of this kind may be done to a Christian?

Again, things in their own nature indifferent cannot, by any human authority, be made any part of the worship of God—for this very reason: because they are indifferent. For, since indifferent things are not capable, by any virtue of their own, to propitiate the Deity, no human power or authority can confer on them so much dignity and excellency as to enable them to do it. In the common affairs of life that use of indifferent things which God has not forbidden is free and lawful, and therefore in those things human authority has place. But it is not so in matters of religion. Things indifferent are not otherwise lawful in the worship of God than as they are instituted by God Himself and as He, by some positive command, has ordained them to be made a part of that worship which He will vouchsafe to accept at the hands of poor sinful men. Nor, when an incensed Deity shall ask us, "Who has required these, or such-like things at your hands?" will it be enough to answer Him that the magistrate commanded them. If civil jurisdiction extend thus far, what might not lawfully be introduced into religion? What hodgepodge of ceremonies, what superstitious inventions, built upon the magistrate's authority, might not (against conscience) be imposed upon the worshippers of God? For the greatest part of these ceremonies and superstitions consists in the religious use of such things as are in their own nature indifferent; nor are they sinful upon any other account than because God is not the author of them. The sprinkling of water and the use of bread and wine are both in their own nature and in the ordinary occasions of life altogether indifferent. Will any man, therefore, say that these things could have been introduced into religion and made a part of divine worship if not by divine institution? If any human authority or civil power could have done this, why might it not also enjoin the eating of fish and drinking of ale in the holy banquet as a part of divine worship? Why not the sprinkling of the blood of beasts in churches, and expiations by water or fire, and abundance more of this kind? But these things, how indifferent soever they be in common uses, when they come to be annexed unto divine worship, without divine authority, they are as abominable to God as the sacrifice of a dog. And why is a dog so abominable? What difference is there between a dog and a goat, in respect of the divine nature, equally and infinitely distant from all affinity with matter, unless it be that God required the use of one in His worship and not of the other? We see, therefore, that indifferent things, how much soever they be under the power of the civil magistrate, yet cannot, upon that pretence, be introduced into religion and imposed upon religious assemblies, because, in the worship of God, they wholly cease to be indifferent. He that worships God does it with design to please Him and procure His favour. But that cannot be done by him who, upon the command of another, offers unto God that which he knows will be displeasing to Him, because not commanded by Himself. This is not to please God, or appease his wrath, but willingly and knowingly to provoke Him by a manifest contempt, which is a thing absolutely repugnant to the nature and end of worship.

But it will be here asked: "If nothing belonging to divine worship be left to human discretion, how is it then that Churches themselves have the power of ordering anything about the time and place of worship and the like?" To this I answer that in religious worship we must distinguish between what is part of the worship itself and what is but a circumstance. That is a part of the worship which is believed to be appointed by God and to be well-pleasing to Him, and therefore that is necessary. Circumstances are such things which, though in general they cannot be separated from worship, yet the particular instances or modifications of them are not determined, and therefore they are indifferent. Of this sort are the time and place of worship, habit and posture of him that worships. These are circumstances, and perfectly indifferent, where God has not given any express command about them. For example: amongst the Jews the time and place of their worship and the habits of those that officiated in it were not mere circumstances, but a part of the worship itself, in which, if anything were defective, or different from the institution, they could not hope that it would be accepted by God. But these, to Christians under the liberty of the Gospel, are mere circumstances of worship, which the prudence of every Church may bring into such use as shall be judged most subservient to the end of order, decency, and edification. But, even under the Gospel, those who believe the first or the seventh day to be set apart by God, and consecrated still to His worship, to them that portion of time is not a simple circumstance, but a real part of Divine worship, which can neither be changed nor neglected.

In the next place: As the magistrate has no power to impose by his laws the use of any rites and ceremonies in any Church, so neither has he any power to forbid the use of such rites and ceremonies as are already received, approved, and practised by any Church; because, if he did so, he would destroy the Church itself: the end of whose institution is only to worship God with freedom after its own manner.

You will say, by this rule, if some congregations should have a mind to sacrifice infants, or (as the primitive Christians were falsely accused) lustfully pollute themselves in promiscuous uncleanness, or practise any other such heinous enormities, is the magistrate obliged to tolerate them, because they are committed in a religious assembly? I answer: No. These things are not lawful in the ordinary course of life, nor in any private house; and therefore neither are they so in the worship of God, or in any religious meeting. But, indeed, if any people congregated upon account of religion should be desirous to sacrifice a calf, I deny that that ought to be prohibited by a law. Meliboeus, whose calf it is, may lawfully kill his calf at home, and burn any part of it that he thinks fit. For no injury is thereby done to any one, no prejudice to another man's goods. And for the same reason he may kill his calf also in a religious meeting. Whether the doing so be well-pleasing to God or no, it is their part to consider that do it. The part of the magistrate is only to take care that the commonwealth receive no prejudice, and that there be no injury done to any man, either in life or estate. And thus what may be spent on a feast may be spent on a sacrifice. But if peradventure such were the state of things that the interest of the commonwealth required all slaughter of beasts should be forborne for some while, in order to the increasing of the stock of cattle that had been destroyed by some extraordinary murrain, who sees not that the magistrate, in such a case, may forbid all his subjects to kill any calves for any use whatsoever?

Only it is to be observed that, in this case, the law is not made about a religious, but a political matter; nor is the sacrifice, but the slaughter of calves, thereby prohibited.

By this we see what difference there is between the Church and the Commonwealth. Whatsoever is lawful in the Commonwealth cannot be prohibited by the magistrate in the Church. Whatsoever is permitted unto any of his subjects for their ordinary use, neither can nor ought to be forbidden by him to any sect of people for their religious uses. If any man may lawfully take bread or wine, either sitting or kneeling in his own house, the law ought not to abridge him of the same liberty in his religious worship; though in the Church the use of bread and wine be very different and be there applied to the mysteries of faith and rites of Divine worship. But those things that are prejudicial to the commonweal of a people in their ordinary use and are, therefore, forbidden by laws, those things ought not to be permitted to Churches in their sacred rites. Only the magistrate ought always to be very careful that he do not misuse his authority to the oppression of any Church, under pretence of public good.

It may be said: "What if a Church be idolatrous, is that also to be tolerated by the magistrate?" I answer: What power can be given to the magistrate for the suppression of an idolatrous Church, which may not in time and place be made use of to the ruin of an orthodox one? For it must be remembered that the civil power is the same everywhere, and the religion of every prince is orthodox to himself. If, therefore, such a power be granted unto the civil magistrate in spirituals as that at Geneva, for example, he may extirpate, by violence and blood, the religion which is there reputed idolatrous, by the same rule another magistrate, in some neighbouring country, may oppress the reformed religion and, in India, the Christian. The civil power can either change everything in religion, according to the prince's pleasure, or it can change nothing. If it be once permitted to introduce anything into religion by the means of laws and penalties, there can be no bounds put to it; but it will in the same manner be lawful to alter everything, according to that rule of truth which the magistrate has framed unto himself. No man whatsoever ought, therefore, to be deprived of his terrestrial enjoyments upon account of his religion. Not even Americans, subjected unto a Christian prince, are to be punished either in body or goods for not embracing our faith and worship. If they are persuaded that they please God in observing the rites of their own country and that they shall obtain happiness by that means, they are to be left unto God and themselves. Let us trace this matter to the bottom. Thus it is: An inconsiderable and weak number of Christians, destitute of everything, arrive in a Pagan country; these foreigners beseech the inhabitants, by the bowels of humanity, that they would succour them with the necessaries of life; those necessaries are given them, habitations are granted, and they all join together, and grow up into one body of people. The Christian religion by this means takes root in that country and spreads itself, but does not suddenly grow the strongest. While things are in this condition peace, friendship, faith, and equal justice are preserved amongst them. At length the magistrate becomes a Christian, and by that means their party becomes the most powerful. Then immediately all compacts are to be broken, all civil rights to be violated, that idolatry may be extirpated; and unless these innocent Pagans, strict observers of the rules of equity and the law of Nature and no ways offending against the laws of the society, I say, unless they will forsake their ancient religion and embrace a new and strange one, they are to be turned out of the lands and possessions of their forefathers and perhaps deprived of life itself. Then, at last, it appears what zeal for the Church, joined with the desire of dominion, is capable to produce, and how easily the pretence of religion, and of the care of souls, serves for a cloak to covetousness, rapine, and ambition.

Now whosoever maintains that idolatry is to be rooted out of anyplace by laws, punishments, fire, and sword, may apply this story to himself. For the reason of the thing is equal, both in America and Europe. And neither Pagans there, nor any dissenting Christians here, can, with any right, be deprived of their worldly goods by the predominating faction of a court-church; nor are any civil rights to be either changed or violated upon account of religion in one place more than another. . . .

But some may ask: "What if the magistrate should enjoin anything by his authority that appears unlawful to the conscience of a private person?" I answer that, if government be faithfully administered and the counsels of the magistrates be indeed directed to the public good, this will seldom happen. But if, perhaps, it do so fall out, I say, that such a private person is to abstain from the action that he judges unlawful, and he is to undergo the punishment which it is not unlawful for him to bear. For the private judgement of any person concerning a law enacted in political matters, for the public good, does not take away the obligation of that law, nor deserve a dispensation. But if the law, indeed, be concerning things that lie not within the verge of the magistrate's authority (as, for example, that the people, or any party amongst them, should be compelled to embrace a strange religion, and join in the worship and ceremonies of another Church), men are not in these cases obliged by that law, against their consciences. For the political society is instituted for no other end, but only to secure every man's possession of the things of this life. The care of each man's soul and of the things of heaven, which neither does belong to the commonwealth nor can be subjected to it, is left entirely to every man's self. Thus the safeguard of men's lives and of the things that belong unto this life is the business of the commonwealth; and the preserving of those things unto their owners is the duty of the magistrate. And therefore the magistrate cannot take away these worldly things from this man or party and give them to that; nor change propriety amongst fellow subjects (no not even by a law), for a cause that has no relation to the end of civil government, I mean for their religion, which whether it be true or false does no prejudice to the worldly concerns of their fellow subjects, which are the things that only belong unto the care of the commonwealth.

But what if the magistrate believe such a law as this to be for the public good? I answer: As the private judgement of any particular person, if erroneous, does not exempt him from the obligation of law, so the private judgement (as I may call it) of the magistrate does not give him any new right of imposing laws upon his subjects, which neither was in the constitution of the government granted him, nor ever was in the power of the people to grant, much less if he make it his business to enrich and advance his followers and fellow-sectaries with the spoils of others. But what if the magistrate believe that he has a right to make such laws and that they are for the public good, and his subjects believe the contrary? Who shall be judge between them? I answer: God alone. For there is no judge upon earth between the supreme magistrate and the people. God, I say, is the only Judge in this case, who will retribute unto every one at the last day according to his deserts; that is, according to his sincerity and uprightness in endeavouring to promote piety, and the public weal, and peace of mankind. But what shall be done in the meanwhile? I answer: The principal and chief care of every one ought to be of his own soul first, and, in the next place, of the public peace; though yet there are very few will think it is peace there, where they see all laid waste.

There are two sorts of contests amongst men, the one managed by law, the other by force; and these are of that nature that where the one ends, the other always begins. But it is not my business to inquire into the power of the magistrate in the different constitutions of nations. I only know what usually happens where controversies arise without a judge to determine them. You will say, then, the magistrate being the stronger will have his will and carry his point. Without doubt; but the question is not here concerning the doubtlessness of the event, but the rule of right.

But to come to particulars. I say, first, no opinions contrary to human society, or to those moral rules which are necessary to the preservation of civil society, are to be tolerated by the magistrate. But of these, indeed, examples in any Church are rare. For no sect can easily arrive to such a degree of madness as that it should think fit to teach, for doctrines of religion, such things as manifestly undermine the foundations of society and are, therefore, condemned by the judgement of all mankind; because their own interest, peace, reputation, everything would be thereby endangered.

Another more secret evil, but more dangerous to the commonwealth, is when men arrogate to themselves, and to those of their own sect, some peculiar prerogative covered over with a specious show of deceitful words, but in effect opposite to the civil right of the community. For example: we cannot find any sect that teaches, expressly and openly, that men are not obliged to keep their promise; that princes may be dethroned by those that differ from them in religion; or that the dominion of all things belongs only to themselves. For these things, proposed thus nakedly and plainly, would soon draw on them the eye and hand of the magistrate and awaken all the care of the commonwealth to a watchfulness against the spreading of so dangerous an evil. But, nevertheless, we find those that say the same things in other words. What else do they mean who teach that faith is not to be kept with heretics? Their meaning, forsooth, is that the privilege of breaking faith belongs unto themselves; for they declare all that are not of their communion to be heretics, or at least may declare them so whensoever they think fit. What can be the meaning of their asserting that kings excommunicated forfeit their crown̲ and kingdoms? It is evident that they thereby arrogate unto themselves the power of deposing kings, because they challenge the power of excommunication, as the peculiar right of their hierarchy. That dominion is founded in grace is also an assertion by which those that maintain it do plainly lay claim to the possession of all things. For they are not so wanting to themselves as not to believe, or at least as not to profess themselves to be the truly pious and faithful. These, therefore, and the like, who attribute unto the faithful, religious, and orthodox, that is, in plain terms, unto themselves, any peculiar privilege or power above other mortals, in civil concernments; or who upon pretence of religion do challenge any manner of authority over such as are not associated with them in their ecclesiastical communion, I say these have no right to be tolerated by the magistrate; as neither those that will not own and teach the duty of tolerating all men in matters of mere religion. For what do all these and the like doctrines signify, but that they may and are ready upon any occasion to seize the Government and possess themselves of the estates and fortunes of their fellow subjects; and that they only ask leave to be tolerated by the magistrate so long until they find themselves strong enough to effect it?

Again: That Church can have no right to be tolerated by the magistrate which is constituted upon such a bottom that all those who enter into it do thereby *ipso facto* deliver themselves up to the protection and service of another prince. For by this means the magistrate would give way to the settling of a foreign jurisdiction in his own country and suffer his own people to be listed, as it were, for soldiers against his own Government. Nor does the frivolous and fallacious distinction between the Court and the Church afford any remedy to this inconvenience; especially when both the one and the other are equally subject to the absolute authority of the same person, who has not only power to persuade the members of his Church to whatsoever he lists, either as purely religious, or in order thereunto, but can also enjoin it them on pain of eternal fire. It is ridiculous for any one to profess himself to be a Mahometan only in his religion, but in everything else a faithful subject to a Christian magistrate, whilst at the same time he acknowledges himself bound to yield blind obedience to the Mufti of Constantinople, who himself is entirely obedient to the Ottoman Emperor and frames the feigned oracles of that religion according to his pleasure. But this Mahometan living amongst Christians would yet more apparently renounce their government if he acknowledged the same person to be head of his Church who is the supreme magistrate in the state.

Lastly, those are not at all to be tolerated who deny the being of a God. Promises, covenants, and oaths, which are the bonds of human society, can have no hold upon an atheist. The taking away of God, though but even in thought, dissolves all; besides also, those that by their atheism undermine and destroy all religion, can have no pretence of religion whereupon to challenge the privilege of a toleration. As for other practical opinions, though not absolutely free from all error, if they do not tend to establish domination over others, or civil impunity to the Church in which they are taught, there can be no reason why they should not be tolerated.

Part Two
THE AMERICAN EXPERIENCE

—————————————— **SIX** ——————————————

Freedom of Conscience and Religious Establishments in a Revolutionary Age

VIRGINIA

VIRGINIA WAS SPECIAL—the most populous state in America, the home of a remarkable galaxy of political leaders, a community in which the claims of an established church and dissenters from it were in sharp conflict and had to be resolved.

1. "QUOTA OF IMPS": THE AWAKENING OF JAMES MADISON

Baptized as an infant in the Church of England, James Madison attended a Presbyterian institution, the College of New Jersey in Princeton, from 1769 to 1772. Back in Virginia, aged twenty-two, he wrote his fellow Princetonian William Bradford on September 25, 1773, on Bradford's choice of a career:

You forbid any recommendation of Divinity by suggesting that you have insuperable objections therefore I can only condole with the Church on the loss of a fine Genius and persuasive Orator. I cannot however suppress thus much of my advice on that head that you would always keep the Ministry obliquely in View whatever your profession be. This will lead you to cultivate an acquaintace [sic] occasionally with the most sublime of all Sciences and will qualify you for a change of public character if you should hereafter desire it. I have sometimes thought there could not be a stronger testimony in favor of Religion or against temporal Enjoyments even the most rational and manly than for men who occupy the most honorable and gainful departments and are rising in reputation and wealth, publicly to declare their unsatisfatoriness [sic] by becoming fervent Advocates in the cause of Christ, & I wish you may give in your Evidence in this way. Such Instances have seldom occurred, therefore they would be more striking and would be instead of a "Cloud of Witnesses" [Madison, *Papers,* ed. William T. Hutchinson and William M. E. Rachal (1962) 1, 96].

"Cloud of Witnesses" was a reference to Hebrews 12:1–2: "With a cloud of witnesses to faith around us, we must throw off every encumbrance, every sin to which we cling, and run with resolution the race for which we are entered, our eyes fixed on Jesus. . . ." The allusions chimed with Madison's interest in "Advocates for Christ" and the admonition (surely self-directed?) to "keep the Ministry obliquely in view." See also William Lee Miller, "The Vocation of Jemmy Madison" in Miller, *The First Liberty: Religion and the American Republic* (1986) 79–96.

Bradford replied on November 5, 1773: Madison had decided him for the law. (He later became attorney general of the United States.) Writing from Philadelphia, he added: "Yet in a place *where* deistical *sentiments* almost universally prevail I look upon it as absolutely *necessary* to be *able to defend as well as believe the Christian religion*" (*ibid.* at 1, 98).

Madison wrote back on December 1, 1773. His question marked his first interest in the great subject on which he was to leave his imprint: "Is an Ecclesiastical Establishment absolutely necessary to support civil society in a supream Government? & how far is it hurtful to a dependant State?" (*ibid.* at 1, 101).

The next letter to Bradford, January 24, 1774, linked religion with politics:

However Political Contests are necessary sometimes as well as military to afford exercise and practise and to instruct in the Art of defending Liberty and property. I verily believe the frequent Assaults that have been made on America[,] Boston, especially, will in the end prove of real advantage. If the Church of England had been the established and general Religion in all the Northern Colonies as it has been among us here and uninterrupted tranquility had prevailed throughout the Continent, It is clear to me that slavery and Subjection might and would have been gradually insinuated among us. Union of Religious Sentiments begets a surprizing confidence and Ecclesiastical Establishments tend to great ignorance and Corruption all of which facilitate the Execution of mischievous Projects [*ibid.* at 1, 105].

The letter continued:

I have indeed as good an Atmosphere at home as the Climate will allow: but have nothing to brag of as to the State and Liberty of my Country. Poverty and Luxury prevail among all sort: Pride ignorance and Knavery among the Priesthood and Vice and Wickedness among the Laity. This is bad enough But It is not the worst I have to tell you. That diabolical Hell conceived principle of persecution rages among some and to their eternal Infamy the Clergy can furnish their Quota of Imps for such business. This vexes me the most of any thing whatever. There are at this [time] in the adjacent County not less than 5 or 6 well meaning men in close Gaol for publishing their religious Sentiments which in the main are very orthodox. I have neither patience to hear talk or think of any thing relative to this matter, for I have squabbled and scolded abused and ridiculed so long about it, to so little purpose that I am without common patience. So I to pity me and pray for Liberty of Conscience [*ibid.* at 1, 106].

Madison was stirred to what his editors describe as this "unaccustomed fervor" by the imprisonment of a half-dozen Baptist preachers in Culpepper County, Virginia. Quakers, Presbyterians, and Regular Baptists existed in the colony, as did smaller groups of Lutherans, Dunkers, and Methodists. The English Act of Toleration of 1689 had been accepted by the colony, and those Protestant churches conforming to its terms, while not on a par with the Church of England, were not persecuted, H. J. Eckenrode, *Separation of Church and State in Virginia* (1910) 30–34. The tolerated churches applied for permits to preach and to build meetinghouses. The Separate Baptists, present in force since the 1750s, did not. Their missionary methods were itinerant. They already had an independent attitude toward British law. Appealing with evangelical enthusiasm to the less affluent part of the white community, they were socially unsettling and, from 1770 on, were persecuted, *ibid.* at 36–37.

In 1771, for example, a Baptist preacher in Caroline County had been hauled off in the middle of his sermon and flogged by the sheriff. Baptists met at Blue Run church in Orange County (Madison's home) and protested this outrage; the crowd of 4,000 was the largest mass meeting ever assembled in Virginia to that date. (*See* Rhys Isaac, " 'The Rage of Malice of the Old Serpent Devil': The Dissenters and the Making and Remaking of the Virginia Statute for Religious Freedom," forthcoming in 1987). Madison's indignation responded to feelings widespread in the community.

In the words of Isaac Backus, the New England Baptist leader: "In Virginia they [the Episcopalians] cruelly imprisoned Baptist ministers, only for preaching the gospel to perishing souls without license from their courts," Backus, *A History of New England with Particular Reference to the Baptists* (1871) 2, 197. Imps, in the eighteenth century, were a species of devil—in the words of Samuel Johnson's *Dictionary*, "subaltern devils" or "puny devils." Madison's characterization of the persecutors is theological. Madison's editors observe: "Apparently it was religious issues, more than tax and trade regulation disputes with England, which were rapidly luring JM away from his beloved studies," *Papers* at 1, 107.

Bradford replied on March 4, 1774, extolling the religious freedom of Pennsylvania, whose "inhabitants think, speak and act with a freedom unknown," *ibid.* at 1, 109. Besides Roger Williams's pioneering views on tolerance in Rhode Island, three colonies had moved toward acceptance of all Christians. Cecil Lord Baron of Baltimore, propietary ruler of Maryland, had on August 26, 1650, approved an act providing that no person "professing to believe in Jesus Christ" should henceforth be molested "for or in respect of his or her religion nor in the free exercise thereof," "An Act Concerning Religion," *Archives of Maryland: Proceedings and Acts of the General Assembly of Maryland, January 1637–September 1664*, ed. William Hand Browne (1883) 244. New York in 1683 had provided that those professing "faith in God by Jesus Christ" should not be molested "for any difference in opinion or matter of religious concernment" if they did not "actually disturb the civill peace of the Province," Hugh Hastings, *Ecclesiastical Records of the State of New York* (1901) 2, 864. William Penn had gone the furthest, providing in 1701 that no one acknowledging "One Almighty God, the Creator, Upholder, and Ruler of the World" should be molested because of his "conscientious Persuasion or Practice, nor be compelled to frequent or maintain any religious Worship, Place or Ministry." However, only those professing to "believe in Jesus Christ, the Saviour of the World" were eligible for public office, *Pennsylvania Charter of Privileges*, Thorpe, ed., *The Federal and State Constitutions* (1909) 5, 3077. For a study in depth of the religious situation, *see* Curry, *The First Freedoms*. For a summary, *see* Forrest McDonald, *Novus Ordo Seclorum: The Intellectual Origins of the Constitution.* (1985) 42–44.

Madison answered Bradford on April 1, 1774:

Our Assembly is to meet the first of May When It is expected something will be done in behalf of the Dissenters: Petitions I hear are already forming among the Persecuted Baptists and I fancy it is in the thoughts of the Presbyterians also to intercede for greater liberty in matters of Religion. For my part I can not help being very doubtful of their succeeding in the attempt. The Affair was on the Carpet during the last Session; but such incredible and extravagant stories were told in the House of the monstrous effects of the Enthusiasm prevalent among the Sectaries and so greedily swallowed by their Enemies that I believe they lost footing by it and the bad name they still have with those who pretend too much contempt to examine into their principles and Conduct and are too much devoted to the ecclesiastical establishment to hear of the Toleration of Dissentients, I am apprehensive, will be again made a pretext for rejecting their requests. The Sentiments of our people of Fortune & fashion on this subject are vastly different from what you have been used to. That liberal catholic and equitable way of thinking as to the rights of Conscience, which is one of the Characteristics of a free people and so strongly marks the People of your province, is but little known among the Zealous adherents to our Hierarchy. We have it is true some persons in the Legislature of generous Principles both in Religion & Politicks but number not merit you know is necessary to carry points there. Besides[,] the Clergy are a numerous and powerful body[,] have great influence at home by reason of their connection with & dependence on the Bishops and Crown and will naturally employ all their art & Interest to depress their rising Adversaries; for such they must consider dissenters who rob them of the good will of the people and may in time endanger their livings & security.

You are happy in dwelling in a Land where those inestimable privileges are fully enjoyed and public has long felt the good effects of their religious as well as Civil Liberty [*ibid.* at 1, 112].

On November 26, 1774, as the First Continental Congress met, Madison wrote Bradford: "I was told by a Quaker Gentleman from Philad^a that a complaint of being persecuted in New-England was laid before the Congress by the People called baptists. Did Truth or prejudice dictate to the Quaker in his report?" [*ibid.* at 1, 130]. As in Virginia, the sufferers were Baptists (*see infra,* section 2).

On July 28, 1775, Madison, now an active rebel, wrote Bradford about the day set by the Continental Congress as one of "public humiliation, fasting and prayer":

A Scotch Parson in an adjoining County refused to observe the fast or preach on that day. When called on he pleaded Conscience, alledging that it was his duty to pay no regard to any such appointments made by unconstitutional authority. The Committee it seems have their Consciences too: they have ordered his Church doors to be shut and his salary to be stopped, and have sent to the convention for their advice. If the Convention should connive at their proceedings I question, should his insolence not abate if he does not get ducked in a coat of Tar & surplice of feathers and then he may go in his new Canonicals and act under the lawful Authority of Gen. Gage if he pleases. We have one of the same Kidney in the parish I live in. He was sometime ago published in the Gazette for his insolence and had liked to have met with sore treatment; but finding his protection to be not so much in the law as the favor of the people he is grown very supple & obsequious [*ibid.* at 1, 161].

Madison's reaction on this occasion should be compared with his later view (*infra,* Chap. VII) on government-sponsored prayers.

Madison was named on May 6, 1776, to a committee to prepare "a declaration of rights for revolutionary Virginia." George Mason, the senior member, a devout Anglican, proposed the following on religious freedom:

That as Religion, or the Duty which we owe to our divine and omnipotent Creator, and the Manner of discharging it, can be governed only by Reason and Conviction, not by Force or Violence; and therefore that all Men shou'd enjoy the fullest Toleration in the Exercise of Religion, according to the Dictates of Conscience, unpunished and unrestrained by the Magistrate, unless, under Colour of Religion, any Man disturb the Peace, the Happiness, or Safety of Society, or of Individuals. And that is the mutual

Duty of all, to practice Christian Forbearance, Love and Charity towards Each other [*ibid.* at 1, 172–173].

Madison, the youngest member, was not only characterized by "extreme modesty" (Jefferson, *Autobiography, Writings* (1907) 1, 61) but was without legal training. Nonetheless, wanting to go beyond toleration, he proposed a crucial change. He eliminated the restriction about disturbing the peace, and he attacked state support of religion:

That religion or the duty which we owe to our Creator, and the manner of discharging it, being under the direction of reason and conviction only, not of violence or compulsion; all men are equally entitled to the full and free exercise of it accordg to the dictates of Conscience; and therefore that no man or class of men ought, on account of religion to be invested with peculiar emoluments or privileges, nor subjected to any penalties or disabilities unless under &c. [Madison 1, 174].

Patrick Henry, in the past a defender of imprisoned Baptists, introduced the amendment to the Convention. But when asked if he intended to disestablish the Episcopal Church, he "disclaimed such an object." The amendment was doomed (*ibid.* at 1, 171). Madison drafted a second proposal, which, slightly altered, was almost completely accepted:

That religion, or the duty which we owe to our Creator, and the manner of discharging it, can be directed only by reason and conviction, not by force or violence; and therefore, all men are equally entitled to the free exercise of religion, according to the dictates of conscience; and that it is the mutual duty of all to practise Christian forbearance, love, and charity, towards each other [*ibid.* at 1, 175].

The magic words "free exercise of religion"—so much stronger than "toleration"—were fixed in a public document of great importance.

2. "COMFORTABLE LIBERTY": JEFFERSON ENTERS THE BATTLE

In Virginia, Madison was overshadowed by Thomas Jefferson. Jefferson, as a young lawyer, had made a short investigation into the question, "Whether Christianity is part of the common law?" His conclusion conveyed the anticlericalism—not anti-Christianity—that was to be characteristic of him:

In truth, the alliance between church and state in England, has ever made their judges accomplices in the frauds of the clergy; and even bolder than they are; for instead of being contented with the surreptitious introduction of these four chapters of Exodus, they have taken the whole leap, and declared at once that the whole Bible and Testament, in a lump, make a part of the common law of the land; the first judicial declaration of which was by this Sir Matthew Hale. And thus they have incorporate into the English code, laws made for the Jews alone, and the precepts of the gospel, intended by their benevolent author as obligatory only in foro conscientiae; and they arm the whole with the coercions of municipal law. They do this, too, in a case where the question was, not at all, whether Christianity was a part of the law of England, but simply how far the ecclesiastical law was to be respected by the common law courts of England, in the special case of a right of presentment. Thus identifying Christianity with the ecclesiastical law of England. [Printed as an Appendix to *Jefferson's Reports* in *Virginia Reports Annotated* (1903)].

NOTE. The Position of Jews in Colonial America. Jews were subjected to a variety of religious discriminations. In Maryland they were subject to the laws against blasphemy, in Virgnia they could not employ Christian servants, and in eight states they had to pay taxes to support the established Christian church, Jacob R. Marcus, *The Colonial Jew in America* (1970) 1, 507–508. An insistence on Christian oaths made it impossible for Jews to be lawyers in most colonies and prevented them from being instructors in some schools and colleges, *ibid.* at 508. In all the colonies the Jews were ineligible for public office, *ibid.* at 511. In Connecticut, Delaware, Maryland, Pennsylvania, Rhode Island, South Carolina, and Virginia, they could not vote, *ibid.* at 510. Rhode Island was an especially ironic example. Roger Williams, its founder, had believed in religious freedom for all (*supra*, Chapter V). There were traces of Jewish life in Newport in the seventeenth century, and by 1763 there was a synagogue and a Jewish community equal to about 1 percent of the population of this town of 6,000, Marcus 1, 319. But in Rhode Island, Jews were denied both office and the vote. They were not emancipated until the Rhode Island Constitution of 1842! *ibid.* at 1, 438.

NOTE. The Protestant Episcopal Church. The legal status of the Church of England, whose legal head was the King of England, was peculiarly affected by the Revolution and the severing of all legalities with the old country. Central to the organization of the Church was the episcopate, but prior to the Revolution no bishops had existed in America. New England Congregationalists and the dissenters in England had worked on the English government to prevent the introduction of bishops in America, despite the strenuous efforts of the Reverend Samuel Johnson of Connecticut to create an American diocese. Nelson Rollin Burr, *The Story of the Diocese of Connecticut*, (1962) 127–130. During the Revolution, on November 14, 1784, the Reverend Samuel Seabury, a native of Connecticut, was consecrated a bishop by three Scottish bishops who did not require him to swear allegiance to George III. *Id.* 138. A national convention, held in Philadelphia in September 1785, announced the formation of the Protestant Episcopal Church, distinct in its independent legal organization and to be ruled by elected bishops. *Id.* 148–149. Parliament enacted a statute permitting the bishops of England to consecrate without requiring the oath of allegiance to the crown, and in late 1786 two more Americans, Samuel Provoost and William White, sailed to England to be ordained as bishops. *Id.* 151. In October 1789 Seabury, White, and Provoost joined in consecrating Edward Bass of Newbury as a bishop. The episcopal line of succession was established. The church, no longer under the crown, now stood as an independent ecclesiastical entity.

In October 1776 Jefferson, as a member of the Virginia House of Delegates, threw himself into what he described as "the severest contest in which I have ever been engaged," Jefferson, *Autobiography, Writings*, ed. Albert E. Bergh (1907) 57. The following notes, prepared for a speech in the House of Delegates, show the thrust of his thought about Christianity ("Xty") and the State:

Hs. *State Right* to adopt an Opn. in mattr. Relign.
  whn. mn. ent. Socty. Surrendr. litt. as posble.
  Civl. rts. all yt. r. nec. to Civl. govmt. Religs.
  rts. nt. nec. surrd.
    Individ. cnt. surrdr.—answble. to God
      If is *unalienable right,* [. . .] is Religs.
  God reqres. evy. act acdg. to *Belief*
    yt. Belf. foundd. on Evdce. offd. to his mind.
      as yngs. appr. to hims. nt. to anoth.

Obj. oth. mens Undstgs. *better.*
Ans. hs. own Undstg., wh. mo. or less. judics. only faclty. god
True line betw. Opn. or tendcy. of opn.—& *Overt* act.
  humn. 1. nothg. t. d. wth. Opn. or tendcy.—only
  Overt acts. if magistr. restrn. prins. bec. of
  tendcy. & h. judge yn.
    Relign. no longer *free.*
    Coercn. exercd. by *fallible men.*
Obj. Belief of *Future State* necess.
Ans. Jewish theocrcy.
  God dd. nt. revl. in *Bible.*
  Sadducees.

<*Obj. Religion will decline if not supported*
Ans. Gates of Hell shall not prevail . . .>

Is a Relign. of State <*Use*> *Expedt.*
  Purpose mst. be *Uniformty.*
(a) Is *Uniformty. desirble?*
  if evr. cd. b. obtd. wd. be b. suffoctg. free
  enqry.
    all imprvmts. in Relign. or Philos. hve. bn.
    frm. settg. up privte. jdmt. agt. Public—
    ventrg. dept. Uniformty.
    Monksh. imposns.—ignorce.—darknss. suppd. on
    ruins Enqry.
    Glorious Reformn. effect of shakg. off Pub. opn.
      Mahomsm. supprtd. by stiflg. *free enqry.*
    Philos. reformd by *free* enq.
      Galileo. Newton
  Unifmty. no. mo. nec. in *Relign.* yn. *Philos.*
    no consqce. if Newtonn. or Cartesn.
    Overt acts all yt. nec.
  Diffc. in Religs. opn. supplies place *Censor Morum*
    Teachrs. evy. sect. inculcte. sa. mor. princ. wh. yn.
    gve. peculr. priv. to any?
(b) Is *Unifmty. Attainable?*
  by *Inquisn.*
  by lessr. Punmts.—Burng heretic—Fine. Impr. Abjurn.
  Constrt. m. prodce. Hippocr.—nt. prevt. sentimt.
  Coercn. mst. b. xrcd. by *fallib.* men—abused
    Experce. hs. provd. *Unattnb.*
  Millns. burnt—tortd.—find.—imprisd. yet men *differ.*
  in Romn. Cath. countr. most infidelty.
  If Relign. of sta. mst b. stabld. *Is ours right?*
    Zealot wll. an. *yes.*
    1/10,000 of men of our Relign.
  Obj. all states have *establmt.*
  Ans. then all religions have been established
  <*Ans*> hve Govng. pwrs. of earth shewn *Infallibility.* by this?
      nevr. pretendd. to it till Xty.
      Exam. effects since
    hs. God *stampd.* us wth. mark
      r.w. whiter—handsmr.—athletc.—wisr.

if n. sch. *Ear-mark* whence ys. *Confidence?*
  ans. Reason.
    true evy. mn's *Reasn.* judge fr. hms. presbn. fr.
      Presbn.—Episcn. for Episcn.
    bt. wh. m. reasn. step int. jdmt. seat of yours?
Advantags to *Relign.* to put all on footg.
  Strengthn. Church.
  oblige it's ministers to be *Industrs. Exemplary*
  Northern clergy
  wh. depdce. or Indepdce. mst. likely to mke. industrs.
    Lawyers—Physicns.
  Xty. florshd. 300.y. witht. establmt.
  soon as establd. *declind.* frm. *Purity*
  betrays wnt. confdce. in doctrnes. of chch. to
    suspct. yt. reasn. or intrinsck. xcllce. insfft.
    wtht. seculr. prop.
    Gates of hell shall never prevail
Attach People
  20,000 beyd. & adjg. Blue ridge.
  55,000 in all.
  ceding wll. attach.
Obj. *Fixd. Contribn.*
  inequalty. of Parishes
  no. of dissentrs. difft. in difft. parish.
  Contribn. wll. nt. supprt. Preachrs. in some Chch.
    min. in other
  Contribn. of sme. yn. wll. be lost or givn. agt.
  Conscce.
  Decln. of rts. is *freedm.* of *Religion*
    force mn. to contribte. wn. n. teachr. of sect to
    recve. is t. force to supprt. heresy
  Quakrs. give no Contribns.
  Disgorge. fornrs.
    N. Engld.
[Jefferson, *Papers,* ed. Julian P. Boyd (1950) I, 537–539.]

The arguments were practical and political (the numbers given under "Attach People" are estimates of voters who are religious dissenters); Lockean (the nature of government; constitutional [the Declaration of Rights]); conscientious (the duty owed God); and Christian (the gates of Hell shall not prevail, Matt. 16:18). Jefferson's efforts to effect disestablishment had limited success, as he observed eight years later in Paris in his *Notes on Virginia, Works,* ed. Bergh, 2, 217–225:

Query XVII
The different religions received into that state?

The first settlers in this country were emigrants from England, of the English church, just at a point of time when it was flushed with complete victory over the religious of all other persuasions. Possessed, as they became, of the powers of making, administering and executing the laws, they shewed equal intolerance in this country with their Presbyterian brethren, who had emigrated to the northern government. The poor Quakers were flying from persecution in England. They cast their eyes on these new countries as aslyums of civil and religious freedom; but they found them free only for the reigning sect. Several acts of the Virginia assembly of 1659, 1662, and 1693, had made it penal in parents to refuse to have their children baptized; had prohibited the unlawful assembling of Quakers; had made it penal for any master of a vessel to bring a Quaker into the state; had ordered those already here, and such as should come thereafter, to be imprisoned till they should abjure the country; provided a milder punishment for their first and second return, but death for their third; had inhibited all persons from suffering their meetings in or near their houses, entertaining them individually, or disposing of books which supported their tenets. If no capital execution took place here, as did in New England, it was not owing to the moderation of the church, or spirit of the legislature, as may be inferred from the law itself; but to historical circumstances which have not been handed down to us. The Anglicans retained full possession of the country about a century. Other opinions began then to creep in, and the great care of the government to support their own church, having begotten an equal degree of indolence in its clergy, two thirds of the people had become dissenters at the commencement of the present revolution. The laws indeed were still oppressive on them, but the spirit of the one party had subsided into moderation, and of the other had risen to a degree of determination which commanded respect.

The present state of our laws on the subject of religion is this. The convention of May 1776, in their declaration of rights, declared it to be a truth, and a natural right, that the exercise of religion should be free; but when they proceeded to form on that declaration the ordinance of government, instead of taking up every principle declared in the bill of rights, and guarding it by legislative sanction, they passed over that which asserted our religious rights, leaving them as they found them. The same convention, however, when they met as a member of the general assembly in October 1776, repealed all acts of parliament which had rendered criminal the maintaining any opinions in matters of religion, the forbearing to repair to church, and the exercising any mode of worship; and suspended the laws giving salaries to the clergy, which suspension was made perpetual in October 1779. Statutory oppressions in religion being thus wiped away, we remain at present under those only imposed by the common law, or by our own acts of assembly. At the common law, heresy was a capital offence, punishable by burning. Its definition was left to the ecclesiastical judges, before whom the conviction was, till the statute of the I El. c. I. circumscribed it, by declaring that nothing should be deemed heresy but what had been so determined by authority of the canonical scriptures, or by one of the four first general councils, or by some other council having for the grounds of their declaration the express and plain words of the scriptures. Heresy, thus circumscribed, being an offence at the common law, our act of assembly of October 1777, c. 17 gives cognizance of it to the general court, by declaring that the jurisdiction of that court shall be general in all matters at the common law. The execution is by the writ *De haeretico comburendo.* By our own act of assembly of 1705, c. 30, if a person brought up in the christian religion denies the being of a God, or the trinity, or asserts there are more Gods than one, or denies the christian religion to be true, or the scriptures to be of divine authority, he is punishable on the first offence by incapacity to hold any office or employment ecclesiastical, civil, or military; on the second by disability to sue, to take any gift or legacy, to be guardian, executor or administrator, and by three years imprisonment, without bail. A father's right to the custody of his own children being founded in law on his right of guardianship, this being taken away, they may of course be severed from him and put, by the authority of a court, into more orthodox hands. This is a summary view of that religious slavery under which a people have been willing to remain who have lavished their lives and fortunes for the establishment of their civil freedom. The error seems not sufficiently eradicated, that the operations of the mind, as well as the acts of the body, are subject to the coercion of the laws. But our rulers can have authority over such natural rights, only as we have submitted to them. The rights of conscience we never submitted, we could not submit. We are answerable for them to our God. The legitimate powers of government extend to such acts only as are injurious to others. But it does me no injury for my neighbor to say there are twenty gods, or no god. It neither picks my pocket nor breaks my leg. If it be said his testimony in a court of justice cannot be relied on, reject it then, and be the stigma on him. Constraint may make him worse by making him a hypocrite, but it will never make him a truer man. It may fix him obstinately in his errors, but will not cure them. Reason and free inquiry are the only effectual agents against error. Give a loose to them, they will support the true religion by bringing every false one to their tribunal, to the test of their investigation. They are the natural enemies of error, and of error only. Had not the Roman government permitted free inquiry, christianity could never have been introduced. Had not free inquiry been indulged, at the era of the reformation, the corruptions of christianity could not have been purged away. If it be restrained now, the present corruptions will be protected, and new ones encouraged. Was the government to prescribe to us our medicine and diet, our bodies would be in such keeping as our souls are now. Thus in France the emetic was once forbidden as a medicine, and the potatoe as an article of food. Government is just as infallible, too, when it fixes systems in physics. Galileo was sent to the inquisition for affirming that the earth was a sphere; the government had declared it to be as flat as a trencher, and Galileo was obliged to abjure his error. This error however at length prevailed, the earth became a globe, and Descartes declared it was whirled round its axis by a vortex. The government in which he lived was wise enough to see that this was no question of civil jurisdiction, or we should all have been involved by authority in vortices. In fact the vortices have been exploded, and the Newtonian principle of gravitation is now more firmly established, on the basis of reason, than it would be were the government to step in and to make it an article of necessary faith. Reason and experiment have been indulged, and error has fled before them. It is error alone which needs the support of government. Truth can stand by itself. Subject opinion to coercion: who will you make your inquisitors? Fallible men; men governed by bad passions, by private as well as public reasons. And why subject it to coercion? To produce uniformity. But is uniformity of opinion desireable? No more than of face and stature. Introduce the bed of Procrustes then, and as there is danger that the large men may beat the small, make us all of a size, by lopping the former and stretching the latter. Difference of opinion is advantageous in religion. The several sects perform the office of a Censor morum over each other. Is uniformity attainable? Millions of innocent men, women and children, since the introduction of Christianity, have been burnt, tortured, fined, imprisoned: yet we have not advanced one inch towards uniformity. What has been the effect of coercion? To make one half the world fools, and the other half hypocrites. To support roguery and error all over the earth. Let us reflect that it is inhabited by a thousand millions of people. That these profess probably a thousand different systems of religion. That ours is but one of that thousand. That if there be but one right, and ours that one, we should wish to see the 999 wandering sects gathered into the fold of truth. But against such a majority we cannot effect this by force. Reason and persuasion are the only practicable instruments. To make way for these, freer inquiry must be indulged; and how can we wish others to indulge it while we refuse it ourselves. But every state, says an inquisitor, has established some religion. "No two, say I, have established the same." Is this a proof of the infallibility of establishment? Our sister states of Pennsylvania and New York, however, have long subsisted without any establishment at all. The experiment was new and doubtful when they made it. It has answered beyond conception. They flourish infinitely. Religion is well supported; of various kinds indeed, but all good enough; all sufficient to preserve peace and order: or if a sect arises whose tenets would subvert morals, good sense has fair play, and reasons and laughs it out of doors, without suffering the state to be troubled with it. They do not hang more malefactors than we do. They are not more disturbed with religious dissentions. On the contrary, their harmony is unparallelled, and can be ascribed to nothing but their unbounded tolerance, because there is no other circumstances in which they differ from every nation on earth. They have made the happy discovery, that the way to silence religious disputes, is to take no notice of them. Let us too give this experiment fair play, and get rid, while we may, of those tyrannical laws. It is true we are as yet secured against them by the spirit of the times. I doubt whether the people of this country would suffer an execution for heresy, or a three years imprisonment for not comprehending the mysteries of the trinity. But is the spirit of the people an infallible, a permanent reliance? Is it government? Is this the kind of protection we receive in return for the rights we give up? Besides, the spirit of the times may alter, will alter. Our rulers will become corrupt, our people careless. A single zealot may commence persecuter, and better men be his victims. It can never be too often repeated, that the time for fixing every essential right on a legal basis is while our rulers are honest, and ourselves united. From the conclusion of this war we shall be going down hill. It will not then be necessary to resort every moment to the people for support. They will be forgotten therefore, and their rights disregarded. They will forget themselves, but in the sole faculty of making money, and will never think of uniting to effect a due respect for their rights. The shackles, therefore, which shall not be knocked off at the conclusion of this war, will remain on us long, will be made heavier and heavier, till our rights shall revive or expire in a convulsion.

If Jefferson's estimate of religious denominations in Virginia was correct, the Episcopalians were a minority. But "although the majority of our citizens were dissenters, as has been observed, a majority of the legislature were churchmen," Jefferson, *Autobiography, Works* 1, 58. In 1779, Jefferson penned "A Bill for Establishing Religious Freedom"—"establishing" here being neatly turned to the advantage of liberty. The bill was introduced in the General Assembly in May 1779 and its author was certainly acceptable to many legislators: on June 1 the General Assembly, 67 to 61, elected Jefferson governor of the commonwealth (*Papers* 2, 278). His bill read as follows:

A Bill for Establishing Religious Freedom

Well aware that the opinions and belief of men depend not on their own will, but follow involuntarily the evidence proposed to their minds; that Almighty God hath created the mind free, *and manifested his supreme will that free it shall remain by making it altogether insusceptible of restraint;* that all attempts to influence it by temporal punishments, or burthens, or by civil incapacitations, tend only to beget habits of hypocrisy and meanness, and are a departure from the plan of the holy author of our religion, who being lord both of body and mind, yet chose not to propagate it by coercions on either, as was in his Almighty power to do, *but to extend it by its influence on reason alone;* that the impious presumption of legislators and rulers, civil as well as ecclesiastical, who, being themselves but fallible and uninspired men, have assumed dominion over the faith of others, setting up their own opinions and modes of thinking as the only true and infallible, and as such endeavoring to impose them on others, hath established and maintained false religions over the greatest part of the world and through all time: That to compel a man to furnish contributions of money for the propagation of opinions which he disbelieves *and abhors,* is sinful and tyrannical; that even the forcing him to support this or that teacher of his own religious persuasion, is depriving him of the comfortable liberty of giving his contributions to the particular pastor whose morals he would make his pattern, and whose powers he feels most persuasive to righteousness; and is withdrawing from the ministry those temporary rewards, which proceeding from an approbation of their personal conduct, are an additional incitement to earnest and unremitting labours for the instruction of mankind; that our civil rights have no dependance on our religious opinions, any more than our opinions in physics or geometry; that therefore the proscribing any citizen as unworthy the public confidence by laying upon him an incapacity of being called to offices of trust and emolument, unless he profess or renounce this or that religious opinion, is depriving him injuriously of those privileges and advantages to which, in common with his fellow citizens, he has a natural right; that it tends also to corrupt the principles of that *very* religion it is meant to encourage, by bribing, with a monopoly of worldly honours and emoluments, those who will externally profess and conform to it; that though indeed these are criminal who do not withstand such temptation, yet neither are those innocent who lay the bait in their way; *that the opinions of men are not the object of civil government, nor under its jurisdiction,* that to suffer the civil magistrate to intrude his powers into the field of opinion and to restrain the profession or propagation of principles on supposition of their ill tendency is a dangerous fallacy, which at once destroys all religious liberty, because he being of course judge of that tendency will make his opinions the rule of judgment, and approve or condemn the sentiments of others only as they shall square with or differ from his own; that it is time enough for the rightful purposes of civil government for its officers to interfere when principles break out into overt acts against peace and good order; and finally, that truth is great and will prevail if left to herself; that she is the proper and sufficient antagonist to error, and has nothing to fear from the conflict unless by human interposition disarmed of her natural weapons, free argument and debate; errors ceasing to be dangerous when it is permitted freely to contradict them.

We the General Assembly of Virginia do enact that no man shall be compelled to frequent or support any religious worship, place, or ministry whatsoever, nor shall be enforced, restrained, molested, or burthened in his body or goods, nor shall otherwise suffer, on account of his religious opinions or belief; but that all men shall be free to profess, and by argument to maintain, their opinions in matters of religion, and that the same shall in no wise diminish, enlarge, or affect their civil capacities.

And though we well know that this Assembly, elected by the people for the ordinary purposes of legislation only, have no power to restrain the acts of succeeding Assemblies, constituted with powers equal to our own, and that therefore to declare this act irrevocable would be of no effect in law; yet we are free to declare, and do declare, that the rights hereby asserted are of the natural rights of mankind, and that if any act shall be hereafter passed to repeal the present or to narrow its operation, such act will be an infringement of natural right.

The bill was read twice, and was killed in August 1779, a death that reflected the political skill and strength of the establishment Jefferson had attempted to destroy.

3. THE "GREAT BARRIER"

On April 25, 1784, Madison reported to Jefferson, now the American minister in Paris, that Patrick Henry, "the old fox," was friendly to a "general assessment" on behalf of the Christian religion (Madison, *Papers* 8, 20). Petitions in favor of such a bill were introduced in the Virginia House of Delegates, but their supporters were nervous about the outcome and did not push for enactment, *ibid.* at 8, 93. On November 11, 1784, the House, 47–32, called for a tax for "the support of the Christian religion," but no tax was actually passed, *ibid.* at 8, 155. Jefferson on December 8, 1784, wrote from Paris: "I am glad the *Episcopalians* have again shown their teeth and fangs. The *dissenters* had almost forgotten them," *ibid.* at 8, 178. Finally, on Christmas Eve 1784, a tax was put before the House:

A Bill Establishing a Provision for Teachers of the Christian Religion

Whereas the general diffusion of Christian knowledge hath a natural tendency to correct the morals of men, restrain their vices, and preserve the peace of society; which cannot be effected without a competent provision for learned teachers, who may be thereby enabled to devote their time and attention to the duty of instructing such citizens, as from their circumstances and want of education, cannot otherwise attain such knowledge; and it is judged that such provision may be made by the Legislature, without counteracting the liberal principle heretofore adopted and intended to be preserved by abolishing all distinctions of pre-eminence amongst the different societies or communities of Christians;

Be it herefore enacted by the General Assembly, That for the support of Christian teachers,   per centum on the amount, or   in the pound on the sum payable for tax on the property within this Commonwealth, is hereby asessed, and shall be paid by every person chargeable with the said tax at the time the same shall become due; and the Sheriffs of the several Counties shall have power to levy and collect the same in the same manner and under the like restrictions and limitations, as are or may be prescribed by the laws for raising the Revenues of this State.

And be it enacted, That for every sum so paid, the Sheriff or Collector shall give a receipt, expressing therein to what society of Christians the person from whom he may receive the same shall direct the money to be paid, keeping a distinct account thereof in his books. The Sheriff of every County, shall, on or before the   day of   in every year, return to the Court, upon oath, two alphabetical lists of the payments to him made, distinguishing in columns opposite to the names of the persons who shall have paid the same, the society to which the money so paid was by them appropriated; and one column for the names where no appropriation shall be made. One of which lists, after being recorded in a book to be kept for that purpose, shall be filed by the Clerk in his office; the other shall by the Sheriff be fixed up in the Court-house, there to remain for the inspection of all concerned. And the Sheriff, after deducting five per centum for the collection, shall forthwith pay to such person or persons as shall be appointed to receive the same by the Vestry, Elders, or Directors, however denominated of each such society, the sum so stated to be due to that society; or in default thereof, upon the motion of such person or person to the next or any succeeding Court, execution shall be awarded for the same against the Sheriff and his security, his and their executors or administrators; provided that ten days previous notice be given of such motion. And upon every such execution, the Officer serving the same shall proceed to immediate sale of the estate taken, and shall not accept of security for payment at the end of three months, nor to have the goods forthcoming at the day of sale; for his better direction wherein, the Clerk shall endorse upon every such execution that no security of any kind shall be taken.

And be it further enacted, That the money to be raised by virtue of this Act, shall be by the Vestries, Elders, or Directors of each religious society, appropriated to a provision for a Minister or Teacher of the Gospel of their denomination, or the providing places of divine worship, and to none other use whatsoever; except in the denomination of Quakers and Menonists, who may receive what is collected from their members, and place it in their general fund, to be disposed of in a manner which they shall think best calculated to promote their particular mode of worship.

And be it enacted, That all sums which at the time of payment to the Sheriff or Collector may not be appropriated by the person paying the same, shall be accounted for with the Court in manner as by this Act is directed; and after deducting for his collection, the Sheriff shall pay the amount thereof (upon account certified by the Court to the Auditors of Public Accounts, and by them to the Treasurer) into the public Treasury, to be disposed of under the direction of the General Assembly, for the encouragement of seminaries of learning within the Counties whence such sums shall arise, and to no other use or purpose whatsoever.

THIS Act shall commence, and be in force, from and after the   day of in the year   .

A Copy from the Engrossed Bill.

JOHN BECKLEY, C.H.D.

Madison's notes indicate his argument against it (*Papers* 8, 197–199):

[Outline A]

[23–24 December 1784]

Debate on Bill for Relig. Estabt proposed by Mr. Henry

1. limited
2. in particular
3. What is Christianity? Courts of law to Judge
4. What edition, Hebrew, Septuagint, or vulgate? What copy—what translation?
5. What books canonical, what apochryphal? the papists holding to be the former what protestants the latter, the Lutherans the latter what other protestants & papists the former
6. In What light are they to be viewed, as dictated every letter by inspiration, or the essential parts only? or the matter in generall not the words?
7. What sense the true one, for if some doctrines be essential to *Christiantiy,* those who reject these, whatever name they take are no *Christian* Society?
8. Is it Trinitarianism, arianism, Socinianism? Is it salvation by faith or works also— by free grace, or free will–&c &c &c–
9. What clue is to guide Judge thro' this labyrinth? When the question comes before them whether any particular Society is a Christian Society?
10. Ends in what is orthodoxy, what heresy?

[Outline B]

[23–24 December 1784]

I. *Rel:* not within purview of Civil Authority.
tendency of Estabg. Christianity

                              1. to project of Uniformity
                              2. to penal laws for supportg. it.

_____

Progres[s] of Gen: Assest. proves this tendency

_____

difference between estabg. & tolerating errour—

II. True question not—Is Rel: necesy.?
are Religs. Estabts. necessy. for Religion? no.
1. propensity of man to Religion.
2. Experience shews Relig: corrupted by Estabt.
3. downfal of States, mentioned by Mr. H[enry]. happened where there was Estabts.
4. Experience gives no model of Gel. Asst?
5. Case of Pa. explained—not solitary. N.J.
See Const: of it. R.I.N.Y.D.

_____

   factions greater in S.C.
6. Case of primitive Christianity.
of Reformation
of Dissenters formerly.

III. Decl: Rig[hts].7.Progress of Religious Liberty

IV. Policy.
1. promote emigrations from State
2. prevent [immigration] into it as *asylum*

V. Necessity of Estabts. inferred from State of Conty.

---

true causes of disease
1. War   common to other States &
2. bad laws produce same complts. in N.E.
3. pretext from taxes
4. State of Administration of Justice.
5. transition from old to new plan.
6. policy & hopes of friends to G. Asst.

---

true remedies not Estabt. but being out war
1. laws cherish virtue
2. Administ: justice
3. personal example—Association for R.
4. By present vote cut off hope of G. Asst.
5. Education of youth

Probable defects of Bill
   dishonor Christianity

---

   panegyric on it on our side

Decl: Rights.

By one vote the House voted to delay the bill, and then by a vote of 45–37, put off a third reading till next November, *ibid.* at 8, 200. Madison, writing Lafayette on March 20, 1785, rejoiced at the defeat of what he called "the Act for corrupting our Religious system," *ibid.* at 8, 254.

In the spring, writing James Monroe on April 12, 1785, Madison analyzed the situation: "The Episcopal people are generally for it, tho' I think the zeal of some of them has cooled. The laity of the other sects are equally unanimous on the other side. So are all the Clergy except the Presbyterians. . . .," *ibid.* at 8, 261. George Nicholas urged Madison to organize petitions to show the true feeling of the "great majority," *ibid.* at 8, 264 and 328. Madison wrote Jefferson, April 27, 1785, that the bill had "produced some fermentation below the Mountains and a violent one beyond them," *ibid* at 8, 268. By the end of June 1785 Madison had prepared a petition for general use:

To the Honorable the General Assembly of the Commonwealth of Virginia
A Memorial and Remonstrance

We the subscribers, citizens of the said Commonwealth, having taken into serious consideration, a Bill printed by order of the last Session of General Assembly, entitled "A Bill establishing a provision for Teachers of the Christian Religion," and conceiving that the same if finally armed with the sanctions of a law, will be a dangerous abuse of power, are bound as faithful members of a free State to remonstrate against it, and to declare the reasons by which we are determined. We remonstrate against the said Bill,

1. Because we hold it for a fundamental and undeniable truth, "that Religion or the duty which we owe to our Creator and the manner of discharging it, can be directed only by reason and conviction, not by force or violence." The Religion then of every man must be left to the conviction and conscience of every man; and it is the right of every man to exercise it as these may dictate. This right is in its nature an unalienable right. It is unalienable, because the opinions of men, depending only on the evidence contemplated by their own minds cannot follow the dictates of other men: It is unalienable also, because what is here a right towards men, is a duty towards the Creator. It is the duty of every man to render to the Creator such homage and such only as he believes to be acceptable to him. This duty is precedent, both in order of time and in degree of obligation, to the claims of Civil Society. Before any man can be considered as a member of Civil Society, he must be considered as a subject of the Governour of the Universe: And if a member of Civil Society, who enters into any subordinate Association, must always do it with a reservation of his duty to the General Authority; much more must every man who becomes a member of any particular Civil Society, do it with a saving of his allegiance to the Universal Sovereign. We maintain therefore that in matters of Religion, no mans right is abridged by the institution of Civil Society and that Religion is wholly exempt from its cognizance. True it is, that no other rule exists, by which any question which may divide a Society, can be ultimately determined, but the will of the majority; but it is also true that the majority may trespass on the rights of the minority.

2. Because if Religion be exempt from the authority of the Society at large, still less can it be subject to that of the Legislative Body. The latter are but the creatures and vicegerents of the former. Their jurisdiction is both derivative and limited: it is limited with regard to the co-ordinate departments, more necessarily is it limited with regard to the constituents. The preservation of a free Government requires not merely, that the metes and bounds which separate each department of power be invariably maintained; but more especially that neither of them be suffered to overleap the great Barrier which defends the rights of the people. The Rulers who are guilty of such an encroachment, exceed the commission from which they derive their authority, and are Tyrants. The People who submit to it are governed by laws made neither by themselves nor by an authority derived from them, and are slaves.

3. Because it is proper to take alarm at the first experiment on our liberties. We hold this prudent jealousy to be the first duty of Citizens, and one of the noblest characteristics of the late Revolution. The free men of America did not wait till usurped power had strengthened itself by exercise, and entangled the question in precedents. They saw all the consequences in the principle, and they avoided the consequences by denying the principle. We revere this lesson too much soon to forget it. Who does not see that the same authority which can establish Christianity, in exclusion of all other Religions, may establish with the same ease any particular sect of Christians, in exclusion of all other Sects? that the same authority which can force a citizen to contribute three pence only of his property for the support of any one establishment, may force him to conform to any other establishment in all cases whatsoever?

4. Because the Bill violates that equality which ought to be the basis of every law, and which is more indispensible, in proportion as the validity or expediency of any law is more liable to be impeached. If "all men are by nature equally free and independent," all men are to be considered as entering into Society on equal conditions; as relinquishing no more, and therefore retaining no less, one than another, of their natural rights. Above all are they to be considered as retaining an "*equal* title to the free exercise of Religion according to the dictates of Conscience." Whilst we assert for ourselves a freedom to embrace, to profess and to observe the Religion which we believe to be of divine origin, we cannot deny an equal freedom to those whose minds have

not yet yielded to the evidence which has convinced us. If this freedom be abused, it is an offence against God, not against man: To God, therefore, not to man, must an account of it be rendered. As the Bill violates equality by subjecting some to peculiar burdens, so it violates the same principle, by granting to others peculiar exemptions. Are the Quakers and Menonists the only sects who think a compulsive support of their Religions unnecessary and unwarrantable? Can their piety alone be entrusted with the care of public worship? Ought their Religions to be endowed above all others with extraordinary privileges by which proselytes may be enticed from all others? We think too favorably of the justice and good sense of these denominations to believe that they either covet pre-eminences over their fellow citizens or that they will be seduced by them from the common opposition to the measure.

5. Because the Bill implies either that the Civil Magistrate is a competent Judge of Religious Truth; or that he may employ Religion as an engine of Civil policy. The first is an arrogant pretension falsified by the contradictory opinions of Rulers in all ages, and throughout the world: the second an unhallowed perversion of the means of salvation.

6. Because the establishment proposed by the Bill is not requisite for the support of the Christian Religion. To say that it is, is a contradiction to the Christian Religion itself, for every page of it disavows a dependence on the powers of this world: it is a contradiction to fact; for it is known that this Religion both existed and flourished, not only without the support of human laws, but in spite of every opposition from them, and not only during the period of miraculous aid, but long after it had been left to its own evidence and the ordinary care of Providence. Nay, it is a contradiction in terms; for a Religion not invented by human policy, must have pre-existed and been supported, before it was established by human policy. It is moreover to weaken in those who profess this Religion a pious confidence in its innate excellence and the patronage of its Author; and to foster in those who still reject it, a suspicion that its friends are too conscious of its fallacies to trust it to its own merits.

7. Because experience witnesseth that ecclesiastical establishments, instead of maintaining the purity and efficacy of Religion, have had a contrary operation. During almost fifteen centuries has the legal establishment of Christianity been on trial. What have been its fruits? More or less in all places, pride and indolence in the Clergy, ignorance and servility in the laity, in both, superstition, bigotry and persecution. Enquire of the Teachers of Christianity for the ages in which it appeared in its greatest lustre; those of every sect, point to the ages prior to its incorporation with Civil policy. Propose a restoration of this primitive State in which its Teachers depended on the voluntary rewards of their flocks, many of them predict its downfall. On which Side ought their testimony to have greatest weight, when for or when against their interest?

8. Because the establishment in question is not necessary for the support of Civil Government. If it be urged as necessary for the support of Civil Government only as it is a means of supporting Religion, and it be not necessary for the latter purpose, it cannot be necessary for the former. If Religion be not within the cognizance of Civil Government how can its legal establishment be necessary to Civil Government? What influence in fact have ecclesiastical establishments had on Civil Society? In some instances they have been seen to erect a spiritual tyranny on the ruins of the Civil authority; in many instances they have been seen upholding the thrones of political tyranny: in no instance have they been seen the guardians of the liberties of the people. Rulers who wished to subvert the public liberty, may have found an established Clergy convenient auxiliaries. A just Government instituted to secure & perpetuate it needs them not. Such a Government will be best supported by protecting every Citizen in the enjoyment of his Religion with the same equal hand which protects his person and his property; by neither invading the equal rights of any Sect, nor suffering any Sect to invade those of another.

9. Because the proposed establishment is a departure from the generous policy, which, offering an Asylum to the persecuted and oppressed of every Nation and Religion,

promised a lustre to our country, and an accession to the number of its citizens. What a melancholy mark is the Bill of sudden degeneracy? Instead of holding forth an Asylum to the persecuted, it is itself a signal of persecution. It degrades from the equal rank of Citizens all those whose opinions in Religion do not bend to those of the Legislative authority. Distant as it may be in its present form from the Inquisition, it differs from it only in degree. The one is the first step, the other the last in the career of intolerance. The magnanimous sufferer under this cruel scourge in foreign Regions, must view the Bill as a Beacon on our Coast, warning him to seek some other haven, where liberty and philanthrophy in their due extent, may offer a more certain repose from his Troubles.

10. Because it will have a like tendency to banish our Citizens. The allurements presented by other situations are every day thinning their number. To superadd a fresh motive to emigration by revoking the liberty which they now enjoy, would be the same species of folly which has dishonoured and depopulated flourishing kingdoms.

11. Because it will destroy that moderation and harmony which the forbearance of our laws to intermeddle with Religion has produced among its several sects. Torrents of blood have been spilt in the old world, by vain attempts of the secular arm, to extinguish Religious discord, by proscribing all difference in Religious opinion. Time has at length revealed the true remedy. Every relaxation of narrow and rigorous policy, wherever it has been tried, has been found to assuage the disease. The American Theatre has exhibited proofs that equal and compleat liberty, if it does not wholly eradicate it, sufficiently destroys its malignant influence on the health and prosperity of the State. If with the salutary effects of this system under our own eyes, we begin to contract the bounds of Religious freedom, we know no name that will too severely reproach our folly. At least let warning be taken at the first fruits of the threatened innovation. The very appearance of the Bill has transformed "that Christian forbearance, love and charity," which of late mutually prevailed, into animosities and jealousies, which may not soon be appeased. What mischiefs may not be dreaded, should this enemy to the public quiet be armed with the force of a law?

12. Because the policy of the Bill is adverse to the diffusion of the light of Christianity. The first wish of those who enjoy this precious gift ought to be that it may be imparted to the whole race of mankind. Compare the number of those who have as yet received it with the number still remaining under the dominion of false Religions; and how small is the former! Does the policy of the Bill tend to lessen the disproportion? No; it at once discourages those who are strangers to the light of revelation from coming into the Region of it; and countenances by example the nations who continue in darkness, in shutting out those who might convey it to them. Instead of Levelling as far as possible, every obstacle to the victorious progress of Truth, the Bill with an ignoble and unchristian timidity would circumscribe it with a wall of defence against the encroachments of error.

13. Because attempts to enforce by legal sanctions, acts obnoxious to so great a proportion of Citizens, tend to enervate the laws in general, and to slacken the bands of Society. If it be difficult to execute any law which is not generally deemed necessary or salutary, what must be the case, where it is deemed invalid and dangerous? And what may be the effect of so striking an example of impotency in the Government, on its general authority?

14. Because a measure of such singular magnitude and delicacy ought not to be imposed, without the clearest evidence that it is called for by a majority of citizens, and no satisfactory method is yet proposed by which the voice of the majority in this case may be determined, or its influence secured. "The people of the respective counties are indeed requested to signify their opinion respecting the adoption of the Bill to the next Session of Assembly." But the representation must be made equal, before the voice either of the Representatives or of the Counties will be that of the people. Our hope is that neither of the former will, after due consideration, espouse the dangerous principle

of the Bill. Should the event disappoint us, it will still leave us in full confidence, that a fair appeal to the latter will reverse the sentence against our liberties.

15. Because finally, "the equal right of every citizen to the free exercise of his Religion according to the dictates of conscience" is held by the same tenure with all our other rights. If we recur to its origin, it is equally the gift of nature; if we weigh its importance, it cannot be less dear to us; if we consult the "Declaration of those rights which pertain to the good people of Virginia, as the basis and foundation of Government," it is enumerated with equal solemnity, or rather studied emphasis. Either then, we must say, that the Will of the Legislature is the only measure of their authority; and that in the plenitude of this authority, they may sweep away all our fundamental rights; or, that they are bound to leave this particular right untouched and sacred: Either we must say, that they may controul the freedom of the press, may abolish the Trial by Jury, may swallow up the Executive and Judiciary Powers of the State; nay that they may despoil us of our very right of suffrage, and erect themselves into an independent and hereditary Assembly or, we must say, that they have no authority to enact into law the Bill under consideration. We the Subscribers say, that the General Assembly of this Commonwealth have no such authority: And that no effort may be omitted on our part against so dangerous an usurpation, we oppose to it, this remonstrance; earnestly praying, as we are in duty bound, that the Supreme Lawgiver of the Universe, by illuminating those to whom it is addressed, may on the one hand, turn their Councils from every act which would affront his holy prerogative, or violate the trust committed to them: and on the other, guide them into every measure which may be worthy of his [blessing, may re]dound to their own praise, and may establish more firmly the liberties, the prosperity and the happiness of the Commonwealth.

Madison, not anxious to alienate allies on other subjects who were in favor of this bill, had the petition circulated anonymously; it gained 1,552 signatures. Another anonymous petition, asserting the General Assessment to be against "the Spirit of the Gospel," obtained 4,899. In all, 10,929 persons indicated opposition to the measure, which died in the November 1785 session, *ibid.* at 8, 295–298. Madison provided the political leadership. The evangelicals, especially the Baptists, provided the decisive numbers, Thomas E. Buckley, S.J., *Church and State in Revolutionary Virginia, 1776–1787* (1977) 175.

The aftermath was glorious for Madison and Jefferson. Jefferson's bill, defeated in 1779, now passed. As Madison wrote Jefferson in Paris on January 22, 1786:

The steps taken throughout the Country to defeat the Genl. Assessment, had produced all the effect that could have been wished. The table was loaded with petitions & remonstrances from all parts against the interposition of the Legislature in matters of Religion. A General convention of the Presbyterian church prayed expressly that the bill in the Revisal might be passed into a law, as the best safeguard short of a constitutional one, for their religious rights. The bill was carried thro' the H of Delegates, without alteration. The Senate objected to the preamble, and sent down a proposed substitution of the 16th art: of the Declaration of Rights. The H. of D. disagreed. The Senate insisted and asked a Conference. Their objections were frivolous indeed. In order to remove them as they were understood by the Managers of the H. of D. the preamble was sent up again from the H. of D. with one or two verbal alterations. As an amendment to these the Senate sent down a few others; which as they did not affect the substance though they somewhat defaced the composition, it was thought better to agree to than to run further risks, especially as it was getting late in the Session and the House growing thin. The enacting clauses past without a single alteration, and I flatter myself have in this Country extinguished for ever the ambitious hope of making laws for the human mind. [Madison, *Papers* 8, 473–474].

The changes made by the legislature are indicated by italics in the copy of Jefferson's bill, *supra*, VI, 2. "Comfortable liberty" was established, even if Madison's estimation of the victory—the end of "making laws for the human mind"—was exaggerated.

When Jefferson had attacked the belief that Christianity was part of the common law, he had found one ancient ecclesiastical phrase acceptable: *in foro conscientiae*, "in the forum of conscience" or internal tribunal where the old canonists said each one had to judge his own acts. Jefferson had abandoned external judgment of the morality of an act while retaining the sanction of conscience. That sanction, coupled with the idea of an avenging God, he invoked in his reflections on slavery, another portion of his *Notes on Virginia*, 266–267:

Query XVIII

The particular customs and manners that may happen to be received in that State:

It is difficult to determine on the standard by which the manners of a nation may be tried, whether *catholic* or *particular*. It is more difficult for a native to bring to that standard the manners of his own nation, familiarized to him by habit. There must doubtless by an unhappy influence on the manners of our people produced by the existence of slavery among us. The whole commerce between master and slave is a perpetual exercise of the most boisterous passions, the most unremitting despotism on the one part, and degrading submissions on the other. Our children see this, and learn to imitate it; for man is an imitative animal. This quality is the germ of all education in him. From his cradle to his grave he is learning to do what he sees others do. If a parent could find no motive either in his philanthropy or his self-love, for restraining the intemperance of passion towards his slave, it should always be a sufficient one that his child is present. But generally it is not sufficient. The parent storms, the child looks on, catches the lineaments of wrath, puts on the same airs in the circle of smaller slaves, gives a loose to the worst of passions, and thus nursed, educated, and daily exercised in tyranny, cannot but be stamped by it with odious peculiarities. The man must be a prodigy who can retain his manners and morals undepraved by such circumstances. And with what execrations should the statesman be loaded, who permitting one half the citizens thus to trample on the rights of the other, transforms those into despots, and these into enemies, destroys the morals of the one part, and the amor patriae of the other. For if a slave can have a country in this world, it must be any other in preference to that in which he is born to live and labour for another: in which he must lock up the faculties of his nature, contribute as far as depends on his individual endeavours to the evanishment of the human race, or entail his own miserable condition on the endless generations proceeding from him. With the morals of the people, their industry also is destroyed. For in a warm climate, no man will labour for himself who can make another labour for him. This is so true, that of the proprietors of slaves a very small proportion indeed are ever seen to labour. And can the liberties of a nation be thought secure when we have removed their only firm basis, a conviction in the minds of the people that these liberties are the gift of God? That they are not to be violated but with his wrath? Indeed I tremble for my country when I reflect that God is just: that his justice cannot sleep forever: that considering numbers, nature and natural means only, a revolution of the wheel of fortune, an exchange of situation, is among possible events: that it may become probable by supernatural interference! The Almighty has no attribute which can take side with us in such a contest—But it is impossible to be temperate and to pursue this subject through the various considerations of policy, of morals, of history natural and civil. We must be contented to hope they will force their way into every one's mind. I think a change already perceptible, since the origin of the present revolution. The spirit of the master is abating, that of the slave rising from the dust, his condition mollifying, the way I hope preparing, under the auspices of heaven, for a total emancipation, and that this is disposed, in the order of events, to be with the consent of the masters rather than by their extirpation.

The slaves were one large class of human beings whose minds were not permitted to be free. Slaves worshipped on the terms their masters and the commonwealth of Virginia allowed. Slaves learned what religious doctrine their masters thought suitable. Slaves supported the churches to which their masters contributed the income from their labor. Freeing the free population from external religious restraints, Madison and Jefferson did not acknowledge that they left at least half the population bound, religiously as well as physically. Was the price of religious liberty for one half of the population in Virginia in 1785 slavery for the other half?

MASSACHUSETTS

Meanwhile in Massachusetts, lawmaking had taken a different turn. The Baptists in Massachusetts had sent Isaac Backus to the Continental Congress in 1775 to complain of their being "obliged to support a ministry we cannot attend." The following took place between Backus and the Massachusetts delegates to the Congress:

In their plea, S. Adams tried to represent that *regular* Baptists were quite easy among us; and more than once insinuated that these complaints came from enthusiasts who made it a merit to suffer persecution; and also that enemies had a hand therein. Paine said, there was nothing of conscience in the matter; it was only a contending about paying a little money; and also that we would not be neighborly and let them know who we were, which was all they wanted, and they would readily exempt us.

In answer, I told them they might call it enthusiasm or what they pleased; but I freely own, before all these gentlemen, that it is absolutely a point of conscience with me; for I cannot give in the certificates they require without implicitly acknowledging that power in man which I believe belongs only to God. This shocked them; and Cushing said: "*It quite altered the case;* for if it were a point of conscience, he had nothing to say to that." And the conference of about four hours continuance, closed with their promising to do what they could for our relief; though to deter us from thinking of their coming upon equal footing with us as to religion, John Adams at one time said, we might as well expect a change in the solar system, to expect they would give up their establishment [Isaac Backus, *A History of New England with particular reference to the denomination of Christians called Baptists* (1871; 1969) 2, 201–202].

A state constitution proposed in 1778 had been rejected partly because it lacked a declaration of rights. In 1780 a new Convention remedied this defect. The chief author of the consititution of 1780—a prototype of written American constitutions—was John Adams, who has described his part: "I was by the Convention put upon the Committee—by the Committee upon the Subcommittee—and by the Subcommittee appointed a Sub Sub Committee—so that I had the honor to be principal Engineer," Adams to Edmund Jennings, June 7, 1800, quoted in *Diary and Autobiography of John Adams*, ed. L. H. Butterfield, Leonard C. Faber, Wendell D. Garrett (1961) 2, 401.

The constitution of 1780 opened with a preamble that acknowledged "the goodness of the Great Legislature of the Universe" and prayed for his guidance. Part I proceeded as follows:

A Declaration of the Rights of the Inhabitants of the Commonwealth of Massachusetts

Art. I. All men are born free and equal, and have certain natural, essential, and unalienable rights; among which may be reckoned the right of enjoying and defending their lives and liberties; that of acquiring, possessing, and protecting property; in fine, that of seeking and obtaining their safety and happiness.

II. It is the right as well as the duty of all men in society, publicly, and at stated seasons, to worship the SUPREME BEING, the great creator and preserver of the universe. And no subject shall be hurt, molested, or restrained, in his person, liberty, or estate, for worshipping GOD in the manner and season most agreeable to the dictates of his own conscience; or for his religious profession or sentiments; provided he doth not disturb the public peace, or obstruct others in their religious worship.

III. As the happiness of a people, and the good order and preservation of civil government, essentially depend upon piety, religion and morality; and as these cannot be generally diffused through a community, but by the institution of the public worship of GOD, and of public instructions in piety, religion and morality: Therefore, to promote their happiness and to secure the good order and preservation of their government, the people of this Commonwealth have a right to invest their legislature with power to authorize and require, and the legislature shall, from time to time, authorize and require, the several towns, parishes, precincts, and other bodies-politic, or religious societies, to make suitable provision, at their own expense, for the institution of the public worship of GOD, and for the support and maintenance of public protestant teachers of piety, religion and morality, in all cases where such provision shall not be made voluntarily.

And the people of this Commonwealth have also a right to, and do, invest their legislature with authority to enjoin upon all the subjects an attendance upon the instructions of the public teachers aforesaid, at stated times and seasons, if there be any on whose instructions they can conscientiously and conveniently attend.

Provided notwithstanding, that the several towns, parishes, precincts, and other bodies-politic, or religious societies, shall, at all times, have the exclusive right of electing their public teachers, and of contracting with them for their support and maintenance.

And all monies paid by the subject to the support of public worship, and of the public teachers aforesaid, shall, if he require it, be uniformly applied to the support of the public teacher or teachers of his own religious sect or denomination, provided there be any on whose instructions he attends: otherwise it may be paid towards the support of the teacher or teachers of the parish or precinct in which the said monies are raised.

And every denomination of christians, demeaning themselves peaceably, and as good subjects of the Commonwealth, shall be equally under the protection of the law: And no subordination of any one sect or denomination to another shall ever be established by law.

At the convention, Article III—an article that Adams accepted but did not draft—had been the most controversial. In effect it "virtually established Congregationalism as the state religion of Massachusetts," Samuel Eliot Morison, "The Struggle over the Adoption of the Constitution of Massachusetts, 1780," Massachusetts Historical Society *Proceedings 1916–1917*, 50:368. This establishment resulted from a "parish" being governed by the same male taxpayers who governed a town, and these taxpayers being Congregationalists. The "public teachers" who were to receive public support were Congregationalist ministers, *ibid.* at 370.

Four compromises, of arguable value, had been won by the dissenters in the Convention:

1. Provision for church support could be "voluntary" (Article III, Paragraph 1, last clause). This provision acknowledged the system prevalent in Boston, where the churches supported

themselves by pew rent, not public taxes. Baptists said they wanted no greater liberty (Morison 375).

2. The choice of the minister could be made by the town, parish, or *religious society* (Article III, Paragraph 3). How extensive a concession this provision was depended on what "religious society" included.

3. One's tax money went to one's own minister (Article III, Paragraph 4), but with two qualifications. One had to attend his services. Who counted as a minister or public teacher depended on what was a "religious society."

4. No sect was to be subordinated to another (Article III, Paragraph 5).

The didactic part of Article III, explaining why the preservation of civil government was owed to the worship of God, gained the "full concurrence" of Isaac Backus (Backus, *A History of New England* 2, 228). Article III as a whole was still opposed by the Baptists. A petition gave these reasons for the electorate to reject it:

First, because it asserts a right in the people to give away a power they never had themselves; for no man has a right to judge for others in religious matters; yet this article would give the majority of each town and parish the exclusive right of covenanting for the rest with religious teachers and so of excluding the minority from the liberty of choosing for themselves in that respect.

Second, Because this power is given entirely into the hands of men who vote only by virtue of *money* qualifications; without any regard to the Church of Christ.

Third, Because said article contradicts itself; for it promises *equal* protection of all sects, with an exemption from any subordination of one religious denomination to another; when it is impossible for the majority of any community to govern in any affair, unless the minority are in subordination to them in that affair [Petition, October 1780, Morison 376].

The town meetings voted on the constitution. Twenty-nine towns objected that Article III interfered "in Matters that belong to Christ & Conscience" (*e.g.*, Town of Granville, ibid. 407; *cf.* 379). The popular vote was only 8,885 to 6,225 in favor of the Article (*ibid.* at 411). In terms of the total population of Massachusetts—about 378,000 (Massachusetts Historical Society *Proceedings*, 50:55)—a tiny fragment approved. The convention itself had specified that two-thirds of those voting must agree (Convention of 1780, *Journal* 169). By the convention's own criteria Article III had not been adopted. Nevertheless, the convention and everyone else proceeded to treat Article III as if it had been approved. The Declaration of Rights in Massachusetts thus entrenched the system that Adams had told Backus he might as well expect to change as the solar system.

The constitution of 1780 had further provisions bearing on religion in Part II, "The Frame of Government." Two oaths were required:

ART. I. Any person chosen Governor, Lieutenant-Governor, Counsellor, Senator, or Representative, and accepting the trust, shall, before he proceed to execute the duties of his place or office, make and subscribe the following declaration, viz—

I, A.B. do declare, that I believe the christian religion, and have a firm persuasion of its truth. . . .

And every person chosen to either of the places or offices aforesaid, as also any person appointed or commissioned to any judicial, executive, military, or other office under the government, shall, before he enters on the discharge of the business of his place or office, take and subscribe the following declaration, and oaths or affirmations, viz—

. . .

And that I do renounce and adjure all allegiance, subjection and obedience to the King, Queen or Government of Great Britian, (as the case may be) and every other foreign power whatsoever: And that no foreign Prince, Person, Prelate, State or Potentate, hath, or ought to have, any jurisdiction, superiority, pre-eminence, authority, dispensing or other power, in any matter, civil, ecclesiastical or spiritual, within this Commonwealth; except the authority and power which is or may be vested by their Constituents in the Congress of the United States: And I do further testify and declare, that no man or body of men hath or can have any right to absolve or discharge me from the obligation of this oath, declaration or affirmation; and that I do make this acknowledgement, profession, testimony, declaration, denial, renunciation and abjuration, heartily and truly, according to the common meaning and acceptation of the foregoing words, without any equivocation, mental evasion, or secret reservation whatsoever. So help me GOD. [Constitution of Massachusetts, 1780, Part II, Chapter VI].

The convention did not acknowledge inconsistency between the first oath and the right of conscience recognized by Part I, Article II. However, the convention did express concern over the relation of the second oath to Article III's final clause about not subordinating one sect to another. Addressing the electorate, the convention declared:

Your Delegates did not conceive themselves to be vested with Power to set up one Denomination of Christians above another; Religion must at all Times be a matter between GOD and individuals: But we have nevertheless, found ourselves obliged by a Solemn Test, to provide for the exclusion of those from Offices who will not disclaim those Principles of Spiritual Jurisdiction which Roman Catholicks *in some Countries* have held, and which are subversive of a free Government established by the People [*Journal* 220–221].

That only some Catholics believed in the spiritual preeminence of the pope was a delusion the convention readily entertained to free itself from the implication of bigotry.

Finally, the constitution made provision for the college that it acknowledged as valuable to both "Church and State":

Chapter V. *The University at Cambridge, and Encouragement of Literature, etc.*
Section I. *The University*
Art. I. Whereas our wise and pious ancestors, so early as the year one thousand six hundred and thirty six, laid the foundation of Harvard-College, in which University many persons of great eminence have, by the blessing of GOD, been initiated in those arts and sciences, which qualified them for public employments, both in Church and State: And whereas the encouragement of Arts and Sciences, and all good literature, tends to the honor of GOD, the advantage of the christian religion, and the great benefit of this, and the other United States of America—It is declared, That the PRESIDENT AND FELLOWS OF HARVARD-COLLEGE, in their corporate capacity, and their successors in that capacity, their officers and servants, shall have, . . . all the powers, . . . which they now have, or are entitled to have, hold, use, exercise and enjoy . . . forever. . . .

And it being necessary, in this new Constitution of Government, to ascertain who shall be deemed successors to the said Governor, Deputy-Governor and Magistrates: IT IS DECLARED, That the Governor, Lieutenant-Governor, Council and Senate of this Commonwealth, are, and shall be deemed, their successors; who, with the President of Harvard-College, for the time being, together with the ministers of the congregational churches in the towns of Cambridge, Watertown, Charlestown, Boston, Roxbury, and Dorchester, mentioned in the said act, shall be, and hereby are, vested with all the powers and authority belonging, or in any way appertaining to the Overseers of Harvard College. . . . [Constitution of Massachusetts, 1780, Part II, Chapter V].

Divinity was part of the college curriculum. Congregationalist ministers were trained by instruction in the college courses. The constitution gave the legislature a basis for further encouraging, by the appropriation of tax money, this key institution of the religious establishment.

THE UNITED STATES OF AMERICA

The Massachusetts system was with minor variations the system of Connecticut and New Hampshire. South Carolina had its own distinctive Episcopalian establishment. None of these states accepted the anti-establishment views of Virginia. The makers of the new nation had to form it for constituents who came from both camps.

1. THE DECLARATION OF INDEPENDENCE

Thomas Jefferson, the principal draftsman of the Declaration of Independence, referred to "the equal and independent station to which the laws of nature & of nature's god entitle [Americans]." He went on to say: "We hold these truths to be sacred & undeniable: that all Men are created equal and independent, that from that creation they derive rights inherent and inalienable," Jefferson's "original Rough draught," *Papers* 1, 423. Equality was derived from creation; God was invoked as the author of nature's laws.

The draft was then revised by John Adams, Benjamin Franklin, Roger Sherman, and Robert R. Livingston, *ibid.* at 1, 414 and read:

When in the Course of human events, it becomes necessary for one people to dissolve the political bonds which have connected them with another, and to assume among the powers of the earth, the separate and equal station to which the Laws of Nature and of Nature's God entitle them, a decent respect to the opinions of mankind requires that they should declare the causes which impel them to the separation. We hold these truths to be self-evident, that all men are created equal, that they are endowed by their Creator with certain unalienable Rights, that among these are Life, Liberty and the pursuit of Happiness.

The theology embedded in this opening paragraph was acceptable to a wide spectrum of Christians and Deists. Congress added two ideas taken more specifically from a Judeo-Christian theology:

We, therefore, the Representatives of the united States of America, in General Congress, Assembled, appealing to the Supreme Judge of the world for the rectitude of our intentions, do, in the Name, and by Authority of the good People of these Colonies, solemnly publish and declare, That these United Colonies are, and of Right ought to be Free and Independent States; that they are Absolved from all Allegiance to the British Crown, and that all political connection between them and the State of Great Britain, is and ought to be totally dissolved; and that as Free and Independent States, they have full Power to levy War, conclude Peace, contract Alliances, establish Commerce, and to do all other Acts and Things which Independent States may of right do. And for the support of this Declaration, with a firm reliance on the protection of divine

Providence, we mutually pledge to each other our Lives, our Fortunes and our sacred Honor.

The Supreme Judge stepped out of Scripture. The belief in a superintending Providence was biblical. And, although the Declaration charged the king of England with many crimes, nothing was said about his fostering religious establishments or permitting the persecution of religious dissenters. The national consensus agreed on God, His bestowal of inalienable rights, His role as Judge, His help. Virginian ideas about religious freedom were postponed.

2. THE OATH OF OFFICE

Religion first reached the floor of the convention that made the Constitution of the United States on August 20, 1787, when Charles Pinckney of South Carolina, aged twenty-four, put forward the proposition:

No religious test or qualification shall ever be annexed to any oath of office under the authority of the U.S. [Madison's Notes, *Records of the Federal Convention of 1787,* ed. Max Farrand (1911) 2, 342].

On August 30, 1787, Pinckney saw his opportunity to move this language as an addition to the article on the oath of office to support the Constitution. According to the fullest account of what happened next—Luther Martin's to the legislature of Maryland:

The part of the system which provides, that *no religious test* shall ever be required as a qualification to any office or public trust under the United States, was adopted by a great majority of the convention, and without much debate; however, there were some members *so unfashionable* as to think, that a *belief of the existence of a Deity,* and of a *state of future rewards and punishments* would be some security for the good conduct of our rulers, and that, in a Christian country, it would be *at least decent* to hold out some distinction between the professors of Christianity and downright infidelity or paganism. [Farrand 3, 227, note 100].

According to Madison, Roger Sherman of Connecticut opposed the proposal as "unnecessary, the prevailing liberality being a sufficient security against such tests." Gouverneur Morris of Pennsylvania and Charles Cotesworth Pinckney supported young Pinckney. The provision was then adopted unanimously (Madison's Notes 2, 468).

Article VI of the Constitution accordingly ran:

The Senators and Representatives before mentioned, and the Members of the several State Legislatures, and all executive and judicial Officers, both of the United States and of the several States, shall be bound by Oath or Affirmation, to support this Constitution; but no religious Test shall ever be required as a Qualification to any Office or public Trust under the United States.

The oath as a special ritual required of officeholders rested on the assumption that an oath-taker believed in God and would out of respect, love, or fear not call on Him to witness his words unless he spoke the truth. Article VI employed this religious device.

3. THE PROPOSED NATIONAL UNIVERSITY

On September 14, 1787, James Madison and Charles Pinckney moved to give Congress a power "to establish an University, in which no preferences or distinctions should be made on account of religion" (Madison's Notes 2, 616).

A national university had the potential of bringing the religious differences of the nation to the fore. The motion, however, was not opposed on that ground, but on the ground that the power was superfluous; Congress would be free to establish educational institutions in the federal district. The motion failed 4–6.

4. WRITTEN SECURITY: THE FIRST AMENDMENT

Thomas Jefferson, who had been abroad while the Constitution was being drafted, wrote to James Madison from Paris on December 20, 1787:

I will now add what I do not like. First, the omission of a bill of rights providing clearly and without the aid of sophisms for freedom of religion, freedom of the press, protection against standing armies, restrictions against monopolies, the eternal and unremitting force of the habeas corpus laws, and trials by jury in all matters of fact triable by the laws of the land and not by the laws of Nations. . . . Let me add that a bill of rights is what the people are entitled to against every government on earth, general or particular, and what no just government should refuse or rest on inference. [Madison, *Papers* 10, 336–337].

A second letter from Jefferson on February 6, 1788, called the absence of a declaration of rights the Constitution's "principal defect," and he hoped that the first nine states would ratify and the last four refuse to ratify until the defect had been cured, *ibid.* at 10, 474. Connecticut, Delaware, Georgia, Maryland, New Jersey, and Pennsylvania in fact asked for no amendments. Massachusetts asked for none relating to religion. South Carolina asked for a minor clarification of Article VI, Chester J. Antieau, Arthur T. Downey, and Edward C. Roberts, *Freedom from Federal Establishment* (1964) 112–113, 117. The five other states made substantive proposals for amendments relating to religion.

New Hampshire, on June 21, 1788, proposed a single sentence:

Congress shall make no laws touching religion, or to infringe the rights of conscience. [Jonathan Elliot, *The Debates in the Several State Conventions on the Adoption of the Federal Constitution* (1836) 1, 326.

In New Hampshire, the Congregationalist churches were established by a provision in the New Hampshire Bill of Rights almost identical with Article III of the Massachusetts constitution. Asking that Congress not "touch religion," New Hampshire wanted the hands of the national government off its state religion.

Virginia, on June 27, 1788 proposed:

That any person religiously scrupulous of bearing arms ought to be exempted, upon payment of an equivalent to employ another to bear arms in his stead.

That religion, or the duty which we owe to our Creator, and the manner of discharging it, can be directed only by reason and conviction, not by force or violence; and therefore all men *have an equal, natural, and unalienable right to the free* exercise of religion, according to the dictates of conscience; and *that no particular religious sect or society ought to be favored or established, by law, in preference to others.* [*ibid.* at 3, 659].

Italics indicate additions to the Virginia Declaration of Rights of 1776. That declaration's last clause as to the Christian duty of mutual charity was omitted.

North Carolina, on August 1, 1788, adopted the language of Virginia, *ibid.* at 4, 244. So did Rhode Island on June 16, 1790, *ibid.* at 1, 334–335. New York, on July 26, 1788, also used language almost identical with the last clause of Virginia's proposal (*ibid.* at 1, 328). All of the proposals, including New Hampshire's, treated freedom of conscience as essential. The Virginia language forbade preference for one religion over another.

\ James Madison, so active in securing religious liberty in Virginia, had shown much more interest in getting the Constitution adopted than amended by any bill of rights. On June 12, 1788, in the Virginia convention on the Constitution, he answered Patrick Henry, an opponent of ratification, who had invoked Jefferson's known desire for a bill of rights:

The honorable member has introduced the subject of religion. Religion is not guarded— there is no bill of rights declaring that religion should be secure. Is a bill of rights a security for religion? Would the bill of rights in this state exempt the people from paying for the support of one particular sect, if such sect were exclusively established by law? If there were a majority of one sect, a bill of rights would be a poor protection for liberty. Happily for the states, they enjoy the utmost freedom of religion. This freedom arises from that multiplicity of sects, which pervades America, and which is the best and only security for religious liberty in any society. For where there is such a variety of sects, there cannot be a majority of any one sect to oppress and persecute the rest. Fortunately for this commonwealth, a majority of the people are decidedly against any exclusive establishment—I believe it to be so in the other states. There is not a shadow of right in the general government to intermeddle with religion. Its least interference with it would be a most flagrant usurpation. I can appeal to my uniform conduct on this subject, that I have warmly supported religious freedom. It is better that this security should be depended upon from the general legislature, than from one particular state. A particular state might concur in one religious project. But the United States abound in such a variety of sects, that it is a strong security against religious persecution, and is sufficient to authorise a conclusion, that no one sect will ever be able to out-number or depress the rest.

Madison's argument paralleled his argument in *The Federalist* #10, that the great security against oppression by a political factor was a multiplicity of interests each contending with the other.

When Virginia finally proposed several amendments, including the one on religion, Madison referred to them globally, saying that a number were "highly objectionable," Madison to George Washington, June 27, 1788 *Papers* 11, 182. On October 17, 1788, he wrote to Thomas Jefferson in Paris giving his views a little more explicitly:

One of the objections in New England was the Constitution by prohibiting religious tests opened a door for Jews Turks & infidels. 3. because the limited powers of the federal Government and the jealousy of the subordinate Governments, afford a security which has not existed in the case of the State Governments, and exists in no other. 4. because experience proves the inefficacy of a bill of rights on those occasions when its controul is most needed. Repeated violations of these parchment barriers have been committed by overbearing majorities in every State. In Virginia I have seen the bill of rights violated in every instance where it has been opposed to a popular current. Notwithstanding the explicit provision contained in that instrument for the rights of Conscience it is well known that a religious establishment wd. have taken place in that State, if the legislative majority had found as they expected, a majority of the people in favor of the measure; and I am persuaded that if a majority of the people were now of one sect, the measure would still take place and on narrower ground than was then proposed, notwithstanding the additional obstacle which the law has since created. Wherever the real power in a Government lies, there is the danger of oppression.

Supposing a bill of rights to be proper the articles which ought to compose it, admit of much discussion. I am inclined to think that *absolute* restrictions in cases that are doubtful, or where emergencies may overrule them, ought to be avoided. The restrictions however strongly marked on paper will never be regarded when opposed to the decided sense of the public; and after repeated violations in extraordinary cases, they will lose even their ordinary efficacy.

Jefferson replied firmly on November 18, 1788: "As to the bill of rights however I still think it should be added," *ibid.* at 11, 353.

Madison's attitude changed when he ran for the House of Representatives in November 1788–February 1789. On January 2, 1789, he wrote to George Eve, the Baptist pastor of Blue Run Church in Orange County:

Sir,   January 2d. 1789
Being informed that reports prevail not only that I am opposed to any amendments whatever to the new federal Constitution; but that I have ceased to be a friend to the rights of Conscience; and inferring from a conversation with my brother William, that you are disposed to contradict such reports as far as your knowledge of my sentiments may justify, I am led to trouble you with this communication of them. As a private Citizen it could not be my wish that erroneous opinions should by entertained, with respect to either of those points, particularly, with respect to religious liberty. But having been induced to offer my services to this district as its representative in the federal Legislature, considerations of a public nature make it proper that, with respect to both, my principles and views should be rightly understood.

I freely own that I have never seen in the Constitution as it now stands those serious dangers which have alarmed many respectable Citizens. Accordingly whilst it remained unratified, and it was necessary to unite the States in some one plan, I opposed all previous alterations as calculated to throw the States into dangerous contentions, and to furnish the secret enemies of the Union with an opportunity of promoting its dissolution. Circumstances are now changed: The Constitution is established on the ratifications of eleven States and a very great majority of the people of America; and amendments, if pursued with a proper moderation and in a proper mode, will be not only safe, but may serve the double purpose of satisfying the minds of well meaning opponents, and of providing additional guards in favour of liberty. Under this change of circumstances, it is my sincere opinion that the Constitution ought to be revised, and that the first Congress meeting under it, ought to prepare and recommend to the States for ratification, the most satisfactory provisions for all essential rights, particularly the rights of Conscience in the fullest latitude, the freedom of the press, trials by jury, security against general warrants &c.

Madison's adviser, George Nicholas, urged him by letter on the same day to make further appeals to Reuben Ford, the Baptist minister at Goochland Church, and to get John Leland, the leader of the Virginia Baptists, to "exert himself," *ibid.* at 11, 407–408. Leland had had his greatest success in converts that year—300 baptized—and was based in Orange, Madison's home county, *ibid.* at 10, 516. The Reverend Eve responded by holding an election meeting at the Baptist church, taking "a very spirited and decided part" for Madison and recalling his "many important services" to the Baptists, Benjamin Johnson to Madison, January 19, 1789, *ibid.* at 11, 423–424. Madison continued to campaign, announcing in the Fredericksburg, Virginia, *Herald* his view that the Constitution should have "specific provisions made on the subject of the Rights of Conscience," *ibid.* at 11, 428. On February 2, 1789, Madison was elected to Congress. John Leland wrote him at once, congratulating him, reminding him that he had voted for him, and concluding: "One Thing I shall expect; that if religious Liberty is anywise threatened, that I shall receive the earliest Intelligence," *ibid.* at 11, 442–443.

On June 8, 1789, true to his campaign promises, Madison moved for amendments to the Constitution, including this one:

That in article 1st, section 9, between clauses 3 and 4, be inserted these clauses, to wit: The civil rights of none shall be abridged on account of religious belief or worship, nor shall any national religion be established, nor shall the full and equal rights of conscience be in any manner, or on any pretext, infringed [*Annals of Congress,* 1, 451].

Fisher Ames, the most brilliant New Englander in the House, reacted to Madison's ideas:

We have had the amendments on the *tapis,* and referred them to a committee of one from a state. I hope much debate will be avoided by this mode, and that the amendments will be more rational, and less *ad populum,* than Madison's. It is necessary to conciliate, and I would have amendments. But they should not be trash, such would dishonor the Constitution, without pleasing its enemies [Ames to George Richards Minot, July 23, 1789, Ames, *Works,* ed. W. B. Allen (1983) 1, 694].

Quakers and Mennonites had been exempted from bearing arms by the revolutionary convention at Richmond in 1775; their exemption had been protested, R. K. MacMaster, S. L. Holste, and R. F. Ulle, *Conscience in Crisis: Mennonite and Other Peace Churches in America, 1739–1789* (1979) 273. The Schweckfelders and Amish were equally opposed to fighting, *ibid* at 225. A proposed amendment reflected these constituencies, chiefly in Pennsylvania and Virginia:

Monday, August 17
Amendments to the Constitution

The House again resolved itself into a committee, Mr. BOUDINOT in the chair, on the proposed amendments to the constitution. The third clause of the fourth proposition in the report was taken into consideration, being as follows: "A well regulated militia, composed of the body of the people, being the best security of a free state, the right of the people to keep and bear arms shall not be infringed; but no person religiously scrupulous shall be compelled to bear arms."

Mr. GERRY.—This declaration of rights, I take it, is intended to secure the people against the mal-administration of the Government; if we could suppose that, in all cases, the rights of the people would be attended to, the occasion for guards of this kind would be removed. Now, I am apprehensive, sir, that this clause would give an opportunity to the people in power to destroy the constitution itself. They can declare who are those religiously scrupulous, and prevent them from bearing arms. . . .

Mr. JACKSON did not expect that all the people of the United States would turn Quakers or Moravians; consequently, one part would have to defend the other in case of invasion. Now this, in his opinion, was unjust, unless the constitution secured an equivalent: for this reason he moved to amend the clause, by inserting at the end of it, "upon paying an equivalent, to be established by law."

Mr. SMITH, of South Carolina, inquired what were the words used by the conventions respecting this amendment. If the gentleman would conform to what was proposed by Virginia and Carolina, he would second him. He thought they were to be excused provided they found a substitute.

Mr. JACKSON was willing to accommodate. He thought the expression was, "No one, religiously scrupulous of bearing arms, shall be compelled to render military service, in person, upon paying an equivalent."

Mr. SHERMAN conceived it difficult to modify the clause and make it better. It is well known that those who are religiously scrupulous of bearing arms, are equally scrupulous of getting substitutes or paying an equivalent. Many of them would rather die than do either one or the other; but he did not see an absolute necessity for a clause of this kind. We do not live under an arbitrary Government, said he, and the States, respectively, will have the government of the militia, unless when called into actual service; besides, it would not do to alter it so as to exclude the whole of any sect, because there are men amongst the Quakers who will turn out, notwithstanding the religious principles of the society, and defend the cause of their country. Certainly it will be improper to prevent the exercise of such favorable dispositions, at least whilst it is the practice of nations to determine their contests by the slaughter of their citizens and subjects.

Mr. VINING hoped the clause would be suffered to remain as it stood, because he saw no use in it if it was amended so as to compel a man to find a substitute, which, with respect to the Government, was the same as if the person himself turned out to fight.

Mr. STONE inquired what the words "religiously scrupulous" had reference to: was it of bearing arms? If it was, it ought so to be expressed.

Mr. BENSON moved to have the words "but no person religiously scrupulous shall be compelled to bear arms," struck out. He would always leave it to the benevolence of the Legislature, for, modify it as you please, it will be impossible to express it in such a manner as to clear it from ambiguity. No man can claim this indulgence of right. It may be a religious persuasion, but it is no natural right, and therefore ought to be left to the discretion of the Government. If this stands part of the constitution, it will be a question before the Judiciary on every regulation you make with respect to the organization of the militia, whether it comports with this declaration or not. It is extremely injudicious to intermix matters of doubt with fundamentals.

I have no reason to believe but the Legislature will always possess humanity enough to indulge this class of citizens in a matter they are so desirous of; but they ought to be left for their discretion.

The motion for striking out the whole clause being seconded, was put, and decided in the negative—22 members voting for it, and 24 against it. [*Annals* 1, 778–780].

Meanwhile another important amendment had also been adopted by the House:

Saturday, August 15
Amendments to the Constitution

The House again went into a Committee of the whole on the proposed amendments to the constitution, Mr. BOUDINOT in the chair.

The fourth proposition being under consideration, as follows:

Article 1. Section 9. Between paragraphs two and three insert "no religion shall be established by law, nor shall the equal rights of conscience be infringed."

Mr. SYLVESTER had some doubts of the propriety of the mode of expression used in this paragraph. He apprehended that it was liable to a construction different from what had been made by the committee. He feared it might be thought to have a tendency to abolish religion altogether.

Mr. VINING suggested the propriety of transposing the two members of the sentence.

Mr. GERRY said it would read better if it was, that no religious doctrine shall be established by law.

Mr. SHERMAN thought the amendment altogether unnecessary, inasmuch as Congress had no authority whatever delegated to them by the constitution to make religious establishments; he would, therefore, move to have it struck out.

Mr. CARROLL—As the rights of conscience are, in their nature, of peculiar delicacy, and will little bear the gentlest touch of governmental hand; and as many sects have concurred in opinion that they are not well secured under the present constitution, he said he was much in favor of adopting the words. He thought it would tend more towards conciliating the minds of the people to the Government than almost any other amendment he had heard proposed. He would not contend with gentlemen about the phraseology, his object was to secure the substance in such a manner as to satisfy the wishes of the honest part of the community.

Mr. MADISON said, he apprehended the meaning of the words to be, that Congress should not establish a religion, and enforce the legal observation of it by law, nor compel men to worship God in any manner contrary to their conscience. Whether the words are necessary or not, he did not mean to say, but they had been required by some of the State Conventions, who seemed to entertain an opinion that under the clause of the constitution, which gave power to Congress to make all laws necessary and proper to carry into execution the constitution, and the laws made under it, enabled them to make laws of such a nature as might infringe the rights of conscience, and establish a national religion; to prevent these effects he presumed the amendment was intended, and he thought it as well expressed as the nature of the language would admit.

Mr. HUNTINGTON said that he feared, with the gentleman first up on this subject, that the words might be taken in such latitude as to be extremely hurtful to the cause of religion. He understood the amendment to mean what had been expressed by the gentleman from Virginia; but others might find it convenient to put another construction upon it. The ministers of their congregations to the Eastward were maintained by the contributions of those who belonged to their society; the expense of building meeting-houses was contributed in the same manner. These things were regulated by by-laws. If an action was brought before a Federal Court on any of these cases, the person who had neglected to perform his engagements could not be compelled to do it; for a support of ministers, or building of places of worship might be construed into a religious establishment.

By the charter of Rhode Island, no religion could be established by law; he could give a history of the effects of such a regulation; indeed the people were now enjoying the blessed fruits of it. He hoped, therefore, the amendment would be made in such a way as to secure the rights of conscience, and a free exercise of the rights of religion, but not to patronize those who professed no religion at all.

Mr. MADISON thought, if the word national was inserted before religion, it would satisfy the minds of honorable gentlemen. He believed that the people feared one sect might obtain a pre-eminence, or two combine together, and establish a religion to which they would compel others to conform. He thought if the word national was introduced, it would point the amendment directly to the object it was intended to prevent.

Mr. LIVERMORE was not satisfied with that amendment; but he did not wish them to dwell long on the subject. He thought it would be better if it was altered, and made to read in this manner, that Congress shall make no laws touching religion, or infringing the rights of conscience.

Mr. GERRY did not like the term national, proposed by the gentleman from Virginia, and he hoped it would not be adopted by the House. It brought to his mind some observations that had taken place in the conventions at the time they were considering the present constitution. It had been insisted upon by those who were called antifederalists, that this form of Government consolidated the Union; the honorable gentleman's motion shows that he considers it in the same light. Those who were called antifederalists at that time complained that they had injustice done them by the title, because they were in favor of a Federal Government, and the others were in favor of a national one; the federalists were for ratifying the constitution as it stood, and the others not until amendments were made. Their names then ought not to have been distinguished by federalists and antifederalists, but rats and antirats.

Mr. MADISON withdrew his motion, but observed that the words "no national religion shall be established by law," did not imply that the Government was a national one; the question was then taken on Mr. Livermore's motion, and passed in the affirmative, thirty-one for, and twenty against it [*Annals* 1, 757–759].

On August 17, the House proceeded to the fifth proposition:

Article I. section 10. between the first and second paragraph, insert, "no State shall infringe the equal rights of conscience, nor the freedom of speech or of the press, nor of the right of trial by jury in criminal cases."

Mr. TUCKER.—This is offered, I presume, as an amendment to the constitution of the United States, but it goes only to the alteration of the constitutions of particular States. It will be much better, I apprehend, to leave the State Governments to themselves, and not to interfere with them more than we already do; and that is thought by many to be rather too much. I therefore move, sir, to strike out these words.

Mr. MADISON conceived this to be the most valuable amendment in the whole list. If there was any reason to restrain the Government of the United States from infringing upon these essential rights, it was equally necessary that they should be secured against the State Governments. He thought that if they provided against the one, it was as necessary to provide against the other, and was satisfied that it would be equally grateful to the people.

Mr. LIVERMORE had no great objection to the sentiment, but he thought it not well expressed. He wished to make it an affirmative proposition; "the equal rights of conscience, the freedom of speech or of the press, and the right of trial by jury in criminal cases, shall not be infringed by any State" [*ANNALS* 1, 783–784].

The proposition ultimately adopted by the House on August 20, 1789, was formulated by Fisher Ames.

Congress shall make no law establishing religion, or to prevent the free exercise thereof, or to infringe the rights of conscience.

The Senate killed the provision on conscientious objection while keeping the right of the people to bear arms, *Journal of the First Session of the Senate,* September 4, 1789 (1820) 71. It also killed the article that Madison had thought "the most valuable," the resolution against interference with conscience by the States, *ibid.* at 72. A revised form of the establishment and freedom proposal, advanced by Oliver Ellsworth of Connecticut, was adopted:

Congress shall make no law establishing *articles of faith or a mode of worship,* or prohibiting the free exercise *of religion. Ibid.* 70. [Italics indicate changes from the House version.]

The House refused to concur and asked for a conference. Senators Ellsworth, Charles Carroll of Maryland, William Paterson of New Jersey, and Representatives Madison, Roger Sherman of Connecticut, and John Vining of Delaware were the conferees. From their deliberations emerged what became the First Amendment clause on religion:

Congress shall make no law respecting an establishment of religion, nor prohibiting the free exercise thereof.

SEVEN

Multiple Establishments, 1790–1840

A multitude of Christian beliefs, presuppositions, and practices were incorporated into the laws of the United States and of the individual states. A number of them were so ingrained and generally accepted as to have been uncontroverted; others were the subject of doubt, debate, or denial.

1. PRAYER

In the House of Representatives, on September 24, 1789, the day on which the House concurred with the Senate in adopting the First Amendment, the following debate occurred:

Day of Thanksgiving

Mr. BOUDINOT said, he could not think of letting the session pass over without offering an opportunity to all the citizens of the United States of joining, with one voice, in returning to Almighty God their sincere thanks for the many blessings he had poured down upon them. With this view, therefore, he would move the following resolution:

Resolved, That a joint committee of both Houses be directed to wait upon the President of the United States, to request that he would recommend to the people of the United States a day of public thanksgiving and prayer, to be observed by acknowledging, with grateful hearts, the many signal favors of Almighty God, especially by affording them an opportunity peaceably to establish a Constitution of government for their safety and happiness.

Mr. BURKE did not like this mimicking of European customs, where they made a mere mockery of thanksgivings. Two parties at war frequently sung *Te Deum* for the same event, though to one it was a victory, and to the other a defeat.

Mr. BOUDINOT was sorry to hear arguments drawn from the abuse of a good thing against the use of it. He hoped no gentleman would make a serious opposition to a measure both prudent and just.

Mr. TUCKER thought the House had no business to interfere in a matter which did not concern them. Why should the President direct the people to do what, perhaps, they have no mind to do? They may not be inclined to return thanks for a Constitution until they have experienced that it promotes their safety and happiness. We do not yet know but they may have reason to be dissatisfied with the effects it has already produced;

but whether this be so or not, it is a business with which Congress have nothing to do; it is a religious matter, and, as such, is proscribed to us. If a day of thanksgiving must take place, let it be done by the authority of the several States; they know best what reason their constituents have to be pleased with the establishment of this Constitution.

Mr. SHERMAN justified the practice of thanksgiving, on any signal event, not only as a laudable one in itself, but as warranted by a number of precedents in holy writ: for instance, the solemn thanksgivings and rejoicings which took place in the time of Solomon, after the building of the temple, was a case in point. This example, he thought, worthy of Christian imitation on the present occasion; and he would agree with the gentleman who moved the resolution.

Mr. BOUDINOT quoted further precedents from the practice of the late Congress; and hoped the motion would meet a ready acquiescence.

The question was now put on the resolution, and it was carried in the affirmative; and Messrs. BOUDINOT, SHERMAN, and SYLVESTER were appointed a committee on the part of the House. [*Annals* 1, 949–950].

George Washington issued the requested proclamation, James D. Richardson, ed., *Messages and Papers of the Presidents 1789–1897* (1896) 1, 64:

Proclamation
A National Thanksgiving

Whereas it is the duty of all nations to acknowledge the providence of Almighty God, to obey His will, to be grateful for His benefits, and humbly to implore His protection and favor; and

Whereas both Houses of Congress have, by their joint committee, requested me "to recommend to the people of the United States a day of public thanksgiving and prayer, to be observed by acknowledging with grateful hearts the many and signal favors of Almighty God, especially by affording them an opportunity peaceably to establish a form of government for their safety and happiness:"

Now, therefore, I do recommend and assign Thursday, the 26th day of November next, to be devoted by the people of these States to the service of that great and glorious Being who is the beneficent author of all the good that was, that is, or that will be; that we may then all unite in rendering unto Him our sincere and humble thanks for His kind care and protection of the people of this country previous to their becoming a nation; for the signal and manifold mercies and the favorable interpositions of His providence in the course and conclusion of the late war; for the great degree of tranquillity, union, and plenty which we have since enjoyed; for the peaceable and rational manner in which we have been enabled to establish constitutions of government for our safety and happiness, and particularly the national one now lately instituted; for the civil and religious liberty with which we are blessed, and the means we have of acquiring and diffusing useful knowledge; and, in general, for all the great and various favors which He has been pleased to confer upon us.

And also that we may then unite in most humbly offering our prayers and supplications to the great Lord and Ruler of Nations, and beseech Him to pardon our national and other trangressions; to enable us all, whether in public or private stations, to perform our several and relative duties properly and punctually; to render our National Government a blessing to all the people by constantly being a Government of wise, just, and constitutional laws, discreetly and faithfully executed and obeyed; to protect and guide all sovereigns and nations (especially such as have shown kindness to us), and to bless them with good governments, peace, and concord; to promote the knowledge and practice of true religion and virtue, and the increase of science among them and us; and, generally, to grant unto all mankind such a degree of temporal prosperity as He alone knows to be best.

Given under my hand, at the city of New York, the 3d day of October, A. D. 1789.

G. WASHINGTON

John Adams issued a similar proclamation, referring to the Holy Spirit and the Redeemer as well as the Father (Richardson 1, 268–270):

As the safety and prosperity of nations ultimately and essentially depend on the protection and the blessing of Almighty God, and the national acknowledgment of this truth is not only an indispensable duty which the people owe to Him, but a duty whose natural influence is favorable to the promotion of that morality and piety without which social happiness can not exist nor the blessings of a free government be enjoyed; and as this duty, at all times incumbent, is so especially in seasons of difficulty or of danger, when existing or threatening calamities, the just judgments of God against prevalent iniquity, are a loud call to repentance and reformation; and as the United States of America are at present placed in a hazardous and afflictive situation by the unfriendly disposition, conduct, and demands of a foreign power, evinced by repeated refusals to receive our messengers of reconciliation and peace, by depredations on our commerce, and the infliction of injuries on very many of our fellow-citizens while engaged in their lawful business on the seas—under these considerations it has appeared to me that the duty of imploring mercy and benediction of Heaven on our country demands at this time a special attention from its inhabitants.

I have therefore thought fit to recommend, and I do hereby recommend, that Wednesday, the 9th day of May next, be observed throughout the United States as a day of solemn humiliation, fasting, and prayer; that the citizens of these States, abstaining on that day from their customary worldly occupations, offer their devout addresses to the Father of Mercies agreeably to those forms or methods which they have severally adopted as the most suitable and becoming; that all religious congregations do, with the deepest humility, acknowledge before God the manifold sins and transgressions with which we are justly chargeable as individuals and as a nation, beseeching Him at the same time, of His infinite grace, through the Redeemer of the World, freely to remit all our offenses, and to incline us by His Holy Spirit to that sincere repentance and reformation which may afford us reason to hope for his inestimable favor and heavenly benediction; that it be made the subject of particular and earnest supplication that our country may be protected from all the dangers which threaten it; that our civil and religious privileges may be preserved inviolate and perpetuated to the latest generations; that our public councils and magistrates may be especially enlightened and directed at this critical period; that the American people may be united in those bonds of amity and mutual confidence and inspired with that vigor and fortitude by which they have in times past been so highly distinguished and by which they have obtained such invaluable advantages; that the health of the inhabitants of our land may be preserved, and their agriculture, commerce, fisheries, arts, and manufactures be blessed and prospered; that the principles of genuine piety and sound morality may influence the minds and govern the lives of every description of our citizens, and that the blessings of peace, freedom, and pure religion may be speedily extended to all the nations of the earth.

And finally, I recommend that on the said day the duties of humiliation and prayer be accompanied by fervent thanksgiving to the Bestower of Every Good Gift, not only for His having hitherto protected and preserved the people of these United States in the independent enjoyment of their religious and civil freedom, but also for having prospered them in a wonderful progress of population, and for conferring on them many and great favors conducive to the happiness and prosperity of a nation.

Given under my hand and the seal of the United States of America, at Philadelphia,
[SEAL.]   this 23d day of March, A.D. 1798, and of the Independence of the said States
the twenty-second.

JOHN ADAMS

By the President:
TIMOTHY PICKERING,
Secretary of State

Thomas Jefferson made reference to the need for the nation to worship in his First Inaugural, March 4, 1801:

Kindly separated by nature and a wide ocean from the exterminating havoc of one quarter of the globe; too high-minded to endure the degradations of the others; possessing a chosen country, with room enough for our descendants to the thousandth and thousandth generation; entertaining a due sense of our equal right to the use of our own faculties, to the acquisitions of our own industry, to honor and confidence from our fellow-citizens, resulting not from birth, but from our actions and their sense of them; enlightened by a benign religion, professed, indeed, and practiced in various forms, yet all of them inculcating honesty, truth, temperance, gratitude, and the love of man; acknowledging and adoring an overruling Providence, which by all its dispensations proves that it delights in the happiness of man here and his greater happiness hereafter—with all these blessings, what more is necessary to make us a happy and a prosperous people? [*ibid.* 1, 323].

Jefferson had occasion to reply to an address voted later in the year by the Danbury Baptist Association, twenty-six churches mostly in the Connecticut Valley. Yale, a more conservative institution than Harvard, was under the presidency of Timothy Dwight, a Congregationalist minister, known to the irreverent as "the Pope." At the start of the nineteenth century the Congregationalist dominance of Connecticut was a fundamental fact of political life, to the great discomfort of Baptist, Episcopalian, and Methodist minorities. "Connecticut," wrote an Episcopalian priest, "is more completely under the administration of a Pope than Italy," Burr, *The Story of the Diocese of Connecticut* 163. By 1800 Connecticut was split between the ruling Congregationalist Federalist party and the Republican or Toleration Party favorable to the presidential aspirations of Thomas Jefferson, *ibid.* The Danbury Baptist Association wrote Jefferson, "We have reason to believe that America's God has raised you up to fill the chair of state," William G. McLoughlin, *New England Dissent 1630–1833*, (1971) 2, 1004–1005. Jefferson replied on New Year's Day, 1802 (*Works*, 281–282):

Messrs. Nehemiah Dodge, Ephraim Robbins, and Stephen S. Nelson, a committee of the Danbury Baptist Association, in the state of Connecticut

Washington, January 1, 1802.
GENTLEMEN,—The affectionate sentiments of esteem and approbation which you are so good as to express towards me, on behalf of the Danbury Baptist Association, give me the highest satisfaction. My duties dictate a faithful and zealous pursuit of the interests of my constituents, and in proportion as they are persuaded of my fidelity to those duties, the discharge of them becomes more and more pleasing.
Believing with you that religion is a matter which lies solely between man and his God, that he owes account to none other for his faith or his worship, that the legislative powers of government reach actions only, and not opinions, I contemplate with sovereign reverence that act of the whole American people which declared that their legislature should "make no law respecting an establishment of religion, or prohibiting the free

exercise thereof," thus building a wall of separation between Church and State. Adhering to this expression of the supreme will of the nation in behalf of the rights of conscience, I shall see with sincere satisfaction the progress of those sentiments which tend to restore to man all his natural rights, convinced he has no natural right in opposition to his social duties.

I reciprocate your kind prayers for the protection and blessing of the common Father and Creator of man, and tender you for yourselves and your religious association, assurances of my high respect and esteem.

This letter contained the phrase destined to become famous: "a wall of separation between Church and State." It also ended with the president joining the Baptists in prayer to the Father and Creator.

Jefferson ended his Second Inaugural with a request for prayer as specific as Washington's Proclamation and with an explicit invocation of the Old Testament and God's deliverance of Israel after the Exodus:

I shall now enter on the duties to which my fellow-citizens have again called me, and shall proceed in the spirit of those principles which they have approved. I fear not that any motives of interest may lead me astray; I am sensible of no passion which could seduce me knowingly from the path of justice, but the weaknesses of human nature and the limits of my own understanding will produce errors of judgment sometimes injurious to your interests. I shall need, therefore, all the indulgence which I have heretofore experienced from my constituents; the want of it will certainly not lessen with increasing years. I shall need, too, the favor of that Being in whose hands we are, who led our fathers, as Israel of old, from their native land and planted them in a country flowing with all the necessaries and comforts of life; who has covered our infancy with His providence and our riper years with His wisdom and power, and to whose goodness I ask you to join in supplications with me that He will so enlighten the minds of your servants, guide their councils, and prosper their measures that whatsoever they do shall result in your good, and shall secure to you the peace, friendship, and approbation of all nations [Richardson 1, 382].

James Madison, as he revealed after he ceased to be president, believed that religious proclamations by the president were objectionable. Members of the government might speak "in their individual capacities as distinct from their official station," Madison, Posthumously Published Essay, *Harper's*, March 1914. As president, however, he acted differently. The war with Great Britain was proceeding disastrously for the Americans. Congress asked the president to recommend a day of public humiliation and prayer, to be observed "with religious solemnity." On July 23, 1813, Madison responded:

I do, therefore, issue this my Proclamation, recommending to all, who shall be piously disposed to unite their hearts and voices in addressing, at one and the same time, their vows and adorations to the Great Parent and Sovereign of the Universe, that they assemble, on the second Thursday of September next, in their respective religious congregations, to render Him thanks for the many blessings He has bestowed on the people of the United States; that He has blessed them with a land capable of yielding all the necessaries and requisites of human life, with ample means for convenient exchanges with foreign countries; that He has blessed the labors employed in its cultivation and improvement; that He is now blessing the exertions to extend and establish the arts and manufactures, which will secure within ourselves supplies too important to remain dependent on the precarious policy, on the peaceable dispositions of other nations; and, particularly, that He has blessed the United States with a political Constitution, founded on the will and authority of the whole people, and guaranteeing to each individual the security, not only of his person and his property, but of those sacred rights of conscience, so essential to his present happiness, and so dear to his future hopes. [*Annals* 27, 2673-2674].

Other equally religious proclamations of Madison as president were issued on July 9, 1812; July 23, 1813; November 16, 1814; and March 4, 1815, Richardson 1, 513, 532, 558, 561. Subsequent presidents issued proclamations asking for public prayer without apparent hesitation.

In the second month of the first session of Congress, April 1789, the House and Senate set up committees to select chaplains, and in September 1789, as Congress adopted the First Amendment, a statute was enacted to pay the chaplains, 1 Stat. 70-71; see *Marsh v. Chambers, infra*, XIII, 4.

2. OATHS

George Washington's Farewell Address, on September 17, 1796, took up, among several subjects on which he offered counsel to his fellow citizens, the place of religion and specifically of oaths:

Of all the dispositions and habits which lead to political prosperity, religion and morality are indispensable supports. In vain would that man claim the tribute of patriotism who should labor to subvert these great pillars of human happiness—these firmest props of the duties of men and citizens. The mere politician, equally with the pious man, ought to respect and to cherish them. A volume could not trace all their connections with private and public felicity. Let it simply be asked, Where is the security for property, for reputation, for life, if the sense of religious obligation *desert* the oaths which are the instruments of investigation in the courts of justice? And let us with caution indulge the supposition that morality can be maintained without religion. Whatever may be conceded to the influence of refined education on minds of peculiar structure, reason and experience both forbid us to expect that national morality can prevail in exclusion of religious principle.

It is substantially true that virtue or morality is a necessary spring of popular government. The rule indeed extends with more or less force to every species of free government. Who that is a sincere friend to it can look with indifference upon attempts to shake the foundation of the fabric? Promote, then, as an object of primary importance, institutions for the general diffusion of knowledge. In proportion as the structure of a government gives force to public opinion, it is essential that public opinion should be enlightened. . . .

Observe good faith and justice toward all nations. Cultivate peace and harmony with all. Religion and morality enjoin this conduct. And can it be that good policy does not equally enjoin it? It will be worthy of a free, enlightened, and at no distant period a great nation to give to mankind the magnanimous and too novel example of a people always guided by an exalted justice and benevolence. Who can doubt that in the course of time and things the fruits of such a plan would richly repay any temporary advantages which might be lost by a steady adherence ot it? Can it be that Providence has not connected the permanent felicity of a nation with its virtue? The experiment, at least, is recommended by every sentiment which ennobles human nature. Alas! is it rendered impossible by its vices? [Richardson 1, 220-221].

In the most important case ever decided by the Supreme Court, *Marbury v. Madison*, asserting the Court's power and duty to pronounce on the constitutionality of federal law, Chief Justice John Marshall, at the penultimate phase of the opinion, wrote:

Why otherwise does it [the Constitution] direct the judges to take an oath to support it? This oath certainly applies in an especial manner, to their conduct in their official character. How immoral to impose it on them, if they were to be used as the instruments, and the knowing instruments, for violating what they swear to support!

The oath of office, too, imposed by the legislature, is completely demonstrative of the legislative opinion on this subject. It is in these words: "I do solemnly swear, that I will administer justice, without respect to persons, and do equal right to the poor and to the rich; and that I will faithfully and impartially discharge all the duties incumbent on me as ————, according to the best of my abilities and understanding, agreeably to the constitution and laws of the United States." Why does a judge swear to discharge his duties agreeably to the constitution of the United States, if that constitution forms no rule for his government? if it is closed upon him, and cannot be inspected by him? If such be the real state of things, this is worse than solemn mockery. To prescribe, or to take this oath, becomes equally a crime [5 U.S. (1 Cranch) 179–180 (1803)].

The oath invoked by Marshall incorporated the ancient standard of Deuteronomy 16:19 "without respect to persons," an English translation of the Hebrew "without lifting faces." God, to whom the oath was sworn, was a Being believed to be living, intelligent, attentive to human actions, and punishing promise-breakers.

Other governmentally prescribed oaths required not only belief in a caring God but doctrinal beliefs. Oaths of this kind were outlawed by the federal Constitution, *supra*, but the states did not understand that the federal prohibition applied to them. The two oaths required by the Massachusetts constitution of 1780, *supra*, VI, were retained for forty years. Under the anti-Catholic oath, no Catholic was "capable of holding any public office in this Commonwealth," Robert E. Lord, *History of the Archdiocese of Boston*, (1945) 1, 776. Both oaths were finally abolished when the Massachusetts constitution was amended in 1820, Massachusetts Constitutional Convention, 1820, *Journal* 284, 630–634.

3. SWEARING AND BLASPHEMY

Cursing and swearing, acts that are the mirror opposite of oath-taking, took significance from their use of God's name or invocation of His power. Even a state with as much religious freedom as Virginia treated cursing or swearing as an offense, albeit minor, providing:

That, if any person or persons shall profanely swear or curse, or shall be drunk . . . [they] shall forfeit and pay the sum of eighty-three cents for every such offense [*Virginia Revised Laws*, c. 142 (*Statute* of 1792)].

Other states had stiffer laws for what was classified as "blasphemy," that is, contemptuous public comments about God or matters held sacred by Christians. Without a statute, blasphemy was held to be a crime at common law and was so punished in New York in 1811. The opinion by Chief Judge James Kent, one of the most influential American authorities on the common law, became a classic:

The People against Ruggles
8 Johns. 225 (1811)

The defendant was indicted at the General Sessions of the Peace, held at *Kingsbury*, in the county of *Washington*, in *December*, 1810, for that he did, on the 2d day of *September*, 1810, at *Salem, &c. wickedly, maliciously,* and *blasphemously*, utter, and with a loud voice publish, in the presence and hearing of divers good and christian people, &c. of and concerning the christian religion, and of and concerning JESUS CHRIST, the false, scandalous, malicious, wicked and blasphemous words following, to wit, *"Jesus Christ* was a bastard, and his mother must be a whore," in contempt of the christian religion, and the laws of this state, to the evil and pernicious example of all others, &c. The indictment was removed into the Court of Oyer and Terminer and gaol delivery, held on the 11th *June,* 1811 in *Washington* county, before Mr. Justice *Spencer,* and the judges of the Common Pleas, when the defendant was tried and found guilty and was sentenced by the court to be imprisoned for three months, and to pay a fine of 500 dollars.

The record of the proceedings and conviction, &c. having been removed to this court,

Wendell, for the prisoner, now contended, that the offence charged in the indictment was not punishable by the law of this state, though, he admitted, it was punishable by the common law of *England,* where *christianity* makes part of the law of the land, on account of its connection with the established church. In *England,* apostacy, heresy, reviling the ordinances of the established church, and nonconformity, are made punishable by statute. But from the preamble, and the provisions of the constitution of this state, and the silence of the legislature, it was to be inferred that *christianity* did not make a part of the common law of this state. There are no statutes concerning religion, except those relative to the Sabbath, and to suppress immorality. The constitution allows a free toleration to all religions and all kinds of worship. The exception as to *licentiousness,* refers to conduct, not opinions. *Judaism* and *Mahometanism* may be preached here without any legal animadversion. For aught that appears, the prisoner may have been a *Jew,* a *Mahometan,* or a *Socinian;* and if so, he had a right by the constitution, to declare his opinions.

Kent, Ch. J., delivered the opinion of the Court. The offence charged is, that the defendant below did"wickedly, maliciously, and blasphemously utter, in the presence and hearing of divers good and christian people, these false, feigned, scandalous, malicious, wicked and blasphemous words, to wit, "Jesus Christ was a bastard, and his mother must be a whore;" and the single question is, whether this be a public offence by the law of the land. After conviction, we must intend that these words were uttered in a wanton manner, and, as they evidently import, with a wicked and malicious disposition, and not in a serious discussion upon any controverted point in religion. The language was blasphemous not only in a popular, but in a legal sense; for blasphemy, according to the most precise definitions, consists in maliciously reviling God, or religion, and this was reviling christianity through its author. (*Emlyn's Preface to the State Trials,* p. 8. See, also, *Whitlock's Speech, State Trials,* vol 2, 273.) The jury have passed upon the intent or quo anima and if those words spoken, in any case, will amount to a misdemeanor, the indictment is good.

Such words, uttered with such a disposition, were an offence at common law. In *Taylor's* case (1 *Vent.* 293, 3 *Keb.* 607. *Tremaine's Pleas of the Crown,* 226. S.C.) the defendant was convicted upon information of speaking similar words, and the court of K.B. said, that christianity was parcel of the law, and to cast contumelious reproaches upon it, tended to weaken the foundation of moral obligation, and the efficacy of oaths. And in the case of *Rex v. Woolston* (Str. 834. *Fitzg.* 64) on a like conviction, the court said they would not suffer it to be debated whether defaming christianity in general was not an offence at common law, for that whatever strikes at the root of christianity, tends manifestly to the dissolution of civil government. But the court were careful to say, that they did not intend to include disputes between learned men upon particular controverted points. The same doctrine was laid down in the late case of *The King v. Williams,* for the publication of *Paine's* "Age of Reason," which was tried before Lord Kenyon in July, 1797. The authorities show that blasphemy against God, and contumelious reproaches and profane ridicule of Christ or the Holy Scriptures, (which are equally treated as blasphemy) are offences punishable at common law, whether uttered by words or writings. (*Taylor's* case 1 *Vent.* 293. 4 *Black, Com.* 59. 1 *Hawk* b.1 c.5. 1 *East's* P.C. 3. *Tremaine's Entries,* 225. *Rex v. Doyley.*) The consequences may be less extensively pernicious in the one case than in the other, but in both instances, the reviling is still an offence, because it tends to corrupt the morals of the people, and to destroy good order. Such offences have always been considered independent of any religious establishment or the rights of the church. They are treated as affecting the essential interests of civil society.

And why should not the language contained in the indictment be still an offence with us? There is nothing in our manners or institutions which has prevented the application or the necessity of this part of the common law. We stand equally in need, now as formerly, of all that moral discipline, and of those principles of virtue, which help to bind society together. The people of this state, in common with the people of this country, profess the general doctrines of christianity, as the rule of their faith and practice; and to scandalize the author of these doctrines is not only, in a religious point of view, extremely impious, but, even in respect to the obligations due to society, is a gross violation of decency and good order. Nothing could be more offensive to the virtuous part of the community, or more injurious to the tender morals of the young, than to declare such profanity lawful. It would go to confound all distinction between things sacred and profane. . . . The act concerning oaths (*Laws,* vol. 1. p, 405. [2 R.S. 407, s. 82,]) recognises the common law mode of administering an oath, "by laying the hand on and kissing the gospels." Surely, then, we are bound to conclude, that wicked and malicious words, writings and actions which go to vilify those gospels, continue, as at common law, to be an offence against the public peace and safety. They are inconsistent with the reverence due to the administration of an oath, and among their other evil consequences, they tend to lessen, in the public mind, its religious sanction.

The court are accordingly of opinion that the judgment below must be affirmed.

Judgment affirmed.

Massachusetts punished blasphemy under a statute enacted in 1782. According to Chief Justice Lemuel Shaw, the statue was "frequently enforced" for at least the next fifty years. There were "many prosecutions and convictions," *Commonwealth v. Kneeland,* 37 Mass. (20 Pick.) 206, 217 (1838). The statute reflected trinitarian theology—"reproaching Jesus Christ or the Holy Ghost" was as bad as "denying God"—but its constitutionality, when finally challenged in 1838, was upheld by Unitarians, *ibid.* at 220–221. Abner Kneeland, a newspaper editor, had jeered Jesus' Virgin Birth—how sensitive a subject this was *People v. Ruggles* had shown. Kneeland had also denied belief in the truth of the Gospels and the reality of the resurrection of the dead. His oral appeal to the Supreme Court of the United States was quickly denied by Chief Justice Shaw, and he spent sixty days in the Suffolk County Jail for his forceful assertions of skepticism about Christianity, Abner Kneeland, *A Review of the Trial, Conviction and Final Imprisonment in the Common Jail of the County of Suffolk, of Abner Kneeland, for the Alleged Crime of Blasphemy* (1838) reproduced in Leonard W. Levy, *Blasphemy in Massachusetts* (1973) 493–505.

4. THE LORD'S DAY

Observance of the Lord's Day—Sunday, the day associated with the Resurrection of Christ—was an early concern of the New York legislature, *see Ruggles, supra*. Virginia, in the same 1792 statute that punished swearing, forbade laboring "on a sabbath day" under pain of paying $1.67 for the offense. Employing a slave was treated as sabbath-breaking too, *Virginia, Revised Laws* (1819) c. 141. The majority of Baptists in Virginia, as in Massachusetts, supported the measure, which imposed "the beliefs and values of the dominant Protestant churches upon the inhabitants of the state," Thomas P. Buckley, *Church and State in Revolutionary Virginia*, 1776–1787 (1977) 181–182. Massachusetts, by a statute enacted October 22, 1782, provided:

WHEREAS the observance of the Lord's Day is highly promotive of the welfare of a community, by affording necessary seasons for relaxation from labour and the cares of business; for moral reflections and conversation on the duties of life, and the frequent errors of human conduct; for publick and private worship of the Maker, Governour and Judge of the world, and for those acts of charity which support and adorn a Christian society: . . .

I. Be it therefore enacted by the Senate and House of Representatives, in General Court assembled, and by the authority of the same, That no person or persons whatsoever shall keep open his or their shop, ware-house or work-house, nor shall upon land or water do any manner of labour, business or work, nor be present at any concert of musick, dancing or any publick diversion, shew or entertainment, nor use any sport, game, play or recreation on the Lord's Day, or any part thereof (works of necessity and charity only excepted) upon penalty that every person so offending, shall forfeit and pay a sum not exceeding twenty shillings nor less than ten shillings.

. . .

III. And be it further enacted, That no person shall recreate, disport or unnecessarily walk or loiter, or assemble themselves in the streets, lanes, wharves, highways, common fields, pastures or orchards of any town or place within this State, on the said day, or any part thereof, on penalty of the sum of five shillings.

. . .

VII. . . . And whereas the publick worship of Almighty God is esteemed by Christians an essential part of the due observance of the Lord's Day, and requires the greatest decency and reverence for a due performance of the same.

VIII. Be it therefore enacted, That each person being able of body, and not otherwise necessarily prevented, who shall for the space of one month together, absent him or herself from the publick worship of God on the Lord's Day, shall forfeit and pay the sum of ten shillings, provided there be any place of worship on which they can conscientiously and conveniently attend [Massachusetts, *Perpetual Laws* 198–199].

Compulsory church attendance was reduced to once every three months in 1792, Act of March 8, 1792, *Massachusetts Laws* 2, 538, (Nov. 1780 to Feb. 1807). The state constitutional convention of 1820 proposed taking away altogether the power to force attendance, Massachusetts Constitution Convention, 1820, *Journal* (1853) 623; but the amendment was rejected when the people vetoed any tampering with Article III (*ibid.* at 634). Finally, in 1833, the Constitution was amended to abolish the legislature's power over the subject, Mass. Const. Amend. XI.

Observance of the Lord's Day continued to require the prohibition of secular work or play. Well after the Civil War the criminal law forbidding work on the Lord's Day was enforced by preventing persons injured by Sabbath-breaking from recovering compensation for their injuries: Timothy McGrath helped a mill owner fix his wheel pit on Sunday so that the mill could get started on Monday; injured, he was denied an action for negligence, because his "illegal act . . . was inseparably connected with the cause of action and contributed to his injury," *McGrath v. Merwin,* 112 Mass. 467 (1873).

5. MARRIAGE AND SEXUAL ACTIVITY

Without any special awareness that they were enacting Christian doctrine, all the states treated marriage as a privileged institution and punished various forms of sexual activity outside of monogamy. In Massachusetts only a justice of the peace for the county or the "stated and ordained Minister of the Gospel" of the town could perform a marriage. In 1784, for example, John Murray, the Universalist minister in Gloucester, was prosecuted for performing a marriage; in 1787 he was found liable under the statute to a fine of fifty pounds (John D. Cushing, "Notes of Disestablishment in Massachusetts, 1780–1833," 26 *William and Mary Quarterly* 169, 174 (1969).

Monogamy was protected by statutes making bigamy a crime punishable by public whipping, Act of February 17, 1785, Massachusetts, *Perpetual Laws* 203 (Oct. 1780 to May 1789), or by death, Virginia, *Acts in Force* ch. 104, 270, 274 (1814). Later legislation reduced the Virginia penalty to a penitentiary term, *Warner v. Commonwealth,* 4 Va. (2 Va. Cas.) 95 (1817). Adultery was punishable in Massachusetts by the man or woman being put on the gallows "for the space of one hour" and "publickly whipped, not exceeding thirty-nine stripes," Act of February 17, 1785, Massachusetts, *Perpetual Laws* 203 (Oct. 1780 to May 1789). Whipping was also prescribed for "open gross lewdness and lascivious behaviour," *ibid.* at 204. Homosexual intercourse was punished by death, An Act against Sodomy, March 3, 1785, *ibid.* at 182, a punishment reduced in 1804 to "not more than twenty years" in the state prison, Massachusetts, *Revised Statutes,* Ch. 130, Sect. 14, 741 (1835). The statute of 1785 took its inspiration from Leviticus; like it, it prescribed the death penalty for sex with an animal and the burning of the beast. Except for bigamy, sexual crimes were less severely treated in Virginia. Fornication by a free person there was a crime punishable by a fine; in 1845 the statute was interpreted to apply to a free person fornicating with a slave, *Commonwealth v. Jones,* 43 Va. (2 Gratt.) 555 (1845).

6. FINANCIAL SUPPORT

Federal Aid to Religious Education

Among the actions of Congress taken to further the religious education of Americans in general or the religious education provided by particular churches was the Northwest Ordinance:

Religion, morality, and knowledge, being necessary to good government and the happiness of mankind, schools and the means of education shall forever be encouraged [Article III of "An ordinance for the Government of the Territory of the United States north-west of the river Ohio," a statute of the Continental Congress of 1787, reproduced in ch. 8, 1 Stat. 50, 51–53 (1789)].

This declaration linking religion and the schools co-existed with the Northwest Ordinance's statement of purpose to extend "the fundamental principles of civil and religious liberty" to the new federal domain and with Article I of the Ordinance which provided:

No person, demeaning himself in a peacable and orderly manner, shall ever be molested on account of his mode of worship or religious sentiments, in the said territory.

On August 7, 1789, the same First Congress that a month later adopted the First Amendment took steps to adapt the Northwest Ordinance "to the present Constitution of the United States." No changes were made in the Ordinance's provision connecting schools and religion, Act of Aug. 7, 1789, ch. 8, 1 Stat. 50 (1789).

Grant to the Ohio Company. The Continental Congress gave the Ohio Company an enormous grant of land, specifying that a substantial acreage be reserved and used for the support of religion. Congress, during the presidency of Washington, confirmed this grant and reservation for religion on April 21, 1792, Act of Apr. 21, 1792, ch. 25, 1 Stat. 257 (1792). In 1833, during Jackson's presidency, Congress authorized the state of Ohio to sell the land appropriated "for the support of religion" and to use the proceeds "for ever" for "the support of religion," Act of Feb. 20, 1833, ch. 42, 4 Stat. 618 (1833).

Grant to Columbian College. In 1822 the Baptists founded a national university, Columbian College (later George Washington University), in the District of Columbia (McLoughlin 2, 1264). The Baptists were by now famous for their opposition to religious establishments. Ten years after its founding, during Jackson's presidency, Columbian College received a land grant from Congress, Act of July 14, 1832, ch. 248, 4 Stat. 603 (1832).

Grant to Georgetown College. Georgetown College, an institution for the education of Catholic boys, was owned and directed by the Society of Jesus; its president and directors were all Jesuits. In 1833 Congress granted Georgetown $25,000 worth of land in the District of Columbia for the establishment of such professorships as its president and directors should decide, Act of March 2, 1833, ch. 86, 6 Stat. 538 (1833).

Federal Missionaries. In 1819, Congress passed, and President James Monroe affirmed, an act appropriating $10,000 in order that the president might employ "capable persons of good moral character" to instruct the Indians, Act of March 3, 1819, ch. 85, 3 Stat. 516 (1819). In 1831 Samuel Worcester was found guilty by the state of Georgia of residing in the Cherokee nation without a license from Georgia. He was sentenced to four years at hard labor in the penitentiary, *Worcester v. Georgia,* 31 U.S. (6 Pet.) 515 (1832).

Worcester pointed out that "he entered the aforesaid Cherokee nation, in the capacity of a duly authorized missionary of the American Board of Commissioners for Foreign Missions, under the authority of the President of the United States . . . that he was, at the time of his arrest, engaged in preaching the Gospel to the Cherokee Indians, and in translating the sacred Scriptures into their language," *ibid.* at 529.

Chief Justice Marshall gave the opinion of the Court:

Will these powerful considerations avail the plaintiff in error? We think they will. He was seized, and forcibly carried away, while under guardianship of treaties guarantying the country in which he resided, and taking it under the protection of the United States. He was seized, while performing, under the sanction of the chief magistrate of the Union, those duties which the humane policy adopted by congress had recommended. He was apprehended, tried and condemned, under color of a law which has been shown to be repugnant to the constitution, laws and treaties of the United States. Had a judgment, liable to the same objections, been rendered for property, none would question the jurisdiction of this court. It cannot be less clear, when the judgment affects personal liberty, and inflicts disgraceful punishment—if punishment could disgrace, when inflicted on innocence. The plaintiff in error is not less interested in the operation of this unconstitutional law, than if it affected his property. He is not less entitled to the protection of the constitution, laws and treaties of his country. This point has been elaborately argued, and after deliberate consideration, decided, in the case of *Cohens v. Commonwealth of Virginia,* 6 Wheat. 264.

It is the opinion of this court, that the judgment of the superior court for the county of Gwinnett, in the state of Georgia, condemning Samuel A. Worcester to hard labor in the penitentiary of the state of Georgia, for four years, was pronounced by that court under color of a law which is void, as being repugnant to the constitution, treaties and laws of the United States, and ought, therefore, to be reversed and annulled [6 Pet. at 562–563].

State Aid to Religious Education

At the state level, the key to the religious establishment in Massachusetts was Harvard College, first a Congregationalist, then a Unitarian institution for boys, from whom came the clergy of the establishment. The Massachusetts legislature in 1811, at the behest of the new Unitarian rulers of Harvard, altered the composition of the board of overseers. This alteration was debated in the Masschusetts Constitutional Convention of 1820. How, it was asked, could an institution that was "partly the property of the State" be put outside "the control of the State"? Convention, *Journal* (1853) 71.

Harvard, the recipient of many earlier bounties from the commonwealth, was at the time enjoying an annual grant of $10,000, voted for ten years in 1814. The sum loomed large in comparison with the college's own income of $17,000 (Daniel Webster, Report, January 4, 1821, Massachusetts Constitutional Convention, *Journal* (1853) 527–531). Joseph Richardson of Hingham observed:

This provision appears to me to place all the other denominations of christians in a degree of *subordination* to one, as if all others were disqualified for the high trust. What are the inferences naturally following such a provision? That this State from the first institution of this government and (as a province) long before, has with liberal munificence fostered Harvard University, for the encouragement of arts and sciences, and all good literature, (as expressed by the constitution) tending to the honor of God, the advantage of the christian religion, and the great benefit of this and the other United States—but entrusted, so far as depending on the care of the ministers of religion, to one denomination only. Does not the inference follow, from the exclusive words, or rather from the implied and actual exclusion, that ministers of other denominations are, in the view of the State, unworthy to be trusted with the care of an institution on which the "honor of God, and the advantage of christian religion depend?" It appears that all other denominations are taxed with large appropriations to support the character and dignity of an institution, which, as the constitution now stands, is a sort of holy of holies, which even the clergy of other denominations are not permitted to approach, only in subordination. Are there not respectable clergymen of other denominations in the several towns mentioned (admitting that the board of overseers must be limited to these towns) who might be safely permitted to share in the management of that University? In these several towns there are Episcopalians, Baptists, Methodists, Universalists, and perhaps other denominations, who have formed societies of high reputation, possessing great numbers and wealth, who have long contributed in the same proportion that others have done, to erect the numerous superb buildings, to endow liberally the many professorships, or at least to aid them, and in varous ways to dignify this renowned institution. But these denominations are all excluded from the least participation in that department of trust assigned to the ministers of religion. If, sir, my views of this subject are erroneous, I hope to be convinced by fair arguments that they are so. But every feature of a free government that tends to cherish and perpetuate a spirit of intolerance among different denominations of christians, is inconsistent, in my view, with liberty, both civil and religious. I am constrained to view this policy of preference and exclusion as verging too much towards a national establishment of religion, and who has been conversant in history, and does not admit that religious establishments on narrow principles, maintained by civil power and authority, have not proved instruments of great calamity? Sir, I oppose the provision of the constitution on another ground. This partiality to Congregational tenets, in my view, is to render this denomination a spoiled child of the State.

The voters of Massachusetts, 20,123–8,020, rejected any change in Harvard's place in the Constitution, *ibid.* 633–634.

State Subsidy of Ministers of the Gospel

No state did more to identify an official clergy and support it than Massachusetts. A generation after the adoption of the Constitution of 1780, litigation began to show the nature of the religious establishment and to test its limits.

Joseph Avery had been chosen minister in 1788 by a majority vote at "a legal town meeting" of Tyringham. The town meeting had agreed that if he would "settle with, and preach the gospel to said inhabitants, and instruct them in the principles and doctrines of the Christian religion," the town would provide him a parsonage and pay him 70 pounds annually in produce. In May 1803 a majority vote of a town meeting dissolved the contract. Avery sued for his salary:

Avery v. Inhabitants of Tyringham
3 Mass. 160 (1807)

PARSONS, C.J. In this cause, after a verdict for the plaintiff, the defendants move for a new trial, and also in arrest of judgment.

On the motion for a new trial, we are called upon to decide a question of the first importance to the good order and peace of society, and to the best interests of our fellow-citizens. The defendants' counsel insists that a Congregational minister of any parish, regularly called, ordained, and settled, according to the ancient usages of the country, and faithfully executing the duties of his office, according to his capacity, holds his office at the will of his parish, who may remove him at their pleasure. The plaintiff's counsel contend that he holds his office for life, determinable on sufficient cause exhibited and proved before a proper tribunal. If the office be holden at will, the evidence rejected ought to have been admitted, and the action must be sent to a new trial, otherwise the verdict must stand.

It is a general rule that an office is holden at the will of either party, unless a different tenure be expressed in the appointment, or is implied by the nature of the office, or results from ancient usage. A consideration of the nature and duties of the ministerial office is important in determining its tenure. It is the duty of a minister to adapt his religious and moral instructions to the various classes comprising his congregation. He ought, therefore, to have a knowledge of their situation, circumstances, habits, and characters, which is not to be obtained, but by a long and familiar acquaintance with them.

Vice is to be reproved by him in public and private; and the more prevalent and fashionable are any bad habits, the more necessary is it for the faithful minister to censure them, and to rebuke those who indulge them. But if it be a principle that his office and support depend on the will of his people, the natural tendency of such a principle, by operating on his fears, will be to restrain him from a full and plain discharge of his official duties. And it may be added, that the same principle, by diminishing his weight and influence, will render his exhortations and rebukes unavailing and ineffectual. And as it cannot be for the interest of the people to hold a power, probably dangerous, and certainly inconvenient to themselves, I cannot believe that a tenure at will, whence this power results, can accord with the nature and duties of the office. And it may be also observed, that if the tenure of his office be at will, a minister, after a life of exemplary diligence in the exercise of his official duties, may, when oppressed with the infirmities of age, be removed from office and be dismissed to poverty and neglect. A consequence of this power in a parish, will be the deterring of young men of information and genius, from entering into the clerical profession; and devolving the public instruction in religion and morals, on incompetent persons, without talents, education, or any suitable qualifications. Thus an office, which, to be useful, ought to attract our respect and veneration, will be the subject of general contempt and disgrace. And an effect of this kind, surely every good citizen would wish the laws to prevent, so far as the laws may have power.

But considerations of irresistible weight result from the ancient usages established by our pious ancestors, and wisely continued to this day.

In the settlement of a minister, the parish invite some candidate to preach on probation, that they may have an opportunity to judge of his qualifications, and that he may have some knowledge of the state, temper, and principles of the people. If a settlement be agreed upon by both parties, it is the general practice of parishes, not having parsonages, to grant a sum of money, or other property, to the minister, exclusive of his annual salary, which is emphatically called his *settlement*. This name was derived from the uses to which it was intended the money should be applied by the minister. With it he usually purchased in his town some domicil, where he might have a permanent abode among his people, and be conveniently situated to attend to all the duties of his office.

But if the tenure of his office be at will, it is unquestionably at the will of either party. The minister, therefore, if the parish can remove him at their pleasure, may, at his own pleasure, immediately after he has availed himself of the grant, abandon his office, and carry away his settlement, to the great loss and damage of the parish. The usage of granting a settlement is satisfactory evidence that the tenure of his office is not at will, but that the ministerial relation must continue until it be dissolved for good cause.

As an encouragement to settle ministers in new towns where the property of the inhabitants is not large, the practice of granting permanent settlements had been long confirmed by grants from the former provincial legislature, and from the General Court of the commonwealth.

When new townships are sold, two rights are reserved by the government, one as a parsonage for the minister and his successors, and the other for the absolute use of the first settled minister and his heirs. Unwise indeed, and negligent, must have been the legislature, in making this charitable provision, if the first minister, soon after his settlement, might resign his office at his own will, and retain, for himself and his heirs, the fruits of the public beneficence.

But in forming my opinion I am not confined to inferences drawn from the practice of towns or parishes in the settlement of ministers, or from the intent of legislative grants. Before and since the revolution, this question has been considered by the courts of law, in many actions sued by ministers for the recovery of their salaries. And it has been the uniform opinion of all the judges, who have successively filled the bench of our highest judicial court, that when no tenure was annexed to the office of a minister by the terms of settlement, he did not hold the office at will, but for life, determinable for some good and sufficient cause, or by the consent of both parties; and many cases have been mentioned, where this opinion was declared. And no case has been produced or referred to, by the counsel for the defendants, where a different opinion has been given.

The counsel for the defendants have contended that, admitting the contract of settlement before the revolution, was not at will, the constitution has altered the law; and that now the tenure of the minister must be at will. The part of the constitution relied on, is the provision in the *third* article of the declaration of rights, which secures to towns, &c., the exclusive right, *at all times,* of electing their public teachers, and of contracting with them for their support and maintenance. The argument is in this form; a town shall at all times elect its public teacher; but if, after one be elected, the town cannot remove him at pleasure, then there will be a time when the town cannot elect a public teacher, the office being full.

This argument certainly will prove much. If the town, in the election of a public teacher, contracts with him for a certain number of years, by this construction it must have a right to break its contract solemnly made. A conclusion so unreasonable and unjust, it is supposed, the counsel for the defendants are not willing to admit. The fair and natural construction of this provision is, that a town, &c, shall at all times, when it has no public teacher, have the exclusive right of election, but no right to violate its own contracts solemnly and deliberately made.

This article of the constitution has, without doubt, made some alteration in the ecclesiastical establishments of the state. Under the colonial laws, the church members in full communion had the exclusive right of electing and settling their minister, to whose support all the inhabitants of the town were obliged to contribute. And when the town neglected or refused suitably to maintain the minister, the county court was authorized to assess on the inhabitants a sum of money adequate to his support. Under the colony charter no man could be a freeman, unless he was a church member, until the year 1662; and a majority of the church constituted a majority of the legal voters of the town. After that time, inhabitants, not church members, if freeholders, and having certain other qualifications, might be admitted to the rights of freemen. In consequence of this alteration, a different method of settling a minister was adopted, under the provincial charter. The church made the election, and sent their proceedings to the town for their approbation. If the town approved the election, it also voted the salary and settlement. When the candidate accepted, he was solemnly introduced to the office by ordination, and became the settled minister, entitled to his salary and settlement under the votes of the town. If the town disapproved, and the church insisted on its election, it might call an ecclesiastical council; and if the council approved the election, the town was obliged to maintain the person chosen, as the settled minister of the town, by the interference of the Court of Sessions, if necessary; but if the council disapproved, the church must have proceeded to a new election.

By the constitution the rights of the town are enlarged, if it choose to exercise them, and those of the church impaired. If the church, when their election has been disapproved by the town, shall unwisely refuse to make a new election, or the town, for any cause, shall abandon the ancient usages of the country in settling a minister, it may, without or against the consent of the church, elect a public teacher, and contract to support him. And such teacher will have a legal right to the benefit of the contract, although he cannot be considered as the settled minister of the gospel, agreeably to the usages and practice of the Congregational churches in the state. An adherence to these usages so manifestly tends to the preservation of good order, peace, and harmony among the people, in the exercise of their religious privileges, it may be presumed that a departure from them will never be admitted by any town, but in cases of necessity.

It has been objected that a minister holds his office at his own will, because his town have no legal remedy, if he abandon his office, and therefore that he should also hold at the will of the town. The conclusion is certainly just, if the premises were correct. But a minister does not hold his office at his own will; and if he abandon it without cause, and without the consent of his town, the inhabitants may recover at law such damages as they have sustained by his injurious conduct. In *Cumberland,* before the revolution, Mr. *Wiswall,* a settled minister of the parish of *New Casco,* in the town of *Falmouth,* left his parish without its consent, and was ordained over the Episcopal church in that town. The parish brought an action against him to recover damages for his leaving his office. There was no objection made by the court, or the defendant's counsel, to the action, as not lying in such a case; but the cause went off from a variance between the declaration and the contract of settlement.

It is further objected that the minister ought to hold his office at the will of either party, because there is no jurisdiction competent to declare when the office is forfeited, or when the contract may be dissolved; and that the custom of applying to an ecclesiastical council may be rendered nugatory by either party refusing to concur in the appointment.

This objection deserves a particular consideration. It is the duty of a minister to teach by precept and example. If his example is vicious, he is worse than useless. Immoral conduct is then such misfeasance, as amounts to a forfeiture of his office. I do not mean to include mere infirmities incident to human nature, and to which an habitually good man is sometimes liable. Negligence also, or a willful and faulty neglect of public preaching, or of adminsitering the ordinances, or of performing other usual parochial duties, is such a non-feasance, as will cause a forfeiture of the office. In either of these cases, or in both, the town may, at a legal meeting, declare the office forfeited, assigning in their votes the causes of the forfeiture, and of their dismission. If the minister do not resist, no further question will arise; if he still claim the office, and sue for his salary, the charges made by the town, as creating a forfeiture, are questions of fact properly to be submitted to the jury. If they find the allegations true, the minister will not be considered as holding his office after the vote of dismission. If the allegations are false, justice requires that he shall recover his salary. These allegations the jury are competent to inquire into, and on such inquiry ultimately to decide. And doubtless they would be as willing to relieve a town from the burden of supporting a vicious and unworthy minister, as they would to aid an exemplary and faithful one in recovering his stipulated salary.

There are also objections to a minister founded in questions of doctrine and discipline. A town may sometimes desire a dissolution of the ministerial contract, from its impoverishment, by a great part of its inhabitants annexing themselves to other de-nominations of Christians, or from other causes. A minister may also desire his dismission from various causes. In all these cases, therefore, and also on charges of immorality and neglect in the minister, the parties, if they cannot agree to dissolve the contract, may call to their assistance an ecclesiastical council mutually chosen; and their advice, technically called their result, is so far of the nature of an award made by the arbitrators, that either party conforming thereto will be justified. If, in a proper case for the meeting of an ecclesiastical council to be mutually chosen, either party should, unreasonably and without good cause, refuse their concurrence to a mutual choice, the aggrieved party may choose an impartial council, and will be justified in conforming to the result.

In 1810, the Supreme Judicial Court spoke in a case that had large implications for the nonestablished churches, *Barnes v. First Parish in Falmouth.* Thomas Barnes was the Universalist minister in Falmouth (now Portland, Maine, then part of Massachusetts). In 1807 he sued to recover from the town "the ministerial taxes" paid from 1798 to 1805 by two Universalists. Barnes claimed that under the Massachusetts constitution he was entitled to ministerial taxes paid by members of his denomination. The town had two defenses. First, the Universalists were not a separate denomination, for they agreed with the Congregationalists in discipline, though not in doctrine—the Universalists, unlike orthodox Congregationalists, believed in the certainty of the salvation of every human being. The second was that the Universalists of Falmouth were not an incorporated society and so their minister was ineligible for tax support.

The case was argued twice before the Supreme Judicial Court and finally decided in May 1810:

Barnes v. First Parish in Falmouth
6 Mass. 400 (1810)

PARSONS, C.J. The plaintiff claims to be a public teacher of piety, religion, and morality, within the third article of the declaration of rights prefixed to the constitution of this commonwealth, but of a sect of Christians different from the inhabitants of the first parish in Falmouth, and publicly instructing several of the said inhabitants, who are of the same sect with himself, who usually attend on his preaching, and who have directed their taxes, paid for supporting public worship in the parish, to be paid over for his support; and he has instituted this suit to recover those taxes of the parish.

Not pretending to be the public teacher of any incorporated religious society obliged by law to maintain a public teacher, to maintain the issue on his part, he offered evidence, that in fact he was the teacher of a voluntary society of Universalists, who usually attended on his instruction. This evidence was rejected by the judge, on the ground that no person could maintain this action but a Protestant teacher of piety, religion, and morality, of some incorporated religious society; and to this rejection the plaintiff excepts.

The legal effect of evidence of this kind, in cases of this nature, has been often a subject of discussion; and among judges there have been different opinions. The subject certainly requires a diligent examination, exempt, as far as possible, from the influence of any prepossessions, or preconceived opinions. For this purpose, we shall consider the motives which induced this people to introduce into the constitution a religious establishment, the nature of the establishment introduced, and the rights and privileges it secured to the people, and to their teachers. If these points shall be clearly and justly explained, it will be easy to infer the principles by which the present action must be decided.

The object of a free civil government is the promotion and security of the happiness of the citizens. These effects cannot be produced, but by the knowledge and practice of our moral duties, which comprehend all the social and civil obligations of man to man, and of the citizen to the state. If the civil magistrate in any state could procure by his regulations a uniform practice of these duties, the government of that state would be perfect.

To obtain that perfection, it is not enough for the magistrate to define the rights of the several citizens, as they are related to life, liberty, property, and reputation, and to punish those by whom they may be invaded. Wise laws, made to this end, and faithfully executed, may leave the people strangers to many of the enjoyments of civil and social life, without which their happiness will be extremely imperfect. Human laws cannot oblige to the performance of the duties of imperfect obligation; as the duties of charity and hospitality, benevolence and good neighborhood; as the duties resulting from the relation of husband and wife, parent and child; of man to man, as children of a common parent; and of real patriotism, by influencing every citizen to love his country, and to obey all its laws. These are moral duties, flowing from the disposition of the heart, and not subject to the control of human legislation.

Neither can the laws prevent, by temporal punishment, secret offences, committed without witness, to gratify malice, revenge, or any other passion, by assailing the most important and most estimable rights of others. For human tribunals cannot proceed against any crimes, unless ascertained by evidence; and they are destitute of all power to prevent the commission of offences, unless by the feeble examples exhibited in the punishment of those who may be detected.

Civil government, therefore, availing itself only of its own powers, is extremely defective; and unless it could derive assistance from some superior power, whose laws extend to the temper and disposition of the human heart, and before whom no offence is secret, wretched indeed would be the state of man under a civil constitution of any form.

This most manifest truth has been felt by legislators in all ages; and as man is born, not only a social, but a religious being, so, in the pagan world, false and absurd systems of religion were adopted and patronized by the magistrate, to remedy the defects necessarily existing in a government merely civil.

On these principles, tested by the experience of mankind, and by the reflections of reason, the people of Massachusetts, in the frame of their government, adopted and patronized a religion, which, by its benign and energetic influences, might cooperate with human institutions, to promote and secure the happiness of the citizens, so far as might be consistent with the imperfections of man.

In selecting a religion, the people were not exposed to the hazard of choosing a false and defective religious system. Christianity had long been promulgated, its pretensions and excellences well known, and its divine authority admitted. This religion was found to rest on the basis of immortal truth; to contain a system of morals adopted to man, in all possible ranks and conditions, situations and circumstances, by conforming to which he would be meliorated and improved in all the relations of human life; and to furnish the most efficacious sanctions, by bringing to light a future state of retribution. And this religion, as understood by Protestants, tending, by its effects, to make every man submitting to its influence, a better husband, parent, child, neighbor, citizen, and magistrate, was by the people established as a fundamental and essential part of their constitution.

The manner in which this establishment was made, is liberal, and consistent with the rights of conscience on religious subjects. As religious opinions, and the time and manner of expressing the homage due to the Governor of the universe, are points depending on the sincerity and belief of each individual, and do not concern the public interest, care is taken, in the second article of the declaration of rights, to guard these points from the interference of the civil magistrate; and no man can be hurt, molested, or restrained, in his person, liberty, or estate, for worshipping God in the manner and season most agreeable to the dictates of his own conscience, or for his religious profession or sentiment, provided he does not disturb the public peace, or obstruct others in their religious worship in which case he is punished, not for his religious opinions or worships, but because he interrupts others in the enjoyment of the rights he claims for himself, or because he has broken the public peace.

Having secured liberty of conscience, on the subject of religious opinion and worship, for every man, whether Protestant or Catholic, Jew, Mahometan, or Pagan, the constitution then provides for the public teaching of the precepts and maxims of the religion, of Protestant Christians to all the people. And for this purpose it is made the right and the duty of all corporate religious societies, to elect and support a public Protestant teacher of piety, religion, and morality; and the election and support of the teacher depend exclusively on the will of a majority of each society incorporated for those purposes. As public instruction requires persons who may be taught, every citizen may be enjoined to attend on some one of these teachers, at times and seasons to be stated by law, if there be any on whose instructions he can conscientiously attend.

In the election and support of a teacher, every member of the corporation is bound by the will of the majority; but as the great object of this provision was to secure the election and support of public Protestant teachers by corporate societies, and as some members of any corporation might be of a sect or denomination of Protestant Christians different from the majority of the members, and might choose to unite with other Protestant Christians of their own sect or denomination, in maintaining a public teacher, who by law was entitled to support, and on whose instructions they usually attended, indulgence was granted, that persons thus situated might have the money they contributed to the support of public worship, and of the public teachers aforesaid, appropriated to the support of the teacher on whose instructions they should attend.

Several objections have at times been made to this establishment, which may be reduced to three: that when a man disapproves of any religion, or of any supported doctrines of any religion, to compel him by law to contribute money for public instruction in such religion or doctrine, is an infraction of his liberty of conscience; that to compel a man to pay for public religious instructions, on which he does not attend, and from which he can therefore derive no benefit, is unreasonable and intolerant; and that it is anti-christian for any state to avail itself of the precepts and maxims of Christianity, to support civil government, because the Founder of it has declared that his kingdom is not of this world.

These objections go to the authority of the people to make this constitution, which is not proper nor competent for us to bring into question. And although we are not able, and have no inclination, to assume the character of theologians, yet it may not be improper to make a few short observations, to defend our constitution from the charges of persecution, intolerance, and impiety.

When it is remembered that no man is compellable to attend on any religious instruction, which he conscientiously disapproves and that he is absolutely protected in the most perfect freedom of conscience in his religious opinions and worship, the first objection seems to mistake a man's conscience for his money and to deny the state a right of levying and of appropriating the money of the citizens, at the will of the legislature, in which they all are represented. But as every citizen derives the security of his property, and the fruits of his industry, from the power of the state, so, as the price of this protection, he is bound to contribute, in common with his fellow-citizen, for the public use, so much of his property, and for such public uses, as the state shall direct. And if any individual can lawfully withhold his contribution, because he dislikes the appropriation, the authority of the state to levy taxes would be annihilated; and without money it would soon cease to have any authority. But all money raised and appropriated for public uses, by any corporation, pursuant to powers derived from the state, are raised and appropriated substantially by the authority of the state. And the people, in their constitution, instead of devolving the support of public teachers on the corporations, by whom they should be elected, might have directed their support to be defrayed out of the public treasure to be reimbursed by the levying and collection of state taxes. And against this mode of support, the objection of an individual, disapproving of the object of the public taxes, would have the same weight it can have against the mode of public support through the medium of corporate taxation. In either case, it can have no weight to maintain a charge of persecution for conscience' sake. The great error lies in not distinguishing between liberty of conscience in religious opinions and worship, and the right of appropriating money by the state. The former is an unalienable right; the latter is surrendered to the state, as the price of protection.

The second objection is, that it is intolerant to compel a man to pay for religious instruction, from which, as he does not hear it, he can derive no benefit. This objection is founded wholly in mistake. The object of public religious instruction is to teach, and to enforce by suitable arguments, the practice of a system of correct morals among the people, and to form and cultivate reasonable and just habits and manners; by which every man's person and property are protected from outrage, and his personal and social enjoyments promoted and multiplied. From these effects every man derives the most important benefits; and whether he be, or be not, an auditor of any public teacher, he receives more solid and permanent advantages from this public instruction, than the administration of justice in courts of law can give him. The like objection may be made by any man to the support of public schools, if he have no family who attend; and any man, who has no lawsuit, may object to the support of judges and jurors on the same ground; when, if there were no courts of law, he would unfortunately find that causes for lawsuits would sufficiently abound.

The last objection is founded upon the supposed antichristian conduct of the state, in availing itself of the precepts and maxims of Christianity, for the purposes of a more excellent civil government. It is admitted that the Founder of this religion did not intend to erect a temporal dominion, agreeable to the prejudices of his countrymen; but to reign in the hearts of men, by subduing their irregular appetites and propensities, and by moulding their passions to the noblest purposes. And it is one great excellence of his religion, that, not pretending to worldly pomp and power, it is calculated and accommodated to meliorate the conduct and condition of man, under any form of civil government.

The objection goes further, and complains that Christianity is not left, for its promulgation and support, to the means designed by its Author, who requires not the assistance of man to effect his purposes and intentions. Our constitution certainly provides for the punishment of many breaches of the laws of Christianity, not for the purpose of propping up the Christian religion, but because those breaches are offences against the laws of the state; and it is a civil as well as a religious duty of the magistrate, not to bear the sword in vain. But there are many precepts of Christianity, of which the violation cannot be punished by human laws; and as obedience to them is beneficial to civil society, the state has wisely taken care that they should be taught, and also enforced by explaining their moral and religious sanctions, as they cannot be enforced by temporal punishments. And from the genius and temper of this religion, and from the benevolent character of its Author, we must conclude that it is his intention that man should be benefited by it in his civil and political relations, as well as in his individual capacity. And it remains for the objector to prove, that the patronage of Christianity by the civil magistrate, induced by the tendency of its precepts to form good citizens, is not one of the means by which the knowledge of its doctrines was intended to be disseminated and preserved among the human race.

The last branch of the objection rests on the very correct position that the faith and precepts of the Christian religion are so interwoven, that they must be taught together; whence it is inferred that the state, by enjoining instruction in its precepts, interferes with its doctrines, and assumes a power not intrusted to any human authority.

If the state claimed the absurd power of directing or controlling the faith of its citizens, there might be some ground for the objection. But no such power is claimed. The authority derived from the constitution extends no further than to submit to the understanding of the people the evidence of truths deemed of public utility, leaving the weight of the evidence, and the tendency of those truths, to the conscience of every man.

Indeed, this objection must come from a willing objector; for it extends, in its consequences, to prohibit the state from providing for public instruction in many branches of useful knowledge which naturally tend to defeat the arguments of infidelity, to illustrate the doctrines of the Christian religion, and to confirm the faith of its professors.

As Christianity has the promise not only of this, but of a future life, it cannot be denied that public instruction in piety, religion, and morality, by Protestant teachers, may have a beneficial effect beyond the present state of existence. And the people are to be applauded, as well for their benevolence as for their wisdom, that, in selecting a religion whose precepts and sanctions might supply the defects in civil government, necessarily limited in its power, and supported only by temporal penalties, they adopted a religion founded in truth; which in its tendency will protect our property here, and may secure to us an inheritance in another and a better country.

These objections to our constitution cannot be made by the plaintiff, who, having sought his remedy by an action at law, must support it as resting on our religious establishment, or his claim can have no legal foundation.

The last point for our consideration is, whether this establishment, according to the true intent and design of its provisions, will, or will not, enable the plaintiff to maintain his claim to the money he demands.

The objection against his claim is substantially this: that the constitution has not provided in any way for the legal support of any teacher of piety, religion, and morality, unless he be a public Protestant teacher of some incorporated religious society. It is admitted by the parties, that the plaintiff is a Protestant teacher of a voluntary society not incorporated, and which is under no legal obligation to elect or support a teacher; that he and his hearers are of a denomination of Christians different from that of the inhabitants of the first parish in Falmouth; and all other facts, necessary to support the action, may be presumed.

After a consideration of these facts, we are all of opinion that the constitution has not authorized any teacher to recover, by action at law, any money assessed pursuant to the third article of the declaration of rights, but a public Protestant teacher of some legally incorporated society; and that the objection must prevail. The societies, who may be enjoined to elect and support teachers of this description, are described as "towns, parishes, precincts, or other bodies politic, or religious societies," which last expression is merely explanatory of the words, "bodies politic," and confines them to bodies politic incorporated to act as religious societies. If we are to consider the words "religious societies" as descriptive of a class of societies not included in the words "bodies politic," the consequences would be, that all bodies politic, for whatever purposes incorporated, would be obliged to elect and maintain a teacher of religion—a consequence too absurd to be admitted. Indeed, the words "religious societies" must, from the nature of the duty imposed of them, necessarily mean societies having corporate powers; because, without those powers, the duty cannot be legally performed, a voluntary association having no legal authority to assess money on all the members, or to compel payment, or to elect a teacher by a vote of the greater part.

The plaintiff's claim is endeavored to be supported by the fourth paragraph of the third article, in which it is declared that "all moneys paid by the subject to the support of public worship, and of the public teachers aforesaid, shall, if he require it, be uniformly applied to the support of the teacher of his own religious denomination, on whose instruction he attends." And it is contended, that in this paragraph two descriptions of teachers are included—the first referring to the teachers of incorporated societies provided for in the first paragraph, and the latter embracing teachers of any voluntary society, who, in fact, have a teacher, although not obliged to elect and support one. We are, however, satisfied, that in every part of the third article, but one class of public teachers is contemplated, and which is particularly described in the first paragraph; and that, whenever teachers are mentioned, such teachers alone are intended, who by law are entitled to support. For, although the constitution contemplates different denominations of Protestant Christians, yet no religious societies are referred to, unless incorporated; and no teachers are mentioned as existing, who are not entitled to a maintenance.

If the construction which was contended for was right, then a Roman Catholic teacher might maintain an action similar to the plaintiff's. But in the case of *Matignon v. The Inhabitants of Newcastle,* in the county of Lincoln, decided some years since by this Court in Suffolk, it was determined, that the teacher mentioned in the latter part of the fourth paragraph so far referred to the first paragraph, as that he must be a Protestant teacher. And if a reference must be made to any part of the description, we know not why it must not be made to the whole of it, as the article has drawn no line of distinction.

In the latter part of this fourth paragraph, the teachers to whom the money may be applied, are described as public teachers. But a public teacher must be a teacher of some public, and not of any private religious society. And what society must be deemed a public society, is certainly a question of law, whether it be settled by a judge or by a jury. When, therefore, the facts, describing the nature or circumstances of any society, are established by evidence, from those facts the law must conclude whether the society be, in legal contemplation, public or private. Now, if the society be not incorporated, what rules are prescribed by law, by which its character may be defined? Does it depend on the number of the associates, or on the notoriety of the association? If on the former, what number is sufficient? If on the latter, what degree of notoriety is necessary? On these points the law is silent. But there is a legal principle applicable to this subject, and which can at all times be applied with certainty. A public society is a society known in law, formed by the public authority of the state; and a private society is formed by the voluntary association of private persons, the powers of which are derived from the individual consent of each member.

To admit the plaintiff's construction, would render the first paragraph unreasonable and unjust. By that paragraph, a corporate religious society is obliged to support a public teacher; but by his construction, the means of support may be taken from it, without any fault on its own part. Any number of members, whether five or five hundred, (for a voluntary society may consist of any number, large or small,) may associate together, assume the denomination of Protestant Christians, and at their own pleasure withdraw their assistance from the corporation whose duty remains, by engaging a teacher upon any or no terms, and whom they are not obliged by law to maintain.

By this last paragraph, a reasonable indulgence is in particular cases granted. When there are teachers of two incorporated religious societies of different denominations, a member of one, who is of the sect and worships with the other, may direct his parish tax to be paid to the teacher on whose instructions he attends. This can be attended with little inconvenience, as both the teachers are entitled by law to a support, and the exchange of hearers may be mutual.

But to extend this indulgence to a teacher of an unincorporated society, who is entitled to no support, would be to grant him a remedy where he has no right, and to encourage disaffection and divisions in regular parishes, thereby also lessening or defeating the means they have of supporting a public teacher, to which they are obliged by this very article. . . .

To the further objection of Article III's caveat that "no subordination of one sect or denomination to another shall ever be established by law," Chief Justice Parsons replied that this provision's "object was to prevent any hierarchy, or ecclesiastical jurisdiction of one sect of Christians over any other." But here "the only inferiority is founded on a social principle, essential to the existence of any society, the submission of the minority to the majority," *ibid.* at 416–417. The Baptists had made the same point when they made objection to the adoption of the constitution in 1780, *supra* VI, B.

Barnes, in the words of Governor Elbridge Gerry, "produced a great excitement," McLoughlin 2, 1098. Its author, Chief Justice Theophilus Parsons, was a leading Federalist, prominent in the Massachusetts constitutional convention of 1780 and active in assuring the ratification of the federal Constitution by Massachusetts. In the eyes of his admirers, he was "the great man of his time," Isaac Parker, "Address to the Grand Jury of Suffolk County, November 23, 1813," 10 Mass. 522. To his Jeffersonian enemies, he was "the Goliath of the Massachusetts Gentile-Army, a man as cunning as Lucifer and about half as good," Benjamin Waterhouse to Thomas Jefferson, March 20, 1813, printed in Samuel Eliot Morison, "The Great Rebellion in Harvard College, and the Resignation of President Kirkland," Colonial Society of America, 27 *Transactions* 59 (1920). He was also—as Chief Justice Parker later had inserted in the Massachusetts Reports—a convinced Christian believer in the Resurrection and a member of a Unitarian congregation, 10 Mass. 536. His enthusiastic exposition of how Massachusetts had "adopted a religion" showed how little the Federalists of the first generation thought that religious freedom and religious establishment were incompatible.

The practical effect of Parsons's decision was to require religious societies to incorporate if their members were not to be forced to support the established church of the town. Many Baptists and other dissenters had scruples about recognizing the legislature's power over their churches and accepting from the state a power to share in taxes. Less than half the Baptist societies were incorporated; even fewer of other dissenters' societies had applied for such legitimation by the state, McLoughlin 2, 1088. In the legislature, the dissenters presented a bill to override Parsons. John Leland (Madison's Baptist constituent now back in New England) declared that the Baptists did not want "the mischievous dagger" of civil power: governmental support of religion normally was "the first step in the case which leads in regular progression to inquisition," *ibid.* at 2, 1097. The dissenters wanted only not to have to pay taxes to maintain a faith they did not believe in. Joseph W. Cannon, a Methodist from Nantucket, denounced the system outlined by Parsons as "an eternal disgrace to the state," *ibid.* at 2, 1100. Religion became a political issue. A Federalist Unitarian judge had spoken in *Barnes*. A Republican, non-Unitarian legislature passed "An Act respecting Publick Worship and Religious Freedom," which put unincorporated religious societies on a par with incorporated ones, *Laws of Massachusetts from February 21, 1807 to December 14, 1816*, 227. The Baptists, despite their disclaimers, were given power to participate in tax revenues.

"Churches" were not mentioned in the Constitution of Massachusetts. The time came when it was necessary to define them legally. Jonathan Burr, the minister in Sandwich, had become more Calvinist than the parish. At a parish meeting, called by a warrant addressed to the town constable, Burr was dismissed by a vote of 83–80. Nine-tenths of "the church" supported Burr, and he sued for his salary, Jacob C. Meyer, *Church and States in Massachusetts from 1740 to 1833* (1930) 168. Chief Justice Parsons held for the defendants. The case was appealed to the Supreme Judicial Court. Another Unitarian, Isaac Parker, wrote the opinion:

Burr v. The Inhabitants of the First Parish in Sandwich
9 Mass. 276 (1812)

The last cause assigned by the plaintiff for his refusal, and the only cause stated by him to the committee, was, that his church would not concur with him in the choice of a mutual council; and it is in evidence that the church had refused their concurrence.

The sufficiency of this cause has had much attention, because the law on this point may have a general influence. And we have to decide upon the nature and powers of a Congregational church, as distinct from a parish. Formerly a question of this kind could not have arisen; because all the legal voters of any parish were members of the church. For no man was privileged to vote but a freeman; and for many years after the first settlement of the colony, church membership was an indispensable qualification of a freeman.

Now, a parish and church are bodies with different powers. A regularly-gathered Congregational church is composed of a number of persons, associated by a covenant or agreement of church fellowship, principally for the purpose of celebrating the rites of the supper and of baptism. They elect deacons: and the minister of the parish is also admitted a member. The deacons are made a corporation, to hold property for the use of the church, and they are accountable to the members. The members of a church are generally inhabitants of the parish: but this inhabitancy is not a necessary qualification for a church member. This body has no power to contract with or to settle a minister, that power residing wholly in the parish, of which the members of the church, who are inhabitants, are a part. The parish, when the ministerial office is vacant, from an ancient and respectable usage, wait until the church have made choice of a minister, and have requested the concurrence of the parish. If the parish do not concur, the election of the church is a nullity. If the parish concur, then a contract of settlement is made wholly between the parish and the minister, and is obligatory only on them. The proceedings of the church, so far as they relate to the settlement, are only a nomination of a minister to the parish, which may be concurred in or rejected. This view of the subject must be confined to parishes created by the general laws of the land, and not extended to parishes incorporated specially with different powers.

When, therefore, the parish should have a reasonable claim to a dissolution of their contract with the minister, on grounds proper to be inquired into by an ecclesiastical council, if the church, who have no pecuniary interest in this contract, could, by refusing their assent to the convening of a council, justify the minister in rejecting the offer of a mutual council, the parish would be without remedy. The parish could not legally dissolve the contract by their own vote, for a difference with their minister merely relating to points of doctrine, because a court of law has no means of deciding on those points. The minister refusing to join in calling a mutual council, the parish could not proceed to choose one *ex parte,* because the non-concurrence of the church would be sufficient cause of his refusal.

If, therefore, this cause of refusal, assigned by the plaintiff, were to be adjudged sufficient, the consequence would be, either the parish had no remedy, which would be unreasonable; or that they might dissolve the ministerial contract by their own vote, thus reducing the office of a minister to a mere tenure at will, which would be repugnant to the nature of the office, and the intent of the parties when the contract was made; or disputes in theology must come into courts of law for decision, when the law has not furnished the jury with weapons of polemic divinity. The conclusion is, therefore, necessary, that no interference of the church can justify the minister in refusing a mutual council; and this last cause assigned, resting on the non-concurrence of the church, cannot be admitted as sufficient.

This conclusion cannot be affected by an inference from a supposed peculiar relation between the plaintiff and his church. Although minister of his parish, it seems to have been supposed that he is emphatically the pastor of his church. This use of the terms may be adopted in common parlance, but we must look to the fact. A minister has no peculiar relation to his church, but as a member of it; and his right to adminster the ordinances he claims from his ordination, which right may remain after his dismission from the church. The term pastor is correlative to flock, and is an expressive metaphor. Now, of whom is the flock composed? Of all whom it is the minister's duty to instruct and reprove. And these are the inhabitants of the parish; they compose the flock, of which the minister is the pastor.

We have the less regret in admitting this conclusion, because we are satisfied, from attending to the result of the very respectable council in this case, that the peace and happiness of both parties will be promoted by a separation; and we are satisfied, from all the facts which have been disclosed in this cause, that Mr. Burr's moral character remains fair and unimpeached. When he was settled, he and his people believed the same religious doctrines, which both parties then considered as essential. Mr. Burr has since, from honest conviction, as we trust, changed his opinion as to some of those doctrines; and, believing the doctrines which he has recently adopted to be essential, he has endeavored to support them in his public preaching, to the great pain and dissatisfaction of a majority of his parish, who for this cause have sought a separation.

Judgment is to be entered for the defendants on the verdict.

The parish appeared to rule the church. The Baptists of Bellingham drew the inference that when they became a majority in the town they owned the meeting house and the Congregationalists would have to go elsewhere. Their logic was unassailable, their sense of the allocation of power in the commonwealth deficient. A court ruled against their claim, Meyer, *Church and State in Massachusetts* 213. Only Unitarians had a chance of taking over the Congregationalist town establishment. But the Unitarian view of the relation of the church to the parish was scandalous to Trinitarian Congregationalists. Their basic theological position was expressed by Lyman Beecher (1775–1863), a graduate of Yale College, then, under Timothy Dwight, a Trinitarian stronghold. Beecher, ordained as a Presbyterian in 1799, had served as the minister in East Hampton, Long Island, and then in Litchfield, Connecticut. As the conflict between Trinitarians and Unitarians grew, it attracted his attention, and eventually in 1826 he was called as a minister by Trinitarians anxious to fortify their thinned ranks in Boston. Their approval was won by the views he set out in this excerpt from his *Autobiography*. Note the recurrence of the "wall" metaphor:

Lyman Beecher, The Local Church

The Unitarian controversy involved, in its progress, a discussion, not only of the principal doctrines of theology, but also of the principles of Congregational Church organization, which are but the outgrowth of that theology. According to the primitive Puritan faith, a local Church is not a voluntary association on purely human principles, but a divine family, a household of children spiritually born of God, heirs of God and joint heirs with Christ. "One is your Master, even Christ, and all ye are brethren," is the organic law of the local Church. God creates the Church by creating the spiritual children who are *ipso facto* its members. True sonship to God constitutes membership in the visible church, as really as natural birth in the natural family. All that the local Church can do, according to this view, is to recognize as members, on suitable evidence, those who are such by birth divine. All she can require of candidates she must require in the form of evidence of present spiritual sonship to God.

Now, in proportion as a system of theology is adopted which extenuates human guilt, explains away regeneration, and divests the Christian character of its distinctive supernatural peculiarity, in that proportion it tends to destroy that form of organization which avowedly depends on such peculiarity as its fundamental organic law.

This, however, was precisely what the system of Unitarianism did, and, as a natural consequence, the whole system of the local Church was shaken. By the inevitable operation of the laws of logical consistency, attempts were made to efface the distinction between the regenerate and the unregenerate, and enlarge the circle of Church fellowship to include the whole congregation. In progress of controversy, the endeavor was pushed in various ways, beyond the bounds of argument and moral influence, until the churches felt themselves invaded, robbed of their rights, and in peril of utter destruction.

It was the object of the sermon on "the Design, Rights, and Duties of Local Churches," given at Salem, Massachusetts in 1819, to meet the onset, and sound a note of defensive war so loud and clear that "all the churches of the land might feel the assault made upon their Christian liberty, and stand together upon the defensive."

Extracts from Sermon

"Wherever, therefore, a number of individuals, possessing the required qualifications, associate to maintain the ordinances of the Gospel, they become *a society incorporated by the God of heaven with specific chartered privileges.*

"The requisite qualifications for membership in a Church of Christ are *personal holiness in the sight of God, and a credible profession of holiness before men.* *** The commission given by our Savior to His apostles at His ascension directs them first to make disciples and then to baptize them, inculcating universal obedience. The qualifications for discipleship Jesus has before disclosed. They were love to Christ above father or mother; daily self-denial; real religion. ***

"A regularly ordained ministry, an orthodox creed, and devout forms of worship, can not constitute a Church of Christ without personal holiness in the members. *** The attempt which is making to confound the scriptural distinction between the regenerate and the unregenerate blots out practically, as has been long done in theory, the doctrine of regeneration by the special influence of the Holy Ghost. To abolish the revealed terms of membership in the Church of God, and to form churches without reference to doctrinal opinion or experimental religion, and only by location within certain parish limits, and by certain civil qualifications, is the most pernicious infidelity that was ever broached. It breaks the spring of motion in the centre of God's system of good will to men and stops the work of salvation. * * *

"That system of aggression which would break down the sacred inclosures about the Church, and throw the Church and the world together in one common field, and which, to accomplish its purpose, would bring into competition the rights of churches and of congregations, and, by designed invidious excitement, arouse and direct the stream of popular indignation against the Church, is a system of practical infidelity armed with the principles of the most efficient persecution. * * * All the churches of our Lord, and all ecclesiastical societies, and all men who wish well to the civil as promoted by the religious order of our fathers, have more cause to fear and to execrate such a system of aggression than all the infidel books that ever were printed. * * *

"Local churches have the right to require a confession of faith and a satisfactory account of Christian experience as the condition of membership in their communion. A belief of the truth, attended by corresponding affection of heart, is a part of the evidence which is indispensable to constitute a profession of religion credible. If, then, churches have no right to interrogate a candidate for admission concerning the articles of his belief and the exercises of his heart, they are deprived of the only means of preserving the Church as a society of faithful men; for external actions, without any reference to belief or experience, do not furnish credible evidence of piety. * * *

"Notwithstanding the current of invective poured out against creeds, after the most deliberate attention to the subject I have not been able to perceive any rational ground of objection against them. * * * It is not the object of creeds to supplant the Bible, but to ascertain, for purposes of concentrated effort in the propagation of truth, how pastors and churches understand the Bible. * * *

"If men attached invariably the same ideas to the language of the Bible, creeds would be superfluous, and the profession of a general belief in the Bible would suffice. But as men differ indefinitely as to the import of scripture language, a profession of a belief in the Bible, as a means of informing those who have a right to know in what particular sense the Bible is understood, has now become an intelligible profession of no one truth which it contains. And to profess that *Jesus is the Christ, the Son of God*—a phrase which in the apostolic age had known a definite meaning—does not now, when different circumstances exist and opposite meanings are attached to it, communicate any intelligible profession of our belief on that point; and all pretension of giving an account of our faith in that manner is an artifice for concealment unworthy of honest men, and an indignity offered to the understandings of those who desire to know in what manner we understand and doctrines of the Bible. * * *

Baker v. Fales
16 Mass. 488 (1820)

In 1820, the Massachusetts constitutional convention recognized that Article III was central to the legal controversy and proposed adopting the principle of the Republican legislation of 1811 as a kind of constitutional compromise. But country Trinitarians of one denomination or another combined to defeat the proposed amendment, Convention of 1820, *Journal* 613–614, 634. Article III of the constitution of 1780 continued in force. Meanwhile a new case decided by the Unitarian-dominated Supreme Judicial Court fueled the fire of controversy.

The minister in Dedham resigned in 1818. The *parish* chose Alvan Lamson, a Unitarian, to replace him. The *church,* 17 to 15, rejected Lamson. The *parish* called an ecclesiastical council dominated by such Unitarian luminaries as William Ellery Channing; Henry Ware, Hollis Professor of Divinity at Harvard; and John Thornton Kirkland, the president of Harvard. The council, unsurprisingly, approved Lamson, Meyer, *Church and State in Massachusetts* 174–175. In the person of Eiphalet Baker, represented by Daniel Webster, the *church* sued the deacons of the *parish* for possession of the money and documents that belonged to "the First Church in Dedham." Deacon Samuel Fales spent $3,000 of his own money to defend the parish's possession, *ibid.* at 177.

Chief Justice Parker traced the history of grants to the church in Dedham since the seventeenth century and held that the grants had created a trust, of which the church was the trustee, and that the beneficiary for whose benefit the trustee must act was the parish. The parish, he continued, was "the assembly of Christians in Dedham." This assembly he equated with the inhabitants of the town. Specifically, "as the particular trusts intended must have been the providing for the public worship of God in Dedham, the inhabitants at large of that town, as parishioners or members of the religious society" were the proper beneficiaries of the trust, [*Baker* at 497–498].

The Chief Justice continued:

If a church may subsist unconnected with any congregation or religious society, as has been urged in argument, it is certain that it has no legal qualities, and more especially that it cannot exercise any control over property which it may have held in trust for the society with which it had been formerly connected. That any number of the members of a church who disagree with their brethren, or with the minister, or with the parish, may withdraw from fellowship with them, and act as a church in a religious point of view, having the ordinances administered and other religious offices performed, it is not necessary to deny; indeed, this would be a question proper for an ecclesiastical council to settle, if any should dispute their claim. But as to all civil purposes, the secession of a whole church from the parish would be an extinction of the church; and it is competent to the members of the parish to institute a new church, or to engraft one upon the old stock if any of it should remain; and this new church would succeed to all the right of the old, in relation to the parish [*ibid.* at 503–504]. . . .

It is said, in argument, that churches may subsist without connection with any parish or religious society; and the churches of Harvard College, Dartmouth College, and the Andover Institution, are cited as instances. We have before said that it was not intended to deny that there may be such churches in an ecclesiastical sense; but there is not appertaining to them, as churches, any civil rights or privileges, by virtue merely of their association as members of a church. These very churches may possibly be religious societies under the statute of 1811, called the religious freedom act, and may, as such, exercise power, *quasi* a body politic, to a certain extent; but this does not tend to show that a church, which had existed within a parish, and as such has had the custody and the disposition of property for parish purposes, can disunite itself from the parish, and retain, nevertheless, all the property, and dispose of it to other uses, or to similar uses, in another parish. If all the members of a church so situated should withdraw, leaving not even the deacons, or members enough to elect them, it might be necessary, perhaps, to apply to the legislature, in the absence of a court of chancery, to appoint some new trustee of the property, until a new church should be organized within the parish. But where members enough are left to execute the objects for which a church is gathered, choose deacons, &c., no legal change has taken place; the body remains, and the secession of a majority of the members would have no other effect than a temporary absence would have upon a meeting which had been regularly summoned.

That a church cannot subsist without some religious community to which it is attached, with the exceptions before stated, is not a new theory. It has, we believe, been the understanding of the people of New England, from the foundation of the colonies. A few anomalous cases can have no bearing on the question. All the numerous laws, which were passed by the colonial and provincial legislature, in relation to churches, are predicated upon a supposed connection with some body politic; and, in the year 1800, a decisive expression of the public opinion was given in an act of the legislature, which provides for the public worship of God and for other purposes; for, by the first section of that statute, it is enacted, "That the respective churches, connected and associated in public worship with the several towns, parishes, precincts, districts, and other bodies politic, being religious societies, shall at all times have, use, exercise, and enjoy, all their accustomed privileges and liberties, respecting divine worship, church order and discipline, not repugnant to the constitution."

The consequences of the doctrine contended for by the defendant, will glaringly show the unsoundness of the principle upon which the argument is founded. The position is that, whenever property is given to a church, it has the sole control of it, and the members, for the time being, may remove to any other place, even without the commonwealth, and carry the property with them.

Now, property bestowed upon churches has always been given for some pious or benevolent purpose, and with a particular view to some associated body of Christians. The place in which the church is located, is generally had in view by the donor, either because he there had enjoyed the preaching of the gospel and the ordinances, or because it was the place where his ancestors or his family and friends had assembled together for religious purposes. These associations will be found to be the leading motive for the particular direction which his charity has received. If he gives to a church for the general purpose of promoting piety, or for the use of the poor of the church, he generally designates the body by the place where it is accustomed to worship. Thus, if a donation were made to the Old South church, Park-street church, Brattle-street church, or any other that might be thus designated by local qualities, it must be supposed that the donor had in view the society of Christians worshipping in those places; and as his donation is intended to be perpetual, that he had regard to the welfare of successive generations, who might become worshipping Christians and church members in the same place. If the whole society should find occasion to remove to some other place in the same town, the identity might be preserved, and the bounty enjoyed as he intended it. But if the church alone should withdraw, and unite itself to some other church, or to a new and different congregation, it would be defeating his intentions to carry the property with them, and distribute the proceeds in a community for the members of which he may have never entertained any particular feelings of kindness.

To divert the charity from the poor of the Old South church, to the poor of the church in Park-street, would be to violate the will and design of the donor, as effectually as to apply it to the support of the town's or state's poor. So, of property given for the support of public worship in any particular place.

It being, as we think, established that the members of the church, who withdrew from the parish, ceased to be the first church in Dedham, and that all the rights and duties of that body, relative to property intrusted to it, devolved upon those members who remained with and adhered to the parish; it remains to be considered whether the plaintiffs were duly chosen deacons of that church, and so became entitled to the possession of the property, as the trustees under the statute of 1754, as stated by the judge in his charge to the jury. And, as this was thought to depend upon the validity of the settlement and ordination of Mr. Lamson, which took place in November, 1818, it has seemed to become necessary to look into the facts which led the judge to state to the jury, "that Mr. Lamson was legally ordained, as minister of said first parish, and that those members of the church who adhered to the parish and united with them on this occasion, must be considered as the church in said first parish in Dedham, and the successors of said ancient church, and that those members of the church who withdrew from the parish and refused to concur in the proceedings of the majority of the inhabitants of said parish in the ordination of Mr. Lamson, could not, in law, be considered as a church, so as to entitle them (through a majority) to hold, appropriate, or control, said ministerial or church fund or property."

The objection to the settlement of Mr. Lamson rests altogether upon the supposition that there could be no legal settlement and ordination, unless the church, as a distinct body from the parish or congregation, had assented to his call, and concurred in the proceedings preliminary to his settlement; and it is upon this ground, also, that the ordaining council are supposed to have had no authority in the matter, they being invited by the parish and a minority of the members of the church, but not by the church itself, to which body, it is alleged, belongs solely the right of convening a council upon such occasions.

That the proceedings of the parish and the council were not conformable to the general usage of the country, cannot be denied. But the parish alleged, in vindication of their departure from this usage, their constitutional right to elect and contract with their minister, exclusively of any concurrence or control of the church; and the necessity they were under to proceed as they did, because the church had refused to concur with them in the choice, and in the invitation to the ordaining council. That the parish have the constitutional right contended for, cannot be questioned by those who will pursue the clause of the third article of the Declaration of Rights, upon which this claim is asserted. It is there provided, "that the several towns, parishes, precincts, and other bodies politic or religious societies, shall at all times have the exclusive right of electing their public teachers, and of contracting with them, for their support and maintenance." This is too explicit to admit of cavilling or to require explanation, as every constitutional provision for the security of civil or religious liberty ought to be. All preexisting laws or usages must bow before this fundamental expression of the public will; and however convenient or useful it might be to continue the old form of electing or settling a minister, whenever a parish determines to assert its constitutional authority, there is no power in the state to oppose their claim.

It has been supposed by counsel in the argument, that there is a distinction between a public teacher, whose election is thus provided for in the Declaration of Rights, and a minister or pastor of a church, in the ecclesiastical or clerical sense of these terms; and that, although a civil contract may be made with the former, binding upon the parish, he is not vested with a religious character or office, so as to be entitled to the privileges of a minister of the gospel. But we see no ground for such distinction. A teacher of piety, religion and morality, is a minister of the gospel within the meaning of the Declaration of Rights; and it is a strange supposition, that the framers of the constitution, or the people, had respect, in this provision, to a class of men not known at the time the constitution was formed; to whom should belong only a part of the character, duties and privileges of ministers of the gospel. The term "teacher" was made use of as *nomen generalissimum,* to embrace the clerical head of every denomination of Christians in the state. It was well-known, that, in early times, certain titles used in the established church were offensive to our modest ancestors, as savoring of ecclesiastical distinction, and that the terms "teacher, teaching elder, teaching officer," &c., were commonly used, in lieu of other official designations known in the English church. By a colonial law of 1668, it is provided, that teaching officers of churches should be the ministers to all the inhabitants of the towns in which the churches over which they are placed shall be planted. If a teacher of piety, religion and morality, in the sense of the Declaration of Rights, does not mean ministers of the gospel, then the provision is senseless and nugatory; for there was not then, not is there now, any such officer known in the parishes or churches. It was supposed that this distinction was countenanced by the late Chief Justice Parsons, in the opinion delivered by him in the case of *Avery vs. The Inhabitants of Tyringham, 3 Mass Rep.* 160. His words are, "By the constitution, the rights of the town are enlarged, if it choose to exercise them, and those of the church impaired. If the church, when the election has been disapproved by the town, shall unwisely refuse to make a new election, or the town, for any cause, shall abandon the ancient usages of the country in settling a minister, it *may, without or against* the consent of the church, elect a public teacher, and contract to support him; and such a teacher will have a legal right to the benefit of the contract, although he cannot be considered a settled minister of the gospel, agreeably to the usages and practice of the Congregational churches in the state." He then goes on to recommend an adherence to those usages, and to deprecate a departure from them, except in cases of necessity.

We agree with him in estimating highly these ancient usages, protected as the people are by the constitutional provision, and in hoping they may be observed in future, as they have been in past times. But we cannot think, nor can it be inferred from his observations that he thought, that a teacher chosen by the parish, without the consent of the church, and publicly set apart by ordination over the parish, would not be a settled minister of the gospel; although he would not be so according to the usages and practice of the Congregational churches in the state. For the constitution supersedes those usages, where the parties do not choose to observe them; and to deny the character of ministers of the gopsel to those who are chosen according to the constitution, would be to repeal the constitution and render it nugatory.

There is one religious society in the state at least [Brattle-street church, Boston], probably there are many, which, from its foundations, even before the adoption of the constitution, has departed from the general usage in the mode of settling their ministers. In this society there has been a long line of able, pious, learned ministers, teaching their flock for many generations, administering the holy ordinances of baptism and the Lord's supper, associating with the reverend clergy who may have been settled according to the common usage, and interchanging official duties with them. Will any one refuse to these teachers the character of ministers of the gospel, because they were not settled "according to the usages and practice of Congregational churches in the state?" We apprehend not. The practice in this society has been, immemorially, for the parish only to choose the minister, church members acting only as parishioners; and the church is requested, as a matter of courtesy, to invite the ordaining council. As in former times, particularly at the period of forming our constitution, many distinguished citizens belonged to this society, it is not improbable that the constitutional provision emanated from them, for it is exactly conformable to the practice of this society since its foundation. And, if uninterrupted harmony for near a century between church and society, and repeated unanimity in the choice of a minister, is any evidence of the merits of any system, there need be no apprehension of those disorders, which some have imagined will follow a general execution of the constitutional privilege. The distinction suggested is founded upon the hypothesis that the people, in establishing the provision in the third article, meant only to secure the right in towns, &c., to elect certain civil officers to be called teachers of piety, religion, and morality, like schoolmasters, who were not to be vested with a sacred or religious character or privileges; and that, in order to endow them with these, there must still be an appointment by the church, or some other body foreign to the town or parish. But this would have been going only half way in establishing the right of the people; for the most interesting, if not the principal, office of a minister is of a religious nature; such as administering the holy ordinances to those who should seek them; and of this benefit the people would be deprived at the will of the church, if such is to be the construction of the constitution. Indeed, if the church and congregation should concur in the choice of a minister, and other churches should, from disagreement with their creed, decline to advise to, and assist in the ordination; upon this close construction, the person chosen might be a teacher, but he could not be a minister of the gospel, because not settled according to the usages and practice of the Congregational churches; for those usages require a council, composed of the ministers and delegates of other churches, to give validity to an ordination.

What is the essential virtue and public benefit of an ordination? Surely, it is nothing but setting apart, installing or inaugurating, one who has been chosen to the office, and tendering to him the fellowship of the churches who assist in the ceremony. It will not now be contended, that any spiritual or temporal power is conferred by the imposition of hands. Ordination, according to the Platform, is nothing else but the solemn putting a man into his place and office in the church, whereunto he had a right before by election; being like the installation of a magistrate in the commonwealth. "Ordination is therefore not to go before, but to follow election." Again;—"Ordination doth not constitute an office, nor give him the essentials of his office." *Cambridge Platform,* ch. ix. sec. 2. It is true, that the election here spoken of is an election by the church; but whenever, by change of law or usage, the right of election come to the congregation, the principles in regard to ordination are applicable. The people having the constitutional right to choose, they must have the right to have the minister of their choice set over them, or the former right would be in many important respects useless. If, then, the church would obstruct their wishes, by refusing to concur in calling a council, they have a right to invite one themselves; or if, upon prudential motives, or from adherence to old forms, they could find no ministers or churches to aid them, they would have the right, by some public solemn act, to carry into full effect their constitutional privilege, and thus to secure to their pastor all the privileges and immunities of a public teacher of piety, religion and morality, and of a minister of the gospel. This doctrine is as old as the history of the New England churches; for the first minister of Salem was set apart by the lay brethren, accident having prevented the clergy who were expected from attending; and though, after they arrived, they participated in the ceremony by giving the right hand of fellowship, this act was not an essential part of ordination. They seem not to have doubted the right of the people to give publicity to their choice; for although, after they formed themselves into a church state, they installed their ministers anew, it does not appear that any council was called in for this purpose. And the *Cambridge Platform* recognizes the principle; for in sec. 4, ch. 9, it is said, if the people may elect officers, which is the greater, and wherein the substance of the office doth consist, they may much more (need so requiring) impose hands in ordination, which is the less, and but the accomplishment of the other.

We consider, then, the non-concurrence of the church in the choice of the minister, and in the invitation to the ordaining council, as in no degree impairing the constitutional right of the parish. That council might have refused to proceed, but the parish could not by that have been deprived of their minister. It was right and proper, as they could not proceed according to ancient usage, because of the dissent of the church, to approach as near to it as possible by calling a respectable council, and having their sanction in the ordination. And it was certainly wise in that council, finding that the points of disagreement were such as would be likely to cause a permanent separation, to yield to the wishes of the parish, and give their sanction to proceedings which were justified by the constitution and laws of the land. They ordained him over the parish only; but, by virtue of that act, founded upon the choice of the people, he became not only the minister of the parish, but of the church still remaining there, notwithstanding the secession of a majority of the members. Mr. Lamson thus became the lawful minister of the first parish in Dedham, and of the church subsisting therein; and he had a right to call church meetings, and do all other acts pertaining to a settled and ordained minister of the gospel. The church had a right to choose deacons, finding that the former deacons had abdicated their office, and thus no legal objection is found to exist against their right to maintain this action. . . .

Indeed, we apprehend those are mistaken, who imagine that the cause of religion would be served, public worship promoted, or instruction in piety, religion and morality more extensively encouraged, by restoring to the churches the power they once enjoyed, of electing the minister without concurrence of the people of the congregation, or by the aid of a council which they might select to sanction their choice. Nothing would tend more directly to break up the whole system of religious instruction; for the people never would consent to be taxed for the support of men in whose election they had no voice. It is an undoubted fact, that the male members of the churches form but a small part of the corporation which makes the contract, and is obliged to perform it; and it is not at all consistent with the spirit of the times, that the great majority should, in this particular, be subject to the minority. To arrogate such a power, would be to break up, in no distant period, every parish in the commonwealth.

The authority of the church should be of that invisible, but powerful nature, which results from superior gravity, piety, and devout example. It will then have its proper effect upon the congregation, who will cheerfully yield to the wishes of those who are best qualified to select the candidate. But as soon as it is challenged as a right, it will be lost. The condition of the members of a church is thought to be hard, where the minister elected by the parish is not approved by them. This can only be because they are a minority; and it is one part of the compensation paid for the many blessings resulting from a state of society. A difficulty of this nature surely would not be cured by returning to the old provincial system of letting the minority rule the majority; unless we suppose that the doctrines of a minister are of no consequence to any but church members. Besides, in the present state of our laws, and as they are likely to continue, there is no hardship, although there may be some inconvenience; for dissenting members of the church, as well as of the parish, may join any other church and society, or they may institute a new society; so that they are neither obliged to hear nor to pay a minister, in whose settlement they did not concur. It is true, if there are any parish funds, they will lose the benefit of them by removal; but an inconvenience of this sort will never be felt, when a case of conscience is in question.

Having established the points necessary to settle this cause, viz., that the property sued for belongs to the first church in Dedham, *sub modo;* that is, to be managed by its deacons under the superintendence of the church, for the general good of the inhabitants of the first parish, in the support of the public worship of God,—that the members of the church now associated and worshipping with the first parish, constitute the first church,—and that the plaintiffs are duly appointed deacons of that church; it follows that the verdict of the jury is right, and that judgment must be entered accordingly.

The court, it has been observed, avoided "abstruse problems of 'theology,' " and did its best "to make the litigants realize that the court was deciding nothing more than a controversy with respect to the control of property," Howe, *The Garden and the Wilderness* 37, 40. But are not the nature of a church, its relations to a parish, and the status of a minister "abstruse questions of theology?" The Supreme Judicial Court could not help being embroiled in religious controversy when Massachusetts had adopted a religion.

Baker v. Fales was a blow to the Trinitarian Congregationalists. It was not made sweeter to them by the Chief Justice's unctuous words on their loss of the parish funds: "an inconvenience of this sort will never be felt, when a case of conscience is in question." Inconvenience of this sort, and feeling about it, were just what had led Deacon Eliphalet Baker to defend the suit and hire the great Daniel as his lawyer. The Congregationalists did not feel better when, as the controversy continued in the political arena, Chief Justice Parker issued a long defense of his opinion in the *Christian Examiner,* an organ of the Unitarians, Meyer 205–206.

Between 1820 and 1834 nearly one hundred Congregationalist parishes fell under Unitarian control—over one-quarter of the Congregationalist parishes in the commonwealth, McLoughlin 2, 1175 n. 22, 1196. The Trinitarians estimated that the Unitarians took $608,000 worth of property, Meyer 177. The Trinitarians, as they watched the process, became champions of abolishing Article III. The entrenched Unitarians defended the establishment. "The government of this Commonwealth has uniformly distinguished itself by the spirit of religious freedom," declared their leader, William Ellery Channing, in the election sermon of 1830. "Intolerance, however rife abroad, has found no shelter in our halls of legislation," Meyer 217.

Reopening the issue of *Baker v. Fales,* the Trinitarian Congregationalists were again defeated in an opinion by the new Chief Justice, Lemuel Shaw, also a Unitarian, *Stebbins v. Jennings,* 27 Mass. (10 Pick.) 172 (1830). The Trinitarians now sounded the note the Baptists had been sounding for generations: "To say that our religion cannot be supported without the aid of establishments and law is to disgrace it in the eyes of the world, and to cast reproach on its maker, *Spirit of the Pilgrims* (1831) 629-648, excerpted in Meyer 218.

Universalists, denouncing diehard Unitarians, took the lead in moving for constitutional reform, McLoughlin 2, 1245-1254. Triniarian Congregationalists, Baptists, dissenters of every kind then voted for the eleventh amendment of the state constitution abolishing the right to tax for public worship. It was passed in 1833 by a vote of 32,324-3,273, *ibid.* 2, 1259.

The Eleventh Amendment left intact Article III's premise: The "public worship of GOD" promotes "the security of a republican government." It gave every religious society, incorporated or not, the right to elect "their pastors or religious teachers" and to raise money to support them. What it did not decide was who owned the property of the parishes. Legislation enacted in 1834 declared that all parishes continued to enjoy their existing rights, Massachusetts, *Revised Statutes,* 1835, c. 20, sec. 2. The churches, "connected and associated in public worship with such parishes," were to continue to "enjoy all their accustomed privileges", *ibid.* sec. 3.

Under the principle established in *Baker v. Fales* it would have appeared that the voters of a parish could dispossess the churches and devote the church property to whatever Christian creed the majority of voters wanted. But the Trinitarian churches kept their church property and the Unitarians kept the property they had already won. On what basis? "That question has never been satisfactorily answered," Meyer 181. The result of the eleventh amendment and the 1834 legislation was to transfer a large amount of property, hitherto public, to the control of the two denominations. A kind of golden handshake was extended by the commonwealth to both the Trinitarian Congregationalist ministers and the Unitarian ministers no longer supported by public taxes. They took over as their own what had been trusts for "public worship." Disestablished in one sense, they were publicly endowed with the meeting-houses and parish funds of the towns of Massachusetts.

7. "THE FOREMOST OF THE POLITICAL INSTITUTIONS"

In 1830 a Frenchman, Alexis de Tocqueville, aged twenty-five, began a nine-month tour of America. By training he was a lawyer, and he had had experience as a minor judge at Versailles. By temperament and intuition, he was a great observer, and he possessed, to the degree of genius, a Gallic capacity to generalize. His nine-month trip led in 1835 to the first volume of a masterpiece on the mores and government of the United States, *La Démocratie en l'Amérique,* subsequently translated by Henry Reeve as *Democracy in America.*

Religion and its relation to government were of great concern to Tocqueville. Their relationship was indeed of paramount concern:

You seem to me to have well understood the general ideas on which my programme rests. What has most struck me about my country, more especially these last few years, is to see ranged on one side men who prize morality, religion, and order; and upon the other, those who love liberty and the equality of men before the law. This spectacle has struck me as the most extraordinary and the most deplorable ever offered to the eyes of a man; for all the things that we separate in this way, are, I am certain, united indissolubly in the eyes of God. They are *holy* things, if I may so express myself, because the greatness and the happiness of man in this world can result only from their simultaneous union. From this I believe to have perceived that one of the finest enterprises of our time would be to demonstrate that these things are not at all incompatible; that, on the contrary, they are bound together by a necessary tie, so that each of them is weakened in being separated from the others. Such is my general idea [Tocqueville to Eugene Stoffels, July 24, 1836; Tocqueville, *Oeuvres et correspondance inédites* (1861) 1, 432 (emphasis in original)].

Tocqueville's comments on religion in America are a mixture of observation, exhortations to his own countrymen, and prophecy of what was to come in America. As Reeve's translation of *Democracy in America,* pp. 306-317, reads:

Religion Considered as a Political Institution, Which Powerfully Contributes to the Maintenance of the Democratic Republic Amongst the Americans

North America peopled by men who professed a democratic and republican Christianity—Arrival of the Catholics—For what reason the Catholics form the most democratic and the most republican class at the present time.

Every religion is to be found in juxtaposition to a political opinion which is connected with it by affinity. If the human mind be left to follow its own bent, it will regulate the temporal and spiritual institutions of society upon one uniform principle; and man will endeavor, if I may use the expression, to harmonize the state in which he lives upon earth with the state which he believes to await him in heaven. The greatest part of British America was peopled by men who, after having shaken off the authority of the Pope, acknowledged no other religious supremacy; they brought with them into the New World a form of Christianity which I cannot better describe than by styling it a democratic and republican religion. This sect contributed powerfully to the establishment of a democracy and a republic, and from the earliest settlement of the emigrants politics and religion contracted an alliance which has never been dissolved.

About fifty years ago Ireland began to pour a Catholic population into the United States; on the other hand, the Catholics of America made proselytes, and at the present moment more than a million of Christians professing the truths of the Church of Rome are to be met with in the Union. The Catholics are faithful to the observances of their religion; they are fervent and zealous in the support and belief of their doctrines. Nevertheless they constitute the most republican and the most democratic class of citizens which exists in the United States; and although this fact may surprise the observer at first, the causes by which it is occasioned may easily be discovered upon reflection. . . .

I happened to be staying in one of the largest towns in the Union, when I was invited to attend a public meeting which had been called for the purpose of assisting the Poles, and of sending them supplies of arms and money. I found two or three thousand persons collected in a vast hall which had been prepared to receive them. In a short time a priest in his ecclesiastical robes advanced to the front of the hustings: the spectators rose, and stood uncovered, whilst he spoke in the following terms:—

"Almighty God! the God of Armies! Thou who didst strengthen the hearts and guide the arms of our fathers when they were fighting for the sacred rights of national independence; Thou who didst make them triumph over a hateful oppression, and hast granted to our people the benefits of liberty and peace; Turn, O Lord, a favorable eye upon the other hemisphere; pitifully look down upon that heroic nation which is even now struggling as we did in the former time, and for the same rights which we defended with our blood. Thou, who didst create Man in the likeness of the same Image, let not tyranny mar Thy work, and establish inequality upon the earth. Almighty God! do Thou watch over the destiny of the Poles, and render them worthy to be free. May Thy wisdom direct their councils, and may Thy strength sustain their arms! Shed forth Thy terror over their enemies, scatter the powers which take counsel against them; and vouchsafe that the injustice which the world has witnessed for fifty years, be not consummated in our time. O Lord, who holdest alike the hearts of nations and of men in Thy powerful hand; raise up allies to the sacred cause of right; arouse the French nation from the apathy in which its rulers retain it, that it go forth again to fight for the liberties of the world.

"Lord, turn not Thou Thy face from us, and grant that we may always be the most religious as well as the freest people of the earth. Almighty God, hear our supplications this day. Save the Poles, we beseech Thee, in the name of Thy well-beloved Son, our Lord Jesus Christ, who died upon the cross for the salvation of men. Amen."

The whole meeting responded "Amen!" with devotion.

Indirect Influence of Religious Opinions Upon Political Society in the United States

Christian morality common to all sects—Influence of religion upon the manners of the Americans—Respect for the marriage tie—In what manner religion confines the imagination of the Americans within certain limits, and checks the passion of innovation—Opinion of the Americans on the political utility of religion—Their exertions to extend and secure its predominance.

I have just shown what the direct influence of religion upon politics is in the United States, but its indirect influence appears to me to be still more considerable, and it never instructs the Americans more fully in the art of being free than when it says nothing of freedom.

The sects which exist in the United States are innumerable. They all differ in respect to the worship which is due from man to his Creator, but they all agree in respect to the duties which are due from man to man. Each sect adores the Deity in its own peculiar manner, but all the sects preach the same moral law in the name of God. If it be of the highest importance to man, as an individual, that his religion should be true, the case of society is not the same. Society has no future life to hope for or to fear; and provided the citizens profess a religion, the peculiar tenets of that religion are of very little importance to its interests. Moreover, almost all the sects of the United States are comprised within the great unity of Christianity, and Christian morality is everywhere the same.

It may be believed without unfairness that a certain number of Americans pursue a peculiar form of worship, from habit more than from conviction. In the United States the sovereign authority is religious, and consequently hypocrisy must be common; but there is no country in the whole world in which the Christian religion retains a greater influence over the souls of men than in America; and there can be no greater proof of its utility, and of its conformity to human nature, than that its influence is most powerfully felt over the most "enlightened" and "free" nation of the earth.

I have remarked that the members of the American clergy in general, without even excepting those who do not admit religious liberty, are all in favor of civil freedom; but they do not support any particular political system. They keep aloof from parties and from public affairs. In the United States religion exercises but little influence upon the laws and upon the details of public opinion, but it directs the manners of the community, and by regulating domestic life it regulates the State.

I do not question that the great austerity of manners which is observable in the United States, arises, in the first instance, from religious faith. Religion is often unable to restrain man from the numberless temptations of fortune; nor can it check that passion for gain which every incident of his life contributes to arouse, but its influence over the mind of woman is supreme, and women are the protectors of morals. There is certainly no country in the world where the tie of marriage is so much respected as in America, or where conjugal happiness is more highly or worthily appreciated. In Europe almost all the disturbances of society arise from the irregularities of domestic life. To despise the natural bonds and legitimate pleasures of home, is to contract a taste for excesses, a restlessness of heart, and the evil of fluctuating desires. Agitated by the tumultuous passions which frequently disturb his dwelling, the European is galled by the obedience which the legislative powers of the State exact. But when the American retires from the turmoil of public life to the bosom of his family, he finds in it the image of order and of peace. There his pleasures are simple and natural, his joys are innocent and calm; and as he finds that an orderly life is the surest path to happiness, he accustoms himself without difficulty to moderate his opinions as well as his tastes. Whilst the European endeavors to forget his domestic troubles by agitating society, the American derives from his own home that love of order which he afterwards carries with him into public affairs.

In the United States the influence of religion is not confined to the manners, but it extends to the intelligence of the people. Amongst the Anglo-Americans, there are some who profess the doctrines of Christianity from a sincere belief in them, and others who do the same because they are afraid to be suspected of unbelief. Christianity, therefore, reigns without any obstacle, by universal consent; the consequence is, as I have before observed, that every principle of the moral world is fixed and determinate, although the political world is abandoned to the debates and the experiments of men. Thus the human mind is never left to wander across a boundless field; and, whatever may be its pretensions, it is checked from time to time by barriers which it cannot surmount. Before it can perpetrate innovation, certain primal and immutable principles are laid down, and the boldest conceptions of human device are subjected to certain forms which retard and stop their completion.

The imagination of the Americans, even in its greatest flights, is circumspect and undecided; its impulses are checked, and its works unfinished. These habits of restraint recur in political society, and are singularly favorable both to the tranquillity of the people and to the durability of the institutions it has established. Nature and circumstances concurred to make the inhabitants of the United States bold men, as is sufficiently attested by the enterprising spirit with which they seek for fortune. If the mind of the Americans were free from all trammels, they would very shortly become the most daring innovators and the most implacable disputants in the world. But the revolutionists of America are obliged to profess an ostensible respect for Christian morality and equity, which does not easily permit them to violate the laws that oppose their designs; nor would they find it easy to surmount the scruples of their partisans, even if they were able to get over their own. Hitherto no one in the United States has dared to advance the maxim, that everything is permissible with a view to the interests of society; an impious adage which seems to have been invented in an age of freedom to shelter all the tyrants of future ages. Thus whilst the law permits the Americans to do what they please, religion prevents them from conceiving, and forbids them to commit, what is rash or unjust.

Religion in America takes no direct part in the government of society, but it must nevertheless be regarded as the foremost of the political institutions of that country; for if it does not impart a taste for freedom, it facilitates the use of free institutions. Indeed, it is in this same point of view that the inhabitants of the United States themselves look upon religious belief. I do not know whether all the Americans have a sincere faith in their religion, for who can search the human heart? but I am certain that they hold it to be indispensable to the maintenance of republican institutions. This opinion is not peculiar to a class of citizens or to a party; but it belongs to the whole nation, and to every rank of society.

In the United States, if a political character attacks a sect, this may not prevent even the partisans of that very sect from supporting him; but if he attacks all the sects together, everyone abandons him, and he remains alone.

Whilst I was in America, a witness, who happened to be called at the assizes of the county of Chester (State of New York), declared that he did not believe in the existence of God, or in the immortality of the soul. The judge refused to admit his evidence, on the ground that the witness had destroyed beforehand all the confidence of the Court in what he was about to say. The newspapers related the fact without any further comment.

The Americans combine the notions of Christianity and of liberty so intimately in their minds, that it is impossible to make them conceive the one without the other; and with them this conviction does not spring from that barren traditionary faith which seems to vegetate in the soul rather than to live.

I have known of societies formed by the Americans to send out ministers of the Gospel into the new Western States to found schools and churches there, lest religion should be suffered to die away in those remote settlements, and the rising States be less fitted to enjoy free institutions than the people from which they emanated. I met with wealthy New Englanders who abandoned the country in which they were born in order to lay the foundations of Christianity and of freedom on the banks of the Missouri, or in the prairies of Illinois. Thus religious zeal is perpetually stimulated in the United States by the duties of patriotism. These men do not act from an exclusive consideration of the promises of a future life; eternity is only one motive of their devotion to the cause; and if you converse with these missionaries of Christian civilization, you will be surprised to find how much value they set upon the goods of this world, and that you meet with a politician where you expected to find a priest. They will tell you that "all the American republics are collectively involved with each other; if the republics of the West were to fall into anarchy, or to be mastered by a despot, the republican institutions which now flourish upon the shores of the Atlantic Ocean would be in great peril. It is, therefore, our interest that the new States should be religious, in order to maintain our liberties."

Such are the opinions of the Americans, and if any hold that the religious spirit which I admire is the very thing most amiss in America, and that the only element wanting to the freedom and happiness of the human race is to believe in some blind cosmogony, or to assert with Cabanis the secretion of thought by the brain, I can only reply that those who hold this language have never been in America, and that they have never seen a religious or a free nation. When they return from their expedition, we shall hear what they have to say.

There are persons in France who look upon republican institutions as a temporary means of power, of wealth, and distinction; men who are the *condottieri* of liberty, and who fight for their own advantage, whatever be the colors they wear: it is not to these that I address myself. But there are others who look forward to the republican form of government as a tranquil and lasting state, towards which modern society is daily impelled by the ideas and manners of the time, and who sincerely desire to prepare men to be free. When these men attack religious opinions, they obey the dictates of their passions to the prejudice of their interests. Despotism may govern without faith, but liberty cannot. Religion is much more necessary in the republic which they set forth in glowing colors than in the monarchy which they attack; and it is more needed in democratic republics than in any others. How is it possible that society should escape destruction if the moral tie be not strengthened in proportion as the political tie is relaxed? and what can be done with a people which is its own master, if it be not submissive to the Divinity?

Principal Causes Which Render Religion Powerful in America

Care taken by the Americans to separate the Church from the State—The laws, public opinion, and even the exertions of the clergy concur to promote this end—Influence of religion upon the mind in the United States attributable to this cause—Reason of this—What is the natural state of men with regard to religion at the present time—What are the peculiar and incidental causes which prevent men, in certain countries, from arriving at this state.

The philosophers of the eighteenth century explained the gradual decay of religious faith in a very simple manner. Religious zeal, said they, must necessarily fail, the more generally liberty is established and knowledge diffused. Unfortunately, facts are by no means in accordance with their theory. There are certain populations in Europe whose unbelief is only equalled by their ignorance and their debasement, whilst in America one of the freest and most enlightened nations in the world fulfils all the outward duties of religious fervor.

Upon my arrival in the United States, the religious aspect of the country was the first thing that struck my attention; and the longer I stayed there the more did I perceive the great political consequences resulting from this state of things, to which I was unaccustomed. In France I had almost always seen the spirit of religion and the spirit of freedom pursuing courses diametrically opposed to each other; but in America I found that they were intimately united, and that they reigned in common over the same country. My desire to discover the causes of this phenomenon increased from day to day. In order to satisfy it I questioned the members of all the different sects; and I more especially sought the society of the clergy, who are the depositaries of the different persuasions, and who are more especially interested in their duration. As a member of the Roman Catholic Church I was more particularly brought into contact with several of its priests, with whom I became intimately acquainted. To each of these men I expressed my astonishment and I explained my doubts; I found that they differed upon matters of detail alone; and that they mainly attributed the peaceful dominion of religion in their country to the separation of Church and State. I do not hesitate to affirm that during my stay in America I did not meet with a single individual, of the clergy or of the laity, who was not of the same opinion upon this point.

This led me to examine more attentively than I had hitherto done, the station which the American clergy occupy in political society. I learned with surprise that they filled no public appointments; not one of them is to be met with in the administration, and they are not even represented in the legislative assemblies. In several States the law excludes them from political life, public opinion in all. And when I came to inquire into the prevailing spirit of the clergy I found that most of its members seemed to retire of their own accord from the exercise of power, and that they made it the pride of their profession to abstain from politics.

I heard them inveigh against ambition and deceit, under whatever political opinions these vices might chance to lurk; but I learned from their discourses that men are not guilty in the eye of God for any opinions concerning political government which they may profess with sincerity, any more than they are for their mistakes in building a house or in driving a furrow. I perceived that these ministers of the gospel eschewed all parties with the anxiety attendant upon personal interest. These facts convinced me that what I had been told was true; and it then became my object to investigate their causes, and to inquire how it happened that the real authority of religion was increased by a state of things which diminished its apparent force: these causes did not long escape my researches.

The short space of threescore years can never content the imagination of man; nor can the imperfect joys of this world satisfy his heart. Man alone, of all created beings, displays a natural contempt of existence, and yet a boundless desire to exist; he scorns life, but he dreads annihilation. These different feelings incessantly urge his soul to the contemplation of a future state, and religion directs his musings thither. Religion, then, is simply another form of hope; and it is no less natural to the human heart than hope itself. Men cannot abandon their religious faith without a kind of aberration of intellect, and a sort of violent distortion of their true natures; but they are invincibly brought back to more pious sentiments; for unbelief is an accident, and faith is the only permanent state of mankind. If we only consider religious institutions in a purely human point of view, they may be said to derive an inexhaustible element of strength from man himself, since they belong to one of the constituent principles of human nature.

I am aware that at certain times religion may strengthen this influence, which originates in itself, by the artificial power of the laws, and by the support of those temporal institutions which direct society. Religions, intimately united to the governments of the earth, have been known to exercise a sovereign authority derived from the twofold source of terror and of faith; but when a religion contracts an alliance of this nature, I do not hesitate to affirm that it commits the same error as a man who should sacrifice his future to his present welfare; and in obtaining a power to which it has no claim, it risks that authority which is rightfully its own. When a religion founds its empire upon the desire of immortality which lives in every human heart, it may aspire to universal dominion; but when it connects itself with a government, it must necessarily adopt maxims which are only applicable to certain nations. Thus, in forming an alliance with a political power, religion augments its authority over a few, and forfeits the hope of reigning over all.

As long as a religion rests upon those sentiments which are the consolation of all affliction, it may attract the affections of mankind. But if it be mixed up with the bitter passions of the world, it may be constrained to defend allies whom its interests, and not the principle of love, have given to it; or to repel as antagonists men who are still attached to its own spirit, however opposed they may be to the powers to which it is allied. The Church cannot share the temporal power of the State without being the object of a portion of that animosity which the latter excites.

The political powers which seem to be most firmly established have frequently no better guarantee for their duration than the opinions of a generation, the interests of the time, or the life of an individual. A law may modify the social condition which seems to be most fixed and determinate; and with the social condition everything else must change. The powers of society are more or less fugitive, like the years which we spend upon the earth; they succeed each other with rapidity, like the fleeting cares of life; and no government has ever yet been founded upon an invariable disposition of the human heart, or upon an imperishable interest.

As long as a religion is sustained by those feelings, propensities, and passions which are found to occur under the same forms, at all the different periods of history, it may defy the efforts of time; or at least it can only be destroyed by another religion. But when religion clings to the interests of the world, it becomes almost as fragile a thing as the powers of earth. It is the only one of them all which can hope for immortality; but if it be connected with their ephemeral authority, it shares their fortunes, and may fall with those transient passions which supported them for a day. The alliance which religion contracts with political powers must needs be onerous to itself; since it does not require their assistance to live, and by giving them its assistance it may be exposed to decay.

The danger which I have just pointed out always exists, but it is not always equally visible. In some ages governments seem to be imperishable; in others, the existence of society appears to be more precarious than the life of man. Some constitutions plunge the citizens into a lethargic somnolence, and others rouse them to feverish excitement. When governments appear to be so strong, and laws so stable, men do not perceive the dangers which may accrue from a union of Church and State. When governments display so much weakness, and laws so much inconstancy, the danger is self-evident, but it is no longer possible to avoid it; to be effectual, measures must be taken to discover its approach.

In proportion as a nation assumes a democratic condition of society, and as communities display democratic propensities, it becomes more and more dangerous to connect religion with political institutions; for the time is coming when authority will be bandied from hand to hand, when political theories will succeed each other, and when men, laws, and constitutions will disappear, or be modified from day to day, and this, not for a season only, but unceasingly. Agitation and mutability are inherent in the nature of democratic republics, just as stagnation and inertness are the law of absolute monarchies.

If the Americans, who change the head of the Government once in four years, who elect new legislators every two years, and renew the provincial officers every twelvemonth; if the Americans, who have abandoned the political world to the attempts of innovators, had not placed religion beyond their reach, where could it abide in the ebb and flow of human opinions? where would that respect which belongs to it be paid, amidst the struggles of faction? and what would become of its immortality, in the midst of perpetual decay? The American clergy were the first to perceive this truth, and to act in conformity with it. They saw that they must renounce their religious influence, if they were to strive for political power; and they chose to give up the support of the State, rather than to share its vicissitudes.

In America, religion is perhaps less powerful than it has been at certain periods in the history of certain peoples; but its influence is more lasting. It restricts itself to its own resources, but of those none can deprive it: its circle is limited to certain principles, but those principles are entirely its own, and under its undisputed control.

EIGHT

Emancipation, 1834–1870

AT THE VERY TIME that the churches of Massachusetts were being emancipated from tax support by the state, the energy of a nucleus of Christian laity and clergy was being turned to the emancipation of the slaves in the American South. The "abolitionist crusade"—an enterprise more religious in its origins and more single-minded in its object than the crusades to save the Holy Land—began in the administration of Andrew Jackson and reached its climax with the enactment of the Thirteenth Amendment in 1865. Christian motivation and fervor and biblical arguments and imagery created a massive religious intervention in American politics that could be read to confirm Tocqueville's observations on the role of religion in America.

1. THE BIBLE AGAINST SLAVERY

In 1834, 124 ministers of the Gospel, predominantly from Massachusetts and predominantly Congregationalist, but with a sprinkling of names from other denominations and other northern states, issued an address to the public which declared:

We believe,
1. That Slavery in our land is a great and threatening evil.
2. That it is a great and crying national sin.
3. That every man whether he live at the North, South, East, or West, is personally responsible, and has personal duties to discharge in respect to it.
4. That every man, who adopts opinions or pursues practices, which adopted and pursued by all others, would go to perpetuate this sin, does thereby become personally guilty in respect to it.
5. We believe that slavery, like other sins, ought to be remedied as soon as the nature of the case admits; and further, that the nature of the case admits the *possibility* and therefore imposes the obligation of Immediate Emancipation [Amos A. Phelps, *Lectures on Slavery and Its Remedy* (1834; republished 1970) v-vi].

In this manifesto, slavery is a religious, not a political issue; cooperation with the sin becomes sin, too; emancipation is not a far-off goal but a present duty. These themes were to be the themes of the abolitionist minority for the next thirty years.

A minister, once converted to the cause, addressed other ministers "because this subject has been woefully and criminally overlooked and forgotten by ministers, who, of all other men, ought ever to be alive to it" (ibid. at 13). Ministers were already organizing for another great cause, "Temperance." Emancipation, like temperance, should be the work of all Christian denominations, "a common cause," *ibid.* at xi. Ministers were the key to public opinion. "Once get the public sentiment of the ministry right, and then inspire them with courage to speak that sentiment out, and you revolutionize the public sentiment of the community in a trice," *ibid.* at 14–15. Some clergymen pleaded it was "a political subject" that they should not touch; as to which the pulpit should be silent, *ibid.* at 15. But like Jeremiah, the minister should not hesitate to pull down "the strong holds of Satan." Like Jesus Christ, he should "preach deliverance to the captives," *ibid.* at 16, 24.

The Christian attack on slavery was met with the Christian answer that slavery was sanctioned in the Old Testament, never criticized by Christ, and expressly approved by St. Paul. To these excuses, the answer was that servitude among the Jews was not like slavery in America, and that the entire spirit of the Bible condemned slavery, *ibid.* at 65–80. Slavery as practiced in America was clearly sinful because it denied God's moral government, reducing the slave from an intelligent, responsible human being to a chattel, William Goodell, "Slavery Tested by Its Own Code," 1 *Quarterly Anti-Slavery Magazine* 23–24 (1836). American slavery, moreover, denied the slave his religious rights by denying him literacy and with it the possibility of reading the Bible, *ibid.* at 25. American slave law also denied that slaves could marry. Doing so, "it blots out the seventh commandment" and "renders all this promiscuous concubinage inevitably certain!" *ibid.* at 26–27.

The ministers struck a vital spark, even though they were only a minority of the clergy, and the main church bodies—Methodist, Baptist, Presbyterian, Episcopalian, Roman Catholic— took no stand against the institution. The ministers alone would not have succeeded if their words had not influenced laymen who provided much of the leadership. Among the latter was Theodore Dwight Weld, the son of a Congregationalist minister in Utica, New York, and the descendant of a long line of New England ministers. Weld, like others in the antislavery cause, was first active as a temperance advocate. Under the influence of Charles Finney, a Presbyterian revivalist, Weld took the lead in bringing students to a new Presbyterian seminary, Lane, in Cincinatti, that became a center of abolitionist thought. He brought the gospel of emancipation to the Middle West, *Dictionary of American Biography* 19, 625. The title of his first book, *The Bible Against Slavery* (1837) shows the religious center of his zeal.

The most controversial of all the abolitionists, William Lloyd Garrison, had been crusading against intoxication and Sabbath-breaking before he was converted to the new cause by a Quaker, Benjamin Lundy. The first speech of his antislavery career was delivered on July 4, 1829, in the Park Street Church, Boston—a characteristic association of the celebration of American independence with religion and freedom for all human beings. Later, angry at the apathy of the mainline churches—"cages of unclean birds," as he described them—Garrison was less than orthodox but well within the doctrine of liberal Bostonian Christianity. For him as for the other leaders, the wicked wilderness of the world was a challenge to Christian reform.

Christian belief also inspired the agents of abolitionism and provided a model for their martyrdom. In 1835 Amos Dresser, a student at Lane, brought abolitionist tracts into Nashville and was apprehended. At his trial he declared "slaveholding to be inconsistent with the Gospel, and a constant transgression of God's law." He was sentenced to a public whipping of twenty lashes. Dresser's narrative of what happened, much circulated in the North, continues:

I knelt to receive the punishment which was inflicted by Mr. Braughton, the city officer, with a heavy cowskin. When the infliction ceased, an involuntary feeling of thanksgiving to God for the fortitude with which I had been enabled to endure it arose in my soul, to which I began aloud to give utterance. The death-like silence that prevailed for a moment was suddenly broken with loud exclamations, G-d d--n him, stop his praying" [The Narrative of Amos Dresser," in John L. Thomas, ed., *Slavery Attacked: The Abolitionist Crusade* (1965) 43–44].

No reader familiar with stories of Christian endurance under Roman persecution could ignore the analogies.

The Christians for emancipation did not propose that force be used to effect it. Their program was to arouse ministers of the Gospel and stir the conscience of the community. Slaveholders, however, could not endure this kind of religious upbraiding; and they feared that the doctrines of the abolitionists would stir the slaves to armed rebellion. As early as 1835 President Andrew Jackson's postmaster general unofficially sought to close the United States mails in the South to abolitionist literature, *see* Thomas 41, 52. In 1836 the House of Representatives adopted "the gag rule" refusing to listen to or print petitions for the end of slavery in the District of Columbia.

The abolitionists' Christian critique had made the issue inflammatory. The dynamism of the situation was this: the more religious condemnation was heaped upon the institution, the more aggressive its beneficiaries became in asserting its rightness. They could not stand being put down as bad Christians and morally inferior beings. Their critics did not mind the effect of their words; they saw themselves as physicians provoking a crisis in an unhealthy body. The discomfort of the South would not alter their prescriptions. As Jefferson had done half a century ago, abolitionists appealed to the judgments of a "sin-avenging God," Phelps 150. They also appealed to the Last Judgment in the Gospel of Matthew, chapter 25, where Christ asks each what he has done for the needy, *e.g.*, Beriah Green, "Letter to a Minister of the Gospel," 1 *Quarterly Anti-Slavery Magazine* 340 (1836).

2. NO COMPROMISE WITH SIN

The question of the annexation of Texas made slavery a major issue of national politics in the 1840s. Mexico had abolished slavery in Texas; but Texas wished to enter the Union as a slave state from which other slave states could be formed, giving the slave side preponderance in the United States Senate. The center of opposition was New England where the "Conscience Whigs"—their name betraying their religious scruples—joined actual abolitionists in issuing *How to Settle the Texas Question* (1845) telling voters how to act and adding this direction: "To clergymen: You are entreated in the name of God and Christ to pray for the slave; and preach at least one sermon against the admission of Texas as a slave state, as soon as may be" [Thomas, *Slavery Attacked*, 105–106.]

When the United States actually went to war with Mexico, the war was seen by the abolitionists and their allies as a war to extend slavery. In Boston in 1846 it was denounced by the Reverend Theodore Parker, one of the purest products of the Unitarian culture of Harvard Divinity School and its Emersonian development. Too liberal for the established Unitarians, yet revering Jesus as "the highest known representative of God," Parker was the pastor of the Twenty-Eighth Congregationalist Society in Boston. As a mass meeting at Faneuil Hall he said:

Men and brothers, I call on you all to protest against this most infamous war, in the name of the States, in the name of the country, in the name of man—yes, in the name of God. . . .

Leave not your memory infamous among the nations, because you feared men, feared the Government . . . because you loved slavery, loved war, but loved not the eternal justice of all-judging God [Parker, "The Mexican War," in Parker, *The Slave Power* (1969) 31].

The Wilmot Proviso, banning slavery in land acquired from Mexico, failed of passage in Congress in 1847. After the war the terms on which California and New Mexico would become states had to be decided; by 1850 passions ran high over whether they should be slave or free. The sectional division was deep. Southern fire-eaters talked secession. General Winfield Scott, commander of the army, thought the country "on the eve of a terrible civil war," James Ford Rhodes, *History of the United States* (1910) 1, 131. In this crisis Henry Clay outlined a compromise, which, embodied in a series of bills, preserved the Union for another decade. California was admitted as a free state. The question of slavery in New Mexico was left open. The Texas boundary was drawn not to include New Mexico. The slave trade in the District of Columbia was abolished. A new and harsher Fugitive Slave Act gave slaveholders more legal resources in the North in recapturing escaped slaves, Rhodes 182–183.

Slavery was now the single issue by which the religious abolitionists judged public men. A key speech in support of Clay's compromise was delivered on March 7, 1850, by Daniel Webster who, for three decades, had been a force in Massachusetts—a leader at the constitutional convention of 1820; a congressman from Boston in 1822; United States senator, 1828–1840; secretary of state, 1840–1843; senator again since 1846; a perennial prospect for the presidency. No past glory could outweigh the offense of his speech of March 7, 1850. Again addressing a meeting in Faneuil Hall, Boston, on March 25, 1850, Theodore Parker declared (*Works* 3, 37):

Parker, Mr. Webster's Speech

. . . Four great men in the Senate of the United States have given us their decision; the four most eminent in the party politics of the nation—two great whigs, two great democrats. The Shibboleth of their party is forgotten by each; there is a strange unanimity in their decision. The Herod of free trade and the Pilate of protection are "made friends," when freedom is to be crucified. All four decide adverse to freedom; in favor of slavery; against the people. Their decisions are such as you might look for in the politicians of Austria and Russia. Many smaller ones have spoken on this side or on that. Last of all, but greatest, the most illustrious of the four, so far as great gifts of the understanding are concerned, a son of New England, long known, and often and deservedly honored, has given his decision. We waited long for his words; we held our peace in his silence; we listened for his counsel. Here it is; adverse to freedom beyond the fears of his friends, and the hopes even of his foes. He has done wrong things before, cowardly things more than once; but this, the wrongest and most cowardly of them all; we did not look for it. No great man in America has had his faults or his failings so leniently dealt with; private scandal we will not credit, public shame we have tried to excuse, or, if inexcusable, to forget. We have all of us been proud to go forward and honor his noble deeds, his noble efforts, even his noble words. I wish we could take a mantle big and black enough, and go backward and cover up the shame of the great man who has fallen in the midst of us, and hide him till his honor and his conscience shall return. But no, it cannot be; his deed is done in the face of the world, and nothing can hide it.

We have come together to-night in Faneuil Hall, to talk the matter over, in our New England way; to look each other in the face; to say a few words of warning, a few of counsel, perhaps something which may serve for guidance. We are not met here to-night to "calculate the value of the Union," but to calculate the worth of freedom and the rights of man; to calculate the value of the Wilmot Proviso. Let us be cool and careful, not violent, not rash; true and firm, not hasty or timid. . . .

Now, Mr. Foote of Mississippi—"Hangman Foote," as he has been called—understands the laws of the formation of the earth as well as the distinguished senator from

Massachusetts. Why, the inhabitants of that part of the Northwest Territory, which now forms the States of Indiana and Illinois, repeatedly asked Congress to allow them to introduce slaves north of the Ohio; and but for the ordinance of '87, that territory would now be covered with the mildew of slavery!

But I have not yet adduced all the testimony of Mr. Foote. Last year, on the 23d of February, 1849, he declared: "No one acquainted with the vast mineral resources of California and New Mexico, and who is aware of the peculiar adaptedness of slave labor to the development of mineral treasures, can doubt for a moment, that were slaves introduced into California and New Mexico, being employed in the mining operations there in progress, their labor would result in the acquisition of pecuniary profits not heretofore realized by the most successful cotton or sugar planter of this country?" Does not Mr. Webster know this? Perhaps he did not hear Mr. Foote's speech last year; perhaps he has a short memory, and has forgotten it. Then let us remind the nation of what its Senator forgets. Not know this—forget it? Who will credit such a statement? Mr. Webster is not an obscure clergyman, busy with far different things, but the foremost politician of the United States.

But why do I mention the speeches of Mr. Foote, a year ago? Here is something hardly dry from the printing-press. Here is an advertisement from the "Mississippian" of March 7th, 1850, the very day of that speech. The "Mississippian" is published at the city of Jackson, in Mississippi.

"CALIFORNIA,
"THE SOUTHERN SLAVERY COLONY.

"Citizens of the slave States, desirous of emigrating to California with their slave property, are requested to send their names, number of slaves, and period of contemplated departure, to the address of 'SOUTHERN SLAVE COLONY,' Jackson, Miss. . . .

"It is the desire of the friends of this enterprise to settle in the richest mining and agricultural portions of California, and to have the uninterrupted enjoyment of slave property. It is estimated that, by the first of May next, the members of this Slave Colony will amount to about five thousand, and the slaves to about ten thousand. The mode of effecting organization, &c., will be privately transmitted to actual members.

"Jackson (Miss), Feb. 24, 1850.   dtf."

What does Mr. Webster say in view of all this? "If a proposition were now here for a government for New Mexico, and it was moved to insert a provision for the prohibition of slavery, I would not vote for it." Why not vote for it? There is a specious pretence, which is publicly proclaimed, but there is a real reason for it which is not mentioned!

In the face of all these facts, Mr. Webster says that these men would wish "to protect the everlasting snows of Canada from the pest of slavery by the same overspreading wing of an act of Congress." Exactly so. If we ever annex Labrador—if we "re-annex" Greenland, and Kamskatka, I would extend the Wilmot Proviso there, and exclude slavery forever and forever.

But Mr. Webster would not "reaffirm an ordinance of nature," nor "reenact the will of God." I would. I would reaffirm nothing else, enact nothing else. What is justice but the "ordinance of nature?" What is right but "the will of God?" When you make a law, "Thou shalt not kill," what do you but "reenact the will of God?" When you make laws for the security of the "unalienable rights" of man, and protect for every man the right to life, liberty, and the pursuit of happiness, are you not re-affirming an ordinance of nature? Not reenact the will of God? Why, I would enact nothing else. The will of God is a theological term; it means truth and justice, in common speech. What is the theological opposite to "The will of God?" It is "the will of the devil." One of the two you must enact—either the will of God, or of the devil. The two are the only theological categories for such matters. *Aut Deus aut Diabolus.* There is no other alternative, "Choose you which you will serve." . . .

It is a great question before us, concerning the existence of millions of men. To many men in politics, it is merely a question of party rivalry; a question of in and out, and nothing more. To many men in cities, it is a question of commerce, like the establishment of a bank, or the building of one railroad more or less. But to serious men, who love man and love their God, this is a question of morals, a question of religion, to be settled with no regard to party rivalry, none to fleeting interests of to-day, but to be settled under the awful eye of conscience, and by the just law of God.

Shall we shut up slavery or extend it? It is for us to answer. Will you deal with the question now, or leave it to your children, when the evil is ten times greater? In 1749, there was not a slave in Georgia; now, two hundred and eighty thousand. In 1750, in all the United States, but two hundred thousand; now, three millions. In 1950, let Mr. Webster's counsels be followed, there will be thirty millions. Thirty millions! Will it then be easier for your children to set limits to this crime against human nature, than now for you? Our fathers made a political, and a commercial, and a moral error—shall we repeat it? They did a wrong; shall we extend and multiply the wrong? Was it an error in our fathers; not barely a wrong—was it a sin? No, not in them; they knew it not. But what in them to establish was only an error, in us to extend or to foster is a sin!

Perpetuate Slavery, we cannot do it. Nothing will save it. It is girt about by a ring of fire which daily grows narrower, and sends terrible sparkles into the very centre of the shameful thing. "Joint resolutions" cannot save it; annexations cannot save it—not if we re-annex all the West Indies; delinquent representatives cannot save it; uninstructed senators, refusing instructions, cannot save it, no, not with all their logic, all their eloquence, which smites as an earthquake smites the sea. No, slavery cannot be saved; by no compromise, no non-intervention, no Mason's Bill in the Senate. It cannot be saved in this age of the world until you nullify every ordinance of nature, until you repeal the will of God, and dissolve the union He has made between righteousness and the welfare of a people. Then, when you displace God from the throne of the world, and instead of his eternal justice, reenact the will of the Devil, then you may keep Slavery; keep it forever, keep it in peace. Not till then.

The question is, not if slavery is to cease, and soon to cease, but shall it end as it ended in Massachusetts, in New Hampshire, in Pennsylvania, in New York; or shall it end as in St. Domingo? Follow the counsel of Mr. Webster—it will end in fire and blood. God forgive us for our cowardice, if we let it come to this, that three millions or thirty millions of degraded human beings, degraded by us, must wade through slaughter to their unalienable rights.

Mr. Webster has spoken noble words—at Plymouth, standing on the altar-stone of New England; at Bunker Hill, the spot so early reddened with the blood of our fathers. But at this hour, when we looked for great counsel, when we forgot the paltry things which he has often done, and said, "Now he will rouse his noble soul, and be the man his early speeches once bespoke," who dared to fear that Olympian head would bow so low, so deeply kiss the ground? Try it morally, try it intellectually, try it by the statesman's test, world-wide justice; nay, try it by the politician's basest test, the personal expediency of to-day—it is a speech "not fit to be made," and when made, not fit to be confirmed.

> "We see dimly in the distance what is small and what is great,
>   Slow of faith how weak an arm may turn the iron helm of fate;
>   But the soul is still oracular; amid the market's din,
>   List the ominous stern whisper from the Delphic cave within—
> 'They enslave their children's children, who make compromise with sin.' "

The Compromise of 1850—"compromise with sin" to its religious critics—settled nothing, because more states applied for admission and the terms of their admission had to be settled. Moreover, the new Fugitive Slave Act of 1850 virtually assured that outrages to northern opinion would occur: persons would be carried off, under the authority of the law, from freedom to slavery. When Chief Justice Lemuel Shaw sustained the constitutionality of the act in 1851, he satisfied the mercantile class of Boston, anxious for concord with the South, but did nothing to reconcile religious antislavery feeling, *Sims' Case,* 61 Mass. (7 Cush.) 285 (1851). His son-in-law, Herman Melville, wrote *Billy Budd,* showing a scrupulously legalistic Captain Vere putting to death an innocent Billy Budd in defiance of a higher law.

By 1854 the issue of the terms on which Kansas and Nebraska would be admitted divided the country. The Missouri Compromise of 1820, long taken to be untouchable, prohibited slavery in the entire area. Stephen Douglas proposed the Kansas-Nebraska Act, letting Kansas determine by "popular sovereignty" whether it entered the Union as a free or a slave state. Northern moderates, who were not abolitionists but were against extension of slavery, took alarm. A petition against Douglas's bill was presented to the Senate by Hamilton Fish, senator from New York. The bishop of the Episcopal diocese of New York headed the signatories, and a majority of the clergymen of New York were reported to have signed it. The next day Edward Everett, senator from Massachusetts, presented a protest signed by 3,500 of the 3,800 clergymen in New England. Among them were not only names like Theodore Parker and Lyman Beecher but also those of the clergymen presidents of Amherst, Brown, Williams, and Yale. The statement read:

The undersigned, clergymen of different religious denominations in New England, hereby, in the name of Almighty God, and in his presence, do solemnly protest against the passage of what is known as the Nebraska bill. . . . We protest against it as a great moral wrong, as a breach of faith eminently unjust to the moral principles of the community, and subversive of all confidence in national engagements; as a measure full of danger to the peace and even the existence of our beloved Union, and exposing us to the righteous judgments of the Almighty [Rhodes, *History of the United States* 478].

The intrusion of the clergy was strongly resented by Christians in favor of slavery, compromise, peace. A third petition of 500 clergymen from Illinois and neighboring states was read aloud by Stephen Douglas, a sponsor of the bill. He added that he understood that in New England alone on one day between 1,500 and 2,000 sermons had been preached against the proposed legislation. He continued:

It is well known that there is an organization by which a copy of the New England protest has been sent to every preacher of every denomination, in all the free States of the Union, for his signature. Every minister has been appealed to, and yet they have been able to bring to their support but comparatively a small number. This shows that the great mass of the Christian ministers, the great mass of preachers of the Gospel, abhor this attempt to prostitute religion into the means of elevating men into power. The great mass are unwilling in the pulpit to utter a slander, and falsehood, and calumny against public men in a place where no answer can be made, and no vindication can be put forth. I submit, sir, whether it is fair as between man and man, whether it is honest, on the part of ministers of the Gospel towards their congregations, to pursue such a course. They take a partisan view of the subject in these sermons. They fix the character of each public man. They indorse this man; they condemn that. They indorse this political party; they excommunicate that. They give what pretends to be a true statement of the facts of the question; when that statement is derived from the address and speeches of the Abolition confederates, and contradicted by the records of the country, and these records are not allowed to be produced. If these statements are put forth upon the stump, we can refute them. If they should be put forth anywhere else than in the pulpit, or except upon the Sabbath day, we can disprove them. What would these gentlemen think of me if I were to violate the Holy Sabbath day by going into Chicago, and on that day making a stump speech in vindication of the Nebraska bill?

If they have a right to discuss it on the Sabbath day in opposition, may I not expose their slanders by vindicating the truth? Sir, this is an attempt to convert the Sabbath into the great day of the hustings, to make it a great day of electioneering, to get people out on the Sabbath for the purpose of hearing stump speeches; and in the most convenient of all modes, for if you wish to blacken the character of a man, you can do it then with security and with impunity, because no man can rise up and expose the slander, although a dozen living witnesses may be present and know it to be a slander.

I say, sir, that the purity of the Christian church, the purity of our holy religion, and the preservation of our free institutions, require that Church and State shall be separated; that the preacher on the Sabbath day shall find his text in the Bible; shall preach "Jesus Christ and him crucified," shall preach from the Holy Scriptures, and not attempt to control the political organizations and political parties of the day [*Congressional Globe* 29, 656].

The bill passed the House by three votes on May 22, 1854, and was signed by President Franklin Pierce on May 30.

While the bill was awaiting the president's signature, Anthony Burns was arrested in Boston on May 24. Burns was a black Baptist preacher, who in February had escaped from his master in Richmond. The convergence of the application of the Fugitive Slave Act to Burns with passage of the Kansas-Nebraska Act excited the strongest emotions. At a meeting at Faneuil Hall on May 26, Theodore Parker cried:

I have heard many hurrahs and cheers for liberty many times; I have not seen a great many *deeds* done for liberty. I ask you are we to have *deeds* as well as words? . . . Gentlemen, there was a Boston once, and you and I had fathers—brave fathers; and mothers who stirred up fathers to manly deeds. . . . They did not obey the stamp act. . . . You know what they did with the *tea* [Rhodes 502].

The crowd attempted to storm the court house; a marshal's aide was killed.

Escorted by troops ready to fire without notice, Burns on May 31 was taken to a Treasury cutter and shipped back to Virginia (details of the military preparations in *Ela v. Smith*, 71 Mass. 121 [1855]. Burns himself was subsequently purchased by Bostonians from a new owner, set free, and financed for study at Oberlin. He became a Baptist pastor in Indianapolis and later in Canada, *Dictionary of American Biography* 3, 308. The role of the authorities in Massachusetts became the subject of impassioned religious criticism at a mass meeting of 10,000 persons in Framingham on Independence Day, 1854.

"We have degenerated," William Lloyd Garrison told the meeting, "in our reverence for the higher law of God." In a scene modeled on the Old Testament, Garrison picked up a copy of the Fugitive Slave Act, set it on fire, and said, "And let the people say Amen." They did. He then set fire to a copy of the decision returning Burns and again asked the people to say amen. A third time he took up the Constitution itself. He described it as "the parent of all other atrocities," "a covenant with death," "an agreement with hell." He lit the paper and called out, "So perish all compromises with tyranny!" "And let the people say Amen." They did, Phillip S. Paludan, *A Covenant with Death* (1975) 2–3. The scene was permeated by theology. The Constitution was seen as the reverse of Israel's lifegiving covenant with God. The whole ritual was modeled on Deuteronomy 27 in which Moses tells the Levites to intone a curse "upon him who slights his father or his mother" and adds, "Let the people say Amen," and so on through several commandments of the Law. With the same solemnity Garrison cursed the Constitution.

3. THE GOSPEL TO KANSAS

In 1820, it will be recalled, Lyman Beecher had been a defender of the Congregational establishment. In 1826 he had been called to the new Hanover Street Church in Boston and conducted a powerful evangelical ministry there. In 1831 his zealous attacks on Catholicism were generally regarded as contributing to the state of mind in which a mob burned down a convent belonging to the Ursuline nuns in Charleston. Beecher then left Massachusetts to become the president of Lane in Cincinatti. So his career reflected the times. He was now an antislavery man. When the Kansas-Nebraska Act passed, he was among the leaders organizing an influx of antislavery men into Kansas, the prelude to a kind of civil war in the state. Beecher's appeal read:

Education, Temperance, Freedom, Religion in Kansas

Dear Sir:

We are engaged in an effort to have all the "clergymen of New England," the life members of the New England Emigrant Aid Company.

By insuring thus their cooperation in the direction of this Company, and by engaging its funds at this period of its highest uefulness, we are satisfied that the Christians of New England will bring to bear a stronger influence in sustaining the principles of what was last year called the "Ministers' Memorial," than by any other means which Providence puts in their hands. We ask such cooperation as you can give us; supposing that you may have been one of those 3,050 ministers, who in the Senate of the United States were pronounced to know nothing of the facts, laws and votes involved in the Nebraska bill and to have "no time to understand them." We are certain that you belong to that body of Northern ministers who have been prohibited from entering northwestern Missouri Kansas, by those mobs of men who have attempted to take the law of that region in their own hands.

We beg your attention to the great work the New England Emigrant Aid Company has in hand. We ask your particular attention in the encouragement which divine providence has given to its efforts. We beg you to observe all the facts in the case, before you give way to the false and discouraging impressions, assiduously circulated before the pretended election in Kansas, of March 30, which was the work, simply, of an invading army. You may rely on the following statements of the work of the Emigrant Aid Company, since it was established:

1. For Freedom—It has assisted in establishing at commanding points the towns of Lawrence, Topeka, Osawatomie, Boston, Hampden, and Wabounse. In some of these towns it has mills—in most of them some investment of value to the settlers. These towns are all peopled by "Free-State men," whose whole influence goes to make Kansas free. There are other towns already started of similar character. The only "Slave-State" town of commanding influence in Kansas is Leavenworth, on the Missouri frontier, separated from the other settled parts of the Territory by Indian reservations. We may say, therefore, that all the most important centers of influence have been established or assisted by the Emigrant Aid Company, and that their influence tells for the cause of Freedom. This Company has, in fact, directly transported between two and three thousand emigrants to Kansas. Not one man of them is known to have ever given a "Slave-State" vote. More than ten thousand, from free States of the Northwest, have been led there by its indirect influence here. To prevent the return of this tide, and to provide those who go with the assistance which capital only can provide, this Company wishes to supply saw-mills at important points, and other conveniences. For such purposes will it use any enlargement of its funds. The emigration is still very large; and whenever this Company can establish a saw-mill, with other conveniences, a "Free-

State" town can be gathered. From the best sources of information, from the officers of the Company, and well-informed persons in Kansas and Missouri, we are convinced, as the result of what has been done, that the great proportion of settlers now in Kansas wish it to become a free State. At the election held on the 22d ult., to fill vacancies in the Legislature, nine "Free-State" members were chosen, and only three "Slave-State" members—the last in Leavenworth, which is separated by a ferry only from Missouri.

2. *For Religion.*—The officers of this Company have understood that, to make a free State, they needed, first of all, the Gospel. Every missionary sent there by different boards has received their active assistance. Divine service is regularly maintained in the towns where the company has influence, and, we believe, no where else. Every Sabbath school in the Territory has been formed with the assistance of the Company, or its officers. Every church organized has been organized with their cooperation.

3. *For Education.*—Schools will be in operation at Lawrence, at Topeka, at Osawatomie and Hampden before the end of July. These, which are the only schools in the Territory of which we have any account, are due to the exertions of the New England Emigrant Aid Company and its officers.

4. *For Temperance.*—The traffic in intoxicating liquors scarcely exists in any one of the towns founded with the Company's assistance, and any attempt to introduce it will be resisted by their citizens. This prohibition, intended in the first instance for the benefit of the towns, will approve itself to you as the only hope for the Indians still remaining in that Territory.

Such has been the work of this Company in one year. To carry further such operations in these towns, and to plant more towns at once in Kansas, so as to secure its future destiny before next January, the Company needs $150,000. We think it highly desirable that that sum shall be furnished by those who will continue to the Company the Christian direction which has always guided it. We address this statement of facts, therefore, to every clergyman in New England, asking for it their careful attention. . . .

In 1857 the Supreme Court decided the Dred Scott case, denying that a descendant of black slaves could ever be a citizen of the United States and denying the power of Congress to exclude slavery from the territories, *Dred Scott v. Sandford* 60 U. S. (19 How.) 393. The dissenting opinion of Justice John McLean was read from the pulpit. George B. Cheever, author of *God Against Slavery* and pastor of the Church of the Puritans in New York City, declared that when sin and the devil usurped power, it was everyone's duty to disobey. *The Independent,* a Congregationalist weekly, edited by Henry Ward Beecher (Lyman's son) and other ministers, declared that the justices had "achieved only their own infamy." If the people obeyed, the paper said, "they disobey God," Don E. Fehrenbacher, *The Dred Scott Case: Its Significance in American Law and Politics* (1978) 422–423. Compromise with sin was once more denounced.

4. "GOD IS MARCHING ON"

When the war came, religious support for the contestants was a major factor in morale on both sides. The identification of the war as God's battle was more intense in the North. Julia Ward Howe, a New Yorker married to a New Englander, made the Howes' Boston home, Green Peace, a center of Unitarian causes, editing from there the antislavery journal, *The Commonwealth.* Visiting Washington at the end of 1861, as the first year of war drew to a close, she wrote religious words to the tune of the popular song "John Brown's Body." Published in February 1862 in *The Atlantic Monthly,* her poem perfectly expressed the sense of religious mission that brought together God's judgment and Christ's redemptive sacrifice and perceived victory for the Union as both divine judgment and liberation:

Battle-Hymn of the Republic

Mine eyes have seen the glory of the coming
of the Lord:
He is trampling out the vintage where the
grapes of wrath are stored;
He hath loosed the fateful lightning of His
terrible swift sword;
His truth is marching on.

I have seen Him in the watch-fires of a hundred circling camps;
They have builded Him an altar in the evening dews and damps;
I can read His righteous sentence by the dim
and flaring lamps:
His day is marching on.

I have read a fiery gospel writ in burnished
rows of steel:
"As ye deal with my contemners, so with you
my grace shall deal;
Let the Hero, born of woman, crush the serpent with his heel,
Since God is marching on."

He has sounded forth the trumpet that shall
never call retreat;
He is sifting out the hearts of men before His
judgment-seat;
Oh, be swift, my soul, to answer Him! be
jubiliant, my feet!
Our God is marching on.

In the beauty of the lilies Christ was born
across the sea,
With a glory in his bosom that transfigures
you and me:
As he died to make men holy, let us die to
make men free,
While God is marching on.

The idea that God had a special interest in the cause was held in higher official quarters. Gideon Welles, secretary of the navy, described in his diary this meeting of Lincoln's cabinet, shortly after the quasi-victory of the Union at Antietam:

September 22. A special Cabinet-meeting. The subject was the Proclamation for emancipating the slaves after a certain date, in States that shall then be in rebellion. For several weeks the subject has been suspended, but the President says never lost sight of. When it was submitted, and now in taking up the Proclamation, the President stated that the question was finally decided, the act and the consequences were his, but that he felt it due to us to make us acquainted with the fact and to invite criticism on the paper which he had prepared. There were, he had found, not unexpectedly, some differences in the Cabinet, but he had, after ascertaining in his own way the views of each and all, individually and collectively, formed his own conclusions and made his own decisions. In the course of the discussion on this paper, which was long, earnest, and, on the general principle involved, harmonious, he remarked that he had made a vow, a covenant, that if God gave us the victory in the approaching battle, he would consider it an indication of Divine will, and that it was his duty to move forward in the cause of emancipation. It might be thought strange, he said, that he had in this way submitted the disposal of matters when the way was not clear to his mind what he should do. God had decided this question in favor of the slaves. He was satisfied it was right, was confirmed and strengthened in his action by the vow and the results. His mind was fixed, his decision made, but he wished his paper announcing his course as correct in terms as it could be made without any change in his determination [Diary of Gideon Welles (Sept. 20, 1862)].

Victory at Gettysburg was announced by the president in terms that incorporated a portion of the Lord's Prayer:

Announcement of News from Gettysburg
Washington City, July 4, 10 A.M. 1863

The President announces to the country that news from the Army of the Potomac, up to 10 P.M. of the 3rd is such as to cover that Army with the highest honor, to promise a great success to the cause of the Union, and to claim the condolence of all for the many gallant fallen. And that for this, he especially desires that on this day, He whose will, not ours, should ever be done, be everywhere remembered and reverenced with profoundest gratitude.

Abraham Lincoln

[Lincoln, *Collected Works,* ed. Roy P. Basler (1953) 6, 314.]

Eleven days later the president issued this proclamation:

Proclamation of Thanksgiving

July 15, 1863

By the President of the United States of America
A Proclamation

It has pleased Almighty God to hearken to the supplications and prayers of an afflicted people, and to vouchsafe to the army and the navy of the United States victories on land and on the sea so signal and so effective as to furnish reasonable grounds for augmented confidence that the Union of these States will be maintained, their constitution preserved, and their peace and prosperity permanently restored. But these victories have been accorded not without sacrifices of life, limb, health and liberty incurred by brave, loyal and patriotic citizens. Domestic affliction in every part of the country follows in the train of these fearful bereavements. It is meet and right to recognize and confess the presence of the Almighty Father and the power of His Hand equally in these triumphs and in these sorrows:

Now, therefore, be it known that I do set apart Thursday the 6th. day of August next, to be observed as a day for National Thanksgiving, Praise and Prayer, and I invite the People of the United States to assemble on that occasion in their customary places of worship, and in the forms approved by their own consciences, render the homage due to the Divine Majesty, for the wonderful things he has done in the Nation's behalf, and invoke the influence of His Holy Spirit to subdue the anger, which has produced, and so long sustained a needless and cruel rebellion, to change the hearts of the insurgents, to guide the counsels of the Government with wisdom adequate to so great a national emergency, and to visit with tender care and consolation throughout the length and breadth of our land all those who, through the vicissitudes of marches, voyages, battles and sieges, have been brought to suffer in mind, body or estate, and finally to lead the whole nation, through the paths of repentance and submission to the Divine Will, back to the perfect enjoyment of Union and fraternal peace.

In witness whereof, I have hereunto set my hand and caused the seal of the United States to be affixed.

Done at the city of Washington, this fifteenth day of July, in the year of our Lord one thousand eight hundred and sixty-three, and of the Independence of the United States of America the eighty-eighth.

By the President: ABRAHAM LINCOLN

WILLIAM H. SEWARD, Secretary of State.

[*Ibid.* at 6, 332.]

On November 19, 1863, the president gave the Gettysburg Address, classic in its compact statement of principle, and concluding "that we here highly resolve these dead shall not have died in vain—that this nation, under God, shall have a new birth of freedom—and that government of the people, by the people, for the people, shall not perish from the earth," *ibid.* at 7, 23.

In March 1865, Lincoln delivered his Second Inaugural Address, a small summa of theology on the war, its divine cause, and the proper scriptural response to it:

Second Inaugural Address
March 4, 1865

At this second appearing to take the oath of the presidential office, there is less occasion for an extended address than there was at the first. Then a statement, somewhat in detail, of a course to be pursued, seemed fitting and proper. Now, at the expiration of four years, during which public declarations have been constantly called forth on every point and phase of the great contest which still absorbs the attention, and engrosses the enerergies [*sic*] of the nation, little that is new could be presented. The progress of our arms, upon which all else chiefly depends, is as well known to the public as to myself; and it is, I trust, reasonably satisfactory and encouraging to all. With high hope for the future, no prediction in regard to it is ventured.

On the occasion corresponding to this four years ago, all thoughts were anxiously directed to an impending civil war. All dreaded it—all sought to avert it. While the inaugeral [*sic*] address was being delivered from this place, devoted altogether to *saving* the Union without war, insurgent agents were in the city seeking to *destroy* it without war—seeking to dissole [*sic*] the Union, and divide effects, by negotiation. Both parties deprecated war; but one of them would *make* war rather than let the nation survive; and the other would *accept* war rather than let it perish. And the war came.

One eighth of the whole population were colored slaves, not distributed generally over the Union, but localized in the Southern part of it. These slaves constituted a peculiar and powerful interest. All knew that this interest was, somehow, the cause of the war. To strengthen, perpetuate, and extend this interest was the object for which the insurgents would rend the Union, even by war; while the government claimed no right to do more than to restrict the territorial enlargement of it. Neither party expected for the war, the magnitude, or the duration, which it has already attained. Neither anticipated that the *cause* of the conflict might cease with, or even before, the conflict itself should cease. Each looked for an easier triumph, and a result less fundamental and astounding. Both read the same Bible, and pray to the same God; and each invokes

His aid against the other. It may seem strange that any men should dare to ask a just God's assistance in wringing their bread from the sweat of other men's faces; but let us judge not that we be not judged. The prayers of both could not be answered; that of neither has been answered fully. The Almighty has His own purposes. "Woe unto the world because of offences! for it must needs be that offences come; but woe to that man by whom the offence cometh!" If we shall suppose that American Slavery is one of those offences which, in the providence of God, must needs come, but which, having continued through His appointed time, He now wills to remove, and that He gives to both North and South, this terrible war, as the woe due to those by whom the offence came, shall we discern therein any departure from those divine attributes which the believers in a Living God always ascribe to Him? Fondly do we hope—fervently do we pray—that this mighty scourge of war may speedily pass away. Yet, if God wills that it continue, until all the wealth piled by the bond-man's two hundred and fifty years of unrequited toil shall be sunk, and until every drop of blood drawn with the lash, shall be paid by another drawn with the sword, as was said three thousand years ago, so still it must be said "the judgments of the Lord, are true and righteous altogether."

With malice toward none; with charity for all; with firmness in the right, as God gives us to see the right, let us strive on to finish the work we are in; to bind up the nation's wounds; to care for him who shall have borne the battle, and for his widow, and his orphan—to do all which may achieve and cherish a just and lasting peace, among ourselves, and with all nations.

Presidential prayer; quotation of Psalm 19:9 (on the judgments of the Lord); invocation of duty to the widow and the orphan as in Deuteronomy 10:16–18; Jesus' words on not judging lest one be judged (Matt. 7:1–2); Jesus' words of woe to him by whom scandal comes (Matt. 18:7); finally an expression of charity reflecting the deepest of biblical doctrines—these were the themes of the president's formal message as the war neared its close. Less than six weeks later, on Good Friday, the president was assassinated. "Over and over again were the parallels drawn of Lincoln and Christ in blood of atonement dying for mankind," Carl Sandburg, *Abraham Lincoln* (1939) 4, 361. In the clerical-political interpretation of his death Lincoln legitimated the emancipation and confirmed the religious reading of its rightness.

5. TWO MAINLINE CHURCHES AND THE WAR

The Methodist Church had an early history of antipathy to slavery. John Wesley had formed a "Society for the Suppression of the Slave Trade." Several eighteenth-century Methodist ministers in the South denounced slavery and freed their own slaves. The "Christmas Conference" of the American Methodist Church in 1784 forbade the purchase of slaves. But most Methodists lived in the slaveholding states, and many resisted the rule laid down without any religious sanctions being applied against them. By the time of the General Conference of 1808, the Methodists were willing to compromise and accept slaveholding, Charles Baumer Swaney, *Episcopal Methodism and Slavery* (1926; reprint 1962) 1–19. When abolitionist sentiment mounted in New England, southern Methodists were advised to "shun abolition as you would the DEVIL," *ibid.* at 50). By 1839 the church had taken strong disciplinary steps to crush the abolitionists within it, *ibid.* at 100. Northern abolitionist ministers threatened secession, but in 1844 it was at the instance of Southerners that the General Conference divided the church, *ibid.* at 143. The church's prosperous publishing house, the Book Concern, was not divided without litigation. In two circuit court cases, Supreme Court Justice Samuel Nelson, a New York proslavery Presbyterian, decided for the Southern Church; while Supreme Court Justice John McLean, the most prominent Methodist in the country and an antislavery man, decided for the Northern Church. Both justices urged compromise. When one case finally reached the

Supreme Court itself, Justice Nelson wrote the opinion upholding the authority of the General Conference as "the sovereign power" in the church to divide it, *Smith v. Swormstedt*, 57 U.S. 288, 307 (1853). Justice McLean acquiesced but the disappointed side voiced its distrust of a court dominated by slaveholders, Swaney 184.

Northern Methodist journals such as *Zion's Herald* condemned the Compromise of 1850, denouncing politicians who were "pro-slavery men" or "dough-faces." The *Western Christian Advocate* sommoned "the religious press" to condemn politicians favoring the Compromise, *ibid.* at 264-265. The *Dred Scott* decision was condemned by Northern Methodist conferences, the New Hampshire Conference stigmatizing it as contrary to "the Constitution, justice and religion," *ibid.* at 277. When the war came, the bishops of the church in the North vigorously supported the government against "this infernal rebellion, the most hellish since Satan seceded from the government of Heaven," *ibid.* at 300.

The Upper Iowa Conference of the Church in 1863 noted that there were 100,000 Methodists in the Union armies, and the General Conference of 1864 wrote Lincoln stating the Church's support for the Union cause, *ibid.* at 299. Lincoln replied:

May 18, 1864

Gentlemen:

In response to your address, allow me to attest the accuracy of it's historical statements; indorse the sentiments it expresses; and thank you, in the nation's name, for the sure promise it gives.

I would utter nothing which might, in the least, appear invidious against any. Yet, without this, it may fairly be said that the Methodist Episcopal Church, not less devoted than the best, is by it's greatest numbers, the most important of all. It is no fault in others that the Methodist Church sends more soldiers to the field, more nurses to the hospital, and more prayers to Heaven than any. God bless the Methodist Church— bless all the churches—and blessed be God, Who in this our great trial, giveth us the churches [Lincoln, *Collected Works* 7, 350–351].

As a historian of Methodism notes: "One of the most important addresses delivered in behalf of Lincoln during the campaign of 1864 was that of Bishop [Matthew] Simpson, November 3, 1864. Before an immense New York audience, he gave his great lecture on 'Our Country' which had created such an intense spirit of loyalty in many other cities. This speech was reported by the leading New York papers so that he spoke to the whole nation. It probably had a large part in completing the splendid victory obtained by the President in the November election," Swaney 306. At the direction of the secretary of war, Edward Stanton, Methodist churches in the South that did not have "loyal ministers" were turned over to bishops of the Northern Church, *ibid.* at 303-305.

The General Assembly of the Presbyterian Church in 1818 declared:

We consider the voluntary enslaving of one part of the human race by another, as a gross violation of the most precious and sacred rights of human nature; as utterly inconsistent with the law of God, which requires us to love our neighbour as ourselves and as totally irreconcilable with the spirit and principles of the Gospel of Christ, which enjoin that, "all things whatsoever ye would that men should do to you, do ye even so to them." Slavery creates a paradox in the moral system—it exhibits rational, accountable, and immortal beings, in such circumstances as scarcely to leave them the power of moral action. It exhibits them as dependent on the will of others, whether they shall receive religious instruction; whether they shall know and worship the true God; whether they shall enjoy the ordinances of the Gospel; whether they shall perform the duties and cherish the endearments of husbands and wives, parents and children, neighbours and friends; whether they shall preserve their chastity and purity, or regard the dictates of justice and humanity [Robert Ellis Thompson, *A History of the Presbyterian Churches in the United States* (1895) 364].

By 1845 the General Assembly took a different view:

The Church of Christ is a spiritual body, whose jurisdiction extends only to the religious faith, and moral conduct of her members. She cannot legislate where Christ has not legislated, nor make terms of membership which he has not made. The question, therefore, which this Assembly is called upon to decide, is this: Do the Scriptures teach that the holding of slaves, without regard to circumstances, is a sin, the renunciation of which should be made a condition of membership in the church of Christ.

It is impossible to answer this question in the affirmative, without contradicting some of the plainest declarations of the word of God [*ibid.* at 369–370]

When the war came, however, the Assembly, over a strong minority protest, opted for the Union:

Resolved, 2. That this General Assembly, in the spirit of that Christian partriotism which the Scriptures enjoin, and which has always characterized this Church, do hereby acknowledge and declare our obligation to promote and perpetuate, so far as in us lies, the integrity of these United States, and to strengthen, uphold, and encourage the Federal Government in the exercise of all its functions under our noble Constitution; and to this Constitution, in all its provisions, requirements, and principles, we profess our unabated loyalty [*ibid.* at 380].

The Southern Presbyteries formed the Presbyterian Church in the Confederate States of America, declaring:

The first thing which roused our Presbyteries to look the question of separation seriously in the face, was the course of the Assembly in venturing to determine, as a Court of Jesus Christ, which it did by necessary implication, the true interpretation of the Constitution of the United States as to the kind of government it intended to form. A political theory was, to all intents and purposes, propounded, which made secession a crime, the seceding States rebellious, and the citizens who obeyed them traitors. We say nothing here as to the righteousness or unrighteousness of these decrees. What we maintain is, that, whether right or wrong, the Church had no right to make them— she transcended her sphere, and usurped the duties of the State [*ibid.*].

The services to the Confederate States of the moderator of this church were said to have been "worth more to the cause than a soldiery of ten thousand men," *ibid.* at 156.

After the war the 1866 Assembly of the northern Presbyteries declared secession a crime and made rejection of slavery as a divine institution a condition of membership in the Church. These resolutions deeply divided the Presbyteries in border states such as Missouri and Kentucky. Fifty-four ministers and 173 elders signed a "Declaration and Testimony" accusing the Assembly of acting on political questions. The Synods of Missouri and Kentucky supported this protest. The Assembly cut off these synods. The case of the Walnut Street Church in Louisville became a test as to which group should control the church property, *ibid.* at 167–169. The case reached the Supreme Court. The majority opinion was written by Samuel Miller, a Lincoln appointee and a Unitarian:

Watson v. Jones
80 U.S. (13 Wall.) 679 (1871)

This was a litigation which grew out of certain disturbances in what is known as the "Third or Walnut Street Presbyterian Church," of Louisville, Kentucky, and which resulted in a division of its members into two distinct bodies, each claiming the exclusive use of the property held and owned by that local church. The case was thus:

The Presbyterian Church in the United States is a voluntary religious organization, which has been in existence for more than three-quarters of a century. It has a written Confession of Faith, Form of Government, Book of Discipline, and Directory for Worship. The government of the church is exercised by and through an ascending series of "judicatories," known as Church Sessions, Presbyteries, Synods, and a General Assembly. . . .

The General Assembly, consisting of ministers and elders commissioned from each Presbytery under its care, is the highest judicatory of the Presbyterian Church, representing in one body all the particular churches of the denomination. Besides the power of receiving and issuing appeals and references from inferior judicatories, to review the records of Synods, and to give them advice and instruction in all cases submitted to them in conformity with the constitution of the church, it is declared that it "shall constitute the bond of union, peace, correspondence, and mutual confidence among all our churches." "To the General Assembly also belongs the power of deciding in all controversies respecting doctrine and discipline; of reproving, warning, or hearing testimony against any error in doctrine or immorality in practice, in any Church, Presbytery, or Synod; . . . of superintending the concerns of the whole church; . . . of suppressing schismatical contentions and disputations; and, in general, of recommending and attempting reformation of manners, and the promotion of charity, truth, and holiness through all the churches under their care." . . .

We have already adverted to the war of the insurrection, its action on the subject of slavery, and the feeling engendered by this action in the special congregation of the Walnut Street Church.

We now speak of the same subject of the war, of slavery, &c., in its more general relation with the judicatories above that local church, and of the way in which this local church was affected by and identified itself with the action of the more general church. From the beginning of the war to its close, the General Assembly of the Presbyterian Church at its annual meetings expressed in Declaratory Statements or Resolutions, its sense of the obligation of all good citizens to support the Federal government in that struggle; and when, by the proclamation of President Lincoln, emancipation of the slaves of the States in insurrection was announced, that body also expressed views favorable to emancipation, and adverse to the institution of slavery. At its meeting in Pittsburg in May, 1865, instructions were given to the Presbyteries, the Board of Missions, and to the Sessions of the churches, that when any person from the Southern States should make application for employment as missionary or for admission as members, or ministers of churches, inquiry should be made as to their sentiments in regard to loyalty to the government and on the subject of slavery; and if it was found that they had been guilty of voluntarily aiding the war of the rebellion, or held the doctrine announced by the large body of the churches in the insurrectionary States which had organized a new General Assembly, that "the system of negro slavery in the South is a divine institution, and that it is the peculiar mission of the Southern church to conserve that institution," they should be required to repent and forsake these sins before they could be received.

In the month of September thereafter the Presbytery of Louisville, under whose immediate jurisdiction was the Walnut Street Church, adopted and published in pamphlet form, what it called *"A Declaration and Testimony against the erroneous and heretical doctrines and practices which have obtained and been propagated in the Presbyterian Church of the United States during the last five years."* This Declaration denounced, in the severest terms, the action of the General Assembly in the matters we have just mentioned, declared an intention to refuse to be governed by that action, and invited the co-operation of all members of the Presbyterian Church who shared the sentiments of the Declaration, in a concerted resistance to what they called "the usurpation of authority" by the Assembly.

The General Assembly of 1866, denounced in turn the Declaration and Testimony and declared that every Presbytery which refused to obey its order should be *ipso facto* dissolved, and called to answer before the next General Assembly; giving the Louisville Presbytery an opportunity for repentance and conformity. The Louisville Presbytery divided, and the adherents of the Declaration and Testimony sought and obtained admission, in 1868, into "the Presbyterian Church of the Confederate States," a body which had several years previously withdrawn from the General Assembly of the United States and set up a new organization. . . .

On the 1st of June, 1867, the Presbytery and Synod recognized by *Watson and his party,* were declared by the General Assembly to be "in no sense a true and lawful Synod and Presbytery in connection with and under the care and authority of the General Assembly of the Presbyterian Church in the United States of America;" and were permanently excluded from connection with or representation in the Assembly. By the same resolution the Synod and Presbytery adhered to by those whom *Watson and his party* opposed were declared to be the true and lawful Presbytery of Louisville and Synod of Kentucky.

Justice Miller now delivered the opinion of the court.

This case belongs to a class, happily rare in our courts, in which one of the parties to a controversy, essentially ecclesiastical, resorts to the judicial tribunals of the State for the maintenance of rights which the church has refused to acknowledge, or found itself unable to protect. Much as such dissensions among the members of a religious society should be regretted, a regret which is increased when passing from the control of the judicial and legislative bodies of the entire organization to which the society belongs, an appeal is made to the secular authority; the courts when so called on must perform their functions as in other cases.

Religious organizations come before us in the same attitude as other voluntary associations for benevolent or charitable purposes, and their rights of property, or of contract, are equally under the protection of the law, and the actions of their members subject to its restraints. Conscious as we may be of the excited feeling engendered by this controversy, and of the extent to which it has agitated the intelligent and pious body of Christians in whose bosom it originated, we enter upon its consideration with the satisfaction of knowing that the principles which we are to decide so much of it as is proper for our decision, are those applicable alike to all of its class, and that our duty is the simple one of applying those principles to the facts before us. . . .

But the third of these classes of cases is the one which is oftenest found in the courts, and which, with reference to the number and difficulty of the questions involved, and to other considerations, is every way the most important.

It is the case of property acquired in any of the usual modes for the general use of a religious congregation which is itself part of a large and general organization of some religious denomination, with which it is more or less intimately connected by religious views and ecclesiastical government.

The case before us is one of this class, growing out of a schism which has divided the congregation and its officers, and the presbytery and synod, and which appeals to the courts to determine the right to the use of the property so acquired. Here is no case of property devoted forever by the instrument which conveyed it, or by any specific declaration of its owner, to the support of any special religious dogmas, or any peculiar form of worship, but of property purchased for the use of a religious congregation, and so long as any existing religious congregation can be ascertained to be that congregation, or its regular and legitimate successor, it is entitled to the use of the property. In the case of an independent congregation we have pointed out how this identity, or succession, is to be ascertained, but in cases of this character we are bound to look at the fact that the local congregation is itself but a member of a much larger and more important religious organization, and is under its government and control, and is bound by its orders and judgments. There are in the Presbyterian system of ecclesiastical government, in regular succession, the presbytery over the session or local church, the synod over the presbytery, and the General Assembly over all. These are called, in the language of the church organs, "judicatories," and they entertain appeals from the decisions of those below, and prescribe corrective measures in other cases.

In this class of cases we think the rule of action which should govern the civil courts, founded in a broad and sound view of the relations of church and state under our system of laws, and supported by a preponderating weight of judicial authority is, that, whenever the questions of discipline, or of faith, or ecclesiastical rule, custom, or law have been decided by the highest of these church judicatories to which the matter has been carried, the legal tribunals must accept such decisions as final, and as binding on them, in their application to the case before them. . . .

In this country the full and free right to entertain any religious belief, to practice any religious principle, and to teach any religious doctrine which does not violate the laws of morality and property, and which does not infringe personal rights, is conceded to all. The law knows no heresy, and is committed to the support of no dogma, the establishment of no sect. The right to organize voluntary religious associations to assist in the expression and dissemination of any religious doctrine, and to create tribunals for the decision of controverted questions of faith within the association, and for the ecclesiastical government of all the individual members, congregations, and officers within the general association, is unquestioned. All who unite themselves to such a body do so with an implied consent to this government, and are bound to submit to it. But it would be a vain consent and would lead to the total subversion of such religious bodies, if any one aggrieved by one of their decisions could appeal to the secular courts and have them reversed. It is of the essence of these religious unions, and of their right to establish tribunals for the decision of questions arising among themselves, that those decisions should be binding in all cases of ecclesiastical cognizance, subject only to such appeals as the organism itself provides for.

Nor do we see that justice would be likely to be promoted by submitting those decisions to review in the ordinary judicial tribunals. Each of these large and influential bodies (to mention no others, let reference be had to the Protestant Episcopal, the Methodist Episcopal, and the Presbyterian churches), has a body of constitutional and ecclesiastical law of its own, to be found in their written organic laws, their books of discipline, in their collections of precedents, in their usage and customs, which as to each constitute a system of ecclesiastical law and religious faith that tasks the ablest minds to become familiar with. It is not to be supposed that the judges of the civil courts can be as competent in the ecclesiastical law and religious faith of all these bodies as the ablest men in each are in reference to their own. It would therefore be an appeal from the more learned tribunal in the law which should decide the case, to one which is less so.

The Court of Appeals of Kentucky, in the case of *Watson v. Avery,* before referred to, while admitting the general principle here laid down, maintains that when a decision of an ecclesiastical tribunal is set up in the civil courts, it is always open to inquiry whether the tribunal acted within its jurisdiction, and if it did not, its decision could not be conclusive.

There is, perhaps, no word in legal terminology so frequently used as the word jurisdiction, so capable of use in a general and vague sense, and which is used so often by men learned in the law without a due regard to precision in its application. As regards its use in the matters we have been discussing it may very well be conceded that if the General Assembly of the Presbyterian Church should undertake to try one of its members for murder, and punish him with death or imprisonment, its sentence would be of no validity in a civil court or anywhere else. Or if it should at the instance of one of its members entertain jurisdiction as between him and another member as to their individual right to property, real or personal, the right in no sense depending on ecclesiastical questions, its decision would be utterly disregarded by any civil court where it might be set up. And it might be said in a certain general sense very justly, that it was because the General Assembly had no jurisdiction of the case. Illustrations of this character could by multiplied in which the proposition of the Kentucky court would be strictly applicable.

But it is a very different thing where a subject-matter of dispute, strictly and purely ecclesiastical in its character,—a matter over which the civil courts exercise no juris-diction,—a matter which concerns theological controversy, church discipline, ecclesiast-ical government, or the conformity of the members of the church to the standard of morals required of them,—becomes the subject of its action. It may be said here, also, that no jurisdiction has been conferred on the tribunal to try the particular case before it, or that, in its judgment, it exceeds the powers conferred upon it, or that the laws of the church do not authorize the particular form of proceeding adopted; and, in a sense often used in the courts, all of those may be said to be questions of jurisdiction. But it is easy to see that if the civil courts are to inquire into all these matters, the whole subject of the doctrinal theology, the usages and customs, the written laws, and fundamental organization of every religious denomination may, and must, be examined into with minuteness and care, for they would become, in almost every case, the *criteria* by which the validity of the ecclesiastical decree would be determined in the civil court.

. . .

The novelty of the questions presented to this court for the first time, their intrinsic importance and far-reaching influence, and the knowledge that the schism in which the case originated has divided the Presbyterian churches throughout Kentucky and Missouri, have seemed to us to justify the careful and laborious examination and discussion which we have made of the principles which should govern the case. For the same reasons we have held it under advisement for a year; not uninfluenced by the hope, that since the civil commotion, which evidently lay at the foundation of the trouble, has passed away, that charity, which is so large an element in the faith of both parties, and which, by one of the apostles of that religion, is said to be the greatest of all the Christian virtues, would have brought about a reconciliation. But we have been dis-appointed. It is not for us to determine or apportion the moral responsibility which attaches to the parties for this result. We can only pronounce the judgment of the law as applicable to the case presented to us, and that requires us to affirm the decree of the Circuit Court as it stands.

DECREE AFFIRMED.

The Chief Justice did not sit on the argument of this case, and took no part in its decision.

Mr. Justice Clifford with whom concurred Mr. Justice Davis, dissented.

NOTE: *Bouldin v. Alexander,* 82 U.S. (15 Wall.) 131 (1872). Albert Bouldin, a black minister, founded the Third Colored Baptist Church in Washington, D.C. Some years later the congregation divided, each faction claiming to be the Third Colored Baptist Church. In June 1867 Bouldin and a minority of the congregation voted to "turn out" four of the seven trustees who had been elected in February 1867. The Bouldin group gained control of the building. The Philadelphia Baptist Association, described in the statement of the case as "an ancient authoritative body of the Baptist Church," recognized the trustees aligned with the majority. In an action by these trustees to recover the money of the church from Bouldin, the Supreme Court held for the majority trustees. The trustees, the Court said, might be excommunicated but they could not be turned out as trustees "by a minority of the church society or meeting, without warning, and acting without charges, without citation or trial, and in direction contravention of the church rules." The case came on appeal from the District of Columbia. The First Amendment was not mentioned in the opinion by Justice William Strong for a unanimous Court.

6. THE FOURTEENTH AMENDMENT

In the immediate aftermath of the war, the Fourteenth Amendment passed Congress in the first half of 1866 and was found to be ratified by the requisite number of states by the summer of 1868. As the Fourteenth Amendment was to become, much later, the chief vehicle for applying the First Amendment to the states, it is appropriate to note its terms and contemporaneous understanding of them:

Section 1. All persons born or naturalized in the United States, and subject to the jurisdiction thereof, are citizens of the United States and of the State wherein they reside. No State shall make or enforce any law which shall abridge the privileges or immunities of citizens of the United States; nor shall any State deprive any person of life, liberty, or property, without due process of law; nor deny to any person within its jurisdiction the equal protection of the laws.

While the Fourteenth Amendment was pending ratification, a case illustrated the existing narrow understanding of the protection accorded by the Constitution to the free exercise of religion. In 1865, Missouri by popular vote had amended its constitution and prescribed an oath to be taken by every officeholder, lawyer, teacher, and clergyman that declared that he had not "ever, by act or word, manifested his adherence to the cause of such enemies [the Confederate States] or his desire for their triumph over the arms of the United States or his sympathy with those engaged in exciting or carrying on rebellion against the United States," *Cummings v. Missouri,* 71 U.S. (4 Wall.) 277, 279–281 (1866). Father Cummings, a Catholic priest, was convicted of preaching without having taken the oath and fined $500; the Supreme Court of Missouri affirmed. On appeal to the Supreme Court of the United States, Cummings, represented by David Dudley Field, attacked the law as violating the Constitution of the United States, Article I, section 10, which provides "No State shall . . . pass any Bill of Attainder, ex post facto Law or Law impairing the Obligation of Contracts." This provision had been applied by Chief Justice John Marshall in regard to contracts and described by him as "what may be deemed a bill of rights for the people of each state," *Fletcher v. Peck,* 10 U.S. (6 Cranch) 87 at 137 (1810). Field made little of the statute's intrusion on religion except to say: "It would be strange, indeed, if a minister of the Gospel, whose sympathies are with all the children of men—the good and the sinful, the happy and the sorrowing—might not manifest such sympathy by an act of charity or a word of consolation." *Cummings* at 285.

Four pre-Civil War appointees voted against the statute. The swing vote was that of Stephen Field, whose brother David Dudley argued for Father Cummings. The Fields were sons of a country Congregationalist, a Massachusetts minister in Stockbridge. Stephen Field voted to uphold his brother's contention that Article I, section 10, had been violated, *Cummings* at 325, 327. Justice Field made no reference to religion as such having any special protection. The decision came down in the spring of 1867 and underscored the contemporary view that the Constitution did not extend the Bill of Rights to the states.

Four of five of Lincoln's appointees to the Court voted to uphold the statute. Their dissent was attached to *Ex parte Garland,* 71 U.S. (4 Wall.) at 397 (1866). Samuel F. Miller, a Unitarian and religious liberal, wrote apropos religious rights:

In regard to the case of *Cummings v. The State of Missouri,* allusions have been made in the course of argument to the sanctity of the ministerial office, and to the inviolability of religious freedom in this country.

But no attempt has been made to show that the Constitution of the United States interposes any such protection between the State governments and their own citizens. Nor can anything of this kind be shown. The Federal Constitution contains but two provisions on this subject. One of these forbids Congress to make any law respecting the establishment of religion, or prohibiting the free exercise thereof. The other is, that no religious test shall ever be required as a qualification to any office or public trust under the United States.

No restraint is placed by that instrument on the action of the States; but on the contrary, in the language of Story, "the whole power over the subject of religion is left exclusively to the State governments, to be acted upon according to their own sense of justice and the State constitutions."

If there ever was a case calling upon this court to exercise all the power on this subject which properly belongs to it, it was the case of the Rev. B. Permoli.

An ordinance of the first municipality of the city of New Orleans imposed a penalty on any priest who should officiate at any funeral, in any other church than the obituary chapel. Mr. Permoli, a Catholic priest, performed the funeral services of his church over the body of one of his parishioners, inclosed in a coffin, in the Roman Catholic Church of St. Augustine. For this he was fined, and relying upon the vague idea advanced here, that the Federal Constitution protected him in the exercise of his holy functions, he brought the case to this court.

But hard as that case was, the court replied to him in the following language: "The Constitution (of the United States) makes no provision for protecting the citizens of the respective States in their religious liberties; this is left to the State constitutions and laws; nor is there any inhibition imposed by the Constitution of the United States in this respect on the States." Mr. Permoli's writ of error was, therefore, dismissed for want of jurisdiction.

In that case an ordinance of a mere local corporation forbids a priest, loyal to his government, from performing what he believed to be the necessary rites of his church over the body of his departed friend. This court said it could give him no relief.

In this case the constitution of the State of Missouri, the fundamental law of the people of that State, adopted by their popular vote, declares that no priest of any church shall exercise his ministerial functions, unless he will show, by his own oath, that he has borne a true allegiance to his government. This court now holds this constitutional provision void, on the ground that the Federal Constitution forbids it. I leave the two cases to speak for themselves.

That the Fourteenth Amendment was chiefly intended to protect the rights of the recently freed slaves is incontestable. The first sentence of section 1 denied the doctrine of *Dred Scott* that descendants of black slaves could never be citizens. The second sentence gave a constitutional basis for condemning laws discriminating against blacks. But did the amendment have implications for religious freedom and religious establishment?

Senator Jacob M. Howard, reporting the amendment to the Senate from the Joint Committee on Reconstruction had this to say:

Such is the character of the privileges and immunities spoken of in the second section of the fourth article of the Constitution. To these privileges and immunities, whatever they may be—for they are not and cannot be fully defined in their entire extent and precise nature—to these should be added the personal rights guarantied and secured by the first eight amendments of the Constitution; such as the freedom of speech and of the press; the right of the people peaceably to assemble and petition the Government for a redress of grievances, a right appertaining to each and all the people; the right to keep and to bear arms; the right to be exempted from the quartering of soldiers in a house without the consent of the owner; the right to be exempt from unreasonable searches and seizures, and from any search or seizure except by virtue of a warrant issued upon a formal oath or affidavit; the right of an accused person to be informed of the nature of the accusation against him, and his right to be tried by an impartial jury of the vicinage; and also the right to be secure against excessive bail and against cruel and unusual punishments [*Congressional Globe,* 39th Congress, 1st Session, 2765].

This statement does not mention freedom of religion, but purports to be illustrative, not comprehensive.

In contrast, Senator Luke Poland, former chief justice of Vermont, declared:

The clause of the first proposed amendment, that "no State shall make or enforce any law which shall abridge the privileges or immunities of citizens of the United States," secures nothing beyond what was intended by the original provision in the Constitution, that "the citizens of each State shall be entitled to all privileges and immunities of citizens in the several States" [*ibid.* at 296].

The "original Constitution" does not contain the First Amendment.

The most explicit statement as to the meaning of section 1 was made by Representative John A. Bingham of Ohio, a member of the Joint Committee on Reconstruction and the actual draftsman of section 1, Charles Fairman, "Does the Fourteenth Amendment Incorporate the Bill of Rights?" 2 *Stan. L. Rev.* 5, 19, 21 (1949). Five years after his drafting, Bingham in debate in the House declared:

Mr. Speaker, that the scope and meaning of the limitations imposed by the first section, fourteenth amendment of the Constitution may be more fully understood, permit me to say that the privileges and immunities of citizens of the United States, as contra-distinguished from citizens of a State, are chiefly defined in the first eight amendments to the Constitution of the United States [*Congressional Globe,* 42nd Congress, 1st Session (1871) 151].

On the other hand, Representative Bingham, running for reelection in 1866, had explained section 1 in a speech at Bowerstown, Ohio, on August 24:

It is the spirit of Christianity embodied in your legislation. It is a simple, strong, plain declaration that equal laws and equal and exact justice shall hereafter be secured within every State of this Union by the combined power of all the people of every State. It takes from no State any right which hitherto pertained to the several States of the Union, but it imposes a limitation upon the States to correct their abuses of power, which hitherto did not exist within the letter of your Constitution, and which is essential to the nation's life. Look at that simple proposition. No State shall deny to any person, no matter whence he comes, or how poor, how weak, how simple—no matter how friendless—no State shall deny to any person within its jurisdiction the equal protection of the laws. If there be any man here who objects to a proposition as just as that, I would like him to rise in his place and let his neighbors look at him and see what manner of man he is. That proposition, I think, my fellow-citizens, needs no argument. No man can look his fellow-man in the face, surrounded by this clear light of heaven in which we live, and dare to utter the proposition that of right any State in the Union shall deny to any human being who behaves himself well the equal protection of the laws. Paralysis ought to strangle the utterance upon the tongue before a man should be guilty of the blasphemy of saying that he himself to the exclusion of his fellow man, should enjoy the protection of the laws. I hazard nothing, I think, in saying to the American people that the adoption of that amendment by the people, and its enforcement by the laws of the nation is, in the future, as essential to the safety and peace of this Republic, as is the air which surrounds us essential to the life of the people of the nation. Hereafter the American people can not have peace, if, as in the past, States are permitted to take away freedom of speech, and to condemn men, as felons, to the penitentiary for teaching their fellow men that there is a hereafter, and a reward for those who learn to do well [Fairman 76].

The reference to penalizing persons who teach "that there is a hereafter" probably is to slave-state laws against preaching to slaves. No reference is made to the establishment part of the First Amendment. Rather, Bingham endorses a kind of establishment: the embodiment in legislation of "the spirit of Christianity."

Howard's statement in 1866 and Bingham's in 1871 are the strongest evidence that the Fourteenth Amendment was meant to incorporate the Bill of Rights wholesale. Against this understanding, the amendment was ratified by states whose own constitutions were inconsistent with the Bill of Rights. Connecticut, the first to ratify, did not require indictment by grand jury as the Bill of Rights (Amendment VI) does. New Jersey did not require a jury trial in all civil suits as the Bill of Rights (Amendment VII) does. Most relevantly for our purposes, New Hampshire—the second state to ratify—had a Constitution modeled on that of Massachusetts of 1780, empowering the legislature to make provision through the towns for the support of "public Protestant teachers of piety, religion, and morality," and only Protestants were eligible to be governor or to sit in the legislature.

On December 14, 1875, James G. Blaine, a leader of the Republican Party, introduced the following amendment to the Constitution:

No State shall make any law respecting an establishment of religion or prohibiting the free exercise thereof; and no money raised by taxation in any State for the support of public schools, or derived from any public fund therefor, nor any public lands devoted thereto, shall ever be under the control of any religious sect, nor shall any money so raised or lands so devoted by divided between religious sects or denominations [4 *Congressional Record* (1875) 205].

The timing indicated that the Republicans saw the Blaine amendment as a campaign issue for 1876. It passed the House 116–5, *ibid.* at 5192.

The Senate Judiciary Committee made it much stronger:

Article XVI

No State shall make any law respecting an establishment of religion, or prohibiting the free exercise thereof; and no religious test shall ever be required as a qualification to any office or public trust under any State. No public property, and no public revenue of, nor any loan of credit by or under the authority of the United States, or any State, Territory, District, or municipal corporation, shall be appropriated to, or made or used for, the support of any school, educational or other institution, under the control of any religious or anti-religious sect, organization, or denomination, or wherein the particular creed or tenets of any religious or anti-religious sect, organization, or denomination shall be taught; and no such particular creed or tenets shall be read or taught in any school or institution supported in whole or in part by such revenue or loan of credit; and no such appropriation or loan of credit shall be made to any religious or anti-religious sect, organization, or denomination, or to promote its interests or tenets. This article shall not be construed to prohibit the reading of the Bible in any school or institution, and it shall not have the effect to impair rights of property already voted.

Sec. 2. Congress shall have power, by appropriate legislation, to provide for the prevention and punishment of violations of this article [*ibid.* at 5580].

In debate, Senator George F. Edmunds read from the encyclical letter *Quanta cura* of Pius IX, of December 8, 1864:

Contrary to the teaching of the Holy Scriptures, of the Church, and of the holy fathers, these persons do not hesitate to assert that "the best condition of human society is that wherein no duty is recognized by the Government of correcting by enacted penalties the violators of the Catholic religion, except when the maintenance of the public peace requires it." From this totally false notion of social government they fear not to uphold that erroneous opinion most pernicious to the Catholic Church and to the salvation of souls which was called by our predecessor Gregory XVI . . . "insanity" . . . (*deliramentum*), namely, that "liberty of conscience and of worship is the right of every man; and that this right ought in every well governed state, to be proclaimed and asserted by law; and that the citizens possess the right of being unrestrained in the exercise of every kind of liberty, by any law, ecclesiastical or civil, so that they are authorized to publish and put forward openly all their ideas whatsoever, either by speaking, in print, or by any other method." But while these men make these rash assertions, they do not reflect or consider that they preach the liberty of perdition, (St. Augustine, Epistle 105, al. 106) and that, "if it is always free to human arguments to discuss men will never be wanting who will dare to resist the truth, and to rely upon the loquacity of human wisdom, when we know from the command of our Lord Jesus Christ how faith and Christian wisdom ought to avoid this most mischievous vanity" (St. Leo, Epistle 164, al. 133, section 2, Boll. edition).

Edmunds added a quotation from the *Syllabus of Errors*, a compendium of propositions also condemned by Pius IX:

45. The entire direction of public schools in which the youth of Christian states are educated, except (to a certain extent) in the case of episcopal seminaries, may and must appertain to the civil power, and belong to it so far that no other authority whatsoever shall be recognized as having any right to interfere in the discipline of the schools, the arrangement of the studies, the taking of degrees, or the choice and approval of the teachers.

In the light of this doctrine, Edmunds asked how the Democrats could oppose the amendment, *Congressional Record* 4, 5587–5588. The Democrats contended that the amendment would harm religious activities in all government hospitals, orphanages, prisons, and veterans' homes, *ibid.* at 5595. The amendment was rejected by the Senate, *ibid.* at 5595.

Both sides assumed and stated that without an amendment no federal constitutional provision controlled the states' support of religion, *e.g., ibid.* at 5561 (Senator Freylinghuysen); 5589 (Senator Adlai Stevenson).

NINE

"The Civilization That Christianity Has Produced": Marriage, 1852–1890

ON SEPTEMBER 21, 1823, according to Mormon belief, the angel Moroni appeared to Joseph Smith telling him of the existence of a book of divine revelations, written by Moroni's father, Mormon. From this beginning came the organization, in 1830 in Fayette, New York, of the Church of Christ, later known as the Church of Jesus Christ of Latter-Day Saints, Richard L. Bushman, *Joseph Smith and the Beginnings of Mormonism* (1984) 143; Leonard J. Arrington and Davis Bitton, *The Mormon Experience: A History of the Latter Day Saints* (1979) 8, 20–21. Tolerance, by now fairly general in the United States toward every variety of Protestant Christianity, was not extended to this church. It was hounded out of Missouri and Illinois. Joseph Smith was killed by a mob. Under Brigham Young, the Mormons emigrated West and founded a new "kingdom" where, at first, religious services and civic meetings were generally combined (Arrington and Bitton 116). In 1850, their community became a territory of the United States with Young as governor.

The novelty of a book added to Scripture, and the corporate enterprise of the Mormons and its substantial success, were irritants to their non-Mormon neighbors. But what led to the religious clash resulting in federal legislation challenging the church was more fundamental. In 1852 a general conference of the church announced that plural marriage should, if possible, be practiced by Mormon males. In fact only a minority of 7 or 8 percent did, chiefly those higher up in the church, Thomas O'Dea, *The Mormons* (1957) 246. As late as 1880 the population of Utah consisted of 74,509 males and 69,454 females, a ratio suggesting how impractical widespread practice would have been. Polygamy, however, became the focal point of religious attention. It was opposed to the understanding of Scripture of virtually all other Christian denominations. Like slavery, the practice in the minds of its critics carried with it sinister suggestions of sexual licentiousness. Worse than slavery, it formally challenged the accepted sexual code of the rest of the country. Like the split on slavery, the division was deep; theological; past compromise. Either the Mormons were right about the relationship between the sexes or the challenged religious view was. The use of governmental power by those who believed in the traditional Christian sexual norms was seen as the way to meet the challenge.

The Republican Platform of 1856 read:

Resolved that the Constitution confers upon Congress sovereign power over the Territories of the United States for their government, and that in the exercise of this power it is both the right and the imperative duty of Congress to prohibit in the Territories those twin relics of barbarianism, polygamy and slavery [*Platforms of the Two Great Political Parties,* comp. George D. Ellis (1928) 13].

The Democrats also saw political possibilities in the situation. Robert Taylor, a champion of southern rights, wrote President James Buchanan on April 27, 1857: "I believe that we can supersede the Negro-Mania with the almost universal excitements of an Anti-Mormon crusade," quoted in Norman F. Furniss, *The Mormon Conflict, 1850–1859* (1960) 74–75. When Buchanan later in 1857 ordered federal troops into the territory, it was seen by many as an effort to "root out polygamy as an affront to Christian morality," *ibid.* at 82.

Not until the Civil War, however, did Congress actually legislate. It then passed "An Act to punish and prevent the Practice of Polygamy in the Territories of the United States . . . ," 12 *Stat.* 501–502 (1862). Bigamy was subjected to a $500 fine or five years' imprisonment. Acts of the territorial legislature incorporating the Church of Jesus Christ of the Latter-Day Saints and countenancing polygamy were annulled, with the proviso that the act was to be "so limited and constructed" as not to affect existing property rights nor "the right 'to worship God according to the dictates of conscience.'" A further provision—"in the nature of a mortmain law," as Senator James Bayard told the Senate, *Congressional Globe,* (June 3, 1862) 2506—limited future acquisitions by churches of real estate in any territory to $50,000. The measure had originated in the House, which had framed a bill as early as 1860. The sponsor in 1862 was Justin Morrill of Vermont; his measure passed the House without a record vote, *ibid.* (April 28, 1862) 1847. The most significant change made in the Senate was removal of a penalty for mere cohabitation without marriage. It was the formal institution of plural marriage to which Congress objected, *ibid.* (June 3, 1862) 2506. On July 2, 1862, Abraham Lincoln signed the bill into law, *ibid.* at 3082.

The statute was not enforced. But the completion of the Union Pacific in 1869 brought more non-Mormons—"Gentiles" to the Saints—into Utah. By 1869 there was also internal dissent. William Godbe was tried by the Church for heresy and was expelled, leading him to form the independent Church of Zion. The dissension encouraged Schuyler Colfax, vice-president of the United States, to go to Utah and in a public speech in Salt Lake City to urge the Mormons to give way on polygamy, Leonard J. Arrington, *Brigham Young: American Moses* (1985) 355–361, 374–375. John Taylor, an apostle of the Church of Latter-Day Saints, replied in the New York *Tribune*:

Loyola did not invent and put into use the faggot, the flame, the sword, the thumbscrews, the rack and gibbet to persecute anybody; it was to purify the Church of heretics, as others would purify Utah. "Ours," says Mr. Colfax, "is a land of civil and religious liberty, and the faith of every man is a matter between himself and God alone,"—providing God don't shock our moral ideas by introducing something we don't believe in. If He does, let Him look out.

The religious issue was central. In 1870, for example, the chaplain for the Senate, John P. Newman, a leading Methodist, traveled to Salt Lake City to debate Brigham Young for three days in the Tabernacle. The subject: "Does the Bible Sanction Polygamy?," Arrington and Bitton 178. Methodists and Presbyterians urged Congress to act. In 1874 Congress passed the proposal of another Vermont congressman, Luke Poland, extending direct federal control over most legal cases in the territory, *ibid.* at 177.

In 1875 George Reynolds, secretary to Brigham Young, was indicted under the Morrill Act. Married to Mary Ann Tuddenham, he had also married Amelia Jane Schofield. Reynolds was convicted and sentenced to two years at hard labor. He appealed to the Supreme Court of the United States.

Morrison R. Waite, Chief Justice, delivered the opinion of the unanimous Court:

Reynolds v. United States
98 U.S. 145 (1879)

. . .

As to the defence of religious belief or duty.

On the trial, the plaintiff in error, the accused, proved that at the time of his alleged second marriage he was, and for many years before had been, a member of the Church of Jesus Christ of Latter-Day Saints, commonly called the Mormon Church, and a believer in its doctrines; that it was an accepted doctrine of that church "that it was the duty of male members of said church, circumstances permitting, to practise polygamy; . . . that this duty was enjoined by different books which the members of said church believed to be of divine origin, and among others the Holy Bible, and also that the members of the church believed that the practice of polygamy was directly enjoined upon the male members thereof by the Almighty God, in a revelation to Joseph Smith, the founder and prophet of said church; that the failing or refusing to practise polygamy by such male members of said church, when circumstances would admit, would be punished, and that the penalty for such failure and refusal would be damnation in the life to come." He also proved "that he had received permission from the recognized authorities in said church to enter into polygamous marriage; . . . that Daniel H. Wells, one having authority in said church to perform the marriage ceremony, married the said defendant on or about the time the crime is alleged to have been committed, to some woman by the name of Schofield, and that such marriage ceremony was performed under and pursuant to the doctrines of said church."

Upon this proof he asked the court to instruct the jury that if they found from the evidence that he "was married as charged—if he was married—in pursuance of and in conformity with what he believed at the time to be a religious duty, that the verdict must be 'not guilty.'" This request was refused, and the court did charge "that there must have been a criminal intent, but that if the defendant, under the influence of a religious belief that it was right,—under an inspiration, if you please, that it was right,—deliberately married a second time, having a first wife living, the want of consciousness of evil intent—the want of understanding on his part that he was committing a crime—did not excuse him; but the law inexorably in such case implies the criminal intent."

Upon this charge and refusal to charge the question is raised, whether religious belief can be accepted as a justification of an overt act made criminal by the law of the land. The inquiry is not as to the power of Congress to prescribe criminal laws for the Territories, but as to the guilt of one who knowingly violates a law which has been properly enacted, if he entertains a religious belief that the law is wrong.

Congress cannot pass a law for the government of the Territories which shall prohibit the free exercise of religion. The first amendment to the Constitution expressly forbids such legislation. Religious freedom is guaranteed everywhere throughout the United States, so far as congressional interference is concerned. The question to be determined is, whether the law now under consideration comes within this prohibition.

The word "religion" is not defined in the Constitution. We must go elsewhere, therefore, to ascertain its meaning, and nowhere more appropriately, we think, than to the history of the times in the midst of which the provision was adopted. The precise point of the inquiry is, what is the religious freedom which has been guaranteed.

Before the adoption of the Constitution, attempts were made in some of the colonies and States to legislate not only in respect to the establishment of religion, but in respect to its doctrines and precepts as well. The people were taxed, against their will, for the support of religion, and sometimes for the support of particular sects to whose tenets they could not and did not subscribe. Punishments were prescribed for a failure to attend upon public worship, and sometimes for entertaining heretical opinions. The controversy upon this general subject was animated in many of the States, but seemed at last to culminate in Virginia. In 1784, the House of Delegates of that State having under consideration "a bill establishing provision for teachers of the Christian religion," postponed it until the next session, and directed that the bill should be published and distributed, and that the people be requested "to signify their opinion respecting the adoption of such a bill at the next session of assembly."

This brought out a determined opposition. Amongst others, Mr. Madison prepared a "Memorial and Remonstrance," which was widely circulated and signed, and in which he demonstrated "that religion, or the duty we owe the Creator," was not within the cognizance of civil government. Semple's Virginia Baptists, Appendix. At the next session the proposed bill was not only defeated, but another, "for establishing religious freedom," drafted by Mr. Jefferson, was passed. 1 Jeff. Works, 45; 2 Howison, Hist. of Va. 298. In the preamble of this act (12 Hening's Stat. 84) religious freedom is defined; and after a recital "that to suffer the civil magistrate to intrude his powers into the field of opinion, and to restrain the profession or propagation of principles on supposition of their ill tendency, is a dangerous fallacy which at once destroys all religious liberty," it is declared "that it is time enough for the rightful purposes of civil government for its officers to interfere when principles break out into overt acts against peace and good order." In these two sentences is found the true distinction between what properly belongs to the church and what to the State.

In a little more than a year after the passage of this statute the convention met which prepared the Constitution of the United States. Of this convention Mr. Jefferson was not a member, he being then absent as minister to France. As soon as he saw the draft of the Constitution proposed for adoption, he, in a letter to a friend, expressed his disappointment at the absence of an express declaration insuring the freedom of religion (2 Jeff. Works, 855), but was willing to accept it as it was, trusting that the good sense and honest intentions of the people would bring about the necessary alterations.1 Jeff. Works, 79. Five of the States, while adopting the Constitution, proposed amendments. Three—New Hampshire, New York, and Virginia—included in one form or another a declaration of religious freedom in the changes they desired to have made, as did also North Carolina, where the convention at first declined to ratify the Constitution until the proposed amendments were acted upon. Accordingly, at the first session of the first Congress the amendment now under consideration was proposed with others by Mr. Madison. It met the views of the advocates of religious freedom, and was adopted. Mr. Jefferson afterwards, in reply to an address to him by a committee of the Danbury Baptist Association (8 id. 113), took occasion to say: "Believing with you that religion is a matter which lies solely between man and his God; that he owes account to none other for his faith or his worship; that the legislative powers of the government reach actions only, and not opinions,—I contemplate with sovereign reverence that act of the whole American people which declared that their legislature should 'make no law respecting an establishment of religion or prohibiting the free exercise thereof,' thus building a wall of separation between church and State. Adhering to this expression of the supreme will of the nation in behalf of the rights of conscience, I shall see with sincere satisfaction the progress of those sentiments which tend to restore man to all his natural rights, convinced he has no natural right in opposition to his social duties." Coming as this does from an acknowledged leader of the advocates of the measure, it may be accepted almost as an authoritative declaration of the scope and effect of the amendment thus secured. Congress was deprived of all legislative power over mere opinion, but was left free to reach actions which were in violation of social duties or subversive of good order.

Polygamy has always been odious among the northern and western nations of Europe, and, until the establishment of the Mormon Church, was almost exclusively a feature of the life of Asiatic and of African people. At common law, the second marriage was always void (2 Kent, Com. 79), and from the earliest history of England polygamy has been treated as an offence against society. After the establishment of the ecclesiastical courts, and until the time of James I, it was punished through the instrumentality of those tribunals, not merely because ecclesiastical rights had been violated, but because upon the separation of the ecclesiastical courts from the civil the ecclesiastical were supposed to be the most appropriate for the trial of matrimonial causes and offences against the rights of marriage, just as they were for testamentary causes and the settlement of the estates of deceased persons.

By the statute of 1 James I. (c.11), the offence, if committed in England or Wales, was made punishable in the civil courts, and the penalty was death. As this statute was limited in its operation to England and Wales, it was at a very early period re-enacted, generally with some modifications, in all the colonies. In connection with the case we are now considering, it is a significant fact that on the 8th of December, 1788, after the passage of the act establishing religious freedom, and after the convention of Virginia had recommended as an amendment to the Constitution of the United States the declaration in a bill of rights that "all men have an equal, natural, and unalienable right to the free exercise of religion, according to the dictates of conscience," the legislature of that State substantially enacted the statute of James I., death penalty included, because, as recited in the preamble, "it hath been doubted whether bigamy or polygamy be punishable by the laws of this Commonwealth." 12 Hening's Stat. 691. From that day to this we think it may safely be said there never has been a time in any State of the Union when polygamy has not been an offence against society, cognizable by the civil courts and punishable with more or less severity. In the face of all this evidence, it is impossible to believe that the constitutional guaranty of religious freedom was intended to prohibit legislation in respect to this most important feature of social life. Marriage, while from its very nature a sacred obligation, is nevertheless, in most civilized nations, a civil contract, and usually regulated by law. Upon it society may be said to be built, and out of its fruits spring social relations and social obligations and duties, with which government is necessarily required to deal. In fact, according as monogamous or polygamous marriages are allowed, do we find the principles on which the government of the people, to a greater or less extent, rests. Professor Lieber says, polygamy leads to the patriarchal principle, and which, when applied to large communities, fetters the people in stationary despotism, while that principle cannot long exist in connection with monogamy. Chancellor Kent observes that this remark is equally striking and profound. 2 Kent, Com. 81, note (e). An exceptional colony of polygamists under an exceptional leadership may sometimes exist for a time without appearing to disturb the social condition of the people who surround it; but there cannot be a doubt that, unless restricted by some form of constitution, it is within the legitimate scope of the power of every civil government to determine whether polygamy or monogamy shall be the law of social life under its dominion.

In our opinion, the statute immediately under consideration is within the legislative power of Congress. It is constitutional and valid as prescribing a rule of action for all those residing in the Territories, and in places over which the United States have exclusive control. This being so, the only question which remains, is, whether those who make polygamy a part of their religion are excepted from the operation of the statute. If they are, then those who do not make polygamy a part of their religious belief may be found guilty and punished, while those who do, must be acquitted and go free. This would be introducing a new element into criminal law. Laws are made for the government of actions, and while they cannot interfere with mere religious belief and opinions, they may with practices. Suppose one believed that human sacrifices were a necessary part of religious worship, would it be seriously contended that the civil government under which he lived could not interfere to prevent a sacrifice? Or if a wife religiously believed it was her duty to burn herself upon the funeral pile of her dead husband, would it be beyond the power of the civil government to prevent her carrying her belief into practice?

So here, as a law of the organization of society under the exclusive dominion of the United States, it is provided that plural marriages shall not be allowed. Can a man excuse his practices to the contrary because of his religious belief? To permit this would be to make the professed doctrines of religious belief superior to the law of the land, and in effect to permit every citizen to become a law unto himself. Government could exist only in name under such circumstances.

A criminal intent is generally an element of crime, but every man is presumed to intend the necessary and legitimate consequences of what he knowingly does. Here the accused knew he had been once married, and that his first wife was living. He also knew that his second marriage was forbidden by law. When, therefore, he married the second time, he is presumed to have intended to break the law. And the breaking of the law is the crime. Every act necessary to constitute the crime was knowingly done, and the crime was therefore knowingly committed. Ignorance of a fact may sometimes be taken as evidence of a want of criminal intent, but not ignorance of the law. The only defence of the accused in this case is his belief that the law ought not to have been enacted. It matters not that his belief was a part of his professed religion: it was still belief, and belief only.

In *Regina* v. *Wagstaff* (10 Cox Crim. Cases, 531), the parents of a sick child, who omitted to call in medical attendance because of their religious belief that what they did for its cure would be effective, were held not to be guilty of manslaughter, while it was said the contrary would have been the result if the child had actually been starved to death by the parents, under the notion that it was their religious duty to abstain from giving it food. But when the offence consists of a positive act which is knowingly done, it would be dangerous to hold that the offender might escape punishment because he religiously believed the law which he had broken ought never to have been made. No case, we believe, can be found that has gone so far.

As to that part of the charge which directed the attention of the jury to the consequences of polygamy.

The passage complained of is as follows: "I think it not improper, in the discharge of your duties in this case, that you should consider what are to be the consequences to the innocent victims of this delusion. As this contest goes on, they multiply, and there are pure-minded women and there are innocent children,—innocent in a sense even beyond the degree of the innocence of childhood itself. These are to be the sufferers; and as jurors fail to do their duty, and as these cases come up in the Territory of Utah, just so do these victims multiply and spread themselves over the land."

While every appeal by the court to the passions or the prejudices of a jury should be promptly rebuked, and while it is the imperative duty of a reviewing court to take care that wrong is not done in this way, we see no just cause for complaint in this case. Congress, in 1862 (12 Stat. 501), saw fit to make bigamy a crime in the Territories. This was done because of the evil consequences that were supposed to flow from plural marriages. All the court did was to call the attention of the jury to the peculiar character of the crime for which the accused was on trial, and to remind them of the duty they had to perform. There was no appeal to the passions, no instigation of prejudice. Upon the showing made by the accused himself, he was guilty of a violation of the law under which he had been indicted: and the effort of the court seems to have been not to withdraw the minds of the jury from the issue to be tried, but to bring them to it; not to make them partial, but to keep them impartial.

Upon a careful consideration of the whole case, we are satisfied that no error was committed by the court below.

Judgment affirmed.

After a petition for rehearing, the judgment was remanded to enter the same verdict, except to the extent that it required imprisonment at hard labor.

Consider the function of the Court's citation to "Professor Lieber," a citation entirely derived from Chancellor James Kent's *Commentaries* (1844) 2, 81, which stated that polygamy was prohibited because of "the precepts of Christianity and the laws of our social nature." Kent added, "Polygamy may be regarded as exclusively the feature of Asiatic manners, and of half civilized life, and to be incompatible with civilization, refinement and domestic felicity." In a footnote Kent referred to "Mr. Lieber", *i.e.*, to the *Manual of Political Ethics* (1839) of Francis Lieber, a learned German immigrant who was professor of political science at South Carolina College.

Lieber and Kent both wrote before the Mormon experience of polygamy had been observed. By 1855, however, Lieber was asserting that polygamous Utah and its "theo-democratic" government be denied statehood until the Church's power was broken. In 1865, now teaching at Columbia in New York, Lieber proposed a constitutional amendment outlawing polygamy, (Lieber, *Contributions to Political Science; Miscellaneous Writings* (1881) 2, 173, 534). Lieber taught that the Mormons "deny the very first principles . . . of our whole western civilization, as distinguished from oriental life," Lieber, *On Civil Liberty and Self-Government* (1869) 101. This pop sociology—scarcely more than the hearty assertion of prejudice—was supplemented by another guide, whom Waite did not acknowledge in the opinion: the historian George Bancroft, to whom he wrote on January 17, 1879: "As you gave me the information on which the judgment in the late polygamy case rests, I send you a copy of the opinion that you may see what use has been made of your facts," Bruce R. Trimble, *Chief Justice Waite* (1938), 244–245. It may reasonably be surmised that Waite owed to him the references to Jefferson's letter, now destined to be famous. Waite was an Episcopalian, regular and reverent in his practice. He described his opinion to a clergyman as "my sermon on the religion of polygamy," (Trimble 18 and 244). Was not Waite's use of Jefferson's metaphor of the wall intended to suppress the suggestion that he, Morrison Waite, might be guilty of breaking it?

Note the reappearance of Locke's distinction between belief and acts. Most people would concede that the religious practices Waite mentions by way of analogy need to be restrained. Does he unfairly weight the argument by not noticing that the acts he mentions involve irremediable physical injury, while the act the statute condemns is a consensual sexual relation?

The Republicans in 1880 pressed on the nation the duty to "extirpate that relic of barbarism, polygamy" (*Platforms* 46). Protestant criticism mounted. A new law was added in 1882, proposed by Senator George F. Edmunds (another Vermonter!). The 1862 act was amended: Persons practicing polygamy or even believing it to be "right" were disqualified from sitting as jurors on polygamy prosecution cases. Practicing polygamists were disqualified from office and from voting. Cohabitation was made a misdemeanor, and persons cohabiting with more than one woman were disqualified like polygamists. A federal commission was created to supervise elections in Utah. Two provisions held out the carrot with the stick. The president was authorized to amnesty polygamists. Their offspring born before January 1, 1883, were declared legitimate. Finally, careful provision was made that no one should be excluded from voting because of "any opinion" on polygamy, 22 Stat. 31–32.

The Republicans in 1884 called for more action specifically affecting the Church:

Resolved: That it is the duty of Congress to enact such laws as shall promptly and effectually suppress the system of polygamy within our Territories and divorce the political from the ecclesiastical power of the so-called Mormon Church; and that the laws so enacted shall be rigidly enforced by the civil authorities, if possible, and by the military if need be [*Platforms* 65].

Under the new law, Angus M. Cannon—a Mormon who lived with two women, Amanda and Clara, each of whom was known as "Mrs. Cannon" and each of whom alternated in sharing meals with him—was convicted in 1885. The Supreme Court, reviewing the conviction immediately, upheld the conviction, interpreting "cohabit" to mean "to live together as husband and wife." Proof of actual sexual intercourse was irrelevant, *Cannon v. United States*, 116 U.S. 55 (1885). Justices Miller and Field dissented. Prominent churchmen in Utah went into hiding. Arrests and prosecutions increased, Arrington and Bitton 181.

Congress was now determined to push further. The Tucker Act, with a Virginian as sponsor, proposed to declare forfeit the property of the Church itself. John T. Caine, a native of the Isle of Man and Utah's delegate to Congress, spoke warmly against the bill, emphasizing the honesty, prosperity, and patriotism of the Mormons and comparing their plight to persecuted English Puritans, Irish Catholics, and French Huguenots, 18 *Congressional Record* 585–586 (January 12, 1887). Congressmen supporting the bill did not disguise their target: the Church itself. Ezra B. Taylor of Ohio said:

That church governs all things with a steady and relentless hand; it disposes of liberty; it dictates laws and practices. . . . This people and this church defy the moral sense of the civilized world and are of necessity antagonistic to the principles and institution of the Republic [*ibid.* at 584].

In favor of the bill, Lucien Bonaparte Caswell of Wisconsin declared: "The bill strikes at the very root of the church. It absolutely repeals the charter which gave it existence," *ibid.* at 592. John R. Tucker, closing on behalf of the Committee on the Judiciary, declared:

I do not care what the Mormon believes. But he must not believe and act upon his belief if it violates the right of any other man or violates the power of the Government and its laws for the peace and good order of society. That is all. I do not object to his saying that he or some other man ought to have two wives or more; but I do not intend to let him or that other man have more than one. If you are not a polygamist in act I do not care what you believe; but I do care very much what you do. When religious belief breaks out into the overt act of polygamy it is time for the civil government to interfere to preserve the peace, purity, and good order of society.

Now, Mr. Speaker, that being the power of Congress, what is it the duty of Congress to do? What is polygamy? It is a crime by the law of every state in Christendom. Ever since Christ interpreted the Judaic law and gave it to us in His own express words it has been not only a sin against God, but has been made a crime by every Christian society. Mark His words:

"For this cause shall a man leave his father and mother, and cleave to his wife; and they twain—not a whole bundle of them, but they twain—shall be one flesh: so then they are no more twain, but one flesh."

Ever since Christ uttered that language all of the Japhetic race have adopted monogamy as the only foundation of a decent civilization [*ibid.* at 593].

The bill passed without a record vote and, unsigned by President Grover Cleveland, became law.

The authorities were now to rely on three devices with an old pedigree in ecclesiastical controversies: oaths; charges of conspiracy; and a ban on speech. Samuel D. Davis was prosecuted for conspiracy to violate section 501 of the Revised Statutes of the Territory of Idaho, which barred from holding office or even from voting any "bigamist or polygamist, or [one] who teaches, advises, counsels, or encourages any person or persons to become bigamists or polygamists."

Conspiracy was charged on the theory that Davis and other Mormons had agreed to take falsely the oath which the territorial statute prescribed. The oath-taker was required to swear:

I am not a bigamist or polygamist. . . . I am not a member of any order, organization, or association . . . which practices bigamy or polygamy or plural or celestial marriage as a doctrinal rite of such organization. I do not and will not, publicly or privately, or in any manner whatever, teach, advise, counsel, or encourage any person to commit the crime of bigamy or polygamy. . . .

Like the anti-Catholic oath of the Massachusetts Constitution of 1780, this oath proscribed the objectionable belief, delicately avoiding mention of the Church whose beliefs were being condemned. Like that other oath, it anticipated evasion and tried to prevent it. Unlike that other oath, it even forbade advocacy.

Davis was found guilty and sentenced to a $500 fine or 250 days in jail. He applied at once for habeas corpus. Counsel before the Supreme Court assailed the Idaho territorial statute (law enacted by federal authority) as infringing the First Amendment by preventing the free exercise of religion and as infringing Article VI of the Constitution by requiring the oath.

Author of the unanimous opinion of the Court was Stephen J. Field. The new issues the case raised were scarcely noticed, but, unlike Waite, Field candidly acknowledged the relevance of Christianity:

Davis v. Beason
133 U.S. 333 (1890)

. . .

On this appeal our only inquiry is whether the District Court of the Territory had jurisdiction of the offence charged in the indictment of which the defendant was found guilty. If it had jurisdiction, we can go no farther. We cannot look into any alleged errors in its rulings on the trial of the defendant. The writ of *habeas corpus* cannot be turned into a writ of error to review the action of that court. Nor can we inquire whether the evidence established the fact alleged, that the defendant was a member of an order or organization known as the Mormon Church, called the Church of Jesus Christ of Latter-Day Saints, or the fact that the order or organization taught and counselled its members and devotees to commit the crimes of bigamy and polygamy as duties arising from membership therein. On this hearing we can only consider whether, these allegations being taken as true, an offence was committed of which the territorial court had jurisdiction to try the defendant. And on this point there can be no serious discussion or difference of opinion. Bigamy and polygamy are crimes by the laws of all civilized and Christian countries. They are crimes by the laws of the United States, and they are crimes by the laws of Idaho. They tend to destroy the purity of the marriage relation, to disturb the peace of families, to degrade woman and to debase man. Few crimes are more pernicious to the best interests of society and receive more general or more deserved punishment. To extend exemption from punishment for such crimes would be to shock the moral judgment of the community. To call their advocacy a tenet of religion is to offend the common sense of mankind. If they are crimes, then to teach, advise and counsel their practice is to aid in their commission, and such teaching and counselling are themselves criminal and proper subjects of punishment, as aiding and abetting crime are in all other cases.

The term "religion" has reference to one's views of his relations to his Creator, and to the obligations they impose of reverence for his being and character, and of obedience to his will. It is often confounded with the *cultus* or form of worship of a particular sect, but is distinguishable from the latter. The first amendment to the Constitution, in declaring that Congress shall make no law respecting the establishment of religion, or forbidding the free exercise thereof, was intended to allow every one under the jurisdiction of the United States to entertain such notions respecting his relations to his Maker and the duties they impose as may be approved by his judgment and conscience, and to exhibit his sentiments in such form of worship as he may think proper, not injurious to the equal rights of others, and to prohibit legislation for the support of any religious tenets, or the modes of worship of any sect. The oppressive measures adopted, and the cruelties and punishments inflicted by the governments of Europe for many ages, to compel parties to conform, in their religious beliefs and modes of worship, to the views of the most numerous sect, and the folly of attempting in that way to control the mental operations of persons, and enforce an outward conformity to a prescribed standard, led to the adoption of the amendment in question. It was never intended or supposed that the amendment could be invoked as a protection against legislation for the punishment of acts inimical to the peace, good order and morals of society. With man's relations to his Maker and the obligations he may think they impose, and the manner in which an expression shall be made by him of his belief on those subjects, no interference can be permitted, provided always the laws of society, designed to secure its peace and prosperity, and the morals of its people, are not interfered with. However free the exercise of religion may be, it must be subordinate to the criminal laws of the country, passed with reference to actions regarded by general consent as properly the subjects of punitive legislation. There have been sects which denied as part of their religious tenets that there should be any marriage tie, and advocated promiscuous intercourse of the sexes as prompted by the passions of its members. And history discloses the fact that the necessity of human sacrifices, on special occasions, has been a tenet of many sects. Should a sect of either of these kinds ever find its way into this country, swift punishment would follow the carrying into effect of its doctrines, and no heed would be given to the pretence that, as religious beliefs, their supporters could be protected in their exercise by the Constitution of the United States. Probably never before in the history of this country has it been seriously contended that the whole punitive power of the government for acts recognized by the general consent of the Christian world in modern times as proper matters for prohibitory legislation, must be suspended in order that the tenets of a religious sect encouraging crime may be carried out without hindrance. . . .

It is assumed by counsel of the petitioner, that because no mode of worship can be established or religious tenets enforced in this country, therefore any form of worship may by followed and any tenets, however destructive of society, may be held and advocated, if asserted to be a part of the religious doctrines of those advocating and practising them. But nothing is further from the truth. Whilst legislation for the establishment of a religion is forbidden, and its free exercise permitted, it does not follow that everything which may be so called can be tolerated. Crime is not the less odious because sanctioned by what any particular sect may designate as religion. . . .

In the same year *Davis* was decided, a case involving forfeiture of the property of the Church reached the Supreme Court. The government had proceeded with a certain gradualness. The statute itself exempted buildings used for worship from confiscations. The government valued the rest of the Church's property at $3,000,000 but had seized only $381,812, mostly cash on hand, *see* Thomas E. Kauper, "Religious Corporations and the Law," 71 *Michigan Law Review* (1973) at 1517. After argument in January 1889, the Supreme Court postponed decision, a suspended execution bringing pressure on the Church to prepare to conform. In May 1890, Joseph Bradley wrote the majority opinion. Bradley had been brought up in the Dutch Reformed Church, but his religious opinions had evolved to the point where he believed that Christ "taught no dogmas but one—that God is our Father and that we are all brethren," Bradley, "Esoteric Thoughts on Religion and Religionism" (1876), in Bradley, *Miscellaneous Writings,* ed. Charles Bradley (1902) 431. The heart of his opinion was his view of polygamy in relation to Christian civilization:

The Late Corporation of the Church of Jesus Christ of Latter Day Saints v. United States
Romney v. United States
136 U.S. 1 (1890)

. . . The next question is, whether Congress or the court had the power to cause the property of the said corporation to be seized and taken possession of, as was done in this case.

When a business corporation, instituted for the purposes of gain, or private interest, is dissolved, the modern doctrine is, that its property, after payment of its debts, equitably belongs to its stockholders. But this doctrine has never been extended to public or charitable corporations. As to these, the ancient and established rule prevails, namely: that when a corporation is dissolved, its personal property, like that of a man dying without heirs, ceases to be the subject of private ownership, and becomes subject to the disposal of the sovereign authority; whilst its real estate reverts or escheats to the grantor or donor, unless some other course of devolution has been directed by positive law, though still subject as we shall hereafter see to the charitable use. To this rule the corporation in question was undoubtedly subject. But the grantor of all, or the principal part, of the real estate of the Church of Jesus Christ of Latter-Day Saints was really the United States, from whom the property was derived by the church, or its trustees, through the operation of the town site act. Besides, as we have seen, the act of 1862 expressly declared that all real estate acquired or held by any of the corporations or associations therein mentioned, (of which the Church of Jesus Christ of Latter-Day Saints was one), contrary to the provisions of that act, should be forfeited and escheat to the United States, with a saving of existing vested rights. The act prohibited the acquiring or holding of real estate of greater value than $50,000 in a Territory, and no legal title had vested in any of the lands in Salt Lake City at that time, as the town site act was not passed until March 2, 1867. There can be no doubt, therefore, that the real estate of the corporation in question could not, on its dissolution, revert or pass to any other person or persons than the United States.

If it be urged that the real estate did not stand in the name of the corporation, but in the name of a trustee or trustees, and therefore was not subject to the rules relating to corporate property, the substance of the difficulty still remains. It cannot be contended that the prohibition of the act of 1862 could have been so easily evaded as by putting the property of the corporation into the hands of trustees. The equitable or trust estate was vested in the corporation. The trustee held it for no other purpose; and the corporation being dissolved that purpose was at an end. The trust estate devolved to the United States in the same manner as the legal estate would have done had it been in the hands of the corporation. The trustee became trustee for the United States instead of trustee for the corporation. We do not now speak of the religious and charitable uses for which the corporation, through its trustee, held and managed the property.

That aspect of the subject is one which places the power of the government and of the court over the property on a distinct ground.

Where a charitable corporation is dissolved, and no private donor, or founder, appears to be entitled to its real estate (its personal property not being subject to such reclamation,) the government, or sovereign authority, as the chief and common guardian of the State, either through its judicial tribunals or otherwise, necessarily has the disposition of the funds of such corporation, to be exercised, however, with due regard to the objects and purposes of the charitable uses to which the property was originally devoted, so far as they are lawful and not repugnant to public policy. This is the general principle, which will be more fully discussed further on. In this direction, it will be pertinent, in the meantime to examine into the character of the corporation of the Church of Jesus Christ of Latter-Day Saints, and the objects which, by its constitution and principles, it promoted and had in view.

It is distinctly stated in the pleadings and findings of fact, that the property of the said corporation was held for the purpose of religious and charitable uses. But it is also stated in the findings of fact, and is a matter of public notoriety, that the religious and charitable uses intended to be subserved and promoted are the inculcation and spread of the doctrines and usages of the Mormon Church, or Church of Latter-Day Saints, one of the distinguishing features of which is the practice of polygamy—a crime against the laws, and abhorrent to the sentiments and feelings of the civilized world. Notwithstanding the stringent laws which have been passed by Congress—notwithstanding all the efforts made to suppress this barbarous practice—the sect or community composing the Church of Jesus Christ of Latter-Day Saints perseveres, in defiance of law, in preaching, upholding, promoting and defending it. It is a matter of public notoriety that its emissaries are engaged in many countries in propagating this nefarious doctrine, and urging its converts to join the community in Utah. The existence of such a propaganda is a blot on our civilization. The organization of a community for the spread and practice of polygamy is, in a measure, a return to barbarism. It is contrary to the spirit of Christianity and of the civilization which Christianity has produced in the Western world. The question, therefore, is whether the promotion of such a nefarious system and practice, so repugnant to our laws and to the principles of our civilization, is to be allowed to continue by the sanction of the government itself; and whether the funds accumulated for that purpose shall be restored to the same unlawful uses as heretofore, to the detriment of the true interests of civil society.

It is unnecessary here to refer to the past history of the sect, to their defiance of the government authorities, to their attempt to establish an independent community, to their efforts to drive from the territory all who were not connected with them in communion and sympathy. The tale is one of patience on the part of the American government and people, and of contempt of authority and resistance to law on the part of the Mormons. Whatever persecutions they may have suffered in the early part of their history, in Missouri and Illinois, they have no excuse for their persistent defiance of law under the government of the United States.

One pretense for this obstinate course is, that their belief in the practice of polygamy, or in the right to indulge in it, is a religious belief, and, therefore, under the protection of the constitutional guaranty of religious freedom. This is altogether a sophistical plea. No doubt the Thugs of India imagined that their belief in the right of assassination was a religious belief; but their thinking so did not make it so. The practice of suttee by the Hindu widows may have sprung from a supposed religious conviction. The offering of human sacrifices by our own ancestors in Britain was no doubt sanctioned by an equally conscientious impulse. But no one, on that account, would hesitate to brand these practices, now, as crimes against society, and obnoxious to condemnation and punishment by the civil authority.

The State has a perfect right to prohibit polygamy, and all other open offenses against the enlightened sentiment of mankind, notwithstanding the pretense of religious conviction by which they may be advocated and practised. *Davis v. Beason,* 133 U.S. 333. And since polygamy has been forbidden by the laws of the United States, under severe penalties, and since the Church of Jesus Christ of Latter-Day Saints has persistently used and claimed the right to use, and the unincorporated community still claims the same right to use the funds with which the late corporation was endowed for the purpose of promoting and propagating the unlawful practice as an integral part of their religious usages, the question arises, whether the government, finding these funds without legal ownership, has or has not, the right, through its courts, and in due course of administration, to cause them to be seized and devoted to objects of undoubted charity and usefulness—such for example as the maintenance of schools—for the benefit of the community whose leaders are now misusing them in the unlawful manner above described; setting apart, however, for the exclusive possession and use of the church, sufficient and suitable portions of the property for the purposes of public worship, parsonage buildings and burying grounds, as provided in the law.

. . .

As to the constitutional question, we see nothing in the act which, in our judgment, transcends the power of Congress over the subject. We have already considered the question of its power to repeal the charter of the corporation. It certainly also had power to direct proceedings to be instituted for the forfeiture and escheat of the real estate of the corporation; and, if a judgment should be rendered in favor of the government in these proceedings, the power to dispose of the proceeds of the lands thus forfeited and escheated, for the use and benefit of common schools in the Territory, is beyond dispute. It would probably have power to make such a disposition of the proceeds if the question were merely one of charitable uses, and not of forfeiture. Schools and education were regarded by the Congress of the Confederation as the most natural and obvious appliances for the promotion of religion and morality. In the ordinance of 1787, passed for the government of the Territory Northwest of the Ohio, it is declared, Art. 3, "Religion, morality and knowledge, being necessary to good government and the happiness of mankind, schools and the means of education shall forever be encouraged." Mr. Dane, who is reputed to have drafted the said ordinance, speaking of some of the statutory provisions of the English law regarding charities as inapplicable to America, says: "But in construing these laws, rules have been laid down, which are valuable in every State; as that the erection of schools and the relief of the poor are always right, and the law will deny the application of private property only as to uses the nation deems superstitious." 4 Dane's Abridg. 239.

The only remaining constitutional question arises upon that part of the 17th section of the act, under which the present proceedings were instituted. We do not well see how the constitutionality of this provision can be seriously disputed, if it be conceded or established that the corporation ceased to exist, and that its property thereupon ceased to have a lawful owner, and reverted to the care and protection of the government as *parens patriae.* The point has already been fully discussed. We have no doubt that the state of things referred to existed, and that the right of the government to take possession of the property followed thereupon.

The application of Romney and others, representing the unincorporated members of the Church of Jesus Christ of Latter-Day Saints, is fully disposed of by the considerations already adduced. The principal question discussed has been, whether the property of the church was in such a condition as to authorize the government and the court to take possession of it and hold it until it shall be seen what final disposition of it should be made; and we think it was in such a condition, and that it is properly held in the custody of the receiver. The rights of the church members will necessarily be taken into consideration in the final disposition of the case. There is no ground for granting their present application. The property is in the custody of the law, awaiting the judgment of the court as to its final disposition in view of the illegal uses to which it is subject in the hands of the Church of Latter-Day Saints, whether incorporated or unincorporated.

The conditions for claiming possession of it by the members of the sect or community under the act do not at present exist.

The attempt made, after the passage of the act on February 19, 1887, and whilst it was in the president's hands for his approval or rejection, to transfer the property from the trustee then holding it to other persons, and for the benefit of different associations, was so evidently intended as an evasion of the law, that the court below justly regarded it as void and without force or effect.

We have carefully examined the decree, and do not find anything in it that calls for a reversal. It may perhaps require modification in some matters of detail, and for that purpose only the case is reserved for further consideration.

Chief Justice Fuller, with whom concurred Justice Field and Justice Lamar, dissented as to the power of Congress to confiscate the property.

The Mormons had been confident that they were protected by the Constitution, which they believed to be divinely inspired. Joseph Smith in 1833 had received a revelation that God "established the constitution of this land, by the hands of wise men whom [He] raised up unto this very purpose," *Book of Doctrine and Covenants, Reorganized Church of Jesus Christ of Latter-Day Saints* (1970) 98:10. The doctrine did not impose polygamy at all costs but only when practicable. When the Supreme Court permitted the Church's property to be confiscated, they were confronted with circumstances that made polygamy impracticable. On September 25, 1890, Wilford Woodruff, the presiding officer of the Church, announced what became known as "the Manifesto."

Inasmuch as laws have been enacted by Congress forbidding plural marriages, which laws have been pronounced constitutional by the court of last resort, I hereby declare my intention to submit to those laws, and to use any influence with the members of the Church over which I preside to have them do likewise [Arrington and Bitton 183].

Without conceding a doctrinal change, President Woodruff acknowledged that circumstances no longer made the old rule applicable. Federal law, applied directly against a church, had altered that church's perception of what was morally practicable. In 1894 Congress returned the Church's property; in 1896 it admitted Utah as a state.

TEN

"The Mass of Organic Utterances": Governmental Benevolence, 1890–1940

1. "A RELIGIOUS PEOPLE"

JUSTICE DAVID J. BREWER, grandson of a New England Congregationalist minister and son of a Congregationalist missionary to Turkey, spoke for a unanimous Court in a trivial case that he made the vehicle for affirmation of what he declared to be the religion of America:

Holy Trinity Church v. United States
143 U.S. 457 (1892)

Plaintiff in error is a corporation, duly organized and incorporated as a religious society under the laws of the State of New York. E. Walpole Warren was, prior to September 1887, an alien residing in England. In that month the plaintiff in error made a contract with him, by which he was to remove to the city of New York and enter into its service as rector and pastor; and in pursuance of such contract, Warren did so remove and enter upon such service. It is claimed by the United States that this contract on the part of the plaintiff in error was forbidden by the act of February 26, 1885, 23 Stat. 332, c. 164, and an action was commenced to recover the penalty prescribed by that act. The Circuit Court held that the contract was within the prohibition of the statute, and rendered judgment accordingly, (36 Fed. Rep. 303;) and the single question presented for our determination is whether it erred in that conclusion.

The first section describes the act forbidden, and is in these words:

"Be it enacted by the Senate and House of Representatives of the United States of America in Congress assembled, That from and after the passage of this act it shall be unlawful for any person, company, partnership, or corporation, in any manner whatsoever, to prepay the transportation, or in any way assist or encourage the importation or migration of any alien or aliens, any foreigner or foreigners, into the United States, its Territories, or the District of Columbia, under contract or agreement, parol or special, express or implied, made previous to the importation or migration of such alien or

aliens, foreigner or foreigners, to perform labor or service of any kind in the United States, its Territories, or the District of Columbia."

It must be conceded that the act of the corporation is within the letter of this section, for the relation of rector to his church is one of service, and implies labor on the one side with compensation on the other. Not only are the general words labor and service both used, but also, as it were to guard against any narrow interpretation and emphasize a breadth of meaning, to them is added "of any kind;" and, further, as noticed by the Circuit Judge in his opinion, the fifth section, which makes specific exceptions, among them professional actors, artists, lecturers, singers and domestic servants, strengthens the idea that every other kind of labor and service was intended to be reached by the first section. While there is great force to this reasoning, we cannot think Congress intended to denounce with penalties a transaction like that in the present case. It is a familiar rule, that a thing may be within the letter of the statute and yet not within the statute, because not within its spirit, nor within the intention of its makers. This has been often asserted, and the reports are full of cases illustrating its application. This is not the substitution of the will of the judge for that of the legislator, for frequently words of general meaning are used in a statute, words broad enough to include an act in question, and yet a consideration of the whole legislation, or of the circumstances surrounding its enactment, or of the absurd results which follow from giving such broad meaning to the words, makes it unreasonable to believe that the legislator intended to include the particular act. . . .

We find, therefore, that the title of the act, the evil which was intended to be remedied, the circumstances surrounding the appeal to Congress, the reports of the committee of each house, all concur in affirming that the intent of Congress was simply to stay the influx of this cheap unskilled labor.

But beyond all these matters no purpose of action against religion can be imputed to any legislation, state or national, because this is a religious people. This is historically true. From the discovery of this continent to the present hour, there is a single voice making this affirmation. The commission to Christopher Columbus, prior to his sail westward, is from "Ferdinand and Isabella, by the grace of God, King and Queen of Castile," etc., and recites that "it is hoped that by God's assistance some of the continents and islands in the ocean will be discovered," etc. The first colonial grant, that made to Sir Walter Raleigh in 1584, was from Elizabeth, by the grace of God, of England, Fraunce and Ireland, queene, defender of the faith," etc.; and the grant authorizing him to enact statutes for the government of the proposed colony provided that "they be not against the true Christian faith nowe professed in the Church of England." The first charter of Virginia, granted by King James I in 1606, after reciting the application of certain parties for a charter, commenced the grant in these words: "We, greatly commending, and graciously accepting of, their Desires for the Furtherance of so noble a Work, which may, by the Providence of Almighty God, hereafter tend to the Glory of his Divine Majesty, in propagating of Christian Religion to such People, as yet live in Darkness and miserable Ignorance of the true Knowledge and Worship of God, and may in time bring the Infidels and Savages, living in those parts, to human Civility, and to a settled and quiet Government; DO, by these our Letters-Patents, graciously accept of, and agree to, their humble and well-intended Desires."

Language of similar import may be found in the subsequent charters of that colony, from the same king, in 1609 and 1611; and the same is true of the various charters granted to the other colonies. In language more or less emphatic is the establishment of the Christian religion declared to be one of the purposes of the grant. The celebrated compact made by the Pilgrims in the Mayflower, 1620, recites: "Having undertaken for the Glory of God, and Advancement of the Christian Faith, and the Honour of our King and Country, a Voyage to plant the first Colony in the northern Parts of Virginia; Do by these Presents, solemnly and mutually, in the Presence of God and one another, covenant and combine ourselves together into a civil Body Politick, for our better Ordering and Preservation, and Furtherance of the Ends aforesaid."

The fundamental orders of Connecticut, under which a provisional government was instituted in 1638–1639, commence with this declaration: "Forasmuch as it hath pleased the All-mighty God by the wise disposition of his diuyne pruidence so to Order and dispose of things that we the Inhabitants and Residents of Windsor, Hartford and Wethersfield are now cohabiting and dwelling in and vppon the River of Conectecotte and the Lands thereunto adioyneing; And well knowing where a people are gathered togather the word of God requires that to mayntayne the peace and vnion of such a people there should be an orderly and decent Gouerment established according to God, to order and dispose of the affayres of the people at all seasons as occation shall require; doe therefore assotiate and conioyne our selues to be as one Publike State or Comonwelth; and doe, for our selues and our Successors and such as shall be adioyned to vs att any tyme hereafter, enter into Combination and Confederation togather, to mayntayne and presearue the liberty and purity of the gospell of our Lord Jesus wch we now p^{r}fesse, as also the disciplyne of the Churches, wch according to the truth of the said gospell is now practised amongst vs."

In the charter of privileges granted by William Penn to the province of Pennsylvania, in 1701, it is recited: "Because no People can be truly happy, though under the greatest Enjoyment of Civil Liberties, if abridged of the Freedom of their Consciences, as to their Religious Profession and Worship; And Almighty God being the only Lord of Conscience, Father of Lights and Spirits; and the Author as well as Object of all divine Knowledge, Faith and Worship, who only doth enlighten the Minds, and persuade and convince the Understandings of People, I do hereby grant and declare," etc.

Coming nearer to the present time, the Declaration of Independence recognizes the presence of the Divine in human affairs. . . .

. . . And in the famous case of *Vidal v. Girard's Executors,* 2 How. 127, 198, this court, while sustaining the will of Mr. Girard, with its provision for the creation of a college into which no minister should be permitted to enter, observed: "It is also said, and truly, that the Christian religion is a part of the common law of Pennsylvania."

If we pass beyond these matters to a view of American life as expressed by its laws, its business, its customs and its society, we find everywhere a clear recognition of the same truth. Among other matters note the following: The form of oath universally prevailing, concluding with an appeal to the Almighty; the custom of opening sessions of all deliberative bodies and most conventions with prayer; the prefatory words of all wills, "In the name of God, amen;" the laws respecting the observance of the Sabbath, with the general cessation of all secular business, and the closing of courts, legislatures, and other similar public assemblies on that day; the churches and church organizations which abound in every city, town and hamlet; the multitude of charitable organizations existing everywhere under Christian auspices; the gigantic missionary associations, with general support, and aiming to establish Christian missions in every quarter of the globe. These, and many other matters which might be noticed, add a volume of unofficial declarations to the mass of organic utterances that this is a Christian nation. In the face of all these, shall it be believed that a Congress of the United States intended to make it a misdemeanor for a church of this country to contract for the services of a Christian minister residing in another nation?

Suppose in the Congress that passed this act some member had offered a bill which in terms declared that, if any Roman Catholic church in this country should contract with Cardinal Manning to come to this country and enter into its service as pastor and priest; or any Episcopal church should enter into a like contract with Canon Farrar; or any Baptist church should make similar arrangements with Rev. Mr. Spurgeon; or any Jewish synagogue with some eminent Rabbi, such contract should be adjudged unlawful and void, and the church making it be subject to prosecution and punishment, can it be believed that it would have received a minute of approving thought or a single vote? Yet it is contended that such was in effect the meaning of this statute. The construction invoked cannot be accepted as correct. It is a case where there was presented a definite evil, in view of which the legislature used general terms with the purpose of reaching all phases of that evil, and thereafter, unexpectedly, it is developed that the general language thus employed is broad enough to reach cases and acts which the whole history and life of the country affirm could not have been intentionally legislated against. It is the duty of the courts, under those circumstances, to say that, however broad the language of the statute may be, the act, although within the letter, is not within the intention of the legislature, and therefore cannot be within the statute.

The judgment will be reversed, and the case remanded for further proceedings in accordance with this opinion.

2. THE FIRST CHURCH AID CASE

Federal aid to a hospital owned and operated by a Catholic religious order was litigated in the 1890s. The petitioner, Joseph Bradfield, appearing in his own behalf, won in the supreme court of the District of Columbia, but lost in the Court of Appeals. He appealed to the Supreme Court of the United States. The Republican administration of William McKinley vigorously defended the propriety of the grant. The opinion for a unanimous Court was delivered by Rufus W. Peckham, an upstate New Yorker of long-established Protestant stock:

Bradfield v. Roberts
175 U.S. 291 (1899)

This was a suit in equity, brought by the appellant to enjoin the defendant from paying any moneys to the directors of Providence Hospital in the city of Washington, under an agreement entered into between the Commissioners of the District of Columbia and the directors of the hospital, by virtue of the authority of an act of Congress, because of the alleged invalidity of the agreement for the reasons stated in the bill of complaint. In that bill complainant represents that he is a citizen and taxpayer of the United States and a resident of the District of Columbia, that the defendant is the Treasurer of the United States, and the object of the suit is to enjoin him from paying to or on account of Providence Hospital, in the city of Washington, District of Columbia, any moneys belonging to the United States, by virtue of a contract between the Surgeon General of the Army and the directors of that hospital, or by virtue of an agreement between the Commissioners of the District of Columbia and such directors, under the authority of an appropriation contained in the sundry civil appropriation bill for the District of Columbia, approved June 4, 1897.

Complainant further alleged in his bill:

"That the said Providence Hospital is a private eleemosynary corporation, and that to the best of the complainant's knowledge and belief it is composed of members of a monastic order or sisterhood of the Roman Catholic Church, and is conducted under the auspices of said church; that the title to its property is vested in the 'Sisters of Charity of Emmitsburg, Maryland;' that it was incorporated by a special act of Congress approved April 8, 1864, whereby, in addition to the usual powers of bodies corporate and politic, it was invested specially with 'full power and all the rights of opening and keeping a hospital in the city of Washington for the care of such sick and invalid persons as may place themselves under the treatment and care of said corporation.'

"That in view of the sectarian character of said Providence Hospital and the specific and limited object of its creation, the said contract between the same and the Surgeon General of the Army and also the said agreement between the same and the Commissioners of the District of Columbia are unauthorized by law, and, moreover, involve a principle and a precedent for the appropriation of the funds of the United States for the use and support of religious societies, contrary to the article of the Constitution which declares that Congress shall make no law respecting a religious establishment, and also a precedent for giving to religious societies a legal agency in carrying into effect a public and civil duty which would, if once established, speedily obliterate the essential distinction between civil and religious functions.

"That the complainant and all other citizens and taxpayers of the United States are injured by reason of the said contract and the said agreement, in virtue whereof the public funds are being used and pledged for the advancement and support of a private and sectarian corporation, and that they will suffer irreparable damage if the same are allowed to be carried into full effect by means of payments made through or by the said defendant out of the Treasury of the United States, contrary to the Constitution and declared policy of the Government." . . .

Mr. Joseph Bradfield, appellant, in person for appellant.

Mr. Assistant Attorney General Hoyt for appellee. *Mr. Attorney General* was on his brief.

Justice Peckham, after stating the facts, delivered the opinion of the court.

Passing the various objections made to the maintenance of this suit on account of an alleged defect of parties, and also in regard to the character in which the complainant sues, merely that of a citizen and taxpayer of the United States and a resident of the District of Columbia, we come to the main question as to the validity of the agreement between the Commissioners of the District and the directors of the hospital, founded upon the appropriation contained in the act of Congress, the contention being that the agreement if carried out would result in an appropriation by Congress of money to a religious society, thereby violating the constitutional provision which forbids Congress from passing any law respecting an establishment of religion. Art. I of the Amendments to Constitution.

The appropriation is to be found in the general appropriation act for the government of the District of Columbia, approved March 3, 1897, c. 387, 29 Stat. 665, 679. It reads: "For two isolating buildings, to be constructed, in the discretion of the Commissioners of the District of Columbia, on the grounds of two hospitals, and to be operated as a part of such hospitals, thirty thousand dollars." Acting under the authority of this appropriation the Commissioners entered into the agreement in question.

As the bill alleges that Providence Hospital was incorporated by an act of Congress, approved April 8, 1864, c. 50, 13 Stat. 43, and assumes to give some of its provisions, the act thus referred to is substantially made a part of the bill, and it is therefore set forth in the margin.

The act shows that the individuals named therein and their successors in office were incorporated under the name of "The Directors of Providence Hospital," with power to receive, hold and convey personal and real property, as provided in its first section. By the second section the corporation was granted "full power and all the rights of opening and keeping a hospital in the city of Washington for the care of such sick and invalid persons as may place themselves under the treatment and care of the said corporation." The third section gave it full power to make such by-laws, rules and regulations that might be necessary for the general accomplishment of the objects of the hospital, not inconsistent with the laws in force in the District of Columbia. Nothing is said about religion or about the religious faith of the incorporators of this institution in the act of incorporation. It is simply the ordinary case of the incorporation of a hospital for the purposes for which such an institution is generally conducted. It is claimed that the allegation in the complainant's bill, that the said "Providence Hospital is a private eleemosynary corporation, and that to the best of complainant's knowledge and belief it is composed of members of a monastic order or sisterhood of the Roman Catholic Church, and is conducted under the auspices of said church; that the title to its property is vested in the Sisters of Charity of Emmitsburg, Maryland," renders the agreement void for the reason therein stated, which is that Congress has no power to make "a law respecting a religious establishment," a phrase which is not synonymous with that used in the Constitution, which prohibits the passage of a law "respecting an establishment of religion."

If we were to assume, for the purpose of this question only, that under this appropriation an agreement with a religious corporation of the tenor of this agreement would be invalid, as resulting indirectly in the passage of an act respecting an establishment of religion, we are unable to see that the complainant in his bill shows that the corporation is of the kind described, but on the contrary he has clearly shown that it is not.

The above-mentioned allegations in the complainant's bill do not change the legal character of the corporation or render it on that account a religious or sectarian body. Assuming that the hospital is a private eleemosynary corporation, the fact that its members, according to the belief of the complainant, are members of a monastic order or sisterhood of the Roman Catholic Church, and the further fact that the hospital is conducted under the auspices of said church, are wholly immaterial, as is also the allegation regarding the title to its property. The statute provides as to its property and makes no provision for its being held by any one other than itself. The facts above stated do not in the least change the legal character of the hospital, or make a religious corporation out of a purely secular one as constituted by the law of its being. Whether the individuals who compose the corporation under its charter happen to be all Roman Catholics, or all Methodists, or Presbyterians, or Unitarians, or members of any other religious organization, or of no organization at all, is of not the slightest consequence with reference to the law of its incorporation, nor can the individual beliefs upon religious matters of the various incorporators be inquired into. Nor is it material that the hospital may be conducted under the auspices of the Roman Catholic Church. To be conducted under the auspices is to be conducted under the influence or patronage of that church. The meaning of the allegation is that the church exercises great and perhaps controlling influence over the management of the hospital. It must, however, be managed pursuant to the law of its being. That the influence of any particular church may be powerful over the members of a non-sectarian and secular corporation, incorporated for a certain defined purpose and with clearly stated powers, is surely not sufficient to convert such a corporation into a religious or sectarian body. That fact does not alter the legal character of the corporation, which is incorporated under an act of Congress, and its powers, duties and character are to be solely measured by the charter under which it alone has any legal existence. There is no allegation that its hospital work is confined to members of that church or that in its management the hospital has been conducted so as to violate its charter in the smallest degree. It is simply the case of a secular corporation being managed by people who hold to the doctrines of the Roman Catholic Church, but who nevertheless are managing the corporation according to the law under which it exists. The charter itself does not limit the exercise of its corporate powers to the members of any particular religious denomination, but on the contrary those powers are to be exercised in favor of any one seeking the ministrations of that kind of an institution. All that can be said of the corporation itself is that it has been incorporated by an act of Congress, and for its legal powers and duties that act must be exclusively referred to. As stated in the opinion of the Court of Appeals, this corporation "is not declared the trustee of any church or religious society. Its property is to be acquired in its own name and for its own purposes; that property and its business are to be managed in its own way, subject to no visitation, supervision or control by any ecclesiastical authority whatever, but only to that of the Government which created it. In respect then of its creation, organization, management and ownership of property it is an ordinary private corporation whose rights are determinable by the law of the land, and the religious opinions of whose members are not subjects of inquiry."

It is not contended that Congress has no power in the District to appropriate money for the purpose expressed in the appropriation, and it is not doubted that it has power to authorize the Commissioners of the District of Columbia to enter into a contract with the trustees of an incorporated hospital for the purposes mentioned in the agreement in this case, and the only objection set up is the alleged "sectarian character of the hospital and the specific and limited object of its creation."

The other allegations in complainant's bill are simply statements of his opinion in regard to the results necessarily flowing from the appropriation in question when connected with the agreement mentioned.

The act of Congress, however, shows there is nothing sectarian in the corporation, and "the specific and limited object of its creation" is the opening and keeping a hospital in the city of Washington for the care of such sick and invalid persons as may place themselves under the treatment and care of the corporation. To make the agreement was within the discretion of the Commissioners, and was a fair exercise thereof.

The right reserved in the third section of the charter to amend, alter or repeal the act leaves full power in Congress to remedy any abuse of the charter privileges.

Without adverting to any other objections to the maintenance of this suit, it is plain that complainant wholly fails to set forth a cause of action, and the bill was properly dismissed by the Court of Appeals, and its decree will, therefore, be

Affirmed.

3. THE FIRST SCHOOL CASE

In the 1870s, during the Grant administration, the government set out to educate the Indians by "contract schools," federally funded schools largely operated under religious auspices. Catholic schools came to predominate. The Indian Rights Association, a philanthropic Protestant enterprise founded in 1882, proposed, as an alternative, compulsory federal education, where the Indians would be "Americanized" and the educational influence would be mainline Protestant American. The Indian Rights Association's leader, Herbert Welsh, painted an unfavorable contrast between "Roman control of our Indian schools" and "the American Public School idea," Francis P. Prucha, *The Churches and the Indian Schools 1888–1912* (1979) 3–31.

The American Protective Association (APA), founded in 1887 in reaction to Catholic immigration, made the Catholic influence on the Indian schools one of its major issues. In 1894, after the Catholic schools had received over $3 million of federal money, the APA attacks led to congressional attacks on the annual appropriation. The Cleveland administration met the outcry by a plan to phase out the contract schools in favor of federal schools. In 1896, Daniel M. Browning, Commissioner for Indian Affairs, instructed an Indian agent: "It is your duty first to build up and maintain the Government Day Schools . . . the Indian parents have no right to designate which school their children shall attend." [*ibid.* at 58]. The ruling was seen as a near-fatal blow to the Catholic schools.

In a pattern familiar to students of American politics, the Cleveland administration—Democrats and so confident of the Catholic vote—cultivated the Protestants. The Roosevelt administration—Republican and anxious to woo Catholics—revoked the Browning ruling in 1902, *ibid.* 62. In 1904 the Bureau of Catholic Indian Missions, the first national Catholic lobby, proposed to the administration that the United States use tribal funds to support the mission schools. Roosevelt agreed if the Indians would petition for this use. The Catholic Bureau drew up formal legal petitions. Many Indians affixed their mark. The Indian Rights Association and the American Baptist Home Missionary Society protested to the President. William Hare, the Episcopal bishop of South Dakota, suggested that the Sioux sue. His efforts resulted in a letter signed by a Sioux, Reuben Quick Bear, asking the Indian Rights Association for legal assistance. The association estimated the cost of a suit to be between $500 and $1,000 and hesitated, *ibid.* at 84–92.

Rebuffed in Congress and by the Roosevelt administration, the association's law committee in 1905 finally voted to bring suit against Francis Leupp, Roosevelt's Commissioner for Indian Affairs, and to pay for the litigation. Reuben Quick Bear was chosen and two other Sioux were recruited as plaintiffs, *ibid.* at 151–157. The Justice Department turned over defense of the case to special counsel chosen and compensated by the Catholic Bureau, *ibid.* at 153–154. A prototypical civil rights case, *Quick Bear v. Leupp*, set nominal plaintiffs against a nominal defendant while the interested ideological parties paid for the litigation and directed the strategy.

The history was set out in the answer filed by the United States:

1. The United States had approved the creation of Catholic Mission Schools in order "to encourage the education and civilization of the Indians through the work of religious organizations. The Act of 1819 appropriated $10,000 for such schools as the War Department approved (see *supra*, VII).

2. From 1819 to 1870 "the principal educational work" among the Indians was conducted by religious societies "aided more or less by the Government."

3. In 1870 Congress appropriated $100,000 which was used for contracts with various denominations to educate the Indians. In 1876 Congress began to make a general appropriation each year for the same purpose.

4. In 1894 objection was made to appropriating money for education "in sectarian institutions." The secretary of the interior agreed with the "intense feeling of opposition to sectarian education, which is showing itself all over the land," but concluded it would be impracticable to abandon the policy instantly; he recommended a decrease of 20 percent per year. General appropriation of public money for the sectarian schools stopped in 1899.

5. The money now being paid by the United States came from "Trust Funds" set up when the government bought land from the Indians and "Treaty Funds" set up by treaty. Appropriation of money for admittedly "sectarian schools" was classed under the heading "Fulfilling Treaty Stipulations with and Support of Indian Tribes." The money was regarded as the Indians' but was disbursed for their benefit by the secretary of the interior.

6. The treaty with the Sioux, made April 29, 1868, bound the United States to provide a schoolhouse and teacher for every thirty children.

7. On February 3, 1905, President Theodore Roosevelt wrote the Interior Department that the Indians "were entitled as a matter of moral right to have the moneys coming to them used for the education of their children at the schools of their choice." When petitions were signed by 212 Sioux Indians indicating that they wanted the Catholic schools to continue, the Department accordingly executed a contract with the Bureau of Catholic Indian Missions, using the 212 Sioux' proportionate share of the Trust Fund and Treaty Fund.

8. The amount in litigation was $27,000 due under such contract, executed July 1, 1905, for the education of 250 Indian pupils at St. Francis Mission School, Rosebud Reservation, South Dakota, at $108 per pupil per year, *Quick Bear v. Leupp, infra*, 58–71.

On appeal to the Supreme Court, defendants argued:

1. "A religious establishment, however, is not synonymous with an establishment of religion." See *Bradfield v. Roberts* [*supra*, this section]. A school, like a hospital, is neither an establishment of religion nor a religious establishment, although along with secular education

there might be, as there commonly is, instruction in morality and religion, just as in a hospital there would be religious ministrations, *ibid* at 74.

2. Not to let the Indians choose their own schools "perverts the supposed general spirit of the constitutional provisions into a means of prohibiting the free exercise of religion," *ibid.* 77.

The opinion of a unanimous Court was delivered by Chief Justice Melville W. Fuller, a fairly high-church Episcopalian:

Quick Bear v. Leupp
210 U.S. 50 (1908)

We concur in the decree of the Court of Appeals of the District and the reasoning by which its conclusion is supported, as set forth in the opinion of Wright, J., speaking for the court. Washington Law Rep., v. 35, p. 766.

The validity of the contract for $27,000 is attacked on the ground that all contracts for sectarian education among the Indians are forbidden by certain provisos contained in the Indian Appropriation Acts of 1895, 1896, 1897, 1898 and 1899. But if those provisos relate only to the appropriations made by the Government out of the public moneys of the United States raised by taxation from persons of all creeds and faiths, or none at all, and appropriated gratuitously for the purpose of education among the Indians, and not to "Tribal Funds," which belong to the Indians themselves, then the contract must be sustained. The difference between one class of appropriations and the other has long been recognized in the annual appropriation acts. The gratuitous appropriation of public moneys for the purpose of Indian education has always been made under the heading "Support of Schools," whilst the appropriation of the "Treaty Fund" has always been under the heading "Fulfilling Treaty Stipulations and Support of Indian Tribes," and that from the "Trust Fund" is not in the Indian Appropriation Acts at all. One class of appropriations relates to public moneys belonging to the Government; the other to moneys which belong to the Indians and which is administered for them by the Government. . . .

As has been shown, in 1868 the United States made a treaty with the Sioux Indians, under which the Indians made large cessions of land and other rights. In consideration of this the United States agreed that for every thirty children a house should be provided and a teacher competent to teach the elementary branches of our English education should be furnished for twenty years. In 1877, in consideration of further land cessions, the United States agreed to furnish all necessary aid to assist the Indians in the work of civilization and furnish them schools and instruction in mechanical and agricultural arts, as provided by the Treaty of 1868. In 1889 Congress extended the obligation of the treaty for twenty years, subject to such modifications as Congress should deem most effective, to secure the Indians equivalent benefits of such education. Thereafter, in every annual Indian appropriation act, there was an appropriation to carry out the terms of this treaty, under the heading "Fulfilling Treaty Stipulations with and Support of Indian Tribes."

These appropriations rested on different grounds from the gratuitous appropriations of public moneys under the heading "Support of Schools." The two subjects were separately treated in each act, and, naturally, as they are essentially different in character. One is the gratuitous appropriation of public moneys for the purpose of Indian education, but the "Treaty Fund" is not public money in this sense. It is the Indians' money, or at least is dealt with by the Government as if it belonged to them, as morally it does. It differs from the "Trust Fund" in this: The "Trust Fund" has been set aside for the Indians and the income expended for their benefit, which expenditure required no annual appropriation. The whole amount due the Indians for certain land cessions was appropriated in one lump sum by the act of 1889, 25 Stat. 888, chap. 405. This "Trust Fund" is held for the Indians and not distributed *per capita,* being held as property in common. The money is distributed in accordance with the discretion of the Secretary of the Interior, but really belongs to the Indians. The President declared it to be the moral right of the Indians to have this "Trust Fund" applied to the education of the Indians in the schools of their choice, and the same view was entertained by the Supreme Court of the District of Columbia and the Court of Appeals of the District. But the "Treaty Fund" has exactly the same characteristics. They are moneys belonging really to the Indians. They are the price of land ceded by the Indians to the Government. The only difference is that in the "Treaty Fund" the debt to the Indians created and secured by the treaty is paid by annual appropriations. They are not gratuitous appropriations of public moneys, but the payment, as we repeat, of a treaty debt in installments. We perceive no justification for applying the proviso or declaration of policy to the payment of treaty obligations, the two things being distinct and different in nature and having no relation to each other, except that both are technically appropriations.

Some reference is made to the Constitution, in respect to this contract with the Bureau of Catholic Indian Missions. It is not contended that it is unconstitutional, and it could not be. *Roberts* v. *Bradfield,* 12 App. D.C. 475; *Bradfield* v. *Roberts,* 175 U.S. 291. But it is contended that the spirit of the Constitution requires that the declaration of policy that the Government "shall make no appropriation whatever for education in any sectarian schools" should be treated as applicable, on the ground that the actions of the United States were to always be undenominational, and that, therefore, the Government can never act in a sectarian capacity, either in the use of its own funds or in that of the funds of others, in respect of which it is a trustee; hence that even the Sioux trust fund cannot be applied for education in Catholic schools, even though the owners of the fund so desire it. But we cannot concede the proposition that Indians cannot be allowed to use their own money to educate their children in the schools of their own choice because the Government is necessarily undenominational, as it cannot make any law respecting an establishment of religion or prohibiting the free exercise thereof. The Court of Appeals well said:

"The 'Treaty' and 'Trust' moneys are the only moneys that the Indians can lay claim to as matter of right; the only sums on which they are entitled to rely as theirs for education; and while these moneys are not delivered to them in hand, yet the money must not only be provided, but be expended, for their benefit and in part for their education; it seems inconceivable that Congress should have intended to prohibit them from receiving religious education at their own cost if they so desired it; such an intent would be one 'to prohibit the free exercise of religion' amongst the Indians, and such would be the effect of the construction for which the complainants contend."

The *cestuis que trust* cannot be deprived of their rights by the trustee in the exercise of power implied.

Decree affirmed.

4. THE CHURCHES AND THE FEDERAL INCOME TAX

The first income tax after passage of the Sixteenth Amendment exempted from tax the income of any "corporation or association organized and operated exclusively for religious, charitable, scientific or educational purposes, no part of the net income of which inures to the benefit of any private stockholder or individual," 38 Stat. 172 (1913). In *Brushaber* v. *Union Pacific Railroad* 240 U.S. 1 (1916), the case that upheld the power of Congress under the Sixteenth Amendment to set different rates of income tax for different classes, Chief Justice Edward Douglas White, a Catholic, writing for the Court swept away all objections to the lines drawn by Congress; no special mention was made of the charitable exemption or the benefits thereby accorded to religious groups.

5. THE CHURCHES AND THE DRAFT

Selective Draft Law Cases
245 U.S. 366 (1918)

Chief Justice White delivered the opinion of the court.

. . .The act exempted from subjection to the draft designated United States and state officials as well as those already in the military or naval service of the United States, regular or duly ordained ministers of religion and theological students under the conditions provided for, and, while relieving from military service in the strict sense the members of religious sects as enumerated whose tenets excluded the moral right to engage in war, nevertheless subjected such persons to the performance of service of a non-combatant character to be defined by the President. . . .

It remains only to consider contentions which, while not disputing power, challenge the act because of the repugnancy to the Constitution supposed to result from some of its provisions. . . . And we pass without anything but statement the proposition that an establishment of a religion or an interference with the free exercise thereof repugnant to the First Amendment resulted from the exemption clauses of the act to which we at the outset referred, because we think its unsoundness is too apparent to require us to do more. . . .

6. PROHIBITION

During World War I the movement to eliminate the general consumption of alcohol culminated in Congress on December 22, 1917, with the submission of the Eighteenth Amendment to the states for ratification. By January 1919, ratification had been voted by forty-six states. The amendment provided:

After one year from the ratification of this article the manufacture, sale or transportation of intoxicating liquors within . . . the United States . . . for beverage purposes is hereby prohibited.

The Eighteenth Amendment was the triumph of a movement with strong religious roots reaching back to the temperance reformers of the 1820s like Lyman Beecher and William Lloyd Garrison. After the Civil War, reformers who believed alcoholism to be a national menace called for delegates from churches and Sunday schools, and from state temperance groups, to form a Prohibition Party; its first national convention was in 1872, Norman H. Clark, *Deliver Us from Evil: An Interpretation of American Prohibition* (1976) 69–70. Thereafter the movement was largely sustained by Baptists, Presbyterians, Scandinavian Lutherans, and, above all, by Methodists, *ibid.*, at 89. A "Women's Crusade" in the 1870s attacked saloons with demonstrations and prayers in the street. In 1874 the Women's Christian Temperance Union was formed and in 1879, under President Frances Willard, it began to change the consciousness of the nation in a war against saloons. From New York to Kansas, the Republican party was affected by Prohibitionist pressures, usually identified with the churches, *ibid.*, at 74, 89. In 1887, H. H. Rutherford, a minister using "individual Protestant churches as his basic organizational unit," led the way in designing legislation letting local governments abolish the saloon, *ibid.* at 94. The Anti-Saloon League was self-identified as "the Protestant church in action," Andrew Sinclair, *Prohibition: The Era of Excess* (1962) 65. The leader of the league's educational work, Ernest Cherrington, wrote that "The church voters' lists . . . constituted the real key," Ernest Cherrington, *History of the Anti-Saloon League* (1913) 59.

The evils at which the Anti-Saloon League aimed—essentially the evils of alcoholism—were palpable: broken homes and broken lives, the loss of employment and the loss of self-esteem by those who became addicted. In addition, the anti-alcohol crusaders played on the association of alcohol with sexual sin, arguing that alcohol lowered inhibitions and facilitated lust, while the saloons themselves were often centers for prostitution, Sinclair 51. Just as in the crusade against slavery, the danger to chastity—a high value in Western Christianity—gave added impetus to the preachers against the evil.

As in the case of slavery, there was a biblical argument against the reformers. Wine had an honored place in Scripture; Jesus himself had turned water into wine at Cana (John 2). The biblical arguments were met as the scriptural arguments for slavery had been met, by saying that the wine accepted by the Jews was different from modern beverages, Sinclair 70. A more serious religious problem that divided the religious camp was that Catholics used wine to celebrate Mass, Episcopalian and various Protestant churches to celebrate Holy Communion, and Jews to observe Passover and other religious commemorations. Complete prohibition of all alcohol intruded sharply into basic liturgical practices. A lower court did enforce an Oklahoma statute literally to prevent shipment of sacramental wine to a Catholic priest, but the decision was reversed by the Oklahoma Supreme Court, Clark 126. Making an exception for liturgical use was politic. In some cases the Catholic vote was crucial in closing saloons locally—for example, in Los Angeles and San Jose in 1916, *ibid.,* at 108. These local victories underscored how important the role of religious fervor was to the outcome. In general, none of the adherents of the more liturgical religions—Catholics, Episcopalians, Jews—showed the appetite for the suspension of alcohol that characterized the more pietistic churches.

The Eighteenth Amendment, on its face, exacerbated the religious problem. A ban on "intoxicating liquors . . . for beverage purposes," read literally, included all wine. No one could pretend that wine was not drunk when it was used liturgically; and it was capable of intoxicating. The National Prohibition Act (the Volstead Act) made criminal the manufacture, sale, delivery, or possession of any beverage containing over .5 percent alcohol, but it wrote a discreet gloss, for the sake of religion, on the Amendment. The statute excepted "liquor for nonbeverage purposes and wine for sacramental purposes" and went on to say:

Nothing in this title shall be held to apply to the manufacture, importation, possession or distribution of wine for sacramental purposes, or like religious rites [41 Stat. 311 (1919)].

The sale of such wine, however, was forbidden "to any person not a rabbi, minister of the gospel, priest, or an officer duly authorized for the purpose by any church or congregation." Like the Income Tax and the Selective Draft Acts, the Volstead Act gave a special privilege to the clergy.

Prohibition did not divide the country as profoundly as slavery had divided it, because self-image and basic views of humanity were not at issue. A type of sumptuary law was at stake; but the seriousness with which the movement developed was owed above all to religion.

7. THE PRIVATE SCHOOLS CASE

In 1922 the voters of Oregon passed an initiative into law whose effect would have been to end religious and other private schools in the state. A three-judge federal court held the law unconstitutional, unreasonably encroaching on the lawful business of the schools, *Society of the Sisters of the Holy Names of Jesus and Mary v. Pierce; Hill Military Academy v. Pierce*, 296 F. 928 (D. Ore. 1924). On appeal, counsel for Governor Pierce argued:

The voters of Oregon who adopted this law had the right to act on the belief that the fact that the great increase in juvenile crime in the United States followed so closely after the great increase in the number of children in the United States who were not attending public schools, was more than a coincidence. The voters in Oregon might also have based their action in adopting this law upon the alarm which they felt at the rising tide of religious suspicions in this country, and upon their belief that the basic cause of such religious feelings was the separation of children along religious lines during the most susceptible years of their lives, with the inevitable awakening of a consciousness of separation, and a distrust and suspicion of those from whom they were so carefully guarded. The voters of Oregon might have felt that the mingling together, during a portion of their education, of the children of all races and sects, might be the best safeguard against future internal dissentions and consequent weakening of the community against foreign dangers [*Pierce v. Society of Sisters*, 268 U.S. 510 (1925), at 524–525].

It was also argued:

The statute does not interfere with religious identity. *Permoli v. New Orleans*, 3 How. 589.—The American people as a whole have unalterably determined that there shall be an absolute and unequivocal separation of church and state, and that the public schools shall be maintained and conducted free from influences in favor of any religious organization, sect, creed or belief. [*ibid.* at 512–513].

In reply for the Sisters, William D. Guthrie, an old Wall Street lawyer and a Catholic, argued the historic contribution of religious schools and colleges—all, in principle, he contended, threatened by the act. He went on to invoke the rights of parents—"those rights, which the statute seriously abridges and impairs, are of the very essence of personal liberty and freedom," *ibid.* at 518. He said these rights were not held today in the slight esteem they were by Plato and by the Spartans, except in "Soviet Russia."

For a unanimous Court, Justice James McReynolds, a Protestant, delivered an opinion, which, like the court below and Guthrie's general line of argument, avoided invoking the First Amendment.

Pierce v. Society of Sisters
268 U.S. 510 (1925)

. . .

The challenged Act, effective September 1, 1926, requires every parent, guardian or other person having control or charge or custody of a child between eight and sixteen years to send him "to a public school for the period of time a public school shall be held during the current year" in the district where the child resides; and failure so to do is declared a misdemeanor. There are exemptions—not specially important here—for children who are not normal, or who have completed the eighth grade, or who reside at considerable distances from any public school, or whose parents or guardians hold special permits from the County Superintendent. The manifest purpose is to compel general attendance at public schools by normal children, between eight and sixteen, who have not completed the eighth grade. And without doubt enforcement of the statute would seriously impair, perhaps destroy, the profitable features of appellees' business and greatly diminish the value of their property.

Appellee, the Society of Sisters, is an Oregon corporation, organized in 1880, with power to care for orphans, educate and instruct the youth, establish and maintain academies or schools, and acquire necessary real and personal property. It has long devoted its property and effort to the secular and religious education and care of children, and has acquired the valuable good will of many parents and guardians. It conducts interdependent primary and high schools and junior colleges, and maintains orphanages for the custody and control of children between eight and sixteen. In its primary schools many children between those ages are taught the subjects usually pursued in Oregon public schools during the first eight years. Systematic religious instruction and moral training according to the tenets of the Roman Catholic Church are also regularly provided. All courses of study, both temporal and religious, contemplate continuity of training under appellee's charge; the primary schools are essential to the system and the most profitable. It owns valuable buildings, especially constructed and equipped for school purposes. The business is remunerative—the annual income from primary schools exceeds thirty thousand dollars—and the successful conduct of this requires long time contracts with teachers and parents. The Compulsory Education Act of 1922 has already caused the withdrawal from its schools of children who would otherwise continue, and their income has steadily declined. The appellants, public officers, have proclaimed their purpose strictly to enforce the statute.

After setting out the above facts the Society's bill alleges that the enactment conflicts with the right of parents to choose schools where their children will receive appropriate mental and religious training, the right of the child to influence the parents' choice of a school, the right of schools and teachers therein to engage in a useful business or profession, and is accordingly repugnant to the Constitution and void. And, further, that unless enforcement of the measure is enjoined the corporation's business and property will suffer irreparable injury.

Appellee, Hill Military Academy, is a private corporation organized in 1908 under the laws of Oregon, engaged in owning, operating and conducting for profit an elementary, college preparatory and military training school for boys between the ages of five and twenty-one years. The average attendance is one hundred, and the annual fees received for each student amount to some eight hundred dollars. The elementary department is divided into eight grades, as in the public schools; the college preparatory department has four grades, similar to those of the public high schools; the courses of study conform to the requirements of the State Board of Education. Military instruction and training are also given, under the supervision of an Army officer. It owns considerable real and personal property, some useful only for school purposes. The business and incident good will are very valuable. In order to conduct its affairs long time contracts must be made for supplies, equipment, teachers and pupils. Appellants, law officers of the State and County, have publicly announced that the Act of November 7, 1922, is valid and have declared their intention to enforce it. By reason of the statute and threat of enforcement appellee's business is being destroyed and its property depreciated; parents and guardians are refusing to make contracts for the future instruction of their sons, and some are being withdrawn.

The Academy's bill states the foregoing facts and then alleges that the challenged Act contravenes the corporation's rights guaranteed by the Fourteenth Amendment and that unless appellants are restrained from proclaiming its validity and threatening to enforce it irreparable injury will result. The prayer is for an appropriate injunction.

No answer was interposed in either cause, and after proper notices they were heard by three judges (Jud. Code § 266) on motions for preliminary injunctions upon the specifically alleged facts. The court ruled that the Fourteenth Amendment guaranteed appellees against the deprivation of their property without due process of law consequent upon the unlawful interference by appellants with the free choice of patrons, present and prospective. It declared the right to conduct schools was property and that parents and guardians, as a part of their liberty, might direct the education of children by selecting reputable teachers and places. Also, that these schools were not unfit or harmful to the public, and that enforcement of the challenged statute would unlawfully deprive them of patronage and thereby destroy their owners' business and property. Finally, that the threats to enforce the Act would continue to cause irreparable injury; and the suits were not premature.

No question is raised concerning the power of the State reasonably to regulate all schools, to inspect, supervise and examine them, their teachers and pupils; to require that all children of proper age attend some school, that teachers shall be of good moral character and patriotic disposition, that certains studies plainly essential to good citizenship must be taught, and that nothing be taught which is manifestly inimical to the public welfare.

The inevitable practical result of enforcing the Act under consideration would be destruction of appellees' primary schools, and perhaps all other private primary schools for normal children within the State of Oregon. These parties are engaged in a kind of undertaking not inherently harmful, but long regarded as useful and meritorious. Certainly there is nothing in the present records to indicate that they have failed to discharge their obligations to patrons, students or the State. And there are no peculiar circumstances or present emergencies which demand extraordinary measures relative to primary education.

Under the doctrine of *Meyer* v. *Nebraska*, 262 U.S. 390, we think it entirely plain that the Act of 1922 unreasonably interferes with the liberty of parents and guardians to direct the upbringing and education of children under their control. As often heretofore pointed out, rights guaranteed by the Constitution may not be abridged by legislation which has no reasonable relation to some purpose within the competency of the State. The fundamental theory of liberty upon which all governments in this Union repose excludes any general power of the State to standardize its children by forcing them to accept instruction from public teachers only. The child is not the mere creature of the State; those who nurture him and direct his destiny have the right, coupled with the high duty, to recognize and prepare him for additional obligations.

. . . *Affirmed.*

8. THE FIRST DIVISION ON SEXUAL MORALS

Protestants and Catholics had in general agreed on what Christian sexual morality required. They had differed on divorce, but as far back as 1906 Edward Douglass White, a Catholic, had written a majority opinion for the Supreme Court limiting a state's right to grant divorce to a nonresident of the state, but recognizing the "inherent power" of the state "over the marriage relation, its formation and dissolutions." *Haddock* v. *Haddock*, 201 U.S. 562 at 569 (1906). White's view differed from the teaching of Pope Leo XIII in the encyclical *Arcanum*, February 10, 1880, *Acta Sanctae Sedis* 12, 385, at 390–391; but White's position reflected an American consensus.

Statutes permitting sterilization became popular in the 1920s. Catholic moralists denounced the laws. In 1927 the Virginia statute authorizing compulsory sterilization of the feeble-minded came before the Supreme Court in the case of Carrie Buck. The majority opinion was written by Oliver Wendell Holmes, Jr. Holmes was one of the few members ever appointed to the

Court who was openly agnostic about God and skeptical of revealed religion. As he wrote Harold Laski on January 11, 1929, "I regard [man] as I do the other species (except that my private interests are with his) having for his main business to live and propagate, and for his main interests food and sex" (*Holmes–Laski Letters,* ed. Mark De Wolfe Howe (1953) 2, 1125). As Holmes worked on the case, he wrote Laski on April 25, 1927: "My lad tells me the religious are astir," *ibid.* 2, 938. However, when Holmes upheld the statute, there was but one dissenter: Pierce Butler, the only Catholic on the Court, who dissented without opinion, *Buck v. Bell,* 274 U.S. 200 (1927). Holmes confided to Laski, May 12, 1927: "[I] felt that I was getting near to the first principle of real reform. I say merely getting near. I don't mean that the surgeon's knife is the ultimate symbol," *Letters* 2, 942.

9. ENFORCEMENT OF CHURCH LAW

The proper interpretation of a trust to celebrate mass was litigated in the Supreme Court of the Philippines, from whose decision an appeal lay to the Supreme Court of the United States. The unanimous opinion of the Court was delivered by Louis Brandeis. Brandeis was of Jewish antecedents and for that reason had been opposed by anti-Semites when named to the Court by President Wilson. He was a devoted Zionist, but he was not religiously Jewish, *see* Allon Gal, *Brandeis of Boston* (1980) 188–207. His opinion deferred to the canon law of the Catholic church, at the same time insisting that the secular courts had jurisdiction of the controversy and could override a church tribunal where there was "fraud, collusion, or arbitrariness":

Gonzalez v. Roman Catholic Archbishop of Manila
280 U.S. 1 (1929)

Justice Brandeis delivered the opinion of the Court.

This case is here on certiorari to the Supreme Court of the Philippine Islands. 278 U.S. 588. The subject matter is a collative chaplaincy in the Roman Catholic Archdiocese of Manila, which has been vacant since December 1910. The main question for decision are whether the petitioner is legally entitled to be appointed the chaplain and whether he shall recover the surplus income accrued during the vacancy.

Raul Rogerio Gonzalez, by his guardian *ad litem,* brought the suit against the Archbishop in the Court of First Instance of Manila, on August 5, 1924. He prayed for judgment declaring the petitioner the lawful heir to the chaplaincy and its income; establishing the right of the petitioner and his successors to be appointed to and receive the income of the chaplaincy during their infancy whenever it may be vacant and, pending such appointment, to receive the income for their maintenance and support; declaring the trust character of the property and ordering it to be so recorded; directing the Archbishop to appoint the petitioner chaplain and to account to him for the income of the property from 1910 on; and directing the defendant to pay the petitioner 1,000 pesos a month pending the final determination of the case. The trial court directed the Archbishop to appoint the petitioner chaplain; and ordered payment to him of 173,725 pesos ($86,862.50), that sum being the aggregate net income of the chaplaincy during the vacancy, less the expense of having the prescribed masses celebrated in each year. It reserved the petitioner any legal right he may have to proceed in the proper court for cancellation of the certificate of registration of the property in the name of the Archbishop. The Supreme Court of the Philippine Islands reversed the judgment on February 4, 1928, and absolved the Archbishop from the complaint, "without prejudice to the right of proper persons in interest to proceed for independent relief," in respect to the income accured during the vacancy, or in respect to the reformation of the certificate of registration so as to show the fiduciary character of the title. As the amount in controversy exceeds $25,000, this Court has jurisdiction on certiorari, Act of February 13, 1925, c. 229, § 7, 43 Stat. 936, 940.

The chaplaincy was founded in 1820, under the will of Doña Petronila de Guzman. By it, she requested "the Father chaplain to celebrate sixty masses annually" in behalf of the souls of her parents, brothers, sisters and herself. The deed of foundation, which was executed by the testamentary executor of Doña Petronila, provided that "said property is segregated from temporal properties and transferred to the spiritual properties of this Archbishopric, without its being possible to alienate or convert the property as such into any other estate for any cause, even though it be of a more pious character, . . . so that by virtue of this Deed of Foundation canonical collation may be conferred on the said appointed chaplain." By appropriate proceedings an ecclesiastical decree approved "the foundation of the chaplaincy with all the circumstances and conditions provided for in said clause (of the will) and in the deed of foundation, as well as the imposition (charge) of seventeen hundred pesos against said building, converting said sum into spiritual property of a perpetual character subject to the ecclesiastical forum and jurisdiction."

The will provided that the foundation should effect the immediate appointment as chaplain of D. Esteban de Guzman, the great-grandson of the testatrix; and "in his default, the nearest relative, and in default of the latter, a collegian (colegial) of San Juan de Letran, who should be an orphan *mestizo*, native of this said town." It named the president of that college as the patron of the chaplaincy. Esteban was appointed chaplain in 1820. From time to time thereafter four other descendants of the testatrix were successively appointed. The latest of these renounced the chaplaincy in December, 1910; married soon thereafter; and in 1912 became the father of the petitioner, Raul Rogerio Gonzalez, who is a legitimate son of the fifth chaplain and claims to be the nearest relative in descent from the first chaplain and the foundress.

Raul was presented to the Archibishop for appointment in 1922. The Archbishop refused to appoint him, on the ground that he did not then have "the qualifications required for chaplain of the said chaplaincy." He added: "The grounds of my conclusion are the very canons of the new Code of Canon Law. Among others, I can mention canon 1442 which says: 'Simple chaplaincies or benefices are conferred upon clergymen of the secular clergy,' in connection with canon 108, paragraph 1, 'Clergymen are those already initiated in the first tonsure' and canon 976, paragraph 1, 'No one can be promoted to first tonsure before he has begun the course in theology.' In view of the Canon as above mentioned, and other reasons which may be adduced, I believe that the boy, Raul Gonzalez, is not legally (ecclesiastically speaking) capacitated to the enjoyment of a chaplaincy."

Ever since the Council of Trent (1545–1563), it has been the law of the church that no one can be appointed to a collative chaplaincy before his fourteenth year. When Raul was presented for appointment, he was in his tenth year. He was less than twelve when this suit was begun. He was fourteen when the trial court entered its judgment. It is also urged on behalf of the Archbishop that at no time since that Council could one be lawfully appointed who lacked elementary knowledge of Christian Doctrine.

The new Codex Juris Canonici, which was adopted in Rome in 1917 and was promulgated by the Church to become effective in 1918, provides that no one shall be appointed to a collative chaplaincy who is not a cleric, Can. 1442. It requires students for the priesthood to attend a seminary; and prescribes their studies, Can. 1354, 1364. It provides that in order to be a cleric one must have had "prima tonsura," Can. 108, par. 1; that in order to have "prima tonsura" one most have begun the study of theology, Can. 976, par. 1; and that in order to study theology one must be a "bachiller," that is, must have obtained the first degree in the sciences and liberal arts, Can. 1365. It also provides that no one may validly receive ordination unless in the opinion of the ordinary he has the necessary qualifications, Can. 968, par. 1, 1464. Petitioner concedes that the chaplaincy here involved is a collative one; and that Raul lacked, at the time of his presentment and of the commencement of the suit, the age qualification required by the Canon Law in force when the chaplaincy was founded. It is also conceded that he lacked, then, and at the time of the entry of the judgment, other qualifications of a candidate for a collative chaplaincy essential, if the new Codex was applicable.

Raul's contention, in effect, is that the nearest male relative in descent from the foundress and the first chaplain, willing to be appointed chaplain, is entitled to enjoy the revenues of the foundation, subject only to the duty of saying himself the sixty masses in each year, if he is qualified so to do, or of causing them to be said by a qualified priest and paying the customary charge therefor out of the income. He claims that the provisions of the new Codex are not applicable and that his rights are to be determined by the Canon Law in force at the time the chaplaincy was founded; and that the judgment of the trial court should be reinstated, because he possessed at the time of the entry of the judgment all the qualifications required by the Canon Law in force in 1820. Raul argues that contemporaneous construction and long usage have removed any doubt as to what these qualifications were; that when the foundation was established, and for a long time thereafter, the ecclesiastical character of the incumbent was a minor consideration; that this is shown by the administration of this chaplaincy; and that his own ecclesiastical qualifications, at the time of the entry of the judgment in the trial court, were not inferior to those of the prior incumbents. He asserts that, although chaplaincies were disamortized in Spain prior to 1867, Alcubilla, Diccionario, Vol. II, p. 118, they had in the Philippines remained undisturbed by any legislation of Spain; and that the rights of the church were preserved by Article VIII of the Treaty of Paris. 30 Stat. 1754, 1758. *Ponce* v. *Roman Catholic Church,* 210 U.S. 296, 315–322. He contends that to deprive him of his alleged right to the chaplaincy because of a change made in 1918 in the Canon Law would violate the Constitution of the United States, the Treaty with Spain of 1898, and the Organic Act of the Philippine Islands.

The trial court rested its judgment for Raul largely on the ground that he possessed, at the time of its entry, the qualifications required by the Canon Law in force when the chaplaincy was founded; and that, hence, he was entitled both to be appointed chaplain and to recover the income accrued during the vacancy, even though he did not possess the qualifications prescribed by the new Codex then otherwise in force. The Supreme Court held that to give effect to the provisions of the new Codex would not impair the obligation of the contract made in 1820, as it was an implied term of the deed of foundation that the qualifications of a chaplain should be such as the church authorities might prescribe from time to time; and that, since Raul confessedly did not possess the qualifications prescribed by the new Codex which had been promulgated before he was presented, he could not be appointed.

First. The Archbishop interposes here, as he did below, an objection to the jurisdiction of the Philippine courts. He insists that, since the chaplaincy is confessedly a collative one, its property became spiritual property of a perpetual character subject to the jurisdiction of the ecclesiastical forum; and that thereby every controversy concerning either the right to appointment or the right to the income was removed from the jurisdiction of secular courts. The objection is not sound. The courts have jurisdiction of the parties. For the Archbishop is a juristic person amenable to the Philippine courts for the enforcement of any legal right; and the petitioner asserts such a right. There is jurisdiction of the subject matter. For the petitioner's claim is, in substance, that he is entitled to the relief sought as the beneficiary of a trust.

The fact that the property of the chaplaincy was transferred to the spiritual properties of the Archbishopric affects not the jurisdiction of the court, but the terms of the trust. *Watson* v. *Jones,* 13 Wall. 679, 714, 729. The Archbishop's claim in this respect is that by an implied term of the gift, the property, which was to be held by the church, should be administered in such manner and by such persons as may be prescribed by the church from time to time. Among the church's laws which are thus claimed to be applicable are those creating tribunals for the determination of ecclesiastical controversies. Because the appointment is a canonical act, it is the function of the church authorities to determine what the essential qualifications of a chaplain are and whether the candidate possesses them. In the absence of fraud, collusion, or arbitrariness, the decisions of the proper church tribunals on matters purely ecclesiastical, although affecting civil rights, are accepted in litigation before the secular courts as conclusive, because the parties in interest made them so by contract or otherwise. Under like circumstances, effect is given in the courts to the determinations of the judicatory bodies established by clubs and civil associations.

Second. The Archbishop contended that Raul lacked even the minimum of training and knowledge of Christian Doctrine made indispensable by the Canon Law in force in 1820; that his confessed lack of the essential age at the time of the presentment and also at the time of the institution of the suit were unsurmountable obstacles to the granting of the prayer for appointment to the chaplaincy; and, moreover, that the failure to take an appeal to the Pope from the decision of the Archbishop, as provided by the Canon Law, precluded resort to legal proceedings. We have no occasion to consider the soundness of these contentions. For we are of opinion that the Canon Law in force at the time of the presentation governs, and the lack of the qualification prescribed by it is admitted. Neither the foundress, nor the church authorities, can have intended that the perpetual chaplaincy created in 1820 should, in respect to the qualifications of an incumbent, be forever administered according to the canons of the church which happened to be in force at that date. The parties to the foundation clearly contemplated that the Archbishop would, before ordination, exercise his judgment as to the fitness of the applicant; and they must have contemplated that, in the course of the centuries, the standard of fitness would be modified.

When the new Codex was promulgated in 1918 Raul was only six years old and had not yet been presented. If he had been presented, he obviously could not have been appointed. No right was then being enjoyed by him of which the promulgation of the new Codex deprived him. When he was presented later, he was ineligible under the then existing Canon Law. In concluding that Raul lacked the qualifications essential for a chaplain the Archbishop appears to have followed the controlling Canon Law. There is not even a suggestion that he exercised his authority arbitrarily.

Third. Raul urges that, even though he is not entitled to be appointed chaplain, he is entitled to recover the surplus net income earned during the vacancy. Indeed, it is the property rights involved that appear to be his main consideration. The value of the property in 1820 was about 1,700 pesos. The annual net income was then 180 pesos, a sum sufficient only to defray the annual expense of sixty masses. The annual net income has grown to about 12,000 pesos; and the annual expense of the sixty masses does not now exceed 300 pesos. In each year during the vacancy the masses have been duly celebrated. The surplus income accruing during the vacancy has been used by the Archbishop currently for pious purposes, namely, education. By canon 1481 of the new Codex the surplus income of a chaplaincy, after deducting expenses of the acting chaplain, must one-half be added to the endowment or capital and one-half to the repair of the church, unless there is a custom of using the whole for some common good to the diocese. The use made of the surplus of this chaplaincy was in accordance with what was claimed to be the long established custom of the Archdiocese. Both the custom and the specific application made of this surplus have been approved by the Holy See. The Supreme Court held that since Raul had sought the income only as an incident of the chaplaincy, he could not recover anything.

Raul's claim, which is made even in respect to income accured prior to his birth, is rested upon some alleged right by inheritance, although his father is still living. The intention of the foundress, so far as expressed, was that the income should be applied to the celebration of masses and to the living of the chaplain, who should preferably be the nearest male relative in the line of descent from herself or the first chaplain. The claim that Raul individually is entitled as nearest relative to the surplus by inheritance is unsupported by anything in the deed of gift or the applicable law. Since Raul is not entitled to be appointed chaplain, he is not entitled to a living from the income of the chaplaincy.

Raul urges also an alleged right as representative of the heirs of the testatrix as a class. This suggestion was, we think, properly met by the ruling of the Supreme Court that the suit was not brought as a class suit. Whether the surplus income earned during the vacancy has been properly disposed of by the Archbishop and what disposition shall be made of it in the future we have no occasion to enquire. The entry of the judgment without prejudice "to the right of proper persons in interest to proceed for independent relief" leaves any existing right of that nature unaffected.

Affirmed.

10. THE SCHOOL BOOKS CASE

Louisiana in 1928 supplied free school books to all school children in the state. Taxpayers in Shreveport and Baton Rouge challenged the constitutionality of the action and appealed from a decision of the Louisiana Supreme Court to the United States Supreme Court. They argued:

if the furnishing of text-books free to children attending private schools is not considered an aid to such private schools, but as incidental to the state educational system, then it logically follows that the tuition of the children attending such schools could be paid; their transportation to and from such schools could be provided; the salaries of the instructors could be paid in part or in whole; and finally, the buildings themselves could be erected,—with state funds; all of which, under the reasoning evinced in the statutes of Louisiana, might be justified on the ground that it is the interest of the State to see that its youth are educated [*Cochran v. Board of Education, infra* at 372.].

The opinion of a unanimous Supreme Court was delivered by Justice Charles Evans Hughes, the son of a Baptist minister:

Cochran v. Board of Education
281 U.S. 370 (1930)

. . .

Act No. 100 of 1928 provided that the severance tax fund of the State, after allowing funds and appropriations as required by the state constitution, should be devoted "first, to supplying school books to the school children of the State." The Board of Education was directed to provide "school books for school children free of cost to such children." Act No. 143 of 1928 made appropriations in accordance with the above provisions.

The Supreme Court of the State, following its decision in *Borden* v. *Louisiana State Board of Education,* 168 La. 1005, held that these acts were not repugnant to either the state or the Federal Constitution.

No substantial Federal question is presented under section 4 of Article IV of the Federal Constitution guaranteeing to every State a republican form of government, as questions arising under this provision are political, not judicial, in character. *State of*

Ohio ex rel. Bryant v. *Akron Metropolitan Park District, ante,* p. 74, and cases there cited.

The contention of the appellant under the Fourteenth Amendment is that taxation for the purchase of school books constituted a taking of private property for a private purpose. *Loan Association* v. *Topeka,* 20 Wall. 655. The purpose is said to be to aid private, religious, sectarian, and other schools not embraced in the public educational system of the State by furnishing text-books free to the children attending such private schools. The operation and effect of the legislation in question were described by the Supreme Court of the State as follows (168 La., p. 1020):

"One may scan the acts in vain to ascertain where any money is appropriated for the purchase of school books for the use of any church, private, sectarian or even public school. The appropriations were made for the specific purpose of purchasing school books for the use of the school children of the state, free of cost to them. It was for their benefit and the resulting benefit to the state that the appropriations were made. True, these children attend some school, public or private, the latter, sectarian or non-sectarian, and that the books are to be furnished them for their use, free of cost, whichever they attend. The schools, however, are not the beneficiaries of these appropriations. They obtain nothing from them, nor are they relieved of a single obligation, because of them. The school children and the state alone are the beneficiaries. It is also true that the sectarian schools, which some of the children attend, instruct their pupils in religion, and books are used for that purpose, but one may search diligently the acts, though without result, in an effort to find anything to the effect that it is the purpose of the state to furnish religious books for the use of such children. . . . What the statutes contemplate is that the same books that are furnished children attending public schools shall be furnished children attending private schools. This is the only practical way of interpreting and executing the statutes, and this is what the state board of education is doing. Among these books, naturally, none is to be expected, adapted to religious instruction."

The Court also stated, although the point is not of importance in relation to the Federal question, that it was "only the use of the books that is granted to the children, or, in other words, the books are lent to them."

Viewing the statute as having the effect thus attributed to it, we can not doubt that the taxing power of the State is exerted for a public purpose. The legislation does not segregate private schools, or their pupils, as its beneficiaries or attempt to interfere with any matters of exclusively private concern. Its interest is education, broadly; its method, comprehensive. Individual interests are aided only as the common interest is safeguarded.

Judgment affirmed.

11. CONSCIENTIOUS OBJECTORS

Rosika Schwimmer, a forty-nine-year-old Hungarian immigrant applying for naturalization, declared, "I am not willing to bear arms." She asserted, "My 'cosmic consciousness of belonging to the human family' is shared by all those who believe that all human beings are the children of God," *United States* v. *Schwimmer,* 279 U.S. 644 (1929). Denial of her naturalization application was upheld by Pierce Butler, writing for a majority of six that the duty of citizens to defend their government by arms was a "fundamental principle of the Constitution," *ibid.* at 650. Justice Holmes, joined in his dissent by Justice Brandeis, noted:

I would suggest that the Quakers have done their share to make the country what it is, that many citizens agree with the applicant's belief and that I had not supposed hitherto that we regretted our inability to expel them because they believe more than some of us do in the teachings of the Sermon on the Mount [*ibid.* at 655; Justice Sanford also dissented].

United States v. Macintosh
283 U.S. 605 (1931)

In 1929 Douglas Clyde Macintosh, a Canadian, applied for naturalization. He was a Baptist minister who had served as chaplain at the front in World War I; he was now Dwight Professor of Theology at Yale. He declared he would not support the United States "right or wrong" or promise to take up arms in its defense. He "could not put allegiance to the government of any country before allegiance to the will of God."

The Second Circuit, per Judge Martin Manton, ordered him admitted to citizenship, 42 F.2d 845 (1930). The government took the case to the Supreme Court, arguing it was indistinguishable from *Schwimmer.* On Macintosh's behalf, John W. Davis argued that the free exercise of religion "embraces human conduct expressive of the relation between man and God," *United States v. Macintosh,* at 612. Davis asserted there was a constitutional immunity against bearing arms in a war if one has "conscientious religious scruples against doing so," *ibid.* at 623.

For the Court, Justice George Sutherland characterized Davis's argument as astonishing: "Of course, there is no such principle in the Constitution, fixed or otherwise," *ibid.* at 623. Sutherland continued:

When he speaks of putting his allegiance to the will of God above his allegiance to the government, it is evident, in the light of his entire statement, that he means to make his own *interpretation* of the will of God the decisive test which shall conclude the government and stay its hand. We are a Christian people (*Holy Trinity Church v. United States,* 143 U.S. 457, 470–471), according to one another the equal right of religious freedom, and acknowledging with reverence the duty of obedience to the will of God. But, also, we are a Nation with the duty to survive; a Nation whose Constitution contemplates war as well as peace; whose government must go forward upon the assumption, and safely can proceed upon no other, that unqualified allegiance to the Nation and submission and obedience to the laws of the land, as well those made for war as those made for peace, are not inconsistent with the will of God.

Chief Justice Hughes, joined by Justices Holmes, Brandeis, and Stone—a weighty minority—dissented:

The essence of religion is belief in a relation to God involving duties superior to those arising from any human relation. As was stated by Mr. Justice Field, in *Davis v. Beason,* 133 U.S. 333, 342: "The term 'religion' has reference to one's views of his relations to his Creator, and to the obligations they impose of reverence for his being and character, and of obedience to his will." One cannot speak of religious liberty, with proper appreciation of its essential and historic significance, without assuming the existence of a belief in supreme allegiance to the will of God. Professor Macintosh, when pressed by the inquiries put to him, stated what is axiomatic in religious doctrine. And, putting aside dogmas with their particular conceptions of deity, freedom of conscience itself implies respect for an innate conviction of paramount duty. The battle for religious liberty has been fought and won with respect to religious beliefs and practices, which are not in conflict with good order, upon the very ground of the supremacy of conscience within its proper field. What that field is, under our system of government, presents in part a question of constitutional law and also, in part, one of legislative policy in avoiding unnecessary clashes with the dictates of conscience. There is abundant room for enforcing the requisite authority of law as it is enacted and requires obedience, and for maintaining the conception of the supremacy of law as essential to orderly government, without demanding that either citizens or applicants for citizenship shall assume by oath an obligation to regard allegiance to God as subordinate to allegiance to civil power. The attempt to exact such a promise, and thus to bind one's conscience by the taking of oaths or the submission to tests, has been the cause of many deplorable conflicts. The Congress has sought to avoid such conflicts in this country by respecting our happy tradition. In no sphere of legislation has the intention to prevent such clashes been more conspicuous than in relation to the bearing of arms. It would require strong evidence that the Congress intended a reversal of its policy in prescribing the general terms of the naturalization oath. I find no such evidence.

Nor is there ground, in my opinion, for the exclusion of Professor Macintosh because his conscientious scruples have particular reference to wars believed to be unjust. There is nothing new in such an attitude. Among the most eminent statesmen here and abroad have been those who condemned the action of their country in entering into wars they thought to be unjustified. Agreements for the renunciation of war presuppose a preponderant public sentiment against wars of aggression. If, while recognizing the power of Congress, the mere holding of religious or conscientious scruples against all wars should not disqualify a citizen from holding office in this country, or an applicant otherwise qualified from being admitted to citizenship, there would seem to be no reason why a reservation of religious or conscientious objection to participation in wars believed to be unjust should constitute such a disqualification.

Apart from the terms of the oath, it is said that the respondent has failed to meet the requirement of "attachment to the principles of the Constitution." Here, again, is a general phrase which should be construed, not in opposition to, but in accord with, the theory and practice of our Government in relation to freedom of conscience. What I have said as to the provisions of the oath I think applies equally to this phase of the case.

The Regents of the University of California required all male students to complete one course in military service and tactics. The Methodist Episcopal church in its General Conference of 1928 had declared, "We renounce war as an instrument of national policy." Two Methodist students, sons of ministers, asserting their religious belief "that war, training for war, and military training are immoral," were suspended from the university for failing to take the prescribed course. The supreme court of California sustained the Regents. The two Methodists appealed to the Supreme Court, contending that free exercise of religion was protected against the states by the First Amendment and that the principle of free exercise "must afford protection to outward manifestations of religious belief."

Pierce Butler, a Catholic, delivered the opinion of the Supreme Court, citing the naturalization cases of *Schwimmer* and *Macintosh* to show that there was no unconstitutional infringement of religious belief for a government to require willingness to bear arms, *Hamilton v. Regents of the University of California*, 293 U.S. 245 (1934). Concurring in the opinion, Justice Benjamin Cardozo—a humanist of Jewish background—found nothing contrary to "the free exercise of religion as the phrase was understood by the founders of the nation, and by the generations that have followed," *ibid.* at 265. He added at 268: "One who is a martyr to a principle—which may turn out in the end to be a delusion or an error—does not prove by his martyrdom that he has kept within the law."

Part Three
CONTEMPO-
RARY
CONTRO-
VERSIES

ELEVEN

Sacred Duties

1. PREACHING FROM HOUSE TO HOUSE

CONSTITUTIONAL CHALLENGES by a single religious group to state regulation of religion were the catalyst that brought the United States Supreme Court to bear upon the subject. The challenges occurred at a time when the Court was reading other First Amendment freedoms into the meaning of "the due process of law" guarantee of the Fourteenth Amendment. The challenges were made by the Jehovah's Witnesses, a group that, like the eighteenth-century Baptists, was evangelical and outside the mainline Protestant churches; tightly knit like the nineteenth-century Mormons; and ruled by a supreme authority like twentieth-century Catholics. Like the Mennonites, the Witnesses were pioneers of civil liberty while being severe in maintaining orthodoxy within their own ranks, *see* M. James Penton, *Apocalypse Delayed* (1985) 62-68. Paradoxically they were to attack the hypocrisy of all "religionists" while claiming their own freedom from regulation that interfered with their own free exercise of "religion."

In 1880, in Pittsburgh, Charles Taze Russell began the publication of *Zion's Watch Tower and Herald of Christ's Presence,* teaching that the Second Coming of Christ was imminent. Book salesmen who were believers—"colporteurs," to use the term earlier applied to evangelical distributors of the Bible—sold Russell's works throughout the United States and Britain. By the eve of World War I, the *Watch Tower* had 45,000 subscribers, James A. Beckford, *The Trumpet of Prophecy: A Sociological Study of Jehovah's Witnesses* (1975) 1-18.

On Russell's death in 1916, Joseph Franklin Rutherford succeeded him as president of the Watch Tower Bible and Tract Society, the New York corporation that held title to all church property. Rutherford was a lawyer, once a special judge in Missouri, and customarily called Judge Rutherford. The next year Rutherford was indicted under the Espionage Act of 1917 for conspiracy to obstruct recruiting and to cause insubordination in the armed forces. Evidence supporting the charge was his publication of *The Finished Mystery,* a book that attacked "patriotism" as one of "the great untruths" of Satan, denounced war as murder, and declared that no issue was worth a single life. At the trial the government clinched its case by showing Rutherford's activity "advising men subject to the draft to claim their exemption and to refuse to perform any duty in camp if they were drafted," *Rutherford v. United States,* 258 F. 855, 865 (2nd Cir. 1919). For his book and his advice, Rutherford and six other defendants were sentenced to twenty years in the federal penitentiary. On appeal, by a vote of 2-1, the convictions were set aside on the ground of a prejudicial act by the trial judge (sentencing an evasive witness for contempt), *ibid.* at 863. The First Amendment was not invoked. The government did not renew the prosecution. Other Jehovah's Witnesses received long prison sentences for distributing *The Finished Mystery, e.g., Stephens v. United States,*

261 F. 590 (9th Cir. 1919) (distributors had "a disloyal and wicked" purpose). But Judge Rutherford himself had had an unforgettable experience of the justice administered by the appellate courts of the United States.

Jehovah's Witnesses were prosecuted for selling their literature without a license as early as 1928. Prior to this time, the Witnesses had accepted the conventional view that Paul, in Romans 13:1, commanding obedience to the "powers," had meant the civil authorities, *supra*, I, 4. Now in 1929 Judge Rutherford interpreted "the powers" to be obeyed as being God and Christ, Penton 139. In the 1930s the conflict between the Witnesses and local licensing authorities increased, and Rutherford in 1933 ordered that all adverse court decisions be appealed. In 1935 he set up a legal department under Olin R. Moyle, a Witness, to coordinate the defense of Witnesses, David R. Manwaring, *Render unto Caesar: The Flag-Salute Controversy* (1962) 26–27.

The Witnesses saturated communities—usually on Sundays, their day off from their ordinary occupation—with their tracts, ignoring local restrictions as infringements of their duty to carry out a divine command. In 1937 the Supreme Court, invoking the Mormon cases, unanimously dismissed for want of federal jurisdiction, leaving religiously motivated distributors of literature unprotected, *Coleman v. City of Griffin*, 302 U.S. 636 (1937). The next year, however, by a vote of 8-0, the Supreme Court invalidated the Griffin ordinance on the ground that it unconstitutionally abridged the Witnesses' freedom of speech and the freedom of the press, *Lovell v. City of Griffin*, 303 U.S. 444 (1938). These freedoms were characterized by Chief Justice Charles Evans Hughes as "among the fundamental personal rights" protected by the Fourteenth Amendment, while the Court still left a purely religious right without protection. The victory was largely the work of the American Civil Liberties Union (then called the American Liberties Union), which had come to the Witnesses' assistance. In 1939 the Court, 8-1, struck down four more municipal ordinances as abridgments of the freedom of speech and of the press, *Schneider v. Irvington*, 308 U.S. 147 (1939). Not, however, until 1940 did the Supreme Court address affirmatively the claim of free exercise of religion.

The Witnesses were now represented by Hayden C. Covington, a young Texan Witness, with whom Rutherford had replaced Moyle; he was to have a remarkable career in Supreme Court litigation, in the next fifteen years winning thirty-six cases, Penton 88. Without mentioning *Coleman*—unanimously decided only three years earlier—the Supreme Court in effect overruled it. More remarkably, the Court—composed of Hughes, McReynolds, Stone, and Roberts, whose appointments antedated the New Deal, and Roosevelt's appointees Black, Reed, Frankfurter, Douglas, and Murphy—was in complete agreement.

Cantwell v. Connecticut
310 U.S. 696 (1940)

Mr. Hayden C. Covington, with whom *Mr. Joseph F. Rutherford* was on the brief, for appellants and petitioner.

Messrs. Francis A. Pallotti, Attorney General, and *Mr. Edwin S. Pickett*, with whom *Messrs. William L. Hadden, Richard F. Corkey*, Assistant Attorney General, and *Luke H. Stapleton* were on the brief, for the State of Connecticut, appellee and respondent.

. . .

Justice Roberts delivered the opinion of the Court.

Newton Cantwell and his two sons, Jesse and Russell, members of a group known as Jehovah's Witnesses, and claiming to be ordained ministers, were arrested in New Haven, Connecticut, and each was charged by information in five counts, with statutory and common law offenses. After trial in the Court of Common Pleas of New Haven

County each of them was convicted on the third count, which charged a violation of § 6294 of the General Statutes of Connecticut, and on the fifth count, which charged commission of the common law offense of inciting a breach of the peace. On appeal to the Supreme Court the conviction of all three on the third count was affirmed. The conviction of Jesse Cantwell, on the fifth count, was also affirmed, but the conviction of Newton and Russell on that count was reversed and a new trial ordered as to them. . . .

The facts adduced to sustain the convictions on the third count follow. On the day of their arrest the appellants were engaged in going singly from house to house on Cassius Street in New Haven. They were individually equipped with a bag containing books and pamphlets on religious subjects, a portable phonograph and a set of records, each of which, when played, introduced, and was a description of, one of the books. Each appellant asked the person who responded to his call for permission to play one of the records. If permission was granted he asked the person to buy the book described and, upon refusal, he solicited such contribution towards the publication of the pamphlets as the listener was willing to make. If a contribution was received a pamphlet was delivered upon condition that it would be read.

Cassius Street is in a thickly populated neighborhood, where about ninety per cent of the residents are Roman Catholics. A phonograph record, describing a book entitled "Enemies," included an attack on the Catholic religion. None of the persons interviewed were members of Jehovah's Witnesses.

The statute under which the appellants were charged provides:

"No person shall solicit money, services, subscriptions or any valuable thing for any alleged religious, charitable or philanthropic cause, from other than a member of the organization for whose benefit such person is soliciting or within the county in which such person or organization is located unless such cause shall have been approved by the secretary of the public welfare council. Upon application of any person in behalf of such cause, the secretary shall determine whether such cause is a religious one or is a bona fide object of charity or philanthropy and conforms to reasonable standards of efficiency and integrity, and, if he shall so find, shall approve the same and issue to the authority in charge a certificate to that effect. Such certificate may be revoked at any time. Any person violating any provision of this section shall be fined not more than one hundred dollars or imprisoned not more than thirty days or both." . . .

First. We hold that the statute, as construed and applied to the appellants, deprives them of their liberty without due process of law in contravention of the Fourteenth Amendment. The fundamental concept of liberty embodied in that Amendment embraces the liberties guaranteed by the First Amendment. The First Amendment declares that Congress shall make no law respecting an establishment of religion or prohibiting the free exercise thereof. The Fourteenth Amendment has rendered the legislatures of the states as incompetent as Congress to enact such laws. The constitutional inhibition of legislation on the subject of religion has a double aspect. On the one hand, it forestalls compulsion by law of the acceptance of any creed or the practice of any form of worship. Freedom of conscience and freedom to adhere to such religious organization or form of worship as the individual may choose cannot be restricted by law. On the other hand, it safeguards the free exercise of the chosen form of religion. Thus the Amendment embraces two concepts,—freedom to believe and freedom to act. The first is absolute but, in the nature of things, the second cannot be. Conduct remains subject to regulation for the protection of society. The freedom to act must have appropriate definition to preserve the enforcement of that protection. In every case the power to regulate must be so exercised as not, in attaining a permissible end, unduly to infringe the protected freedom. No one would contest the proposition that a State may not, by statute, wholly deny the right to preach or to disseminate religious views. Plainly such a previous and absolute restraint would violate the terms of the guarantee. It is equally clear that a State may by general and non-discriminatory legislation regulate the times, the places, and the manner of soliciting upon its streets, and of holding meetings thereon; and may in other respects safeguard the peace, good order and comfort of the community, without unconstitutionally invading the liberties protected by the Fourteenth Amendment. The appellants are right in their insistence that the Act in question is not such a regulation. If a certificate is procured, solicitation is permitted without restraint but, in the absence of a certificate, solicitation is altogether prohibited.

The appellants urge that to require them to obtain a certificate as a condition of soliciting support for their views amounts to a prior restraint on the exercise of their religion within the meaning of the Constitution. The State insists that the Act, as construed by the Supreme Court of Connecticut, imposes no previous restraint upon the dissemination of religious views or teaching but merely safeguards against the perpetration of frauds under the cloak of religion. Conceding that this is so, the question remains whether the method adopted by Connecticut to that end transgresses the liberty safeguarded by the Constitution.

The general regulation, in the public interest, of solicitation, which does not involve any religious test and does not unreasonably obstruct or delay the collection of funds, is not open to any constitutional objection, even though the collection be for a religious purpose. Such regulation would not constitute a prohibited previous restraint on the free exercise of religion or interpose an inadmissible obstacle to its exercise.

It will be noted, however, that the Act requires an application to the secretary of the public welfare council of the State; that he is empowered to determine whether the cause is a religious one, and that the issue of a certificate depends upon his affirmative action. If he finds that the cause is not that of religion, to solicit for it becomes a crime. He is not to issue a certificate as a matter of course. His decision to issue or refuse it involves appraisal of facts, the exercise of judgment, and the formation of an opinion. He is authorized to withhold his approval if he determines that the cause is not a religious one. Such a censorship of religion as the means of determining its right to survive is a denial of liberty protected by the First Amendment and included in the liberty which is within the protection of the Fourteenth.

The State asserts that if the licensing officer acts arbitrarily, capriciously, or corruptly, his action is subject to judicial correction. Counsel refer to the rule prevailing in Connecticut that the decision of a commission or an administrative official will be reviewed upon a claim that "it works material damage to individual or corporate rights, or invades or threatens such rights, or is so unreasonable as to justify judicial intervention, or is not consonant with justice, or that a legal duty has not been performed." It is suggested that the statute is to be read as requiring the officer to issue a certificate unless the cause in question is clearly not a religious one; and that if he violates his duty his action will be corrected by a court.

To this suggestion there are several sufficient answers. The line between a discretionary and a ministerial act is not always easy to mark and the statute has not been construed by the state court to impose a mere ministerial duty on the secretary of the welfare council. Upon his decision as to the nature of the cause, the right to solicit depends. Moreover, the availability of a judicial remedy for abuses in the system of licensing still leaves that system one of previous restraint which, in the field of free speech and press, we have held inadmissible. A statute authorizing previous restraint upon the exercise of the guaranteed freedom by judicial decision after trial is as obnoxious to the Constitution as one providing for like restraint by administrative action.

Nothing we have said is intended even remotely to imply that, under the cloak of religion, persons may, with impunity, commit frauds upon the public. Certainly penal laws are available to punish such conduct. Even the exercise of religion may be at some slight inconvenience in order that the State may protect its citizens from injury. Without doubt a State may protect its citizens from fraudulent solicitation by requiring a stranger in the community, before permitting him publicly to solicit funds for any purpose, to establish his identity and his authority to act for the cause which he purports to represent. The State is likewise free to regulate the time and manner of solicitation generally, in the interest of public safety, peace, comfort or convenience. But to condition the solicitation of aid for the perpetuation of religious views or systems upon a license, the grant of which rests in the exercise of a determination by state authority as to what is a religious cause, is to lay a forbidden burden upon the exercise of liberty protected by the Constitution.

Second. We hold that, in the circumstances disclosed, the conviction of Jesse Cantwell on the fifth count must be set aside. Decision as to the lawfulness of the conviction demands the weighing of two conflicting interests. The fundamental law declares the interest of the United States that the free exercise of religion be not prohibited and that freedom to communicate information and opinion be not abridged. The State of Connecticut has an obvious interest in the preservation and protection of peace and good order within her borders. We must determine whether the alleged protection of the State's interest, means to which end would, in the absence of limitation by the Federal Constitution, lie wholly within the State's discretion, has been pressed, in this instance, to a point where it has come into fatal collision with the overriding interest protected by the federal compact.

Conviction on the fifth count was not pursuant to a statute evincing a legislative judgment that street discussion of religious affairs, because of its tendency to provoke disorder, should be regulated, or a judgment that the playing of a phonograph on the streets should in the interest of comfort or privacy be limited or prevented. Violation of an Act exhibiting such a legislative judgment and narrowly drawn to prevent the supposed evil, would pose a question differing from that we must here answer. Such a declaration of the State's policy would weigh heavily in any challenge of the law as infringing constitutional limitations. Here, however, the judgment is based on a common law concept of the most general and undefined nature. The court below has held that the petitioner's conduct constituted the commission of an offense under the state law, and we accept its decision as binding upon us to that extent.

The offense known as breach of the peace embraces a great variety of conduct destroying or menacing public order and tranquility. It includes not only violent acts but acts and words likely to produce violence in others. No one would have the hardihood to suggest that the principle of freedom of speech sanctions incitement to riot or that religious liberty connotes the privilege to exhort others to physical attack upon those belonging to another sect. When clear and present danger of riot, disorder, interference with traffic upon the public streets, or other immediate threat to public safety, peace, or order, appears, the power of the State to prevent or punish is obvious. Equally obvious is it that a State may not unduly suppress free communication of views, religious or other, under the guise of conserving desirable conditions. Here we have a situation analogous to a conviction under a statute sweeping in a great variety of conduct under a general and indefinite characterization, and leaving to the executive and judicial branches too wide a discretion in its application.

Having these considerations in mind, we note that Jesse Cantwell, on April 26, 1938, was upon a public street, where he had a right to be, and where he had a right peacefully to impart his views to others. There is no showing that his deportment was noisy, truculent, overbearing or offensive. He requested of two pedestrians permission to play to them a phonograph record. The permission was granted. It is not claimed that he intended to insult or affront the hearers by playing the record. It is plain that he wished only to interest them in his propaganda. The sound of the phonograph is not shown to have disturbed residents of the street, to have drawn a crowd, or to have impeded traffic. Thus far he had invaded no right or interest of the public or of the men accosted.

The record played by Cantwell embodies a general attack on all organized religious systems as instruments of Satan and injurious to man; it then singles out the Roman Catholic Church for strictures couched in terms which naturally would offend not only persons of that persuasion, but all others who respect the honestly held religious faith of their fellows. The hearers were in fact highly offended. One of them said he felt like hitting Cantwell and the other that he was tempted to throw Cantwell off the street. The one who testified he felt like hitting Cantwell said, in answer to the question "Did you do anything else or have any other reaction?" "No, sir, because he said he would take the victrola and he went." The other witness testified that he told Cantwell he had better get off the street before something happened to him and that was the end of the matter as Cantwell picked up his books and walked up the street.

Cantwell's conduct, in the view of the court below, considered apart from the effect of his communication upon his hearers, did not amount to a breach of the peace. One may, however, be guilty of the offense if he commit acts or make statements likely to provoke violence and disturbance of good order, even though no such eventuality be intended. Decisions to this effect are many, but examination discloses that, in practically all, the provocative language which was held to amount to a breach of the peace consisted of profane, indecent, or abusive remarks directed to the person of the hearer. Resort to epithets or personal abuse is not in any proper sense communication of information or opinion safeguarded by the Constitution, and its punishment as a criminal act would raise no question under that instrument.

We find in the instant case no assault or threatening of bodily harm, no truculent bearing, no intentional discourtesy, no personal abuse. On the contrary, we find only an effort to persuade a willing listener to buy a book or to contribute money in the interest of what Cantwell, however misguided others may think him, conceived to be true religion.

In the realm of religious faith, and in that of political belief, sharp differences arise. In both fields the tenets of one man may seem the rankest error to his neighbor. To persuade others to his own point of view, the pleader, as we know, at times, resorts to exaggeration, to vilification of men who have been, or are, prominent in church or state, and even to false statement. But the people of this nation have ordained in the light of history, that, in spite of the probability of excesses and abuses, these liberties are, in the long view, essential to enlightened opinion and right conduct on the part of the citizens of a democracy.

The essential characteristics of these liberties is, that under their shield many types of life, character, opinion and belief can develop unmolested and unobstructed. Nowhere is this shield more necessary than in our own country for a people composed of many races and of many creeds. There are limits to the exercise of these liberties. The danger in these times from the coercive activities of those who in the delusion of racial or religious conceit would incite violence and breaches of the peace in order to deprive others of their equal right to the exercise of their liberties, is emphasized by events familiar to all. These and other transgressions of those limits the States appropriately may punish.

Although the contents of the record not unnaturally aroused animosity, we think that, in the absence of a statute narrowly drawn to define and punish specific conduct as constituting a clear and present danger to a substantial interest of the State, the petitioner's communication, considered in the light of the constitutional guarantees, raised no such clear and present menace to public peace and order as to render him liable to conviction of the common law offense in question.

The judgment affirming the convictions on the third and fifth counts is reversed and the cause is remanded for further proceedings not inconsistent with this opinion.

Reversed.

The Religion of the Justices

The religious views of the Justices are a taboo subject in legal analysis. Why? For an exception to the rule, *see* Michael E. Smith, "The Special Place of Religion in the Constitution,"

1983 Sup. Ct. Rev. 83, 105–118. The religious makeup of the Court that took the momentous step of *Cantwell* was as follows. Five members had had Protestant upbringing but were no longer identified with the specific tenets of any church: Chief Justice Hughes's religious evolution is representative. He was the son of a Baptist minister in upstate New York and had himself taught Sunday School at the Fifth Avenue Baptist Church in New York City. But in his own words, "I had long since ceased to attach any importance to what many regard as the distinctive tenets of the denomination. Rather, I cherished the nobler tradition of the Baptists as protagonists in the struggle for religious liberty. I wished to throw what influence I had to the support of Christian institutions," Hughes *infra*, 1, 110. The others were as follows: Black (former Baptist), Stone (former Congregationalist), Douglas (former Presbyterian and ex-born-again Christian), McReynolds and Reed (identified only as "Protestant"). Frankfurter had a Jewish background but belonged to no Jewish congregation. Roberts was an Episcopalian; Murphy was a somewhat anticlerical Catholic. Douglas as well as Hughes was a minister's son. The attitudes toward religion expressed by the Court correspond with fair exactness to the spiritual outlook of the majority of the Court, unchurched, unsympathetic to mainline orthodoxies, open to spiritual currents, basically theistic and in favor of "Christian" ideas.

Sources for the religions of the Justices: Merlo Pusey, *Charles Evans Hughes* (1951) 1, 1–2, 110; Alpheus Thomas Mason, *Harlan Fiske Stone: Pillar of the Law* (1956) 29, 79, 807; Black, *My Father: A Remembrance* (1975) 104, 176; William O. Douglas, *Go East, Young Man* (1974) 4, 109–111; Liva Baker, *Felix Frankfurter* (1969) 18–19; J. Woodford Howard, *Mr. Justice Murphy* (1968) 444–445, 455–456; *Biographical Dictionary of the Federal Judiciary* (1976) (McReynolds, 191, Reed, 231, Roberts, 237).

Murdock v. Pennsylvania
319 U.S. 105 (1943)

Mr. Hayden C. Covington for petitioner.
Mr. Fred B. Tiescher for respondent.
Justice Douglas delivered the opinion of the Court.

. . .

Petitioners spread their interpretations of the Bible and their religious beliefs largely through the hand distribution of literature by full or part time workers. They claim to follow the example of Paul, teaching "publickly, and from house to house." Acts 20:20. They take literally the mandate of the Scriptures, "Go ye into all the world, and preach the gospel to every creature." Mark 16:15. In doing so they believe that they are obeying a commandment of God.

The hand distribution of religious tracts is an age-old form of missionary evangelism— as old as the history of printing presses. It has been a potent force in various religious movements down through the years. This form of evangelism is utilized today on a large scale by various religious sects whose colporteurs carry the Gospel to thousands upon thousands of homes and seek through personal visitations to win adherents to their faith.[7] It is more than preaching; it is more than distribution of religious literature.

---

[7] The General Conference of Seventh-Day Adventists, who filed a brief *amicus curiae* on the reargument of *Jones v. Opelika,* has given us the following data concerning their literature ministry: This denomination has 83 publishing houses throughout the world, issuing publications in over 200 languages. Some 9,256 separate publications were issued in 1941. By printed and spoken word, the Gospel is carried into 412 countries in 824 languages. 1942 Yearbook, p. 287. During December 1941, a total of 1,018 colporteurs operated in North America. They delivered during that month $97,997.19 worth of gospel literature, and for the whole year of 1941 a total of $790,610.36—an average per person of about $65 per month. Some of these were students and temporary workers.

It is a combination of both. Its purpose is as evangelical as the revival meeting. This form of religious activity occupies the same high estate under the First Amendment as do worship in the churches and preaching from the pulpits. It has the same claim to protection as the more orthodox and conventional exercises of religion. It also has the same claim as the others to the guarantees of freedom of speech and freedom of the press.

The integrity of this conduct or behavior as a religious practice has not been challenged. Nor do we have presented any question as to the sincerity of petitioners in their religious beliefs and practices, however misguided they may be thought to be. Moreover, we do not intimate or suggest in respecting their sincerity that any conduct can be made a religious rite and by the zeal of the practitioners swept into the First Amendment. *Reynolds v. United States*, 98 U.S. 145, 161–167, and *Davis v. Beason*, 133 U.S. 333 denied any such claim to the practice of polygamy and bigamy. Other claims may well arise which deserve the same fate. We only hold that spreading one's religious beliefs or preaching the Gospel through distribution of religious literature and through personal visitations is an age-old type of evangelism with as high a claim to constitutional protection as the more orthodox types. The manner in which it is practiced at times gives rise to special problems with which the police power of the states is competent to deal. See for example *Cox v. New Hampshire*, 312 U.S. 569, and *Chaplinsky v. New Hampshire*, 315 U.S. 568. But that merely illustrates that the rights with which we are dealing are not absolutes. *Schneider v. State*, 308 U.S. 147, 160–161. We are concerned, however, in these cases merely with one narrow issue. There is presented for decision no question whatsoever concerning punishment for any alleged unlawful acts during the solicitation. Nor is there involved here any question as to the validity of a registration system for colporteurs and other solicitors. The cases present a single issue—the constitutionality of an ordinance which as construed and applied requires religious colporteurs to pay a license tax as a condition to the pursuit of their activities.

The alleged justification for the exaction of this license tax is the fact that the religious literature is distributed with a solicitation of funds. Thus it was stated, in *Jones v. Opelika, supra*, p. 597, that when a religious sect uses "ordinary commercial methods of sales of articles to raise propaganda funds," it is proper for the state to charge "reasonable fees for the privilege of canvassing." Situations will arise where it will be difficult to determine whether a particular activity is religious or purely commercial. The distinction at times is vital. As we stated only the other day, in *Jamison v. Texas*, 318 U.S. 413, 417, "The states can prohibit the use of the streets for the distribution of purely commercial leaflets, even though such leaflets may have 'a civic appeal, or a moral platitude' appended. *Valentine v. Chrestensen*, 316 U.S. 52, 55. They may not prohibit the distribution of handbills in the pursuit of a clearly religious activity merely because the handbills invite the purchase of books for the improved understanding of the religion or because the handbills seek in a lawful fashion to promote the raising of funds for religious purposes." But the mere fact that the religious literature is "sold" by itinerant preachers rather than "donated" does not transform evangelism into a commercial enterprise. If it did, then the passing of the collection plate in church would make the church service a commercial project. The constitutional rights of those spreading their religious beliefs through the spoken and printed word are not to be gauged by standards governing retailers or wholesalers of books. The right to use the press for expressing one's views is not to be measured by the protection afforded commercial

---

Colporteurs of this denomination receive half of their collections, from which they must pay their traveling and living expenses. Colporteurs are specially trained and their qualifications equal those of preachers. In the field, each worker is under the supervision of a field missionary secretary to whom a weekly report is made. After fifteen years of continuous service, each colporteur is entitled to the same pension as retired ministers. And see Howell, The Great Advent Movement (1935), pp. 72–75.

handbills. It should be remembered that the pamphlets of Thomas Paine were not distributed free of charge. It is plain that a religious organization needs funds to remain a going concern. But an itinerant evangelist, however misguided or intolerant he may be, does not become a mere book agent by selling the Bible or religious tracts to help defray his expenses or to sustain him. Freedom of speech, freedom of the press, freedom of religion are available to all, not merely to those who can pay their own way. As we have said, the problem of drawing the line between a purely commercial activity and a religious one will at times be difficult. On this record it plainly cannot be said that petitioners were engaged in a commercial rather than a religious venture. It is a distortion of the facts of record to describe their activities as the occupation of selling books and pamphlets. And the Pennsylvania court did not rest the judgments of conviction on that basis, though it did find that petitioners "sold" the literature. The Supreme Court of Iowa in *State v. Mead,* 230 Iowa 1217, 300 N.W. 523, 524, described the selling activities of members of this same sect as "merely incidental and collateral" to their "main object which was to preach and publicize the doctrines of their order." And see *State v. Meredith,* 197 S.C. 351, 15 S. E. 2d 678; *People v. Barber,* 289 N.Y. 378, 385–386, 46 N. E. 2d 329. That accurately summarizes the present record.

We do not mean to say that religious groups and the press are free from all financial burdens of government. See *Grosjean v. American Press Co.,* 297 U.S. 233, 250. We have here something quite different, for example, from a tax on the income of one who engages in religious activities or a tax on property used or employed in connection with those activities. It is one thing to impose a tax on the income or property of a preacher. It is quite another thing to exact a tax from him for the privilege of delivering a sermon. . . .

Reversed.

Justices Reed, Roberts, Frankfurter and Jackson dissented.

. . .

Justice Jackson, concurring in the result in *Douglas v. City of Jeannette,* 319 U.S. 157 (1943) and dissenting in *Murdock v. Pennsylvania [supra]:*

From the record in *Douglas* we learn:

In 1939, a "Watch Tower Campaign" was instituted by Jehovah's Witnesses in Jeannette, Pennsylvania, an industrial city of some 10,000 inhabitants.[1] Each home was visited, a bell was rung or the door knocked upon, and the householder advised that the Witness had important information. If the householder would listen, a record was played on the phonograph. Its subject was "Snare and Racket." The following words are representative of its contents: "Religion is wrong and a snare because it deceives the people, but that does not mean that all who follow religion are willingly bad. Religion is a racket because it has long been used and is still used to extract money from the people upon the theory and promise that the paying over of money to a priest will serve to relieve the party paying from punishment after death and further insure

---

[1] Sixteenth Annual Census of the United States (1940), Population, Volume 1 (Census Bureau of the United States Department of Commerce) p. 922. The City of Jeannette is included in Westmoreland County, shown by the 1940 Census to have a population of 303,411, an increase over 1930 and 1920. *Ibid.* The 1930 Census of Religious Bodies shows that of the people in Westmoreland County 168,008 were affiliated with some religious body, 80,276 of them with the Roman Catholic Church. Census of Religious Bodies (1930), Volume I (Census Bureau of the United States Department of Commerce) pp. 809–814. According to unpublished information in the files of the Census Bureau, the 1936 Census of Religious Bodies shows that there were in the City of Jeannette 5,520 Roman Catholics. Thus it appears that the percentage of Catholics in the City is somewhat higher than in the County as a whole.

his salvation." This line of attack is taken by the Witnesses generally upon all denominations, especially the Roman Catholic. The householder was asked to buy a variety of literature for a price or contribution. The price would be twenty-five cents for the books and smaller sums for the pamphlets. Oftentimes, if he was unwilling to purchase, the book or pamphlet was given to him anyway.

When this campaign began, many complaints from offended householders were received, and three or four of the Witnesses were arrested. Thereafter, the "zone servant" in charge of the campaign conferred with the Mayor. He told the Mayor it was their right to carry on the campaign and showed him a decision of the United States Supreme Court, said to have that effect, as proof of it. The Mayor told him that they were at liberty to distribute their literature in the streets of the city and that he would have no objection if they distributed the literature free of charge at the houses, but that the people objected to their attempt to force these sales, and particularly on Sunday. The Mayor asked whether it would not be possible to come on some other day and to distribute the literature without selling it. The zone servant replied that that was contrary to their method of "doing business" and refused. He also told the Mayor that he would bring enough Witnesses into the City of Jeannette to get the job done whether the Mayor liked it or not. The Mayor urged them to await the outcome of an appeal which was then pending in the other cases and let the matter take its course through the courts. This, too, was refused, and the threat to bring more people than the Mayor's police force could cope with was repeated.

On Palm Sunday of 1939, the threat was made good. Over 100 of the Witnesses appeared. They were strangers to the city and arrived in upwards of twenty-five automobiles. The automobiles were parked outside the city limits, and headquarters were set up in a gasoline station with telephone facilities through which the director of the campaign could be notified when trouble occurred. He furnished bonds for the Witnesses as they were arrested. As they began their work, around 9:00 o'clock in the morning, telephone calls began to come in to the Police Headquarters, and complaints in large volume were made all during the day. They exceeded the number that the police could handle, and the Fire Department was called out to assist. The Witnesses called at homes singly and in groups, and some of the homes complained that they were called upon several times. Twenty-one Witnesses were arrested. Only those were arrested where definite proof was obtainable that the literature had been offered for sale or a sale had been made for a price. Three were later discharged for inadequacies in this proof, and eighteen were convicted. The zone servant furnished appeal bonds.

The national structure of the Jehovah's Witness movement is also somewhat revealed in this testimony. At the head of the movement in this country is the Watch Tower Bible & Tract Society, a corporation organized under the laws of Pennsylvania, but having its principal place of business in Brooklyn, N.Y. It prints all pamphlets, manufactures all books, supplies all phonographs and records, and provides other materials for the Witnesses. It "ordains" these Witnesses by furnishing each, on a basis which does not clearly appear, a certificate that he is a minister of the Gospel. Its output is large and its revenues must be considerable. Little is revealed of its affairs. One of its "zone servants" testified that its correspondence is signed only with the name of the corporation and anonymity as to its personnel is its policy. The assumption that it is a "non-profit charitable" corporation may be true, but it is without support beyond mere assertion. In none of these cases has the assertion been supported by such usual evidence as a balance sheet or an income statement. What its manufacturing costs and revenues are, what salaries or bonuses it pays, what contracts it has for supplies or services we simply do not know. The effort of counsel for Jeannette to obtain information, books and records of the local "companies" of Witnesses engaged in the Jeannette campaign in the trial was met by contradictory statements as to the methods and meaning of such meager accounts as were produced.

The publishing output of the Watch Tower corporation is disposed of through converts, some of whom are full-time and some part-time ministers. These are organized into groups or companies under the direction of "zone servants." It is their purpose to carry on in a thorough manner so that every home in the communities in which they work may be regularly visited three or four times a year. The full-time Witnesses acquire their literature from the Watch Tower Bible & Tract Society at a figure which enables them to distribute it at the prices printed thereon with a substantial differential. Some of the books they acquire for 5¢ and dispose of for a contribution of 25¢. On others, the margin is less. Part-time ministers have a differential between the 20¢ which they remit to the Watch Tower Society and the 25¢ which is the contribution they ask for the books. We are told that many of the Witnesses give away a substantial quantity of the literature to people who make no contributions. Apart from the fact that this differential exists and that it enables the distributors to meet in whole or in part their living expenses, it has proven impossible in these cases to learn the exact results of the campaigns from a financial point of view. There is evidence that the group accumulated a substantial amount from the differentials, but the tracing of the money was not possible because of the failure to obtain records and the failure, apparently, to keep them.

The literature thus distributed is voluminous and repetitious. Characterization is risky, but a few quotations will indicate something of its temper.

Taking as representative the book "Enemies," of which J. F. Rutherford, the lawyer who long headed this group, is the author, we find the following: "The greatest racket ever invented and practiced is that of religion. The most cruel and seductive public enemy is that which employs religion to carry on the racket, and by which means the people are deceived and the name of Almighty God is reproached. There are numerous systems of religion, but the most subtle, fraudulent and injurious to humankind is that which is generally labeled the 'Christian religion,' because it has the appearance of a worshipful devotion to the Supreme Being, and thereby easily misleads many honest and sincere persons." *Id.* at 144–145. It analyzes the income of the Roman Catholic hierarchy and announces that it is "the great racket, a racket that is greater than all other rackets combined." *Id.* at 178. It also says under the chapter heading "Song of the Harlot," "Referring now to the foregoing Scriptural definition of *harlot:* What religious system exactly fits the prophecies recorded in God's Word? There is but one answer, and that is, The Roman Catholic Church organization." *Id.* at 204–205. "Those close or nearby and dependent upon the main organization, being of the same stripe, picture the Jewish and Protestant clergy and other allies of the Hierarchy who tag along behind the Hierarchy at the present time to do the bidding of the old 'whore'." *Id.* at 222. "Says the prophet of Jehovah: 'It shall come to pass in that day, that Tyre (modern Tyre, the Roman Catholic Hierarchy organization) shall be forgotten.' Forgotten by whom? By her former illicit paramours who have committed fornication with her." *Id.* at 264. Throughout the literature, statements of this kind appear amidst scriptural comment and prophecy, denunciation of demonology, which is used to characterize the Roman Catholic religion, criticism of government and those in authority, advocacy of obedience to the law of God instead of the law of man, and an interpretation of the law of God as they see it.

The spirit and temper of this campaign is most fairly stated perhaps in the words, again of Rutherford, in his book "Religion," pp. 196–198:

"God's faithful servants go from house to house to bring the message of the kingdom to those who reside there, omitting none, not even the houses of the Roman Catholic Hierarchy, and there they give witness to the kingdom because they are commanded by the Most High to do so. "They shall enter in at the windows like a thief.' They do not loot nor break into the houses, but they set up their phonographs before the doors and windows and send the message of the kingdom right into the houses into the ears of those who might wish to hear; and while those desiring to hear are hearing, some of the 'sourpusses' are compelled to hear. Locusts invade the homes of the people and even eat the varnish off the wood and eat the wood to some extent. Likewise God's faithful witnesses, likened unto locusts, get the kingdom message right into the house and they take the veneer off the religious things that are in that house, including candles and 'holy water', remove the superstition from the minds of the people, and show them that the doctrines that have been taught to them are wood, hay and stubble, destructible by fire, and they cannot withstand the heat. The people are enabled to learn that 'purgatory' is a bogeyman, set up by the agents of Satan to frighten the people into the religious organizations, where they may be fleeced of their hard-earned money. Thus the kingdom message plagues the religionists, and the clergy find that they are unable to prevent it. Therefore, as described by the prophet, the message comes to them like a thief that enters in at the windows, and this message is a warning to those who are on the inside that Jesus Christ has come, and they remember his warning words, to wit: 'Behold, I come as a thief.' (Revelation 16:15.) The day of Armageddon is very close, and that day comes upon the world in general like a thief in the night."

The day of Armageddon, to which all of this is prelude, is to be a violent and bloody one, for then shall be slain all "demonologists," including most of those who reject the teachings of Jehovah's Witnesses.

In the *Murdock* case, on another Sunday morning of the following Lent, we again find the Witnesses in Jeannette, travelling by twos and threes and carrying cases for the books and phonographs. This time eight were arrested, as against the 21 arrested on the preceding Palm Sunday involved in the *Douglas* case.

In the *Struthers* case, we find the Witness knocking on the door of a total stranger at 4:00 on Sunday afternoon, July 7th. The householder's fourteen year old son answered, and, at the Witness's request, called his mother from the kitchen. His mother had previously become "very much disgusted about going to the door" to receive leaflets, particularly since another person had on a previous occasion called her to the door and told her, as she testified, "that I was doomed to go to hell because I would not let this literature in my home for my children to read." She testified that the Witness "shoved in the door" the circular being distributed, and that she "couldn't do much more than take" it, and she promptly tore it up in the presence of the Witness, for while she believed "in the worship of God," she did not "care to talk to everybody" and did not "believe that anyone needs to be sent from door to door to tell us how to worship." The record in the *Struthers* case is even more sparse than that in the *Murdock* case, but the householder did testify that at the time she was given the circular the Witness "told me that a number of them were in jail and would I call the Chief of Police and ask that their workers might be released."

Such is the activity which it is claimed no public authority can either regulate or tax. This claim is substantially, if not quite, sustained today. I dissent—a disagreement induced in no small part by the facts recited.

NOTE. *Compare Prince v. Massachusetts*, 321 U.S. 158 (1944): Massachusetts law prohibited children from selling newspapers or magazines on the streets. Sarah Prince, an ordained Jehovah's Witness, permitted her ward Betty, a girl of nine, "to engage in the preaching work" receiving contributions for the *Watch Tower* on the streets of Brockton. Betty believed that failure to do the work would condemn her "to everlasting destruction at Armageddon." Convicted of aiding a minor to violate the statute, Sarah Prince contended that her own freedom to raise the child and Betty's free exercise of religion had been unconstitutionally compromised. Citing *Reynolds* and *Davis, supra* IX, Justice Wiley B. Rutledge for the Supreme Court wrote at 166: "But the family itself is not beyond regulation in the public interest, as against a claim of religious liberty." He upheld the state's right to protect children from work on the streets, adding at 170: "Parents may be free to become martyrs themselves. But it

does not follow they are free, in identical circumstances, to make martyrs of their children.
. . ."

Justices Jackson, Roberts, and Frankfurter agreed with the result but not with the opinion making age the criterion for regulation of religion. Justice Murphy dissented:

No chapter in human history has been so largely written in terms of persecution and intolerance as the one dealing with religious freedom. From ancient times to the present day, the ingenuity of man has known no limits in its ability to forge weapons of oppression for use against those who dare to express or practice unorthodox religious beliefs. And the Jehovah's Witnesses are living proof of the fact that even in this nation, conceived as it was in the ideals of freedom, the right to practice religion in unconventional ways is still far from secure. Theirs is a militant and unpopular faith, pursued with a fanatical zeal. They have suffered brutal beatings; their property has been destroyed; they have been harassed at every turn by the resurrection and enforcement of little used ordinances and statutes. See Mulder and Comisky, "Jehovah's Witnesses Mold Constitutional Law," 2 *Bill of Rights Review,* No. 4, p. 262. To them, along with other present-day religious minorities, befalls the burden of testing our devotion to the ideals and constitutional guarantees of religious freedom. We should therefore hesitate before approving the application of a statute that might be used as another instrument of oppression. Religious freedom is too sacred a right to be restricted or prohibited in any degree without convincing proof that a legitimate interest of the state is in grave danger [*ibid.* at 175].

NOTE. *Heffron v. International Society for Krishna Consciousness, Inc.,* 452 U.S. 640 (1981). The International Society for Krishna Consciousness, Inc., a religious society, teaches its members the practice of Sankirtan, a religious ritual in which its members greet members of the public by giving them flowers or small American flags, distribute or sell the society's religious literature, and seek donations to support the Krishna religion. The society and Joseph Beca, head of its temple in Minneapolis, sought an injunction against the application to the society and its members of a rule of the Minnesota Agricultural Society governing the state fair. The rule required all persons or groups selling or distributing literature to do so in licensed booths. Represented by Laurence Tribe, the Krishna believers prevailed in the supreme court of Minnesota, which held the rule an unconstitutional restriction of Sankirtan. 299 N.W. 2d 79 (1980). The United States Supreme Court, 5-4, reversed.

The Court, per Justice Byron R. White, held that speech could be subjected to reasonable restrictions as to time, place, and manner, and that here the restrictions were a reasonable expression of the state's interest in the orderly movement of over 100,000 persons daily in a space of 125 acres.

The Minnesota Supreme Court had seen little danger of disorder resulting from an exception for the followers of Krishna. But the Supreme Court said that they had no claim to a special exemption as compared to the claims of

other religious who also distribute literature and solicit funds. None of our cases suggest that the inclusion of peripatetic solicitation as part of a church ritual entitles church members to solicitation rights in a public forum superior to those of members of other religious groups that raise money but do not purport to ritualize the process. Nor for present purposes do religious organizations enjoy rights to communicate, distribute, and solicit on the fairgrounds superior to those of other organizations having social, political, or other ideological messages to proselytize. These nonreligious organizations seeking support for their activities are entitled to rights equal to those of religious groups to enter a public forum and spread their views, whether by soliciting funds or by distributing literature [*ibid.* at 652–653].

Justices Brennan, Blackmun, Marshall, and Stevens dissented. Justice Brennan contended that the Court's treatment of the Sankirtan issue was "seemingly inconsistent with prior case law. . . . Our cases are clear that governmental regulations which interfere with the exercise of specific religious beliefs or principles should be scrutinized with particular care" (*ibid.* at 659, citing *Sherbert v. Verner* [XI, 4] and *Wisconsin v. Yoder* [XI, 5]).

Query. Is Heffron consistent with *Cantwell?* With *Murdoch?*

2. WORSHIP OF A GRAVEN IMAGE

At the same time that the Jehovah's Witnesses were challenging restrictions on the evangelizing activity, they were challenging laws and regulations requiring their children to salute the flag. They succeeded where other religious groups had failed. As early as 1918 a Mennonite in Ohio was convicted of not keeping his nine-year-old daughter in school when she was sent home for refusing to salute; a school teacher in Nebraska who was a member of the Church of God was also fired for refusing. In 1925 the state of Washington committed a nine-year-old boy to a juvenile home when he obeyed his parents, members of the Elijah Voice Society, in not saluting at school. In 1928 in Delaware thirty-eight Mennonite children were expelled for not saluting, *see* Manwaring, *Render unto Caesar* 11–14.

Jehovah's Witnesses did not take a militant stand against saluting until 1935. In that year Judge Rutherford denounced the exaltation of Hitler in Germany (where the Witnesses were being persecuted) and eventually Rutherford singled out the salute "Heil Hitler" as idolatry. On October 6, 1935, in a national radio broadcast, Rutherford praised Carleton B. Nicholls, Jr., a third-grade student in Lynn, Massachusetts, who had refused to salute the flag, "declaring himself," Rutherford said, "for Jehovah God and his kingdom" (Manwaring 30–31). The Witnesses cited as controlling: "You shall have no other gods before me. You shall not make yourself a graven image, or any likeness of anything . . . you shall not bow down to them or serve them" (Ex. 20:3–5).

In at least thirty states the salute of the flag was required by statute or custom. After Rutherford's speech the children of Witnesses throughout the country refused to conform. By mid-1936, 120 such children had been expelled; by 1939, the number had passed 200 (Manwaring 56). The state courts universally refused to recognize that the Witnesses had a protected constitutional right. Chief Justice Arthur Rugg's opinion upholding Carleton Nicholls's expulsion was typical. He wrote: "The pledge of allegiance to the flag . . . has nothing to do with religion. . . . There is nothing in the salute or the pledge of allegiance which constitutes an act of idolatry, or which approaches to any religious observance," *Nicholls v. Lynn,* 297 Mass. 65, 71, 7 N.E. 2d 577, 580 (1937). When twelve-year-old Dorothy Leoles was expelled in Georgia for failure to salute, the Supreme Court dismissed her appeal "for the want of a substantial federal question," *Leoles v. Landers,* 302 U.S. 656 (1937). The American Civil Liberties Union aided the Witnesses and actually handled most of their cases, and in New Jersey provided a model brief; but New Jersey, too, upheld an expulsion, and the Supreme Court dismissed the appeal, *Hering v. State Board of Education,* 303 U.S. 624 (1938).

The first full-dress treatment of the issue in the Supreme Court began with the action of the school board in Minersville, Pennsylvania, a depressed coal town (pop. 8,686). In October 1935 the board expelled Lillian Gobitis, twelve, and William Gobitis, ten, for failing to salute. The children then attended a Kingdom School, run by the Witnesses, thirty miles distant. Their father, Walter, sought legal help to reinstate the children, and in May 1937, Olin R. Moyle and the ACLU initiated a federal suit to reinstate them. Outside groups such as the Patriotic Order of the Sons of America helped finance the school board in its opposition, Manwaring 81–93. District Judge Albert B. Maris, a Quaker, ruled on June 18, 1938, that the school board had violated the Fourteenth Amendment, 24 F. Supp. 27 (E.D. Pa. 1938). The Third Circuit affirmed, in an opinion by William Clark, a Presbyterian, 108 F. 2d 683 (3rd Cir. 1939).

In the Supreme Court, Rutherford argued for the Gobitises that "the issue" was "the arbitrary totalitarian rule of the State versus full devotion and obedience to the THEOCRATIC GOVERNMENT or Kingdom of Jehovah God under Christ Jesus His anointed King." An ACLU *amicus* brief, written by George K. Gardner of Harvard Law School, argued that under *Reynolds v. United States* an innocuous religious belief could not be punished. The brief of the Bill of Rights Committee of the American Bar Association—another *amicus curiae*—was written by Grenville Clark and Louis Lusky; it invoked a famous footnote by Justice Harlan Stone in *United States v. Carolene Products Co.*, 304 U.S. 144, 152 n.4 (1938), calling for "more searching judicial inquiry" in cases of "prejudice against discrete and insular minorities." The distinction between judicial intervention to invalidate economic regulations—a type of intervention long criticized by liberals—and intervention on behalf of discrete and insular minorities was crucial if a Supreme Court already half made up of New Dealers was to respond.

Two weeks before *Gobitis* was decided, the Court held unanimously for the Witnesses in *Cantwell, supra*. But it was not an augury. Chief Justice Hughes dominated the Court's discussion of the case, and he denied that there was any infringement of religion, *see* Merlo Pusey, *Charles Evans Hughes* (1951) 2, 672–673. Hughes assigned the writing of the opinion to Felix Frankfurter. Frankfurter was to describe himself in the sequel to *Gobitis* as one "who belongs to the most vilified and persecuted minority in history," the Jews. He was also an immigrant from Austria-Hungary to the United States and a zealous upholder of judicial restraint in approaching the constitutionality of legislation. As he put it himself on December 5, 1942, "As one who has no ties with any formal religion, perhaps the feelings that underlie religious forms for me run into intensification of my feelings about American citizenship," quoted in Baker, *Felix Frankfurter* (1969), 290.

Note, in particular, that the Court's opinion states that the Fourteenth Amendment not only absorbed the free exercise clause of the First Amendment but also the prohibition on the establishment of religion. This statement, uncontested by any member of the Court, was to survive long after *Gobitis* was gone.

Minersville School District v. Gobitis
310 U.S. 586 (1940)

. . .

Centuries of strife over the erection of particular dogmas as exclusive or all-comprehending faiths led to the inclusion of a guarantee for religious freedom in the Bill of Rights. The First Amendment, and the Fourteenth through its absorption of the First, sought to guard against repetition of those bitter religious struggles by prohibiting the establishment of a state religion and by securing to every sect the free exercise of its faith. So pervasive is the acceptance of this precious right that its scope is brought into question, as here, only when the conscience of individuals collides with the felt necessities of society.

Certainly the affirmative pursuit of one's convictions about the ultimate mystery of the universe and man's relation to it is placed beyond the reach of law. Government may not interfere with organized or individual expression of belief or disbelief. Propagation of belief—or even of disbelief—in the supernatural is protected, whether in church or chapel, mosque or synagogue, tabernacle or meeting-house. Likewise the Constitution assures generous immunity to the individual from imposition of penalties for offending, in the course of his own religious activities, the religious views of others, be they a minority or those who are dominant in government. *Cantwell* v. *Connecticut* [*supra*, XI].

But the manifold character of man's relations may bring his conception of religious duty into conflict with the secular interests of his fellow-men. When does the constitutional guarantee compel exemption from doing what society thinks necessary for the promotion of some great common end, or from a penalty for conduct which appears dangerous to the general good? To state the problem is to recall the truth that no single principle can answer all of life's complexities. The right to freedom of religious belief, however dissident and however obnoxious to the cherished beliefs of others—even of a majority—is itself the denial of an absolute. But to affirm that the freedom to follow conscience has itself no limits in the life of a society would deny that very plurality of principles which, as a matter of history, underlies protection of religious toleration. Compare Mr. Justice Holmes in *Hudson Water Co.* v. *McCarter*, 209 U.S. 349, 355. Our present task, then, as so often the case with courts, is to reconcile two rights in order to prevent either from destroying the other. But, because in safeguarding conscience we are dealing with interests so subtle and so dear, every possible leeway should be given to the claims of religious faith.

In the judicial enforcement of religious freedom we are concerned with a historic concept. See Mr. Justice Cardozo in *Hamilton* v. *Regents* [*supra*, X, 11]. The religious liberty which the Constitution protects has never excluded legislation of general scope not directed against doctrinal loyalties of particular sects. Judicial nullification of legislation cannot be justified by attributing to the framers of the Bill of Rights views for which there is no historic warrant. Conscientious scruples have not, in the course of the long struggle for religious toleration, relieved the individual from obedience to a general law not aimed at the promotion or restriction of religious beliefs. The mere possession of religious convictions which contradict the relevant concerns of a political society does not relieve the citizen from the discharge of political responsibilities. The necessity for this adjustment has again and again been recognized. In a number of situations the exertion of political authority has been sustained, while basic considerations of religious freedom have been left inviolate. *Reynolds* v. *United States, Davis* v. *Beason* [*supra*, IX] *Selective Draft Law Cases, Hamilton* v. *Regents* [*supra*, X, 11]. In all these cases the general laws in question, upheld in their application to those who refused obedience from religious conviction, were manifestations of specific powers of government deemed by the legislature essential to secure and maintain that orderly, tranquil, and free society without which religious toleration itself is unattainable. Nor does the freedom of speech assured by Due Process move in a more absolute circle of immunity than that enjoyed by religious freedom. Even if it were assumed that freedom of speech goes beyond the historic concept of full opportunity to utter and to disseminate views, however heretical or offensive to dominant opinion, and includes freedom from conveying what may be deemed an implied but rejected affirmation, the question remains whether school children, like the Gobitis children, must be excused from conduct required of all the other children in the promotion of national cohesion. We are dealing with an interest inferior to none in the hierarchy of legal values. National unity is the basis of national security. To deny the legislature the right to select appropriate means for its attainment presents a totally different order of problem from that of the propriety of subordinating the possible ugliness of littered streets to the free expression of opinion through distribution of handbills. Compare *Schneider* v. *State*, 308 U.S. 147.

Situations like the present are phases of the profoundest problem confronting a democracy—the problem which Lincoln cast in memorable dilemma: "Must a government of necessity be too *strong* for the liberties of its people, or too *weak* to maintain its own existence?" No mere textual reading or logical talisman can solve the dilemma. And when the issue demands judicial determination, it is not the personal notion of judges of what wise adjustment requires which must prevail.

Unlike the instances we have cited, the case before us is not concerned with an exertion of legislative power for the promotion of some specific need or interest of secular society—the protection of the family, the promotion of health, the common defense, the raising of public revenues to defray the cost of government. But all these specific activities of government presuppose the existence of an organized political society. The ultimate foundation of a free society is the binding tie of cohesive sentiment. Such a sentiment is fostered by all those agencies of the mind and spirit which may serve to gather up the traditions of a people, transmit them from generation to generation, and thereby create that continuity of a treasured common life which constitutes a civilization. "We live by symbols." The flag is the symbol of our national unity, transcending all internal differences, however large, within the framework of the Constitution. This Court has had occasion to say that ". . . the flag is the symbol of the Nation's power, the emblem of freedom in its truest, best sense. . . . it signifies government resting on the consent of the governed; liberty regulated by law; the protection of the weak against the strong; security against the exercise of arbitrary power; and absolute safety for free institutions against foreign aggression." *Halter* v. *Nebraska,* 205 U. S. 34, 43. And see *United States* v. *Gettysburg Electric Ry. Co.,* 160 U.S. 668.

The case before us must be viewed as though the legislature of Pennsylvania had itself formally directed the flag-salute for the children of Minersville; had made no exemption for children whose parents were possessed of conscientious scruples like those of the Gobitis family; and had indicated its belief in the desirable ends to be secured by having its public school children share a common experience at those periods of development when their minds are supposedly receptive to its assimilation, by an exercise appropriate in time and place and setting, and one designed to evoke in them appreciation of the nation's hopes and dreams, its sufferings and sacrifices. The precise issue, then, for us to decide is whether the legislatures of the various states and the authorities in a thousand counties and school districts of this country are barred from determining the appropriateness of various means to evoke that unifying sentiment without which there can ultimately be no liberties, civil or religious. To stigmatize legislative judgment in providing for this universal gesture of respect for the symbol of our national life in the setting of the common school as a lawless inroad on that freedom of conscience which the Constitution protects, would amount to no less than the pronouncement of pedagogical and psychological dogma in a field where courts possess no marked and certainly no controlling competence. The influences which help toward a common feeling for the common country are manifold. Some may seem harsh and others no doubt are foolish. Surely, however, the end is legitimate. And the effective means for its attainment are still so uncertain and so unauthenticated by science as to preclude us from putting the widely prevalent belief in flag-saluting beyond the pale of legislative power. It mocks reason and denies our whole history to find in the allowance of a requirement to salute our flag on fitting occasions the seeds of sanction for obeisance to a leader.

The wisdom of training children in patriotic impulses by those compulsions which necessarily pervade so much of the educational process is not for our independent judgment. Even were we convinced of the folly of such a measure, such belief would be no proof of its unconstitutionality. For ourselves, we might be tempted to say that the deepest patriotism is best engendered by giving unfettered scope to the most crochety beliefs. Perhaps it is best, even from the standpoint of those interests which ordinances like the one under review seek to promote, to give to the least popular sect leave from conformities like those here in issue. But the courtroom is not the arena for debating issues of educational policy. It is not our province to choose among competing considerations in the subtle process of securing effective loyalty to the traditional ideals of democracy, while respecting at the same time individual idiosyncracies among a people so diversified in racial origins and religious allegiances. So to hold would in effect make us the school board for the country. That authority has not been given to this Court, nor should we assume it.

We are dealing here with the formative period in the development of citizenship. Great diversity of psychological and ethical opinion exists among us concerning the best way to train children for their place in society. Because of these differences and because of reluctance to permit a single, iron-cast system of education to be imposed upon a nation compounded of so many strains, we have held that, even though public education is one of our most cherished democratic institutions, the Bill of Rights bars a state from compelling all children to attend the public schools. *Pierce* v. *Society of Sisters* [*supra*, X, 6]. But it is a very different thing for this Court to exercise censorship over the conviction of legislatures that a particular program or exercise will best promote in the minds of children who attend the common schools an attachment to the institutions of their country.

What the school authorities are really asserting is the right to awaken in the child's mind considerations as to the significance of the flag contrary to those implanted by the parent. In such an attempt the state is normally at a disadvantage in competing with the parent's authority, so long—and this is the vital aspect of religious toleration— as parents are unmolested in their right to counteract by their own persuasiveness the wisdom and rightness of those loyalties which the state's educational system is seeking to promote. Except where the transgression of constitutional liberty is too plain for argument, personal freedom is best maintained—so long as the remedial channels of the democratic process remain open and unobstructed—when it is ingrained in a people's habits and not enforced against popular policy by the coercion of adjudicated law. That the flag-salute is an allowable portion of a school program for those who do not invoke conscientious scruples is surely not debatable. But for us to insist that, though the ceremony may be required, exceptional immunity must be given to dissidents, is to maintain that there is no basis for a legislative judgment that such an exemption might introduce elements of difficulty into the school discipline, might cast doubts in the minds of the other children which would themselves weaken the effect of the exercise.

The preciousness of the family relation, the authority and independence which give dignity to parenthood, indeed the enjoyment of all freedom, presuppose the kind of ordered society which is summarized by our flag. A society which is dedicated to the preservation of these ultimate values of civilization may in self-protection utilize the educational process for inculcating those almost unconscious feelings which bind men together in a comprehending loyalty, whatever may be their lesser differences and difficulties. That is to say, the process may be utilized so long as men's right to believe as they please, to win others to their way of belief, and their right to assemble in their chosen places of worship for the devotional ceremonies of their faith, are all fully respected.

Judicial review, itself a limitation on popular government, is a fundamental part of our constitutional scheme. But to the legislature no less than to courts is committed the guardianship of deeply-cherished liberties. See *Missouri, K. & T. Ry. Co.* v. *May*, 194 U. S. 267, 270. Where all the effective means of inducing political changes are left free from interference, education in the abandonment of foolish legislation is itself a training in liberty. To fight out the wise use of legislative authority in the forum of public opinion and before legislative assemblies rather than to transfer such a contest to the judicial arena, serves to vindicate the self-confidence of a free people.

Reversed

Justice McReynolds concurred in the result. Justice Stone dissented.

NOTE. *Repercussions.* The *New Republic*, which Frankfurter had helped found, said the Court had come "dangerously close" to being the victim of war hysteria. *Christian Century*, a liberal Protestant magazine, said, "Courts that will not protect even Jehovah's Witnesses will not long protect anybody." *America*, the Jesuits' journal, said that the Court had permitted destruction of "one of the most precious rights under the Federal and our State Constitutions." The *Harvard Educational Review* said the decision subordinated the civil liberties of minorities to "the will of the majority." Thirty-nine law reviews discussed the decision, thirty-one of them critically. Few decisions of the Court in modern times have met with such across-the-board intellectual rejection, Manwaring 149–157.

The Jehovah's Witnesses were already unpopular. Before the decision came down on June 3, 1940, they had been victims of several incidents of mob violence in Texas. After the decision, individual Witnesses were attacked in Maine (beatings, burning of the Kingdom Hall in Kennebunk); West Virginia (forced drinking of castor oil); Wyoming (tarring and feathering); Nebraska (castration); Arkansas (shooting); Illinois, Indiana, Maryland, Mississippi, Oregon (mob attacks). Forty percent of the incidents occurred in two states, Oklahoma and Texas. Small towns, not tolerant of outsiders, were the usual sites, *ibid.* 163–173.

Legal measures against the Witnesses added to their woes. Many communities adopted new flag salute requirements. In Indiana two women Witnesses were sentenced to 2-to-10 years in prison for "flag desecration" because they had distributed literature opposing the salute; their convictions were ultimately overturned, *McKee v. State*, 219 Ind. 247, 37 N.E.2d 940 (1941). The Mississippi legislature, declaring that "the very life and existence of these United States and the state of Mississippi are threatened" by Germany, Italy, and Japan, made it a felony, punishable by imprisonment until the end of the war, to teach or distribute literature "which reasonably tends to create an attitude of stubborn refusal to salute, honor, or respect the flag." A Witness, R. E. Taylor, was sentenced under the statute. Affirming his conviction, 3–3, the supreme court of Mississippi rejected Taylor's claim of free exercise of religion, declaring that religion's "primary object is a haven of rest after 'life's fitful fever is over.' It is a fallacy of the rankest kind to assume that loyalty to one's country and its flag is attributing to them any aspect of divinity or omnipotent power," *Taylor v. State*, 194 Miss. 1, 34, 11 So. 2d 663, 673 (1943), *rev'd.*, *Taylor v. Mississippi*, 319 U.S. 583 (1943). In at least thirty-one states legal steps were taken to expel nonsaluting Witness children from the public schools, Manwaring 187. Planned by no central authority, unintended by the Supreme Court, overshadowed by World War II, the legal and illegal persecution of Witnesses from 1941 to 1943 was the greatest outbreak of religious intolerance in twentieth-century America.

Three state courts (Kansas, Minnesota, and Washington) refused to follow the reasoning of *Gobitis* and excused nonsaluters. The Civil Rights Section of the Justice Department on May 4, 1942, advised United States attorneys that they should take steps with local officials "to the end that official vigilantism violative of freedom of worship may be avoided," *ibid.* 181. In the Supreme Court itself, dissenting in *Jones v. Opelika*, 316 U.S. 584 (1942), Justices Black, Douglas, and Murphy went out of their way to say: "Since we joined in the opinion in the Gobitis case, we think this is an appropriate occasion to state that we now believe that it was also wrongly decided . . .," *ibid.* at 623–624.

Hayden Covington saw the opportunity. Two months after this dissent, in August 1942, a class action was filed on behalf of Witnesses challenging the constitutionality of an order of the West Virginia Board of Education. The order had been adopted earlier in the year, quoted liberally from *Gobitis,* and required the salute from school children; a number of Witnesses had already been expelled. Walter Barnette, the father of two such children, was enlisted as the plaintiff, Manwaring 208–211. A three-judge federal court, in an opinion by John J. Parker, enjoined enforcement of the board's order, 47 F. Supp. 251 (S.D. W. Va. 1942). The state appealed, unenthusiastically.

Hayden Covington drew on the earlier briefs in *Gobitis*, invoked Daniel 3 and Esther 3 on the duty to obey God and not worship idols, and boldly attacked Frankfurter's opinion. In oral argument he compared *Gobitis* to *Dred Scott*. The Bill of Rights Committee of the

American Bar Association and the ACLU filed strong supporting briefs, Manwaring 217–224. The decision was announced on June 13, 1943, Flag Day:

West Virginia State Board of Education v. Barnette
319 U.S. 624 (1943)

Mr. Hayden C. Covington for appellees.
Mr. W. Holt Wooddell, Assistant Attorney General of West Virginia, with whom *Mr. Ira J. Partlow* was on the brief, for appellants.

Briefs of *amici curiae* were filed on behalf of the Committee on the Bill of Rights, of the American Bar Association, consisting of *Messrs. Douglas Arant, Julius Birge, William D. Campbell, Zechariah Chafee, Jr., L. Stanley Ford, Abe Fortas, George I. Haight, H. Austin Hauxhurst, Monte M. Lemann, Alvin Richards, Earl F. Morris, Burton W. Musser,* and *Basil O'Connor;* and by *Messrs. Osmond K. Fraenkel, Arthur Garfield Hays,* and *Howard B. Lee,* on behalf of the American Civil Liberties Union,—urging affirmance; and by *Mr. Ralph B. Gregg,* on behalf of the American Legion, urging reversal.

Justice Jackson delivered the opinion of the Court.

Following the decision by this Court on June 3, 1940, in *Minersville School District v. Gobitis,* 310 U. S. 586, the West Virginia legislature amended its statutes to require all schools therein to conduct courses of instruction in history, civics, and in the Constitutions of the United States and of the State "for the purpose of teaching, fostering and perpetuating the ideals, principles and spirit of Americanism, and increasing the knowledge of the organization and machinery of the government." Appellant Board of Education was directed, with advice of the State Superintendent of Schools, to "prescribe the courses of study covering these subjects" for public schools. The Act made it the duty of private, parochial and denominational schools to prescribe courses of study "similar to those required for the public schools."

The Board of Education on January 9, 1942, adopted a resolution containing recitals taken largely from the Court's *Gobitis* opinion and ordering that the salute to the flag become "a regular part of the program of activities in the public schools," that all teachers and pupils "shall be required to participate in the salute honoring the Nation represented by the Flag; provided, however, that refusal to salute the Flag be regarded as an act of insubordination, and shall be dealt with accordingly."

The resolution originally required the "commonly accepted salute to the Flag" which it defined. Objections to the salute as "being too much like Hitler's" were raised by the Parent and Teachers Association, the Boy and Girl Scouts, the Red Cross, and the Federation of Women's Clubs. Some modification appears to have been made in deference to these objections, but no concession was made to Jehovah's Witnesses. What is now required is the "stiff-arm" salute, the saluter to keep the right hand raised with palm turned up while the following is repeated: "I pledge allegiance to the Flag of the United States of America and to the Republic for which it stands; one Nation, indivisible, with liberty and justice for all."

Failure to conform is "insubordination" dealt with by expulsion. Readmission is denied by statute until compliance. Meanwhile the expelled child is "unlawfully absent" and may be proceeded against as a delinquent. His parents or guardians are liable to prosecution, and if convicted are subject to fine not exceeding $50 and jail term not exceeding thirty days.

Appellees, citizens of the United States and of West Virginia, brought suit in the United States District Court for themselves and others similarly situated asking its injunction to restrain enforcement of these laws and regulations against Jehovah's

Witnesses. The Witnesses are an unincorporated body teaching that the obligation imposed by law of God is superior to that of laws enacted by temporal government. Their religious beliefs include a literal version of Exodus, Chapter 20, verses 4 and 5, which says: "Thou shalt not make unto thee any graven image, or any likeness of anything that is in heaven above, or that is in the earth beneath, or that is in the water under the earth; thou shalt not bow down thyself to them nor serve them." They consider that the flag is an "image" within this command. For this reason they refuse to salute it. . . .

The very purpose of a Bill of Rights was to withdraw certain subjects from the vicissitudes of political controversy, to place them beyond the reach of majorities and officials and to establish them as legal principles to be applied by the courts. One's right to life, liberty, and property, to free speech, a free press, freedom of worship and assembly, and other fundamental rights may not be submitted to vote; they depend on the outcome of no elections.

In weighing arguments of the parties it is important to distinguish between the due process clause of the Fourteenth Amendment as an instrument for transmitting the principles of the First Amendment and those cases in which it is applied for its own sake. The test of legislation which collides with the Fourteenth Amendment, because it also collides with the principles of the First, is much more definite than the test when only the Fourteenth is involved. Much of the vagueness of the due process clause disappears when the specific prohibitions of the First become its standard. The right of a State to regulate, for example, a public utility may well include, so far as the due process test is concerned, power to impose all of the restrictions which a legislature may have a "rational basis" for adopting. But freedoms of speech and of press, of assembly, and of worship may not be infringed on such slender grounds. They are susceptible of restriction only to prevent grave and immediate danger to interests which the State may lawfully protect. It is important to note that while it is the Fourteenth Amendment which bears directly upon the State it is the more specific limiting principles of the First Amendment that finally govern this case.

Nor does our duty to apply the Bill of Rights to assertions of official authority depend upon our possession of marked competence in the field where the invasion of rights occurs. True, the task of translating the majestic generalities of the Bill of Rights, conceived as part of the pattern of liberal government in the eighteenth century, into concrete restraints on officials dealing with the problems of the twentieth century, is one to disturb self-confidence. These principles grew in soil which also produced a philosophy that the individual was the center of society, that his liberty was attainable through mere absence of governmental restraints, and that government should be entrusted with few controls and only the mildest supervision over men's affairs. We must transplant these rights to a soil in which the *laissez-faire* concept or principle of non-interference has withered at least as to economic affairs, and social advancements are increasingly sought through closer integration of society and through expanded and strengthened governmental controls. These changed conditions often deprive precedents of reliability and cast us more than we would choose upon our own judgment. But we act in these matters not by authority of our competence but by force of our commissions. We cannot, because of modest estimates of our competence in such specialties as public education, withhold the judgment that history authenticates as the function of this Court when liberty is infringed.

4. Lastly, and this is the very heart of the *Gobitis* opinion, it reasons that "National unity is the basis of national security," that the authorities have "the right to select appropriate means for its attainment," and hence reaches the conclusion that such compulsory measures toward "national unity" are constitutional. *Id.* at 595. Upon the verity of this assumption depends our answer in this case.

National unity as an end which officials may foster by persuasion and example is not in question. The problem is whether under our Constitution compulsion as here employed is a permissible means for its achievement.

Struggles to coerce uniformity of sentiment in support of some end thought essential to their time and country have been waged by many good as well as by evil men. Nationalism is a relatively recent phenomenon but at other times and places the ends have been racial or territorial security, support of a dynasty or regime, and particular plans for saving souls. As first and moderate methods to attain unity have failed, those bent on its accomplishment must resort to an ever-increasing severity. As governmental pressure toward unity becomes greater, so strife becomes more bitter as to whose unity it shall be. Probably no deeper division of our people could proceed from any provocation than from finding it necessary to choose what doctrine and whose program public educational officials shall compel youth to unite in embracing. Ultimate futility of such attempts to compel coherence is the lesson of every such effort from the Roman drive to stamp out Christianity as a disturber of its pagan unity, the Inquisition, as a means to religious and dynastic unity, the Siberian exiles as a means to Russian unity, down to the fast failing efforts of our present totalitarian enemies. Those who begin coercive elimination of dissent soon find themselves exterminating dissenters. Compulsory unification of opinion achieves only the unanimity of the graveyard.

It seems trite but necessary to say that the First Amendment to our Constitution was designed to avoid these ends by avoiding these beginnings. There is no mysticism in the American concept of the State or of the nature or origin of its authority. We set up government by consent of the governed, and the Bill of Rights denies those in power any legal opportunity to coerce that consent. Authority here is to be controlled by public opinion, not public opinion by authority.

The case is made difficult not because the principles of its decision are obscure but because the flag involved is our own. Nevertheless, we apply the limitations of the Constitution with no fear that freedom to be intellectually and spiritually diverse or even contrary will disintegrate the social organization. To believe that patriotism will not flourish if patriotic ceremonies are voluntary and spontaneous instead of a compulsory routine is to make an unflattering estimate of the appeal of our institutions to free minds. We can have intellectual individualism and the rich cultural diversities that we owe to exceptional minds only at the price of occasional eccentricity and abnormal attitudes. When they are so harmless to others or to the State as those we deal with here, the price is not too great. But freedom to differ is not limited to things that do not matter much. That would be a mere shadow of freedom. The test of its substance is the right to differ as to things that touch the heart of the existing order.

If there is any fixed star in our constitutional constellation, it is that no official, high or petty, can prescribe what shall be orthodox in politics, nationalism, religion, or other matters of opinion or force citizens to confess by word or act their faith therein. If there are any circumstances which permit an exception, they do not now occur to us.

We think the action of the local authorities in compelling the flag salute and pledge transcends constitutional limitations on their power and invades the sphere of intellect and spirit which it is the purpose of the First Amendment to our Constitution to reserve from all official control.

The decision of this Court in *Minersville School District* v. *Gobitis* and the holdings of those few *per curiam* decisions which preceded and foreshadowed it are overruled, and the judgment enjoining enforcement of the West Virginia Regulation is

Affirmed.

Justices Roberts and Reed adhere to the views expressed by the Court in *Minersville School District v. Gobitis,* 310 U.S. 586, and are of the opinion that the judgment below should be reversed. Justice Frankfurter dissented.

NOTE. *Not Being Photographed.* In *Quaring v. Peterson,* 728 F.2d 1121 (8th Cir. 1984), Frances J. Quaring, a Christian, held the belief that the commandment, "You shall not make any graven image or likeness of anything . . ." (Ex. 20:4; Deut. 5:8) prohibited her from having a likeness of anything in creation. She possessed no photographs, did not own a television set, and would permit no pictures of any kind, even on canned food, within her home. She refused to comply with Nebraska's requirement that her driver's license carry her photograph. In an action to obtain the license without complying, the Eighth Circuit, 2–1, held that the statute burdened Quaring's free exercise of religion (she needed the car in her work) and that Nebraska had not shown a compelling state interest in requiring the photograph. Quaring's claim was upheld. The Supreme Court, 4–4, affirmed, 105 S.Ct. 3492 (1985).

3. NOT KILLING, NOT HELPING, NOT REGISTERING IN WAR

The Selective Draft Act of 1940 read:

Nothing contained in this Act shall be construed to require any person to be subject to combatant training and service in the land or naval forces of the United States who, by reason of religious training and belief, is conscientiously opposed to participation in war in any form. Any such person claiming such exemption from combatant training and service because of such conscientious objections whose claim is sustained by the local board shall, if he is inducted into the land or naval forces under this Act, be assigned to noncombatant service as defined by the President, or shall, if he is found to be conscientiously opposed to participation in such noncombatant service, in lieu of such induction, be assigned to work of national importance under civilian direction [54 *Stat.* 885 (1940)].

Between 25,000 and 50,000 men who objected to bearing arms in war were assigned in the armed services to noncombatant duty in food supply, communications, or the Medical Corps; the largest single religious group were some 12,000 Seventh Day Adventists, Mulford Q. Sibley and Philip E. Jacob, *Conscription of Conscience: The American State and the Conscientious Objector, 1940–1947* (1952) 86–90. Those who qualified under the statute but were unwilling to be in the military—about 12,000 in all—worked for the Civilian Public Service (CPS). CPS work was in forestry and conservation camps; in hospitals and mental institutions; on government survey teams and on private farms. The work was 40 to 96 hours a week and was without pay, *ibid.* at 112, 124. The better CPS camps were run by "the Historic Peace Churches"—the Friends, the Mennonites, and the Brethren—as agents of the government, *ibid.* at 111. The camp programs included religious indoctrination by the churches in charge of the camps, *ibid.* at 173. The constitutional problem involved in making men labor without pay was brushed aside by the courts, *e.g., Roodenko v. United States,* 147 F.2d 752 (10th Cir. 1944), *cert. den.* 324 U.S. 860 (1945). The constitutional problem of letting churches act as custodial agencies of the government does not seem to have been judicially addressed. The majority but by no means all of those in the CPS were themselves members of the Peace Churches. The Peace Churches as government agents were, in the eyes of one academic authority, mice yoked to a cat, Sibley and Jacob, 471.

The Selective Draft Act of 1940 was substantially broader than that of 1917. Instead of exempting only members of "any well-recognized religious sect," all that it required was "religious training and belief." The Circuit Courts divided on what constituted "religious training and belief." In a dictum in *United States v. Kauten,* 133 F.2d 703, 708 (2nd Cir. 1943), Judge Augustus N. Hand said:

Religious belief arises from a sense of the inadequacy of reason as a means of relating the individual to his fellow-men and to his universe—a sense common to men in the most primitive and in the most highly civilized societies. It accepts the aid of logic but refuses to be limited by it. It is a belief finding expression in a conscience which categorically requires the believer to disregard elementary self-interest and to accept martyrdom in preference to transgressing its tenets. . . .

There is a distinction between a course of reasoning resulting in a conviction that a particular war is inexpedient or disastrous and a conscientious objection to participation in any war under any circumstances. The latter, and not the former, may be the basis of exemption under the Act. The former is usually a political objection, while the latter, we think, may justly be regarded as a response of the individual to an inward mentor, call it conscience or God, that is for many persons at the present time the equivalent of what has always been thought a religious impulse.

The dictum was applied in *United States ex rel. Phillips v. Downer*, 135 F.2d 521 (2nd Cir. 1943), in recognizing as a conscientious objector Randolph G. Phillips, who said he had been influenced to oppose "the killing of men" by the Lord's Prayer, the Ten Commandments, and the Sermon on the Mount, and by "historians and poets from Plato to Shaw." Arguably to the contrary, the Ninth Circuit en banc upheld denial of conscientious objector status to Herman Berman, whose objections to war had been learned from two Socialists, Norman Thomas and Eugene Debs, who were serious Christians, *Berman v. United States*, 156 F.2d 377 (9th Cir. 1946). The Supreme Court, denying certiorari, declined the opportunity of clarifying the law, 329 U.S. 795 (1946).

The Supreme Court grappled with conscientious objection only indirectly. In *In re Summers*, 325 U.S. 561 (1945), 5–4, per Justice Stanley F. Reed, it upheld the right of Illinois to deny Clyde Wilson Summers admission to the bar because he refused to take an oath to support the constitution of Illinois. Summers had refused because of his conscientious objection to bearing arms as the Illinois constitution required in time of war; his refusal had led the bar's Committee on Character and Fitness to refuse to certify him. Invoking *Hamilton v. Regents, supra*, X, 10, Justice Reed said that any exemption from military service for conscientious objectors was "by grace of Congressional recognition of their beliefs." He found no violation of "the principles of religious freedom." Dissenting, Justice Black quoted the Sermon on the Mount, the Holmes dissent in *Schwimmer, supra*, X, 10, and the Hughes dissent in *Macintosh, supra*, X, 10.

Less than a year later, in *Girouard v. United States*, 328 U.S. 61 (1946), the *Schwimmer* and *Macintosh* dissents became the law as the Court, 5–3, per Justice Douglas, interpreted the Nationality Act of 1940 not to bar a conscientious objector from citizenship. The successful petitioner was James Louis Girouard, a Seventh Day Adventist, opposed only to combatant service.

During the war the law was clear that only those who could come within the terms of the draft law's exemption would be exempted. But the exemption was sometimes interpreted by local boards with prejudice toward particular religious groups, *e.g.*, in Oklahoma, toward the Mennonites and Brethren, Sibley and Jacob 65. In other cases boards acted capriciously, *see* Francis Heiser (a lawyer who represented many conscientious objectors), "The Law Versus the Conscientious Objector," 20 *University of Chicago Law Review* 441 (1953). Administrative appeal corrected some injustices but was limited. Judicial review of classifications by local boards was extremely narrow until in 1946, at the behest of a Jehovah's Witness represented by Hayden Covington, the Supreme Court permitted challenge of a classification as a defense in a criminal prosecution, *Estep v. United States*, 327 U.S. 114 (1946).

Beyond prejudice and caprice, there was the inadequacy of the exemption. It did not extend to those who refused to register at all. Of these, 300 were criminally prosecuted, one-third of them Black Muslims, Sibley and Jacob, 334. Roman Catholics who objected to the war as "unjust" but did not object to war "in any form" were occasionally prosecuted. Above all, the Jehovah's Witnesses did not fit the exemption. Witnesses did not object to the wars ordered by God in the Bible and so appeared not to object to war "in any form." They did object to fighting "Satan's war" for America. They regularly made the claim that each Witness was a minister of the Gospel, Herbert Hewitt Stroup, *The Jehovah's Witnesses* (1945) 165–166. They pitched their main constitutional case during the war on this point and lost, *Cox v. United States, infra,* XII, 2. In Germany at the same time the Witnesses were being sent to lunatic asylums or to Dachau for refusal to serve, M. James Penton, *Apocalypse Delayed* (1985) 142. The United States was not as harsh, but over 5,000 Witnesses were imprisoned for their refusal to serve; no other church produced so many martyrs to conscience, Sibley and Jacob 84.

Well after World War II, the Court was prepared to back the draft law without greater sensitivity to scruples of religion. In *Gara v. United States,* 340 U.S. 857 (1950), a student at a Mennonite college had decided not to register for the draft. When the FBI came to arrest him, Gara, the dean of men, a practicing Quaker, told him, "Stand by your principles. Don't let them coerce you into registering." Gara was convicted of the felony of aiding and abetting a refusal to register. His free exercise claim was overriden by the government's interest in draft registration, 178 F.2d 38 (6th Cir. 1949). The Supreme Court, 4–4, affirmed without opinion.

In 1955 the Witnesses made a notable breach in the draft law in *Sicurella v. United States,* 348 U.S. 385 (1955), where a Witness willing to engage in theocratic war commanded by God was held to be opposed to participation in war "in any form" within the meaning of the draft act. The Court's conclusion suggested how constitutional issues could be avoided by imaginative construction of the congressional exemption. Justice Tom C. Clark wrote the opinion; Justices Reed and Minton dissented.

Sicurella was apt precedent when a new kind of conscientious objector appeared in litigation. The cases, significantly, arose in the 1950s when the United States was at peace. Equally significantly, they were decided when the Vietnam War was becoming unpopular.

United States v. Seeger
380 U.S. 163 (1965)

Solicitor General Cox argued the cause for the United States in all cases. *Assistant Attorney General Miller* was with him on the briefs in all cases. *Ralph S. Spritzer* was with him on the briefs in Nos. 50 and 51, and *Marshall Tamor Golding* was with him on the briefs in No. 50.

Duane B. Beeson argued the cause and filed a brief for petitioner in No. 29.

Kenneth W. Greenawalt argued the cause and filed a brief for respondent in No. 50.

Herman Alderstein argued the cause and filed a brief for respondent in No. 51.

Briefs of *amici curiae,* urging affirmance in Nos. 50 and 51 and reversal in No. 29, were filed by *Alfred Lawrence Toombs* and *Melvin L. Wulf* for the American Civil Liberties Union, and by *Leo Pfeffer, Shad Polier, Will Maslow* and *Joseph B. Robison* for the American Jewish Congress. Briefs of *amici curiae,* urging affirmance in No. 50, were filed by *Herbert A. Wolff, Leo Rosen, Nanette Dembitz* and *Nancy F. Wechsler* for the American Ethical Union, and by *Tolbert H. McCarroll, Lester Forest* and *Paul Blanshard* for the American Humanist Association.

Justice Clark delivered the opinion of the Court. . . .

No. 50: Seeger was convicted in the District Court for the Southern District of New York of having refused to submit to induction in the armed forces. He was originally classified 1–A in 1953 by his local board, but this classification was changed in 1955 to 2–S (student) and he remained in this status until 1958 when he was reclassified 1–A. He first claimed exemption as a conscientious objector in 1957 after successive annual renewals of his student classification. Although he did not adopt verbatim the printed Selective Service System form, he declared that he was conscientiously opposed to participation in war in any form by reason of his "religious" belief; that he preferred to leave the question as to his belief in a Supreme Being open, "rather than answer 'yes' or 'no' "; that his "skepticism or disbelief in the existence of God" did "not necessarily mean lack of faith in anything whatsoever"; that his was a "belief in and devotion to goodness and virtue for their own sakes, and a religious faith in a purely ethical creed." R.69–70, 73. He cited such personages as Plato, Aristotle and Spinoza for support of his ethical belief in intellectual and moral integrity "without belief in God, except in the remotest sense." R.73. His belief was found to be sincere, honest, and made in good faith; and his conscientious objection to be based upon individual training and belief, both of which included research in religious and cultural fields. Seeger's claim, however, was denied solely because it was not based upon a "belief in a relation to a Supreme Being" as required by § 6 (j) of the Act. At trial Seeger's counsel admitted that Seeger's belief was not in relation to a Supreme Being as commonly understood, but contended that he was entitled to the exemption because "under the present law Mr. Seeger's position would also include definitions of religion which have been stated more recently," R. 49, and could be "accommodated" under the definition of religious training and belief in the Act, R. 53. He was convicted and the Court of Appeals reversed, holding that the Supreme Being requirement of the section distinguished "between internally derived and externally compelled beliefs" and was, therefore, an "impermissible classification" under the Due Process Clause of the Fifth Amendment. 326 F.2d 846.

No. 51: Jakobson was also convicted in the Southern District of New York on a charge of refusing to submit to induction. On his appeal the Court of Appeals reversed on the ground that rejection of his claim may have rested on the factual finding, erroneously made, that he did not believe in a Supreme Being as required by § 6 (j). 325 F.2d 409.

Jakobson was originally classified 1–A in 1953 and intermittently enjoyed a student classification until 1956. It was not until April 1958 that he made claim to noncombatant classification (1–A–O) as a conscientious objector. He stated on the Selective Service System form that he believed in a "Supreme Being" who was "Creator of Man" in the sense of being "ultimately responsible for the existence of" man and who was "the Supreme Reality" of which "the existence of man is the *result.*" R. 44. (Emphasis in the original.) He explained that his religious and social thinking had developed after much meditation and thought. He had concluded that man must be "partly spiritual" and, therefore, "partly akin to the Supreme Reality"; and that his "most important religious law" was that "no man ought ever to willfully sacrifice another man's life as a means to any other end. . . ." R. 45–46. In December 1958 he requested a 1–O classification since he felt that participation in any form of military service would involve him in "too many situations and relationships that would be a strain on [his] conscience that [he felt he] must avoid." R. 70. He submitted a long memorandum of "notes on religion" in which he defined religion as the *"sum and essence of one's basic attitudes to the fundamental problems of human existence,"* R. 72 (emphasis in the original); he said that he believed in "Godness" which was "the Ultimate Cause for the fact of the Being of the Universe"; that to deny its existence would but deny the existence of the universe because "anything that Is, has an Ultimate Cause for its Being." R. 73. There was a relationship to Godness, he stated, in two directions, *i.e.,* "vertically, towards Godness directly," and "horizontally, towards Godness through Mankind and the World." R. 74. He accepted the latter one. The Board classified him 1–A–O and Jakobson appealed. The hearing officer found that the claim was based upon a personal moral code and that he was not sincere in his claim. The Appeal Board classified him 1–A. It did not indicate upon what ground it based its decision, *i.e.,* insincerity or a conclusion that his belief was only a personal moral code. The Court of Appeals reversed, finding that his claim came within the requirements of § 6 (j). Because it could not determine whether the Appeal Board had found that Jakobson's beliefs failed to come within the statutory definition, or whether it had concluded that he lacked sincerity, it directed dismissal of the indictment.

No. 29: Forest Britt Peter was convicted in the Northern District of California on a charge of refusing to submit to induction. In his Selective Service System form he stated that he was not a member of a religious sect or organization; he failed to execute section VII of the questionnaire but attached to it a quotation expressing opposition to war, in which he stated that he concurred. In a later form he hedged the question as to his belief in a Supreme Being by saying that it depended on the definition and he appended a statement that he felt it a violation of his moral code to take human life and that he considered this belief superior to his obligation to the state. As to whether his conviction was religious, he quoted with approval Reverend John Haynes Holmes' definition of religion as "the consciousness of some power manifest in nature which helps man in the ordering of his life in harmony with its demands . . . [; it] is the supreme expression of human nature; it is man thinking his highest, feeling his deepest, and living his best." R. 27. The source of his conviction he attributed to reading and meditation "in our democratic American culture, with its values derived from the western religious and philosophical tradition." *Ibid.* As to his belief in a Supreme Being, Peter stated that he supposed "you could call that a belief in the Supreme Being or God. These just do not happen to be the words I use." R. 11. In 1959 he was classified 1–A, although there was no evidence in the record that he was not sincere in his beliefs. After his conviction for failure to report for induction the Court of Appeals, assuming *arguendo* that he was sincere, affirmed, 324 F. 2d 173.

. . .

Few would quarrel, we think, with the proposition that in no field of human endeavor has the tool of language proved so inadequate in the communication of ideas as it has in dealing with the fundamental questions of man's predicament in life, in death or in final judgment and retribution. This fact makes the task of discerning the intent of Congress in using the phrase "Supreme Being" a complex one. Nor is it made the easier by the richness and variety of spiritual life in our country. Over 250 sects inhabit our land. Some believe in a purely personal God, some in a supernatural deity; others think of religion as a way of life envisioning as its ultimate goal the day when all men can live together in perfect understanding and peace. There are those who think of God as the depth of our being; others, such as the Buddhists, strive for a state of lasting rest through self-denial and inner purification; in Hindu philosophy, the Supreme Being is the transcendental reality which is truth, knowledge and bliss. Even those religious groups which have traditionally opposed war in every form have splintered into various denominations: from 1940 to 1947 there were four denominations using the name "Friends," Selective Service System Monograph No. 11, Conscientious Objection 13 (1950); the "Church of the Brethren" was the official name of the oldest and largest church body of four denominations composed of those commonly called Brethren, *id.,* at 11; and the "Mennonite Church" was the largest of 17 denominations, including the Amish and Hutterites, grouped as "Mennonite bodies" in the 1936 report on the Census of Religious Bodies, *id.,* at 9. This vast panoply of beliefs reveals the magnitude of the problem which faced the Congress when it set about providing an exemption from armed service. It also emphasizes the care that Congress realized was necessary in the fashioning of an exemption which would be in keeping with its long-established policy of not picking and choosing among religious beliefs.

In spite of the elusive nature of the inquiry, we are not without certain guidelines. In amending the 1940 Act, Congress adopted almost intact the language of Chief Justice Hughes in *United States v. Macintosh* [*supra*, X, 11]:

> "The essence of religion is belief in a relation to *God* involving duties superior to those arising from any human relation." At 663–634. (Emphasis supplied.)

By comparing the statutory definition with those words, however, it becomes readily apparent that the Congress deliberately broadened them by substituing the phrase "Supreme Being" for the appellation "God." And in so doing it is also significant that Congress did not elaborate on the form or nature of this higher authority which it chose to designate as "Supreme Being." By so refraining it must have had in mind the admonitions of the Chief Justice when he said in the same opinion that even the word "God" had myriad meanings for men of faith:

> "[P]utting aside dogmas with their particular conceptions of deity, freedom of conscience itself implies respect for an innate conviction of paramount duty. The battle for religious liberty has been fought and won with respect to religious beliefs and practices, which are not in conflict with good order, upon the very ground of the supremacy of conscience within its proper field."   At 634.

Moreover, the Senate Report on the bill specifically states that § 6 (j) was intended to re-enact "substantially the same provisions as were found" in the 1940 Act. That statute, of course, refers to "religious training and belief" without more. Admittedly, all of the parties here purport to base their objection on religious belief. It appears, therefore, that we need only look to this clear statement of congressional intent as set out in the report. Under the 1940 Act it was necessary only to have a conviction based upon religious training and belief; we believe that is all that is required here. Within that phrase would come all sincere religious beliefs which are based upon a power or being, or upon a faith, to which all else is subordinate or upon which all else is ultimately dependent. The test might be stated in these words: A sincere and meaningful belief which occupies in the life of its possessor a place parallel to that filled by the God of those admittedly qualifying for the exemption comes within the statutory definition. This construction avoids imputing to Congress an intent to classify different religious beliefs, exempting some and excluding others, and is in accord with the well-established congressional policy of equal treatment for those whose opposition to service is grounded in their religious tenets. . . .

In summary, Seeger professed "religious belief" and "religious faith." He did not disavow any belief "in a relation to a Supreme Being"; indeed he stated that "the cosmic order does, perhaps, suggest a creative intelligence." He decried the tremendous "spiritual" price man must pay for his willingness to destroy human life. In light of his beliefs and the unquestioned sincerity with which he held them, we think the Board, had it applied the test we propose today, would have granted him the exemption. We think it clear that the beliefs which prompted his objection occupy the same place in his life as the belief in a traditional deity holds in the lives of his friends, the Quakers. We are reminded once more of Dr. Tillich's thoughts:

> "And if that word [God] has not much meaning for you, translate it, and speak of the depths of your life, of the source of your being, of your ultimate concern, *of what you take seriously without any reservation.* Perhaps, in order to do so, you must forget everything traditional that you have learned about God. . . ." Tillich, The Shaking of the Foundations 57 (1948). (Emphasis supplied.)

It may be that Seeger did not clearly demonstrate what his beliefs were with regard to the usual understanding of the term "Supreme Being." But as we have said Congress did not intend that to be the test. We therefore affirm the judgment in No. 50.

In *Jakobson,* No. 51, the Court of Appeals found that the registrant demonstrated that his belief as to opposition to war was related to a Supreme Being. We agree and affirm that judgment.

We reach a like conclusion in No. 29. It will be remembered that Peter acknowledged "some power manifest in nature . . . the supreme expression" that helps man in ordering his life. As to whether he would call that belief in a Supreme Being, he replied, "you could call that a belief in the Supreme Being or God. These just do not happen to be the words I use." We think that under the test we establish here the Board would grant the exemption to Peter and we therefore reverse the judgment in No. 29.

Is Congress entitled to give special protection to freedom of religious conscience, finding in its exercise a particular moral and social value, and citing as justification for its actions the recognition of this value in the free exercise clause of the First Amendment? Is it entitled to extend this protection even though it must frankly be recognized that to do so does result in some advantage to religious belief and does indirectly disadvantage those who do not profess the particular religious belief protected? John H. Mansfield, "Conscientious Objection—1964 Term," 1965 *Religion and Public Order,* ed. Donald A. Gianella, 74–75. In *Seeger,* Mansfield observes at 77, the Supreme Court virtually merged the conscientious and the religious.

An amendment to the Act in 1967, subsequent to the Court's decision in the *Seeger* case, deleted the reference to a "Supreme Being" but continued to provide that "religious training and belief" does not include "essentially political, sociological, or philosophical views, or a merely personal moral code." 81 Stat. 104, 50 U.S.C. App. § 456(j) (1964 ed., Supp. IV). The statute was interpreted as follows:

Welsh v. United States
398 U.S. 333 (1970)

J.B. Tietz argued the cause and filed briefs for petitioner. *Solicitor General Griswold* argued the cause for the United States. With him on the brief were *Assistant Attorney General Wilson, Francis X. Beytagh, Jr.,* and *Beatrice Rosenberg.* Justice Black announced the judgment of the Court and delivered an opinion in which Justice Douglas, Justice Brennan, and Justice Marshall join.

The petitioner, Elliott Ashton Welsh II, was convicted by a United States District Judge of refusing to submit to induction into the Armed Forces in violation of 50 U.S.C. App. § 462 (a), and was on June 1, 1966, sentenced to imprisonment for three years. One of petitioner's defenses to the prosecution was that § 6 (j) of the Universal Military Training and Service Act exempted him from combat and noncombat service because he was "by reason of religious training and belief . . . conscientiously opposed to participation in war in any form." After finding that there was no religious basis for petitioner's conscientious objector claim, the Court of Appeals, Judge Hamley dissenting, affirmed the conviction. 404 F. 2d 1078 (1968). We granted certiorari chiefly to review the contention that Welsh's conviction should be set aside on the basis of this Court's decision in *United States v. Seeger [supra].* For the reasons to be stated, and without passing upon the constitutional arguments that have been raised, we vote to reverse this conviction because of its fundamental inconsistency with *United States v. Seeger, supra.*

The controlling facts in this case are strikingly similar to those in *Seeger.*

. . .

In the case before us the Government seeks to distinguish our holding in *Seeger* on basically two grounds, both of which were relied upon by the Court of Appeals in affirming Welsh's conviction. First, it is stressed that Welsh was far more insistent and explicit than Seeger in denying that his views were religious. For example, in filling out their conscientious objector applications, Seeger put quotation marks around the word "religious," but Welsh struck the word "religious" entirely and later characterized his beliefs as having been formed "by reading in the fields of history and sociology." App. 22. The Court of Appeals found that Welsh had "denied that his objection to war was premised on religious belief" and concluded that "[t]he Appeal Board was entitled to take him at his word." 404 F. 2d, at 1082. We think this attempt to distinguish *Seeger* fails for the reason that it places undue emphasis on the registrant's interpretation of his own beliefs. The Court's statement in *Seeger* that a registrant's characterization of his own belief as "religious" should carry great weight, 380 U.S., at 184, does not imply that his declaration that his views are nonreligious should be treated similarly. When a registrant states that his objections to war are "religious," that information is highly relevant to the question of the function his beliefs have in his life. But very few registrants are fully aware of the broad scope of the word "religious" as used in § 6 (j), and accordingly a registrant's statement that his beliefs are nonreligious is a highly unreliable guide for those charged with administering the exemption. Welsh himself presents a case in point. Although he originally characterized his beliefs as nonreligious, he later upon reflection wrote a long and thoughtful letter to his Appeal Board in which he declared that his beliefs were "certainly religious in the ethical sense of the word." He explained:

> "I believe I mentioned taking of life as not being, for me, a religious wrong. Again, I assumed Mr. [Brady (the Department of Justice hearing officer)] was using the word 'religious' in the conventional sense, and, in order to be perfectly honest did not characterize my belief as 'religious.' " App. 44.

The Government also seeks to distinguish *Seeger* on the ground that Welsh's views, unlike Seeger's, were "essentially political, sociological, or philosophical views or a merely personal moral code." As previously noted, the Government made the same argument about Seeger, and not without reason, for Seeger's views had a substantial political dimension. . . . In this case, Welsh's conscientious objection to war was undeniably based in part on his perception of world politics. In a letter to his local board, he wrote:

> "I can only act according to what I am and what I see. And I see that the military complex wastes both human and material resources, that it fosters disregard for (what I consider a paramount concern) human needs and ends; I see that the means we employ to 'defend' our 'way of life' profoundly change that way of life. I see that in our failure to recognize the political, social, and economic realities of the world, we, *as a nation,* fail our responsibility *as a nation." App. 30.'*

We certainly do not think that § 6 (j)'s exclusion of those persons with "essentially political, sociological, or philosophical views or a merely personal moral code" should be read to exclude those who hold strong beliefs about our domestic and foreign affairs or even those whose conscientious objection to participation in all wars is founded to a substantial extent upon considerations of public policy. The two groups of registrants that obviously do fall within these exclusions from the exemption are those whose beliefs are not deeply held and those whose objection to war does not rest at all upon moral, ethical, or religious principle but instead rests solely upon considerations of policy, pragmatism, or expediency. In applying § 6 (j)'s exclusion of those whose views are "essentially political, sociological, or philosophical" or of those who have a "merely personal moral code," it should be remembered that these exclusions are definitional and do not therefore restrict the category of persons who are conscientious objectors by "religious training and belief." Once the Selective Service System has taken the first step and determined under the standards set out here and in *Seeger* that the registrant is a "religious" conscientious objector, it follows that his views cannot be "essentially political, sociological, or philosophical." Nor can they be a "merely personal moral code." See *United States v. Seeger* [*supra* this section].

Welsh stated that he "believe[d] the taking of life—anyone's life—to be morally wrong." App. 44. In his original conscientious objector application he wrote the following:

> "I believe that human life is valuable in and of itself; in its living; therefore I will not injure or kill another human being. This belief (and the corresponding 'duty' to abstain from violence toward another person) is not 'superior to those arising from any human relation.' On the contrary: *it is essential to every human relation.* I cannot, therefore, conscientiously comply with the Government's insistence that I assume duties which I feel are immoral and totally repugnant." App. 10.

Welsh elaborated his beliefs in later communications with Selective Service officials. On the basis of these beliefs and the conclusion of the Court of Appeals that he held them "with the strength of more traditional religious convictions," 404 F. 2d, at 1081, we think Welsh was clearly entitled to a conscientious objector exemption. Section 6 (j) requires no more. That section exempts from military service all those whose consciences, spurred by deeply held moral, ethical, or religious beliefs, would give them no rest or peace if they allowed themselves to become a part of an instrument of war.

The judgment is

Reversed.

. . .

Justice Harlan concurring in result:

. . .

The constitutional question that must be faced in this case is whether a statute that defers to the individual's conscience only when his views emanate from adherence to theistic religious beliefs is within the power of Congress. Congress, of course, could, entirely consistently with the requirements of the Constitution, eliminate *all* exemptions for conscientious objectors. Such a course would be wholly "neutral" and, in my view, would not offend the Free Exercise Clause, for reasons set forth in my dissenting opinion in *Sherbert v. Verner, infra,* XI, 4; See *Jacobson v. Massachusetts,* 197 U.S. 11, 29 (1905) (dictum); cf. *McGowan v. Maryland, infra,* XIII, 3; *Davis v. Beason, supra,* IX; *Hamilton v. Board of Regents, supra,* X, 10; *Reynolds v. United States, supra,* IX; Kurland, Of Church and State and the Supreme Court, 29 U. Chi. L. Rev. 1 (1961). However, having chosen to exempt, it cannot draw the line between theistic or nontheistic religious beliefs on the one hand and secular beliefs on the other. Any such distinctions are not, in my view, compatible with the Establishment Clause of the First Amendment.

Justice White, with whom The Chief Justice and Justice Stewart join, dissenting.

Whether or not *United States v. Seeger,* 380 U.S. 163 (1965), accurately reflected the intent of Congress in providing draft exemptions for religious conscientious objectors to war, I cannot join today's construction of § 6 (j) extending draft exemption to those who disclaim religious objections to war and whose views about war represent a purely personal code arising not from religious training and belief as the statute requires but from readings in philosophy, history, and sociology. Our obligation in statutory construction cases is to enforce the will of Congress, not our own; and as Mr. Justice Harlan has demonstrated, construing § 6 (j) to include Welsh exempts from the draft a class of persons to whom Congress has expressly denied an exemption.

NOTE. *Marxist Communism as a Religion.* Writers on communism have frequently characterized it as a religion, *e.g.,* Joseph Schumpeter, *Capitalism, Socialism, and Democracy* (1950) 5–8; Robert C. Tucker, *Philosophy and Myth in Karl Marx* (1972) 21–27. Like all serious systems, it claims to be true. It offers a comprehensive account of human relations and a Marxist morality. It propounds a way of life. It is propagated by the Communist party of the Soviet Union and by other communist parties. Analogies are easily drawn between the communist hierarchy, agents, and missionaries and Christian hierarchies, agents, and missionaries. Communism offers "social salvation," where a general elimination of injustice will occur, instead of an after-death salvation where justice will be done. Its founders are its prophets; the end predicted is apocalyptic. Its belief in the inevitability of class warfare and the victory of the proletariat is a form of predestination. Indeed, many of Marx's own images and ideas were drawn from the Bible, Reinhard Buchbinder, *Bibelzitate, Bibelanspielungen, Bibelparodien, theologische Vergleiche und Analogien bei Marx und Engels* (1976) 28–45. Marx, for example, says, "Materialism is the only-begotten son of Great Britain," *ibid.* at 118, parodying John 1:18. "All the important dogmas of the Church—the Trinity, Creation, Original Sin, Incarnation of the Son of God and Redemption of man, the Church or Mystical Body of Christ as a perfect society, the consummation of history through Christ—have been found "transposed in Marxism to a register of atheistic humanism," Jean-Yves Calvez, *La Pensée de Karl Marx* (1950) 594.

Communism is not treated as a religion for purposes of the First Amendment. Once God is eliminated from a definition of religion, why does not communism qualify? The most obvious objection is that it does not claim to be one. But that is true of SCI/TM, *Malnak v. Yogi, infra* XIV, 2. Suppose, in a change of strategy, the Communist Party, U.S.A., should make the claim. Would its political character disqualify it? Is Islam less a religion because of its political importance to many Middle Eastern governments?

Gillette v. United States
401 U.S. 437 (1971)

Conrad J. Lynn argued the cause for petitioner in no. 85. With him on the brief were *Leon Friedman, Marvin M. Karpatkin,* and *Melvin L. Wulf. Richard Harrington,* argued the cause for petitioner in No. 325. With him on the briefs were *Leigh Athearn, Stuart J. Land,* and *John T. Noonan, Jr.*

Solicitor General Griswold argued the cause for the United States and for the other respondents in both cases. With him on the briefs were *Assistant Attorney General Wilson* and *Beatrice Rosenberg.*

George T. Altman, pro se, filed a brief as *amicus curiae* in both cases. *Leo Rosen* filed a brief for the American Ethical Union as *amicus curiae* in No. 85. Briefs of *amici curiae* in No. 325 were filed by *Charles H. Tuttle* and *Thomas A. Shaw, Jr.,* for the National Council of the Churches of Christ in the U.S.A. et al.; by *Peter J. Donnici* for the Executive Board of the National Federation of Priests' Councils; by *Joseph B. Robison, Ephraim Margolin, Stanley J. Friedman, Seymour Farber,* and *Edwin J. Lukas* for the American Jewish Congress; by *Michael N. Pollet* and *Elsbeth Levy Bothe* for Louis P. Font; and by the American Friends Service Committee.

. . .

Justice Marshall delivered the opinion of the Court.

These cases present the question whether conscientious objection to a particular war, rather than objection to war as such, relieves the objector from responsibilities of military training and service. Specifically, we are called upon to decide whether conscientious scruples relating to a particular conflict are within the purview of established provisions relieving conscientious objectors to war from military service. Both petitioners also invoke constitutional principles barring government interference with the exercise of religion and requiring governmental neutrality in matters of religion. . . .

For purposes of determining the statutory status of conscientious objection to a particular war, the focal language of § 6 (j) is the phrase, "conscientiously opposed to participation in war in any form." This language, on a straightforward reading, can bear but one meaning; that conscientious scruples relating to war and military service must amount to conscientious opposition to participating personally in any war and all war. See *Welsh v. United States [supra]* (concurring in result). See also *United States v. Kauten,* 133 F. 2d 703, 707 (CA2 1943). It matters little for present purposes whether the words, "in any form," are read to modify "war" or "participation." On the first reading, conscientious scruples must implicate "war in any form," and an objection involving a particular war rather than all war would plainly not be covered by § 6 (j). On the other reading, an objector must oppose "participation in war." It would strain good sense to read this phrase otherwise than to mean "participation in all war." For the word "war" would still be used in an unqualified, generic sense, meaning war as such. Thus, however the statutory clause be parsed, it remains that conscientious objection must run to war in any form.

. . .

The critical weakness of petitioners' establishment claim arises from the fact that § 6(j), on its face, simply does not discriminate on the basis of religious affiliation or religious belief, apart of course from beliefs concerning war. The section says that anyone who is conscientiously opposed to all war shall be relieved of military service. The specified objection must have a grounding in "religious training and belief," but no particular sectarian affiliation or theological position is required. The Draft Act of 1917, § 4, 40 Stat. 78, extended relief only to those conscientious objectors affiliated with some "well-recognized religious sect or organization" whose principles forbade members' participation in war, but the attempt to focus on particular sects apparently broke down in administrative practice, *Welsh v. United States, [supra]* (concurring in result), and the 1940 Selective Training and Service Act, § 5 (g), 54 Stat. 869, discarded all sectarian restriction. Thereafter Congress has framed the conscientious objector exemption in broad terms compatible with "its long-established policy of not picking and choosing among religious beliefs." *United States v. Seeger [supra].*

Thus, there is no occasion to consider the claim that when Congress grants a benefit expressly to adherents of one *religion,* courts must either nullify the grant or somehow extend the benefit to cover all religions. For § 6 (j) does not single out any religious organization or religious creed for special treatment. Rather petitioners' contention is that since Congress has recognized one sort of conscientious objection concerning war, whatever its religious basis, the Establishment Clause commands that another, different objection be carved out and protected by the courts.

. . .

Apart from the Government's need for manpower, perhaps the central interest involved in the administration of conscription laws is the interest in maintaining a fair system for determining "who serves when not all serve." When the Government exacts so much, the importance of fair, evenhanded, and uniform decisionmaking is obviously intensified. The Goverment argues that the interest in fairness would be jeopardized by expansion of § 6 (j) to include conscientious objection to a particular war. The contention is that the claim to relief on account of such objection is intrinsically a claim of uncertain dimensions, and that granting the claim in theory would involve a real danger of erratic or even discriminatory decisionmaking in administrative practice. A virtually limitless variety of beliefs are subsumable under the rubric, "objection to a particular war."

. . .

To be sure, the Free Exercise Clause bars "governmental regulation of religious beliefs as such," *Sherbert v. Verner [infra,* XI, 4] (1963), or interference with the dissemination of religious ideas. See *Fowler v. Rhode Island [infra,* XIII, 1] (1953); *Follett v. McCormick,* 321 U.S. 573 (1944); *Murdock v. Pennsylvania [supra,* XI, 1]. It prohibits misuse of secular governmental programs "to impede the observance of one or all religions or . . . to discriminate invidiously between religions, . . . even though the burden may be characterized as being only indirect." *Braunfeld v. Brown, [infra,* XIII, 2] (opinion of Warren, C.J.). And even as to neutral prohibitory or regulatory laws having secular aims, the Free Exercise Clause may condemn certain applications clashing with imperatives of religion and conscience, when the burden on First Amendment values is not justifiable in terms of the Government's valid aims. See *id.; Sherbert v. Verner* [*infra*, XI 4]. See generally Clark, Guidelines for the Free Exercise Clause, 83 Harv. L. Rev. 327 (1969). However, the impact of conscription on objectors to particular wars is far from unjustified. The conscription laws, applied to such persons as to others, are not designed to interfere with any religious ritual or practice, and do not work a penalty against any theological position. The incidental burdens felt by persons in petitioners' position are strictly justified by substantial governmental interests that relate directly to the very impacts questioned. And more broadly, of course, there is the Government's interest in procuring the manpower necessary for military purposes, pursuant to the constitutional grant of power to Congress to raise and support armies. Art. I, § 8.

Affirmed.

. . .

Justice Douglas, dissenting:

The question, Can a conscientious objector, whether his objection be rooted in "religion" or in moral values, be required to kill? has never been answered by the Court. *Hamilton v. Regents* [*supra*, X, 11], did no more than hold that the Fourteenth Amendment did not require a State to make its university available to one who would not take military training. *United States v. Macintosh*, [*supra* X, 11] denied naturalization to a person who "would not promise in advance to bear arms in defense of the United States unless he believed the war to be morally justified." *Id.*, at 613. The question of compelling a man to kill against his conscience was not squarely involved. Most of the talk in the majority opinion concerned "serving in the armed forces of the Nation in time of war." *Id.*, at 623. Such service can, of course, take place in noncombatant roles. The ruling was that such service is "dependent upon the will of Congress and not upon the scruples of the individual, except as Congress provides." *Ibid.* The *dicta* of the Court in the *Macintosh* case squint towards the denial of Gillette's claim, though as I have said, the issue was not squarely presented.

Yet if dicta are to be our guide, my choice is the dicta of Chief Justice Hughes who, dissenting in *Macintosh*, spoke as well for Justices Holmes, Brandeis, and Stone [*see supra*, X, 11].

. . .

I had assumed that the welfare of the single human soul was the ultimate test of the vitality of the First Amendment.

NOTE. *Negre v. Larson*, 401 U.S. 437 (1971). Vietnam not only had led to conscientious objection by persons from traditional churches, it—and the spirit of Vatican II—also had led Catholics to be more assertive of their conscientious scruples to a war which some Catholics found to be unjust. Gordon C. Zahn's *In Solitary Witness: The Life and Death of Franz Jägerstätter* (1964), the life of Franz Jägerstätter, an Austrian Catholic executed for refusing to fight for Hitler, had shown that a simple, saintly man could choose death rather than participate in an unjust war.

That the public interest would be served by legislation permitting selective conscientious objection, that the government should prize such independence as the expression "of the integrity which is the ground of other virtues," was argued by a Protestant theologian, Ralph Potter, "Conscientious Objection to Particular Wars," *Religion and the Public Order*, ed. Donald Gianella (1968) 87. Others were unconvinced, see John A. Rohr, *Prophets without Honor: Public Policy and the Selective Conscientious Objector* (1971) (selective conscientious objectors are like the prophets: they must expect to be stoned for their prophecies).

John Courtney Murray, the leading Catholic writer on conscience and the state, would not condemn the Vietnam War himself but would defend the right to conscientiously object to it;

a member of President Johnson's Advisory Commission on Selective Service, he thus took a minority position on the commission, Murray, "War and Conscience," in James Finn, ed., *A Conflict of Loyalties: The Case for Selective Conscientious Objection* (1968), 19–30. As Murray saw, Congress was hostile to the selective objector, and the selective objection was often wrongly read as a political not a religious contention, *ibid.* at 25.

The claim of a Catholic seminarian that the Vietnam War was immoral and that he could not conscientiously serve in it was raised in a separate case, *Negre v. Larson.* The majority in *Gillette* subsumed Negre's claim under *Gillette* and made no analysis of his distinct religious claim. Dissenting alone in both cases, Justice Douglas said:

I approach the facts of this case with some diffidence, as they involve doctrines of the Catholic Church in which I was not raised. But we have on one of petitioner's briefs an authoritative lay Catholic scholar, Dr. John T. Noonan, Jr., and from that brief I deduce the following:

Under the doctrines of the Catholic Church a person has a moral duty to take part in wars declared by his government so long as they comply with the tests of his church for just wars.[1] Conversely, a Catholic has a moral duty not to participate in unjust wars.[2]

The Fifth Commandment, "Thou shall not kill," provides a basis for the distinction between just and unjust wars. In the 16th century Francisco Victoria, Dominican master of the University of Salamanca and pioneer in international law, elaborated on the distinction. "If a subject is convinced of the injustice of a war, he ought not to serve in it, even on the command of his prince. This is clear, for no one can authorize the killing of an innocent person." He realized not all men had the information of the prince and his counsellors on the causes of a war, but where "the proofs and tokens of the injustice of the war may be such that ignorance would be no excuse even to the subjects" who are not normally informed, that ignorance will not be an excuse if they participate.[3] Well over 400 years later, today, the Baltimore Catechism makes an exception to the Fifth Commandment for a "soldier fighting a just war."[4]

No one can tell a Catholic that this or that war is either just or unjust. This is a personal decision that an individual must make on the basis of his own conscience after studying the facts.[5]

---

[1] The theological basis for this was explained by Pope John XXIII in Part II of Pacem in Terris ¶ 46 (Paulist Press 1963): "Human society can be neither well-ordered nor prosperous unless it has some people invested with legitimate authority to preserve its institutions. . . . These however derive their authority from God, as St. Paul teaches in the words, *There exists no authority except from God.* These words of St. Paul are explained thus by St. John Chrysostom: . . . *What I say is, that it is the divine wisdom and not mere chance, that has ordained that there should be government, that some should command and others obey."* ¶ 50 adds: "When, in fact, men obey their rulers, it is not at all as men that they obey them, but through their obedience it is God . . . since He has decreed that men's dealings with one another should be regulated by an order which He Himself has established."

[2] "Since the right to command is required by the moral order and has its source in God, it follows that, if civil authorities legislate for or allow anything that is contrary to that order and therefore contrary to the will of God, neither the laws made nor the authorizations granted can be binding on the consciences of the citizens, since *we must obey God rather than men." Id.,* at ¶ 51.

[3] De Indis Relectio Posterior, sive De Iure Belli Hispanorum in Barbaros, translated in Classics of International Law 173–174 (E. Nys ed. 1917).

[4] P. 205 (official rev. ed. 1949).

[5] Pope Paul VI in § 16 of the Pastoral Constitution on the Church in the Modern World states:

"Deep within his conscience man discovers a law which he has not laid upon himself but which

Like the distinction between just and unjust wars, the duty to obey conscience is not a new doctrine in the Catholic Church. When told to stop preaching by the Sanhedrin, to which they were subordinate by law, "Peter and the apostles answered and said, 'We must obey God rather than men.'" That duty has not changed. Pope Paul VI has expressed it as follows: "On his part, man perceives and acknowledges the imperatives of the divine law through the mediation of conscience. In all his activity a man is bound to follow his conscience, in order that he may come to God, the end and purpose of life."

NOTE. *Compare United States v. Berg,* 310 F. Supp. 1157 (D. Maine, S.D. 1970). Eugene Alfred Berg, a former seminarian and a graduate of the University of Maine, was a practicing Catholic who believed in the Catholic just war doctrine. He also took the position that, given the present means of warfare, the conditions for a just war can no longer be met. Finding him opposed to war "in any form" and no basis in fact for the draft board's denial of his conscientious objector claim, Judge Edward Gignoux found Berg innocent of draft evasion.

NOTE. In *Johnson v. Robison,* 415 U.S. 361 (1974), William Robert Robison was a conscientious objector to all military service; in 1966 he was so classified by his local board and assigned to work at Peter Bent Brigham Hospital, Boston, for two years. When, on the completion of his service, he was denied educational support by the Veterans' Administration, he attacked as unconstitutional the statute that gave such benefits to veterans of military service but denied them to conscientious objectors. The Supreme Court, per Justice Brennan, found the statute neither to deny equal protection of the laws nor to be an unconstitutional burden on Robison's free exercise of religion. Justice Brennan at 385 found only "an incidental burden," adding "if, indeed, any burden exists at all." The government's interest "in raising and supporting armies" was "clearly sufficient" to justify imposition of the burden. Justice Douglas dissented. He thought that the burden was undeniable; he saw no government interest except the financial one of not having to pay the educational benefits and declared, "That in my view is an invidious discrimination and a penalty on those who assert their religious scruples. . . .," *ibid.* at 389 n. 3.

4. KEEPING HOLY THE SABBATH

Like *Gillette* and *Negre,* the case that follows can be seen as the conferral of a benefit on one religion, a benefit considerably less significant than exemption from military duty.

Sherbert v. Verner
374 U.S. 398 (1963)

William D. Donnelly argued the cause and filed briefs for appellant.

Daniel R. McLeod, Attorney General of South Carolina, argued the cause for appellees. With him on the brief was *Victor S. Evans,* Assistant Attorney General.

Briefs of *amici curiae,* urging reversal, were filed by *Morris B. Abram, Edwin J. Lukas, Arnold Forster, Melvin L. Wulf, Paul Hartman, Theodore Leskes* and *Sol Rabkin* for the American Jewish Committee et al., and by *Leo Pfeffer, Lewis H. Weinstein,*

---

he must obey. Its voice, ever calling him to love and to do what is good and avoid evil, tells him inwardly at the right moment to do this or to shun that. For man has in his heart a law inscribed by God. His dignity lies in observing this law, and by it he will be judged."

Albert Wald, Shad Polier, Ephraim S. London, Samuel Lawrence Brennglass and *Jacob Sheinkman* for the Synagogue Council of America et al.

Justice Brennan delivered the opinion of the Court.

Appellant, a member of the Seventh-day Adventist Church, was discharged by her South Carolina employer because she would not work on Saturday, the Sabbath Day of her faith. When she was unable to obtain other employment because from conscientious scruples she would not take Saturday work, she filed a claim for unemployment compensation benefits under the South Carolina Unemployment Compensation Act. That law provides that, to be eligible for benefits, a claimant must be "able to work and . . . available for work"; and, further, that a claimant is ineligible for benefits "[i]f . . . he has failed, without good cause . . . to accept available suitable work when offered him by the employment office or the employer. . . ." The appellee Employment Security Commission, in administrative proceedings under the statute, found that appellant's restriction upon her availability for Saturday work brought her within the provision disqualifying for benefits insured workers who fail, without good cause, to accept "suitable work when offered . . . by the employment office or the employer . . . ." The Commission's finding was sustained by the Court of Common Pleas for Spartanburg County. That court's judgment was in turn affirmed by the South Carolina Supreme Court, which rejected appellant's contention that, as applied to her, the disqualifying provisions of the South Carolina statute abridged her right to the free exercise of her religion secured under the Free Exercise Clause of the First Amendment through the Fourteenth Amendment. The State Supreme Court held specifically that appellant's ineligibility infringed no constitutional liberties because such a construction of the statute "places no restriction upon the appellant's freedom of religion nor does it in any way prevent her in the exercise of her right and freedom to observe her religious beliefs in accordance with the dictates of her conscience." 240 S. C. 286, 303–304, 125 S.E.2d 737, 746. We noted probable jurisdiction of appellant's appeal. 371 U.S. 938. We reverse the judgment of the South Carolina Supreme Court and remand for further proceedings not inconsistent with this opinion. . . .

We turn first to the question whether the disqualification for benefits imposes any burden on the free exercise of appellant's religion. We think it is clear that it does. In a sense the consequences of such a disqualification to religious principles and practices may be only an indirect result of welfare legislation within the State's general competence to enact; it is true that no criminal sanctions directly compel appellant to work a six-day week. But this is only the beginning, not the end, of our inquiry. For "[i]f the purpose or effect of a law is to impede the observance of one or all religions or is to discriminate invidiously between religions, that law is constitutionally invalid even though the burden may be characterized as being only indirect." *Braunfeld v. Brown* [*infra,* XIII, 2], at 607. Here not only is it apparent that appellant's declared ineligibility for benefits derives solely from the practice of her religion, but the pressure upon her to forego that practice is unmistakable. The ruling forces her to choose between following the precepts of her religion and forfeiting benefits, on the one hand, and abandoning one of the precepts of her religion in order to accept work, on the other hand. Governmental imposition of such a choice puts the same kind of burden upon the free exercise of religion as would a fine imposed against appellant for her Saturday worship.

Nor may the South Carolina court's construction of the statute be saved from constitutional infirmity on the ground that unemployment compensation benefits are not appellant's "right" but merely a "privilege." It is too late in the day to doubt that the liberties of religion and expression may be infringed by the denial of or placing of conditions upon a benefit or privilege. *American Communications Assn. v. Douds,* 339 U.S. 382, 390; *Wieman v. Updegraff,* 344 U.S. 183, 191–192; *Hannegan v. Esquire, Inc.,* 327 U.S. 146, 155–156. . . .

We must next consider whether some compelling state interest enforced in the eligibility provisions of the South Carolina statute justifies the substantial infringement of ap-

pellant's First Amendment right. It is basic that no showing merely of a rational relationship to some colorable state interest would suffice; in this highly sensitive constitutional area, "[o]nly the gravest abuses, endangering paramount interests, give occasion for permissible limitation," *Thomas v. Collins,* 323 U.S. 516, 530. . . .
No such abuse or danger has been advanced in the present case. The appellees suggest no more than a possibility that the filing of fraudulent claims by unscrupulous claimants feigning religious objections to Saturday work might not only dilute the unemployment compensation fund but also hinder the scheduling by employers of necessary Saturday work. But that possibility is not apposite here because no such objection appears to have been made before the South Carolina Supreme Court, and we are unwilling to assess the importance of an asserted state interest without the views of the state court. Nor, if the contention had been made below, would the record appear to sustain it; there is no proof whatever to warrant such fears of malingering or deceit as those which the respondents now advance. Even if consideration of such evidence is not foreclosed by the prohibition against judicial inquiry into the truth or falsity of religious beliefs, *United States v. Ballard* [*infra,* XII, 1]—a question as to which we intimate no view since it is not before us—it is highly doubtful whether such evidence would be sufficient to warrant a substantial infringement of religious liberties. For even if the possibility of spurious claims did threaten to dilute the fund and disrupt the scheduling of work, it would plainly be incumbent upon the appellees to demonstrate that no alternative forms of regulation would combat such abuses without infringing First Amendment rights.

In these respects, then, the state interest asserted in the present case is wholly dissimilar to the interests which were found to justify the less direct burden upon religious practices in *Braunfeld v. Brown,* [*infra,* XIII, 2]. The Court recognized that the Sunday closing law which that decision sustained undoubtedly served "to make the practice of [the Orthodox Jewish merchants'] . . . religious beliefs more expensive," 366 U.S., at 605. But the statute was nevertheless saved by a countervailing factor which finds no equivalent in the instant case—a strong state interest in providing one uniform day of rest for all workers. That secular objective could be achieved, the Court found, only by declaring Sunday to be that day of rest. Requiring exemptions for Sabbatarians, while theoretically possible, appeared to present an administrative problem of such magnitude, or to afford the exempted class so great a competitive advantage, that such a requirement would have rendered the entire statutory scheme unworkable. In the present case no such justifications underlie the determination of the state court that appellant's religion makes her ineligible to receive benefits.

In holding as we do, plainly we are not fostering the "establishment" of the Seventh-day Adventist religion in South Carolina, for the extension of unemployment benefits to Sabbatarians in common with Sunday worshippers reflects nothing more than the governmental obligation of neutrality in the face of religious differences, and does not represent that involvement of religious with secular institutions which it is the object of the Establishment Clause to forestall. . . .

In view of the result we have reached under the First and Fourteenth Amendments' guarantee of free exercise of religion, we have no occasion to consider appellant's claim that the denial of benefits also deprived her of the equal protection of the laws in violation of the Fourteenth Amendment.

The judgment of the South Carolina Supreme Court is reversed and the case is remanded for further proceedings not inconsistent with this opinion. . . .

Justice Stewart concurring in result.

. . .

To require South Carolina to so administer its laws as to pay public money to the appellant under the circumstances of this case is thus clearly to require the State to violate the Establishment Clause as construed by this Court. This poses no problem for me, because I think the Court's mechanistic concept of the Establishment Clause is historically unsound and constitutionally wrong. I think the process of constitutional decision in the area of the relationships between government and religion demands considerably more than the invocation of broad-brushed rhetoric of the kind I have quoted. And I think that the guarantee of religious liberty embodied in the Free Exercise Clause affirmatively requires government to create an atmosphere of hospitality and accommodation to individual belief or disbelief. In short, I think our Constitution commands the positive protection by government of religious freedom—not only for a minority, however small—not only for the majority, however large—but for each of us.

South Carolina would deny unemployment benefits to a mother unavailable for work on Saturdays because she was unable to get a babysitter. Thus, we do not have before us a situation where a State provides unemployment compensation generally, and singles out for disqualification only those persons who are unavailable for work on religious grounds. This is not, in short, a scheme which operates so as to discriminate against religion as such. But the Court nevertheless holds that the State must prefer a religious over a secular ground for being unavailable for work—that state financial support of the appellant's religion is constitutionally required to carry out "the governmental obligation of neutrality in the face of religious differences. . . ."

Yet in cases decided under the Establishment Clause the Court has decreed otherwise. It has decreed that government must blind itself to the differing religious beliefs and traditions of the people. With all respect, I think it is the Court's duty to face up to the dilemma posed by the conflict between the Free Exercise Clause of the Constitution and the Establishment Clause as interpreted by the Court. It is a duty, I submit, which we owe to the people, the States, and the Nation, and a duty which we owe to ourselves. For so long as the resounding but fallacious fundamentalist rhetoric of some of our Establishment Clause opinions remains on our books, to be disregarded at will as in the present case, or to be undiscriminatingly invoked as in the *Schempp* case [XIV, 2], so long will the possibility of consistent and perceptive decision in this most difficult and delicate area of constitutional law be impeded and impaired. And so long, I fear, will the guarantee of true religious freedom in our pluralistic society be uncertain and insecure. . . .

Justice Harlan, joined by Justice White, dissenting.

The South Carolina Supreme Court has uniformly applied this law in conformity with its clearly expressed purpose. It has consistently held that one is not "available for work" if his unemployment has resulted not from the inability of industry to provide a job but rather from personal circumstances, no matter how compelling. The reference to "involuntary unemployment" in the legislative statement of policy, whatever a sociologist, philosopher, or theologian might say, has been interpreted not to embrace such personal circumstances. See, *e.g., Judson Mills v. South Carolina Unemployment Compensation Comm'n,* 204 S.C. 37, 28 S.E. 2d 535 (claimant was "unavailable for work" when she became unable to work the third shift, and limited her availability to the other two, because of the need to care for her four children); *Stone Mfg. Co. v. South Carolina Employment Security Comm'n,* 219 S.C. 239, 64 S.E. 2d 664; *Hartsville Cotton Mill v. South Carolina Employment Security Comm'n,* 224 S.C. 407, 79 S.E. 2d 381.

In the present case all that the state court has done is to apply these accepted principles. Since virtually all of the mills in the Spartanburg area were operating on a six-day week, the appellant was "unavailable for work," and thus ineligible for benefits, when personal considerations prevented her from accepting employment on a full-time basis in the industry and locality in which she had worked. The fact that these personal considerations sprang from her religious convictions was wholly without relevance to the state court's application of the law. Thus in no proper sense can it be said that the State discriminated against the appellant on the basis of her religious beliefs or that she was denied benefits *because* she was a Seventh-day Adventist. She was denied benefits just as any other claimant would be denied benefits who was not "available for work" for personal reasons.

With this background, this Court's decision comes into clearer focus. What the Court is holding is that if the State chooses to condition unemployment compensation on the applicant's availability for work, it is constitutionally compelled to *carve out an exception*—and to provide benefits—for those whose unavailability is due to their religious convictions. Such a holding has particular significance in two respects.

First, despite the Court's protestations to the contrary, the decision necessarily overrules *Braunfeld v. Brown,* [*infra,* XIII, 2], which held that it did not offend the "Free Exercise" Clause of the Constitution for a State to forbid a Sabbatarian to do business on Sunday. The secular purpose of the statute before us today is even clearer than that involved in *Braunfeld.* And just as in *Braunfeld*—where exceptions to the Sunday closing laws for Sabbatarians would have been inconsistent with the purpose to achieve a uniform day of rest and would have required case-by-case inquiry into religious beliefs—so here, an exception to the rules of eligibility based on religious convictions would necessitate judicial examination of those convictions and would be at odds with the limited purpose of the statute to smooth out the economy during periods of industrial instability. Finally, the indirect financial burden of the present law is far less than that involved in *Braunfeld.* Forcing a store owner to close his business on Sunday may well have the effect of depriving him of a satisfactory livelihood if his religious convictions require him to close on Saturday as well. Here we are dealing only with temporary benefits, amounting to a fraction of regular weekly wages and running for not more than 22 weeks. See §§ 68–104, 68–105. Clearly, any differences between this case and *Braunfeld* cut against the present appellant.

NOTE. *Compare Trans World Airlines v. Hardison,* 432 U.S. 63 (1967). Title VII of the Civil Rights Act of 1964 makes it unlawful for an employer to discriminate against an employee on account of religion, and religion is defined to include "practice, as well as belief, unless an employer demonstrates that he is unable to reasonably accommodate . . . without undue hardship to [his] business," 42 U.S.C. sec. 2000 e(j). Larry G. Hardison was a new member of the Worldwide Church of God, which teaches that the Sabbath must be observed without work from sunset on Friday to sunset on Saturday. Hardison worked at the central TWA supply depot, which operated 24 hours a day, seven days a week. He refused to work on Saturday, he did not have the seniority necessary to get off on Saturday, the union rejected TWA's request to waive the seniority rules, and he was fired. The District Court ruled for TWA. The Eighth Circuit found that Title VII had been violated. The United States, the American Civil Liberties Union, the Seventh Day Adventists, and Leo Pfeffer for the Central Conference of American Rabbis were among those urging affirmance. The Supreme Court, per Justice Byron R. White, held that TWA could not have accommodated Hardison without undue hardship. Justices Brennan and Marshall dissented. To give him Saturday off, the Court observed at 85, would mean that "the privilege of having Saturday off would be allocated according to religious beliefs." *See also Thorton v. Caldor, Inc., infra* this section.

But see Thomas v. Review Board, 450 U.S. 707 (1981): Eddie C. Thomas, a Jehovah's Witness, was transferred from work fabricating sheet steel for a variety of uses to a department making turrets for tanks. Thomas refused the job and sought unemployment compensation. The supreme court of Indiana held that his unemployment was "voluntary" and not for "good cause." In an opinion by Chief Justice Warren E. Burger, the Supreme Court of the United States held that *Sherbert* controlled and that the state was not entitled to burden Thomas's exercise of religious liberty in this way. Justice Rehnquist dissented:

. . .

The Court correctly acknowledges that there is a "tension" between the Free Exercise and Establishment Clauses of the First Amendment of the United States Constitution. Although the relationship of the two Clauses has been the subject of much commentary, the "tension" is of fairly recent vintage, unknown at the time of the framing and adoption of the First Admendment. The causes of the tension, it seems to me, are threefold. First, the growth of social welfare legislation during the latter part of the 20th century has greatly magnified the potential for conflict between the two Clauses, since such legislation touches the individual at so many points in his life. Second, the decision by this Court that the First Amendment was "incorporated" into the Fourteenth Amendment and thereby made applicable against the States, *Stromberg v. California,* 283 U.S. 359 (1931); *Cantwell v. Connecticut,* [*supra,* XI, 1], similarly multiplied the number of instances in which the "tension" might arise. The third, and perhaps most important, cause of the tension is our overly expansive interpretation of *both* Clauses. By broadly construing both Clauses, the Court has constantly narrowed the channel between the Scylla and Charybdis through which any state or federal action must pass in order to survive constitutional scrutiny.

None of these developments could have been foreseen by those who framed and adopted the First Amendment. The First Amendment was adopted well before the growth of much social welfare legislation and at a time when the Federal Government was in a real sense considered a government of limited delegated powers. Indeed, the principal argument against adopting the Constitution *without* a "Bill of Rights" was not that such an enactment would be *undesirable,* but that it was *unnecessary* because of the limited nature of the Federal Government. So long as the Government enacts little social welfare legislation, as was the case in 1791, there are few occasions in which the two Clauses may conflict. Moreover, as originally enacted, the First Amendment applied only to the Federal Government, not the government of the States. *Barron v. Baltimore,* 7 Pet. 243 (1833). The Framers could hardly anticipate *Barron* being superseded by the "selective incorporation" doctrine adopted by the Court, a decision which greatly expanded the number of statutes which would be subject to challenge under the First Amendment. Because those who drafted and adopted the First Amendment could not have foreseen either the growth of social welfare legislation or the incorporation of the First Amendment into the Fourteenth Amendment, we simply do not know how they would view the scope of the two Clauses.

NOTE. *Estate of Thornton v. Caldor, Inc.,* 105 S.Ct. 2914 (1985). When Connecticut changed its Sunday laws in 1976, it enacted a statute prohibiting an employer requiring more than six days' employment in a calendar week. The statute added, "No person who states that a particular day of the week is observed as his Sabbath may be required by his employer to work on such day." Donald Thornton, a Presbyterian and a department manager for Caldor, Inc., a chain of department stores, was ordered to work on Sundays. He did so on thirty-one Sundays in two years before notifying Caldor that Sunday was his Sabbath and refusing to work on that day. He was demoted, resigned, and sued Caldor. The highest court of Connecticut held the statute to be an unconstitutional establishment of religion, *Caldor, Inc. v. Thorton,* 191 Conn. 336, 464 A.2d 785 (1983). The secular purpose of the Sunday laws upheld in *McGowan; infra,* XIII, 2, the court said, was to establish a *common* day of rest. But here the benefit of being able to choose one's day off was conferred only on religious persons, on those who had a "Sabbath" to observe. Applying the tests set out in *Lemon, infra,* XIV, 1— tests set out in the context of religious education—the court found the statute's impermissible purpose and effect to be to advance religion. The Supreme Court, 8–1, per Chief Justice Burger, affirmed. The Chief Justice emphasized that the statute was weighted in favor of Sabbath observers and made no allowances for inconvenience or economic hardship of the employer. Its primary effect was to advance "a particular religious practice." Justice Rehnquist dissented without opinion.

NOTE. *Accommodation of Religious Beliefs of a Federal Grantee.* The Hill-Burton Act, 42 U.S.C. Sec. 291 *et seq.,* provided substantial federal funds through the states to hospitals, including those operated by religious orders. After a district court in 1972 enjoined St. Vincent's Hospital in Billings, Montana, from prohibiting a sterilization at the hospital, Congress amended the act in 1973 to provide that receipt of Hill-Burton money "does not authorize any court or any public official" to require the recipient to "make its facilities available for the performance of any sterilization procedure or abortion" contrary to the recipient's "religious beliefs or moral convictions" *Stat.* 91, 95 (1973), 42 U.S.C. sec. 300a, 7(a). In *Chrisman v. Sisters of St. Joseph of Peace,* 506 F. 2d 308 (9th Circ. 1974), Barbara Ann Chrisman sued the religious order operating Sacred Heart Hospital in Eugene, Oregon, alleging that refusal to perform a tubal ligation was the deprival of a civil right secured by 28 U.S.C., sec. 1343. Sacred Heart Hospital had received $691,913 in Hill-Burton funds as part of a total construction budget of $8,035,241. The Court of Appeals, per Eugene Wright, held that the congressional proviso was not an unconstitutional establishment of religion. Citing *Sherbert,* Judge Wright concluded that "Congress quite properly sought to protect the freedom of religion of those with religious or moral scruples. . . ."

5. EDUCATING ONE'S CHILDREN

NOTE. *Introduction; State v. Garber.* Not the Jehovah's Witnesses but a smaller and older denomination of Christians was the protagonist in the establishment of the free exercise of religion in regard to education—the right that *Pierce v. Society of Sisters, supra,* X, 6, had stopped short of asserting. The Amish were a branch of the Mennonites who in 1693 under the leadership of Jacob Ammann of Erlanbach, Switzerland, had set up a stricter church community, characterized by the rigorous shunning of sinners. Immigrating to America between 1720 and 1775, they settled chiefly in Pennsylvania, John A. Hostetler, *Amish Society* (1980) 31–57. By the 1960s Amish settlements existed also in Maryland, Ohio, Indiana, Iowa, Kansas, and Wisconsin. The Old Order Amish, a division of the original movement, were the strictest of all, combining a devotion to the Bible with an agricultural way of life, the use of German as their language, a distinctive dress that went back to the eighteenth century, and a commitment to pacifism.

Grouped in nearly self-sufficient units forming small self-governed commonwealths, the Amish conceive of themselves as bodies of Christians "suspended in a tension-field between obedience to an all-knowing and all-powerful Creator on the one hand and the fear of disobedience on the other," *ibid.* at 21. For the Amish, knowledge unrelated to their agricultural life leads to pride, and pride is destructive sin. Learning the world's ways and mingling with the proud endanger salvation. Love requires a close and closed community with like-minded brothers and sisters, the elect of God who are "a chosen generation" (1 Peter 2:9).

Public education as such was not objectionable to the Amish when such education first appeared in the form of rural neighborhood schoolhouses. Amish children generally attended grammar schools in the nineteenth century. In the twentieth century, however, compulsory secondary schools and consolidated high school districts were seen by the Amish as a threat. Secondary schools went beyond the reading, writing, and arithmetic that Amish life found useful. The consolidated districts brought Amish and non-Amish together. In adolescence, when sexual temptations were perceived as acute, the Amish saw their children thrown together with the proud, immodestly dressed, disobedient children of the world. When, in the 1960s, decisions of the Supreme Court banished prayer and the religious reading of the Bible from the schools, and the teaching of evolution became general, Amish distress with the public high school became acute, *see* Joseph Stoll (editor of *The Blackboard Bulletin*, an Amish parochial school journal), "Who Shall Educate Our Children," in Albert N. Keim, ed. *Compulsory Education and the Amish: The Right Not to be Modern* (1975) 27–42.

As early as 1914, Amish were jailed and fined in Ohio for refusing to send their children to a new consolidated high school, Keim, "From Erlanbach to New Glarus," in Keim, 14–15. For the next fifty years similar sporadic persecutions were patiently endured. In the few cases that drew opinions from appellate courts, the Amish claim of religious freedom was almost universally rejected. In 1966 the Kansas Supreme Court upheld the conviction of LeRoy Garber for not sending his fifteen-year-old daughter Sharon to the public school; the Supreme Court of the United States denied review, *State v. Garber*, 197 Kan. 567, 419 P. 2d 896 (1966), *cert. denied and appeal dismissed*, 389 U.S. 51 (1967).

The Amish bore these trials, disliking litigation and usually reluctant to let others litigate in their behalf, Hostetler in Keim 100. In Pennsylvania, a compromise with the state was worked out in 1955. Amish teenagers were permitted to attend an Amish vocational school three hours a week, doing their homework in agricultural or domestic projects under their parents' supervision, Hostetler, *Amish Society* 258. In Iowa local authorities in 1965 used force to take Amish pupils to the public high school. General public outrage led Iowa to compromise, Donald A. Erickson, "Showdown at an Amish Schoolhouse," in Keim, 43–83. The Iowa case led William C. Lindholm, a Lutheran pastor, to form the National Committee for Amish Religious Freedom.

On Christmas Eve, 1968, Pastor Lindholm asked William Ball, a Catholic lawyer, to defend Amish arrested in New Glarus, Wisconsin, for not sending their children to high school. Ball, a Pennsylvanian, proposed that Wisconsin compromise as Pennsylvania had; to his surprise the state refused. He went to trial in Green County, Wisconsin, in March 1969, relying chiefly on *Sherbert, supra*, XI, 4. He was able to introduce John Hostetler as an expert witness on how Amish religious belief required rejection of the high school, and Donald Erickson as a witness on the education accomplished by an Amish upbringing. Erickson also testified, "I have never seen a school that impressed me either as a culturally or religiously neutral school." Hostetler, "the most superb witness we could have had," was asked by the prosecution: "What's the point of education? Isn't it to get ahead in the world?" Hostetler replied: "It all depends on which world." Ball also put on the county sheriff to testify he did not know of any teenage criminals who were Amish, and the county welfare supervisor to testify how little the Amish burdened the welfare system. Ball lost in the local court and the intermediate court, but won in the Wisconsin Supreme Court. Again, to his surprise, the state refused to yield, appealing to the Supreme Court of the United States and arguing that "the religion" whose free exercise was protected by the First Amendment was worship not "a way of life." By the standard of *Reynolds v. United States, supra* IX, the state was right. But Ball had laid the groundwork for a different approach, and the Supreme Court, affirming, virtually tracked the testimony the trial had elicited, *see* William B. Ball, "Building a Landmark Case," in Keim 114–123.

Wisconsin v. Yoder
406 U.S. 205 (1972)

John W. Calhoun, Assistant Attorney General of Wisconsin, argued the cause for petitioner. With him on the briefs were *Robert W. Warren*, Attorney General, and *William H. Wilker*, Assistant Attorney General.

William B. Ball argued the cause for respondents. With him on the brief was *Joseph G. Skelly.*

Briefs of *amici curiae* urging affirmance were filed by *Donald E. Showalter* for the Mennonite Central Committee; by *Boardman Noland* and *Lee Boothby* for the General Conference of Seventh-Day Adventists; by *William S. Ellis* for the National Council of the Churches of Christ; by *Nathan Lewin* for the National Jewish Commission on Law and Public Affairs; and by *Leo Pfeffer* for the Synagogue Council of America et al.

Chief Justice Burger delivered the opinion of the Court.

On petition of the State of Wisconsin, we granted the writ of certiorari in this case to review a decision of the Wisconsin Supreme Court holding that respondents' convictions of violating the State's compulsory school-attendance law were invalid under the Free Exercise Clause of the First Amendment to the United States Constitution made applicable to the States by the Fourteenth Amendment. For the reasons hereafter stated we affirm the judgment of the Supreme Court of Wisconsin.

Respondents Jonas Yoder and Wallace Miller are members of the Old Order Amish religion, and respondent Adin Yutzy is a member of the Conservative Amish Mennonite Church. They and their families are residents of Green County, Wisconsin. Wisconsin's compulsory school-attendance law required them to cause their children to attend public or private school until reaching age 16 but the respondents declined to send their children, ages 14 and 15, to public school after they completed the eighth grade. The children were not enrolled in any private school, or within any recognized exception to the compulsory-attendance law, and they are conceded to be subject to the Wisconsin statute.

On complaint of the school district administrator for the public schools, respondents were charged, tried, and convicted of violating the compulsory-attendance law in Green County Court and were fined the sum of $5 each. Respondents defended on the ground that the application of the compulsory-attendance law violated their rights under the First and Fourteenth Amendments. The trial testimony showed that respondents believed, in accordance with the tenets of Old Order Amish communities generally, that their children's attendance at high school, public or private, was contrary to the Amish religion and way of life. They believed that by sending their children to high school, they would not only expose themselves to the danger of the censure of the church community, but, as found by the county court, also endanger their own salvation and that of their children. The State stipulated that respondents' religious beliefs were sincere.

In support of their position, respondents presented as expert witnesses scholars on religion and education whose testimony is uncontradicted. They expressed their opinions on the relationship of the Amish belief concerning school attendance to the more general tenets of their religion, and described the impact that compulsory high school attendance could have on the continued survival of Amish communities as they exist in the United States today. The history of the Amish sect was given in some detail, beginning with the Swiss Anabaptists of the 16th century who rejected institutionalized churches and sought to return to the early, simple, Christian life de-emphasizing material success, rejecting the competitive spirit, and seeking to insulate themselves from the modern world. As a result of their common heritage, Old Order Amish communities today are characterized by a fundamental belief that salvation requires life in a church community separate and apart from the world and worldly influence. This concept of life aloof from the world and its values is central to their faith.

A related feature of Old Order Amish communities is their devotion to a life in harmony with nature and the soil, as exemplified by the simple life of the early Christian era that continued in America during much of our early national life. Amish beliefs require members of the community to make their living by farming or closely related activities. Broadly speaking, the Old Order Amish religion pervades and determines the entire mode of life of its adherents. Their conduct is regulated in great detail by the *Ordnung,* or rules, of the church community. Adult baptism, which occurs in late adolescence, is the time at which Amish young people voluntarily undertake heavy obligations, not unlike the Bar Mitzvah of the Jews, to abide by the rules of the church community.

Amish objection to formal education beyond the eighth grade is firmly grounded in these central religious concepts. They object to the high school, and higher education generally, because the values they teach are in marked variance with Amish values and the Amish way of life; they view secondary school education as an impermissible exposure of their children to a "worldly" influence in conflict with their beliefs. The high school tends to emphasize intellectual and scientific accomplishments, self-distinction, competitiveness, worldly success, and social life with other students. Amish society emphasizes informal learning-through-doing; a life of "goodness," rather than a life of intellect; wisdom, rather than technical knowledge; community welfare, rather than competition; and separation from, rather than integration with, contemporary worldly society.

Formal high school education beyond the eighth grade is contrary to Amish beliefs, not only because it places Amish children in an environment hostile to Amish beliefs with increasing emphasis on competition in class work and sports and with pressure to conform to the styles, manners, and ways of the peer group, but also because it takes them away from their community, physically and emotionally, during the crucial and formative adolescent period of life. During this period, the children must acquire Amish attitudes favoring manual work and self-reliance and the specific skills needed to perform the adult role of an Amish farmer or housewife. They must learn to enjoy physical labor. Once a child has learned basic reading, writing, and elementary mathematics, these traits, skills, and attitudes admittedly fall within the category of those best learned through example and "doing" rather than in a classroom. And, at this time in life, the Amish child must also grow in his faith and his relationship to the. Amish community if he is to be prepared to accept the heavy obligations imposed by adult baptism. In short, high school attendance with teachers who are not of the Amish faith—and may even be hostile to it—interposes a serious barrier to the integration of the Amish child into the Amish religious community. Dr. John Hostetler, one of the experts on Amish society, testified that the modern high school is not equipped, in curriculum or social environment, to impart the values promoted by Amish society.

The Amish do not object to elementary education through the first eight grades as a general proposition because they agree that their children must have basic skills in the "three R's" in order to read the Bible, to be good farmers and citizens, and to be able to deal with non-Amish people when necessary in the course of daily affairs. They view such a basic education as acceptable because it does not significantly expose their children to worldly values or interfere with their development in the Amish community during the crucial adolescent period. While Amish accept compulsory elementary education generally, wherever possible they have established their own elementary schools in many respects like the small local schools of the past. In the Amish belief higher learning tends to develop values they reject as influences that alienate man from God.

On the basis of such considerations, Dr. Hostetler testified that compulsory high school attendance could not only result in great psychological harm to Amish children, because of the conflicts it would produce, but would also, in his opinion, ultimately result in the destruction of the Old Order Amish church community as it exists in the United States today. The testimony of Dr. Donald A. Erickson, an expert witness on education, also showed that the Amish succeed in preparing their high school age children to be productive members of the Amish community. He described their system of learning through doing the skills directly relevant to their adult roles in the Amish community as "ideal" and perhaps superior to ordinary high school education. The evidence also showed that the Amish have an excellent record as law-abiding and generally self-sufficient members of society.

Although the trial court in its careful findings determined that the Wisconsin compulsory school-attendance law "does interfere with the freedom of the Defendants to act in accordance with their sincere religious belief" it also concluded that the requirement of high school attendance until age 16 was a "reasonable and constitutional" exercise of governmental power, and therefore denied the motion to dismiss the charges. The Wisconsin Circuit Court affirmed the convictions. The Wisconsin Supreme Court, however, sustained respondents' claim under the Free Exercise Clause of the First Amendment and reversed the convictions. A majority of the court was of the opinion that the State had failed to make an adequate showing that its interest in "establishing and maintaining an educational system overrides the defendants' right to the free exercise of their religion." 49 Wis. 2d 430, 447, 182 N. W. 2d 539, 547 (1971).

I

There is no doubt as to the power of a State, having a high responsibility for education of its citizens, to impose reasonable regulations for the control and duration of basic education. See, *e.g., Pierce v. Society of Sisters,* [*supra,* X, 7]. Providing public schools ranks at the very apex of the function of a State. Yet even this paramount responsibility was, in *Pierce,* made to yield to the right of parents to provide an equivalent education in a privately operated system. There the Court held that Oregon's statute compelling attendance in a public school from age eight to age 16 unreasonably interfered with the interest of parents in directing the rearing of their offspring, including their education in church-operated schools. As that case suggests, the values of parental direction of the religious upbringing and education of their children in their early and formative years have a high place in our society. See also *Ginsberg v. New York,* 390 U. S. 629, 639 (1968); *Meyer v. Nebraska,* 262 U. S. 390 (1923); cf. *Rowan v. Post Office Dept.,* 397 U. S. 728 (1970). Thus, a State's interest in universal education, however highly we rank it, is not totally free from a balancing process when it impinges on fundamental rights and interests, such as those specifically protected by the Free Exercise Clause of the First Amendment, and the traditional interest of parents with respect to the religious upbringing of their children so long as they, in the words of *Pierce,* "prepare [them] for additional obligations." 268 U. S., at 535. . . .

II

We come then to the quality of the claims of the respondents concerning the alleged encroachment of Wisconsin's compulsory school-attendance statute on their rights and the rights of their children to the free exercise of the religious beliefs they and their forebears have adhered to for almost three centuries. In evaluating those claims we must be careful to determine whether the Amish religious faith and their mode of life are, as they claim, inseparable and interdependent. A way of life, however virtuous and admirable, may not be interposed as a barrier to reasonable state regulation of education if it is based on purely secular considerations; to have the protection of the Religion Clauses, the claims must be rooted in religious belief. Although a determination of what is a "religious" belief or practice entitled to constitutional protection may present a most delicate question, the very concept of ordered liberty precludes allowing every person to make his own standards on matters of conduct in which society as a whole has important interests. Thus, if the Amish asserted their claims because of their subjective evaluation and rejection of the contemporary secular values accepted by the majority, much as Thoreau rejected the social values of his time and isolated himself at Walden Pond, their claims would not rest on a religious basis. Thoreau's choice was philosophical and personal rather than religious, and such belief does not rise to the demands of the Religion Clauses.

Giving no weight to such secular considerations, however, we see that the record in this case abundantly supports the claim that the traditional way of life of the Amish is not merely a matter of personal preference, but one of deep religious conviction, shared by an organized group, and intimately related to daily living. That the Old Order Amish daily life and religious practice stem from their faith is shown by the fact that it is in response to their literal interpretation of the Biblical injunction from the Epistle of Paul to the Romans, "be not conformed to this world. . . ." This command is fundamental to the Amish faith. Moreover, for the Old Order Amish, religion is not simply a matter of theocratic belief. As the expert witnesses explained, the Old Order Amish religion pervades and determines virtually their entire way of life, regulating it with the detail of the Talmudic diet through the strictly enforced rules of the church community.

The record shows that the respondents' religious beliefs and attitude toward life, family, and home have remained constant—perhaps some would say static—in a period of unparalleled progress in human knowledge generally and great changes in education. The respondents freely concede, and indeed assert as an article of faith, that their religious beliefs and what we would today call "life style" have not altered in fundamentals for centuries. Their way of life in a church-oriented community, separated from the outside world and "worldly" influences, their attachment to nature and the soil, is a way inherently simple and uncomplicated, albeit difficult to preserve against the pressure to conform. Their rejection of telephones, automobiles, radios, and television, their mode of dress, of speech, their habits of manual work do indeed set them apart from much of contemporary society; these customs are both symbolic and practical.

As the society around the Amish has become more populous, urban, industrialized, and complex, particularly in this century, government regulation of human affairs has correspondingly become more detailed and pervasive. The Amish mode of life has thus come into conflict increasingly with requirements of contemporary society exerting a hydraulic insistence on conformity to majoritarian standards. So long as compulsory education laws were confined to eight grades of elementary basic education imparted in a nearby rural schoolhouse, with a large proportion of students of the Amish faith, the Old Order Amish had little basis to fear that school attendance would expose their children to the worldly influence they reject. But modern compulsory secondary education in rural areas is now largely carried on in a consolidated school, often remote from the student's home and alien to his daily home life. As the record so strongly shows, the values and programs of the modern secondary school are in sharp conflict with the fundamental mode of life mandated by the Amish religion; modern laws requiring compulsory secondary education have accordingly engendered great concern and conflict.

. . .

The State's argument proceeds without reliance on any actual conflict between the wishes of parents and children. It appears to rest on the potential that exemption of Amish parents from the requirements of the compulsory-education law might allow some parents to act contrary to the best interests of their children by foreclosing their opportunity to make an intelligent choice between the Amish way of life and that of the outside world. The same argument could, of course, be made with respect to all church schools short of college. There is nothing in the record or in the ordinary course of human experience to suggest that non-Amish parents generally consult with children of ages 14–16 if they are placed in a church school of the parents' faith.

Indeed it seems clear that if the State is empowered, as *parens patriae,* to "save" a child from himself or his Amish parents by requiring an additional two years of compulsory formal high school education, the State will in large measure influence, if not determine, the religious future of the child. Even more markedly than in *Prince* [*supra,* XI, 1], therefore, this case involves the fundamental interest of parents, as contrasted with that of the State, to guide the religious future and education of their children. The history and culture of Western civilization reflect a strong tradition of parental concern for the nurture and upbringing of their children. This primary role of the parents in the upbringing of their children is now established beyond debate as an enduring American tradition. . . .

Affirmed.

Justices Powell and Rehnquist took no part in the case.

Justice Douglas, dissenting in part:

. . .

The views of the two children in question were not canvassed by the Wisconsin courts. The matter should be explicitly reserved so that new hearings can be held on remand of the case.

III

I think the emphasis of the Court on the "law and order" record of this Amish group of people is quite irrelevant. A religion is a religion irrespective of what the misdemeanor or felony records of its members might be. I am not at all sure how the Catholics, Episcopalians, the Baptists, Jehovah's Witnesses, the Unitarians, and my own Presbyterians would make out if subjected to such a test. It is, of course, true that if a group or society was organized to perpetuate crime and if that is its motive, we would have rather startling problems akin to those that were raised when some years back a particular sect was challenged here as operating on a fraudulent basis. *United States v. Ballard* [*infra*, XIII, 1]. But no such factors are present here, and the Amish, whether with a high or low criminal record, certainly qualify by all historic standards as a religion within the meaning of the First Amendment.

The Court rightly rejects the notion that actions, even though religiously grounded, are always outside the protection of the Free Exercise Clause of the First Amendment. In so ruling, the Court departs from the teaching of *Reynolds v. United States,* [*supra*, IX], where it was said concerning the reach of the Free Exercise Clause of the First Amendment, "Congress was deprived of all legislative power over mere opinion, but was left free to reach actions which were in violation of social duties or subversive of good order." In that case it was conceded that polygamy was a part of the religion of the Mormons. Yet the Court said, "It matters not that his belief [in polygamy] was a part of his professed religion: it was still belief, and belief only." *Id.,* at 167.

Action, which the Court deemed to be antisocial, could be punished even though it was grounded on deeply held and sincere religious convictions. What we do today, at least in this respect, opens the way to give organized religion a broader base than it has ever enjoyed; and it even promises that in time *Reynolds* will be overruled.

NOTE. *Compare United States v. Lee,* 455 U. S. 252 (1982). Part of the Amish religious way is to bear one another's burdens (Gal. 6:2) and so to relieve the wants of the old and the enfeebled (1 Tim. 5:8). Consequently they see no need for social security and have the view that as the government's intervention in these matters is wrong, it is sinful to receive social security benefits or pay the social security tax. They challenged the tax as a burden on their religious freedom. The Supreme Court unanimously rejected the challenge. For the Court, Chief Justice Burger wrote that not all governmentally imposed burdens on religion were unconstitutional. He cited *Reynolds, supra,* IX. The government's interest in having a national, compulsory social security system outweighed the rights of religious conscience.

NOTE. *Regulating Parochial Schools. National Labor Relations Board v. Catholic Bishop of Chicago,* 440 U.S. 490 (1979). The NLRB asserted that the National Labor Relations Act gave it jurisdiction over parochial schools. Writing for the Court, Chief Justice Burger indicated that the Court wished to avoid the "serious constitutional questions" that would arise if the Board had to adjudicate unfair labor charges against such schools and had to consider the defense of religious mission that would be raised by religious administrators. Quoting *Lemon, infra,* XIV, 1, the Court said, "Religious authority necessarily pervades the school system."

The "very process of inquiry," the Court said at 502, might "impinge on rights guaranteed by the Religion Clauses." The Board would have to decide what were "terms and conditions of employment" and therefore mandatory subjects of collective bargaining. Again the Court, at 503, raised the possibility of "the Board's inquiry" involving "sensitive issues that open the door to conflicts between clergy, administrators and the Board, or conflicts with negotiators for unions." The Court concluded that Congress had not intended to include church-operated schools within the NLRB's jurisdiction. Justices Brennan, White, Marshall, and Blackmun dissented. Compare *Holy Trinity Church, supra*, X, 1.

In *St. Martin Evangelical Lutheran Church v. South Dakota*, 451 U.S. 772 (1981), the Court unanimously held that an exception in the Federal Unemployment Tax for services performed in the employ of "a church or a convention or association of churches" should be read to include an elementary school that was not a legal entity separate from the parish church and a secondary school owned by the Wisconsin Evangelical Lutheran Synod. The majority opinion, by Justice Blackmun, laid stress on construing the statute "to avoid raising doubts of its constitutionality." Americans United for Separation of Church and State and the United States Catholic Conference were among the incongruously joined *amici* urging this result.

Compare Dolter v. Wahlert High School 483 F. Supp. 266 (N.D. Iowa, 1980). Susan Dolter was an English teacher at a Catholic high school affiliated with the archdiocese of Dubuque. Single, she became pregnant. She was dismissed for this reason. She sued under Title VII of the Civil Rights Act of 1964, 42 U.S.C. Sec. 2000e, *et seq.*, alleging discrimination based on sex. The court denied the defendant's motion to dismiss. It held that the school could dismiss any teacher who violated the Church's moral teaching by engaging in premarital sex, but the school could not discharge only women who did so. If the school was concerned only with the visible effect of pregnancy, it could give a woman teacher a paid leave of absence. The court said the trial would determine whether Susan Dolter's conduct was such that she did not possess the "bona fide occupational qualifications" for the job and so fell within an exception to the law on sex discrimination.

In contrast to *Dolter*, see *McClure v. Salvation Army*, 460 F.2d 553 (5th Cir. 1972), *cert. denied*, 409 U.S. 846 (1972): Mrs. Billie B. McClure, an officer (minister) in the Salvation Army, alleged sex discrimination when the Army terminated her as an officer. Invoking the line of cases from *Watson v. Jones, supra* VIII, 5, to *Kedroff* and *Kreshik* (*infra.* XII, 3), the Court of Appeals, per James P. Coleman, held that a serious constitutional doubt would arise if Title VII were interpreted to apply to the employment relation between a church and a minister. The court quoted *Kedroff's* recognition of "a spirit of freedom for religious organizations." *Accord Maguire v. Marquette University* (E.D. Wis. 1986), 6 *Religious Freedom Reporter* 141 (Title VII claim of sex discrimination by Marjorie Maguire, denied appointment as associate professor of theology at a Jesuit University; *McClure* found applicable; free exercise clause would be violated by ordering the university to hire Maguire.)

NOTE. *Christian Schools.* Biblically based schools, specifically called Christian Schools and generally operated by Baptists, have fared differently in different states, to some degree because of different state statutes, to some degree because of the courts' greater or lesser sensitivity to the Baptists' free exercise claims. Their position has been that the Bible shows that God has given parents the obligation and right of educating their children, *see, e.g.,* Deuteronomy 6:6–7, Proverbs 22:6, Ephesians 6:4; that in the exercise of this religious right they have instituted schools that are pervasively religious and not secular schools with religious instruction tacked on; that the state has no power to regulate the curriculum of the schools or the credentials of those who teach there; and that the school and the church are one, so that the state can no more prescribe for the one than for the other.

In *State v. Faith Baptist Church of Louisville, Nebraska,* 207 Neb. 802, 301 N.W.2d 571 (1981), *appeal dismissed for want of a substantial federal question,* 454 U.S. 803 (1981), the church ran the Faith Christian School, an elementary and secondary educational enterprise that employed a curriculum supplied by Accelerated Christian Education (A.C.E.), consisting of a series of booklets with instructional information and self-test questions, all with a biblical orientation. For example, a social studies booklet was devoted to Chapter 1 of Genesis; a mathematics booklet interspersed biblical citations and sayings with problems in addition and subtraction. The school refused to supply the state with the names of the students at the school; to get approval of its curriculum; or to employ accredited teachers. The court granted the injunction sought by the state against the operation of the school.

The church and the school were one building. In defiance of a court order closing the building on weekdays to prevent its use as a school, a group of parishioners attended the building and conducted a prayer vigil. Police removed them by force. A federal court held that these parishioners had a cause of action against the officers because the officers had interfered with their right of worship, *McCurry v. Tesch,* 738 F.2d 271 (8th Cir. 1984), *cert. denied,* 105 S.Ct. 1180 (1985). For a short summary of the controversy, *see* Shugrue, "An Approach to Mutual Respect: The Christian Schools Controversy," 18 *Creighton Law Review* 219 (1984–85); Comment, *"State v. Faith Baptist Church:* State Regulation of Religious Education," 15 *Creighton Law Review* 183 (1981); *see also* "In Nebraska, the War Between Church and State Rages On," *Christianity Today* 32 (Feb. 17, 1984); "Fundamentalists Leave Jail, But Nebraska Church Schools Are Still in Trouble," *Christianity Today* 64 (Apr. 6, 1984); "Is the Nebraska School Trouble Finally Over?" *Christianity Today* 40 (July 13, 1984). For an account by one of the fundamentalist participants, *see* H. E. Rowe, *The Day They Padlocked the Church* (1983).

Iowa reached a conclusion like Nebraska's, *Johnson v. Charles City Community Schools Board of Education,* 368 N.W.2d 74 (Iowa 1985), *cert. denied, Pruessner v. Benton,* 106 S.Ct. 594 (1985), the court explicitly agreeing with *Faith Baptist, supra,* and rejecting "the Amish exception" to compulsory attendance that the legislature had provided. The court observed at 84: "Sincerity of belief is the only factor wholly common to both the Amish and these plaintiffs. The beliefs of the plaintiffs are greatly less interwoven with their daily mode of life. The Amish culture is greatly more isolated from mainstream American life. Plaintiffs' children, for all the distinctive religious convictions they will be given, will live, compete for jobs, work, and move about in a diverse and complex society."

On the other hand, in *State v. Whisner,* 47 Ohio St. 2d 181, Ohio Opps. 3d 105, 351 N.E.2d 750 (1976), the Reverend Levi Whisner, pastor of Tabernacle Christian Church in Bradford, Ohio, testified that the church and the Tabernacle Christian School were "the same," *ibid.* at 187, 351 N.E.2d at 754. Parents convicted for failing to send their children to a school conforming to minimum state standards were acquitted on appeal. The court cited *Yoder* and found that the state had not ever attempted to justify its interest in applying its minimum standards to a religious school.

Similarly, in *Bangor Baptist Church v. State of Maine, Department of Educational and Cultural Services,* 576 F. Supp. 1299, 1335 (D. Me. 1983), the church and the administrators of the Bangor Christian School were granted an injunction against Maine officials prohibiting the officials from bringing actions against the plaintiffs "on the ground that they have induced habitual truancy through their statements to parents that the education of their children is a religious duty and that the state should have no role in regulating the education of Christian children." Not coincidentally, William Ball represented the successful churches in Ohio and Maine.

Compare State v. Heart Ministries, Inc., 227 Kan. 244, 607 P.2d 1102 (1980), *appeal dismissed for want of a substantial federal question,* 449 U.S. 802 (1980). The Reverend

William Cowell and his wife Carol operated the Victory Village Home for Girls. According to his testimony Cowell believed that corporal punishment (including beating with belts and boards) is required by Scripture. He did not believe in preparing financial statements or an annual audit of accounts, but believed that God would provide. For these reasons he objected to state regulation of the enterprise and to payment of the state license fee of $5 per year. The Court held that "licensing is necessary and the fee reasonable" and found no need to go into the defendants' religious objections to the regulations that affected their discipline of the children and their financial practices.

Accord, Roloff Evangelistic Enterprises, Inc. v. State, 556 S.W.2d 856 (Tex. App. 1977) (Child Care Licensing Act held enforceable against children's home operated by the Reverend Lester Roloff, who contended, "We cannot comply with this standard since we are not responsible to the State in this matter of raising the children"), *appeal dismissed for want of substantial federal question*, 439 U.S. 803 (1978).

NOTE. *Free Exercise Where Parents Disagree or Disappear.* Do constitutional criteria apply where the custody of a child is at stake and the parents are of different religions? Six states say religion is to be considered among elements determining "the best interests" of the child, see Note, "The Establishment Clause and Religion in Child Custody Disputes: Factoring Religion into the Best Interest Equation." 82 *Michigan Law Review* 1702 (1984), a note critical of the statutes. Consider *Schreifels v. Schreifels*, 47 Wash. 2d 409, 287 P.2d 1001 (1955): John and Violet were husband and wife. Violet fell passionately in love with John's brother, Anthony, and left with him, taking with her the four children. In an action by John to recover custody of the children, the court said, "Adultery, whether promiscuous or not, violates the Ten Commandments and the statutes of this state." The court also took note that John was a devout practicing Catholic and observed that the children while with Violet were "not being given religious training in any denomination and that fact should be considered, together with the mother's misconduct, in awarding custody." *Contra, Bonjour v. Bonjour*, 592 P.2d 1233 (Alaska 1979): Randall and Lindsey Bonjour were divorced. Both remarried. Randall and his second wife were devout Protestants; Lindsey was a non-churchgoing Christian and her new husband a non-Christian. The trial judge, applying the Alaska statute that stated that "the best interests" of the child include "religious" needs, gave weight to Randall's religious practice in awarding him custody of five-year-old Michael Joseph Bonjour. The trial judge made no special finding as to the boy's religious needs. The supreme court of Alaska, per Chief Justice Robert Boocheever, remanded, distinguishing between acceptable judicial recognition of the actual religious preference of a "mature child" and unconstitutional decision by a judge based on the judge's own view of what religious beliefs and practices were favorable to the child's welfare.

Is the case different where the issue is the placement of children in orphanages? In *Wilder v. Sugarman*, 385 F. Supp. 1013 (S.D.N.Y. 1974), six children by their guardians *ad litem*, represented by the New York Civil Liberties Union and the Legal Aid Society of Brooklyn, challenged the New York statute on placement, claiming that the statute discriminated against blacks and Protestants. The defendants—over thirty in number—included New York City and a number of individual institutions such as the Hebrew Children's Home, Lutheran Community Services, and the St. Cabrini Home.

The three-judge court (Walter R. Mansfield, Harold R. Tyler, Jr., and Kevin T. Duffy) in a long *per curiam* opinion, traced the care of orphans in New York back to the Dutch colony, where "poor relief [was] provided through ecclesiastical bodies." The pioneering New York statute of 1875, which removed children from almshouses, directed that they be placed with orphanages controlled by "persons of the same religious faith as the parents," as far as practicable; the settled policy of the state became one to care for such children by state payments to the institutions. In 1921 the principle of matching institution to parental religion was made part of the New York constitution, Art. 6, sec. 18; the principle was left in the constitution by popular vote in 1961. By statute in 1970 the religious preference of the parent was to be matched "so far as consistent with the best interest of the child and where practicable." The statutory language was interpreted by the Court of Appeals of New York to mean that religious matching was desirable but not mandatory, *Dickens v. Ernesto*, 30 N.Y.2d 61, 65–66, 330 N.Y.S.2d 346, 348, 281 N.E. 2d 153, 155 (1972), *appeal dismissed for want of a substantial federal question*, 407 U.S. 917 (1972). The present case was different from *Dickens* in that it challenged state funding of the religiously matched institution. The total amount was substantial: the state spent $194 million annually on these programs. The court asked if this expenditure, coupled with the attention given religious matching, did not amount to an impermissible establishment of religion.

At the same time the court recognized that the state was acting as a surrogate parent for the children it placed. As surrogate parent, the state had the duty "of fulfilling the child's Free Exercise rights." To deny the child spiritual training would be governmental interference with religion.

Finding the free exercise and establishment clauses "in conflict," the court said it would opt for the "benevolent neutrality" recommended by *Walz, infra* XIII,3, and so for practical accommodation. In practical terms, the court saw no alternative for the children apart from "the pervasively religious atmosphere" of the institutions that housed many of them: "Although plaintiffs suggest that non-sectarian homes, agencies or institutions be established, no clue is furnished as to where any such existing facilities might be found or how the capital funds for construction and staffing of new facilities might be provided," *ibid.* at 1028. The court held, at 1029, that the New York statutes represent "a fair and reasonable accommodation between the Establishment and Free Exercise clauses of the Constitution." No appeal was taken.

6. WEARING RELIGIOUS GARB

S. Simcha Goldman, an Orthodox Jew and ordained rabbi, was an Air Force captain serving as a psychologist at March Air Force Base. At all times he wore a yarmulke, a head-covering expressing submission to God (see S. R. Hirsch, *Hirsch Siddur* [1969 ed.] 14), a practice followed by some although not all Orthodox Jews, Isaac Klein, *A Guide to Jewish Religious Practice* (1979) 51–52. The Air Force has comprehensive regulations concerning what headgear its personnel may wear and when they can wear it. When Goldman was ordered to stop wearing the yarmulke, he sought an injunction against enforcement of the regulations. The District Court granted the injunction; the Circuit Court reversed, observing that the Air Force regulations were "necessarily arbitrary" and that the Air Force had "no concrete interest separate from the effect of strict enforcement itself," *Goldman v. Secretary of Defense*, 734 F.2d 1531 (D.C. Cir. 1984). The Supreme Court, 5–4, held against Goldman.

Justice Rehnquist delivered the opinion of the Court.

Goldman v. Weinberger
106 S.Ct. 1310 (1986)

. . .

The considered professional judgment of the Air Force is that the traditional outfitting of personnel in standardized uniforms encourages the subordination of personal preferences and identities in favor of the overall group mission. Uniforms encourage a sense of hierarchical unity by tending to eliminate outward individual distinctions except for those of rank. The Air Force considers them as vital during peacetime as during war because its personnel must be ready to provide an effective defense on a moment's notice; the necessary habits of discipline and unity must be developed in advance of trouble. We have acknowledged that "[t]he inescapable demands of military discipline and obedience to orders cannot be taught on battlefields; the habit of immediate compliance with military procedures and orders must be virtually reflex with no time for debate or reflection." *Chappell v. Wallace,* 462 U.S., at 300, 103 S.Ct., at 2365.

To this end, the Air Force promulgated AFR 35-10, a 190-page document, which states that "Air Force members will wear the Air Force uniform while performing their military duties, except when authorized to wear civilian clothes on duty." AFR § 35-10, ¶ 1-6 (1980). The rest of the document describes in minute detail all of the various items of apparel that must be worn as part of the Air Force uniform. It authorizes a few individualized options with respect to certain pieces of jewelry and hair style, but even these are subject to severe limitations. See AFR 35-10, Table 1-1, and ¶ 1-12.b(1)(b) (1980). In general, authorized headgear may be worn only out of doors. See AFR § 35-10, ¶ 1-6.h (1980). Indoors, "[h]eadgear [may] not be worn . . . except by armed security police in the performance of their duties." AFR 35-10, ¶ 1-6.h(2)(f) (1980). A narrow exception to this rule exists for headgear worn during indoor religious ceremonies. See AFR 35-10, ¶ 1-6.h(2)(d) (1980). In addition, military commanders may in their discretion permit visible religious headgear and other such apparel in designated living quarters and nonvisible items generally. See Department of Defense Directive 1300.17 (June 18, 1985).

Petitioner Goldman contends that the Free Exercise Clause of the First Amendment requires the Air Force to make an exception to its uniform dress requirements for religious apparel unless the accoutrements create a "clear danger" of undermining discipline and esprit de corps. He asserts that in general, visible but "unobtrusive" apparel will not create such a danger and must therefore be accommodated. He argues that the Air Force failed to prove that a specific exception for his practice of wearing an unobtrusive yarmulke would threaten discipline. He contends that the Air Force's assertion to the contrary is mere *ipse dixit,* with no support from actual experience or a scientific study in the record and is contradicted by expert testimony that religious exceptions to AFR 35-10 are in fact desirable and will increase morale by making the Air Force a more humane place.

But whether or not expert witnesses may feel that religious exceptions to AFR 35-10 are desirable is quite beside the point. The desirability of dress regulations in the military is decided by the appropriate military officials, and they are under no constitutional mandate to abandon their considered professional judgment. Quite obviously, to the extent the regulations do not permit the wearing of religious apparel such as a yarmulke, a practice described by petitioner as silent devotion akin to prayer, military life may be more objectionable for petitioner and probably others. But the First Amendment does not require the military to accommodate such practices in the face of its view that they would detract from the uniformity sought by the dress regulations. The Air Force has drawn the line essentially between religious apparel which is visible and that which is not, and we hold that those portions of the regulations challenged here reasonably and evenhandedly regulate dress in the interest of the military's perceived need for uniformity. The First Amendment therefore does not prohibit them from being applied to petitioner even though their effect is to restrict the wearing of the headgear required by his religious beliefs.

The judgment of the Court of Appeals is

Affirmed.

Justice Stevens, with whom Justice White and Justice Powell join, concurring.

Captain Goldman presents an especially attractive case for an exception from the uniform regulations that are applicable to all other Air Force personnel. His devotion to his faith is readily apparent. The yarmulke is a familiar and accepted sight. In addition to its religious significance for the wearer, the yarmulke may evoke the deepest respect and admiration—the symbol of a distinguished tradition and an eloquent rebuke to the ugliness of anti-Semitism. Captain Goldman's military duties are performed in a setting in which a modest departure from the uniform regulation creates almost no danger of impairment of the Air Force's military mission. Moreover, on the record before us, there is reason to believe that the policy of strict enforcement against Captain Goldman had a retaliatory motive—he had worn his yarmulke while testifying on behalf of a defendant in a court-martial proceeding. Nevertheless, as the case has been argued, I believe we must test the validity of the Air Force's rule not merely as it applies to Captain Goldman but also as it applies to all service personnel who have sincere religious beliefs that may conflict with one or more military commands.

Justice Brennan is unmoved by the Government's concern "that while a yarmulke might not seem obtrusive to a Jew, neither does a turban to a Sikh, a saffron robe to a Satchidananda Ashram-Integral Yogi, nor do dreadlocks to a Rastafarian." *Post,* at 1319. He correctly points out that "turbans, saffron robes, and dreadlocks are not before us in this case," and then suggests that other cases may be fairly decided by reference to a reasonable standard based on "functional utility, health and safety considerations, and the goal of a polished, professional appearance." *Id.,* at 1319. As the Court has explained, this approach attaches no weight to the separate interest in uniformity itself. Because professionals in the military service attach great importance to that plausible interest, it is one that we must recognize as legitimate and rational even though personal experience or admiration for the performance of the "rag-tag band of soldiers" that won us our freedom in the revolutionary war might persuade us that the Government has exaggerated the importance of that interest.

The interest in uniformity, however, has a dimension that is of still greater importance for me. It is the interest in uniform treatment for the members of all religious faiths. The very strength of Captain Goldman's claim creates the danger that a similar claim on behalf of a Sikh or a Rastafarian might readily be dismissed as "so extreme, so unusual, or so faddish an image that public confidence in his ability to perform his duties will be destroyed." *Post,* at ———. If exceptions from dress code regulations are to be granted on the basis of a multifactored test such as that proposed by Justice Brennan, inevitably the decisionmaker's evaluation of the character and the sincerity of the requestor's faith—as well as the probable reaction of the majority to the favored treatment of a member of that faith—will play a critical part in the decision. For the difference between a turban or a dreadlock on the one hand, and a yarmulke on the other, is not merely a difference in "appearance"—it is also the difference between a Sikh or a Rastafarian, on the one hand, and an Orthodox Jew on the other. The Air Force has no business drawing distinctions between such persons when it is enforcing commands of universal application.

As the Court demonstrates, the rule that is challenged in this case is based on a neutral, completely objective standard—visibility. It was not motivated by hostility against, or any special respect for, any religious faith. An exception for yarmulkes would represent a fundamental departure from the true principle of uniformity that supports that rule. For that reason, I join the Court's opinion and its judgment.

Justice Brennan, with whom Justice Marshall joins, dissenting.

Simcha Goldman invokes this Court's protection of his First Amendment right to fulfill one of the traditional religious obligations of a male Orthodox Jew—to cover his head before an omnipresent God. The Court's response to Goldman's request is to abdicate its role as principal expositor of the Constitution and protector of individual liberties in favor of credulous deference to unsupported assertions of military necessity. I dissent.

. . .

It is not the province of the federal courts to second-guess the professional judgments of the military services, but we are bound by the Constitution to assure ourselves that there exists a rational foundation for assertions of military necessity when they interfere with the free exercise of religion. "The concept of military necessity is seductively broad," *Glines,* 444 U.S., at 369, 100 S.Ct., at 614 (Brennan, J., dissenting), and military decisionmakers themselves are as likely to succumb to its allure as are the courts and the general public. Definitions of necessity are influenced by decisionmakers' experiences and values. As a consequence, in pluralistic societies such as ours, institutions dominated by a majority are inevitably, if inadvertently, insensitive to the needs and values of minorities when these needs and values differ from those of the majority. The military, with its strong ethic of conformity and unquestioning obedience, may be particularly impervious to minority needs and values. A critical function of the Religion Clauses of the First Amendment is to protect the rights of members of minority religions against quiet erosion by majoritarian social institutions that dismiss minority beliefs and practices as unimportant, because unfamiliar. It is the constitutional role of this Court to ensure that this purpose of the First Amendment be realized.

The Court and the military services have presented patriotic Orthodox Jews with a painful dilemma—the choice between fulfilling a religious obligation and serving their country. Should the draft be reinstated, compulsion will replace choice. Although the pain the services inflict on Orthodox Jewish servicemen is clearly the result of insensitivity rather than design, it is unworthy of our military because it is unnecessary. The Court and the military have refused these servicemen their constitutional rights; we must hope that Congress will correct this wrong.

Justice O'Connor, with whom Justice Marshall joins, dissenting. . . .

The first question that the Court should face here, therefore, is whether the interest that the Government asserts against the religiously based claim of the individual is of unusual importance. It is perfectly appropriate at this step of the analysis to take account of the special role of the military. The mission of our armed services is to protect our Nation from those who would destroy all our freedoms. I agree that, in order to fulfill that mission, the military is entitled to take some freedoms from its members. As the Court notes, the military " 'must insist upon a respect for duty and a discipline without counterpart in civilian life.' " *Ante,* at 1313 (quoting *Schlesinger v. Councilman,* 420 U.S. 738, 757, 95 S.Ct. 1300, 1312–13, 43 L.Ed.2d 591 (1975)). The need for military discipline and esprit de corps is unquestionably an especially important governmental interest.

But the mere presence of such an interest cannot, as the majority implicitly believes, end the analysis of whether a refusal by the Government to honor the free exercise of an individual's religion is constitutionally acceptable. A citizen pursuing even the most noble cause must remain within the bounds of the law. So, too, the Government may, even in pursuing its most compelling interests, be subject to specific restraints in doing so. The second question in the analysis of a Free Exercise claim under this Court's precedents must also be reached here: will granting an exemption of the type requested by the individual do substantial harm to the especially important governmental interest?

In the rare instances where the military has not consistently or plausibly justified its asserted need for rigidity of enforcement, and where the individual seeking the exemption establishes that the assertion by the military of a threat to discipline or esprit de corps is in his or her case completely unfounded, I would hold that the Government's policy of uniformity must yield to the individual's assertion of the right of free exercise of religion. On the facts of this case, therefore, I would require the Government to accommodate the sincere religious belief of Captain Goldman. Napoleon may have been correct to assert that, in the military sphere, morale is to all other factors as three is to one, but contradicted assertions of necessity by the military do not on the scales of justice bear a similarly disproportionate weight to sincere religious beliefs of the individual.

I respectfully dissent.

Justice Blackmun also dissented.

NOTE. *Clerical Garb in Court.* In *La Rocca v. Lane*, 37 N.Y. 2d 575, 376 N.Y.S. 2d 93, 338 N.E. 2d 606 (1975), *cert. denied*, 424 U.S. 968 (1976), the exercise of discretion by a trial judge was upheld in barring a Roman Catholic priest-lawyer from wearing his collar while acting as a Legal Defense attorney in a criminal trial. Three years later another New York trial judge refused to bar Father La Rocca from wearing his collar as a defense lawyer, *People v. Rodriguez*, 424 N.Y.S. 2d 600, 101 Misc. 2d 536 (1979). The court invoked *McDaniel v. Paty, infra;* XV, 2, as authorizing it to take a new look. La Rocca cited the canon law mandating the wearing of the collar in a public forum and the recent pronouncement of John Paul II that a priest should manifest his uniqueness by his dress. Responding to the district attorney's claim of prejudice, the court pointed out that the same prosecutor's office had "strenuously opposed a defendant's motion seeking to prevent a Catholic priest from wearing his clerical collar while testifying as a prosecution witness" in *People v. Ramirez*, *N.Y.L.J.*, September 11, 1979.

NOTE. *Exercises of Religion Untreated by the Supreme Court.* The variety of ways in which religion may be exercised are as infinite as the imagination. Only a small number of these exercises have been pronounced on by the Supreme Court and, in relation to a given statute, been given the status of a protected right or been subordinated to the state. Is it fair to suppose that the Court has taken the cases that appeared to it to represent all issues of greatest social significance? It is apparent that to some degree the organizational abilities, attitude toward litigation, and persistence of some religious groups has been a factor in what cases get before the Court. Other exercises of religion may have struck lawyers and judges as so unusual, so eccentric, so bizarre as not to warrant much judicial attention. The prevailing perspective is captured in the title of an article by Beverly Lake, "Freedom to Worship Curiously," 1 *Florida University Law Review* 203 (1948). But from the point of view of the believer a practice that is "curious" to the outsider may be a matter of divine commandment, evangelical precept, holy faith. The following sections look at a few examples of such practices that have been at least adjudicated by courts below the Supreme Court.

7. PRESERVING THE PURITY OF THE MEMBERSHIP

Many churches assert a religious duty to purge their flock of members who offend in doctrine or practice, *cf.* 1 Corinthians 5:12. The refusal of communion and denial of admission to the church building has been held nonactionable, *Carter v. Papineau*, 222 Mass. 464, 111 N.E. 358 (1916) (no defamation, no tort of any kind when an Episcopal priest exercised his authority under the canons to refuse Holy Communion to one whom he deemed among "open, notorious, evil livers, or to have done any wrong to his neighbors by word or deed").

On the other hand, the Pennsylvania Supreme Court ordered a trial when Robert L. Bear sought equitable relief in Cumberland County when the Reformed Mennonite Church excommunicated him, and all members of the church shunned him. Bear alleged that his family was being destroyed because his wife and children could have no social or physical contact with him and that his business was in collapse because he could not hire workers, get a loan, or market his produce. The court refused to hold that the free exercise clause was a complete defense for the church, *Bear v. Reformed Mennonite Church*, 462 Pa. 330, 341 A.2d 105 (1975).

The American Law Institute's *Restatement of Torts, Second* (1977) recognizes a conditional privilege to communicate an otherwise defamatory statement to others sharing a common interest in the subject. Comment *e* to Section 596 recognizes that members of a religious association have a sufficient common interest "to support a privilege for communications among themselves concerning the qualifications of the officers and members and their participation in the activities of the society." The privilege is lost if the one publishing the defamatory matter acts in reckless disregard of its truth or falsity; or acts solely from spite or ill will; or makes excessive publication of the statement. In *Moyle v. Franz*, 293 N.Y. 842, 59 N.E.2d 437 (1944), affirming *per curiam* 267 App. Div. 423, 46 N.Y.S. 2d 667, a libel judgment of $15,000 against the publisher of *The Watchtower* and leaders of the Jehovah's Witnesses was sustained. The plaintiff was Olin R. Moyle, the lawyer who was the architect of the Witnesses' early constitutional litigation; the defendants were represented by Hayden Covington. In 1939 Moyle had written a long letter to Judge Rutherford criticizing him. The defendants published a notice in *The Watchtower* stating that Moyle was no longer in the society due to "his unfaithfulness to the kingdom interests, and to those who serve the kingdom"; and that Moyle now maligned those who trusted him "just as Judas had proved his unfaithfulness to Christ Jesus." The court laid stress on the fact that *The Watchtower* was available not only to Witnesses but to anyone willing to buy it. This "excessive" publication destroyed the "qualified privilege" to defame that the Witnesses as a religious society possessed. The court also held that the jury could find malice because several of the individual defamants had acquiesced in the statements about Moyle with little knowledge of the incidents the statements referred to.

8. NOT EATING BLOOD

"Flesh, with the life thereof, which is the blood thereof, you shall not eat" (Gen. 9:4). The commandment was renewed in apostolic times by the first-century "Council of Jerusalem": "For it has seemed good to the Holy Spirit and to us to lay upon you no greater burden than these necessary things: That you abstain from meat offered to idols, and from blood, and from things strangled, and from sexual impurity" (Acts 15:28–29). *Cf.* Leviticus 17:10, Deuteronomy 12:23. Jehovah's Witnesses, as a consequence of these biblical injunctions, could not eat blood sausages or blood puddings. On July 1, 1945, *The Watchtower* interpreted the texts also to forbid blood tranfusions as a kind of blood-eating, offensive to God, Penton, *Apocalypse Delayed* 153.

In *Application of the President and Directors of Georgetown College*, 331 F.2d 1000 (D.C. Cir. 1964), *cert. denied*, 377 U.S. 978 (1964), Judge Skelly Wright granted an emergency writ authorizing Georgetown Hospital to give a blood transfusion to Mrs. Jesse Jones, a twenty-five-year-old woman and the mother of a seven-month-old child. The opinion of the attending doctors was that she would die without a tranfusion. Both she and her husband were Jehovah's Witnesses. Mrs. Jones refused consent, and when Judge Wright asked Mrs. Jones on her bed, her only audible reply was, "Against my will." Judge Wright balanced against her religious rights the interest of the state in preserving the parent of a child; the possible criminality of suicide; and the hospital and doctors' unwillingness to let her die. He also observed, "It was obvious that the woman was not in a mental condition to make a decision"; and he added that "[i]f the law undertook the responsibility of authorizing the transfusion without her consent, no problem would be raised with respect to her religious practice."

In *Raleigh Fitkin-Paul Morgan Memorial Hospital v. Anderson*, 42 N.J. 421, 201 A.2d 537 (1964), *cert. denied*, 377 U.S. 985 (1964), Willimina Anderson,, a Jehovah's Witness, thirty-two weeks pregnant, refused a blood transfusion. The hospital applied for a court order, showing that it was probable that at some point in the pregnancy she would hemorrhage and that both she and the unborn child would die. Declaring that "[w]e are satisfied that the unborn child is entitled to the law's protection," the court ordered the appointment of a guardian who would consent on behalf of "the infant." *Accord Jefferson v. Griffin Spalding*

County Hospital Authority, 274 S.E.2d 457 (Ga. 1981) (guardian appointed for thirty-nine week-old fetus whose mother, a member of the Shiloh Sanctified Holiness Baptist Church, refused on religious grounds to undergo a caesarean section; the evidence showed that the child stood a 99 percent chance of dying and the mother a 50 percent chance in the absence of a caesarean operation).

If the child is viewed as having a right to protection, the case accords with *Prince v. Massachusetts, supra* XI, 1. Is its rationale undermined by *Roe v. Wade,* 410 U.S. 113 (1973), recognizing a mother's right to abort her child? In *Aste v. Brooks,* 32 Ill. 2d 361, 206 N.E.2d 435 (1965), the court disapproved as a violation of the First Amendment a court-ordered transfusion to an objecting adult Witness, who had no minor children.

9. CARRYING SNAKES AND DRINKING POISON

And He [Jesus] said to them: "Go into the whole world and preach the Gospel to every creature. Whoever believes and is baptized will be saved; but whoever does not believe will be condemned. These signs will attend those who believe: in my name they shall cast out devils, they shall speak in new tongues; if they carry snakes or if they drink a lethal drink, it shall not harm them; they shall lay hands upon the sick and they shall be well" [Mark 16:15–18].

The Dolly Pond Church of God with Signs Following was founded by George Went Hensley in 1909 at Sale Creek in Grasshopper Valley, Tennessee. A Pentecostal offshoot of Methodism, it spread as "The Holiness Church" in the rural South and Southeast. Hensley's conversion had begun with his handling of a rattlesnake without harm. He and his followers took literally the above verses of Mark. They handled rattlesnakes and drank poison as "signs that God said would follow the believers—signs to confirm the Word of God," *State ex rel. Swann v. Pack,* 527 S.W. 2d 99 (Tenn. 1975), *cert. denied,* 424 U.S. 954 (1976). The district attorney at Newport, Tennessee, sought an injunction prohibiting Pastor Liston Pack and certain elders of the Church from handling poisonous snakes or drinking strychnine. The trial court granted the injunction as to the snakes but not as to drinking the poison. The supreme court of Tennessee enjoined both practices.

The court said, "We recognize that to forbid snake handling is to remove the theological heart of the Holiness Church." But the court held that "the handling of snakes in a crowded church sanctuary, with virtually no safeguards" was a serious danger to the public health. The court continued, "Our state and nation have an interest in having a strong, healthy, robust, taxpaying citizenry capable of self-support and of bearing arms and adding to the resources and reserves of manpower." This interest in preserving the life of its citizens was sufficient to support an injunction against drinking poison. The court said it considered and rejected restricting the church's practice to consenting adults only because it was "too fraught with danger to permit its pursuit in the frenzied atmosphere of an emotional church service."

Accord, Harden v. State, 188 Tenn. 17, 216 S.W. 2d 708 (1948), enforcing against members of the Holiness Church a statute specifically criminalizing the displaying of a poisonous snake so as to endanger anyone. *Accord, Hill v. State,* 38 Ala. App. 404, 88 So.2d 880 (1956), *cert. denied,* 264 Ala. 697, 88 So.2d 887, (1956), where the complaining witness was a minister of the same church as the defendant but did not believe in such acts of faith. Accord, *Lawson v. Commonwealth,* 291 Ky. 437, 164 S.W.2d 972 (1942), where the statute forbade handling of even nonpoisonous snakes and directed its prohibition specifically at handling "in connection with any religious service or gathering."

Query: Apart from most people's repugnance to snakes, do these cases fairly balance the religious claims of the believers against the danger the state is preventing? In the absence of a statute against suicide, how persuasive is the court's reason for enjoining the consumption of poison?

10. CONSUMING PEYOTE

People v. Woody, 61 Cal. 2d 716, 40, Cal. Rptr. 69, 394 P.2d 813 (1964): Jack Woody and several other Navajos were arrested by police who had watched them using peyote and were convicted of illegal possession of this substance; they asserted their free exercise rights under the First Amendment. For the California Supreme Court, Justice Mathew O. Tobriner wrote:

. . .

The plant Lophophora williamsii, a small spineless cactus, found in the Rio Grande Valley of Texas and northern Mexico, produces peyote, which grows in small buttons on the top of the cactus. Peyote's principal constituent is mescaline. When taken internally by chewing the buttons or drinking a derivative tea, peyote produces several types of hallucinations, depending primarily upon the user. In most subjects it causes extraordinary vision marked by bright and kaleidoscopic colors, geometric patterns, or scenes involving humans or animals. In others it engenders hallucinatory symptoms similar to those produced in cases of schizophrenia, dementia praecox, or paranoia. Beyond its hallucinatory effect, peyote renders for most users a heightened sense of comprehension; it fosters a feeling of friendliness toward other persons.

Peyote, as we shall see, plays a central role in the ceremony and practice of the Native American Church, a religious organization of Indians. Although the church claims no official prerequisites to membership, no written membership rolls, and no recorded theology, estimates of its membership range from 30,000 to 250,000, the wide variance deriving from differing definitions of a "member." As the anthropologists have ascertained through conversations with members, the theology of the church combines certain Christian teachings with the belief that peyote embodies the Holy Spirit and that those who partake of peyote enter into direct contact with God.

Peyotism discloses a long history. A reference to the religious use of peyote in Mexico appears in Spanish historical sources as early as 1560. Peyotism spread from Mexico to the United States and Canada; American anthropologists describe it as well established in this country during the latter part of the nineteenth century. Today, Indians of many tribes practice Peyotism. Despite the absence of recorded dogma, the several tribes follow surprisingly similar ritual and theology; the practices of Navajo members in Arizona practically parallel those of adherents in California, Montana, Oklahoma, Wisconsin, and Saskatchewan.

The "meeting," a ceremony marked by the sacramental use of peyote, composes the cornerstone of the peyote religion. The meeting convenes in an enclosure and continues from sundown Saturday to sunrise Sunday. To give thanks for the past good fortune or find guidance for future conduct, a member will "sponsor" a meeting and supply to those who attend both the peyote and the next morning's breakfast. The "sponsor," usually but not always the "leader," takes charge of the meeting; he decides the order of events and the amount of peyote to be consumed. Although the individual leader exercises an absolute control of the meeting, anthropologists report a striking uniformity of its ritual.

A meeting connotes a solemn and special occasion. Whole families attend together, although children and young women participate only by their presence. Adherents don their finest clothing, usually suits for men and fancy dresses for the women, but sometimes ceremonial Indian costumes. At the meeting the members pray, sing, and make ritual use of drum, fan, eagle bone, whistle, rattle and prayer cigarette, the symbolic emblems of their faith. The central event, of course, consists of the use of peyote in quantities sufficient to produce an hallucinatory state.

At an early but fixed stage in the ritual the members pass around a ceremonial bag of peyote buttons. Each adult may take four, the customary number, or take none. The participants chew the buttons, usually with some difficulty because of extreme bitterness; later, at a set time in the ceremony any member may ask for more peyote; occasionally a member may take as many as four more buttons. At sunrise on Sunday the ritual ends; after a brief outdoor prayer, the host and his family serve breakfast. Then the members depart. By morning the effects of the peyote disappear; the users suffer no aftereffects.

Although peyote serves as a sacramental symbol similar to bread and wine in certain Christian churches, it is more than a sacrament. Peyote constitutes in itself an object of worship; prayers are directed to it much as prayers are devoted to the Holy Ghost. On the other hand, to use peyote for nonreligious purposes is sacrilegious. Members of the church regard peyote also as a "teacher" because it induces a feeling of brotherhood with other members; indeed, it enables the particpant to experience the Deity. Finally, devotees treat peyote as a "protector." Much as a Catholic carries his medallion, an Indian G.I. often wears around his neck a beautifully beaded pouch containing one large peyote button.

The record thus establishes that the application of the statutory prohibition of the use of peyote results in a virtual inhibition of the practice of defendants' religion. To forbid the use of peyote is to remove the theological heart of Peyotism.

The court held that the state had failed to show any compelling interest to override the religious claim, noting that "Indian children never and Indian teenagers rarely, use peyote." The Navajos were acquitted. In *In re Grady*, 61 Cal. 2d 887, 39, Cal. Rptr. 912, 394 P. 2d 728 (1964) Arthur Charles Grady, the spiritual leader of a small group living in Gerald Kelly's home at Palm Springs, was held entitled to a trial on the question whether he used peyote with the group as part of "a bona fide practice of a religious belief."

11. PRESERVING SACRED LAND

In *Wilson v. Block*, 708 F.2d 735 (1983), *cert. denied*, 464 U.S. 956 (1983), the facts were these:

The Navajo and Hopi Indian tribes are federally recognized tribes of American Indians. The Hopi reservation and most of the Navajo reservation are located in northeastern Arizona and encompass a total area of 25,000 square miles. Approximately 9,000 Hopis and 160,000 Navajos reside on the reservations.

The dominant geological formation visible from the Hopi villages and much of the western Navajo reservation are the San Francisco Peaks. The Peaks, which rise to a height of 12,633 feet, have for centuries played a central role in the religions of the two tribes. The Navajos believe that the Peaks are one of the four sacred mountains which mark the boundaries of their homeland. They believe the Peaks to be the home of specific deities and consider the Peaks to be the body of a spiritual being or god, with various peaks forming the head, shoulders, and knees of a body reclining and facing to the east, while the trees, plants, rocks, and earth form the skin. The Navajos pray directly to the Peaks and regard them as a living deity. The Peaks are invoked in religious ceremonies to heal the Navajo people. The Navajos collect herbs from the Peaks for use in religious ceremonies, and perform ceremonies upon the Peaks. They believe that artificial development of the Peaks would impair the Peaks' healing power.

The Hopis believe that the Creator uses emissaries to assist in communicating with mankind. The emissaries are spiritual beings and are generally referred to by the Hopis as "Kachinas." The Hopis believe that for about six months each year, commencing in late July or early August and extending through mid-winter, the Kachinas reside at the Peaks. During the remaining six months of the year the Kachinas travel to the Hopi villages and participate in various religious ceremonies and practices. The Hopis believe that the Kachinas' activities on the Peaks create the rain and snow storms that sustain the villages. The Hopis have many shrines on the Peaks and collect herbs, plants and animals from the Peaks for use in religious ceremonies. The Hopis believe that use of the Peaks for commercial purposes would constitute a direct affront to the Kachinas and to the Creator.

The San Francisco Peaks are within the Coconino National Forest and are managed by the Forest Service. A 777 acre portion of the Peaks, known as the "Snow Bowl," has been used for downhill skiing since 1937 when the Forest Service built a road and ski lodge. The lodge was destroyed by fire in 1952 and was replaced in 1956. Ski lifts were built at the Snow Bowl in 1958 and 1962. Since 1962 the facilities have changed very little.

In 1979 the Forest Service approved the clearing of fifty acres of forest for new ski runs and authorized expansion of facilities for skiers in the Snow Bowl. The Navajo Medicinemen's Association and the Hopi Tribe sued to enjoin this development, claiming it would violate their free exercise rights under the First Amendment and also the American Indian Religious Freedom Act of 1980.

The Court of Appeals for the District of Columbia, per Judge Edward Lumbard, declared:

. . . The construction approved by the Secretary is, indeed, inconsistent with the plaintiffs' beliefs, and will cause the plaintiffs spiritual disquiet, but such consequences do not state a free exercise claim under *Sherbert, Thomas,* or any other authority.[3] In sum, the plaintiffs have not shown that expansion of the Snow Bowl will burden their freedom to believe. A separate question, to which we now turn, is whether expansion will burden the plaintiffs in the practice of their religions.

The plaintiffs must have access to the San Francisco Peaks to practice their religions. Certain of the plaintiff's ceremonies must be performed upon the Peaks and religious objects must be collected there. Because the plaintiffs' religions are, in this sense, site specific, development of the Peaks would severely impair the practice of the religions if it destroyed the natural conditions necessary for the performance of ceremonies and the collection of religious objects. The plaintiffs claim that the Preferred Alternative will impair their religious practices in precisely that manner. Few courts have considered whether the Free Exercise Clause prohibits the government from permitting land uses

---

[3] *Pillar of Fire v. Denver Urban Renewal Authority,* 181 Colo. 411, 509 P.2d. 1250 (1973), is not to the contrary. In *Pillar of Fire,* the plaintiff church sought to enjoin the condemnation by an urban renewal project of its first permanent church building. The plaintiff alleged that its members revered the building for its historical and symbolic meaning in the birth of their sect. The Colorado Supreme Court held that the plaintiff was entitled to a court hearing at which its interests could be weighed against those of the renewal authority. "(R)eligious faith and tradition," said the court, "can invest certain structures and land sites with significance which deserves First Amendment protection." 181 Colo. at 419, 509 P.2d at 1254. A governmental taking of privately-owned religious property, however, involves different considerations than does a claimed First Amendment right to restrict the government's use of its own land.

that impair specific religious practices. Of the cases which have considered this problem, we find *Sequoyah v. TVA,* 620 F.2d 1159 (6th Cir.), *cert. denied,* 449 U.S. 953, 101 S.Ct. 357, 66 L.Ed.2d 216 (1980), to be particularly instructive.

In *Sequoyah,* a class action brought on behalf of practitioners of the Cherokee religion, the plaintiffs sought to halt construction of the Tellico Dam on the Little Tennessee River. The plaintiffs alleged that the dam, when completed, would flood the Cherokee "sacred homeland" along the river, and would destroy "sacred sites, medicine gathering sites, holy places and cemeteries," and "disturb the sacred balance of the land." 620 F.2d at 1160. The Sixth Circuit affirmed a grant of summary judgment to the defendant, ruling that the plaintiffs, to establish a burden on free exercise, had to prove that the valley to be flooded was indispensable or central to their ceremonies and practices. The plaintiffs' proof was insufficient, held the court, as the evidence indicated that medicines obtainable in the valley could be obtained elsewhere, and that the flooding would not prevent the plaintiffs from engaging in any particular religious observances.[4]

[6]   Judge Richey relied upon the *Sequoyah* analysis in the present case, and held that the plaintiffs had failed to show the indispensability of the Snow Bowl to the practice of their religions. The plaintiffs challenge Judge Richey's reliance upon *Sequoyah* on two grounds. They argue first that *Sherbert* and *Thomas,* [*supra,* XI, 4], and not

---

[4] Four cases in addition to *Sequoyah* have considered free exercise claims seeking to restrict development of government land. In *Badoni v. Higginson,* 638 F.2d 172 (10th Cir.1980), *cert. denied,* 452 U.S. 954, 101 S.Ct. 3099, 69 L.Ed.2d 695 (1981), Navajo religious practitioners believed that the Rainbow natural bridge, a great arch of sandstone located in Rainbow Bridge National Monument in Utah, was sacred. They complained that a government reservoir which had partially inundated the bridge had covered some of their gods and prayer sites, and that the noisy tourists who visited the bridge desecrated the site and made ceremonies impractical. As relief, the plaintiffs requested the court to order the government to lower the reservoir, to issue regulations controlling tourist behavior, and on appropriate notice, to close the monument to tourists so that ceremonies could be conducted. The Tenth Circuit affirmed a district court decision denying relief. The Tenth Circuit held that the government had a compelling interest in filling the reservoir that outweighed any First Amendment right the plaintiffs might assert, and that closing the Monument, or restricting tourist behavior, to accommodate the plaintiffs' beliefs would violate the Establishment Clause. Ruling as it did, the Tenth Circuit never considered in detail whether the Free Exercise Clause can create a right to restrict government land use. The decision in *Badoni* therefore offers little guidance here. In *Crow v. Gullet,* 541 F.Supp. 785 (D.S.D.1982), a class action on behalf of the Lakota and Tsistsistas nations, and Lakota and Tsistsistas religious practitioners, the plaintiffs objected to certain construction projects and park regulations at the Bear Butte State Park in South Dakota. The plaintiffs alleged, *inter alia,* that Bear Butte was a significant site in their religions that would be desecrated by the access roads, parking lot, and viewing platforms that the state had built or was planning to build. The district court denied relief, holding that "the free exercise clause places a duty upon a state to keep from prohibiting religious acts, not to provide the means or the environment for carrying them out." 541 F.Supp. at 791. It is uncertain, however, whether the court believed that the Free Exercise Clause can *never* restrict government land use, since the court specifically noted that the plaintiffs had "failed to establish that particular religious practices were damaged by the construction." *Id.* In *Inupiat Community of Arctic Slope v. United States,* 548 F.Supp. 182, 188–89 (D.Alaska 1982), the Inupiat people of Alaska brought suit to quiet title to portions of the Beaufort and Chukchi Seas in which the United States had issued oil leases. The plaintiffs claimed, *inter alia,* that development would burden their right freely to practice their religion. The court rejected the plaintiffs' claim, finding that the plaintiffs had failed to show impairment of their religious practices, that the government had a compelling interest in developing energy resources, and that the Establishment Clause in any event barred relief. Finally, in *Northwest Indian Cemetery Protective Assoc. v. Peterson,* 552 F.Supp. 951 (N.D.Cal.1982), the plaintiffs, claiming that their religious activities would be disrupted, sought to enjoin the Forest Service from approving construction of a road upon land sacred to several Northwest Indian tribes. The court held for the defendants, and stated that the First Amendment does not obligate the government "to control or limit public access to public lands in order to facilitate" religious practices. 552 F.Supp. at 954.

Sequoyah, establish the standard applicable to their claim. They contend that governmental action which indirectly imposes a burden upon religious practice greater than the burdens involved in *Sherbert* and *Thomas* necessarily violates the First Amendment. Contending that the Snow Bowl ski area effectively prohibits the practice of their religions, the plaintiffs claim that their burden is greater than that of the practitioners in *Sherbert* and *Thomas,* who, the plaintiffs say, could have continued to practice their beliefs simply by choosing to forego government benefits. However, as we previously stated, *Sherbert* and *Thomas* considered only whether the government may legally condition benefits on a decision to forego or to adhere to religious belief or practice. Those cases did not purport to create a benchmark against which to test all indirect burden claims. Second, the plaintiffs argue that *Sequoyah* incorrectly interpreted the First Amendment. They argue that the First Amendment protects all religious practices, whether or not "central," and that courts are not competent to rule upon the centrality of religious belief or practice. We agree that the First Amendment protection of religion "does not turn on the theological importance of the disputed activity," *Unitarian Church West v. McConnell,* 337 F.Supp. 1252, 1257 (E.D. Wis.1972), *affd.,* 474 F.2d 1351 (7th Cir. 1973), *vacated and remanded on other grounds,* 416 U.S. 932, 94 S.Ct. 1927, 40 L.Ed.2d 283 (1974) and that the courts may not "dictate which practices are or are not required in a particular religion." *Geller v. Secretary of Defense,* 423 F.Supp. 16, 17 (D.D.C.1976). *See Thomas,* 450 U.S. at 715–16, 101 S.Ct. at 1430–1431; *Serbian Eastern Orthodox Diocese v. Milivojevich* [*infra,* XII, 3] (1976). These principles, however, are not contrary to *Sequoyah's* analysis. Far from requiring judicial evaluation of religious doctrine, *Sequoyah* focuses inquiry solely upon the importance of the geographic site in question to the practice of plaintiffs' religion. If the plaintiffs cannot demonstrate that the government land at issue is indispensable to some religious practice, whether or not central to their religion, they have not justified a First Amendment claim. We agree with *Sequoyah's* resolution of the conflict between the government's property rights and duties of public management, and a plaintiff's constitutional right freely to practice his religion. We thus hold that plaintiffs seeking to restrict government land use in the name of religious freedom must, at a minimum, demonstrate that the government's proposed land use would impair a religious practice that could not be performed at any other site.[5]

The plaintiffs argue that their proof establishes a denial of First Amendment rights even under the above standard. They rely principally upon the affidavits submitted by Hopi and Navajo religious practitioners, which establish that ceremonies conducted

---

[5] We do not hold that such proof necessarily would establish a burden on free exercise. Instead, we hold only that the First Amendment requires, at a minimum, proof that the religious practice could not be performed at any site other than that to be developed. Because we agree with Judge Richey that the plaintiffs have not satisfied this minimum burden of proof, we need not consider what, if any, additional factors are necessary to establish a free exercise burden. At the same time, we decline to follow those cases which have placed primary reliance upon the government's property interest and which have held, apparently, that the Free Exercise Clause can never supersede the government's ownership rights and duties of public management. *See Crow v. Gullet,* 541 F.Supp. 785, 791 (D.S.D.1982); *Northwest Indian Protective Cemetery Assoc. v. Peterson,* 552 F.Supp. 951, 954 (N.D.Cal.1982). The government must manage its land in accordance with the constitution, *Badoni v. Higginson,* 638 F.2d 172, 176 (10th Cir. 1980), *cert. denied,* 452 U.S. 954, 101 S.Ct. 3099, 69 L.Ed.2d 695 (1981); *Sequoyah v. TVA,* 620 F.2d 1159, 1164 (6th Cir.1980), *cert. denied,* 449 U.S. 953, 101 S.Ct. 357, 66 L.Ed.2d 216 (1980), which nowhere suggests that the Free Exercise Clause is inapplicable to government land. This is not to say that the government's property rights, and its duty to manage its land for the public benefit, have no bearing upon the free exercise analysis. In holding that government land uses can never burden the right to freedom of belief, and can burden the right to freedom of practice only if site-specific religious practices are significantly impaired, we pay due regard to the government's rights and duties in its land. However, we see no basis for completely exempting government land use from the Free Exercise Clause.

upon the Peaks are indispensable to the plaintiffs' religions; that ceremonial objects must be collected from the Peaks to be effective; that some ceremonial objects and medicinal herbs are collected from the Snow Bowl, and that expansion of the ski area could make those objects and herbs more difficult to find; that ceremonies and prayers have occasionally been conducted in the Snow Bowl, but that expansion of the ski area will destroy the natural conditions necessary for prayers and ceremonies to be effective; and that the mountain as a whole, and not just parts thereof, is considered sacred.

The plaintiffs' affidavits, together with other evidence in the record, establish the indispensability of the Peaks to the practice of the plaintiffs' religions. The Forest Service, however, has not denied the plaintiffs access to the Peaks, but instead permits them free entry onto the Peaks and does not interfere with their ceremonies or the collection of ceremonial objects. At the same time, the evidence does not show the indispensability of that small portion of the Peaks encompassed by the Snow Bowl permit area. The plaintiffs have not proven that expansion of the ski area will prevent them from performing ceremonies or collecting objects that can be performed or collected in the Snow Bowl but nowhere else. The record evidence is, in fact, to the contrary. The Forest Service's Final Environmental Statement found, on the basis of comments submitted by Hopi and Navajo practitioners, that "religious practices, including collecting plant materials, may occur in many locations on the sacred mountain." The government submitted affidavits from two experts on Hopi and Navajo religion. One expert stated that expansion of the Snow Bowl should have little "direct" impact on the plaintiffs' religious practices; the other stated with respect to Hopi practices that "(g)uarantee of access to the mountain should permit the continuation of all essential ritual practices," and with respect to Navajo practices that "(n)o ceremonial items . . . are found only in the permit area." It must be remembered that the Snow Bowl permit area comprises only 777 of the 75,000 acres of the Peaks, and that prior construction on the Peaks has not prevented the plaintiffs from practicing their religions. Judge Richey found that "the Snow Bowl operation has been in existence for nearly fifty years and it appears that plaintiffs' religious practices and beliefs have managed to coexist with the diverse developments that have occurred there." (footnote omitted). The plaintiffs simply have not demonstrated that development will prevent them from engaging in any religious practices.

As the plaintiffs have not shown that development will burden them in their religious beliefs or practices, we need not decide whether the ski area expansion is a compelling governmental interest, or whether the Preferred Alternative is the least restrictive means of achieving that interest.

2. *American Indian Religious Freedom Act.*

[7]   The American Indian Religious Freedom Act, 42 U.S.C. § 1996 (Supp. IV 1980) (AIRFA), provides:

> On and after August 11, 1978 it shall be the policy of the United States to protect and preserve for American Indians their inherent right of freedom to believe, express, and exercise the traditional religions of the American Indian, Eskimo, Aleut, and Native Hawaiians, including but not limited to access to sites, use and possession of sacred objects, and the freedom to worship through ceremonials and traditional rites.

The plaintiffs contend that AIRFA proscribes all federal land uses that conflict or interfere with traditional Indian religious beliefs or practices, unless such uses are justified by compelling governmental interests. They argue that the Snow Bowl ski resort expansion is not a compelling governmental interest, and is accordingly proscribed by AIRFA. Judge Richey refused to give AIRFA the broad reading urged by plaintiffs. He found that AIRFA requires federal agencies to evaluate their policies and procedures with the aim of protecting Indian religious freedom, to refrain from prohibiting access, possession and use of religious objects and the performance of religious ceremonies, and to consult with Indian organizations in regard to proposed actions, but that AIRFA does not require "Native traditional religious considerations always [to] prevail to the exclusion of all else." We agree. Judge Richey's interpretation of AIRFA is fully supported by the legislative history, and the record supports his finding of Forest Service compliance.

[8] AIRFA affirms the protection and preservation of traditional Indian religions as a policy of the United States, but the statutory language does not indicate the extent to which Congress intended that policy to override other land use considerations. We therefore look for guidance to the legislative history, and, in particular, to the substantially identical committee reports prepared by the Senate Select Committee on Indian Affairs and the House Committee on Interior and Insular Affairs. These reports reveal that in AIRFA Congress addressed the unwarranted and often unintended intrusions upon Indian religious practices resulting from federal officials' ignorance and the inflexible enforcement of laws and regulations which, though intended to achieve valid secular goals, had directly affected Indian religious practices. The reports identify three areas of concern: (1) denial of access to religious sites; (2) restrictions on the possession of such substances as peyote; and (3) actual interference with religious events. The federal government, the reports note, had sometimes denied Indians access to religious sites on federal land; had failed to accommodate such federal statutes as the drug and endangered species laws to the Indians' religious needs, and had itself interfered, or permitted others to interfere, with religious observances. *See* S.Rep. No. 709, 95th Cong., 2d Sess. 2–4; H.R.Rep. No. 1308, 95th Cong., 2d Sess. 2–3, *reprinted in* 1978 U.S.Code Cong. & Ad.News 1262, 1263–64. Thus, the House Report stated that the purpose of AIRFA is "to insure that the policies and procedures of various Federal agencies, as they may impact upon the exercise of traditional Indian religious practices, are brought into compliance with the constitutional injunction that Congress shall make no laws abridging the free exercise of religion." H.R.Rep. No. 1308, *supra,* at 1, 1978 U.S.Code Cong. & Ad.News at 1262.

It is clear from the reports, and from the statutory preamble, that AIRFA requires federal agencies to learn about, and to avoid unnecessary interference with, traditional Indian religious practices. Agencies must evaluate their policies and procedures in light of the Act's purpose, and ordinarily should consult Indian leaders before approving a project likely to affect religious practices. AIRFA does not, however, declare the protection of Indian religions to be an overriding federal policy, or grant Indian religious practitioners a veto on agency action. "The clear intent of [AIRFA]," the Senate report states, "is to insure for traditional native religions the same rights of free exercise enjoyed by more powerful religions. However, it is in no way intended to provide Indian religions with a more favorable status than other religions, only to insure that the U.S. Government treats them equally." S.Rep. No. 709, *supra,* at 6.

Affirmed.

See Robert S. Michaelsen, "American Indian Religious Freedom Litigation: Promise and Perils," *The Journal of Law and Religion* 3, 47 (1985).

12. AIDING THE ALIEN AND THE OPPRESSED

In *United States v. Elder,* 601 F. Supp 1574 (S.D. Tex., 1985), John Elder was charged with unlawfully transporting three undocumented Salvadoran aliens. Elder was a practicing Catholic, the director of Casa Oscar Romero, which gave shelter to Salvadorans who had fled their country. The land for Casa Romero had been donated by the Catholic diocese of Brownsville. Parishes and congregations of various religious denominations contributed to the shelter's support. Elder believed he was performing his Christian duty in aiding those who fled brutality in El Salvador. John Fitzpatrick, Catholic bishop of Brownsville, and ministers of local

Baptist, Lutheran, Methodist, and Presbyterian churches testified that such assistance was an expression of the Christian Gospel.

District Judge Hayden W. Head, Jr., ruled that Elder had shown that he was fulfilling his Christian duties as he saw them. Judge Head then ruled that the government's interest in a uniform immigration policy overrode Elder's free exercise claim and refused to dismiss the criminal charge against him.

Elder was acquitted by the jury, see Ignatius Bau, *This Ground Is Holy: Church Sanctuary and Central American Refugees* (1985) 81. In another sanctuary case the defendants were convicted. *U.S. v. Aguilar, et al,; U.S. v. Maria Prado del Socorro, appeal pending* (9th Cir., 1986).

13. WORSHIPPING IN PRISON

NOTE. *Lee v. Crouse*, 284 F.Supp. 541 (D. Kan. 1967), *aff'd per curiam*, 396 F.2d 952 (10th Cir. 1968). Vincent 2X, a Black Muslim, brought an action of habeas corpus against the warden of the state pentitentiary claiming that the warden unconstitutionally prohibited the practice of his religion. The court found that the Black Muslims claimed continuity with Islamic religion but had their own distinctive beliefs, among them that Elijah Muhammad was a messenger of Allah; that a white man cannot be a Black Muslim; that the blacks must be separate from the whites and after a final holy war will be supreme over them. The court concluded that the Black Muslims or The Nation of Islam in North America headed by the Honorable Elijah Muhammad was a religion, but it refused to order the warden to permit Black Muslims to meet in large groups and to let Black Muslim ministers conduct services in the prison. The danger of violence from the Black Muslims' teaching, the court said, justified the warden in thus restricting the Muslims' religious activity.

14. HEALING BY PRAYER AND FAITH

In *People v. Cole*, 219 N.Y. 98, 113 N.E. 790 (1916), Willis Vernon Cole was prosecuted for practicing medicine. The evidence was that he had been called on by a prospective client (actually an investigator for the New York Medical Society). She understood him to promise to "cure her eyes"; she had been wearing glasses for ten years. He told her to take off the glasses and prayed silently; he said he himself had worn glasses for many years but had been healed by prayer. His testimony was that he had not said he could cure her, but that God could, that He was the only healer. He told her she could cure herself by cleansing fear, disharmony, and false thoughts from her consciousness, that "disease was like a shadow which flees before the light."

The applicable statute defined practicing medicine to include holding oneself out as able "to diagnose, treat, operate or prescribe for any human disease." The statute also said, "This article shall not be construed to affect . . . the practice of the religious tenets of any church." Cole was a member of the Christian Science Church and a practitioner as defined by its rules. The court held that his good faith practice of Christian Science was a defense to the charge of unlawfully practicing medicine. Judge Benjamin Cardozo joined the court's opinion. Chief Justice Bartlett went beyond the court, declaring in his concurrence: "I deny the power of the Legislature to make it a crime to treat disease by prayer."

The rule has been otherwise as to the treatment of sick children by prayer. In *People v. Pierson*, 176 N.Y. 201, 68 N.E. 243 (1903), Luther Pierson was a member of the Christian Catholic Church of Chicago. He did not believe in physicians; he did believe that prayer would cure disease. His sixteen-month-old daughter contracted whooping cough, then pneumonia, and died. Even when her symptoms became "dangerous," Cole did not call a doctor, believing that divine healing would be accomplished by his prayer. He was convicted of the misdemeanor of willfully failing to provide medical attendance for his child. He invoked the free exercise of religion clause of the New York constitution. The court said, "But the law of nature, as well as the common law, devolves upon the parents the duty of caring for their young. . . ." The court applied the statute.

The California Penal Code, sec. 270, makes it a misdemeanor for a parent willfully not to furnish "necessary clothing, food, shelter or medical attendance or other remedial care for his or her child." A 1976 amendment to the statute reads:

If a parent provides a minor with treatment by spiritual means through prayer alone in accordance with the tenets and practices of a recognized church or religious denomination, by a duly accredited practitioner thereof, such treatment shall constitute "other remedial care," as used in this section.

The amendment had been made after the thirteen-year-old daughter of Florence Arnold, a member of the Church of the First Born, had died after intestinal blockage treated only by prayer; Mrs. Arnold had pleaded no contest to a charge of manslaughter, *Los Angeles Daily Journal*, September 2, 1985, p. 22.

In 1984, in three separate cases in California, parents were charged with second-degree murder or with involuntary manslaughter when their children died from serious illnesses after prayer treatment by Christian Science practitioners and no medical treatment, see *State v. Walker, State v. Glaser, State v. Rippberger, ibid.*, p. 1. The position of the prosecutors was that the definition of remedial care under section 270 did not prevent prosecution under the murder or manslaughter provision of the Penal Code. "Religious freedom is vital, but a balancing act is needed," one prosecutor said. In *Walker*, dismissal of the indictment was denied. *Walker* v. *Superior Court*, 222 Cal. Rptr. 87, 176 Cal. App. 3d 526 (1986).

———— TWELVE ————
Belief and Organization of Belief

1. INVESTIGATION OF BELIEF

THE CASES INVOLVING the attempted regulation of religious activity often approach the question of the truth of a religious belief or the sincerity with which it is held. Analytically, many of them—*e.g.*, the cases on blood transfusions, peyote-chewing, faith-healing—could be classified under "investigation of belief." However, there is a small group of cases where the constitutionality of such investigations has been considered directly.

The I AM movement falls within the general classification of Theosophical religion. Guy Ballard, its founder, born in 1878, said that he had been visited on Mount Shasta, California, by a young man who offered him a cup of "Omnipotent Life" itself. The young man was a seventeenth-century occultist, St. Germain des Prés, an ascended master, that is, a mortal who had become a spirit and communicated with human beings on earth. St. Germain told Ballard about reincarnation, led him on an astral flight into his past lives, and taught him how to escape the wheel of reincarnation by contact with God. Jesus, distinguished from Christ, was perceived as another ascended master, of great help to mortals. Ballard and his wife Edna conveyed this teaching by *Unveiled Mysteries* (1934) and by classes which developed a membership in the movement, *see Encyclopedia of American Religion*, ed. J. Gordon Melton (1978) 2, 155–159.

Ballard died in 1939. The movement faltered. Edna Ballard and the Ballards' son Donald were indicted for mail fraud. Edna Ballard was sentenced to a year in prison and a fine of $8,000; Donald to thirty days and a fine of $400. Both sentences were suspended, *Los Angeles Times*, June 22, 1943. The Ballards appealed.

United States v. Ballard
322 U.S. 78 (1944)

Solicitor General Fahy, with whom *Assistant Attorney General Tom C. Clark, Mr. Robert S. Erdahl,* and *Miss Beatrice Rosenberg* were on the brief, for the United States. *Messrs. Roland Rich Woolley* and *Joseph F. Rank,* with whom *Mr. Ralph C. Curren* was on the brief, for respondents.

Justice Douglas delivered the opinion of the Court.

Respondents were indicted and convicted for using, and conspiring to use, the mails to defraud. § 215 Criminal Code, 18 U.S.C. § 338; § 37 Criminal Code, 18 U.S.C. § 88. The indictment was in twelve counts. It charged a scheme to defraud by organizing and promoting the I Am movement through the use of the mails. The charge was that certain designated corporations were formed, literature distributed and sold, funds solicited, and memberships in the I Am movement sought "by means of false and fraudulent representations, pretenses and promises." The false representations charged were eighteen in number. It is sufficient at this point to say that they covered respondents' alleged religious doctrines or beliefs. They were all set forth in the first count. The following are representative:

that Guy W. Ballard, now deceased, alias Saint Germain, Jesus, George Washington, and Godfre Ray King, had been selected and thereby designated by the alleged "ascertained masters," Saint Germain, as a divine messenger; and that the words of "ascended masters" and the words of the alleged divine entity, Saint Germain, would be transmitted to mankind through the medium of the said Guy W. Ballard;

that Guy W. Ballard, during his lifetime, and Edna W. Ballard, and Donald Ballard, by reason of their alleged high spiritual attainments and righteous conduct, had been selected as divine messengers through which the words of the alleged "ascended masters," including the alleged Saint Germain, would be communicated to mankind under the teachings commonly known as the "I Am" movement;

that Guy W. Ballard, during his lifetime, and Edna W. Ballard and Donald Ballard had, by reason of supernatural attainments, the power to heal persons of ailments and diseases and to make well persons afflicted with any diseases, injuries, or ailments, and did falsely represent to persons intended to be defrauded that the three designated persons had the ability and power to cure persons of those diseases normally classified as curable and also of diseases which are ordinarily classified by the medical profession as being incurable diseases; and did further represent that the three designated persons had in fact cured either by the activity of one, either, or all of said persons, hundreds of persons afflicted with diseases and ailments;

Each of the representations enumerated in the indictment was followed by the charge that respondents "well knew" it was false. After enumerating the eighteen misrepresentations the indictment also alleged:

At the time of making all of the afore-alleged representations by the defendants, and each of them, the defendants, and each of them, well knew that all of said aforementioned representations were false and untrue and were made with the intention on the part of the defendants, and each of them, to cheat, wrong, and defraud persons intended to be defrauded, and to obtain from persons intended to be defrauded by the defendants, money, property, and other things of value and to convert the same to the use and the benefit of the defendants, and each of them;

The indictment contained twelve counts, one of which charged a conspiracy to defraud. The first count set forth all of the eighteen representations, as we have said. Each of the other counts incorporated and realleged all of them and added no additional ones. There was a demurrer and a motion to quash, each of which asserted, among other things, that the indictment attacked the religious beliefs of respondents and sought to restrict the free exercise of their religion in violation of the Constitution of the United States. These motions were denied by the District Court. Early in the trial, however, objections were raised to the admission of certain evidence concerning respondent's religious beliefs. The court conferred with counsel in absence of the jury and with the acquiescence of counsel for the United States and for respondents confined the issues on this phase of the case to the question of the good faith of respondents. At the request of counsel for both sides the court advised the jury of that action in the following language:

Now, gentlemen, here is the issue in this case:

First, the defendants in this case made certain representations of belief in a divinity and in a supernatural power. Some of the teachings of the defendants, representations, might seem extremely improbable to a great many people. For instance, the appearance of Jesus to dictate some of the works that we have had introduced in evidence, as testified to here at the opening transcription, or shaking hands with Jesus, to some people that might seem highly improbable. I point that out as one of the many statements.

Whether that is true or not is not the concern of this Court and is not the concern of the jury—and they are going to be told so in their instructions. As far as this Court sees the issue, it is immaterial what these defendants preached or wrote or taught in their classes. They are not going to be permitted to speculate on the actuality of the happening of those incidents. Now, I think I have made that as clear as I can. Therefore, the religious beliefs of these defendants cannot be an issue in this court.

The issue is: Did these defendants honestly and in good faith believe those things? If they did, they should be acquitted. I cannot make it any clearer than that.

If these defendants did not believe those things, they did not believe that Jesus came down and dictated, or that Saint Germain came down and dictated, did not believe the things that they wrote, the things that they preached, but used the mail for the purpose of getting money, the jury should find them guilty. Therefore, gentlemen, religion cannot come into this case.

The District Court reiterated that admonition in the charge to the jury and made it abundantly clear. The following portion of the charge is typical:

The question of the defendants' good faith is the cardinal question in this case. You are not to be concerned with the religious belief of the defendants, or any of them. The jury will be called upon to pass on the question of whether or not the defendants honestly and in good faith believed the representations which are set forth in the indictment, and honestly and in good faith believed that the benefits which they represented would flow from their belief to those who embraced and followed their teachings, or whether these representations were mere pretenses without honest belief on the part of the defendants or any of them, and, were the representations made for the purpose of procuring money, and were the mails used for this purpose.

As we have said, counsel for the defense acquiesced in this treatment of the matter, made no objection to it during the trial, and indeed treated it without protest as the law of the case throughout the proceedings prior to the verdict. Respondents did not change their position before the District Court after verdict and contend that the truth or verity of their religious doctrines or beliefs should have been submitted to the jury. In their motion for new trial they did contend, however, that the withdrawal of these issues from the jury was error because it was in effect an amendment of the indictment. That was also one of their specifications of errors on appeal. And other errors urged on appeal included the overruling of the demurrer to the indictment and the motion to quash, and the disallowance of proof of the truth of respondents' religious doctrines or beliefs.

The Circuit Court of Appeals reversed the judgment of conviction and granted a new trial, one judge dissenting. 138 F.2d 540. In its view the restriction of the issue in question to that of good faith was error. Its reason was that the scheme to defraud alleged in the indictment was that respondents made the eighteen alleged false representations; and that to prove that defendants devised the scheme described in the indictment "it was necessary to prove that they schemed to make some, at least, of the (eighteen) representations . . . and that some, at least, of the representations which they schemed to make were false." 138 F.2d 545. One judge thought that the ruling of the District Court was also error because it was "as prejudicial to the issue of honest belief as to the issue of purposeful misrepresentation." *Id.,* p. 546.

The case is here on a petition for a writ of certiorari which we granted because of the importance of the question presented.

. . .

As we have noted, the Circuit Court of Appeals held that the question of the truth of the representations concerning respondents' religious doctrines or beliefs should have been submitted to the jury. And it remanded the case for a new trial. It may be that the Circuit Court of Appeals took that action because it did not think that the indictment could be properly construed as charging a scheme to defraud by means other than misrepresentations of respondents' religious doctrines or beliefs. Or that court may have concluded that the withdrawal of the issue of the truth of those religious doctrines or beliefs was unwarranted because it resulted in a substantial change in the character of the crime charged. But on whichever basis that court rested its action, we do not agree that the truth or verity of respondents' religious doctrines or beliefs should have been submitted to the jury. Whatever this particular indictment might require, the First Amendment precludes such a course, as the United States seems to concede. "The law knows no heresy, and is committed to the support of no dogma, the establishment of no sect." *Watson v. Jones* [*supra,* VIII, 4]. The First Amendment has a dual aspect. It not only "forestalls compulsion by law of the acceptance of any creed or the practice of any form of worship" but also "safeguards the free exercise of the chosen form of religion." *Cantwell v. Connecticut* [*supra,* XI, 1]. "Thus the Amendment embraces two concepts,—freedom to believe and freedom to act. The first is absolute but, in the nature of things, the second cannot be." *Id.,* pp. 303–304. Freedom of thought, which includes freedom of religious belief, is basic in a society of free men. *Board of Education v. Barnette* [*supra,* XI, 2]. It embraces the right to maintain theories of life and of death and of the hereafter which are rank heresy to followers of the orthodox faiths. Heresy trials are foreign to our Constitution. Men may believe what they cannot prove. They may not be put to the proof of their religious doctrines or beliefs. Religious experiences which are as real as life to some may be incomprehensible to others. Yet the fact that they may be beyond the ken of mortals does not mean that they can be made suspect before the law. Many take their gospel from the New Testament. But it would hardly be supposed that they could be tried before a jury charged with the duty of determining whether those teachings contained false representations. The miracles of the New Testament, the Divinity of Christ, life after death, the power of prayer are deep in the religious convictions of many. If one could be sent to jail because a jury in a hostile environment found those teachings false, little indeed would be left of religious freedom. The Fathers of the Constitution were not unaware of the varied and extreme views of religious sects, of the violence of disagreement among them, and of the lack of any one religious creed on which all men would agree. They fashioned a charter of government which envisaged the widest possible toleration of conflicting views. Man's relation to his God was made no concern of the state. He was granted the right to worship as he pleased and to answer to no man for the verity of his religious views. The religious views espoused by respondents might seem incredible, if not preposterous, to most people. But if those doctrines are subject to trial before a jury charged with finding their truth or falsity, then the same can be done with the religious beliefs of any sect. When the triers of fact undertake that task, they enter a forbidden domain. The First Amendment does not select any one group or any one type of religion for preferred treatment. It puts them all in that position. *Murdock v. Pennsylvania* [*supra,* XI, 1]. As stated in *Davis v. Beason* [*supra,* IX], "With man's relations to his Maker and the obligations he may think they impose, and the manner in which an expression shall be made by him of his belief on those subjects, no interference can be permitted, provided always the laws of society, designed to secure its peace and prosperity, and the morals of its people, are not interfered with." See *Prince v. Massachusetts* [*supra* XI, 1]. So we conclude that the District Court ruled properly when it withheld from the jury all questions concerning the truth or falsity of the religious beliefs or doctrines of respondents.

. . .

The case was reversed and remanded to the Court of Appeals for consideration of other issues not before the Supreme Court.

Chief Justice Stone, dissenting:

I am not prepared to say that the constitutional guaranty of freedom of religion affords immunity from criminal prosecution for the fraudulent procurement of money by false statements as to one's religious experiences, more than it renders polygamy or libel immune from criminal prosecution. *Davis v. Beason* [*supra*, IX]; see *Chaplinsky v. New Hampshire,* 315 U.S. 568, 572; cf *Patterson v. Colorado,* 205 U.S. 454, 462; *Near v. Minnesota,* 283 U.S. 697, 715. I cannot say that freedom of thought and worship includes freedom to procure money by making knowingly false statements about one's religious experiences. To go no further, if it were shown that a defendant in this case had asserted as a part of the alleged fraudulent scheme, that he had physically shaken hands with St. Germain in San Francisco on a day named, or that, as the indictment here alleges, by the exertion of his spiritual power he "had in fact cured . . . hundreds of persons afflicted with diseases and ailments," I should not doubt that it would be open to the Government to submit to the jury proof that he had never been in San Francisco and that no such cures had ever been effected. In any event I see no occasion for making any pronouncement on this subject in the present case. . . .

Justice Roberts and Justice Frankfurter join in this opinion.

Justice Jackson, dissenting:

I should say the defendants have done just that for which they are indicted. If I might agree to their conviction without creating a precedent, I cheerfully would do so. I can see in their teachings nothing but humbug, untainted by any trace of truth. But that does not dispose of the constitutional question whether misrepresentation of religious experience or belief is prosecutable; it rather emphasizes the danger of such prosecutions.

The Ballard family claimed miraculous communication with the spirit world and supernatural power to heal the sick. They were brought to trial for mail fraud on an indictment which charged that their representations were false and that they "well knew" they were false. The trial judge, obviously troubled, ruled that the court could not try whether the statements were untrue, but could inquire whether the defendants knew them to be untrue; and, if so, they could be convicted.

I find it difficult to reconcile this conclusion with our traditional religious freedoms. In the first place, as a matter of either practice or philosophy I do not see how we can separate an issue as to what is believed from considerations as to what is believable. The most convincing proof that one believes his statements is to show that they have been true in his experience. Likewise, that one knowingly falsified is best proved by showing that what he said happened never did happen. How can the Government prove these persons knew something to be false which it cannot prove to be false? If we try religious sincerity severed from religious verity, we isolate the dispute from the very considerations which in common experience provide its most reliable answer.

In the second place, any inquiry into intellectual honesty in religion raises profound psychological problems. William James, who wrote on these matters as a scientist, reminds us that it is not theology and ceremonies which keep religion going. Its vitality is in the religious experiences of many people. "If you ask what these experiences are, they are conversations with the unseen, voices and visions, responses to prayer, changes of heart, deliverances from fear, inflowings of help, assurances of support, whenever certain persons set their own internal attitude in certain appropriate ways."[1] If religious liberty includes, as it must, the right to communicate such experiences to others, it seems to me an impossible task for juries to separate fancied ones from real ones, dreams from happenings, and hallucinations from true clairvoyance. Such experiences,

---

[1] William James, Collected Essays and Reviews, pp. 427–8; see generally his Varieties of Religious Experience and The Will to Believe. See also Burton, Heyday of a Wizard.

like some tones and colors, have existence for one, but none at all for another. They cannot be verified to the minds of those whose field of consciousness does not include religious insight. When one comes to trial which turns on any aspect of religious belief or representation, unbelievers among his judges are likely not to understand and are almost certain not to believe him.

And then I do not know what degree of skepticism or disbelief in a religious representation amounts to actionable fraud. James points out that "Faith means belief in something concerning which doubt is still theoretically possible." Belief in what one may demonstrate to the senses is not faith. All schools of religious thought make enormous assumptions, generally on the basis of revelations authenticated by some sign or miracle. The appeal in such matters is to a very different plane of credulity than is invoked by representations of secular fact in commerce. Some who profess belief in the Bible read literally what others read as allegory or metaphor, as they read Aesop's fables. Religious symbolism is even used by some with the same mental reservations one has in teaching of Santa Claus or Uncle Sam or Easter bunnies or dispassionate judges. It is hard in matters so mystical to say how literally one is bound to believe the doctrine he teaches and even more difficult to say how far it is reliance upon a teacher's literal belief which induces followers to give him money.

There appear to be persons—let us hope not many—who find refreshment and courage in the teachings of the "I Am" cult. If the members of the sect get comfort from the celestial guidance of their "Saint Germain," however doubtful it seems to me, it is hard to say that they do not get what they pay for. Scores of sects flourish in this country by teaching what to me are queer notions. It is plain that there is wide variety in American religious taste. The Ballards are not alone in catering to it with a pretty dubious product.

The chief wrong which false prophets do to their following is not financial. The collections aggregate a tempting total, but individual payments are not ruinous. I doubt if the vigilance of the law is equal to making money stick by over-credulous people. But the real harm is on the mental and spiritual plane. There are those who hunger and thirst after higher values which they feel wanting in their humdrum lives. They live in mental confusion or moral anarchy and seek vaguely for truth and beauty and moral support. When they are deluded and then disillusioned, cynicism and confusion follow. The wrong of these things, as I see it, is not in the money the victims part with half so much as in the mental and spiritual poison they get. But that is precisely the thing the Constitution put beyond the reach of the prosecutor, for the price of freedom of religion or of speech or of the press is that we must put up with, and even pay for, a good deal of rubbish.

Prosecutions of this character easily could degenerate into religious persecution. I do not doubt that religious leaders may be convicted of fraud for making false representations on matters other than faith or experience, as for example if one represents that funds are being used to construct a church when in fact they are being used for personal purposes. But that is not this case, which reaches into wholly dangerous ground. When does less than full belief in a professed credo become actionable fraud if one is soliciting gifts or legacies? Such inquiries may discomfort orthodox as well as unconventional religious teachers, for even the most regular of them are sometimes accused of taking their orthodoxy with a grain of salt.

I would dismiss the indictment and have done with this business of judicially examining other people's faiths.

NOTE. *Compare Founding Church of Scientology v. United States,* 406 F.2d 1146 (D.C. Cir. 1969), *cert. denied,* 396 U.S. 963 (1969), where Judge Skelly Wright wrote:

Appellants in this case, claimants to the seized materials, are individual and corporate adherents to the movement known as Scientology. The movement apparently rests almost entirely upon the writings of one man, L. Ron Hubbard, an American who maintained the headquarters of the movement in England at the time this action was brought. In the early 1950's, Hubbard wrote tracts elucidating what he called "Dianetics." Dianetics is a theory of the mind which sets out many of the therapeutic techniques now used by Scientologists, including techniques attacked by the Government in this case as false healing.

The basic theory of Dianetics is that man possesses both a reactive mind and an analytic mind. The analytic mind is a superior computer, incapable of error, to which can be attributed none of the human misjudgments which create social problems and much individual suffering. These are traceable rather to the reactive mind, which is made up of "engrams," or patterns imprinted on the nervous system in moments of pain, stress or unconsciousness. These imprinted patterns may be triggered by stimuli associated with the original imprinting, and may then produce unconscious or conditioned behavior which is harmful or irrational.

Dianetics is not presented as a simple description of the mind, but as a practical science which can cure many of the ills of man. It terms the ordinary person, encumbered by the "engrams" of his reactive mind, as a "preclear," by analogy to a computer from which previously programmed instructions have not been erased. The goal of Dianetics is to make persons "clear," thus freeing the rational and infallible analytical mind. The benefits this will bring are set out in considerable and alluring detail. All mental disorders are said to be caused by "engrams," as are all psychosomatic disorders, and that concept is broadly defined.

A process of working toward "clear" is described as "auditing." This process was explicitly characterized as "therapy" in Hubbard's best-selling book DIANETICS: THE MODERN SCIENCE OF MENTAL HEALTH (1950). The process involves conversation with an "auditor" who would lead the subject or "preclear" along his "time track," discovering and exposing "engrams" along the way. Though auditing is represented primarily as a method of improving the spiritual condition of man, rather explicit benefits to bodily health are promised as well. Hubbard has asserted that arthritis, dermatitis, asthma, some coronary difficulties, eye trouble, bursitis, ulcers and sinusitis are psychosomatic and can be cured, and further that tuberculosis is "perpetuated by engrams."

A few years after the appearance of Dianetics, Hubbard began to set forth the broader theories of Scientology. Dianetics was explicitly endorsed as part of Scientology, "that branch * * * that covers Mental Anatomy." Testimony by Scientology adherents at the trial made clear that they continue to uphold the theories of Dianetics, though they feel that there may have been some errors in early formulations.

With Scientology came much of the overlay which lends color to the characterization of the movement as a religious one. Hubbard has claimed kinship between his theories and those espoused by Eastern religions, especially Hinduism and Buddhism. He argues that man is essentially a free and immortal spirit (a "thetan" in Scientological terminology) which merely inhabits the "mest body" ("mest" is an acronym of the words matter, energy, space, time). Man is said to be characterized by the qualities of "beingness," "havingness," and "doingness." The philosophical theory was developed that the world is constructed on the relationships of "Affinity," "Reality" and "Communication," which taken together are denominated "the ARC Triangle."

On the more mundane level, early in the career of Scientology Hubbard's followers—at least those in the United States—began to constitute themselves into formal religious bodies. The Founding Church of Scientology of Washington, D.C., one of the appellants, was incorporated in the District of Columbia in 1955. A formal creed was promulgated and was made part of the Articles of Incorporation. From the literature of the movement in evidence at trial, it appears that the move toward formal religious organization disturbed some adherents of Scientology, who seem to have regarded it is an attempt to provide a legal cloak for the movement's activities. But Hubbard defended the church movement, disavowing mysticism or supernaturalism, but pointing out the kinship of his ideas with those of the Vedas and other Eastern religious doctrines.

From the evidence developed at trial, it appears that a major activity of the Founding Church and its affiliated organizations in the District of Columbia is providing "auditing" at substantial fees (at the time of trial $500 for a 25-hour course), to persons interested in Scientology. The affiliated Academy of Scientology is engaged in training auditors. Auditors are paid directly by the Church. There is no membership in the Church as such; persons are accepted for auditing on the basis of their interest in Scientology (and presumably their ability to pay for its benefits).

The Hubbard Electrometer, or E-meter, plays an essential, or at least important, part in the process of auditing. The E-meter is a skin galvanometer, similar to those used in giving lie detector tests. The subject or "preclear" holds in his hands two tin soup cans, which are linked to the electrical apparatus. A needle on the apparatus registers changes in the electrical resistance of the subject's skin. The auditor asks questions of the subject, and the movement of the needle is apparently used as a check of the emotional reaction to the questions. According to complex rules and procedures set out in Scientology publications, the auditor can interpret the movements of the needle after certain prescribed questions are asked, and use them in diagnosing the mental and spiritual condition of the subject. The E-meters are sold for about $125, and are advertised in Scientology publications available at the Distribution Center adjoining the Church.

The Scientology movement in the District of Columbia also offers the entire range of Scientology publications for sale. Over the years this literature has grown into a formidable *corpus*. Hubbard's two early books on Dianetics are sold, along with later treatises developing Scientology. A large number of pamphlets and tracts supplements the hardcover books. The movement has a monthly magazine, ABILITY, which at the time of trial had published over 100 numbers. In addition, "L. Ron Hubbard's Professional Auditors' Bulletins," numbering at least 80 at the time of trial, are collected and published in pamphlets. Much of this literature is before the court as exhibits in evidence, and a large proportion of it stands condemned by the District Court's decree as "false or misleading labeling" of the E-meter.

. . .

The *Ballard* case does not hold merely that religious belief is protected. The Ballards — engaged in action; they solicited money from their faithful. Rather the holding of the case seems to be that regulation of religious action which involves testing in court the truth or falsity of religious belief is barred by the First Amendment.

The relevance of *Ballard* to the case before us is obvious. Here the E-meter has been condemned, not because it is itself harmful, but because the representations made concerning it are "false or misleading." And the largest part of those representations is contained in the literature of Scientology describing the process of auditing which appellants have claimed, without contest from the Government, is part of the doctrine of their religion and central to its exercise. Thus if their claims to religious status are accepted, a finding that the seized literature misrepresents the benefits from auditing is a finding that their religious doctrines are false.

Judge Skelly Wright concluded that the Church of Scientology had made a prima facie case that it was a religion and that a jury finding of false labeling under the Food, Drug, and Cosmetics Act would not be upheld when the finding was based on the church's "doctrinal religious literature."

In a civil suit by a former member of the church, La Venda Van Schaick alleged she was induced to become a Scientologist by false representation by the church as to "the nature of the Scientology movement" and "the context of Scientology doctrine." The church, invoking

Ballard, moved to dismiss. Judge W. Arthur Garrity, Jr., ruled, "To treat Scientology as a religion . . . would be to ignore the allegations of the complaint." He ordered a hearing as to whether the church was a religion, *Van Schaick v. Church of Scientology,* 535 F. Supp. 1125 (D. Mass. 1982).

Not only believers but nonbelievers were found to be protected by the First Amendment, or as the famous Footnote 11 in the following case suggested, there was a religion called Secular Humanism:

Torcaso v. Watkins
367 U.S. 488 (1961)

Leo Pfeffer and *Lawrence Speiser* argued the cause for appellant. With them on the briefs were *Joseph A. Sickles, Carlton R. Sickles, Bruce N. Goldberg, Rowland Watts* and *George Kaufmann.*

Thomas B. Finan, Attorney General of Maryland, and *Joseph S. Kaufman,* Deputy Attorney General, argued the cause and filed a brief for appellee. *C. Ferdinand Sybert,* former Attorney General of Maryland, and *Stedman Prescott, Jr.,* former Deputy Attorney General, appeared with *Mr. Kaufman* on the motion to dismiss or affirm.

Briefs of *amici curiae,* urging reversal, were filed by *Herbert A. Wolff* and *Leo Rosen* for the American Ethical Union, and by *Herbert B. Ehrmann, Lawrence Peirez, Isaac G. McNatt, Abraham Blumberg, Arnold Forster, Paul Hartman, Theodore Leskes, Edwin J. Lukas* and *Sol Rabkin* for the American Jewish Committee et al.

Justice Black delivered the opinion of the Court.

Article 37 of the Declaration of Rights of the Maryland Constitution provides:

"[N]o religious test ought ever to be required as a qualification for any office of profit or trust in this State, other than a declaration of belief in the existence of God. . . ."
The appellant Torcaso was appointed to the office of Notary Public by the Governor of Maryland but was refused a commission to serve because he would not declare his belief in God. He then brought this action in a Maryland Circuit Court to compel issuance of his commission, charging that the State's requirement that he declare this belief violated "the First and Fourteenth Amendments to the Constitution of the United States. . . ."[1] The Circuit Court rejected these federal constitutional contentions, and the highest court of the State, the Court of Appeals, affirmed, holding that the state constitutional provision is self-executing and requires declaration of belief in God as a qualification for office without need for implementing legislation. The case is therefore properly here on appeal under 28 U.S.C. § 1257 (2).

There is, and can be, no dispute about the purpose or effect of the Maryland Declaration of Rights requirement before us—it sets up a religious test which was designed to and, if valid, does bar every person who refuses to declare a belief in God from holding a public "office of profit or trust" in Maryland. The power and authority of the State of Maryland thus is put on the side of one particular sort of believers—those who are willing to say they believe in "the existence of God."

. . .

We repeat and again reaffirm that neither a State nor the Federal Government can constitutionally force a person "to profess a belief or disbelief in any religion." Neither can constitutionally pass laws or impose requirements which aid all religions as against

---

[1] Appellant also claimed that the State's test oath requirement violates the provision of Art. VI of the Federal Constitution that "no religious Test shall ever be required as a Qualification to any Office or public Trust under the United States." Because we are reversing the judgment on other grounds, we find it unnecessary to consider appellant's contention that this provision applies to state as well as federal offices.

non-believers,[10] and neither can aid those religions based on a belief in the existence of God as against those religions founded on different beliefs.[11]

In upholding the State's religious test for public office the highest court of Maryland said:

"The petitioner is not compelled to believe or disbelieve, under threat of punishment or other compulsion. True, unless he makes the declaration of belief he cannot hold public office in Maryland, but he is not compelled to hold office."

The fact, however, that a person is not compelled to hold public office cannot possibly be an excuse for barring him from office by state-imposed criteria forbidden by the Constitution. This was settled by our holding in *Wieman v. Updegraff,* 344 U.S. 183. We there pointed out that whether or not "an abstract right to public employment exists," Congress could not pass a law providing " '. . . that no federal employee shall attend Mass or take any active part in missionary work.' "

This Maryland religious test for public office unconstitutionally invades the appellant's freedom of belief and religion and therefore cannot be enforced against him.

The judgment of the Court of Appeals of Maryland is accordingly reversed and the cause is remanded for further proceedings not inconsistent with this opinion.

Reversed and remanded.

Justice Frankfurter and Justice Harlan concur in the result.

2. DETERMINATION OF ECCLESIASTICAL STATUS

If religious belief may not be tested, may religious status be tested by the government employing criteria other than those employed by the religion in question?

Consider these cases involving the Mesifta Talmudical Seminary in Brooklyn: *United States ex rel. Levy v. Cain,* 149 F. 2d 338 (2nd Cir. 1945). To determine whether a registrant was entitled to the statutory deferment given students "preparing for the ministry in theological or divinity schools recognized as such," the New York director of Selective Service set up theological "panels" to advise the local draft boards. Irwin S. Levy, fifteen years old, was admitted to study at Mesifta; he was in his third of nine years of study when he became eighteen and eligible for the draft. The advisory panel, composed of "the most prominent men of the Jewish faith in the great City of New York" (according to a draft board member) recommended denial of exemption as a theological student. Irwin Levy contended that the panel favored Reformed and Conservative Judaism over Orthodox Judaism and that out of fifty bona fide seminarians at Mesifta it had recognized only one as deserving exemption. The

---

[10] In discussing Article VI in the debate of the North Carolina Convention on the adoption of the Federal Constitution, James Iredell, later a Justice of this Court, said:

". . .[I]t is objected that the people of America may, perhaps, choose representatives who have no religion at all, and that pagans and Mahometans may be admitted into offices. But how is it possible to exclude any set of men, without taking away that principle of religious freedom which we ourselves so warmly contend for?"

And another delegate pointed out that Article VI "leaves religion on the solid foundation of its own inherent validity, without any connection with temporal authority; and no kind of oppression can take place." 4 Elliot, *op. cit., supra,* at 194, 200.

[11] Among religions in this country that do not teach what would generally be considered a belief in the existence of God are Buddhism, Taoism, Ethical Culture, Secular Humanism, and others. See *Washington Ethical Society v. District of Columbia,* 101 U.S. App. D.C. 371, 249 F.2d 127; *Fellowship of Humanity v. County of Alameda,* 153 Cal. App.2d 673, 315 P.2d 394; II Encyclopaedia of the Social Sciences 293; 4 Encyclopaedia Britannica (1957 ed.) 325–327; 21 *id.,* at 797; Archer, *Faiths Men Live By* (2d ed. revised by Purinton), 120–138, 254–313; 1961 World Almanac 695, 712; *Year Book of American Churches for 1961,* at 29, 47.

Second Circuit, per Judge Learned Hand, felt that the Board had improperly delegated its responsibility to the panel and ordered Levy released from the army. This decision was followed in *United States v. Samuels,* 151 F.2d 801 (3rd Cir. 1945), a case involving two other Mesifta students, Jacob S. Samuels and Henry Horowitz. On appeal, the Supreme Court per Justice Douglas unanimously reversed:

Eagles v. United States ex rel. Samuels
329 U.S. 304 (1946)

Irving S. Shapiro argued the cause for petitioner. *Meyer Kreeger* argued the cause for respondent.

. . .

It appears that the city director, in aid of these functions, established theological panels. It was thought desirable to give the selective service personnel the benefit of the advice of those familiar with the educational practices of various religious groups so that Selective Service might exercise a more informed judgment in evaluating claims to classifications in IV–D. Accordingly, theological panels were constituted, one of which consisted of prominent laymen and rabbis of the Jewish faith who gave advisory opinions on those who sought a IV–D classification on the grounds that they were either rabbis or students preparing for the ministry in the Jewish religion. The members of the panel were volunteers, as permitted by the regulations. Section 602.2, 6 Fed. Reg. 6826. And pursuant to the regulations each took the oath of office. Section 602.4 (a), 6 Fed. Reg. 6826.

Samuels registered under the Act in February, 1942. In May and July, 1942, he filed with his local board questionnaires stating that he had had two years of high school education; that he was a student at the Mesifta Theological Seminary preparing for the rabbinate; that since 1940 his regular occupation was that of a clerk; that for the past two years he had been employed by a textile company; and that the job for which he was best fitted was that of a spiritual leader and a teacher of Hebrew or rabbinical duties. The local board was advised by the seminary that Samuels had attended there since he was six years old, that he had finished the eight-year elementary course and the four-year pre-rabbinical course, that he had been admitted to the rabbinical division in 1937, that he left the school in 1939 to seek employment, that he returned to the evening school in September, 1941, and that he was transferred to the day session in July, 1942, which, as later appeared, was a few days before the school closed for the summer.

In August, 1942, the local board classified him IV–D. Section 622.44 (a), 6 Fed. Reg. 6607, 6610. In May, 1944, he was given a physical examination and found acceptable for military service. Thereafter the city director requested that he appear before the theological panel in respect to his claim to a IV–D classification. He appeared before the panel in June, 1944, stating, *inter alia,* that he expected to graduate from the seminary in 1945, that ill health caused him to leave the school in 1939, that between 1940 and 1942 he worked as a clerk, and that he returned to the seminary as a full-time student at about the time he filed his selective service questionnaire.

The panel reported that the seminary which Samuels attended was not preparing men exclusively for the rabbinate, that orthodox tradition encouraged advanced study of the subjects in which students for the ministry were trained, and that students ultimately intending to enter business or a profession or some non-rabbinic activity in the field of religion may be enrolled in the same classes as those preparing for the rabbinate. The panel stated that it therefore seemed essential to determine in each case what the registrant had in mind in pursuing his course of study; that to make that determination the character of the seminary, the sincerity of the registrant's declared purpose, his demeanor, and the impression as to his candor and honesty should be considered. It concluded that Samuels was not "preparing in good faith for a career of service in the practicing rabbinate."

The Court said that the draft board had not abandoned its functions to the panel. The Court also said that there was evidence supporting the board's doubt that Samuels was "preparing in good faith for the rabbinate. A registrant might seek a theological school as a refuge for the duration of the war. Congress did not create the exemption in sec. 5(d) for him."

Cox v. United States
332 U.S. 442 (1947)

Hayden C. Covington argued the cause and filed a brief for petitioners.
Irving S. Shapiro argued the cause for the United States. With him on the brief were *Solicitor General Perlman* and *Robert S. Erdahl.*
Justice Reed delivered the opinion of the Court.
. . .
Petitioner Cox registered under the Selective Training and Service Act on October 16, 1940, and in his questionnaire stated that he was 22 years old and had been employed as a truck driver since 1936. The local board classified him IV–F, as not physically fit for service, on January 31, 1941, and on March 10, 1942, changed the classification to I–A. Ten days later Cox filed a request for reclassification as IV–E (conscientious objector), stating that he had become a Jehovah's Witness in January 1942. The board at first rejected the claim, but on June 12 of the same year granted him the requested classification. Ten days later petitioner first made his claim for total exemption from service, claiming to be a minister of religion; the local board refused the exemption and its action was sustained by the board of appeal. On May 18, 1944, the board ordered Cox to report to camp, and on May 26 he complied and then immediately left camp and did not return.

Upon trial Cox's selective service file was received in evidence. It contained an ordination certificate from the Watch Tower Bible and Tract Society stating that Cox was "a duly ordained minister of the Gospel" and that his "entire time" was devoted to missionary work. The file also contained an affidavit of a company servant, Cox's church superior, dated October 29, 1942, stating that Cox "regularly and customarily serves as a minister by going from house to house and conducting Bible Studies and Bible Talks." There was also an affidavit by Cox, dated October 28, 1942, stating that he was enrolled in the "Pioneer service" on October 16 and that he was "able to average 150 hours per month to my ministerial duties without secular work." He added that "my entire time will be devoted to preaching the Gospel as a pioneer." Cox testified at the trial in October 1944 as to his duties as a minister that he preached from house to house, conducted funerals, and "instructed the Bible" in homes. No evidence was introduced showing the total amount of time Cox had spent in religious activities since October 16, 1942. Nor was there evidence of the secular activities of Cox nor the time employed in them. Although the selective service file was introduced in evidence, and the trial court denied the motion for a directed verdict, it does not appear that the trial judge examined the file to determine whether the action of the local board was arbitrary and capricious or without basis in fact. At that time the lower federal courts interpreted *Falbo v. United States,* 320 U.S. 549, as meaning that no judicial review of any sort could be had of a selective service order. In *Estep v. United States,* 327 U.S. 114, we held that a limited review could be obtained if the registrant had exhausted his administrative remedies, and the Circuit Court of Appeals in accordance with that decision reviewed the file of Cox and found that the evidence was "substantially in support" of the classification found by the board.

Petitioner Thompson also registered on October 16, 1940, claiming exemption as a minister. He stated in his questionnaire that he was 30 years old and that for the past 13 years he had operated a grocery store and had been a minister since August 1, 1940. At first the local board gave him a deferred classification because of dependency, but then changed his classification to IV–E. Thompson appealed to the board of appeal on November 5, 1943, explaining his duties as a minister and presenting a full statement of his argument that as a colporteur he was within the exemption for ministers as interpreted by selective service regulations.

. . .

Section 5(d) of the Selective Training and Service Act provides that "regular or duly ordained ministers of religion" shall be exempt from training and service under the Act, and § 622.44 of Selective Service Regulations defines the terms "regular minister of religion" and "duly ordained minister of religion." In order to aid the local boards in applying the regulation, the Director of Selective Service issued Opinion No. 14 (amended) on November 2, 1942, which described the tests to be applied in determining whether Jehovah's Witnesses were entitled to exemption as ministers, regular or ordained. The opinion stated that Witnesses who were members of the Bethel Family (producers of religious supplies) or pioneers, devoting all or substantially all of their time to the work of teaching the tenets of their religion, generally were exempt, and appended a list of certain members of the Bethel Family and pioneers who were entitled to this exemption. None of these Witnesses were on the list. The opinion stated that members of the Bethel Family and pioneers whose names did not appear on the list, as well as all other Witnesses holding official titles in the organization, must be classified by the boards according to the facts in each case. The determining criteria were stated to be "whether or not they devote their lives in the furtherance of the beliefs of Jehovah's Witnesses, whether or not they perform functions which are normally performed by regular or duly ordained ministers of other religions, and, finally, whether or not they are regarded by other Jehovah's Witnesses in the same manner in which regular or duly ordained ministers of other religions are ordinarily regarded." The opinion further stated that the local board should place in the registrant's file "a record of all facts entering into its determination for the reason that it is legally necessary that the record show the basis of the local board's decision."

It will be observed that § 622.44 of the regulation makes "ordination" the only practical difference between a "regular" and a "duly ordained minister." This seems consistent with § 5 of the Act. We are of the view that the regulation conforms to the Act and that it is valid under the rule-making power conferred by § 10 (a). We agree, also, that Opinion 14 furnishes a proper guide to the interpretation of the Act and Regulations.

Affirmed.

Mr. Justice Frankfurter concurs in the result.

Mr. Justice Douglas, with whom Mr. Justice Black concurs, dissenting:

It is not disputed that Jehovah's Witnesses constitute a religious sect or organization. We have, moreover, recognized that its door-to-door evangelism is as much religious activity as "worship in the churches and preaching from the pulpits." *Murdock v. Pennsylvania* [*supra,* XI, 1]. The Selective Service files of these petitioners establish, I think, their status as ministers of that sect. Their claims to that status are supported by affidavits of their immediate superiors in the local group and by their national headquarters. And each of them was spending substantial time in the religious activity of preaching their faith. If a person is in fact engaging in the ministry, his motives for doing so are quite immaterial.

To deny these claimants their statutory exemption is to disregard these facts or to adopt a definition of minister which contracts the classification provided by Congress.

The classification as a minister may not be denied because the registrant devotes but a part of his time to religious activity.

Query. Is the relevant distinction between *Cox* and *Samuels,* on the one hand, and *Ballard,* on the other, that in the draft cases a "privilege" or "exemption" was being granted, while in *Ballard* the ordinary criminal law was being applied? How does the Court's view of the nonbinding effect of ecclesiastical determinations relate to the cases that follow, especially *Kedroff v. St. Nicholas Cathedral* (*Infra,* XII, 3) where the opinion is also written by Justice Reed?

Compare *United States v. Moon,* 718 F.2d 1210 (2nd Cir. 1983), *cert. denied,* 466 U.S. 971 (1984). Reverend Sun Myung Moon, the founder and head of the Unification Church, deposited $1.7 million over three years in the Chase Manhattan Bank in his own name. He did not report the interest as income. He was convicted of filing false federal income tax returns and was sentenced to eighteen months in prison. Crucial questions were whether Moon had been given the money as donations to the church and whether he held the money personally or in trust for the church. The jury was instructed:

If you find that the funds in the Chase accounts were the property of International Unification Church Movement or were held in trust by Moon for the International Unification Church Movement and used for church purposes and that the interest on those funds also belonged to the International Unification Church Movement and were used by it, then that interest would not be taxable income to Moon.

The judge refused to give this instruction requested by Moon:

There is evidence in the case tending to prove that the international Unification Church movement existed as an unincorporated association which was personified by Reverend Moon, founder and spiritual leader of the worldwide Unification Church movement, and which supported and directed the activities of the various national church entities in the United States and elsewhere. [Quoted in Brief for Appellant Moon, printed in Herbert Richardson, ed., *Constitutional Issues in the Case of Rev. Moon* (1984) 65–66.]

Moon also objected to the instruction "[i]f he used money for his own purposes that use would indicate lack of a trust relationship." He also argued that the First Amendment was violated because the trial court failed to charge the jury that it must accept as conclusive the Unification Church's definition of what the church considered a religious purpose. The Second Circuit rejected these arguments. It further held that "the doctrine of *Jones v. Wolf* [*infra,* XII, 3] has no application to the facts of this case."

When Moon applied for certiorari, his petition was supported by some forty organizations and individuals, among them the National Council of the Churches of Christ in the U.S.A., the Presbyterians (U.S.A.), the American Baptist Churches in the U.S.A., the African Methodist Episcopal Church, the National Association of Evangelicals, the Southern Christian Leadership Conference, the Catholic League for Religious and Civil Rights, and the Church of Jesus Christ of Latter-Day Saints. The petition was denied, 446 U.S. 971 (1984).

3. TITLE TO CHURCH PROPERTY

NOTE. *The Neutrality of Courts and State Action.* The Fourteenth Amendment rules action by the state. In *Shelley v. Kraemer*, 334 U.S. 1 (1948), the Supreme Court (6–0) held that when a state enforced a racially restrictive covenant, the judicial decree was state action and, as it enforced a discrimination against blacks, it was state action barred by the Fourteenth Amendment.

The Fourteenth Amendment has now been interpreted by the Court to bar state action establishing a religion. When a state court acts to decide an interchurch property dispute — whether or not the court uses the church rule or "neutral principles" — does the court's decree constitute state action? Is it state action establishing a religion? Is such establishment barred by the Fourteenth Amendment? If not, why not?

Shelley v. Kraemer produced much commentary pondering its implications and attempting to limit its logic, *see* Gerald Gunther, *Constitutional Law: Cases and Materials* (1975) 933–938. History not logic has suggested that in the area of religion *Shelley's* clear holding cannot be applied literally.

Compare Gordon v. Gordon, 332 Mass. 197, 124 N.E. 2d 228 (1955) *cert. denied*, 349 U.S. 947 (1955). Joseph Gordon of Attleboro, an Orthodox Jew, provided by will that if any of his children should "marry a person not born in the Hebrew faith," the testamentary gift to that child was revoked. His son Harold married Veronica Albaugh, a woman raised as a Catholic who was undergoing instruction from rabbis at the time of her wedding and who a little later formally became a convert to Judaism. The court found the phrase "Hebrew faith" not to be too vague (disagreeing with modern English trust cases on this point), it found Veronica to be one not born in that faith, and it rejected Harold Gordon's contention that *Shelley v. Kraemer* prevented enforcement of his father's will. The Probate Court's decree excluded him from the beneficiaries under the will. *Accord, United States National Bank v. Snodgrass*, 202 Or. 530, 275 P. 2d 860 (1954) (will enforced denying gift to daughter if she became a Catholic or married a Catholic).

NOTE. *Communist-Controlled Churches.* The Eastern Christian Churches have traditionally had a much closer identification with the state than any church is permitted to have with the American government. In 1721 the Orthodox Church in Russia was put under government control by the Ecclesiastical Regulation of Peter the Great. Its former mode of government by a patriarch and sobors (councils) was replaced by a bureaucratic institution called the Holy Governing Synod, which took an oath to the czar as "Supreme Judge" and which was supervised by a lay administrator, the chief procurator, *see* Robert K. Massie, *Peter the Great* (1980) 782; Dimitry Pospielovsky, *The Russian Church under the Soviet Regime 1917–1982* (1984) 1, 19, 25. With the abdication of Nicholas II, the church lost its temporal head. In November 1917 a sobor elected Tikhon Belavin as patriarch, giving him unrestricted administrative powers in case the new Soviet government made it impossible to convoke another sobor, Pospielovsky 1, 31, 36. In 1923 a schismatic group, the Renovationists, favored by the Soviet government, deposed Tikhon, now in prison, and set up a new administration, *ibid.* at 1, 56–58.

Tikhon had appointed Platon Rozhdestvensky archbishop of North America, with St. Nicholas Cathedral in New York as his seat. The Renovationsts named John Kedrovsky to the same position (although he was married and so canonically ineligible to be a bishop), and on November 7, 1923, he entered the cathedral, announcing that as appointee of "the Soviet All-Living Church" he had come "to take control of all Russian Church property," *New York Times*, November 8, 1923, p. 21, col. 3. Platon was dismissed for counterrevolutionary acts "directed against the Soviet," *see St. Nicholas Cathedral v. Kreshik, infra*, this section. Platon responded by calling a sobor of the North American clergy and faithful in Detroit in 1924. This sobor concluded that the patriarchate in Russia was under the coercion of the communists. The sobor relied on a decree issued by Tikhon in 1920 authorizing archdioceses to organize on a local basis if the activity of the patriarchate should stop and, "until the restitution of the Supreme Church government, decide definitely all affairs," *ibid*. The Detroit sobor recognized Platon as archbishop. However, the courts of New York recognized the Renovationists as the church and gave Kedrovsky possession of St. Nicholas Cathedral, *Kedrovsky v. Rojdesvensky*, 214 App. Div. 483, 212 N.Y.S. 273 (1925), *affirmed* 242 N.Y. 547, 162 N.E. 421 (1926). Most Orthodox churches in America were transferred to boards of trustees headed by Platon and escaped Kedrovsky, Pospielovsky 2, 283, 283 n. 48.

Litigation resumed in 1945. By this time, Kedrovsky was dead, his son John Kedroff had taken over the cathedral, and the Renovationist Church had lost the support of the Soviet government and disappeared. Meanwhile, New York had amended its Religious Corporation Law confirming title in the Russian Orthodox Church in North America (*i.e.*, the Church governed by Platon and his successors since the Detroit sobor) as the lawful owner of all property held by the Orthodox Church before the Russian Revolution. The American group sued for possession of the cathedral.

Kedroff himself, having no defense, sought out a new claimant. This was Venyamin Fedchenkov, whose claim was through Sergii Stragorodsky. Sergii, since his release from prison in 1927 and his comprehensive declaration of loyalty to the Soviet government, had without canonical authority acted as the de facto ecclesiastical head of the Orthodox Church in Russia while his critics saw him as a puppet of the secret police, Pospielovsky 1, 71–72; 2, 485. Sergii removed Platon and appointed Fedchenkov archbishop of North America in 1933, *ibid*. 2, 289. Soviet support shifted from the Renovationists to the Church headed by Sergii. In 1945, at the end of World War II a sobor was held for three days in Moscow, which recognized Aleksii Simansky, Sergii's successor, as patriarch and enacted a new administrative statute to govern the church; its effect was to make the patriarch supreme, *ibid*. at 2, 209–211. Aleksii supported Fedchenkov, and Fedchenkov supported Kedroff. In 1952 the case reached the Supreme Court.

Kedroff v. Saint Nicholas Cathedral of the Russian Orthodox Church in North America
344 U.S. 94 (1952)

Philip Adler argued the cause and filed the briefs for appellants.

Ralph Montgomery Arkush argued the cause and filed the brief for appellee.

Justice Reed delivered the opinion of the Court.

The right to the use and occupancy of a church in the city of New York is in dispute.

The right to such use is claimed by appellee, a corporation created in 1925 by an act of the Legislature of New York, Laws of New York 1925, c. 403, for the purpose of acquiring a cathedral for the Russian Orthodox Church in North America as a central place of worship and residence of the ruling archbishop "in accordance with the doctrine, discipline and worship of the Holy Apostolic Catholic Church of Eastern Confession as taught by the holy scriptures, holy tradition, seven oecumenical councils and holy fathers of that church."

The corporate right is sought to be enforced so that the head of the American churches, religiously affiliated with the Russian Orthodox Church, may occupy the Cathedral. At the present time that head is the Metropolitan of All America and Canada, the Archbishop of New York, Leonty, who like his predecessors was elected to his ecclesiastical office by a sobor of the American churches.

That claimed right of the corporation to use and occupancy for the archbishop chosen by the American churches is opposed by appellants who are in possession. Benjamin Fedchenkoff bases his right on an appointment in 1934 by the Supreme Church Authority of the Russian Orthodox Church, to wit, the Patriarch *locum tenens* of Moscow and all Russia and its Holy Synod, as Archbishop of the Archdiocese of North America and the Aleutian Islands. The other defendant-appellant is a priest of the Russian Orthodox Church, also acknowledging the spiritual and administrative control of the Moscow hierarchy. . . .

The Russian upheaval caused repercussions in the North American Diocese. That Diocese at the time of the Soviet Revolution recognized the spiritual and administrative control of Moscow. White Russians, both lay and clerical, found asylum in America from the revolutionary conflicts, strengthening the feeling of abhorrence of the secular attitude of the new Russian Government. The church members already here, immigrants and native-born, while habituated to look to Moscow for religious direction, were accustomed to our theory of separation between church and state. The Russian turmoil, the restraints on religious activities and the evolution of a new ecclesiastical hierarchy in the form of the "Living Church," deemed noncanonical or schismatic by most churchmen, made very difficult Russian administration of the American diocese. Furthermore, Patriarch Tikhon, on November 20, 1920, issued Decision No. 362 relating to church administration for troublesome times. This granted a large measure of autonomy, when the Russian ruling authority was unable to function, subject to "confirmation later to the Central Church Authority when it is re-established." Naturally the growing number of American-born members of the Russian Church did not cling to a hierarchy identified with their country of remote origin with the same national feeling that moved their immigrant ancestors. These facts and forces generated in America a separatist movement.

That movement brought about the arrangements at the Detroit Sobor of 1924 for a temporary American administration of the church on account of the disturbances in Russia.[8] This was followed by the declarations of autonomy of the successive sobors since that date, a spate of litigation concerning control of the various churches and occupancy of ecclesiastical positions, the New York legislation (known as Article 5–C, notes 2 and 3, *supra*), and this controversy.

Delegates from the North American Diocese intended to be represented at an admittedly canonical Sobor of the Russian Orthodox Church held in 1945 at Moscow. They did not arrive in time on account of delays, responsibility for which has not been fixed. The following stipulation appears as to their later actions while at Moscow:

"It is stipulated that Bishop Alexi and Father Dzvonchik, representing the local group of American Churches under Bishop Theophilus, appeared before the Patriarch and the members of his Synod in Moscow, presented a written report on the condition of the American Church, with a request for autonomy and a few days later received from the Patriarch the Ukase. . . ."

There came to the Russian Church in America this Ukase of the Moscow Patriarchy of February 14 or 16, 1945, covering Moscow's requirements for reunion of the American Orthodox Church with the Russian. It required for reunion that the Russian Church

---

[8] The attitude of the Russian Church in America will be made sufficiently plain by these extracts from their records of action taken at the Detroit Sobor, 1924:

"Point 1. Temporarily, until the convocation of the All Russian Sobor further indicated in Point 5, to declare the Russian Orthodox Diocese in America a self-governed Church so that it be governed by its own elected Archbishop by means of a Sobor of Bishops, a Council composed of those elected from the clergy and laity, and periodic Sobors of the entire American Church.

"Point 5. To leave the final regulation of questions arising from the relationship of the Russian and the American Churches to a future Sobor of the Russian Orthodox Church which will be legally convoked, legally elected, will sit with the participation of representatives of the American Church under conditions of political freedom, guaranteeing the fullness and authority of its decisions for the entire Church, and will be recognized by the entire Oecumenical Orthodox Church as a true Sobor of the Russian Orthodox Church."

in America hold promptly an "all American Orthodox Church Sobor"; that it express the decision of the dioceses to reunite with the Russian Mother Church, declare the agreement of the American Orthodox Church to abstain "from political activities against the U.S.S.R." and so direct its parishes, and elect a Metropolitan subject to confirmation by the Moscow Patriarchy. The decree said, "In view of the distance of the American Metropolitan District from the Russian Mother Church . . . the Metropolitan-Exarch . . . may be given some extended powers by the Moscow Patriarchy. . . ."

The American congregations speaking through their Cleveland Sobor of 1946 refused the proffered arrangement and resolved in part:

"That any administrative recognition of the Synod of the Russian Orthodox Church Abroad is hereby terminated, retaining, however, our spiritual and brotherly relations with all parts of the Russian Orthodox Church abroad. . . ."

This ended the efforts to compose the differences between the Mother Church and its American offspring, and this litigation followed. We understand the above factual summary corresponds substantially with the factual basis for determination formulated by the Court of Appeals of New York. From those circumstances it seems clear that the Russian Orthodox Church was, until the Russian Revolution, an hierarchical church with unquestioned paramount jurisdiction in the governing body in Russia over the American Metropolitanate. Nothing indicates that either the Sacred Synod or the succeeding Patriarchs relinquished that authority or recognized the autonomy of the American church. The Court of Appeals decision proceeds, we understand, upon the same assumption. 302 N.Y., at 5, 23, 24, 96 N.E. 2d, at 57, 68, 69. That court did consider "whether there exists in Moscow at the present time a true central organization of the Russian Orthodox Church capable of functioning as the head of a free international religious body." It concluded that this aspect of the controversy had not been sufficiently developed to justify a judgment upon that ground. 302 N.Y., at 22–24, 96 N.E. 2d, at 67–69.

The Religious Corporations Law.—The New York Court of Appeals depended for its judgment, refusing recognition to Archbishop Benjamin, the appointee of the Moscow Hierachy of the Russian Orthodox Church, upon Article 5-C of the Religious Corporations Law, quoted and analyzed at notes 2 and 3, *supra*.[10] Certainly a legislature is

---

[10] "The Court said, 302 N.Y. 1, 96 N.E. 2d 56:

"The Legislature has made a determination that the 'Russian Church in America' was the one which, to use our words in 249 New York at pages 77–78, was the trustee which 'may be relied upon to carry out more effectively and faithfully the purposes of this religious trust (*Carrier v. Carrier,* 226 N.Y. 114)' by reason of the changed situation of the patriarchate in Russia." 302 N.Y., at 30, 96 N.E. 2d, at 72.

"The courts have always recognized that it is the province of the Legislature to make the underlying findings of fact which give meaning and substance to its ultimate directives. The courts have traditionally refused to consider the wisdom or technical validity of such findings of fact, if there be some reasonable basis upon which they may rest." 302 N.Y., at 31, 96 N.E. 2d, at 72–73.

"The Legislature of the State of New York, like the Congress, must be deemed to have investigated the whole problem carefully before it acted. The Legislature knew that the central authorities of the Russian Orthodox Church in Russia had been suppressed after the 1917 revolution, and that the patriarchate was later resurrected by the Russian Government. The Legislature, like Congress, knew the character and method of operation of international communism and the Soviet attitude toward things religious. The Legislature was aware of the contemporary views of qualified observers who have visited Russia and who have had an opportunity to observe the present status of the patriarchate in the Soviet system. The Legislature realized that the North American church, in order to be free of Soviet interference in its affairs, had declared its temporary administrative autonomy in 1924, pursuant to the ukase of 1920, while retaining full *spiritual* communion with the patriarchate, and that there was a real danger that those properties and temporalities long enjoyed and used by the Russian Orthodox Church worshippers in this State would be taken from them by the representatives of the patriarchate. On the basis of these facts, and the facts stated (*supra*) and no doubt other facts we know not of, our Legislature concluded that the Moscow

free to act upon such information as it may have as to the necessity for legislation. But an enactment by a legislature cannot validate action which the Constitution prohibits, and we think that the statute here in question passes the constitutional limits. We conclude that Article 5-C undertook by its terms to transfer the control of the New York churches of the Russian Orthodox religion from the central governing hierarchy of the Russian Orthodox Church, the Patriarch of Moscow and the Holy Synod, to the governing authorities of the Russian Church in America, a church organization limited to the diocese of North America and the Aleutian Islands. This transfer takes place by virtue of the statute. Such a law violates the Fourteenth Amendment. It prohibits in this country the free exercise of religion. Legislation that regulates church administration, the operation of the churches, the appointment of clergy, by requiring conformity to church statutes "adopted at a general convention (sobor) held in the City of New York on or about or between October fifth to eighth, nineteen hundred thirty-seven, and any amendments thereto," note 3, *supra,* prohibits the free exercise of religion. Although this statute requires the New York churches to "in all other respects conform to, maintain and follow the faith, doctrine, ritual, communion, discipline, canon law, traditions and usages of the Eastern Confession (Eastern Orthodox or Greek Catholic Church)," their conformity is by legislative fiat and subject to legislative will. Should the state assert power to change the statute requiring conformity to ancient faith and doctrine to one establishing a different doctrine, the invalidity would be unmistakable.

. . .

[The Court then analyzed *Watson v. Jones* and concluded at 116:]

The opinion, however, radiates a spirit of freedom for religious organizations, an independence from secular control or manipulation—in short, power to decide for themselves, free from state interference, matters of church government as well as those of faith and doctrine. Freedom to select the clergy, where no improper methods of choice are proven, we think, must now be said to have federal constitutional protection as a part of the free exercise of religion against state interference.

. . .

Legislative Power.—The Court of Appeals of New York recognized, generally, the soundness of the philosophy of ecclesiastical control of church administration and polity but concluded that the exercise of that control was not free from legislative interference. That Court presented forcefully the argument supporting legislative power to act on its own knowledge of "the Soviet attitude toward things religious." 302 N.Y., at 32–33, 96 N.E. 2d, at 74. It was said:

"The Legislature realized that the North American church, in order to be free of Soviet interference in its affairs, had declared its temporary administrative autonomy in 1924, pursuant to the ukase of 1920, while retaining full *spiritual* communion with the patriarchate, and that there was a real danger that those properties and temporalities long enjoyed and used by the Russian Orthodox Church worshippers in this State would be taken from them by the representatives of the patriarchate." 302 N.Y., at 33, 96 N.E. 2d, at 74.

It was thought that *American Communications Assn. v. Douds,* 339 U.S. 382, supported the thesis that where there is some specific evil, found as a fact, "some infringement upon traditional liberties was justifiable" to effect a cure. 302 N.Y., at 31, 96 N.E. 2d, at 73. On that reasoning it was thought permissible, in view "of the changed situation of the patriarchate in Russia," to replace it with the Russian Church in America as the ruling authority over the administration of the church. The legal basis for this legislative substitution was found in the theory that the Russian Church in America

---

Patriarchate was no longer capable of functioning as a true religious body, but had become a tool of the Soviet Government primarily designed to implement its foreign policy. Whether we, as judges, would have reached the same conclusion is immaterial. It is sufficient that the Legislature reached it, after full consideration of all the facts." 302 N.Y., at 32–33, 96 N.E. 2d, at 73–74.

"was the trustee which 'may be relied upon to carry out more effectively and faithfully the purposes of this religious trust *(Carrier v. Carrier,* 226 N.Y. 114).'" 302 N.Y., at 30, 96 N.E. 2d, at 72. Mindful of the authority of the Court of Appeals in its interpretation of the powers of its own legislature and with respect for its standing and ability, we do not agree with its statement as to legislative power over religious organizations.
. . .

In upholding the validity of Article 5–C, the New York Court of Appeals apparently assumes Article 5–C does nothing more than permit the trustees of the Cathedral to use it for services consistent with the desires of the members of the Russian Church in America. Its reach goes far beyond that point. By fiat it displaces one church administrator with another. It passes the control of matters strictly ecclesiastical from one church authority to another. It thus intrudes for the benefit of one segment of a church the power of the state into the forbidden area of religious freedom contrary to the principles of the First Amendment. Such prohibition differs from the restriction of a right to deal with Government allowed in *Douds,* in that the Union in the *Douds* case had no such constitutionally protected right. New York's Article 5–C directly prohibits the free exercise of an ecclesiastical right, the Church's choice of its hierarchy.

We do not think that New York's legislative application of a *cy-pres* doctrine to this trust avoids the constitutional rule against prohibition of the free exercise of religion. *Late Corporation of Latter-Day Saints v. United States,* [*supra,* IX], relied upon by the appellee, does not support its argument. There the Church of Jesus Christ of Latter-Day Saints had been incorporated as a religious corporation by the State of Deseret, with subsequent confirmation by the Territory of Utah. Its property was held for religious and charitable purposes. That charter was revoked by Congress and some of the property of the church was escheated to the United States for the use of the common schools of Utah. This Court upheld the revocation of the charter, relying on the reserved power of the Congress over the acts of territories, 136 U.S., at 45–46. The seizure of the property was bottomed on the general rule that where a charitable corporation is dissolved for unlawful practices, *id.,* at 49–50, the sovereign takes and distributes the property according to the *cy-pres* doctrine to objects of charity and usefulness, *e.g.,* schools. *Id.,* at 47, 50–51. A failure of the charitable purpose could have the same effect. *Id.,* at 59. None of these elements exist to support the validity of the New York statute putting the Russian Orthodox churches of New York under the administration of the Russian Church in America. See notes 2 and 3, *supra.*

The record before us shows no schism over faith or doctrine between the Russian Church in America and the Russian Orthodox Church. It shows administrative control of the North American Diocese by the Supreme Church Authority of the Russian Orthodox Church, including the appointment of the ruling hierarch in North America from the foundation of the diocese until the Russian Revolution. We find nothing that indicates a relinquishment of this power by the Russian Orthodox Church.

Ours is a government which by the "law of its being" allows no statute, state or national, that prohibits the free exercise of religion. There are occasions when civil courts must draw lines between the responsibilities of church and state for the disposition or use of property. Even in those cases when the property right follows as an incident from decisions of the church custom or law on ecclesiastical issues, the church rule controls. This under our Constitution necessarily follows in order that there may be free exercise of religion.

The decision was reversed and the case remanded to the New York Court of Appeals. Justices Frankfurter and Black concurred in the result.

Justice Jackson, dissenting:
I shall not undertake to wallow through the complex, obscure and fragmentary details of secular and ecclesiastical history, theology, and canon law in which this case is

smothered. To me, whatever the canon law is found to be and whoever is the rightful head of the Moscow patriarchate, I do not think New York law must yield to the authority of a foreign and unfriendly state masquerading as a spiritual institution. (See "The Soviet Propaganda Program," Staff Study No. 3, Senate Subcommittee on Overseas Information Programs of the United States, 82d Cong., 2d Sess.)

I have supposed that a State of this Union was entirely free to make its own law, independently of any foreign-made law, except as the Full Faith and Credit Clause of the Constitution might require deference to the law of a sister state or the Supremacy Clause require submission to federal law. I do not see how one can spell out of the principles of separation of church and state a doctrine that a state submit property rights to settlement by canon law. If there is any relevant inference to be drawn, I should think it would be to the contrary, though I see no obstacle to the state allowing ecclesiastical law to govern in such a situation if it sees fit.

Sequels. Kedroff had both academic and judicial consequences. Mark Howe celebrated Justice Reed's recognition that the freedom of religious exercise could reside in a church as well as in an individual. Howe saw this "liberty of self-government" of a church as linked to the institutional pluralism recommended by John Neville Figgis, *see* Howe, "Foreword: Political Theory and the Nature of Liberty, The Supreme Court, 1952 Term," 67 *Harvard Law Review* 91–95 (1953). Howe made nothing of the anomaly that the church whose liberty was affirmed was the kind of church to which the New York courts now turned their attention.

The highest court of New York read *Kedroff* to leave open the question whether "the Patriarchate, though nominally re-established" could function "except as an arm or agent of an antireligious civil government," *St. Nicholas Cathedral v. Kedroff*, 306 N.Y. 38, 53, 114 N.E. 2d 197, 206, (1953). The case was remanded for trial. On appeal from a decision in favor of the Moscow Patriarchate, the Court of Appeals reviewed the evidence and held, 4–3, by Chief Judge Albert Conway, that the Moscow Patriarchate had ceased to exist by 1924 when the Detroit sobor took place; that, pursuant to Tikhon's grant of authority in 1920, the North American archdiocese had acted properly to protect the property held in trust for the Orthodox Church; that the present Moscow Patriarchate was a tool of the Soviet government; and that to permit the Moscow Patriarchate to exercise jurisdiction over St. Nicholas Cathedral would be a "perversion of the implied trust to which it was dedicated." The court further noted that the Moscow Patriarchate in biblical language had attacked the United States as "the fornicatrix of the resurrected Babylon," "the Washington Cain," and "the beast of the Apocalypse." The court saw its duty as protecting seizure of church property "by agents of a foreign atheistic State acting in the name and guise of a church administration they have infiltrated and subverted. What worse violation of the religious liberties of our people can be envisioned than to require that they subject themselves to the ecclesiastical rule of persons acting for a godless foreign regime as the price of continued use of their churches!" *St. Nicholas Cathedral v. Kreshik*, 7 N.Y. 2d 191, 196 N.Y.S. 2d 655, 164 N.E. 2d 687 (1959).

The Supreme Court, summarily and indeed almost contemptuously, reversed *per curiam*. The decision, the Court declared, "rests on the same premises which were found to have underlain the "enactment of the statute struck down in *Kedroff*." The Court cited *Shelley v. Kraemer, supra* this section, to indicate that it made no difference that the state action was by a court rather than the legislature. The ruling in *Kedroff* was "controlling," *Kreshik v. St. Nicholas Cathedral*, 363 U.S. 190 (1960).

Compare Romanian Orthodox Missionary Episcopate of America v. Trutza, 205 F. 2d 107 (6th Cir. 1953), *cert. denied*, 346 U.S. 915 (1953). In 1936 a council of the Romanian Orthodox Church enacted a statute providing that "the Holy Synod" in Bucharest was "the supreme authority" in the Church. In 1947, after the communists had taken over Romania, the Romanian Orthodox Missionary Episcopate of America voted to suspend the 1936 statute as it affected the Church in America. In 1951 it declared the Church in Romania to be "completely enslaved by the political rulers" and itself to be administratively and spiritually autonomous. The court, per Judge Florence Allen, refused to give a bishop named by the church in Romania the property claimed by the now-autonomous American church. Judge Allen wrote: "We also think that this conclusion is in accord with the spirit, if not with the letter, of the *Kedroff* case, which declares that 'Freedom to select the clergy, where no improper methods of choice are proven . . . must now be said to have federal constitutional protection as a part of the free exercise of religion against state interference.' Since this is true as to protection against the interference of an individual American state, we think it should be equally true as to protection against the domination and interference of a foreign state."

Query. Can this case be reconciled with *Kreshik?* If the Nazis had taken over the Vatican, killed the pope, and arranged the election of a new pope, would the *Kreshik* court have turned over Catholic churches in the United States to his nominees?

Presbyterian Church in the United States v. Mary Elizabeth Blue Hull Memorial Presbyterian Church
393 U.S. 440 (1969)

Charles L. Gowen argued the cause for petitioners. With him on the brief were *Robert B. Troutman* and *Frank S. Cheatham, Jr.*

Owen H. Page argued the cause for respondents and filed a brief for respondents Eastern Heights Presbyterian Church et al. *Richard T. Cowan, Frank B. Zeigler,* and *James Edward McAleer* filed a brief for respondent Mary Elizabeth Blue Hull Memorial Presbyterian Church.

Briefs of *amici curiae,* urging reversal, were filed by *George Wilson McKeag* for Thompson, Stated Clerk of the General Assembly of the United Presbyterian Church in the United States et al., and by *Jackson A. Dykman* and *Harry G. Hill, Jr.,* for the Right Rev. John E. Hines, Presiding Bishop of the Protestant Episcopal Church in the United States.

Briefs of *amici curiae,* urging affirmance, were filed by *William J. McLeod, Jr.,* and *W.J. Williamson, pro se,* for Williamson, Secretary of Concerned Presbyterians, Inc., and by *Alfred J. Schweppe* for Laurelhurst United Presbyterian Church, Inc., et al.

Justice Brennan delivered the opinion of the Court.

This is a church property dispute which arose when two local churches withdrew from a hierarchical general church organization. Under Georgia law the right to the property previously used by the local churches was made to turn on a civil court jury decision as to whether the general church abandoned or departed from the tenets of faith and practice it held at the time the local churches affiliated with it. The question presented is whether the restraints of the First Amendment, as applied to the States through the Fourteenth Amendment, permit a civil court to award church property on the basis of the interpretation and significance the civil court assigns to aspects of church doctrine.

Petitioner, Presbyterian Church in the United States, is an association of local Presbyterian churches governed by a hierarchical structure of tribunals which consists of, in ascending order, (1) the Church Session, composed of the elders of the local church; (2) the Presbytery, composed of several churches in a geographical area; (3) the Synod, generally composed of all Presbyteries within a State; and (4) the General Assembly, the highest governing body.

A dispute arose between petitioner, the general church, and two local churches in Savannah, Georgia—the respondents, Hull Memorial Presbyterian Church and Eastern

Heights Presbyterian Church—over control of the properties used until then by the local churches. In 1966, the membership of the local churches, in the belief that certain actions and pronouncements of the general church were violations of that organization's constitution and departures from the doctrine and practice in force at the time of affiliation,[1] voted to withdraw from the general church and to reconstitute the local churches as an autonomous Presbyterian organization. The ministers of the two churches renounced the general church's jurisdiction and authority over them, as did all but two of the ruling elders. In response, the general church, through the Presbytery of Savannah, established an Administrative Commission to seek a conciliation. The dissident local churchmen remained steadfast; consequently, the Commission acknowledged the withdrawal of the local leadership and proceeded to take over the local churches' property on behalf of the general church until new local leadership could be appointed.

The local churchmen made no effort to appeal the Commission's action to higher church tribunals—the Synod of Georgia or the General Assembly. Instead, the churches filed separate suits in the Superior Court of Chatham County to enjoin the general church from trespassing on the disputed property, title to which was in the local churches. The cases were consolidated for trial. The general church moved to dismiss the actions and cross-claimed for injunctive relief in its own behalf on the ground that civil courts were without power to determine whether the general church had departed from its tenets of faith and practice. The motion to dismiss was denied, and the case was submitted to the jury on the theory that Georgia law implies a trust of local church property for the benefit of the general church on the sole condition that the general church adhere to its tenets of faith and practice existing at the time of affiliation by the local churches.[2] Thus, the jury was instructed to determine whether the actions of the general church "amount to a fundamental or substantial abandonment of the original tenets and doctrines of the [general church], so that the new tenets and doctrines are utterly variant from the purposes for which the [general church] was founded." The jury returned a verdict for the local churches, and the trial judge thereupon declared that the implied trust had terminated and enjoined the general church from interfering with the use of the property in question. The Supreme Court of Georgia affirmed, 224 Ga. 61, 159 S. E. 2d 690 (1968). We granted certiorari to consider the First Amendment questions raised. 392 U. S. 903 (1968). We reverse . . .

[T]he First Amendment severely circumscribes the role that civil courts may play in resolving church property disputes. It is obvious, however, that not every civil court decision as to property claimed by a religious organization jeopardizes values protected by the First Amendment. Civil courts do not inhibit free exercise of religion merely

---

[1] The opinion of the Supreme Court of Georgia summarizes the claimed violations and departures from petitioner's original tenets of faith and practice as including the following: "ordaining of women as ministers and ruling elders, making pronouncements and recommendations concerning civil, economic, social and political matters, giving support to the removal of Bible reading and prayers by children in the public schools, adopting certain Sunday School literature and teaching neo-orthodoxy alien to the Confession of Faith and Catechisms, as originally adopted by the general church, and causing all members to remain in the National Council of Churches of Christ and willingly accepting its leadership which advocated named practices, such as the subverting of parental authority, civil disobedience and intermeddling in civil affairs"; also "that the general church has . . . made pronouncements in matters involving international issues such as the Vietnam conflict and has disseminated publications denying the Holy Trinity and violating the moral and ethical standards of the faith." 224 Ga. 61, 62–63, 159 S. E. 2d 690, 692 (1968).

[2] This theory derives from principles fashioned by English courts. See. *e.g., Craigdallie v. Aikman,* 1 Dow 1, 3 Eng. Rep. 601 (II. L. 1813) (Scot.); *Attorney General ex rel. Mander v. Pearson,* 3 Mer. 353, 36 Eng. Rep. 135 (Ch. 1817). For the subsequent development of the implied trust theory in English courts, see Note, Judicial Intervention in Disputes Over the Use of Church Property, 75 Harv. L. Rev. 1142, 1148–1149 (1962).

by opening their doors to disputes involving church property. And there are neutral principles of law, developed for use in all property disputes, which can be applied without "establishing" churches to which property is awarded. But First Amendment values are plainly jeopardized when church property litigation is made to turn on the resolution by civil courts of controversies over religious doctrine and practice. If civil courts undertake to resolve such controversies in order to adjudicate the property dispute, the hazards are ever present of inhibiting the free development of religious doctrine and of implicating secular interests in matters of purely ecclesiastical concern. Because of these hazards, the First Amendment enjoins the employment of organs of government for essentially religious purposes, *Abington School District v. Schempp* [*infra*, XIV, 2]: the Amendment therefore commands civil courts to decide church property disputes without resolving underlying controversies over religious doctrine. Hence, States, religious organizations, and individuals must structure relationships involving church property so as not to require the civil courts to resolve ecclesiastical questions.

The Georgia courts have violated the command of the First Amendment. The departure-from-doctrine element of the implied trust theory which they applied requires the civil judiciary to determine whether actions of the general church constitute such a "substantial departure" from the tenets of faith and practice existing at the time of the local churches' affiliation that the trust in favor of the general church must be declared to have terminated. This determination has two parts. The civil court must first decide whether the challenged actions of the general church depart substantially from prior doctrine. In reaching such a decision, the court must of necessity make its own interpretation of the meaning of church doctrines. If the court should decide that a substantial departure has occurred, it must then go on to determine whether the issue on which the general church has departed holds a place of such importance in the traditional theology as to require that the trust be terminated. A civil court can make this determination only after assessing the relative significance to the religion of the tenets from which departure was found. Thus, the departure-from-doctrine element of the Georgia implied trust theory requires the civil court to determine matters at the very core of a religion—the interpretation of particular church doctrines and the importance of those doctrines to the religion. Plainly, the First Amendment forbids civil courts from playing such a role.

Since the Georgia courts on remand may undertake to determine whether petitioner is entitled to relief on its cross-claims, we find it appropriate to remark that the departure-from-doctrine element of Georgia's implied trust theory can play *no* role in any future judicial proceedings. The departure-from-doctrine approach is not susceptible of the marginal judicial involvement contemplated in *Gonzalez. Gonzalez'* rights under a will turned on a church decision, the Archbishop's, as to church law, the qualifications for the chaplaincy. It was the archbishopric, not the civil courts, which had the task of analyzing and interpreting church law in order to determine the validity of Gonzalez' claim to a chaplaincy. Thus, the civil courts could adjudicate the rights under the will without interpreting or weighing church doctrine but simply by engaging in the narrowest kind of review of a specific church decision—*i.e.,* whether that decision resulted from fraud, collusion, or arbitrariness. Such review does not inject the civil courts into substantive ecclesiastical matters. In contrast, under Georgia's departure-from-doctrine approach, it is not possible for the civil courts to play so limited a role. Under this approach, property rights do not turn on a church decision as to church doctrine. The standard of departure-from-doctrine, though it calls for resolution of ecclesiastical questions, is a creation of state, not church, law. Nothing in the record suggests that this state standard has been interpreted and applied in a decision of the general church. Any decisions which have been made by the general church about the local churches' withdrawal have at most a tangential relationship to the state-fashioned departure-from-doctrine standard. A determination whether such decisions are fraudulent, collusive, or arbitrary would therefore not answer the questions posed by the state standard. To reach those questions would require the civil courts to engage in the forbidden process of interpreting and weighing church doctrine. Even if the general church had attempted to apply the state standard, the civil courts could not review and enforce the church decision without violating the Constitution. The First Amendment prohibits a State from employing religious organizations as an arm of the civil judiciary to perform the function of interpreting and applying state standards. See *Abington School District v. Schempp.* Thus, a civil court may no more review *a* church decision applying a state departure-from-doctrine standard than it may apply that standard itself.

The judgment of the Supreme Court of Georgia is reversed, and the case is remanded for further proceedings not inconsistent with this opinion.

It is so ordered.

Justice Harlan, concurring.

I am in entire agreement with the Court's rejection of the "departure-from-doctrine" approach taken by the Georgia courts, as that approach necessarily requires the civilian courts to weigh the significance and the meaning of disputed religious doctrine. I do not, however, read the Court's opinion to go further to hold that the Fourteenth Amendment forbids civilian courts from enforcing a deed or will which expressly and clearly lays down conditions limiting a religious organization's use of the property which is granted. If, for example, the donor expressly gives his church some money on the condition that the church never ordain a woman as a minister or elder, see *ante,* at 442, n. 1, or never amend certain specified articles of the Confession of Faith, he is entitled to his money back if the condition is not fulfilled. In such a case, the church should not be permitted to keep the property simply because church authorities have determined that the doctrinal innovation is justified by the faith's basic principles. Cf. *Watson v. Jones* [*supra*, VIII, 5].

On this understanding, I join the Court's opinion.

Maryland and Virginia Eldership of the Churches of God v. Church of God at Sharpsburg, Inc.
396 U.S. 367 (1970)

Alfred L. Scanlan, James H. Booser, and *Charles O. Fisher* for appellants. *Arthur G. Lambert* for appellees.

Per Curiam.

In resolving a church property dispute between appellants, representing the General Eldership, and appellees, two secessionist congregations, the Maryland Court of Appeals relied upon provisions of state statutory law governing the holding of property by religious corporations, upon language in the deeds conveying the properties in question to the local church corporations, upon the terms of the charters of the corporations, and upon provisions in the constitution of the General Eldership pertinent to the ownership and control of church property. 254 Md. 162, 254 A. 2d 162 (1969). Appellants argue primarily that the statute, as applied, deprived the General Eldership of property in violation of the First Amendment. Since, however, the Maryland court's resolution of the dispute involved no inquiry into religious doctrine, appellees' motion to dismiss is granted, and the appeal is dismissed for want of a substantial federal question.

It is so ordered.

Justice Brennan, with whom Justice Douglas and Justice Marshall join, concurring.

I join the *per curiam* but add these comments. We held in *Presbyterian Church in the United States v. Mary Elizabeth Blue Hull Memorial Presbyterian Church,* [*supra*], that "First Amendment values are plainly jeopardized when church property litigation is made to turn on the resolution by civil courts of controversies over religious doctrine and practice. If civil courts undertake to resolve such controversies in order to adjudicate the property dispute, the hazards are ever present of inhibiting the free development of religious doctrine and of implicating secular interests in matters of purely ecclesiastical concern. . . . [T]he [First] Amendment therefore commands civil courts to decide church property disputes without resolving underlying controversies over religious doctrine." It follows that a State may adopt *any* one of various approaches for settling church property disputes so long as it involves no consideration of doctrinal matters, whether the ritual and liturgy of worship or the tenets of faith.

Thus the States may adopt the approach of *Watson v. Jones,* [*supra,* VIII, 5], and enforce the property decisions made within a church of congregational polity "by a majority of its members or by such other local organism as it may have instituted for the purpose of ecclesiastical government," *id.,* at 724, and within a church of hierarchical polity by the highest authority that has ruled on the dispute at issue,[1] unless "express terms" in the "instrument by which the property is held" condition the property's use or control in a specified manner.[2] Under *Watson* civil courts do not inquire whether the relevant church governing body has power under religious law to control the property in question. Such a determination, unlike the identification of the governing body, frequently necessitates the interpretation of ambiguous religious law and usage. To permit civil courts to probe deeply enough into the allocation of power within a church so as to decide where religious law places control over the use of church property would violate the First Amendment in much the same manner as civil determination of religious doctrine.[3] Similarly, where the identity of the governing body or bodies that exercise general authority within a church is a matter of substantial controversy, civil courts are not to make the inquiry into religious law and usage that would be essential to the resolution of the controversy. In other words, the use of the *Watson* approach is consonant with the prohibitions of the First Amendment only if the appropriate church governing body can be determined without the resolution of doctrinal questions and without extensive inquiry into religious polity.

"[N]eutral principles of law, developed for use in all property disputes," *Presbyterian Church, supra,* at 449, provide another means for resolving litigation over religious property. Under the "formal title" doctrine, civil courts can determine ownership by studying deeds, reverter clauses, and general state corporation laws. Again, however, general principles of property law may not be relied upon if their application requires civil courts to resolve doctrinal issues. For example, provisions in deeds or in a denomination's constitution for the reversion of local church property to the general church, if conditioned upon a finding of departure from doctrine, could not be civilly enforced.[4]

---

[1] Under the *Watson* definition, *supra,* at 722–723, congregational polity exists when "a religious congregation . . . , by the nature of its organization, is strictly independent of other ecclesiastical associations, and so far as church government is concerned, owes no fealty or obligation to any higher authority." Hierarchical polity, on the other hand, exists when "the religious congregation . . . is but a subordinate member of some general church organization in which there are superior ecclesiastical tribunals with a general and ultimate power of control more or less complete, in some supreme judicatory over the whole membership of that general organization."

[2] *Id.,* at 722. Except that "express terms" cannot be enforced if enforcement is constitutionally impermissible under *Presbyterian Church.* Any language in *Watson, supra,* at 722–723, that may be read to the contrary must be disapproved. Only express conditions that may be effected without consideration of doctrine are civilly enforceable.

[3] Except that civil tribunals may examine church rulings alleged to be the product of "fraud, collusion, or arbitrariness." *Gonzalez v. Roman Catholic Archbishop* [X, 9] (1929).

[4] Thus a State that normally resolves disputes over religious property by applying general principles of property law would have to use a different method in cases involving such provisions, perhaps that defined in *Watson.* By the same token, States following the *Watson* approach would have to

A third possible approach is the passage of special statutes governing church property arrangements in a manner that precludes state interference in doctrine. Such statutes must be carefully drawn to leave control of ecclesiastical polity, as well as doctrine, to church governing bodies.[5] *Kedroff v. St. Nicholas Cathedral* [*supra*].

NOTE. *Serbian Schism.* Serbian Orthodox in the United States were originally a mission within the Russian Orthodox Church, Pospielovsky 2, 281. After the Russian Revolution, the Serbs set up a Serbian Orthodox Church with a patriarch in Belgrade, ruling all the Orthodox in the new state of Yugoslavia. In 1921 the governing body of this new church, the Holy Council of Bishops, set up a diocese in North America. The Constitution of the Church provided that the diocese stand "under the jurisdiction of the Serbian Orthodox Church in spiritual and hierarchical respects." The constitution of the diocese stated that it enjoyed full administrative freedom while belonging "canonically" to the Serbian Orthodox Church, *see* Djuro J. Vrga and Frank J. Fahey, *Changes and Socio-Religious Conflict in an Ethnic Minority Group: The Serbian Orthodox Church in America* (1975), 29.

In 1963, Dionysius, the bishop of the diocese in North America, was suspended by the authorities of the church in Yugoslavia. He declared, "I do not recognize this communist decision from Belgrade." An assembly of the American and Canadian diocese then called for "the cancellation of canonical hierarchical unity with the Mother Church in the Fatherland and the maintenance of only a spiritual unity of prayer," *ibid.* at 30–31. The members of the diocese divided. Over two-thirds of the old immigrants favored canonical unity with the Mother Church and over two-thirds of the post-World War II immigrants, deeply distrustful of the modern Yugoslav state, wanted the break, *ibid.* at 36. Litigation in Illinois finally led to the Supreme Court.

Serbian Eastern Orthodox Diocese for the United States of America and Canada v. Milivojevich
426 U.S. 696 (1976)

Albert E. Jenner, Jr., argued the cause for petitioners. With him on the briefs were *Keith F. Bode, Robert L. Graham, Thomas J. Karacic,* and *Henry D. Fisher.*

Leo J. Sullivan III argued the cause for respondents. With him on the brief were *Richard J. Smith* and *Jerome H. Torshen.*

Justice Brennan delivered the opinion of the Court.

In 1963, the Holy Assembly of Bishops and the Holy Synod of the Serbian Orthodox Church (Mother Church) suspended and ultimately removed respondent Dionisije Milivojevich (Dionisije) as Bishop of the American-Canadian Diocese of that Church, and appointed petitioner Bishop Firmilian Ocokoljich (Firmilian) as Administrator of the Diocese, which the Mother Church then reorganized into three Dioceses. In 1964 the Holy Assembly and Holy Synod defrocked Dionisije as a Bishop and cleric of the Mother Church. In this civil action brought by Dionisije and the other respondents in Illinois Circuit Court, the Supreme Court of Illinois held that the proceedings of the Mother Church respecting Dionisije were procedurally and substantively defective under the internal regulations of the Mother Church and were therefore arbitrary and invalid.

---

find another ground for decision, perhaps the application of general property law, when identification of the relevant church governing body is impossible without immersion in doctrinal issues or extensive inquiry into church polity.

[5] See, *e.g., Goodson v. Northside Bible Church,* 261 F.Supp. 99 (D.C.S.D. Ala. 1966), aff'd, 387 F. 2d 534 (C. A. 5th Cir. 1967).

The State Supreme Court also invalidated the Diocesan reorganization into three Dioceses. 60 Ill. 2d 477, 328 N. E. 2d 268 (1975). We granted certiorari to determine whether the actions of the Illinois Supreme Court constituted improper judicial interference with decisions of the highest authorities of a hierarchical church in violation of the First and Fourteenth Amendments. 423 U. S. 911 (1975). We hold that the inquiries made by the Illinois Supreme Court into matters of ecclesiastical cognizance and polity and the court's actions pursuant thereto contravened the First and Fourteenth Amendments. We therefore reverse.

. . .

The conclusion of the Illinois Supreme Court that the decisions of the Mother Church were "arbitrary" was grounded upon an inquiry that persuaded the Illinois Supreme Court that the Mother Church had not followed its own laws and procedures in arriving at those decisions. We have concluded that whether or not there is room for "marginal civil court review" under the narrow rubrics of "fraud" or "collusion" when church tribunals act in bad faith for secular purposes, no "arbitrariness" exception—in the sense of an inquiry whether the decisions of the highest ecclesiastical tribunal of a hierarchical church complied with church laws and regulations—is consistent with the constitutional mandate that civil courts are bound to accept the decisions of the highest judicatories of a religious organization of hierarchical polity on matters of discipline, faith, internal organization, or ecclesiastical rule, custom, or law. For civil courts to analyze whether the ecclesiastical actions of a church judicatory are in that sense "arbitrary" must inherently entail inquiry into the procedures that canon or ecclesiastical law supposedly requires the church judicatory to follow, or else into the substantive criteria by which they are supposedly to decide the ecclesiastical question. But this is exactly the inquiry that the First Amendment prohibits; recognition of such an exception would undermine the general rule that religious controversies are not the proper subject of civil court inquiry, and that a civil court must accept the ecclesiastical decisions of church tribunals as it finds them. *Watson* itself [*supra,* VIII, 5] requires our conclusion in its rejection of the analogous argument that ecclesiastical decisions of the highest church judicatories need only be accepted if the subject matter of the dispute is within their "jurisdiction." . . .

Indeed, it is the essence of religious faith that ecclesiastical decisions are reached and are to be accepted as matters of faith whether or not rational or measurable by objective criteria. Constitutional concepts of due process, involving secular notions of "fundamental fairness" or impermissible objectives, are therefore hardly relevant to such matters of ecclesiastical cognizance.

The constitutional evils that attend upon any "arbitrariness" exception in the sense applied by the Illinois Supreme Court to justify civil court review of ecclesiastical decisions of final church tribunals are manifest in the instant case. The Supreme Court of Illinois recognized that all parties agree that the Serbian Orthodox Church is a hierarchical church, and that the sole power to appoint and remove Bishops of the Church resides in its highest ranking organs, the Holy Assembly and the Holy Synod.[9]

---

[9] "Plaintiffs argue and defendant Bishop Dionisije does not dispute that the Serbian Orthodox Church is a hierarchical and episcopal church. Moreover, the parties agree that in cases involving hierarchical churches the decisions of the proper church tribunals on questions of discipline, faith or ecclesiastical rule, though affecting civil rights, are accepted as conclusive in disputes before the civil courts. . . . All parties maintain that the sole limitation on this rule, when civil courts may entertain the 'narrowest kind of review,' occurs when the decision of the church tribunal is claimed to have resulted from fraud, collusion or arbitrariness." 60 Ill. 2d 477, 501, 328 N.E. 2d 268, 280 (1975).

Respondents conceded as much at oral argument. Tr. of Oral Arg. 24–25, 39–40. The hierarchical nature of the relationship between the American-Canadian Diocese and the Mother Church is confirmed by the fact that respondent corporations were organized under the provisions of the Illinois Religious Corporations Act governing the incorporation of religious societies that are

Indeed, final authority with respect to the promulgation and interpretation of *all* matters of church discipline and internal organization rests with the Holy Assembly, and even the written constitution of the Mother Church expressly provides:

"The Holy Assembly of Bishops, as the highest hierarchical body, is legislative authority in the matters of faith, officiation, church order (discipline) and internal organization of the Church, as well as the highest church juridical authority within its jurisdiction (Article 69 sec. 28)." Art. 57.

"All the decisions of the Holy Assembly of Bishops and of the Holy Synod of Bishops of canonical and church nature, in regard to faith, officiation, church order and internal organization of the church, are valid and final." Art. 64.

"The Holy Assembly of Bishops, whose purpose is noted in Article 57 of this Constitution:

"9) interprets canonical-ecclesiastical rules, those which are general and obligatory, and particular ones, and publishes their collections;

"12) prescribes the ecclesiastical-judicial procedure for all Ecclesiastical Courts;

"26) settles disputes of jurisdiction between hierarchical and church-self governing organs;

"27) ADJUDGES:

"A) In first and in final instances:

"a) disagreements between bishops and the Holy Synod, and between the bishops and the Patriarch;

"b) canonical offenses of the Patriarch;

"B) In the second and final instance:

"All matters which the Holy Synod of Bishops judged in the first instance." Art. 69.

Nor is there any dispute that questions of church discipline and the composition of the church hierarchy are at the core of ecclesiastical concern; the bishop of a church is clearly one of the central figures in such a hierarchy and the embodiment of the church within his Diocese, and the Mother Church constitution states that "[h]e is, according to the church canonical regulations, chief representative and guiding leader of all church spiritual life and church order in the diocese." Art. 13.

. . .

Similar considerations inform our resolution of the second question we must address— the constitutionality of the Supreme Court of Illinois' holding that the Mother Church's reorganization of the American-Canadian Diocese into three Dioceses was invalid because it was " 'in clear and palpable excess of its own jurisdiction.' " Essentially, the court premised this determination on its view that the early history of the Diocese "manifested

---

subordinate parts of larger church organizations. Similarly, the Diocese's subordinate nature was manifested in resolutions of the Diocese which Dionisije supported, and by Dionisije's submission of corporate bylaws, proposed constitutional changes, and final judgments of the Diocesan Ecclesiastical Court to the Holy Synod or Holy Assembly for approval. Moreover, when Dionisije was originally elevated to Bishop, he signed an Episcopal-Hierarchical Oath by which he swore that he would "always be obedient to the Most Holy Assembly" and:

"Should I transgress against whatever I promised here, or should I be disobedient to the Divine Ordinances and Order of the Eastern Orthodox Church, or to the Most Holy Assembly (of Bishops) I, personally, will become a schismatic and should I make the Diocese entrusted to me in any manner to become disobedient to the Most Holy Assembly (of Bishops), may I, in that case, be defrocked of my rank and divested of the (episcopal) authority without any excuse or gainsay, and (may I) become an alien to the heavenly gift which is being given unto me by the Holy Spirit through the Consecration of the Laying of Hands." App. 1088.

Finally, the hierarchical relationship was confirmed by provisions in the constitutions of both the Diocese and the Mother Church.

a clear intention to retain independence and autonomy in its administrative affairs while at the same time becoming ecclesiastically and judicially an organic part of the Serbian Orthodox Church," and its interpretation of the constitution of the American-Canadian Diocese as confirming this intention. It also interpreted the constitution of the Serbian Orthodox Church, which was adopted after the Diocesan constitution, in a manner consistent with this conclusion. 60 Ill. 2d, at 506–507, 328 N. E. 2d, at 283–284.

This conclusion was not, however, explicitly based on the "fraud, collusion, or arbitrariness" exception. Rather, the Illinois Supreme Court relied on purported "neutral principles" for resolving property disputes which would "not in any way entangle this court in the determination of theological or doctrinal matters." *Id.,* at 505, 328 N. E. 2d, at 282. Nevertheless the Supreme Court of Illinois substituted its interpretation of the Diocesan and Mother Church constitutions for that of the highest ecclesiastical tribunals in which church law vests authority to make that interpretation. This the First and Fourteenth Amendments forbid.

Reversed.

Chief Justice Burger and Justice White concurred in the judgment.

Justice Rehnquist, with whom Justice Stevens joins, dissenting.

The Court's opinion, while long on the ecclesiastical history of the Serbian Orthodox Church, is somewhat short on the procedural history of this case. A casual reader of some of the passages in the Court's opinion could easily gain the impression that the State of Illinois had commenced a proceeding designed to brand Bishop Dionisije as a heretic, with appropriate pains and penalties. But the state trial judge in the Circuit Court of Lake County was not the Bishop of Beauvais, trying Joan of Arc for heresy; the jurisdiction of his court was invoked by petitioners themselves, who sought an injunction establishing their control over property of the American-Canadian Diocese of the church located in Lake County.

The jurisdiction of that court having been invoked for such a purpose by both petitioners and respondents, contesting claimants to Diocesan authority, it was entitled to ask if the real Bishop of the American-Canadian Diocese would please stand up. The protracted proceedings in the Illinois courts were devoted to the ascertainment of who that individual was, a question which the Illinois courts sought to answer by application of the canon law of the church, just as they would have attempted to decide a similar dispute among the members of any other voluntary association. The Illinois courts did not in the remotest sense inject their doctrinal preference into the dispute. They were forced to decide between two competing sets of claimants to church office in order that they might resolve a dispute over real property located within the State. Each of the claimants had requested them to decide the issue. Unless the First Amendment requires control of disputed church property to be awarded solely on the basis of ecclesiastical paper title, I can find no constitutional infirmity in the judgment of the Supreme Court of Illinois.

Unless civil courts are to be wholly divested of authority to resolve conflicting claims to real property owned by a hierarchical church, and such claims are to be resolved by brute force, civil courts must of necessity make some factual inquiry even under the rules the Court purports to apply in this case. We are told that "a civil court must accept the ecclesiastical decisions of church tribunals as it finds them," *ante,* at 713. But even this rule requires that proof be made as to what these decisions are, and if proofs on that issue conflict the civil court will inevitably have to choose one over the other. In so choosing, if the choice is to be a rational one, reasons must be adduced as to why one proffered decision is to prevail over another. Such reasons will obviously be based on the canon law by which the disputants have agreed to bind themselves, but they must also represent a preference for one view of that law over another.

If civil courts, consistently with the First Amendment, may do that much, the question arises why they may not do what the Illinois courts did here regarding the defrockment of Bishop Dionisije, and conclude, on the basis of testimony from experts on the canon law at issue, that the decision of the religious tribunal involved was rendered in violation of its own stated rules of procedure. Suppose the Holy Assembly in this case had a membership of 100; its rules provided that a bishop could be defrocked by a majority vote of any session at which a quorum was present, and also provided that a quorum was not to be less than 40. Would a decision of the Holy Assembly attended by 30 members, 16 of whom voted to defrock Bishop Dionisije, be binding on civil courts in a dispute such as this? The hypothetical example is a clearer case than the one involved here, but the principle is the same. If the civil courts are to be bound by any sheet of parchment bearing the ecclesiastical seal and purporting to be a decree of a church court, they can easily be converted into handmaidens of arbitrary lawlessness.

Query. If the Orthodox in America could not break from the Russian Orthodox Church and be recognized by an American court (*Kedroff, supra*), how can an American court recognize the Serbian Orthodox Church which has no higher pedigree? Are both *Kedroff* and *Milivojevich* cases putting "paper title" above religious realities?

Jones v. Wolf
443 U.S. 595 (1979)

E. Barrett Prettyman, Jr., argued the cause for petitioners. With him on the briefs were *Allen R. Snyder, Walter A. Smith, Jr., John B. Harris, Jr., T. Reese Watkins,* and *H. T. O'Neal, Jr.*

Frank C. Jones argued the cause for respondents. With him on the brief were *Wallace Miller, Jr., W. Warren Plowden, Jr.,* and *Edward S. Sell, Jr.*

Briefs of *amici curiae* urging reversal were filed by *Samuel W. Witwer, Sr.,* and *Samuel W. Witwer, Jr.,* for the General Council on Finance and Administration of the United Methodist Church; by *J. D. Todd, Jr.,* and *David A. Quattlebaum III* for the Presbyterian Church in the United States; and by *George Wilson McKeag* and *Gregory M. Harvey* for William P. Thompson et al.

George E. Reed and *Patrick F. Geary* filed a brief for the United States Catholic Conference as *amicus curiae.*

Justice Blackmun delivered the opinion of the Court.

This case involves a dispute over the ownership of church property following a schism in a local church affiliated with a hierarchical church organization. The question for decision is whether civil courts, consistent with the First and Fourteenth Amendments to the Constitution, may resolve the dispute on the basis of "neutral principles of law," or whether they must defer to the resolution of an authoritative tribunal of the hierarchical church.

I

The Vineville Presbyterian Church of Macon, Ga., was organized in 1904, and first incorporated in 1915. Its corporate charter lapsed in 1935, but was revived and renewed in 1939, and continues in effect at the present time.

The property at issue and on which the church is located was acquired in three transactions, and is evidenced by conveyances to the "Trustees of [or 'for'] Vineville Presbyterian Church and their successors in office," App. 251, 253, or simply to the "Vineville Presbyterian Church." *Id.,* at 249. The funds used to acquire the property were contributed entirely by local church members. Pursuant to resolutions adopted by the congregation, the church repeatedly has borrowed money on the property. This indebtedness is evidenced by security deeds variously issued in the name of the "Trustees of the Vineville Presbyterian Church," *e.g., id.,* at 278, or, again, simply the "Vineville Presbyterian Church." *Id.,* at 299.

In the same year it was organized, the Vineville church was established as a member church of the Augusta-Macon Presbytery of the Presbyterian Church in the United States (PCUS). The PCUS has a generally hierarchical or connectional form of government, as contrasted with a congregational form. Under the polity of the PCUS, the government of the local church is committed to its Session in the first instance, but the actions of this assembly or "court" are subject to the review and control of the higher church courts, the Presbytery, Synod, and General Assembly, respectively. The powers and duties of each level of the hierarchy are set forth in the constitution of the PCUS, the Book of Church Order, which is part of the record in the present case.

On May 27, 1973, at a congregational meeting of the Vineville church attended by a quorum of its duly enrolled members, 164 of them, including the pastor, voted to separate from the PCUS. Ninety-four members opposed the resolution. The majority immediately informed the PCUS of the action, and then united with another denomination, the Presbyterian Church in America. Although the minority remained on the church rolls for three years, they ceased to participate in the affairs of the Vineville church and conducted their religious activities elsewhere.

In response to the schism within the Vineville congregation, the Augusta-Macon Presbytery appointed a commission to investigate the dispute and, if possible, to resolve it. The commission eventually issued a written ruling declaring that the minority faction constituted "the true congregation of Vineville Presbyterian Church," and withdrawing from the majority faction "all authority to exercise office derived from the [PCUS]." App. 235. The majority took no part in the commission's inquiry, and did not appeal its ruling to a higher PCUS tribunal.

Representatives of the minority faction sought relief in federal court, but their complaint was dismissed for want of jurisdiction. *Lucas v. Hope,* 515 F. 2d 234 (CA5 1975), cert. denied, 424 U. S. 967 (1976). They then brought this class action in state court, seeking declaratory and injunctive orders establishing their right to exclusive possession and use of the Vineville church property as a member congregation of the PCUS. The trial court, purporting to apply Georgia's "neutral principles of law" approach to church property disputes, granted judgment for the majority. The Supreme Court of Georgia, holding that the trial court had correctly stated and applied Georgia law, and rejecting the minority's challenge based on the First and Fourteenth Amendments, affirmed. 241 Ga. 208, 243 S.E. 2d 860 (1978). We granted certiorari. 439 U.S. 891 (1978).

. . .

The primary advantages of the neutral-principles approach are that it is completely secular in operation, and yet flexible enough to accommodate all forms of religious organization and polity. The method relies exclusively on objective, well-established concepts of trust and property law familiar to lawyers and judges. It thereby promises to free civil courts completely from entanglement in questions of religious doctrine, polity, and practice. Furthermore, the neutral-principles analysis shares the peculiar genius of private-law systems in general—flexibility in ordering private rights and obligations to reflect the intentions of the parties. Through appropriate reversionary clauses and trust provisions, religious societies can specify what is to happen to church property in the event of a particular contingency, or what religious body will determine the ownership in the event of a schism or doctrinal controversy. In this manner, a religious organization can ensure that a dispute over the ownership of church property will be resolved in accord with the desires of the members.

This is not to say that the application of the neutral-principles approach is wholly free of difficulty. The neutral-principles method, at least as it has evolved in Georgia, requires a civil court to examine certain religious documents, such as a church constitution, for language of trust in favor of the general church. In undertaking such an examination, a civil court must take special care to scrutinize the document in purely secular terms, and not to rely on religious precepts in determining whether the document indicates that the parties have intended to create a trust. In addition, there may be cases where the deed, the corporate charter, or the constitution of the general church incorporates religious concepts in the provisions relating to the ownership of property. If in such a case the interpretation of the instruments of ownership would require the civil court to resolve a religious controversy, then the court must defer to the resolution of the doctrinal issue by the authoritative ecclesiastical body. *Serbian Orthodox Diocese,* [*supra,* this section].

On balance, however, the promise of nonentanglement and neutrality inherent in the neutral-principles approach more than compensates for what will be occasional problems in applications. These problems, in addition, should be gradually eliminated as recognition is given to the obligation of "States, religious organizations, and individuals [to] structure relationships involving church property so as not to require the civil courts to resolve ecclesiastical questions." *Presbyterian Church I,* [*supra*]. We therefore hold that a State is constitutionally entitled to adopt neutral principles of law as a means of adjudicating a church property dispute.

The dissent would require the States to abandon the neutral-principles method, and instead would insist as a matter of constitutional law that whenever a dispute arises over the ownership of church property, civil courts must defer to the "authoritative resolution of the dispute within the church itself." *Post,* at 614. It would require, first, that civil courts review ecclesiastical doctrine and polity to determine where the church has "placed ultimate authority over the use of the church property." *Post,* at 619. After answering this question, the courts would be required to "determine whether the dispute has been resolved within that structure of government and, if so, what decision has been made." *Post,* at 619 n. 6. They would then be required to enforce that decision. We cannot agree, however, that the First Amendment requires the States to adopt a rule of compulsory deference to religious authority in resolving church property disputes, even where no issue of doctrinal controversy is involved.

The dissent suggests that a rule of compulsory deference would somehow involve less entanglement of civil courts in matters of religious doctrine, practice, and administration. Under its approach, however, civil courts would always be required to examine the polity and administration of a church to determine which unit of government has ultimate control over church property. In some cases, this task would not prove to be difficult. But in others, the locus of control would be ambiguous, and "[a] careful examination of the constitutions of the general and local church, as well as other relevant documents, [would] be necessary to ascertain the form of governance adopted by the members of the religious association." *Post,* at 619–620. In such cases, the suggested rule would appear to require "a searching and therefore impermissible inquiry into church polity." *Serbian Orthodox Diocese* [*supra*]. The neutral-principles approach, in contrast, obviates entirely the need for an analysis or examination of ecclesiastical polity or doctrine in settling church property disputes.

The dissent also argues that a rule of compulsory deference is necessary in order to protect the free exercise rights "of those who have formed the association and submitted themselves to its authority." *Post,* at 618. This argument assumes that the neutral-principles method would somehow frustrate the free-exercise rights of the members of a religious association. Nothing could be further from the truth. The neutral-principles approach cannot be said to "inhibit" the free exercise of religion, any more than do other neutral provisions of state law governing the manner in which churches own property, hire employees, or purchase goods. Under the neutral-principles approach, the outcome of a church property dispute is not foreordained. At any time before the dispute erupts, the parties can ensure, if they so desire, that the faction loyal to the hierarchical church will retain the church property. They can modify the deeds or the corporate charter to include a right of reversion or trust in favor of the general church.

Alternatively, the constitution of the general church can be made to recite an express trust in favor of the denominational church. The burden involved in taking such steps will be minimal. And the civil courts will be bound to give effect to the result indicated by the parties, provided it is embodied in some legally cognizable form.

. . .

Neither the trial court nor the Supreme Court of Georgia, however, explicitly stated that it was adopting a presumptive rule of majority representation. Moreover, there are at least some indications that under Georgia law the process of identifying the faction that represents the Vineville church involves considerations of religious doctrine and polity. Georgia law requires that "church property be held according to the terms of the church government," and provides that a local church affiliated with a hierarchical religious association "is part of the whole body of the general church and is subject to the higher authority of the organization and its laws and regulations." *Carnes v. Smith*, 236 Ga., at 33, 38, 222 S. E. 2d, at 325, 328; see Ga. Code §§ 22-5507, 22-5508 (1978). All this may suggest that the identity of the "Vineville Presbyterian Church" named in the deeds must be determined according to terms of the Book of Church Order, which sets out the laws and regulations of churches affiliated with the PCUS. Such a determination, however, would appear to require a civil court to pass on questions of religious doctrine,[7] and to usurp the function of the commission appointed by the Presbytery, which already has determined that petitioners represent the "true congregation" of the Vineville church. Therefore, if Georgia law provides that the identity of the Vineville church is to be determined according to the "laws and regulations" of the PCUS, then the First Amendment requires that the Georgia courts give deference to the presbyterial commission's determination of that church's identity.[8]

This Court, of course, does not declare what the law of Georgia is. Since the grounds for the decision that respondents represent the Vineville church remain unarticulated, the judgment of the Supreme Court of Georgia is vacated, and the case is remanded for further proceedings not inconsistent with this opinion.

It is so ordered.

Justice Powell, with whom the Chief Justice, Justice Stewart, and Justice White join, dissenting.

This case presents again a dispute among church members over the control of a local church's property. Although the Court appears to accept established principles that I have thought would resolve this case, it superimposes on these principles a new structure of rules that will make the decision of these cases by civil courts more difficult. The new analysis also is more likely to invite intrusion into church polity forbidden by the First Amendment.

---

[7] Issues of church doctrine and polity pervade the provisions of the Book of Church Order of the Presbyterian Church (1972) dealing with the identity of the local congregation. The local church corporation consists of "all the communing members on the active roll" of the church. *Id.*, § 6-2; App. 35, The "active roll," in turn, is composed "of those admitted to the Lord's Table who are active in the church's life and work." § 8-7; App. 38. The Session is given the power "to suspend or exclude from the Lord's Supper those found delinquent, according to the Rules of Discipline." § 15-6 (2); App. 51. See § 111-2; App. 124. The Session is subject to "the review and control" of the Presbytery, § 14-5; App. 49, as a part of the Presbytery's general authority to "order whatever pertains to the spiritual welfare of the churches under its care." § 16-7 (19); App. 56.

[8] There is no suggestion in this case that the decision of the commission was the product of "fraud" or "collusion." See *Serbian Orthodox Diocese* v. *Milivojevich, [supra]*. In the absence of such circumstances, "the First and Fourteenth Amendments mandate that civil courts shall not disturb the decisions of the highest ecclesiastical tribunal within a church of hierarchical polity, but must accept such decisions as binding on them, in their application to the religious issues of doctrine or polity before them." *Id.*, at 709.

I

The Court begins by stating that "[t]his case involves a dispute over the ownership of church property," *ante,* at 597, suggesting that the concern is with legal or equitable ownership in the real property sense. But the ownership of the property of the Vineville church is not at issue. The deeds place title in the Vineville Presbyterian Church, or in trustees of that church, and none of the parties has questioned the validity of those deeds. The question actually presented is which of the factions within the local congregation has the right to control the actions of the titleholder, and thereby to control the use of the property, as the Court later acknowledges. *Ante,* at 602.

Since 1872, disputes over control of church property usually have been resolved under principles established by *Watson v. Jones,* [*supra,* VIII, 5]. Under the new and complex, two-stage analysis approved today, a court instead first must apply newly defined "neutral principles of law" to determine whether property titled to the local church is held in trust for the general church organization with which the local church is affiliated. If it is, then the court will grant control of the property to the councils of the general church. If not, then control by the local congregation will be recognized. In the latter situation, if there is a schism in the local congregation, as in this case, the second stage of the new analysis becomes applicable. Again, the Court fragments the analysis into two substeps for the purpose of determining which of the factions should control the property.

As this new approach inevitably will increase the involvement of civil courts in church controversies, and as it departs from long-established precedents, I dissent.

A

The first stage in the "neutral principles of law" approach operates as a restrictive rule of evidence. A court is required to examine the deeds to the church property, the charter of the local church (if there is one), the book of order or discipline of the general church organization, and the state statutes governing the holding of church property. The object of the inquiry, where the title to the property is in the local church, is "to determine whether there [is] any basis for a trust in favor of the general church." *Ante,* at 600. The court's investigation is to be "completely secular," "rel[ying] exclusively on objective, well-established concepts of trust and property law familiar to lawyers and judges." *Ante,* at 603. Thus, where religious documents such as church constitutions or books of order must be examined "for language of trust in favor of the general church," "a civil court must take special care to scrutinize the document in purely secular terms, and not to rely on religious precepts in determining whether the document indicates that the parties have intended to create a trust." *Ante,* at 604. It follows that the civil courts using this analysis may consider the form of religious government adopted by the church members for the resolution of intrachurch disputes *only* if that polity has been stated, in express relation to church property, in the language of trust and property law.[1]

---

[1] Despite the Court's assertion to the contrary, *ante,* at 602–603, this "neutral principles" approach was not approved by the Court in dismissing the appeal in *Maryland & Va. Eldership v. Sharpsburg Church,* [*supra*]. The state court there examined the constitution of the general church, the charters of the local churches, the deeds to the property at issue, and the relevant state statutes. But it did not restrict its inquiry to a search for statements expressed in the language of trust and property law; see 254 Md., at 169–176, 254 A.2d, at 168–170. Rather the state court canvassed all of these sources, and others, see *Maryland & Va. Eldership v. Sharpsburg Church,* 249 Md. 650, 665–668, 241 A.2d 691, 700–701 (1968), for information about the basic polity of the Church of God. Having concluded that the local congregations retained final authority over their property, it awarded judgment accordingly. Contrary to the statement of the Court in the present case that such an inquiry into church polity requires analysis of "ecclesiastical . . . doctrine," *ante,* at 605, "the Maryland court's resolution of the dispute involved no inquiry into religious doctrine." 396

One effect of the Court's evidentiary rule is to deny to the courts relevant evidence as to the religious polity—that is, the form of governance—adopted by the church members. The constitutional documents of churches tend to be drawn in terms of religious precepts. Attempting to read them "in purely secular terms" is more likely to promote confusion than understanding. Moreover, whenever religious polity has not been expressed in specific statements referring to the property of a church, there will be no evidence of that polity cognizable under the neutral-principles rule. Lacking such evidence, presumably a court will impose some rule of church government derived from state law. In the present case, for example, the general and unqualified authority of the Presbytery over the actions of the Vineville church had not been expressed in secular terms of control of its property. As a consequence, the Georgia courts could find no acceptable evidence of this authoritative relationship, and they imposed instead a congregational form of government determined from state law.

This limiting of the evidence relative to religious government cannot be justified on the ground that it "free[s] civil courts completely from entanglement in questions of religious doctrine, polity, and practice." *Ante,* at 603. For unless the body identified as authoritative under state law resolves the underlying dispute in accord with the decision of the church's own authority, the state court effectively will have reversed the decisions of doctrine and practice made in accordance with church law. The schism in the Vineville church, for example, resulted from disagreements among the church members over questions of doctrine and practice. App. 233. Under the Book of Church Order, these questions were resolved authoritatively by the higher church courts, which then gave control of the local church to the faction loyal to that resolution. The Georgia courts, as a matter of state law, granted control to the schismatic faction, and thereby effectively reversed the doctrinal decision of the church courts. This indirect interference by the civil courts with the resolution of religious disputes within the church is no less proscribed by the First Amendment than is the direct decision of questions of doctrine and practice.[2]

When civil courts step in to resolve intrachurch disputes over control of church property, they will either support or overturn the authoritative resolution of the dispute within the church itself. The new analysis, under the attractive banner of "neutral principles," actually invites the civil courts to do the latter. The proper rule of decision, that I thought had been settled until today, requires a court to give effect in all cases

---

U.S., at 368.

In *Presbyterian Church v. Hull Church* [*supra*], "neutral principles" were referred to in passing, but were never described. *Id.,* at 449. What the Court refers to as an "approving reference" to "neutral principles" in *Serbian Orthodox Diocese v. Milivojevich,* [*supra*] (1976), was only an acknowledgment in a footnote that "[n]o claim is made that the 'formal title' doctrine by which church property disputes may be decided in civil courts is to be applied in this case." *Id.,* at 723 n. 15. Nor can the Court find support for its position in *Watson v. Jones* [VIII, 5].

[2] The neutral-principles approach appears to assume that the requirements of the Constitution will be satisfied if civil courts are forbidden to consider certain types of evidence. The First Amendment's Religion Clauses, however, are meant to protect churches and their members from civil law interference, not to protect the courts from having to decide difficult evidentiary questions. Thus, the evidentiary rules to be applied in cases involving intrachurch disputes over church property should be fashioned to avoid interference with the resolution of the dispute within the accepted church government. The neutral-principles approach consists instead of a rule of evidence that ensures that in some cases the courts will impose a form of church government and a doctrinal resolution at odds with that reached by the church's own authority.

The neutral-principles approach creates other difficulties. It imposes on the organization of churches additional legal requirements which in some cases might inhibit their formation by forcing the organizers to confront issues that otherwise might never arise. It also could precipitate church property disputes, for existing churches may deem it necessary, in light of today's decision, to revise their constitutional documents, charters, and deeds to include a specific statement of church polity in the language of property and trust law.

to the decisions of the church government agreed upon by the members before the dispute arose.

B

The Court's basic neutral-principles approach, as a means of isolating decisions concerning church property from other decisions made within the church, relies on the concept of a trust of local church property in favor of the general church. Because of this central premise, the neutral-principles rule suffices to settle only disputes between the central councils of a church organization and a unanimous local congregation. Where, as here, the neutral-principles inquiry reveals no trust in favor of the general church, and the local congregation is split into factions, the basic question remains unresolved: which faction should have control of the local church.

The Court acknowledges that the church law of the Presbyterian Church in the United States (PCUS), of which the Vineville church is a part, provides for the authoritative resolution of this question by the Presbytery. *Ante,* at 608–609, and n. 7. Indeed, the Court indicates that Georgia, consistently with the First Amendment, may adopt the *Watson v. Jones* rule of adherence to the resolution of the dispute according to church law—a rule that would necessitate reversal of the judgment for the respondents. *Ante,* at 609. But instead of requiring the state courts to take this approach, the Court approves as well an alternative rule of state law: the Georgia courts are said to be free to "adop[t] a presumptive rule of majority representation, defeasible upon a showing that the identity of the local church is to be determined by some other means." *Ante,* at 607. This showing may be made by proving that the church has "provid[ed], in the corporate charter or the constitution of the general church, that the identity of the local church is to be established in some other way." *Ante,* at 607–608.

On its face, this rebuttable presumption also requires reversal of the state court's judgment in favor of the schismatic faction. The polity of the PCUS commits to the Presbytery the resolution of the dispute within the local church. Having shown this structure of church government for the determination of the identity of the local congregation, the petitioners have rebutted any presumption that this question has been left to a majority vote of the local congregation.

The Court nevertheless declines to order reversal. Rather than decide the case here in accordance with established First Amendment principles, the Court leaves open the possibility that the state courts might adopt some restrictive evidentiary rule that would render the petitioners' evidence inadequate to overcome the presumption of majority control. *Ante,* at 608 n. 5. But, aside from a passing reference to the use of the neutral-principles approach developed earlier in its opinion, the Court affords no guidance as to the constitutional limitations on such an evidentiary rule; the state courts, it says, are free to adopt any rule that is constitutional.

"Indeed, the state may adopt any method of overcoming the majoritarian presumption, so long as the use of that method does not impair free-exercise rights or entangle the civil courts in matters of religious controversy." *Ante,* at 608.

In essence, the Court's instructions on remand therefore allow the state courts the choice of following the long-settled rule of *Watson v. Jones* or of adopting some other rule— unspecified by the Court—that the state courts view as consistent with the First Amendment. Not only questions of state law but also important issues of federal constitutional law thus are left to the state courts for their decision, and, if they depart from *Watson v. Jones,* they will travel a course left totally uncharted by this Court.

NOTE. *After* Wolf. *Wolf* predictably led to results that would not have been reached before. The First Presbyterian Church of Schenectady, incorporated in 1803, withdrew from the national church because of the latter's alleged support of radical political groups. The local church had title to the property. Following neutral principles, the Court of Appeals awarded the local church the property. The national church argued that the Book of Order said that "whenever a local church is dissolved," the property was to go to the hierarchical organization; but the court said that the local church had not been dissolved. The court said that to find an implied trust for the national church would require a forbidden inquiry into church doctrine, *First Presbyterian Church of Schenectady v. United Presbyterian Church in the United States of America*, 62 N.Y. 2d 110, 476 N.Y.S. 2d 86, 464 N.E. 2d 454 (1984), *cert. denied*, 105 S.Ct. 514 (1984).

Compare this contemporaneous California case: Four Episcopal churches in Los Angeles — St. Matthias, St. Mary's, Our Saviour, and Holy Apostles — left the Protestant Episcopal Church after the Church's general convention accepted the ordination of women. The Protestant Episcopal Diocese and the Protestant Episcopal Church in the United States sued to recover the property. The court found that the most recently incorporated church, Holy Apostles, had articles of incorporation explicitly declaring that on its "dissolution" its property would inure to the benefit of the diocese. The court found that a "constructive dissolution" had occurred and that the diocese now took the property under this "express trust."

The other three churches were incorporated without any such provision but with a provision in their articles that the constitution, canons, and discipline of the diocese would always form part of their articles. The court said, "We think such declarations no more restrictive of future amendments to the articles of incorporation than would be similar statements in an automobile dealer's articles that it would always distribute General Motors products and always be bound by General Motors rules and policies. . . ." The court also said, "If a Kentucky Fried Chicken franchisee secedes from its national affiliation to join a Tennessee Fried Chicken operation, neutral principles of law do not recognize any claim by the ex-franchisor. . . ." Finding no express trust in favor of the diocese or the national church, the court permitted St. Matthias, St. Mary's, and Our Saviour to leave with the property, *Protestant Episcopal Church v. Barker*, 115 Cal. App. 3d 599, 171 Cal. Rptr. 541 (1981), *cert. denied*, 454 U.S. 864 (1981).

In the light of *Wolf*, the Supreme Court of Minnesota applied "neutral principles" to a dispute within the Serbian Eastern Orthodox Church. The majority of parishioners of St. Sava in South St. Paul, Minnesota, had remained loyal to the American diocese headed by Bishop Dionisije Milivojevich. The Minnesota court ruled in their favor, finding that the United States Supreme Court in *Milivojevich, supra*, had explicitly said, "Whether corporate bylaws or other documents governing the individual property-holding corporations may affect any desired disposition of the Diocesan property is a question not before us." The Minnesota court found that title to the property was in the name of the church of St. Sava and that the charter and bylaws of that church gave control to a majority of the congregation. The generally hierarchical constitution of the Serbian Eastern Orthodox Church did not override these local provisions, *Piletich v. Deretich*, 328 N.W. 2d 696 (Minn. 1982). Apparently even *Kedroff v. St. Nicholas Cathedral, supra*, might have been decided differently under *Wolf*. The corporation backed by the American diocese held the title, *see* 344 U.S. 94 at 96 n.1.

As the Supreme Court of Colorado summed up the law in *Bishop of Colorado v. Mote*, 716 P.2d, 85, 96 n. 10 (1986):

Most courts faced with a post-*Jones* church property dispute did not have to choose between the polity approach and the neutral principles approach without precedential guidance. They simply noted that prior case law or statutes in their state required or suggested that one or the other approach be utilized. *E.g., Harris v. Apostolic Overcoming Holy Church of God, Inc.,* 457 So.2d 385, 387 (Ala. 1984) (neutral principles); *Protestant Episcopal Church in the Diocese of Los Angeles v. Barker,* 115 Cal.App.3d 599, 171 Cal.Rptr. 541, 548–49, *cert. denied*, 454 U.S. 864, 102 S.Ct. 323, 70 L.Ed.2d 163 (1981) (neutral principles); *New York Annual Conference of the United Methodist Church v.*

Fisher, 182 Conn. 272, 438 A.2d 62, 68 (1980) (polity approach); *Grutka v. Clifford,* 445 N.E.2d 1015, 1019 (Ind.App.1983), *cert. denied,* 465 U.S. 1006, 104 S.Ct. 998, 79 L.Ed.2d 231 (1984) (neutral principles); *Fluker Community Church v. Hitchens,* 419 So.2d 445, 447–48 (La.1982) (neutral principles); *Graffam v. Wray,* 437 A.2d 627, 634 (Me.1981) (neutral principles); *Babcock Memorial Presbyterian Church v. Presbytery of Baltimore,* 296 Md. 573, 464 A.2d 1008, 1016 (1983), *cert. denied,* 465 U.S. 1027, 104 S.Ct. 1287, 79 L.Ed.2d 689 (1984) (neutral principles); *Antioch Temple, Inc. v. Parekh,* 383 Mass. 854, 422 N.E.2d 1337, 1340–42 (1981) (polity); *Bennison v. Sharp,* 121 Mich.App. 705, 329 N.W.2d 466, 474 (1982) (polity); *Piletich v. Deretich,* 328 N.W.2d 696, 701–02 (Minn.1982) (neutral principles); *Protestant Episcopal Church v. Graves,* 83 N.J. 572, 417 A.2d 19, 23–24 (1980), *cert. denied sub nom. Moore v. Protestant Episcopal Church,* 449 U.S. 1131, 101 S.Ct. 954, 67 L.Ed.2d 119 (1981) (polity); *Southside Tabernacle v. Pentecostal Church of God,* 32 Wash.App. 814, 650 P.2d 231, 235 (1982) (polity); *Church of God of Madison v. Noel,* 318 S.E.2d 920, 923–24 (W.Va. 1984) (polity). A few courts chose a neutral principles approach after deciding not to follow more or less explicit polity precedents. *E.g., York v. First Presbyterian Church of Anna,* 130 Ill. App.3d 611, 85 Ill.Dec. 756, 474 N.E.2d 716 (1984), *cert. denied,* ——— U.S. ———, 106 S.Ct. 183, 88 L.Ed.2d 152 (1985); *Presbytery of Elijah Parish Lovejoy v. Jaeggi,* 682 S.W.2d 465 (Mo.1984), *cert. denied,* ——— U.S. ———, 105 S.Ct. 2361, 86 L.Ed.2d 262 (1985); *Presbytery of Beaver-Butler v. Middlesex Presbyterian Church,* 507 Pa. 255, 489 A.2d 1317, *cert. denied,* ——— U.S. ———, 106 S.Ct. 198, 88 L.Ed.2d 167 (1985); *Foss v. Dykstra,* 319 N.W.2d 499 (S.D.1982). And in *Fonken v. Community Church of Kamrar,* 339 N.W.2d 810 (Iowa 1983), the Iowa Supreme Court had no precedent requiring the selection of one approach over the other, but the court avoided the issue by applying both polity and neutral principles (reaching the same result) without expressing a preference for either one.

Applying this doctrine in this case, the Colorado Court of Appeals opted for majority rule as the neutral principle and held for the majority in a local church seceding from the Protestant Episcopal Church in the United States. The Colorado Supreme Court, invoking another neutral principle it found apposite, reversed: the local church articles of incorporation and by-laws, "along with relevant provisions in the canons of the general church," demonstrated a trust in favor of the general church. Note that the Colorado court saw no difficulty in interpreting church canons as part of its application of neutral property law.

NOTE. *Other Property Rights.* Is the name of a church protected by the law against unfair competition? Yes, according to *Purcell v. Summer,* 145 F.2d 979, 985 (Fourth Circuit, 1944). (The Methodist Episcopal South Church merged with two other churches to form United Methodist Church. Dissident members who formed their own church using the old name were held to infringe the rights of the now merged church.)

Is *Purcell* good law in the light of *Wolf?*

Can religious materials constitute a protectable trade secret? No, according to *Religious Technology Center v. Wollersheim, et. al.* 796 F.2d. 1076 (Ninth Circuit, 1986). (Church of Scientology denied injunction against ex-members who established the Church of the New Civilization using materials taken from the Church of Scientology. The court held that the value of the confidential materials was "spiritual" not commercial.)

THIRTEEN

"Affirmatively to Help Guarantee": Double Effect

The principle of double effect has a long history in moral argumentation. Essentially it is this: If a single act has both good and evil effects, the act is good if one intends the good effect and if the good effect is proportionately greater than the evil effect. A classic example is a person defending himself from an attempt on his life. With a single blow he strikes the aggressor, intending to defend himself. The effects of the blow are the death of the aggressor and the safety of his victim. The good effect of securing the victim's safety outweighs the evil effect of killing the aggressor.

This simple principle applies in a large number of situations where moral judgments must be made, *see* Peter Knauer, "The Hermeneutic Function of the Principle of Double Effect," 12 *Natural Law Forum* 132 (1967).

The following cases suggest that an analogous analysis could be adopted in the many cases where a state practice has the constitutionally protected effect of permitting the free exercise of religion and the constitutionally prohibited effect of establishing religion.

1. DOUBLE DUTY PARKS

Fowler v. Rhode Island
345 U.S. 67 (1953)

Hayden C. Covington argued the cause and filed a brief for appellant.
Raymond J. Pettine, Assistant Attorney General of Rhode Island, argued the cause for appellee. With him on the brief was *William E. Powers,* Attorney General.

Justice Douglas delivered the opinion of the Court.

The City of Pawtucket, Rhode Island, has an ordinance which reads as follows:
"SEC. 11. No person shall address any political or religious meeting in any public park; but this section shall not be construed to prohibit any political or religious club or society from visiting any public park in a body, provided that no public address shall be made under the auspices of such club or society in such park."

Jehovah's Witnesses, a religious sect, assembled in Slater Park of Pawtucket for a meeting which at the trial was conceded to be religious in character. About 400 people attended, 150 being Jehovah's Witnesses. Appellant is a minister of this sect, residing in Arlington, Massachusetts. He was invited to Pawtucket as a visiting minister to give a talk before the Pawtucket congregation of Jehovah's Witnesses. Appellant accepted the invitation, attended the meeting in the park, and addressed it over two loudspeakers. It was a quiet, orderly meeting with no disturbances or breaches of the peace whatsoever.

Appellant's sect has conventions that are different from the practices of other religious groups. Its religious service is less ritualistic, more unorthodox, less formal than some. But apart from narrow exceptions relevant here (*Reynolds v. United States* [*supra,* IX]; *Davis v. Beason* [*supra,* IX]) it is no business of courts to say that what is a religious practice or activity for one group is not religion under the protection of the First Amendment. Nor is it in the competence of courts under our consitutional scheme to approve, disapprove, classify, regulate, or in any manner control sermons delivered at religious meetings. Sermons are as much a part of a religious service as prayers. They cover a wide range and have as great a diversity as the Bible or other Holy Book from which they commonly take their texts. To call the words which one minister speaks to his congregation a sermon, immune from regulation, and the words of another minister an address, subject to regulation, is merely an indirect way of preferring one religion over another. That would be precisely the effect here if we affirmed this conviction in the face of the concession made during oral argument. Baptist, Methodist, Presbyterian, or Episcopal ministers, Catholic priests, Moslem mullahs, Buddhist monks could all preach to their congregations in Pawtucket's parks with impunity. But the hand of the law would be laid on the shoulder of a minister of this unpopular group for performing the same function.

The judgment is reversed and the cause is remanded to the Supreme Court of Rhode Island for proceedings not inconsistent with this opinion.

Reversed.

Justice Frankfurter concurs in the opinion of the Court, except insofar as it may derive support from the First Amendment. For him it is the Equal-Protection-of-the-Laws Clause of the Fourteenth Amendment that condemns the Pawtucket ordinance as applied in this case.

Justice Jackson concurs in the result.

NOTE. *O'Hair v. Andrus,* 613 F. 2d 931 (D.C. Cir. 1979). Madalyn Murray O'Hair, an avowed atheist, sought to enjoin the celebration of mass by Pope John Paul II on the National Mall in Washington, D.C., on October 7, 1979. The cost of the Park Police service for the occasion was estimated to be between $100,000 and $150,000, plus $28,000 for related services; the Catholic Archdiocese of Washington was to pay over $400,000 to construct the platform for the mass and to provide fencing, electrical equipment, etc. The Park Service issued about 100 permits annually for religious services on national park land within the District of Columbia. The court, per Judge Harold Leventhal, found the National Mall to be "a public park that has regularly been made available to all major demonstrations presenting First Amendment values." It refused to issue the injunction.

Compare Gilfillan v. City of Philadelphia, 637 F. 2d 924 (3rd Cir. 1980), *cert. denied,* 451 U.S. 987 (1981). A taxpayer and the Philadelphia branch of the American Civil Liberties Union sought to enjoin Philadelphia from building a platform where the pope would say mass. The construction went ahead, the archdiocese of Philadelphia agreeing that it would pay if the city lost. The plaintiffs did not challenge city expenditures of about $1,000,000 to build a platform to welcome the pope at the airport and provide police on the pope's parade route; nor did they challenge his use of Logan Circle, a public place. They did challenge the $200,000 spent to build the platform and a cross and to surround the platform with shrubbery and flowers.

The city asserted that it had the secular purposes of protecting the pope and of reaping "a public relations bonanza" from his presence. The Third Circuit, 2–1, per Judge Max Rosenn, held that the challenged expenditures were an unconstitutional establishment of religion.

Applying the tests of *Lemon, infra*, XIV, 1, the court held that the purpose and effect of putting up the platform was to advance religion, and that the joint planning of the city with the archdiocese of Philadelphia was "entanglement." Judge Ruggero J. Aldisert dissented, maintaining that the pope was not only a religious leader but the head of a civil, if theocratic, state.

2. DOUBLE DUTY DAYS

McGowan v. Maryland
366 U.S. 420 (1961)

Harry Silbert argued the cause for appellants. With him on the brief were *A. Jerome Diener* and *Sidney Schlachman. John Martin Jones, Jr.,* Special Assistant Attorney General of Maryland, argued the cause for appellee. With him on the brief was *C. Ferdinand Sybert,* Attorney General.

Chief Justice Warren delivered the opinion of the Court.

The issues in this case concern the constitutional validity of Maryland criminal statutes, commonly known as Sunday Closing Laws or Sunday Blue Laws. These statutes, with exceptions to be noted hereafter, generally proscribe all labor, business and other commercial activities on Sunday. The questions presented are whether the classifications within the statutes bring about a denial of equal protection of the law, whether the laws are so vague as to fail to give reasonable notice of the forbidden conduct and therefore violate due process, and whether the statutes are laws respecting an establishment of religion or prohibiting the free exercise thereof.

Appellants are seven employees of a large discount department store located on a highway in Anne Arundel County, Maryland. They were indicted for the Sunday sale of a three-ring loose-leaf binder, a can of floor wax, a stapler and staples, and a toy submarine in violation of Md. Ann. Code, Art. 27, § 521. Generally, this section prohibited, throughout the State, the Sunday sale of all merchandise except the retail sale of tobacco products, confectioneries, milk, bread, fruits, gasoline, oils, greases, drugs and medicines, and newspapers and periodicals. Recently amended, this section also now excepts from the general prohibition the retail sale in Anne Arundel County of all foodstuffs, automobile and boating accessories, flowers, toilet goods, hospital supplies and souvenirs. It now further provides that any retail establishment in Anne Arundel County which does not employ more than one person other than the owner may operate on Sunday.

. . .

However, it is equally true that the "Establishment" Clause does not ban federal or state regulation of conduct whose reason or effect merely happens to coincide or harmonize with the tenets of some or all religions. In many instances, the Congress or state legislatures conclude that the general welfare of society, wholly apart from any religious considerations, demands such regulation. Thus, for temporal purposes, murder is illegal. And the fact that this agrees with the dictates of the Judaeo-Christian religions while it may disagree with others does not invalidate the regulation. So too with the questions of adultery and polygamy. *Davis v. Beason, Reynolds v. United States* [*supra*, IX]. The same could be said of theft, fraud, etc., because those offenses were also proscribed in the Decalogue.

Thus, these broad principles have been set forth by this Court. Those cases dealing with the specific problems arising under the "Establishment" Clause which have reached this Court are few in number. The most extensive discussion of the "Establishment" Clause's latitude is to be found in *Everson v. Board of Education* [*infra*, XIV, 1]. . . .

Sunday Closing Laws, like those before us, have become part and parcel of this great governmental concern wholly apart from their original purposes or connotations. The present purpose and effect of most of them is to provide a uniform day of rest for all citizens; the fact that this day is Sunday, a day of particular significance for the dominant Christian sects, does not bar the State from achieving its secular goals. To say that the States cannot prescribe Sunday as a day of rest for these purposes solely because centuries ago such laws had their genesis in religion would give a constitutional interpretation of hostility to the public welfare rather than one of mere separation of church and State. . . .

Affirmed.

Justice Frankfurter delivered a concurring opinion, Justice Douglas dissented.

NOTE. *Braunfeld v. Brown*, 366 U.S. 599 (1961). Sunday closing laws were challenged as impairing the free exercise of religion. The plaintiffs, Orthodox Jews, sought to enjoin enforcement of the Pennsylvania Sunday law on the grounds that it penalized their observance of their Sabbath. They faced giving up their Sabbath by keeping their businesses open Saturdays or closing Saturdays and Sundays and being at a serious economic disadvantage.

Citing *Reynolds, supra*, IX, and *Prince, supra*, XI, 1, the Court, per Chief Justice Warren, sustained the statute as imposing "only an indirect burden on the exercise of religion" in the course of accomplishing a lawful state purpose that could not be accomplished without imposing the burden. Justice Brennan concurred in part and dissented in part and Justice Stewart dissented, asserting that the state could secure a day of rest while allowing an exception for Sabbatarians. Justice Douglas also dissented.

NOTE. *State Stimulus to a Religious Divorce.* Under Jewish law a woman is validly divorced only if she receives a bill of divorce or *get* from her husband. If she marries again without it, she commits adultery and any child she bears is a bastard. No similar stigmas attach to the undivorced husband. Husbands consequently are in a position to extract concessions from their civilly divorced wives who need the *get* to remarry without religious opprobrium. Tyrannical husbands can even deny the *get* out of malice, keeping their ex-wives forever in a position where they cannot conscientiously marry.

To remedy this situation, New York, at the request of Orthodox and Conservative Jewish groups, enacted in 1983 a statute that provides that a spouse, married by a clergyman or rabbi and seeking an annulment or divorce, must allege that "he or she has taken or . . . will take, prior to the entry of final judgment, all steps solely within his or her power to remove any barrier to the defendant's remarriage following the annulment or divorce," *New York Domestic Relations Law*, sec. 253. The statute further specifies that such steps do not include applying to a church tribunal (thus letting out Catholics) and that barriers include "any religious or conscientious restraint or inhibition imposed on a party to a marriage . . . by reason of the other party's . . . withholding of any voluntary act."

Does the statute have a double effect? Does the secular effect outweigh the religious?

3. DOUBLE DUTY CHURCHES AND SYNAGOGUES

Walz v. Tax Commission of the City of New York
397 U.S. 664 (1970)

Edward J. Ennis argued the cause for appellant.

J. Lee Rankin argued the cause for appellee. With him on the brief were *Stanley Buchsbaum* and *Edith I. Spivack.*

Briefs of *amici curiae* urging reversal were filed by *Osmond K. Fraenkel, Marvin M. Karpatkin, Norman Dorsen, Mr. Ennis,* and *Melvin L. Wulf* for the American Civil Liberties Union, and by *Lola Boswell* for Madalyn Murray O'Hair and *James H. Anderson, Jr.,* for the Society of Separationists, Inc.

Briefs of *amici curiae* urging affirmance were filed by *Louis J. Lefkowitz,* Attorney General, *Samuel A. Hirshowitz,* First Assistant Attorney General, and *Julius Greenfield,* Assistant Attorney General, for the State of New York, joined by the Attorneys General for their respective States as follows: *MacDonald Gallion* of Alabama, *Gary K. Nelson* of Arizona, *Joe Purcell* of Arkansas, *Duke W. Dunbar* of Colorado, *Robert K. Killian* of Connecticut, *David P. Buckson* of Delaware, *Earl Faircloth* of Florida, *Bertram T. Kanbara* of Hawaii, *William J. Scott* of Illinois, *Theodore L. Sendak* of Indiana, *Richard C. Turner* of Iowa, *Kent Frizzel* of Kansas, *John B. Breckinridge* of Kentucky, *Jack P. F. Gremillion* of Louisiana, *James S. Erwin* of Maine, *Francis B. Burch* of Maryland, *Frank J. Kelley* of Michigan, *A. F. Summer* of Mississippi, *John C. Danforth* of Missouri, *Robert L. Woodahl* of Montana, *Clarence A. H. Meyer* of Nebraska, *Arthur J. Sills* of New Jersey, *James A. Maloney* of New Mexico, *Robert B. Morgan* of North Carolina, *Helgi Johanneson* of North Dakota, *Paul W. Brown* of Ohio, *William C. Sennett* of Pennsylvania, *Herbert F. De Simone* of Rhode Island, *Gordon Mydland* of South Dakota, *George F. McCanless* of Tennessee, *Crawford C. Martin* of Texas, *James M. Jeffords* of Vermont, *Robert Y. Button* of Virginia, *Slade Gorton* of Washington, *Robert W. Warren* of Wisconsin, and *James E. Barrett* of Wyoming, and by *Santiago C. Soler-Favale,* Attorney General of Puerto Rico; by *Franklin C. Salisbury* for Protestants and Other Americans United for Separation of Church and State; by *Noel Thompson* for the Parish Hall School, Inc.; by *Charles H. Tuttle* and *Thomas A. Shaw, Jr.,* for the National Council of the Churches of Christ in the United States; by *Anthony L. Fletcher, Stephen B. Clarkson, John Miles Evans, George F. Mackey, William G. Rhines, William Sherman,* and *H. Richard Schumacher* for the Episcopal Diocese of New York et al.; by *William R. Consedine, George E. Reed, Alfred L. Scanlan, Arthur E. Sutherland,* and *Charles M. Whelan* for the United States Catholic Conference; by *Marvin Braiterman* for the Synagogue Council of America et al.; by *Nathan Lewin* and *Julius Berman* for the National Jewish Commission on Law and Public Affairs; by *Joseph B. Friedman* for the Baptist Joint Committee on Public Affairs; and by *Roy L. Cole* for the Baptist General Convention of Texas.

Chief Justice Burger delivered the opinion of the Court.

Appellant, owner of real estate in Richmond County, New York, sought an injunction in the New York courts to prevent the New York City Tax Commission from granting property tax exemptions to religious organizations for religious properties used solely for religious worship. The exemption from state taxes is authorized by Art. 16, § 1, of the New York Constitution, which provides in relevant part:

"Exemptions from taxation may be granted only by general laws. Exemptions may be altered or repealed except those exempting real or personal property used exclusively for religious, educational or charitable purposes as defined by law and owned by any corporation or association organized or conducted exclusively for one or more of such purposes and not operating for profit."

The essence of appellant's contention was that the New York City Tax Commission's grant of an exemption to church property indirectly requires the appellant to make a contribution to religious bodies and thereby violates provisions prohibiting establishment of religion under the First Amendment which under the Fourteenth Amendment is binding on the States.

Appellee's motion for summary judgment was granted and the Appellate Division of the New York Supreme Court, and the New York Court of Appeals affirmed. We noted probable jurisdiction, 395 U.S. 957 (1969), and affirm.

. . .

The Court has struggled to find a neutral course between the two Religion Clauses, both of which are cast in absolute terms, and either of which, if expanded to a logical extreme, would tend to clash with the other. For example, in *Zorach v. Clauson* [*infra,* XIV, 2], Mr. Justice Douglas, writing for the Court, noted:

"The First Amendment, however, does not say that in every and all respects there shall be a separation of Church and State." *Id.,* at 312.

"We sponsor an attitude on the part of government that shows no partiality to any one group and that lets each flourish according to the zeal of its adherents and the appeal of its dogma." *Id.,* at 313.

Mr. Justice Harlan expressed something of this in his dissent in *Sherbert v. Verner* [*supra,* XI, 4] (1963), saying that the constitutional neutrality imposed on us

"is not so narrow a channel that the slightest deviation from an absolutely straight course leads to condemnation." *Id.,* at 422.

The course of constitutional neutrality in this area cannot be an absolutely straight line; rigidity could well defeat the basic purpose of these provisions, which is to insure that no religion be sponsored or favored, none commanded, and none inhibited. The general principle deducible from the First Amendment and all that has been said by the Court is this: that we will not tolerate either governmentally established religion or governmental interference with religion. Short of those expressly proscribed governmental acts there is room for play in the joints productive of a benevolent neutrality which will permit religious exercise to exist without sponsorship and without interference.

Each value judgment under the Religion Clauses must therefore turn on whether particular acts in question are intended to establish or interfere with religious beliefs and practices or have the effect of doing so. Adherence to the policy of neutrality that derives from an accommodation of the Establishment and Free Exercise Clauses has prevented the kind of involvement that would tip the balance toward government control of churches or governmental restraint on religious practice.

Adherents of particular faiths and individual churches frequently take strong positions on public issues including, as this case reveals in the several briefs *amici,* vigorous advocacy of legal or constitutional positions. Of course, churches as much as secular bodies and private citizens have that right. No perfect or absolute separation is really possible; the very existence of the Religion Clauses is an involvement of sorts—one that seeks to mark boundaries to avoid excessive entanglement.

The hazards of placing too much weight on a few words or phrases of the Court is abundantly illustrated within the pages of the Court's opinion in *Everson* [*infra,* XIV, 1]. Mr. Justice Black, writing for the Court's majority, said the First Amendment

"means at least this: Neither a state nor the Federal Government can . . . pass laws which aid one religion, aid all religions, or prefer one religion over another." 330 U.S., at 15.

Yet he had no difficulty in holding that:

"Measured by these standards, we cannot say that the First Amendment prohibits New Jersey from spending tax-raised funds to pay the bus fares of parochial school pupils as a part of a general program under which it pays the fares of pupils attending public and other schools. *It is undoubtedly true that children are helped to get to church schools. There is even a possibility that some of the children might not be sent to the church schools if the parents were compelled to pay their children's bus fares out of their own pockets. . . ." Id.,* at 17. (Emphasis added.)

The Court did not regard such "aid" to schools teaching a particular religious faith as any more a violation of the Establishment Clause than providing "state-paid policemen, detailed to protect children . . . [at the schools] from the very real hazards of traffic. . . ." *Ibid.*

Mr. Justice Jackson, in perplexed dissent in *Everson,* noted that

"the undertones of the opinion, advocating complete and uncompromising separation

. . . seem utterly discordant with its conclusion. . . ." *Id.*, at 19.

Perhaps so. One can sympathize with Mr. Justice Jackson's logical analysis but agree with the Court's eminently sensible and realistic application of the language of the Establishment Clause. In *Everson* the Court declined to construe the Religion Clauses with a literalness that would undermine the ultimate constitutional objective as illuminated by history. Surely, bus transportation and police protection to pupils who receive religious instruction "aid" that particular religion to maintain schools that plainly tend to assure future adherents to a particular faith by having control of their total education at an early age. No religious body that maintains schools would deny this as an affirmative if not dominant policy of church schools. But if as in *Everson* buses can be provided to carry and policemen to protect church school pupils, we fail to see how a broader range of police and fire protection given equally to all churches, along with nonprofit hospitals, art galleries, and libraries receiving the same tax exemption, is different for purposes of the Religion Clauses.

Similarly, making textbooks available to pupils in parochial schools in common with public schools was surely an "aid" to the sponsoring churches because it relieved those churches of an enormous aggregate cost for those books. Supplying of costly teaching materials was not seen either as manifesting a legislative purpose to aid or as having a primary effect of aid contravening the First Amendment. *Board of Education v. Allen* [*infra*, XIV, 1]. In so holding the Court was heeding both its own prior decisions and our religious tradition. Mr. Justice Douglas, in *Zorach v. Clauson,* after recalling that we "are a religious people whose institutions presuppose a Supreme Being," went on to say:

"We make room for as wide a variety of beliefs and creeds as the spiritual needs of man deem necessary. . . . *When the state encourages religious instruction . . . it follows the best of our traditions.* For it then respects the religious nature of our people and accommodates the public service to their spiritual needs." 343 U.S., at 313–314. (Emphasis added.)

With all the risks inherent in programs that bring about administrative relationships between public education bodies and church-sponsored schools, we have been able to chart a course that preserved the autonomy and freedom of religious bodies while avoiding any semblance of established religion. This is a "tight rope" and one we have successfully traversed.

II

The legislative purpose of the property tax exemption is neither the advancement nor the inhibition of religion; it is neither sponsorship nor hostility. New York, in common with the other States, has determined that certain entities that exist in a harmonious relationship to the community at large, and that foster its "moral or mental improvement," should not be inhibited in their activities by property taxation or the hazard of loss of those properties for nonpayment of taxes. It has not singled out one particular church or religious group or even churches as such; rather, it has granted exemption to all houses of religious worship within a broad class of property owned by nonprofit, quasi-public corporations which include hospitals, libraries, playgrounds, scientific, professional, historical, and patriotic groups. The State has an affirmative policy that considers these groups as beneficial and stabilizing influences in community life and finds this classification useful, desirable, and in the public interest. Qualification for tax exemption is not perpetual or immutable; some tax-exempt groups lose that status when their activities take them outside the classification and new entities can come into being and qualify for exemption.

Governments have not always been tolerant of religious activity, and hostility toward religion has taken many shapes and forms—economic, political, and sometimes harshly oppressive. Grants of exemption historically reflect the concern of authors of constitutions and statutes as to the latent dangers inherent in the imposition of property taxes; exemption constitutes a reasonable and balanced attempt to guard against those dangers.

The limits of permissible state accommodation to religion are by no means co-extensive with the noninterference mandated by the Free Exercise Clause. To equate the two would be to deny a national heritage with roots in the Revolution itself. See *Sherbert v. Verner* [*supra*, XI, 4] (Harlan, J., dissenting); *Braunfeld v. Brown*, 366 U.S. 599, 608 (1961). See generally Kauper, The Constitutionality of Tax Exemptions for Religious Activities in The Wall Between Church and State 95 (D. Oaks ed. 1963). We cannot read New York's statute as attempting to establish religion; it is simply sparing the exercise of religion from the burden of property taxation levied on private profit institutions.

We find it unnecessary to justify the tax exemption on the social welfare services or "good works" that some churches perform for parishioners and others—family counselling, aid to the elderly and the infirm, and to children. Churches vary substantially in the scope of such services; programs expand or contract according to resources and need. As public-sponsored programs enlarge, private aid from the church sector may diminish. The extent of social services may vary, depending on whether the church serves an urban or rural, a rich or poor constituency. To give emphasis to so variable an aspect of the work of religious bodies would introduce an element of governmental evaluation and standards as to the worth of particular social welfare programs, thus producing a kind of continuing day-to-day relationship which the policy of neutrality seeks to minimize. Hence, the use of a social welfare yardstick as a significant element to qualify for tax exemption could conceivably give rise to confrontations that could escalate to constitutional dimensions.

Determining that the legislative purpose of tax exemption is not aimed at establishing, sponsoring, or supporting religion does not end the inquiry, however. We must also be sure that the end result—the effect—is not an excessive government entanglement with religion. The test is inescapably one of degree. Either course, taxation of churches or exemption, occasions some degree of involvement with religion. Elimination of exemption would tend to expand the involvement of government by giving rise to tax valuation of church property, tax liens, tax foreclosures, and the direct confrontations and conflicts that follow in the train of those legal processes.

Granting tax exemptions to churches necessarily operates to afford an indirect economic benefit and also gives rise to some, but yet a lesser, involvement than taxing them. In analyzing either alternative the questions are whether the involvement is excessive, and whether it is a continuing one calling for official and continuing surveillance leading to an impermissible degree of entanglement. Obviously a direct money subsidy would be a relationship pregnant with involvement and, as with most governmental grant programs, could encompass sustained and detailed administrative relationships for enforcement of statutory or administrative standards, but that is not this case. The hazards of churches supporting government are hardly less in their potential than the hazards of government supporting churches; each relationship carries some involvement rather than the desired insulation and separation. We cannot ignore the instances in history when church support of government led to the kind of involvement we seek to avoid.

The grant of a tax exemption is not sponsorship since the government does not transfer part of its revenue to churches but simply abstains from demanding that the church support the state. No one has ever suggested that tax exemption has converted libraries, art galleries, or hospitals into arms of the state or put employees "on the public payroll." There is no genuine nexus between tax exemption and establishment of religion. As Mr. Justice Holmes commented in a related context "a page of history is worth a volume of logic." *New York Trust Co. v. Eisner*, 256 U.S. 345, 349 (1921). The exemption creates only a minimal and remote involvement between church and state and far less than taxation of churches. It restricts the fiscal relationship between church and state, and tends to complement and reinforce the desired separation insulating each from the other.

Separation in this context cannot mean absence of all contact; the complexities of modern life inevitably produce some contact and the fire and police protection received by houses of religious worship are no more than incidental benefits accorded all persons or institutions within a State's boundaries, along with many other exempt organizations. The appellant has not established even an arguable quantitative correlation between the payment of an ad valorem property tax and the receipt of these municipal benefits.

All of the 50 States provide for tax exemption of places of worship, most of them doing so by constitutional guarantees. For so long as federal income taxes have had any potential impact on churches—over 75 years—religious organizations have been expressly exempt from the tax. Such treatment is an "aid" to churches no more and no less in principle than the real estate tax exemption granted by States. Few concepts are more deeply embedded in the fabric of our national life, beginning with pre-Revolutionary colonial times, than for the government to exercise at the very least this kind of benevolent neutrality toward churches and religious exercise generally so long as none was favored over others and none suffered interference.

It is significant that Congress, from its earliest days, has viewed the Religion Clauses of the Constitution as authorizing statutory real estate tax exemption to religious bodies. In 1802 the 7th Congress enacted a taxing statute for the County of Alexandria, adopting the 1800 Virginia statutory pattern which provided tax exemptions for churches. 2 Stat. 194.[5] As early as 1813 the 12th Congress refunded import duties paid by religious societies on the importation of religious articles.[6] During this period the City Council of Washington, D.C., acting under congressional authority, Act of Incorporation, § 7, 2 Stat. 197 (May 3, 1802), enacted a series of real and personal property assessments that uniformly exempted church property.[7] In 1870 the Congress specifically exempted all churches in the District of Columbia and appurtenant grounds and property "from any and all taxes or assessments, national, municipal, or county." Act of June 17, 1870, 16 Stat. 153.[8]

It is obviously correct that no one acquires a vested or protected right in violation of the Constitution by long use, even when that span of time covers our entire national existence and indeed predates it. Yet an unbroken practice of according the exemption to churches, openly and by affirmative state action, not covertly or by state inaction, is not something to be lightly cast aside. Nearly 50 years ago Mr. Justice Holmes stated:

"If a thing has been practised for two hundred years by common consent, it will need a strong case for the Fourteenth Amendment to affect it. . . ." *Jackman v. Rosenbaum Co.,* 260 U.S. 22, 31 (1922).

---

[5] In 1798 Congress passed an Act to provide for the valuation of lands and dwelling houses. All existing state exemptions were expressly excluded from the aforesaid valuation and enumeration. Act of July 9, 1798, § 8, 1 Stat. 585. Subsequent levies of direct taxes expressly or impliedly incorporated existing state exemptions. Act of July 14, 1798, § 2, 1 Stat. 598 (express incorporation of state exemption). See Act of Aug. 2, 1813, § 4, 3 Stat. 71; Act of Jan. 9, 1815, § 5, 3 Stat. 166 (express incorporation of state exemptions).

[6] See 6 Stat. 116 (1813), relating to plates for printing Bibles. See also 6 Stat. 346 (1826) relating to church vestments, furniture, and paintings; 6 Stat. 162 (1816), Bible plates; 6 Stat. 600 (1834), and 6 Stat. 675 (1836), church bells.

[7] See, *e. g.,* Acts of the Corporation of the City of Washington, First Council, c. V, approved Oct. 6, 1802, p. 13; Acts of the Corporation of the City of Washington, Second Council, § 1, approved Sept. 12, 1803, p. 13; Acts of the Corporation of the City of Washington, Third Council, § 1, approved Sept 5, 1804, p. 13. Succeeding Acts of the Corporation impliedly renewed the exemption in subsequent assessments. See, *e. g.,* Acts of the Corporation of the City of Washington, Thirteenth Council, c. 19, § 2, approved July 27, 1815, p. 24.

[8] Subsequent Acts of Congress carried over the substance of the exemption. Act of July 12, 1876, § 8, 19 Stat. 85; Act of March 3, 1877, § 8, 19 Stat. 399; Act of August 15, 1916, 39 Stat. 514; D.C. Code Ann. § 47–801a (1967).

Nothing in this national attitude toward religious tolerance and two centuries of uninterrupted freedom from taxation has given the remotest sign of leading to an established church or religion and on the contrary it has operated affirmatively to help guarantee the free exercise of all forms of religious belief. Thus, it is hardly useful to suggest that tax exemption is but the "foot in the door" or the "nose of the camel in the tent" leading to an established church. If tax exemption can be seen as this first step toward "establishment" of religion, as Mr. Justice Douglas fears, the second step has been long in coming. Any move that realistically "establishes" a church or tends to do so can be dealt with "while this Court sits."

Mr. Justice Cardozo commented in The Nature of the Judicial Process 51 (1921) on the "tendency of a principle to expand itself to the limit of its logic"; such expansion must always be contained by the historical frame of reference of the principle's purpose and there is no lack of vigilance on this score by those who fear religious entanglement in government.

The argument that making "fine distinctions" between what is and what is not absolute under the Constitution is to render us a government of men, not laws, gives too little weight to the fact that it is an essential part of adjudication to draw distinctions, including fine ones, in the process of interpreting the Constitution. We must frequently decide, for example, what are "reasonable" searches and seizures under the Fourth Amendment. Determining what acts of government tend to establish or interfere with religion falls well within what courts have long been called upon to do in sensitive areas.

It is interesting to note that while the precise question we now decide has not been directly before the Court previously, the broad question was discussed by the Court in relation to real estate taxes assessed nearly a century ago on land owned by and adjacent to a church in Washington, D.C.[9] At that time Congress granted real estate tax exemptions to buildings devoted to art, to institutions of public charity, libraries, cemeteries, and "church buildings, and grounds actually occupied by such buildings." In denying tax exemption as to land owned by but not used for the church, but rather to produce income, the Court concluded:

"In the exercise of this [taxing] power, Congress, like any State legislature unrestricted by constitutional provisions, may at its discretion wholly exempt certain classes of property from taxation, or may tax them at a lower rate than other property." Gibbons v. District of Columbia, 116 U.S. 404, 408 (1886).

It appears that at least up to 1885 this Court, reflecting more than a century of our history and uninterrupted practice, accepted without discussion the proposition that federal or state grants of tax exemption to churches were not a violation of the Religion Clauses of the First Amendment. As to the New York statute, we now confirm that view.

Affirmed.

. . .

Justice Brennan, concurring:

. . .

The existence from the beginning of the Nation's life of a practice, such as tax exemptions for religious organizations, is not conclusive of its constitutionality. But such practice is a fact of considerable import in the interpretation of abstract constitutional language. On its face, the Establishment Clause is reasonably susceptible of different interpretations regarding the exemptions. This Court's interpretation of the clause, accordingly, is appropriately influenced by the reading it has received in the practices of the Nation. As Mr. Justice Holmes observed in an analogous context, in

---

[9] *Gibbons* v. *District of Columbia,* 116 U.S. 404 (1886). Cf. *Washington Ethical Society* v. *District of Columbia,* 101 U.S. App. D.C. 371, 249 F.2d 127 (1957).

resolving such questions of interpretation "a page of history is worth a volume of logic." *New York Trust Co. v. Eisner,* 256 U.S. 345, 349 (1921). The more longstanding and widely accepted a practice, the greater its impact upon constitutional interpretation. History is particularly compelling in the present case because of the undeviating acceptance given religious tax exemptions from our earliest days as a Nation. Rarely if ever has this Court considered the constitutionality of a practice for which the historical support is so overwhelming.

. . .

Government has two basic secular purposes for granting real property tax exemptions to religious organizations. First, these organizations are exempted because they, among a range of other private, nonprofit organizations contribute to the well-being of the community in a variety of nonreligious ways, and thereby bear burdens that would otherwise either have to be met by general taxation, or be left undone, to the detriment of the community. . . .

Second, government grants exemptions to religious organizations because they uniquely contribute to the pluralism of American society by their religious activities. Government may properly include religious institutions among the variety of private, nonprofit groups that receive tax exemptions, for each group contributes to the diversity of association, viewpoint, and enterprise essential to a vigorous, pluralistic society. See *Washington Ethical Society v. District of Columbia,* 101 U.S. App. D.C. 371, 373, 249 F.2d 127, 129 (1957). To this end, New York extends its exemptions not only to religious and social service organizations but also to scientific, literary, bar, library, patriotic, and historical groups, and generally to institutions "organized exclusively for the moral or mental improvement of men and women." The very breadth of this scheme of exemptions negates any suggestion that the State intends to single out religious organizations for special preference. The scheme is not designed to inject any religious activity into a nonreligious context, as was the case with school prayers. No particular activity of a religious organization—for example, the propagation of its beliefs—is specially promoted by the exemptions. They merely facilitate the existence of a broad range of private, non-profit organizations, among them religious groups, by leaving each free to come into existence, then to flourish or wither, without being burdened by real property taxes.

. . .

Finally, I do not think that the exemptions "use essentially religious means to serve governmental ends, where secular means would suffice." The means churches use to carry on their public service activities are not "essentially religious" in nature. They are the same means used by any purely secular organization—money, human time and skills, physical facilities. It is true that each church contributes to the pluralism of our society through its purely religious activities, but the state encourages these activities not because it champions religion *per se* but because it values religion among a variety of private, nonprofit enterprises that contribute to the diversity of the Nation. Viewed in this light, there is no nonreligious substitute for religion as an element in our societal mosaic, just as there is no nonliterary substitute for literary groups.

. . .

Justice Harlan, concurring:

. . . This legislation neither encourages nor discourages participation in religious life and thus satisfies the voluntarism requirement of the First Amendment. Unlike the instances of school prayers, *Abington School Dist. v. Schempp* [*infra,* XIV, 2], and *Engel v. Vitale,* or "released time" programs, *Zorach v. Clauson* [*infra,* XIV, 2], and *McCollum v. Board of Education* [*infra,* XIV, 2], the State is not "utilizing the prestige, power, and influence" of a public institution to bring religion into the lives of citizens. 374 U.S., at 307 (Goldberg, J., concurring).

The statute also satisfies the requirement of neutrality. Neutrality in its application requires an equal protection mode of analysis. The Court must survey meticulously the circumstances of governmental categories to eliminate, as it were, religious gerrymanders. In any particular case the critical question is whether the circumference of legislation encircles a class so broad that it can be fairly concluded that religious institutions could be thought to fall within the natural perimeter.

The statute that implements New York's constitutional provision for tax exemptions to religious organizations has defined a class of nontaxable entities whose common denominator is their nonprofit pursuit of activities devoted to cultural and moral improvement and the doing of "good works" by performing certain social services in the community that might otherwise have to be assumed by government. Included are such broad and divergent groups as historical and literary societies and more generally associations "for the moral or mental improvement of men." The statute by its terms grants this exemption in furtherance of moral and intellectual diversity and would appear not to omit any organization that could be reasonably thought to contribute to that goal.

To the extent that religious institutions sponsor the secular activities that this legislation is designed to promote, it is consistent with neutrality to grant them an exemption just as other organizations devoting resources to these projects receive exemptions. I think, moreover, in the context of a statute so broad as the one before us, churches may properly receive an exemption even though they do not themselves sponsor the secular-type activities mentioned in the statute but exist merely for the convenience of their interested members. As long as the breadth of exemption includes groups that pursue cultural, moral, or spiritual improvement in multifarious secular ways, including, I would suppose, groups whose avowed tenets may be antitheological, atheistic, or agnostic, I can see no lack of neutrality in extending the benefit of the exemption to organized religious groups.[1]

Justice Douglas dissenting:

. . .

Engel was as disruptive of traditional state practices as was *Stromberg*. Prior to *Stromberg*, a State could arrest an unpopular person who made a rousing speech on the charge of disorderly conduct. Since *Stromberg*, that has been unconstitutional. And so the revolution occasioned by the Fourteenth Amendment has progressed as Article after Article in the Bill of Rights has been incorporated in it and made applicable to the States.

Hence the question in the present case makes irrelevant the "two centuries of uninterrupted freedom from taxation," referred to by the Court. *Ante*, at 678. If history be our guide, then tax exemption of church property in this country is indeed highly suspect, as it arose in the early days when the church was an agency of the state. See W. Torpey, Judicial Doctrines of Religious Rights in America 171 (1948). The question here, though, concerns the meaning of the Establishment Clause and the Free Exercise Clause made applicable to the States for only a few decades at best.

With all due respect the governing principle is not controlled by *Everson v. Board of Education* [XIV, 1]. *Everson* involved the use of public funds to bus children to parochial as well as to public schools. Parochial schools teach religion; yet they are also educational institutions offering courses competitive with public schools. They prepare

---

[1] While I would suppose most churches devote part of their resources to secular community projects and conventional charitable activities, it is a question of fact, a fact that would only be relevant if we had before us a statute framed more narrowly to include only "charities" or a limited class of organizations, and churches. In such a case, depending on the administration of the exemption, it might be that the granting of an exemption to religion would turn out to be improper. This would depend, I believe, on what activities the church in fact sponsored. It would also depend, I think, on whether or to what extent the exemption were accorded to secular social organizations, conceived to benefit their own membership but also engaged in incidental general philanthropic or cultural undertakings.

students for the professions and for activities in all walks of life. Education in the secular sense was combined with religious indoctrination at the parochial schools involved in *Everson*. Even so, the *Everson* decision was five to four and, though one of the five, I have since had grave doubts about it, because I have become convinced that grants to institutions teaching a sectarian creed violate the Establishment Clause. See *Engel v. Vitale* [*infra*, XIV, 2] (Douglas, J., concurring).

This case, however, is quite different. Education is not involved. The financial support rendered here is to the church, the place of worship. A tax exemption is a subsidy. Is my Brother Brennan correct in saying that we would hold that state or federal grants to churches, say, to construct the edifice itself would be unconstitutional? What is the difference between that kind of subsidy and the present subsidy?

. . .

The religiously used real estate of the churches today constitutes a vast domain. See M. Larson & C. Lowell, The Churches: Their Riches, Revenues, and Immunities (1969). Their assets total over $141 billion and their annual income at least $22 billion. *Id.*, at 232. And the extent to which they are feeding from the public trough in a variety of forms is alarming. *Id., c.* 10.

We are advised that since 1968 at least five States have undertaken to give subsidies to parochial and other private schools—Pennsylvania, Ohio, New York, Connecticut, and Rhode Island. And it is reported that under two federal Acts, the Elementary and Secondary Education Act of 1965, 79 Stat. 27, and the Higher Education Act of 1965, 79 Stat. 1219, *billions of dollars* have been granted to parochial and other private schools.

The federal grants to elementary and secondary schools under 79 Stat. 27 were made to the States which in turn made advances to elementary and secondary schools. Those figures are not available.

But the federal grants to private institutions of higher education are revealed in Department of Health, Education, and Welfare (HEW), Digest of Educational Statistics 16 (1969). These show in billions of dollars the following:[15]

1965–66	$1.4
1966–67	$1.6
1967–68	$1.7
1968–69	$1.9
1969–70	$2.1

It is an old, old problem. Madison adverted to it:

"Are there not already examples in the U.S. of ecclesiastical wealth equally beyond its object and the foresight of those who laid the foundation of it? In the U.S. there is a double motive for fixing limits in this case, because wealth may increase not only from additional gifts, but from exorbitant advances in the value of the primitive one. In grants of vacant lands, and of lands in the vicinity of growing towns & Cities the increase of value is often such as if foreseen, would essentially controul the liberality confirming them. The people of the U.S. owe their Independence & their liberty, to the wisdom of descrying in the minute tax of 3 pence on tea, the magnitude of evil comprized in the precedent. Let them exert the same wisdom, in watching

---

[15] These totals include all types of federal aid—physical plants, dormitory construction, laboratories, libraries, lunch programs, fellowships and scholarships, etc.

Of the total federal outlays for education only two-fifths are for programs administered by the Office of Education, other parts of the Department of HEW account for one-fifth. The rest of the outlays are distributed among 24 federal departments and agencies, of which the largest shares are accounted for by the Department of Defense, the Veterans Administration, the National Science Foundation, and the Office of Economic Opportunity. U.S. Bureau of the Budget, Special Analysis, Federal Education Program, 1971 Budget, Special Analysis I, pt. 2, p. 115 (Feb. 1970).

agst every evil lurking under plausible disguises, and growing up from small beginnings."[17]

If believers are entitled to public financial support, so are nonbelievers. A believer and nonbeliever under the present law are treated differently because of the articles of their faith. Believers are doubtless comforted that the cause of religion is being fostered by this legislation. Yet one of the mandates of the First Amendment is to promote a viable, pluralistic society and to keep government neutral, not only between sects, but also between believers and nonbelievers. The present involvement of government in religion may seem *de minimis*. But it is, I fear, a long step down the Establishment path. Perhaps I have been misinformed. But as I have read the Constitution and its philosophy, I gathered that independence was the price of liberty.

I conclude that this tax exemption is unconstitutional.

4. DOUBLE DUTY PRAYER

Marsh v. Chambers
463 U.S. 783 (1983)

Shanler D. Cronk, Assistant Attorney General of Nebraska, argued the cause for petitioners. With him on the briefs was *Paul L. Douglas,* Attorney General.

Herbert J. Friedman argued the cause for respondent. With him on the brief were *Stephen L. Pevar, Burt Neuborne,* and *Charles S. Sims.*

Chief Justice Burger delivered the opinion of the Court.

The question presented is whether the Nebraska Legislature's practice of opening each legislative day with a prayer by a chaplain paid by the State violates the Establishment Clause of the First Amendment.

I

The Nebraska Legislature begins each of its sessions with a prayer offered by a chaplain who is chosen biennially by the Executive Board of the Legislative Council and paid out of public funds.[1] Robert E. Palmer, a Presbyterian minister, has served as chaplain since 1965 at a salary of $319.75 per month for each month the legislature is in session.

Ernest Chambers is a member of the Nebraska Legislature and a taxpayer of Nebraska. Claiming that the Nebraska Legislature's chaplaincy practice violates the Establishment Clause of the First Amendment, he brought this action under 42 U.S.C. § 1983, seeking

---

[17] In 1875 President Grant in his State of the Union Message referred to the vast amounts of untaxed church property.

"In 1850, I believe, the church property of the United States which paid no tax, municipal or State, amounted to about $83,000,000. In 1860 the amount had doubled; in 1875 it is about $1,000,000,000. By 1900, without check, it is safe to say this property will reach a sum exceeding $3,000,000,000. So vast a sum, receiving all the protection and benefits of Government without bearing its proportion of the burdens and expenses of the same, will not be looked upon acquiescently by those who have to pay the taxes."

[1] Rules of the Nebraska Unicameral, Rules 1, 2, and 21. These prayers are recorded in the Legislative Journal and, upon the vote of the legislature, collected from time to time into prayerbooks, which are published at public expense. In 1975, 200 copies were printed; prayerbooks were also published in 1978 (200 copies), and 1979 (100 copies). In total, publication costs amounted to $458.56.

to enjoin enforcement of the practice.[2] After denying a motion to dismiss on the ground of legislative immunity, the District Court held that the Establishment Clause was not breached by the prayers, but was violated by paying the chaplain from public funds. 504 F.Supp. 585 (Neb. 1980). It therefore enjoined the legislature from using public funds to pay the chaplain; it declined to enjoin the policy of beginning sessions with prayers. Cross-appeals were taken.[3]

The Court of Appeals for the Eighth Circuit rejected arguments that the case should be dismissed on Tenth Amendment, legislative immunity, standing, or federalism grounds. On the merits of the chaplaincy issue, the court refused to treat respondent's challenges as separable issues as the District Court had done. Instead, the Court of Appeals assessed the practice as a whole because "[p]arsing out [the] elements" would lead to "an incongruous result." 675 F. 2d 228, 233 (1982).

Applying the three-part test of *Lemon v. Kurtzman* [*infra,* XIV,1], as set out in *Committee for Public Education & Religious Liberty v. Nyquist* [*infra,* XIV, 1] the court held that the chaplaincy practice violated all three elements of the test: the purpose and primary effect of selecting the same minister for 16 years and publishing his prayers was to promote a particular religious expression; use of state money for compensation and publication led to entanglement. 675 F. 2d, at 234–235. Accordingly, the Court of Appeals modified the District Court's injunction and prohibited the State from engaging in any aspect of its established chaplaincy practice.

We granted certiorari limited to the challenge to the practice of opening sessions with prayers by a state-employed clergyman, 459 U.S. 966 (1982), and we reverse.

II

The opening of sessions of legislative and other deliberative public bodies with prayer is deeply embedded in the history and tradition of this country. From colonial times through the founding of the Republic and ever since, the practice of legislative prayer has coexisted with the principles of disestablishment and religious freedom. In the very courtrooms in which the United States District Judge and later three Circuit Judges heard and decided this case, the proceedings opened with an announcement that concluded, "God save the United States and this Honorable Court." The same invocation occurs at all sessions of this Court.

The tradition in many of the Colonies was, of course, linked to an established church,[5] but the Continental Congress, beginning in 1774, adopted the traditional procedure of

---

[2] Respondent named as defendants State Treasurer Frank Marsh, Chaplain Palmer, and the members of the Executive Board of the Legislative Council in their official capacity. All appear as petitioners before us.

[3] The District Court also enjoined the State from using public funds to publish the prayers holding that this practice violated the Establishment Clause. Petitioners have represented to us that they did not challenge this facet of the District Court's decision, Tr. of Oral Arg. 19–20. Accordingly, no issue as to publishing these prayers is before us.

[5] The practice in Colonies with established churches is, of course, not dispositive of the legislative prayer question. The history of Virginia is instructive, however, because that Colony took the lead in defining religious rights. In 1776, the Virginia Convention adopted a Declaration of Rights that included, as Article 16, a guarantee of religious liberty that is considered the precursor of both the Free Exercise and Establishment Clauses. 1 B. Schwartz, The Bill of Rights: A Documentary History 231–236 (1971); S. Cobb, The Rise of Religious Liberty in America 491–492 (1970). Virginia was also among the first to disestablish its church. Both before and after disestablishment, however, Virginia followed the practice of opening legislative sessions with prayer. See, *e.g.,* J. House of Burgesses 34 (Nov. 20, 1712); Debates of the Convention of Virginia 470 (June 2, 1788) (ratification convention); J. House of Delegates of Va. 3 (June 24, 1788) (state legislature).

Rhode Island's experience mirrored that of Virginia. That Colony was founded by Roger Williams, who was among the first of his era to espouse the principle of religious freedom. Cobb, *supra,* at 426. As early as 1641, its legislature provided for liberty of conscience. *Id.,* at 430. Yet the sessions

opening its sessions with a prayer offered by a paid chaplain. See, *e.g.*, 1 J. Continental Cong. 26 (1774); 2 *id.*, at 12 (1775); 5 *id.*, at 530 (1776); 6 *id.*, at 887 (1776); 27 *id.*, at 683 (1784). See also 1 A. Stokes, Church and State in the United States 448–450 (1950). Although prayers were not offered during the Constitutional Convention, [6] the First Congress, as one of its early items of business, adopted the policy of selecting a chaplain to open each session with prayer. Thus, on April 7, 1789, the Senate appointed a committee "to take under consideration the manner of electing Chaplains." S. Jour., 1st Cong., 1st Sess., 10 (1820 ed.). On April 9, 1789, a similar committee was appointed by the House of Representatives. On April 25, 1789, the Senate elected its first chaplain, *id.*, at 16; the House followed suit on May 1, 1789, H. R. Jour., 1st Cong., 1st Sess., 26 (1826 ed.). A statute providing for the payment of these chaplains was enacted into law on September 22, 1789.[7] 2 Annals of Cong. 2180 § 4, 1 Stat. 71.[8]

On September 25, 1789, three days after Congress authorized the appointment of paid chaplains, final agreement was reached on the language of the Bill of Rights, S.Jour., *supra*, at 88; H. R. Jour., *supra*, at 121.[9] Clearly the men who wrote the First Amendment Religion Clause did not view paid legislative chaplains and opening prayers as a violation of that Amendment, for the practice of opening sessions with prayer has continued without interruption ever since that early session of Congress.[10] It has also been followed consistently in most of the states,[11] including Nebraska, where the

---

of its ratification convention, like Virginia's, began with prayers, see W. Staples, Rhode Island in the Continental Congress, 1765–1790, p. 668 (1870) (reprinting May 26, 1790, minutes of the convention).

[6] History suggests that this may simply have been an oversight. At one point, Benjamin Franklin suggested that "henceforth prayers imploring the assistance of Heaven, and its blessings on our deliberations, be held in this Assembly every morning before we proceed to business." 1 M. Farrand, Records of the Federal Convention of 1787 p. 452 (1911). His proposal was rejected not because the Convention was opposed to prayer, but because it was thought that a midstream adoption of the policy would highlight prior omissions and because "[t]he Convention had no funds." *Ibid.*; see also Stokes, at 455–456.

[7] The statute provided:
"[T]here shall be allowed to each chaplain of Congress . . . five hundred dollars per annum during the session of Congress."
This salary compares favorably with the Congressmen's own salaries of $6 for each day of attendance, 1 Stat. 70–71.

[8] It bears note that James Madison, one of the principal advocates of religious freedom in the Colonies and a drafter of the Establishment Clause, see, *e.g.*, Cobb, *supra* n. 5, at 495–497; Stokes, at 537–552, was one of those appointed to undertake this task by the House of Representatives, H.R.Jour., at 11–12; Stokes, at 541–549, and voted for the bill authorizing payment of the chaplains, 1 Annals of Cong. 891 (1789).

[9] Interestingly, September 25, 1789, was also the day that the House resolved to request the President to set aside a Thanksgiving Day to acknowledge "the many signal favors of Almighty God," H.R.Jour., at 123. See also S.Jour., at 88.

[10] The chaplaincy was challenged in the 1850's by "sundry petitions praying Congress to abolish the office of chaplain," S.Rep. No. 376, 32d Cong., 2d Sess., 1 (1853). After consideration by the Senate Committee on the Judiciary, the Senate decided that the practice did not violate the Establishment Clause, reasoning that a rule permitting Congress to elect chaplains is not a law establishing a national church and that the chaplaincy was no different from Sunday Closing Laws, which the Senate thought clearly constitutional. In addition, the Senate reasoned that since prayer was said by the very Congress that adopted the Bill of Rights, the Founding Fathers could not have intended the First Amendment to forbid legislative prayer or viewed prayer as a step toward an established church. *Id.*, at 2–4. In any event, the 35th Congress abandoned the practice of electing chaplains in favor of inviting local clergy to officiate, see Cong. Globe, 35th Cong., 1st Sess., 14, 27–28 (1857). Elected chaplains were reinstituted by the 36th Congress, Cong. Globe, 36th Cong., 1st Sess., 162 (1859); *id.*, at 1016 (1860).

[11] See Brief for National Conference of State Legislatures as *Amicus Curiae.* Although most state legislatures begin their sessions with prayer, most do not have a formal rule requiring this procedure.

institution of opening legislative sessions with prayer was adopted even before the State attained statehood. Neb. Jour. of Council, General Assembly, 1st Sess., 16 (Jan. 22, 1855).

Standing alone, historical patterns cannot justify contemporary violations of constitutional guarantees, but there is far more here than simply historical patterns. In this context, historical evidence sheds light not only on what the draftsmen intended the Establishment Clause to mean, but also on how they thought that Clause applied to the practice authorized by the First Congress—their actions reveal their intent. An Act "passed by the first Congress assembled under the Constitution, many of whose members had taken part in framing that instrument, . . . is contemporaneous and weighty evidence of its true meaning." *Wisconsin v. Pelican Ins. Co.*, 127 U.S. 265, 297 (1888).

. . .

In light of the unambiguous and unbroken history of more than 200 years, there can be no doubt that the practice of opening legislative sessions with prayer has become part of the fabric of our society. To invoke Divine guidance on a public body entrusted with making the laws is not, in these circumstances, an "establishment" of religion or a step toward establishment; it is simply a tolerable acknowledgment of beliefs widely held among the people of this country. As Justice Douglas observed, "[w]e are a religious people whose institutions presuppose a Supreme Being." *Zorach v. Clauson* [*infra*, XIV, 2].

. . .

Nor is the compensation of the chaplain from public funds a reason to invalidate the Nebraska Legislature's chaplaincy; remuneration is grounded in historic practice initiated, as we noted earlier, *supra*, at 788, by the same Congress that drafted the Establishment Clause of the First Amendment. The Continental Congress paid its chaplain, see, *e.g.*, 6 J. Continental Cong. 887 (1776), as did some of the states, see, *e.g.*, Debates of the Convention of Virginia 470 (June 26, 1788). Currently, many state legislatures and the United States Congress provide compensation for their chaplains, Brief for National Conference of State Legislatures as *Amicus Curiae* 3; 2 U.S.C. § § 61d and 84-2 (1982 ed.); H. R. Res. 7, 96th Cong., 1st Sess. (1979).[18] Nebraska has paid

---

But see, *e.g.* Alaska Legislature Uniform Rules 11 and 17 (1981) (providing for opening invocation); Ark. Rule of Senate 18 (1983); Colo. Legislator's Handbook, H. R. Rule 44 (1982); Idaho Rules of H. R. and Joint Rules 2 and 4 (1982); Ind. H. R. Rule 10 (1983); Kan. Rule of Senate 4 (1983); Kan. Rule of H. R. 103 (1983); Ky. General Assembly H. Res. 2 (1982); La. Rules of Order, Senate Rule 10.1. (1983); La. Rules of Order, H.R. Rule 8.1 (1982); Me. Senate and House Register, Rule of H. R. 4 (1983); Md. Senate and House of Delegates Rules 1 (1982 and 1983); Mo. Rules of Legislature, Joint Rule 1-1 (1983); N. H. Manual for the General Court of N. H., Rule of H. R. 52(a) (1981); N. D. Senate and H. R. Rules 101 and 301 (1983); Ore. Rule of Senate 4.01 (1983); Ore. Rule of H. R. 4.01 (1983) (opening session only); 104 Pa. Code § 11.11 (1983), 107 Pa. Code § 21.17 (1983); S. D. Official Directory and Rules of Senate and H. R., Joint Rule of the Senate and House 4-1 (1983); Tenn. Permanent Rules of Order of the Senate 1 and 6 (1981-1982) (provides for admission into Senate chamber of the "Chaplain of the Day"); Tex. Rule of H. R. 2, § 6 (1983); Utah Rules of Senate and H. R. 4.04 (1983); Va. Manual of Senate and House of Delegates, Rule of Senate 21(a) (1982) (session opens with "period of devotions"); Wash. Permanent Rule of H. R. 15 (1983); Wyo. Rule of Senate 4-1 (1983); Wyo. Rule of H. R. 2-1 (1983). See also P. Mason, Manual of Legislative Procedure § 586(2) (1979).

[18] The states' practices differ widely. Like Nebraska, several states choose a chaplain who serves for the entire legislative session. In other states, the prayer is offered by a different clergyman each day. Under either system, some states pay their chaplains and others do not. For States providing for compensation statutorily or by resolution, see, *e.g.*, Cal. Gov't Code Ann. §§ 9170,9171,9320 (West 1980), and S. Res. No. 6, 1983-1984 Sess.; Colo. H. R. J., 54th Gen. Assembly, 1st Sess., 17-19 (Jan. 5, 1983); Conn. Gen. Stat. Ann. § 2-9 (1983-1984); Ga. H. R. Res. No. 3, § 1(e) (1983); Ga. S. Res. No. 3, § 1(c) (1983); Iowa Code § 2.11 (1983); Mo. Rev. Stat. § 21.150 (1978); Nev. Rev. Stat. § 218.200 (1981); N.J. Stat. Ann. § 52:11-2 (West 1970); N.M. Const., Art. IV,

its chaplain for well over a century, see 1867 Neb. Laws 85, § § 2–4 (June 21, 1867), reprinted in Neb. Gen. Stat. 459 (1873). The content of the prayer is not of concern to judges where, as here, there is no indication that the prayer opportunity has been exploited to proselytize or advance any one, or to disparage any other, faith or belief. That being so, it is not for us to embark on a sensitive evaluation or to parse the content of a particular prayer.

Reversed.

. . .

Justice Brennan, with whom Justice Marshall joins, dissenting.

. . .

That the "purpose" of legislative prayer is pre-eminently religious rather than secular seems to me to be self-evident. "To invoke Divine guidance on a public body entrusted with making the laws," *ante*, at 792, is nothing but a religious act. Moreover, whatever secular functions legislative prayer might play—formally opening the legislative session, getting the members of the body to quiet down, and imbuing them with a sense of seriousness and high purpose—could so plainly be performed in a purely nonreligious fashion that to claim a secular purpose for the prayer is an insult to the perfectly honorable individuals who instituted and continue the practice.

. . .

More fundamentally, however, *any* practice of legislative prayer, even if it might look "nonsectarian" to nine Justices of the Supreme Court, will inevitably and continuously involve the State in one or another religious debate.[39] Prayer is serious business—serious theological business—and it is not a mere "acknowledgment of beliefs widely held among the people of this country" for the State to immerse itself in that business.[40] Some religious individuals or groups find it theologically problematic to engage in joint religious exercises predominantly influenced by faiths not their own.[41] Some might object even to the attempt to fashion a "nonsectarian prayer.[42] Some would find it impossible to participate in any "prayer opportunity," *ante*, at 794, marked by Trinitarian references.[43] Some would find a prayer *not* invoking the name of Christ to represent a flawed

---

§ 9; Okla. Stat. Ann., Tit. 74, §§ 291.12 and 292.1 (West Supp. 1982–1983); Vt. Stat. Ann., Tit. 2, § 19 (Supp. 1982); Wis. Stat. Ann. § 13.125 (West Supp. 1982).

[39] See generally Cahn, On Government and Prayer, 37 N. Y. U. L. Rev. 981 (1962); Hearings, ["Prayer in Public Schools and Buildings—Federal Court Jurisdiction, Hearings before the Subcommittee on Courts, Civil Liberties, and the Administration of Justice of the House Committee on the Judiciary," 96th Cong., 2d Sess., 46–47 (1980) (testimony of M. William Howard, President of the National Council of the Churches of Christ in the U.S.A.) (hereinafter Hearings)] ("there is simply no such thing as 'nonsectarian' prayer . . .").

Cf. N. Y. Times, Sept. 4, 1982, p. 8, col. 2 ("Mr. [Jerry] Falwell [founder of the organization "Moral Majority"] is quoted as telling a meeting of the Religious Newswriters Association in New Orleans that because members of the Moral Majority represented a variety of denominations, 'if we ever opened a Moral Majority meeting with prayer, silent or otherwise, we would disintegrate' ").

[40] I put to one side, not because of its irrelevance, but because of its obviousness, the fact that any official prayer will pose difficulties both for nonreligious persons and for religious persons whose faith does not include the institution of prayer, see, *e.g.*, H. Smith, The Religions of Man 138 (Perennial Library ed. 1965) (discussing Theravada Buddhism).

[41] See, *e.g.*, Hearings 46–47 (testimony of M. Howard) ("We are told that [school] prayers could be 'nonsectarian,' or that they could be offered from various religious traditions in rotation. I believe such a solution is least acceptable to those most fervently devoted to their own religion"); S. Freehof, Modern Reform Responsa 71 (1971) (ecumenical services not objectionable in principle, but they should not take place too frequently); J. Bancroft, Communication in Religious Worship with Non-Catholics (1943).

[42] See, *e.g.*, Hearings, at 47 (testimony of M. Howard) (nonsectarian prayer, even if were possible, would likely be "offensive to devout members of all religions").

[43] See, *e.g.*, S. Freehof, Reform Responsa 115 (1960).

view of the relationship between human beings and God.[44] Some might find any petitionary prayer to be improper.[45] Some might find any prayer that lacked a petitionary element to be deficient.[46] Some might be troubled by what they consider shallow public prayer,[47] or nonspontaneous prayer,[48] or prayer without adequate spiritual preparation or concentration.[49] Some might, of course, have *theological* objections to any prayer sponsored by an organ of government.[50] Some might object on theological grounds to the level of political neutrality generally expected of government-sponsored invocational prayer.[51] And some might object on theological grounds to the Court's requirement, *ante*, at 794, that prayer, even though religious, not be proselytizing.[52] If these problems arose in the context of a religious objection to some otherwise decidedly secular activity, then whatever remedy there is would have to be found in the Free Exercise Clause. See n. 13, *supra*. But, in this case, we are faced with potential religious objections to an activity at the very center of religious life, and it is simply beyond the competence of government, and inconsistent with our conceptions of liberty, for the State to take upon itself the role of ecclesiastical arbiter.

IV

The argument is made occasionally that a strict separation of religion and state robs the Nation of its spiritual identity. I believe quite the contrary. It may be true that individuals cannot be "neutral" on the question of religion.[53] But the judgment of the Establishment Clause is that neutrality by the organs of *government* on questions of religion is both possible and imperative. Alexis de Tocqueville wrote the following concerning his travels through this land in the early 1830's:

"The religious atmosphere of the country was the first thing that struck me on arrival in the United States. . . .

---

[44] See, *e.g.*, D. Bloesch, The Struggle of Prayer 36–37 (1980) (hereinafter Bloesch) ("Because our Savior plays such a crucial role in the life of prayer, we should always pray having in mind his salvation and intercession. We should pray not only in the spirit of Christ but also in the name of Christ. . . . To pray in his name means that we recognize that our prayers cannot penetrate the tribunal of God unless they are presented to the Father by the Son, our one Savior and Redeemer"); cf. Fischer, The Role of Christ in Christian Prayer, 41 Encounter 153, 155–156 (1980).

As the Court points out, Reverend Palmer eliminated the Christological references in his prayers after receiving complaints from some of the State Senators. *Ante*, at 793, n. 14. Suppose, however, that Reverend Palmer had said that he could not in good conscience omit some references. Should he have been dismissed? And, if so, what would have been the implications of *that* action under both the Establishment and the Free Exercise Clauses?

[45] See, *e.g.*, Meister Eckhart 88–89 (R. Blakney trans. 1941); T. Merton, Contemplative Prayer (1971); J. Williams, What Americans Believe and How they Worship 412–413 (3d ed. 1969) (hereinafter Williams) (discussing Christian Science belief that only proper prayer is prayer of communion).

[46] See, *e.g.*, Bloesch 72–73; Stump, Petitionary Prayer, 16 Am. Philosophical Q. 81 (1979); Wells, Prayer: Rebelling Against the Status Quo, Christianity Today, Nov. 2, 1979, pp. 32–34.

[47] See, *e.g.*, Matthew 6:6 ("But thou, when thou prayest, enter into thy closet, and when thou hast shut thy door, pray to thy Father which is in secret; and thy Father which seeth in secret shall reward thee openly").

[48] See, *e.g.*, Williams 274–275 (discussing traditional Quaker practice).

[49] See, *e.g.*, Heschel, *Man's Quest for God* (1954) at 53; Heiler, *supra* n. 24, at 283–285.

[50] See, *e.g.*, Williams 256; 3 Stokes 133–134; Hearings, at 65–66 (statement of Baptist Joint Committee on Public Affairs).

[51] See, *e.g.*, R. Niebuhr, Faith and Politics 100 (R. Stone ed. 1968) ("A genuinely prophetic religion speaks a word of judgment against every ruler and every nation, even against good rulers and good nations").

[52] See, *e.g.*, Bloesch 159 ("World evangelization is to be numbered among the primary goals in prayer, since the proclaiming of the gospel is what gives glory to God").

[53] See W. James, The Will to Believe 1–31 (1st ed. 1897).

"In France I had seen the spirits of religion and of freedom almost always marching in opposite directions. In America I found them intimately linked together in joint reign over the same land.

"My longing to understand the reason for this phenomenon increased daily.

"To find this out, I questioned the faithful of all communions; I particularly sought the society of clergymen, who are the depositaries of the various creeds and have a personal interest in their survival. . . . I expressed my astonishment and revealed my doubts to each of them; I found that they all agreed with each other except about details; all thought that the main reason for the quiet sway of religion over their country was the complete separation of church and state. I have no hesitation in stating that throughout my stay in America I met nobody, lay or cleric, who did not agree about that." Democracy in America 295 (G. Lawrence trans., J. Mayer ed., 1969).

More recent history has only confirmed de Tocqueville's observations. If the Court had struck down legislative prayer today, it would likely have stimulated a furious reaction. But it would also, I am convinced, have invigorated both the "spirit of religion" and the "spirit of freedom."

I respectfully dissent.

Justice Stevens also dissented.

NOTE. *Double Duty Chaplains.* West Point, Annapolis, and Colorado Springs all had regulations requiring cadets and midshipmen at the respective service academies to attend weekly Protestant, Catholic, or Jewish chapel services. Conscientious objectors were excused. In a class action on behalf of all the students, the regulations were held to violate the establishment clause. The government's claim was that "the sole purpose of chapel attendance is to develop in the cadets, through observation of the impact of religion on the lives of others during actual worship services, that sensitivity to religious emotion which is required of a military leader." The Court of Appeals doubted that the purpose was "wholly secular," finding in the regulations "an outright encouragement of religious worship," *Anderson v. Laird*, 466 F. 2d 283 (D.C. Cir. 1972) (2-1 decision), *cert. denied*, 409 U.S. 1076 (1972).

In 1985 the premises of *Anderson* were taken further in a challenge to the armed services' chaplaincy programs, *Katcoff v. Marsh*, 755 F. 2d. 223 (2nd Cir. 1985). Judge Walter R. Mansfield wrote:

Appellants, two practicing attorneys who were Harvard Law School students when they commenced this action, appeal from an order of the Eastern District of New York, Joseph M. McLaughlin, Judge, granting summary judgment dismissing their complaint, which seeks declaratory and injunctive relief against continuation of the Army's chaplaincy program as violative of the Establishment Clause. We affirm except to the extent that the order applies to a few specific aspects of the program, which we reverse and remand for further proceedings.

Congress, in the exercise of its powers under Art. I § 8, of the Constitution to provide for the conduct of our national defense, has established an Army for the purpose of "preserving the peace and security, and providing for the defense, of the United States," 10 U.S.C. § 3062(a), and has directed that the "organized peace establishment of the Army" consist of all organizations and persons "necessary to form the basis for a complete and immediate mobilization for the national defense in the event of a national emergency," 10 U.S.C. § 3062(d). It has specifically authorized that as part of this establishment there be "Chaplains in the Army," who shall include the Chief of Chaplains, and commissioned and other officers of the Army appointed as chaplains. 10 U.S.C. § 3073. Under 10 U.S.C § 3547 each chaplain is required, when practicable, to hold religious services for the command to which he is assigned and to perform burial services for soldiers who die while in that command. The statute also obligates the commanding officer to furnish facilities, including transportation, to assist a chaplain in performing his duties. *Id.*

In providing our armed forces with a military chaplaincy Congress has perpetuated a facility that began during Revolutionary days before the adoption of our Constitution, and that has continued ever since then, with the size of the chaplaincy growing larger in proportion to the increase in the size of our Army. When the Continental Army was formed those chaplains attached to the militia of the 13 colonies became part of our country's first national army. P. Thompson, 1 *The United States Army Chaplaincy* xix (1978). On July 29, 1775, the Continental Congress authorized that a Continental Army chaplain be paid, II Cont.Cong.Jour. 220 (1775), and within a year General George Washington directed that regimental Continental Army chaplains be procured. V *The Writings of George Washington From The Original Manuscript Sources* 244–45 (J. Fitzgerald ed. 1932).

Upon the adoption of the Constitution and before the December 1791 ratification of the First Amendment Congress authorized the appointment of a commissioned Army chaplain. Act of March 3, 1791, Ch. XXVIII, § 5,1 Stat. 222. Since then, as the Army has increased in size the military chaplaincy has been extended and Congress has increased the number of Army chaplains. *See, e.g.,* Act of April 12, 1808, 2 Stat. 481; Act of January 11, 1812, 2 Stat. 671; Act of July 5, 1838, Ch. CLXII, § 18, 5 Stat. 259; Act of February 11, 1847, Ch. VIII, § 7,9 Stat. 124; Act of February 11, 1847, 9 Stat. 123; Act of July 22, 1861, Ch. IX, § 9, 12 Stat. 270.

In 1981 the Army had approximately 1,427 active-duty commissioned chaplains, 10 auxiliary chaplains, 1,383 chaplain's assistants, and 48 Directors of Religious Education. These chaplains are appointed as commissioned officers with rank and uniform but without command. 10 U.S.C. §§ 3293, 3581. Before an applicant may be appointed to the position of chaplain he must receive endorsement from an ecclesiastical endorsing agency recognized by the Armed Forces Chaplains Board, of which there are 47 in the United States, representing 120 denominations. In addition to meeting the theological standards of the endorsing agency the applicant must also meet minimum educational requirements established by the Department of Defense, which are more stringent than those of some religious denominations having endorsing agencies and are designed to insure the applicant's ability to communicate with soldiers of all ranks and to administer religious programs. In deciding upon the denominations of chaplains to be appointed the Office of the Chief of Chaplains establishes quotas based on the denominational distribution of the population of the United States as a whole. The entire civilian church population rather than the current military religious population is used in order to assure that in the event of war or total mobilization the denominational breakdown will accurately reflect that of the larger-sized Army.

Upon his appointment the chaplain, except for a number of civilian clerics provided voluntarily or by contract, is subject to the same discipline and training as that given to other officers and soldiers. He is trained in such subjects as Army organization, command relationships, supply, planning, teaching, map-reading, types of warfare, security, battlefield survival, and military administration. When ordered with troops into any area, including a combat zone under fire, he must obey. He must be prepared to meet problems inherent in Army life, including how to handle trauma, death or serious injury of soldiers on the field of battle, marital and family stresses of military personnel, tending the wounded or dying, and psychological treatment of soldiers' drug or alcohol abuse, as well as the alleviation of tensions between soldiers and their commanders. On the other hand, the chaplain is not required to bear arms or receive training in weapons. Under Articles 33 and 35 of the Geneva Conventions Relative to Treatment of Prisoners of War "chaplains" are accorded a non-combatant status, which means that they are not to be considered prisoners of war and they may exercise their ministry among prisoners of war. Promotion of a chaplain within the military ranks is based solely on his military performance and not on his effectiveness as a cleric.

The primary function of the military chaplain is to engage in activities designed to meet the religious needs of a pluralistic military community, including military personnel and their dependents. In view of the Army's huge size (some 788,000 soldiers and 1,300,000 dependents in 1981) and its far-flung distribution (291,000 soldiers stationed abroad and many in remote areas of the United States) the task is an important and formidable one. The Army consists of a wide spectrum of persons of different ethnic, racial and religious backgrounds who go into military service from varied social, economic and educational environments. The great majority of the soldiers in the Army express religious preferences. About 80% are under 30 years of age and a large number are married. As a result it has become necessary to provide religious facilities for soldiers of some 86 different denominations.[1] A sample survey of military personnel made by the Army in 1979 revealed the following religious preferences among enlisted personnel:

---

[1] The Army chaplains have been distributed by denominations as follows:

DENOMINATION	1980	1981	DENOMINATION	1980	1981
Advent Christian	3	3	Conservative Congregational		
African Methodist Episcopal	12	12	Christian Conf.	6	6
African Methodist Episcopal Zion	4	4	Disciples of Christ	48	50
American Baptist Association	2	3	Eastern Orthodox	2	2
American Baptist Churches, USA	54	52	Elim Fellowship	1	1
American Council of Christian			Evangelical Church in America	1	1
Churches	1	1	Evangelical Congregational	4	3
Anglican Orthodox	1	1	Evangelical Free Church	9	9
Assemblies of God	32	34	Evangelical Covenant Church of		
Associated Gospel	5	5	America	4	4
Association of Evangelical			Evangelical Methodist	0	1
Lutherans	2	2	Fellowship of Grace Brethren	3	3
Association Free Lutheran			Fire Baptist Holiness	1	1
Church	1	1	Four Square Gospel	2	2
Association of Reformed			Full Gospel Pentecostal	1	1
Presbyterian	2	2	General Association of General		
Baptist General Conference	13	11	Baptist	6	7
Baptist Missionary	1	1	General Association of Regular		
Brethren Church	0	1	Baptists	17	17
Catholic	243	238	Grace Gospel Fellowship	0	1
Cedar Mill Bible	1	1	Independent Fundamental		
Christian Churches & Churches			Churches of America	12	11
of Christ	12	13	Jewish	23	21
Christian Methodist Episcopal	20	19	Latter-Day Saints	18	20
Christian & Missionary Alliance	7	8	Latter-Day Saints (Reorganized)	1	1
Christian Reformed	8	7	Lutheran Church in America	84	85
Christian Science	8	9	Lutheran Church-Missouri Synod	47	47
Church of Christ	12	14	Methodist Free Church	7	8
Church of Christ in Christian			Missionary Church	1	1
Union	1	1	Moravian	2	3
Church of God, Indiana	8	8	National Association of Free Will		
Church of God, TN	9	9	Baptists	4	4
Church of God in Christ, Inc.	7	8	National Baptist Convention of		
Church of God of Prophecy	3	3	America	6	7
Churches of God, General			National Baptist Convention,		
Conference	1	1	USA	30	33
Congregational Christian			Nazarene	22	23
(National Association)	4	4	No. American Baptist Conference	6	5
Conservative Baptist Association			Open Bible Standard	2	2
of America	15	14	Orthodox Church in America	7	8

Protestant	38.5%
Catholic	22.5%
Mormon	2.5%
Eastern Orthodox	0.5%
Moslem	1.0%
Jewish	0.7%
Buddhist	0.7%
Other religions not listed	19.3%
No religious preference	14.3%

Aside from the problems arising out of the sheer size and pluralistic nature of the Army, its members experience increased needs for religion as the result of being uprooted from their home environments, transported often thousands of miles to territories entirely strange to them, and confronted there with new stresses that would not otherwise have been encountered if they had remained at home. In 1981 approximately 37% of the Army's active duty soldiers, amounting to 293,000 persons, were stationed overseas in locations such as Turkey, Sinai, Greece, or Korea. In most of these areas the Judeo-Christian faiths of most American soldiers are hardly represented at all by local clergy and the average soldier is separated from the local populace by a linguistic and cultural wall. Within the United States the same problem exists in a somewhat different way in that, although the linguistic or cultural barrier may be absent, local civilian clergy in the rural areas where most military camps are centered are inadequate to satisfy the soldiers' religious needs because they are too few in number for the task and are usually of different religious denominations from those of most of the nearby troops.

The problem of meeting the religious needs of Army personnel is compounded by the mobile, deployable nature of our armed forces, who must be ready on extremely short notice to be transported from bases (whether or not in the United States) to distant parts of the world for combat duty in fulfillment of our nation's international defense commitments. Unless there were chaplains ready to move simultaneously with the troops and to tend to their spiritual needs as they face possible death, the soldiers would be left in the lurch, religiously speaking. In the opinion of top generals of the Army and those presently in the chaplaincy, unless chaplains were made available in such circumstances the motivation, morale and willingness of soldiers to face combat would suffer immeasurable harm and our national defense would be weakened accordingly.

Many soldiers in the Army also suffer serious stresses from other causes attributable largely to their military service, which can be alleviated by counseling and spiritual assistance from a leader of their respective faiths. Among these are tensions created by separation from their homes, loneliness when on duty in strange surroundings involving people whose language or customs they do not share, fear of facing combat or new assignments, financial hardships, personality conflicts, and drug, alcohol or family problems. The soldier faced with any of these problems at home would usually be able

DENOMINATION	1980	1981	DENOMINATION	1980	1981
Orthodox Presbyterian	2	2	Reformed Church in America	8	7
Pentecostal Church of God in			Reformed Presbyterian		
America	2	2	Evangelical Synod	8	8
Pentecostal Holiness	4	5	Seventh-Day Adventist	7	7
Plymouth Brethren	4	4	Southern Baptist	176	162
Presbyterian Church in America	2	3	Unitarian-Universalist Assn.	2	2
Presbyterian, Cumberland	11	11	United Church of Christ	38	38
Presbyterian, US	27	27	United Methodist	169	163
Progressive National Baptist			United Pentecostal, International	2	3
Convention	3	5	United Presbyterian, USA	48	47
Protestant Episcopal	39	39	Wesleyan	6	7

to consult his spiritual adviser. The Army seeks to furnish the same services through military chaplains. In doing so the Army has proceeded on the premise that having uprooted the soldiers from their natural habitats it owes them a duty to satisfy their Free Exercise rights, especially since the failure to do so would diminish morale, thereby weakening our national defense.

To meet the religious needs of our armed forces Army chaplains and their assistants engage in a wide variety of services to military personnel and their families who wish to use them. No chaplain is authorized to proselytize soldiers or their families. The chaplain's principal duties are to conduct religious services (including periodic worship, baptisms, marriages, funerals and the like), to furnish religious education to soldiers and their families, and to counsel soldiers with respect to a wide variety of personal problems. In addition the chaplain, because of his close relationship with the soldiers in his unit, often serves as a liaison between the soldiers and their commanders, advising the latter of racial unrest, drug or alcohol abuse, and other problems affecting the morale and efficiency of the unit, and helps to find solutions. In some areas the Army also makes available religious retreats, in which soldiers voluntarily withdraw for a short period from the routine activities of daily living to another location for spiritual reflection and renewal.

For this comprehensive religious program involving hundreds of thousands of soldiers and their families, the Army has a large and fairly elaborate administrative organization, including not only the chaplains but also supporting personnel, facilities, publications, and other supplies. The Chief of Chaplains, a major general of the Army, is in general supervision and management of the Army's chaplaincy. His office contains three divisions: (1) Administration and Management, which, among other things, maintains liaison with religious and secular organizations, (2) Plans, Programs and Policies, and (3) Personnel and Ecclesiastical Relations. These divisions work closely with the Department of Defense Armed Forces Chaplains Board. Over the years the Army has built or acquired more than 500 chapels which are used for the conduct of religious services of many different denominations. In addition it has built more than 100 Religious Educational Facilities, which are used for religious services and classes in religious education for soldiers and members of their families of all ages (including children). The Army has purchased and made available for voluntary use by various denominations numerous chaplain's kits, vocational kits, communion sets and vestments, and religious publications (including Holy Scriptures and Prayer Books for Jewish Personnel, the New Testament of our Lord and Savior Jesus Christ, and a Book of Worship), and has developed a Cooperative Curriculum for Religious Education of the Armed Forces. Professional education and training has also been furnished to Army chaplains.

In view of the huge task faced in providing religion to our armed forces the Army has, in addition to chaplains, employed civilians to assist them in carrying out the program. These include Directors of Religious Education, assistants to chaplains, organists, voluntary religious teachers who participate in its voluntary religious education program, a small number of "auxiliary chaplains" and civilian or "contract clergy" who are employed to perform denominational services for the military community when military and operational requirements permit and chaplains for such denominations or religions are unavailable on the military installation.

The great majority of the chaplaincy's services, facilities, and supplies are procured by the Army through funds appropriated by Congress, which amounted to over $85 million for the fiscal year 1981, of which more than $62 million was used to pay the salaries and other compensation of chaplains, chaplain's assistants and auxiliary chaplains. Much smaller amounts were paid for the services of contract chaplains ($332,000), directors of religious education ($221,000), and organists and choir directors ($412,000). Some $7.7 million of non-appropriated funds, representing voluntary contributions or designated offerings from soldiers and their dependents, were also used in the fiscal year 1981 to provide for the needs of the Army's chaplaincy program. Generally speaking, non-appropriated funds are used for denominational activities such as the purchase of sacred items and literature and the salaries of organists and the choir directors.

The plaintiffs conceded that "some chaplaincy" was essential and proposed a civilian system that the court found so inherently impractical as to border on the frivolous. The court concluded:

Lastly, even if plaintiffs' proposal were feasible it would, assuming the *Lemon* standard advanced by the plaintiffs were held applicable, violate the Establishment Clause. The Army, financed by Congress, would to at least some extent still be commanding the civilian chaplains and supporting them with taxpayer-provided "logistical support, co-ordination and training in military affairs" (Appellants' Reply Br. 18), including transport, food and facilities.

[6]   We find that the more appropriate standard of relevancy to our national defense and reasonable necessity is met by the great majority of the Army's existing chaplaincy activities. The purpose and effect of the program is to make religion, religious education, counseling and religious facilities available to military personnel and their families under circumstances where the practice of religion would otherwise be denied as a practical matter to all or a substantial number. As a result, the morale of our soldiers, their willingness to serve, and the efficiency of the Army as an instrument for our national defense rests in substantial part on the military chaplaincy, which is vital to our Army's functioning.

[7]   In a few areas, however, the reasonable necessity for certain activities of the military chaplaincy is not readily apparent. For instance, it appears that in some large urban centers, such as at the Pentagon in Washington, D.C., in New York City and San Francisco, government funds may be used to provide military chaplains, facilities and retreats to "armchair" military personnel who, like other government civil servants, commute daily to their homes and spend their free hours (including weekends) in locations where civilian clergy and facilities are just as available to them as to other non-military citizens. Plaintiffs also assert that government-financed Army chaplains and facilities are provided to retired military personnel and their families. If the ability of such personnel to worship in their own communities is not inhibited by their military service and funds for these chaplains and facilities would not otherwise be expended, the justification for a governmental program of religious support for them is questionable and, notwithstanding our deference to Congress in military matters, requires a showing that they are relevant to and reasonably necessary for the conduct of our national defense by the Army. A remand therefore becomes necessary to determine whether, according to the standard we have outlined, government financing of a military chaplaincy in these limited areas for the purposes indicated is constitutionally permissible.

5. DOUBLE DUTY DISPLAYS

Lynch v. Donnelly
465 U.S. 668 (1984)

William F. McMahon argued the cause for petitioners. With him on the briefs were *Richard P. McMahon* and *Spencer W. Viner.*

Solicitor General Lee argued the cause for the United States as *amicus curiae* urging reversal. With him on the brief were *Assistant Attorney General McGrath, Deputy Solicitor General Bator, Deputy Assistant Attorney General Kuhl,* and *Kathryn A. Oberly.*

Amato A. DeLuca argued the cause for respondents. With him on the brief were *Sandra A. Blanding, Burt Neuborne, E. Richard Larson,* and *Norman Dorsen.*

Chief Justice Burger delivered the opinion of the Court.

We granted certiorari to decide whether the Establishment Clause of the First Amendment prohibits a municipality from including a crèche, or Nativity scene, in its annual Christmas display.

I

Each year, in cooperation with the downtown retail merchants' association, the city of Pawtucket, R.I., erects a Christmas display as part of its observance of the Christmas holiday season. The display is situated in a park owned by a nonprofit organization and located in the heart of the shopping district. The display is essentially like those to be found in hundreds of towns or cities across the Nation—often on public grounds— during the Christmas season. The Pawtucket display comprises many of the figures and decorations traditionally associated with Christmas, including, among other things, a Santa Claus house, reindeer pulling Santa's sleigh, candy-striped poles, a Christmas tree, carolers, cutout figures representing such characters as a clown, an elephant, and a teddy bear, hundreds of colored lights, a large banner that reads "SEASONS GREETINGS," and the crèche at issue here. All components of this display are owned by the city.

The crèche, which has been included in the display for 40 or more years, consists of the traditional figures, including the Infant Jesus, Mary and Joseph, angels, shepherds, kings, and animals, all ranging in height from 5″ to 5′. In 1973, when the present crèche was acquired, it cost the city $1,365; it now is valued at $200. The erection and dismantling of the crèche costs the city about $20 per year; nominal expenses are incurred in lighting the crèche. No money has been expended on its maintenance for the past 10 years.

Respondents, Pawtucket residents and individual members of the Rhode Island affiliate of the American Civil Liberties Union, and the affiliate itself, brought this action in the United States District Court for Rhode Island, challenging the city's inclusion of the crèche in the annual display. The District Court held that the city's inclusion of the crèche in the display violates the Establishment Clause, 525 F. Supp. 1150, 1178 (1981), which is binding on the states through the Fourteenth Amendment. The District Court found that, by including the crèche in the Christmas display, the city has "tried to endorse and promulgate religious beliefs," *id.,* at 1173, and that "erection of the crèche has the real and substantial effect of affiliating the City with the Christian beliefs that the creche represents." *Id.,* at 1177. This "appearance of official sponsorship," it believed, "confers more than a remote and incidental benefit on Christianity." *Id.,* at 1178. Last, although the court acknowledged the absence of administrative entanglement, it found that excessive entanglement has been fostered as a result of the political divisiveness of including the crèche in the celebration. *Id.,* at 1179–1180. The city was permanently enjoined from including the crèche in the display.

A divided panel of the Court of Appeals for the First Circuit affirmed. 691 F.2d 1029 (1982). We granted certiorari, 460 U.S. 1080 (1983), and we reverse.

. . .The concept of a "wall" of separation is a useful figure of speech probably deriving from views of Thomas Jefferson. The metaphor has served as a reminder that the Establishment Clause forbids an established church or anything approaching it. But the metaphor itself is not a wholly accurate description of the practical aspects of the relationship that in fact exists between church and state.

No significant segment of our society and no institution within it can exist in a vacuum or in total or absolute isolation. . . .

Our history is replete with official references to the value and invocation of Divine guidance in deliberations and pronouncements of the Founding Fathers and contemporary leaders. Beginning in the early colonial period long before Independence, a day of Thanksgiving was celebrated as a religious holiday to give thanks for the bounties of Nature as gifts from God. President Washington and his successors proclaimed Thanksgiving, with all its religious overtones, a day of national celebration and Congress made it a National Holiday more than a century ago. Ch. 167, 16 Stat. 168. That holiday has not lost its theme of expressing thanks for Divine aid any more than has Christmas lost its religious significance.

Executive Orders and other official announcements of Presidents and of the Congress have proclaimed both Christmas and Thanksgiving National Holidays in religious terms. And, by Acts of Congress, it has long been the practice that federal employees are released from duties on these National Holidays, while being paid from the same public revenues that provide the compensation of the Chaplains of the Senate and the House and the military services. See J. Res. 5, 23 Stat. 516. Thus, it is clear that Government has long recognized—indeed it has subsidized—holidays with religious significance.

Other examples of reference to our religious heritage are found in the statutorily prescribed national motto "In God We Trust," 36 U.S.C. § 186, which Congress and the President mandated for our currency, see 31 U.S.C. § 5112(d)(1) (1982 ed.), and in the language "One nation under God," as part of the Pledge of Allegiance to the American flag. That pledge is recited by many thousands of public school children— and adults—every year.

Art galleries supported by public revenues display religious paintings of the 15th and 16th centuries, predominantly inspired by one religious faith. The National Gallery in Washington, maintained with Government support, for example, has long exhibited masterpieces with religious messages, notably the Last Supper, and paintings depicting the Birth of Christ, the Crucifixion, and the Resurrection, among many others with explicit Christian themes and messages.[4] The very chamber in which oral arguments on this case were heard is decorated with a notable and permanent—not seasonal— symbol of religion: Moses with the Ten Commandments. Congress has long provided chapels in the Capitol for religious worship and meditation.

There are countless other illustrations of the Government's acknowledgment of our religious heritage and governmental sponsorship of graphic manifestations of that heritage. Congress has directed the President to proclaim a National Day of Prayer each year "on which [day] the people of the United States may turn to God in prayer and meditation at churches, in groups, and as individuals." 36 U.S.C. § 169h. Our Presidents have repeatedly issued such Proclamations.[5] Presidential Proclamations and messages have also issued to commemorate Jewish Heritage Week, Presidential Proclamation No. 4844, 3 CFR 30 (1982), and the Jewish High Holy Days, 17 Weekly Comp. of Pres. Doc. 1058 (1981). One cannot look at even this brief résumé without finding that our history is pervaded by expressions of religious beliefs such as are found in *Zorach.* Equally pervasive is the evidence of accommodation of all faiths and all forms of religious expression, and hostility toward none. Through this accommodation, as Justice Douglas observed, governmental action has "follow[ed] the best of our traditions" and "respect[ed] the religious nature of our people." 343 U.S., at 314

III

This history may help explain why the Court consistently has declined to take a rigid, absolutist view of the Establishment Clause. We have refused "to construe the Religion Clauses with a literalness that would undermine the ultimate constitutional objective *as illuminated by history." Walz v. Tax Comm'n., supra,* [XIII, 3] (1970) (emphasis added). In our modern, complex society, whose traditions and constitutional underpinnings rest on and encourage diversity and pluralism in all areas, an absolutist approach

---

[4] The National Gallery regularly exhibits more than 200 similar religious paintings.

[5] See, *e. g.,* Presidential Proclamation No. 5017, 48 Fed. Reg. 4261 (1983); Presidential Proclamation No. 4795, 3 CFR 109 (1981); Presidential Proclamation No. 4379, 3 CFR 486 (1971–1975 Comp.); Presidential Proclamation No. 4087, 3 CFR 81 (1971–1975 Comp.); Presidential Proclamation No. 3812, 3 CFR 155 (1966–1970 Comp.); Presidential Proclamation No. 3501, 3 CFR 228 (1959–1963 Comp.).

in applying the Establishment Clause is simplistic and has been uniformly rejected by the Court.

Rather than mechanically invalidating all governmental conduct or statutes that confer benefits or give special recognition to religion in general or to one faith—as an absolutist approach would dictate—the Court has scrutinized challenged legislation or official conduct to determine whether, in reality, it establishes a religion or religious faith, or tends to do so. See *Walz, supra*, at 669. Joseph Story wrote a century and a half ago:
"The real object of the [First] Amendment was . . . to prevent any national ecclesiastical establishment, which should give to an hierarchy the exclusive patronage of the national government." 3 J. Story, Commentaries on the Constitution of the United States 728 (1833).

In each case, the inquiry calls for line-drawing; no fixed, *per se* rule can be framed. The Establishment Clause like the Due Process Clauses is not a precise, detailed provision in a legal code capable of ready application. The purpose of the Establishment Clause "was to state an objective, not to write a statute. *Walz, supra*, at 668. The line between permissible relationships and those barred by the Clause can no more be straight and unwavering than due process can be defined in a single stroke or phrase or test. The Clause erects a "blurred, indistinct, and variable barrier depending on all the circumstances of a particular relationship." *Lemon* [*infra* XIV, 1].

In the line-drawing process we have often found it useful to inquire whether the challenged law or conduct has a secular purpose, whether its principal or primary effect is to advance or inhibit religion, and whether it creates an excessive entanglement of government with religion. *Lemon, supra*. But, we have repeatedly emphasized our unwillingness to be confined to any single test or criterion in this sensitive area.

. . . The narrow question is whether there is a secular purpose for Pawtucket's display of the crèche. The display is sponsored by the city to celebrate the Holiday and to depict the origins of that Holiday. These are legitimate secular purposes. The District Court's inference, drawn from the religious nature of the crèche, that the city has no secular purpose was, on this record, clearly erroneous.

The District Court found that the primary effect of including the crèche is to confer a substantial and impermissible benefit on religion in general and on the Christian faith in particular. Comparisons of the relative benefits to religion of different forms of governmental support are elusive and difficult to make. But to conclude that the primary effect of including the crèche is to advance religion in violation of the Establishment Clause would require that we view it as more beneficial to and more an endorsement of religion, for example, than expenditure of large sums of public money for textbooks supplied throughout the country to students attending church-sponsored schools, *Board of Education v. Allen, supra;* expenditure of public funds for transportation of students to church-sponsored schools, *Everson v. Board of Education* [XIV, 1]; federal grants for college buildings of church-sponsored institutions of higher education combining secular and religious education, *Tilton v. Richardson* [XIV, 3] noncategorical grants to church-sponsored colleges and universities, *Roemer v. Board of Public Works,* [XIV, 3] (1976); and the tax exemptions for church properties sanctioned in *Walz v. Tax Comm'n,* [XIII, 3]. It would also require that we view it as more of an endorsement of religion than the Sunday Closing Laws upheld in *McGowan v. Maryland,* [XIII, 2]; the release time program for religious training in *Zorach v. Clauson* [XIV, 2]; and the legislative prayers upheld in *Marsh v. Chambers* [XIII, 4].

. . .

Of course the crèche is identified with one religious faith but no more so than the examples we have set out from prior cases in which we found no conflict with the Establishment Clause. See, *e.g., McGowan v. Maryland,* [XIII, 2]; *Marsh v. Chambers* [XIII, 4]. It would be ironic, however, if the inclusion of a single symbol of a particular historic religious event, as part of a celebration acknowledged in the Western World for 20 centuries, and in this country by the people, by the Executive Branch, by the

Congress, and the courts for 2 centuries, would so "taint" the city's exhibit as to render it violative of the Establishment Clause. To forbid the use of this one passive symbol—the crèche—at the very time people are taking note of the season with Christmas hymns and carols in public schools and other public places, and while the Congress and legislatures open sessions with prayers by paid chaplains would be a stilted overreaction contrary to our history and to our holdings. If the presence of the crèche in this display violates the Establishment Clause, a host of other forms of taking official note of Christmas, and of our religious heritage, are equally offensive to the Constitution.

. . .

We hold that, notwithstanding the religious significance of the crèche, the city of Pawtucket has not violated the Establishment Clause of the First Amendment. Accordingly, the judgment of the Court of Appeals is reversed.

It is so ordered.

Justice O'Connor concurred.

Justice Brennan, with whom Justices Marshall, Blackmun, and Stevens join, dissenting:

. . .

The inclusion of a crèche in Pawtucket's otherwise secular celebration of Christmas clearly violates these principles. Unlike such secular figures as Santa Claus, reindeer, and carolers, a nativity scene represents far more than a mere "traditional" symbol of Christmas. The essence of the crèche's symbolic purpose and effect is to prompt the observer to experience a sense of simple awe and wonder appropriate to the contemplation of one of the central elements of Christian dogma—that God sent His Son into the world to be a Messiah. Contrary to the Court's suggestion, the crèche is far from a mere representation of a "particular historic religious event." *Ante,* at 686. It is, instead, best understood as a mystical re-creation of an event that lies at the heart of Christian faith. To suggest, as the Court does, that such a symbol is merely "traditional" and therefore no different from Santa's house or reindeer is not only offensive to those for whom the crèche has profound significance,[19] but insulting to those who insist for religious or personal reasons that the story of Christ is in no sense a part of "history" nor an unavoidable element of our national "heritage."[20]

For these reasons, the crèche in this context simply cannot be viewed as playing the same role that an ordinary museum display does. See *ante,* at 676–677, 683, 685. The Court seems to assume that prohibiting Pawtucket from displaying a crèche would be tantamount to prohibiting a state college from including the Bible or Milton's Paradise Lost in a course on English literature. But in those cases the religiously inspired materials are being considered solely as literature. The purpose is plainly not to single out the particular religious beliefs that may have inspired the authors, but to see in these writings the outlines of a larger imaginative universe shared with other forms of literary expression.[21] The same may be said of a course devoted to the study of art; when the course turns to Gothic architecture, the emphasis is not on the religious beliefs which

---

[19] Many Christian commentators have voiced strong objections to what they consider to be the debasement and trivialization of Christmas through too close a connection with commercial and public celebrations. See, *e. g.,* Kelley, Beyond Separation of Church and State, 5 J. Church & State 181 (1963). See generally Barnett [*The American Christmas*] 55–57.

[20] See A. Stokes & L. Pfeffer, Church and State in the United States 383 (rev. ed. 1964); R. Morgan, The Supreme Court and Religion 126 (1972); Barnett 68 (discussing opposition by Jews and other non-Christian religious groups to public celebrations of Christmas). See also Talmage, [*Disputation and Dialogue* (1985)].

[21] See N. Frye, The Secular Scripture 14–15 (1976).

the cathedrals exalt, but rather upon the "aesthetic consequences of [such religious] thought.[22]

In this case, by contrast, the crèche plays no comparable secular role. Unlike the poetry of Paradise Lost which students in a literature course will seek to appreciate primarily for esthetic or historical reasons, the angels, shepherds, Magi, and infant of Pawtucket's nativity scene can only be viewed as symbols of a particular set of religious beliefs. It would be another matter if the crèche were displayed in a museum setting, in the company of other religiously inspired artifacts, as an example, among many, of the symbolic representation of religious myths. In that setting, we would have objective guarantees that the crèche could not suggest that a particular faith had been singled out for public favor and recognition. The effect of Pawtucket's crèche, however, is not confined by any of these limiting attributes. In the absence of any other religious symbols or of any neutral disclaimer, the inescapable effect of the crèche will be to remind the average observer of the religious roots of the celebration he is witnessing and to call to mind the scriptural message that the nativity symbolizes. The fact that Pawtucket has gone to the trouble of making such an elaborate public celebration and of including a crèche in that otherwise secular setting inevitably serves to reinforce the sense that the city means to express solidarity with the Christian message of the crèche and to dismiss other faiths as unworthy of similar attention and support.

. . .

By insisting that such a distinctly sectarian message is merely an unobjectionable part of our "religious heritage," see *ante,* at 676, 685–686, the Court takes a long step backwards to the days when Justice Brewer could arrogantly declare for the Court that "this is a Christian nation." *Church of Holy Trinity v. United States* [X, 1]. Those days, I had thought, were forever put behind us by the Court's decision in *Engel v. Vitale* [XIV, 2], in which we rejected a similar argument advanced by the State of New York that its Regent's Prayer was simply an acceptable part of our "spiritual heritage." *Id.,* at 425.

NOTE. *Scarsdale v. McCreary,* 105 S.Ct. 1859 (1985), *aff.,* 4–4, 739 F:2d 716 (2d Cir. 1984). The Scarsdale Crèche Committee, an association of seven Catholic and Protestant churches, annually displayed during the Christmas season a set of figures, ½ foot to 3½ feet in height, depicting Christ in the manger, sculptured in wood at a cost of $1,600. The display was at Boniface Circle, a public park in the center of the business area. Boniface Circle was also used by Christmas carol singers. Other public buildings of Scarsdale were also used for religious purposes; for example, Wayside Cottage, a publicly owned building, was used for Bahai, Catholic, Jewish, and Unitarian services.

After litigation was begun to ban the placing of the crèche on Boniface Circle as unconstitutional, the Scarsdale authorities became uneasy about it and eventually decided themselves not to allow it; their feeling was "that because the symbol was religious it should not be on *any* public land." The Crèche Committee and twelve others, mainly residents of Scarsdale, sued to override the denial.

Citing *Lynch, supra,* and *Widmar, infra* XIV, 3, the Second Circuit, per Lawrence W. Pierce, ruled that an injunction should issue prohibiting Scarsdale from "relying on the establishment clause as a reason for prohibiting the erection of a crèche at Boniface Circle,

---

[22] O. von Simson, The Gothic Cathedral 27 (1956). See also E. Panofsky, Meaning in the Visual Arts (1974). Compare Justice Jackson's explanation of his view that the study of religiously inspired material can, in the correct setting, be made a part of a secular educational program: "[m]usic without sacred music, architecture minus the cathedral, or painting without the scriptural themes would be eccentric and incomplete, even from a secular point of view." *Illinois ex rel. McCollum v. Board of Education,* [XIV, 2].

a traditional public forum." The court said that the absence of Santa Claus and other secular figures did not distinguish the Scarsdale case from *Lynch;* in each case the context was that of the celebration of Christmas; the advancement of religion was incidental; the erection of a visible sign disclaiming sponsorship by Scarsdale was sufficient disassociation from the government. The court added that any special impact on children as persons unable to understand that the town was being neutral had not been established.

Fox v. City of Los Angeles, 22 Cal.3d 792, 150 Cal. Rptr. 867, 587 P.2d 663 (1978). On Christmas Eve, Christmas night, Easter in the Western calendar, and Easter in the Orthodox calendar, Los Angeles arranged the lights and blinds of the tower of City Hall so that each side formed a large cross, visible across the freeways. The practice, the city said, was "not in religious tribute, but more in a spirit of peace and good fellowship toward all mankind." The city similarly arranged a display of light on the tower showing the Heart and Easter Seal symbols when these funds had their charitable drives. No evidence was offered that the city had ever refused any similar request. The practice had gone on for thirty years as to the Christmas lighting; no evidence was presented that it had had any religious impact. The supreme court of California, 5–2, per Justice Frank Newman, held in a taxpayer's suit that the display violated the California constitution, art. 1, sec. 4: "The Legislature shall make no law respecting an establishment of religion."

Query. Would the result be the same as to the United States Constitution if *Lynch* and *Scarsdale* were followed? *See also Eugene Sand and Gravel, Inc. v. City of Eugene,* 276 Or. 1007, 558 P.2d 338 (1976) (a large cross on the crest of Skinner's Butte, a municipal park overlooking the city, was erected by two businesses and lighted at Christmas and Easter; it was ordered removed as a violation of both state and federal constitutions. The cross was then given to the city. In public ceremonies sponsored by the American Legion it was dedicated as a "Veteran's War Memorial." It was now lighted on national holidays and according to testimony continued to be seen by many people in Eugene as a religious symbol and was regarded by some as offensive for that reason. The Oregon Supreme Court, 4–3, set aside its earlier decree, holding that the purpose of the display was secular, *cert. denied,* 434 U.S. 876 (1977).

FOURTEEN

Education

1. PAROCHIAL SCHOOLS

Everson v. Board of Education of the Township of Ewing
330 U.S. 1 (1947)

Edward R. Burke and *E. Hilton Jackson* argued the cause for appellant. With *Mr. Burke* on the brief were *Challen B. Ellis, W. D. Jamieson* and *Kahl K. Spriggs.*

William H. Speer argued the cause for appellees. With him on the brief were *Porter R. Chandler* and *Roger R. Clisham.*

Briefs of *amici curiae* in support of appellant were filed by *E. Hilton Jackson* for the General Conference of Seventh-Day Adventists et al.; by *Harry V. Osborne, Kenneth W. Greenawalt* and *Whitney N. Seymour* for the American Civil Liberties Union; and by *Milton T. Lasher* for the State Council of the Junior Order of United American Mechanics of New Jersey.

Briefs of *amici curiae* in support of appellees were filed by *George F. Barrett,* Attorney General of Illinois, *William C. Wines,* Assistant Attorney General of Illinois, and *James A. Emmert,* Attorney General of Indiana, for the States of Illinois and Indiana; by *Fred S. LeBlanc,* Attorney General, for the State of Louisiana; by *Clarence A. Barnes,* Attorney General, for the Commonwealth of Massachusetts; by *Edmund E. Shepherd,* Solicitor General, and *Daniel J. O'Hara,* Assistant Attorney General, for the State of Michigan; by *Nathaniel L. Goldstein,* Attorney General, and *Wendell P. Brown,* Solicitor General, for the State of New York; and by *James N. Vaughn* and *George E. Flood* for the National Council of Catholic Men et al.

Justice Black delivered the opinion of the Court.

A New Jersey statute authorizes its local school districts to make rules and contracts for the transportation of children to and from schools. The appellee, a township board of education, acting pursuant to this statute, authorized reimbursement to parents of money expended by them for the bus transportation of their children on regular busses operated by the public transportation system. Part of this money was for the payment of transportation of some children in the community to Catholic parochial schools. These church schools give their students, in addition to secular education, regular religious instruction conforming to the religious tenets and modes of worship of the Catholic Faith. The superintendent of these schools is a Catholic priest.

The appellant, in his capacity as a district taxpayer, filed suit in a state court challenging the right of the Board to reimburse parents of parochial school students. He contended that the statute and the resolution passed pursuant to it violated both the State and the Federal Constitutions. That court held that the legislature was without power to authorize such payment under the state constitution. 132 N. J. L. 98, 39 A. 2d 75. The New Jersey Court of Errors and Appeals reversed, holding that neither the statute nor the resolution passed pursuant to it was in conflict with the State constitution or the provisions of the Federal Constitution in issue. 133 N. J. L. 350, 44 A. 2d 333. The case is here on appeal under 28 U. S. C. § 344 (a).

Since there has been no attack on the statute on the ground that a part of its language excludes children attending private schools operated for profit from enjoying State payment for their transportation, we need not consider this exclusionary language; it has no relevancy to any constitutional question here presented. Furthermore, if the exclusion clause had been properly challenged, we do not know whether New Jersey's highest court would construe its statutes as precluding payment of the school transportation of any group of pupils, even those of a private school run for profit. Consequently, we put to one side the question as to the validity of the statute against the claim that it does not authorize payment for the transportation generally of school children in New Jersey.

The only contention here is that the state statute and the resolution, insofar as they authorized reimbursement to parents of children attending parochial schools, violate the Federal Constitution in these two respects, which to some extent overlap. *First.* They authorize the State to take by taxation the private property of some and bestow it upon others, to be used for their own private purposes. This, it is alleged, violates the due process clause of the Fourteenth Amendment. *Second.* The statute and the resolution forced inhabitants to pay taxes to help support and maintain schools which are dedicated to, and which regularly teach, the Catholic Faith. This is alleged to be a use of state power to support church schools contrary to the prohibition of the First Amendment which the Fourteenth Amendment made applicable to the states.

First. The due process argument that the state law taxes some people to help others carry out their private purposes is framed in two phases. The first phase is that a state cannot tax A to reimburse B for the cost of transporting his children to church schools. This is said to violate the due process clause because the children are sent to these church schools to satisfy the personal desires of their parents, rather than the public's interest in the general education of all children. This argument, if valid, would apply equally to prohibit state payment for the transportation of children to any non-public school, whether operated by a church or any other non-government individual or group. But, the New Jersey legislature has decided that a public purpose will be served by using tax-raised funds to pay the bus fares of all school children, including those who attend parochial schools. The New Jersey Court of Errors and Appeals has reached the same conclusion. The fact that a state law, passed to satisfy a public need, coincides with the personal desires of the individuals most directly affected is certainly an inadequate reason for us to say that a legislature has erroneously appraised the public need.

It is true that this Court has, in rare instances, struck down state statutes on the ground that the purpose for which tax-raised funds were to be expended was not a public one. *Loan Association v. Topeka,* 20 Wall. 655; *Parkersburg v. Brown,* 106 U.S. 487; *Thompson v. Consolidated Gas Utilities Corp.,* 300 U. S. 55. But the Court has also pointed out that this far-reaching authority must be exercised with the most extreme caution. *Green v. Frazier,* 253 U. S. 233, 240. Otherwise, a state's power to legislate for the public welfare might be seriously curtailed, a power which is a primary reason for the existence of states. Changing local conditions create new local problems which may lead a state's people and its local authorities to believe that laws authorizing new types of public services are necessary to promote the general well-being of the people. The Fourteenth Amendment did not strip the states of their power to meet problems previously left for individual solution. *Davidson v. New Orleans,* 96 U.S. 97, 103–104; *Barbier v. Connolly,* 113 U. S. 27, 31–32; *Fallbrook Irrigation District v. Bradley,* 164 U. S. 112, 157–158.

It is much too late to argue that legislation intended to facilitate the opportunity of children to get a secular education serves no public purpose. *Cochran v. Louisiana State Board of Education,* [*supra,* X, 10], Holmes, J., in *Interstate Ry. v. Massachusetts,* 207 U. S. 79, 87. See opinion of Cooley, J., in *Stuart v. School District No. 1 of Kalamazoo,* 30 Mich. 69 (1874). The same thing is no less true of legislation to reimburse needy parents, or all parents, for payment of the fares of their children so that they can ride in public busses to and from schools rather than run the risk of traffic and other hazards incident to walking or "hitchhiking." See *Barbier v. Connolly, supra,* at 31. See also cases collected 63 A. L. R. 413; 118 A. L. R. 806. Nor does it follow that a law has a private rather than a public purpose because it provides that tax-raised funds will be paid to reimburse individuals on account of money spent by them in a way which furthers a public program. See *Carmichael v. Southern Coal & Coke Co.,* 301 U. S. 495, 518. Subsidies and loans to individuals such as farmers and home-owners, and to privately owned transportation systems, as well as many other kinds of businesses, have been commonplace practices in our state and national history.

Insofar as the second phase of the due process argument may differ from the first, it is by suggesting that taxation for transportation of children to church schools constitutes support of a religion by the State. But if the law is invalid for this reason, it is because it violates the First Amendment's prohibition against the establishment of religion by law. This is the exact question raised by appellant's second contention, to consideration of which we now turn.

Second. The New Jersey statute is challenged as a "law respecting an establishment of religion." The First Amendment, as made applicable to the states by the Fourteenth, *Murdock v. Pennsylvania,* [XI, 1], commands that a state "shall make no law respecting an establishment of religion, or prohibiting the free exercise thereof. . . ." These words of the First Amendment reflected in the minds of early Americans a vivid mental picture of conditions and practices which they fervently wished to stamp out in order to preserve liberty for themselves and for their posterity. Doubtless their goal has not been entirely reached; but so far has the Nation moved toward it that the expression "law respecting an establishment of religion," probably does not so vividly remind present-day Americans of the evils, fears, and political problems that caused that expression to be written into our Bill of Rights. Whether this New Jersey law is one respecting an "establishment of religion" requires an understanding of the meaning of that language, particularly with respect to the imposition of taxes.

. . .

This Court has previously recognized that the provisions of the First Amendment, in the drafting and adoption of which Madison and Jefferson played such leading roles, had the same objective and were intended to provide the same protection against governmental intrusion on religious liberty as the Virginia statute. *Reynolds v. United States* [*supra,* IX]; *Watson v. Jones* [VIII, 5]; *Davis v. Beason* [*supra,* IX]. Prior to the adoption of the Fourteenth Amendment, the First Amendment did not apply as a restraint against the states. Most of them did soon provide similar constitutional protections for religious liberty. But some states persisted for about half a century in imposing restraints upon the free exercise of religion and in discriminating against particular religious groups. In recent years, so far as the provision against the establishment of a religion is concerned, the question has most frequently arisen in connection with proposed state aid to church schools and efforts to carry on religious teachings in the public schools in accordance with the tenets of a particular sect. Some churches have either sought or accepted state financial support for their schools. Here again the efforts to obtain state aid or acceptance of it have not been limited to any one particular faith. The state courts, in the main, have remained faithful to the language of their own constitutional provisions designed to protect religious freedom and to separate religions and governments. Their decisions, however, show the difficulty in drawing the line between tax legislation which provides funds for the welfare of the general public and that which is designed to support institutions which teach religion.

. . .

The "establishment of religion" clause of the First Amendment means at least this: Neither a state nor the Federal Government can set up a church. Neither can pass laws which aid one religion, aid all religions, or prefer one religion over another. Neither can force nor influence a person to go to or to remain away from church against his will or force him to profess a belief or disbelief in any religion. No person can be punished for entertaining or professing religious beliefs or disbeliefs, for church attendance or non-attendance. No tax in any amount, large or small, can be levied to support any religious activities or institutions, whatever they may be called, or whatever form they may adopt to teach or practice religion. Neither a state nor the Federal Government can, openly or secretly, participate in the affairs of any religious organizations or groups and *vice versa.* In the words of Jefferson, the clause against establishment of religion by law was intended to erect "a wall of separation between church and State." *Reynolds v. United States* [*supra,* IX].

We must consider the New Jersey statute in accordance with the foregoing limitations imposed by the First Amendment. But we must not strike that state statute down if it is within the State's constitutional power even though it approaches the verge of that power. See *Interstate Ry. v. Massachusetts,* Holmes, J., *supra* at 85, 88. New Jersey cannot consistently with the "establishment of religion" clause of the First Amendment contribute tax-raised funds to the support of an institution which teaches the tenets and faith of any church. On the other hand, other language of the amendment commands that New Jersey cannot hamper its citizens in the free exercise of their own religion. Consequently, it cannot exclude individual Catholics, Lutherans, Mohammedans, Baptists, Jews, Methodists, Non-believers, Presbyterians, or the members of any other faith, *because of their faith, or lack of it,* from receiving the benefits of public welfare legislation. While we do not mean to intimate that a state could not provide transportation only to children attending public schools, we must be careful, in protecting the citizens of New Jersey against state-established churches, to be sure that we do not inadvertently prohibit New Jersey from extending its general state law benefits to all its citizens without regard to their religious belief.

Measured by these standards, we cannot say that the First Amendment prohibits New Jersey from spending tax-raised funds to pay the bus fares of parochial school pupils as a part of a general program under which it pays the fares of pupils attending public and other schools. It is undoubtedly true that children are helped to get to church schools. There is even a possibility that some of the children might not be sent to the church schools if the parents were compelled to pay their children's bus fares out of their own pockets when transportation to a public school would have been paid for by the State. The same possibility exists where the state requires a local transit company to provide reduced fares to school children including those attending parochial schools, or where a municipally owned transportation system undertakes to carry all school children free of charge. Moreover, state-paid policemen, detailed to protect children going to and from church schools from the very real hazards of traffic, would serve much the same purpose and accomplish much the same result as state provisions intended to guarantee free transportation of a kind which the state deems to be best for the school children's welfare. And parents might refuse to risk their children to the serious danger of traffic accidents going to and from parochial schools, the approaches to which were not protected by policemen. Similarly, parents might be reluctant to permit their children to attend schools which the state had cut off from such general government services as ordinary police and fire protection, connections for sewage disposal, public highways and sidewalks. Of course, cutting off church schools from these services, so separate and so indisputably marked off from the religious function, would make it far more difficult for the schools to operate. But such is obviously not the purpose of the First Amendment. That Amendment requires the state to be a neutral in its relations with groups of religious believers and non-believers; it does not require the state to be their adversary. State power is no more to be used so as to handicap religions than it is to favor them.

Affirmed.

Four members of the Court—Frankfurter, Rutledge, Jackson, and Burton—would have gone further and held the bus transportation unconstitutional. Rutledge, the son of a fundamentalist Baptist minister in Kentucky, had in later life become a modern Unitarian, Fred Israel, "Wiley Rutledge," *The Justices of the United States Supreme Court 1789-1969*, ed. Leon Friedman and Fred L. Israel, IV, 2593-2594. He wrote an especially passionate dissent, declaring that "transportation, where it is needed, is as essential to education as any other element. . . . The only line that can be so drawn is one between more dollars and less. Certainly in this realm such a line can be no valid constitutional measure. Now, as in Madison's time, not the amount but the principle of assessment is wrong." As an appendix to his dissent, Rutledge had reprinted the Remonstrance drafted by Madison in 1785 (*supra*, VI, 3).

NOTE. *Plaintiffs and Amici in the School Cases.* Justice Black had in 1925 been a member of the Ku Klux Klan and in 1926 he was the Klan's candidate for the Senate, see Gerald T. Dunne, *Hugo Black and the Judicial Revolution* (1977) 114-121. Commenting on this membership, Black's son has written: "The Ku Klux Klan and Daddy, so far as I could tell, only had one thing in common. He suspected the Catholic Church. He used to read all of Paul Blanshard's books exposing power abuse in the Catholic Church. He thought the popes and bishops had too much power and property" [Hugo Black, Jr., *My Father: A Remembrance* (1975) 104]. Was it a paradox that Justice Black now wrote for the majority upholding the constitutionality of aid to parochial school pupils? Scarcely, if the premises set out in his opinion in *Everson* were developed in litigation.

Paul Blanshard's *American Freedom and Catholic Power* (1949) sold 165,000 copies within two years. The Catholic Church, according to Blanshard, was an alien and authoritarian institution, dominated by its hierarchy, whose power posed a threat to American democracy. Blanshard emphasized the intolerance of the church and its insistence that in an ideal society the state would repress heresy, *ibid.* at 294-296. The "outcome of the struggle between American democracy and the Catholic hierarchy," he wrote, "depends upon the survival and expansion of the public school. . . . [T]he Catholic hierarchy could never make the United States into a clerical state unless it captured the public-school system or regimented a majority of American children into its own parochial-school system," *ibid.* at 286. He added:

It seems clear to me that there is no alternative for champions of traditional American democracy except to build a resistance movement designed to prevent the hierarchy from imposing its social policies upon our schools, hospitals, government and family organization. . . . In the field of culture and information, the platform should stand for the American public school, from kindergarten through college, as the foundation of American democracy [*ibid.* at 303-304].

Part of "the resistance movement" was an organization called Protestants and Other Americans United for Separation of Church and State, in which Blanshard served as a staff member. Founded in 1947, POAU was launched by the Scottish Rite Masons (Southern Jurisdiction), Frank J. Sorauf, *The Wall of Separation* (1976) 54. POAU was a major participant in litigation designed to invalidate school legislation or practices favorable to Catholics. The Masons were the *éminences grises* of this organization. Its broader constituency was fundamentalist

Protestant with a long tradition of antipopery. Its success reflected "a fear of the loss of Protestant hegemony in American society," *ibid.* at 33, 53.

A second major player in schools' litigation was the American Civil Liberties Union (ACLU). Three currents of thought were identifiable in the ACLU—"the separationism of Madison and Jefferson," ironically now most often found in New England Congregationalists and Unitarians; militant atheism rejecting all religion; and the secular humanism of groups like the Ethical Culture Society. The third current was probably the ACLU mainstream. It was antipathetic to "dogmatic and authoritative religions," *ibid.* at 32–33. The feeling of many ACLU members was captured by a leading American philosopher, John Dewey, when he urged no federal aid for Catholic schools lest encouragement be given "a powerful reactionary world organization in the most vital realm of democratic life," John Dewey, "S. 2499, Its Antidemocratic Implications," *The Nation's Schools* 39 (March 1947):20, 21. Funding of parochial schools, Dewey wrote, "would create divisions among our people and would lead to permanent conflict among self-perpetuating blocs." Dewey did not hesitate to say that the encouragement of the schools of the Catholic Church brought with it "the resulting promulgation of principles inimical to democracy."

The third major participant in school litigation was the American Jewish Congress (AJC). Founded to work for Zionist objectives at the end of World War I, the AJC at the end of World War II reflected the concern of many Jews that they might be vulnerable in an America dominated by a Christian majority. Its membership was drawn from Conservative Judaism and Reform Judaism. Acting on its own behalf or for other organizations such as the Synagogue Council of America, the National Community Relations Advisory Committee, and the Committee for Public Education and Religious Liberty (PEARL), the AJC was the most active amicus of the three organizations, Leo Pfeffer, "Amici in Church–State Litigation," 44 *Law & Contemporary Problems* 83 (1981) at 86. The Orthodox did not belong and in 1965 even formed the Jewish Committee on Law and Political Action (COLPA), which opposed the AJC on support to parochial schools, *ibid.* at 94.

NOTE. *The Declaration on Religious Liberty.* An American Jesuit, John Courtney Murray, drew on the American experience of religious liberty to challenge the Catholic theologians who had opposed religious freedom, *see* Murray, "Governmental Repression of Heresy," *Proceedings of the Catholic Theological Society of America* 3, 161 (1948). Although the Catholic Church had accepted the idea of religious toleration in practice, Murray's arguments met resistance from theologians who believed that the church could not formally repudiate the doctrine of the past, *see supra,* II, 4, and IV, 1. In the end, Murray's arguments prevailed. On December 7, 1965, the Second Vatican Council adopted, and Pope Paul VI approved, the *Declaration on Religious Liberty,* known from its opening words as *Dignitatis Humanae Personae* (Of the Dignity of the Person). The vote of the bishops was 2,308 to 70, Second Vatican Council, *Acta Synodalia* (1978) IV, part VII, 860. The declaration read:

This Vatican Synod has decreed that the human person has the right to religious liberty. . . . It further declares that the right to religious liberty is in truth founded on the very dignity of the human person such as it is known both by the revealed Word of God and by reason itself [*Acta apostolicae sedis,* vol. 58, 929].

The declaration made a fundamental commitment to religious freedom for every person. In a companion Declaration on the Relations of the Church to Non-Christian Religions, *Notra aetate* (In Our Time), on October 28, 1965, the Council recognized the common religious questions and aspirations of humankind, spoke with particular respect of Buddhism and Hinduism; acknowledged Islam as a religion that not only worshipped God but venerated Jesus and Mary;

and gave special homage to the "great spiritual patrimony common to Jews and Christians" and condemned and deplored the persecutions in the past of the Jews [*Acta apostolicae sedis* 58, 740–743].

Ironically it was not the contemporary Catholic Church but images derived from words and deeds of Catholics in earlier ages that animated many of those still suspicious of the parochial schools.

NOTE. *Everson* provided the basis for challenging state aid to the parochial schools. But only in the 1960s did a sustained challenge to such aid develop. The great majority of cases where POAU, ACLU, and AJC intervened were education cases, Pfeffer, 44 *Law and Contemporary Problems* 83 at 94.

The first major case was a setback to the challengers: *Board of Education v. Allen*, 392 U.S. 236 (1968). In 1965 New York required local public school boards to lend textbooks, designed for use in the public schools, to all school children in the district. A school board challenged the statute as a violation of the First Amendment. With the AJC, represented by Leo Pfeffer, and POAU as *amici*, on one side, and the United States and eight states, on the other, the case came before the Supreme Court, which, 6–3, upheld the statute. Justice White for the Court said at 245 that "this Court has long recognized that religious schools pursue two goals, religious instruction and secular education." Support of secular education was a legitimate state function. Justices Black, Douglas, and Fortas dissented: "the wall" must be left "high and impregnable."

The case was decided on the pleadings and stipulated facts without a trial. The record, as the Court commented, was bare of information about the subsidized schools. Moreover, the validity of textbook loans had been established in *Cochran, supra*, X, 10, in the days before the First Amendment was applied to the states. It was not an ideal case for the challengers.

Justice Black, dissenting, declared at 254 that the First Amendment was based on the assumption that state aid to religious schools "generates discord, disharmony, hatred, and strife among our people." The idea was slightly reformulated in a note questioning *Board of Education v. Allen* by Paul A. Freund, University Professor at Harvard. He wrote:

While political debate and discussion is normally a wholesome process for reaching viable accommodations, political division on religious lines is one of the principal evils that the first amendment sought to forestall [Freund, "Public Aid to Parochial Schools," 82 *Harvard Law Review* 1680 at 1692 (1969)].

Freund cited no authority for this proposition. It was to have a career in the Supreme Court. Freund also commented on "the elaborate minuet of the individual student's request for specific books and its approval by the public school board," and noted that new Pennsylvania legislation had replaced the minuet with direct aid to the schools: "all is now modern ballet, bold and muscular." He asked, "Will the Court re-score its composition to accommodate the new movement?"

Pennsylvania was not alone in its new legislation. In the late 1960s, Connecticut, Louisiana, Michigan, New Jersey, Pennsylvania, and Rhode Island passed statutes designed to finance the secular parts of the curriculum of the nonpublic schools, *see* Donald A. Giannella, "*Lemon* and *Tilton:* The Bitter and the Sweet of Church–State Entanglement," *1971 Supreme Court Review* 149. All of these states had substantial Catholic populations; and Rhode Island had a Catholic majority. The statutes passed were tailored to anticipate constitutional objections. The objections were made.

NOTE. *Standing (I).* In 1923, *Frothingham v. Mellon*, 262 U.S. 447 (1923), held that a taxpayer had no standing to object to an act of Congress she asserted to be unconstitutional;

the effect of the government carrying out the act had a "remote, fluctuating and uncertain" impact on her tax burden; she had shown no cognizable injury. In *Doremus v. Board of Education*, 342 U.S. 429 (1952), *Frothingham* was followed and standing denied to a taxpayer objecting to a New Jersey statute authorizing Bible-reading in the public schools. In *Flast v. Cohen*, 392 U.S. 83 (1968), however, the Court permitted a taxpayer to sue to enjoin the expenditure of federal funds under the Elementary and Secondary Education Act of 1965. The taxpayer claimed that the funds were being used to support religious schools in violation of the establishment clause. The court recognized a right in a taxpayer to litigate the unconstitutionality "only of exercises of congressional power under the taxing and spending clause of Article I, sec. 8, of the Constitution," and to do so only if the taxpayer could allege a specific constitutional restraint such as the establishment clause. Justice Douglas, concurring, observed: "The mounting federal aid to sectarian schools is notorious and the subterfuges numerous," *ibid.* at 114. He advocated liberality in allowing standing to objecting taxpayers. Justices Stewart and Fortas also saw peculiar virtue in permitting claims by taxpayers raising objections under the establishment clause. Justice Harlan, dissenting, saw no basis for seeing the establishment clause as a more "specific" limitation than other constitutional commands. Only in "some Pickwickian sense" did any constitutional provisions speak to spending, *ibid.* at 127. For later developments, see *Standing II, infra*, XV, 4.

Lemon v. Kurtzman
403 U.S. 602 (1971)
(and *Earley v. DiCenso* and *Robinson v. DiCenso*)

Henry W. Sawyer III argued the cause and filed briefs for appellants in No. 89. *Edward Bennett Williams* argued the cause for appellants in No. 569. With him on the brief were *Jeremiah C. Collins* and *Richard P. McMahon. Charles F. Cottam* argued the cause for appellants in No. 570. With him on the brief were *Herbert F. DeSimone*, Attorney General of Rhode Island, and *W. Slater Allen, Jr.*, Assistant Attorney General.

J. Shane Creamer argued the cause for appellees Kurtzman et al. in No. 89. On the brief were *Fred Speaker*, Attorney General of Pennsylvania, *David W. Rutstein*, Deputy Attorney General, and *Edward Friedman. William B. Ball* argued the cause for appellee schools in No. 89. With him on the brief were *Joseph G. Skelly, James E. Gallagher, Jr., C. Clark Hodgson, Jr., Samuel Rappaport, Donald A. Semisch*, and *William D. Valente. Henry T. Reath* filed a brief for appellee Pennsylvania Association of Independent Schools in No. 89. *Leo Pfeffer* and *Milton Stanzler* argued the cause for appellees in Nos. 569 and 570. With them on the brief were *Harold E. Adams, Jr.*, and *Allan M. Shine*.

Briefs of *amici curiae* urging reversal in No. 89 were filed by *Mr. Pfeffer* for the American Association of School Administrators et al.; by *Henry C. Clausen* for United Americans for Public Schools; by *Samuel Rabinove, Arnold Forster, George Soll, Joseph B. Robison, Paul Hartman*, and *Sol Rabkin* for the American Jewish Committee et al.; by *Franklin C. Salisbury* for Protestants and Other Americans United for Separation of Church and State; by *J. Harold Flannery* for the Center for Law and Education, Harvard University, et al.; and by *Peter L. Costas* and *Paul W. Orth* for the Connecticut State Conference of Branches of the NAACP et al.

Briefs of *amici curiae* urging affirmance in No. 89 were filed by *Acting Solicitor General Friedman, Assistant Attorney General Ruckelshaus, Robert V. Zener*, and *Donald L. Horowitz* for the United States; by *Paul W. Brown*, Attorney General of Ohio, *pro se*, and *Charles S. Lopeman*, First Assistant Attorney General, for the Attorney General of Ohio et al.; by *Levy Anderson* for the City of Philadelphia; by *Robert M. Landis* for the School District of Philadelphia; by the City of Pittsburgh; by *Bruce W. Kauffman*,

John M. Elliott, and *Edward F. Mannino* for the City of Erie; by *James A. Kelly* for the School District of the City of Scranton; by *Charles M. Whelan, William R. Consedine, Alfred L. Scanlan, Arthur E. Sutherland,* and *Harmon Burns, Jr.,* for the National Catholic Educational Association et al.; by *Ethan A. Hitchcock* and *I. N. P. Stokes* for the National Association of Independent Schools, Inc.; by *Jerome H. Gerber* for the Pennsylvania State AFL-CIO, by *Thomas J. Ford, Edward J. Walsh, Jr.,* and *Theodore D. Hoffmann* for the Long Island Conference of Religious Elementary and Secondary School Administrators; by *Nathan Lewin* for the National Jewish Commission on Law and Public Affairs; by *Stuart Hubbell* for Citizens for Educational Freedom; and by *Edward M. Koza, Walter L. Hill, Jr., Thomas R. Balaban,* and *William J. Pinkowski* for the Polish American Congress, Inc., et al.

The National Association of Laymen filed a brief as *amicus curiae* in No. 89.

Briefs of *amici curiae* urging reversal in Nos. 569 and 570 were filed by *Acting Solicitor General Friedman, Assistant Attorney General Gray,* and *Messrs. Zener* and *Horowitz* for the United States, and by *Jesse H. Choper* and *Messrs. Consedine, Whelan,* and *Burns* for the National Catholic Educational Association et al.

Briefs of *amici curiae* urging affirmance in Nos. 569 and 570 were filed by *Messrs. Rabinove, Robison, Forster,* and *Rabkin* for the American Jewish Committee et al.; by *Mr. Salisbury* for Protestants and Other Americans United for Separation of Church and State; by *Mr. Flannery* for the Center for Law and Education, Harvard University, et al.; and by *Messrs. Costas* and *Orth* for the Connecticut State Conference of Branches of the NAACP et al.

Chief Justice Burger delivered the opinion of the Court.

These two appeals raise questions as to Pennsylvania and Rhode Island statutes providing state aid to church-related elementary and secondary schools. Both statutes are challenged as violative of the Establishment and Free Exercise Clauses of the First Amendment and the Due Process Clause of the Fourteenth Amendment.

Pennsylvania has adopted a statutory program that provides financial support to nonpublic elementary and secondary schools by way of reimbursement for the cost of teachers' salaries, textbooks, and instructional materials in specified secular subjects. Rhode Island has adopted a statute under which the State pays directly to teachers in nonpublic elementary schools a supplement of 15% of their annual salary. Under each statute state aid has been given to church-related educational institutions. We hold that both statutes are unconstitutional.

I

The Rhode Island Statute

The Rhode Island Salary Supplement Act was enacted in 1969. It rests on the legislative finding that the quality of education available in nonpublic elementary schools has been jeopardized by the rapidly rising salaries needed to attract competent and dedicated teachers. The Act authorizes state officials to supplement the salaries of teachers of secular subjects in nonpublic elementary schools by paying directly to a teacher an amount not in excess of 15% of his current annual salary. As supplemented, however, a nonpublic school teacher's salary cannot exceed the maximum paid to teachers in the State's public schools, and the recipient must be certified by the state board of education in substantially the same manner as public school teachers.

In order to be eligible for the Rhode Island salary supplement, the recipient must teach in a nonpublic school at which the average per-pupil expenditure on secular education is less than the average in the State's public schools during a specified period. Appellant State Commissioner of Education also requires eligible schools to submit financial data. If this information indicates a per-pupil expenditure in excess of the statutory limitation, the records of the school in question must be examined in order to assess how much of the expenditure is attributable to secular education and how much to religious activity.[2]

The Act also requires that teachers eligible for salary supplements must teach only those subjects that are offered in the State's public schools. They must use "only teaching materials which are used in the public schools." Finally, any teacher applying for a salary supplement must first agree in writing "not to teach a course in religion for so long as or during such time as he or she receives any salary supplements" under the Act.

Appellees are citizens and taxpayers of Rhode Island. They brought this suit to have the Rhode Island Salary Supplement Act declared unconstitutional and its operation enjoined on the ground that it violates the Establishment and Free Exercise Clauses of the First Amendment. Appellants are state officials charged with administration of the Act, teachers eligible for salary supplements under the Act, and parents of children in church-related elementary schools whose teachers would receive state salary assistance.

A three-judge federal court was convened pursuant to 28 U.S.C. §§ 2281, 2284. It found that Rhode Island's nonpublic elementary schools accommodated approximately 25% of the State's pupils. About 95% of these pupils attended schools affiliated with the Roman Catholic church. To date some 250 teachers have applied for benefits under the Act. All of them are employed by Roman Catholic schools.

The court held a hearing at which extensive evidence was introduced concerning the nature of the secular instruction offered in the Roman Catholic schools whose teachers would be eligible for salary assistance under the Act. Although the court found that concern for religious values does not necessarily affect the content of secular subjects, it also found that the parochial school system was "an integral part of the religious mission of the Catholic Church."

The District Court concluded that the Act violated the Establishment Clause, holding that it fostered "excessive entanglement" between government and religion. In addition two judges thought that the Act had the impermissible effect of giving "significant aid to a religious enterprise." 316 F. Supp. 112. We affirm.

The Pennsylvania Statute

Pennsylvania has adopted a program that has some but not all of the features of the Rhode Island program. The Pennsylvania Nonpublic Elementary and Secondary Education Act was passed in 1968 in response to a crisis that the Pennsylvania Legislature found existed in the State's nonpublic schools due to rapidly rising costs. The statute affirmatively reflects the legislative conclusion that the State's educational goals could appropriately be fulfilled by government support of "those purely secular educational objectives achieved through nonpublic education. . . ."

The statute authorizes appellee state Superintendent of Public Instruction to "purchase" specified "secular educational services" from nonpublic schools. Under the "contracts" authorized by the statute, the State directly reimburses nonpublic schools solely for their actual expenditures for teachers' salaries, textbooks, and instructional materials. A school seeking reimbursement must maintain prescribed accounting procedures that identify the "separate" cost of the "secular educational service." These accounts are subject to state audit. The funds for this program were originally derived from a new tax on horse and harness racing, but the Act is now financed by a portion of the state tax on cigarettes.

---

[2] The District Court found only one instance in which this breakdown between religious and secular expenses was necessary. The school in question was not affiliated with the Catholic church. The court found it unlikely that such determinations would be necessary with respect to Catholic schools because, their heavy reliance on nuns kept their wage costs substantially below those of the public schools.

There are several significant statutory restrictions on state aid. Reimbursement is limited to courses "presented in the curricula of the public schools." It is further limited "solely" to courses in the following "secular" subjects: mathematics, modern foreign languages, physical science, and physical education. Textbooks and instructional materials included in the program must be approved by the state Superintendent of Public Instruction. Finally, the statute prohibits reimbursement for any course that contains "any subject matter expressing religious teaching, or the morals or forms of worship of any sect."

The Act went into effect on July 1, 1968, and the first reimbursement payments to schools were made on September 2, 1969. It appears that some $5 million has been expended annually under the Act. The State has now entered into contracts with some 1,181 nonpublic elementary and secondary schools with a student population of some 535,215 pupils—more than 20% of the total number of students in the State. More than 96% of these pupils attend church-related schools, and most of these schools are affiliated with the Roman Catholic church.

Appellants brought this action in the District Court to challenge the constitutionality of the Pennsylvania statute. The organizational plaintiffs-appellants are associations of persons resident in Pennsylvania declaring belief in the separation of church and state; individual plaintiffs-appellants are citizens and taxpayers of Pennsylvania. Appellant Lemon, in addition to being a citizen and a taxpayer, is a parent of a child attending public school in Pennsylvania. Lemon also alleges that he purchased a ticket at a race track and thus had paid the specific tax that supports the expenditures under the Act. Appellees are state officials who have the responsibility for administering the Act. In addition seven church-related schools are defendants-appellees.

A three-judge federal court was convened pursuant to 28 U.S.C. §§ 2281, 2284. The District Court held that the individual plaintiffs-appellants had standing to challenge the Act, 310 F. Supp. 42. The organizational plaintiffs-appellants were denied standing under *Flast* v. *Cohen,* 392 U.S. 83, 99, 101 (1968).

The court granted appellees' motion to dismiss the complaint for failure to state a claim for relief. 310 F. Supp. 35. It held that the Act violated neither the Establishment nor the Free Exercise Clause, Chief Judge Hastie dissenting. We reverse.

. . .

The language of the Religion Clauses of the First Amendment is at best opaque, particularly when compared with other portions of the Amendment. Its authors did not simply prohibit the establishment of a state church or a state religion, an area history shows they regarded as very important and fraught with great dangers. Instead they commanded that there should be "no law *respecting* an establishment of religion." A law may be one "respecting" the forbidden objective while falling short of its total realization. A law "respecting" the proscribed result, that is, the establishment of religion, is not always easily identifiable as one violative of the Clause. A given law might not *establish* a state religion but nevertheless be one "respecting" that end in the sense of being a step that could lead to such establishment and hence offend the First Amendment.

In the absence of precisely stated constitutional prohibitions, we must draw lines with reference to the three main evils against which the Establishment Clause was intended to afford protection: "sponsorship, financial support, and active involvement of the sovereign in religious activity." *Walz v. Tax Commission* [*supra,* XIII, 3]

Every analysis in this area must begin with consideration of the cumulative criteria developed by the Court over many years. Three such tests may be gleaned from our cases. First, the statute must have a secular legislative purpose; second, its principal or primary effect must be one that neither advances nor inhibits religion, *Board of Education v. Allen* [*supra,* XIV, 1]; finally, the statute must not foster "an excessive government entanglement with religion."

. . .

In *Walz v. Tax Commission,* [*supra,* XIII, 3], the Court upheld state tax exemptions for real property owned by religious organizations and used for religious worship. That holding, however, tended to confine rather than enlarge the area of permissible state involvement with religious institutions by calling for close scrutiny of the degree of entanglement involved in the relationship. The objective is to prevent, as far as possible, the intrusion of either into the precincts of the other.

Our prior holdings do not call for total separation between church and state; total separation is not possible in an absolute sense. Some relationship between government and religious organizations is inevitable. *Zorach v. Clauson* [XIV, 2]; *Sherbert v. Verner* [XI, 4] (Harlan, J., dissenting). Fire inspections, building and zoning regulations, and state requirements under compulsory school-attendance laws are examples of necessary and permissible contacts. Indeed, under the statutory exemption before us in *Walz,* the State had a continuing burden to ascertain that the exempt property was in fact being used for religious worship. Judicial caveats against entanglement must recognize that the line of separation, far from being a "wall," is a blurred, indistinct, and variable barrier depending on all the circumstances of a particular relationship.

This is not to suggest, however, that we are to engage in a legalistic minuet in which precise rules and forms must govern. A true minuet is a matter of pure form and style, the observance of which is itself the substantive end. Here we examine the form of the relationship for the light that it casts on the substance.

. . .

In order to determine whether the government entanglement with religion is excessive, we must examine the character and purposes of the institutions that are benefited, the nature of the aid that the State provides, and the resulting relationship between the government and the religious authority. Mr. Justice Harlan, in a separate opinion in *Walz, supra,* echoed the classic warning as to "programs, whose very nature is apt to entangle the state in details of administration. . . ." *Id.,* at 695. Here we find that both statutes foster an impermissible degree of entanglement.

(a) *Rhode Island program*

The District Court made extensive findings on the grave potential for excessive entanglement that inheres in the religious character and purpose of the Roman Catholic elementary schools of Rhode Island, to date the sole beneficiaries of the Rhode Island Salary Supplement Act.

The church schools involved in the program are located close to parish churches. This understandably permits convenient access for religious exercises since instruction in faith and morals is part of the total educational process. The school buildings contain identifying religious symbols such as crosses on the exterior and crucifixes, and religious paintings and statues either in the classrooms or hallways. Although only approximately 30 minutes a day are devoted to direct religious instruction, there are religiously oriented extracurricular activities. Approximately two-thirds of the teachers in these schools are nuns of various religious orders. Their dedicated efforts provide an atmosphere in which religious instruction and religious vocations are natural and proper parts of life in such schools. Indeed, as the District Court found, the role of teaching nuns in enhancing the religious atmosphere has led the parochial school authorities to attempt to maintain a one-to-one ratio between nuns and lay teachers in all schools rather than to permit some to be staffed almost entirely by lay teachers.

On the basis of these findings the District Court concluded that the parochial schools constituted "an integral part of the religious mission of the Catholic Church." The various characteristics of the schools make them "a powerful vehicle for transmitting the Catholic faith to the next generation." This process of inculcating religious doctrine is, of course, enhanced by the impressionable age of the pupils, in primary schools particularly. In short, parochial schools involve substantial religious activity and purpose.[6]

The substantial religious character of these church-related schools gives rise to entangling church-state relationships of the kind the Religion Clauses sought to avoid. Although the District Court found that concern for religious values did not inevitably or necessarily intrude into the content of secular subjects, the considerable religious activities of these schools led the legislature to provide for careful governmental controls and surveillance by state authorities in order to ensure that state aid supports only secular education.

The dangers and corresponding entanglements are enhanced by the particular form of aid that the Rhode Island Act provides. Our decisions from *Everson* to *Allen* have permitted the States to provide church-related schools with secular, neutral, or non-ideological services, facilities, or materials. Bus transportation, school lunches, public health services, and secular textbooks supplied in common to all students were not thought to offend the Establishment Clause. We note that the dissenters in *Allen* seemed chiefly concerned with the pragmatic difficulties involved in ensuring the truly secular content of the textbooks provided at state expense.

In *Allen* the Court refused to make assumptions, on a meager record, about the religious content of the textbooks that the State would be asked to provide. We cannot, however, refuse here to recognize that teachers have a substantially different ideological character from books. In terms of potential for involving some aspect of faith or morals in secular subjects, a textbook's content is ascertainable, but a teacher's handling of a subject is not. We cannot ignore the danger that a teacher under religious control and discipline poses to the separation of the religious from the purely secular aspects of pre-college education. The conflict of functions inheres in the situation.

In our view the record shows these dangers are present to a substantial degree. The Rhode Island Roman Catholic elementary schools are under the general supervision of the Bishop of Providence and his appointed representative, the Diocesan Superintendent of Schools. In most cases, each individual parish, however, assumes the ultimate financial responsibility for the school, with the parish priest authorizing the allocation of parish funds. With only two exceptions, school principals are nuns appointed either by the Superintendent or the Mother Provincial of the order whose members staff the school. By 1969 lay teachers constituted more than a third of all teachers in the parochial elementary schools, and their number is growing. They are first interviewed by the superintendent's office and then by the school principal. The contracts are signed by the parish priest, and he retains some discretion in negotiating salary levels. Religious authority necessarily pervades the school system.

The schools are governed by the standards set forth in a "Handbook of School Regulations," which has the force of synodal law in the diocese. It emphasizes the role and importance of the teacher in parochial schools: "The prime factor for the success or the failure of the school is the spirit and personality, as well as the professional competency, of the teacher. . . ."The Handbook also states that: "Religious formation is not confined to formal courses; nor is it restricted to a single subject area." Finally, the Handbook advises teachers to stimulate interest in religious vocations and missionary work. Given the mission of the church school, these instructions are consistent and logical.

Several teachers testified, however, that they did not inject religion into their secular classes. And the District Court found that religious values did not necessarily affect the content of the secular instruction. But what has been recounted suggests the potential if not actual hazards of this form of state aid. The teacher is employed by a religious

---

[6] See, *e.g.,* J. Fichter, Parochial School: A Sociological Study 77–108 (1958); Giannella, Religious Liberty, Nonestablishment, and Doctrinal Development, pt. II, The Nonestablishment Principle, 81 Harv. L. Rev. 513, 574 (1968).

organization, subject to the direction and discipline of religious authorities, and works in a system dedicated to rearing children in a particular faith. These controls are not lessened by the fact that most of the lay teachers are of the Catholic faith. Inevitably some of a teacher's responsibilities hover on the border between secular and religious orientation.

We need not and do not assume that teachers in parochial schools will be guilty of bad faith or any conscious design to evade the limitations imposed by the statute and the First Amendment. We simply recognize that a dedicated religious person, teaching in a school affiliated with his or her faith and operated to inculcate its tenets, will inevitably experience great difficulty in remaining religiously neutral. Doctrines and faith are not inculcated or advanced by neutrals. With the best of intentions such a teacher would find it hard to make a total separation between secular teaching and religious doctrine. What would appear to some to be essential to good citizenship might well for others border on or constitute instruction in religion. Further difficulties are inherent in the combination of religious discipline and the possibility of disagreement between teacher and religious authorities over the meaning of the statutory restrictions.

We do not assume, however, that parochial school teachers will be unsuccessful in their attempts to segregate their religious beliefs from their secular educational responsibilities. But the potential for impermissible fostering of religion is present. The Rhode Island Legislature has not, and could not, provide state aid on the basis of a mere assumption that secular teachers under religious discipline can avoid conflicts. The State must be certain, given the Religion Clauses, that subsidized teachers do not inculcate religion—indeed the State here has undertaken to do so. To ensure that no trespass occurs, the State has therefore carefully conditioned its aid with pervasive restrictions. An eligible recipient must teach only those courses that are offered in the public schools and use only those texts and materials that are found in the public schools. In addition the teacher must not engage in teaching any course in religion.

A comprehensive, discriminating, and continuing state surveillance will inevitably be required to ensure that these restrictions are obeyed and the First Amendment otherwise respected. Unlike a book, a teacher cannot be inspected once so as to determine the extent and intent of his or her personal beliefs and subjective acceptance of the limitations imposed by the First Amendment. These prophylactic contacts will involve excessive and enduring entanglement between state and church.

There is another area of entanglement in the Rhode Island program that gives concern. The statute excludes teachers employed by nonpublic schools whose average per-pupil expenditures on secular education equal or exceed the comparable figures for public schools. In the event that the total expenditures of an otherwise eligible school exceed this norm, the program requires the government to examine the school's records in order to determine how much of the toal expenditures is attributable to secular education and how much to religious activity. This kind of state inspection and evaluation of the religious content of a religious organization is fraught with the sort of entanglement that the Constitution forbids. It is a relationship pregnant with dangers of excessive government direction of church schools and hence of churches. The Court noted "the hazards of government supporting churches" in *Walz v. Tax Commission* [*supra,* XIII, 3], and we cannot ignore here the danger that pervasive modern governmental power will ultimately intrude on religion and thus conflict with the Religion Clauses.

(b) *Pennsylvania program*

The Pennsylvania statute also provides state aid to church-related schools for teachers' salaries. The complaint describes an educational system that is very similar to the one existing in Rhode Island. According to the allegations, the church-related elementary and secondary schools are controlled by religious organizations, have the purpose of propagating and promoting a particular religious faith, and conduct their operations to fulfill that purpose. Since this complaint was dismissed for failure to state a claim for relief, we must accept these allegations as true for purposes of our review.

As we noted earlier, the very restrictions and surveillance necessary to ensure that teachers play a strictly nonideological role give rise to entanglements between church and state. The Pennsylvania statute, like that of Rhode Island, fosters this kind of relationship. Reimbursement is not only limited to courses offered in the public schools and materials approved by state officials, but the statute excludes "any subject matter expressing religious teaching, or the morals or forms of worship of any sect." In addition, schools seeking reimbursement must maintain accounting procedures that require the State to establish the cost of the secular as distinguished from the religious instruction.

The Pennsylvania statute, moreover, has the further defect of providing state financial aid directly to the church-related school. This factor distinguishes both *Everson* and *Allen,* for in both those cases the Court was careful to point out that state aid was provided to the student and his parents—not to the church-related school. *Board of Education v. Allen; Everson v. Board of Education* [XIV, 1]. In *Walz v. Tax Commission* [XIII, 3], the Court warned of the dangers of direct payments to religious organizations:

"Obviously a direct money subsidy would be a relationship pregnant with involvement and, as with most governmental grant programs, could encompass sustained and detailed administrative relationships for enforcement of statutory or administrative standards. . . ."

The history of government grants of a continuing cash subsidy indicates that such programs have almost always been accompanied by varying measures of control and surveillance. The government cash grants before us now provide no basis for predicting that comprehensive measures of surveillance and controls will not follow. In particular the government's post-audit power to inspect and evaluate a church-related school's financial records and to determine which expenditures are religious and which are secular creates an intimate and continuing relationship between church and state.

IV

A broader base of entanglement of yet a different character is presented by the divisive political potential of these state programs. In a community where such a large number of pupils are served by church-related schools, it can be assumed that state assistance will entail considerable political activity. Partisans of parochial schools, understandably concerned with rising costs and sincerely dedicated to both the religious and secular educational missions of their schools, will inevitably champion this cause and promote political action to achieve their goals. Those who oppose state aid, whether for constitutional, religious, or fiscal reasons, will inevitably respond and employ all the usual political campaign techniques to prevail. Candidates will be forced to declare and voters to choose. It would be unrealistic to ignore the fact that many people confronted with issues of this kind will find their votes aligned with their faith.

Ordinarily political debate and division, however vigorous or even partisan, are normal and healthy manifestations of our democratic system of government, but political division along religious lines was one of the principal evils against which the First Amendment was intended to protect. Freund, Comment, Public Aid to Parochial Schools, 82 Harv. L. Rev. 1680, 1692 (1969). The potential divisiveness of such conflict is a threat to the normal political process. *Walz v. Tax Commission* [XIII, 3] (separate opinion of Harlan, J.). See also *Board of Education v. Allen* [XIV, 1] (Harlan, J., concurring); *Abington School District v. Schempp* [XIV, 2] (Goldberg, J., concurring). To have States or communities divide on the issues presented by state aid to parochial schools would tend to confuse and obscure other issues of great urgency. We have an expanding array of vexing issues, local and national, domestic and international, to debate and divide on. It conflicts with our whole history and tradition to permit questions of the Religion Clauses to assume such importance in our legislatures and in our elections that they could divert attention from the myriad issues and problems that confront every level of government. The highways of church and state relationships are not likely to be one-way streets, and the Constitution's authors sought to protect religious worship from the pervasive power of government. The history of many countries attests to the hazards of religion's intruding into the political arena or of political power intruding into the legitimate and free exercise of religious belief.

Of course, as the Court noted in *Walz,* "[a]dherents of particular faiths and individual churches frequently take strong positions on public issues." *Walz v. Tax Commission* [XIII, 3]. We could not expect otherwise, for religious values pervade the fabric of our national life. But in *Walz* we dealt with a status under state tax laws for the benefit of all religious groups. Here we are confronted with successive and very likely permanent annual appropriations that benefit relatively few religious groups. Political fragmentation and divisiveness on religious lines are thus likely to be intensified.

The potential for political divisiveness related to religious belief and practice is aggravated in these two statutory programs by the need for continuing annual appropriations and the likelihood of larger and larger demands as costs and populations grow.

The judgment of the Rhode Island District Court in the De Censo cases was affirmed; the judgment of the Pennsylvania District Court was reversed.

Justice Douglas concurred in an opinion joined by Black; Justices Brennan and White also wrote separate concurrences. Justice White dissented in *Earley;* Justice Marshall took no part in *Lemon,* but concurred with Justice Douglas in *Earley.*

NOTE. *Parochial Schools Since* Lemon. *Lemon* was a watershed, a substantial departure in analysis and mood from *Allen, supra,* this section. The Chief Justice's opinion picked up Freund's metaphor of a minuet and boldly proclaimed that the Court was committed not to form but to substance. The Court endorsed Freund's idea that a principal evil envisaged by the First Amendment was political division on religious lines. Above all, the Court promulgated the three-pronged test that was to dominate the education cases and affect other First Amendment litigation about religion. The line followed in subsequent cases was as "blurred, indistinct, and variable" as *Lemon* had indicated.

In *Lemon v. Kurtzman,* 411 U.S. 192 (1973) (*Lemon* II), the District Court permitted Pennsylvania to reimburse the nonpublic schools for services rendered in the school year 1970–1971, although the payment would be made after June 28, 1971, when the Supreme Court had held the Pennsylvania statute unconstitutional. The successful parties in *Lemon* I challenged the reimbursement. The Supreme Court, 5–3, per Chief Justice Burger, upheld the District Court's exercise of discretion. The schools had relied on the statute. The decision in *Lemon* I was "not clearly foreshadowed." The burden on the schools not getting reimbursement would be heavy. The "constitutional interests at stake in *Lemon* I" would not be compromised by a single payment and a single and final postaudit of the school's expenditures. Justices Douglas, Brennan, and Stewart dissented, insisting that the establishment clause was violated if any money was paid: "the subsidy today given to sectarian schools out of taxpayers' monies exceeds by far the 'three pence' which Madison condemned in his Remonstrance."

On June 25, 1973, the Supreme Court decided *Committee for Public Education and Religious Liberty v. Nyquist,* 413 U.S. 756. Leo Pfeffer represented PEARL; amici supporting the New York law included the United States, represented by Solicitor General Erwin Griswold. The New York statute, enacted in 1972, provided:

1. Money grants of $30 to $40 per pupil to nonpublic schools serving low-income families to maintain and repair school facilities "to ensure the health" of the students. The grants would not exceed 50 percent of per pupil cost in a public school.
2. Reimbursement of $50 to $100 per nonpublic school pupil to parents with income of less than $5,000. The reimbursement could not exceed 50 percent of the parents' outlay. The

announced legislative purpose was to give educational options to low-income families and to prevent "a massive increase in public school enrollment and costs" by nonpublic school pupils transferring to public schools.

3. A tax deduction per nonpublic school pupil for parents with income of $25,000 or less; the deduction, declining as income increased, amounted at the most to $50 per child. The legislature noted that the nonpublic schools already had tax-exempt status and that voluntary contributions to them were already tax-deductible (*ibid.* at 762–767).

In New York State, there were 2,038 nonpublic schools. Of these, 1,415 were Catholic, 164 Jewish, 59 Lutheran, 49 Episcopal, 37 Seventh-Day Adventist, 18 other religions, *ibid.* at 768.

In an opinion by Justice Powell, the Court held each part of the New York law invalid:

1. The maintenance and repair provisions "violate the Establishment Clause because their effect, inevitably, is to subsidize and advance the religious mission of sectarian schools," *ibid.* at 779–780.
2. The effect of the reimbursement of the low-income parents was "to provide desired financial support for nonpublic, sectarian institutions." That the grants were to the parents, not to the schools; that they were reimbursements, and not prospective; that they paid only 50 percent of the parents' outlay; that they were designed to let low-income parents exercise their religion because "without state assistance their right to have their children educated in a religious environment is diminished or even denied"—all these considerations were taken up by the Court and found insufficient to justify "a step which can only be regarded as one 'advancing' religion," *ibid.* at 780–788.
3. The tax deduction was found to be equally "a charge made upon the state for the purpose of religious education," *ibid.* at 791. The Court rejected the analogy with property tax exemptions for churches. That exemption, it said, was based on history; this one was an innovation. The purpose of the property tax exemption, the Court asserted, was to minimize entanglement with the state; the benefit to the churches was "incidental." The exemption went to all charities; here the benefit was channelled "primarily" to sectarian schools, *ibid.* at 793–794.

Chief Justice Burger and Justice Rehnquist agreed with striking down the "maintenance and repair" provisions. Justice White dissented on all issues, and the Chief Justice and Justice Rehnquist joined him in finding that the decision on reimbursement and tax deduction ran counter to *Everson* (XIV, 1), *Allen* (XIV, 1), *Walz* (XIII, 3), and *Quick Bear* (X, 1). The Chief Justice declared: "The essence of all these decisions, I suggest, is that government aid to individuals generally stands on an entirely different footing from direct aid to religious institutions" (*ibid.* at 801). The same day the Court, 6–3, per Justice Powell, invalidated a similar statute passed by Pennsylvania after *Lemon* I, *supra*, *Sloan v. Lemon*, 413 U.S. 825 (1973).

Levitt v. Committee for Public Education and Religious Liberty, 413 U.S. 472 (1973). By a vote of 8–1 (Justice White dissenting) the Court upheld a challenge by PEARL, again represented by Leo Pfeffer, to a New York statute that gave a cash grant of $27 to $45 per pupil to nonpublic schools to pay them for the cost of administering both examinations prepared by the state and internal examinations prepared by their own teachers. The Court, per Chief Justice Burger, noted at 480 that the internal tests might "be drafted with an eye, unconsciously or otherwise, to inculcate students in the religious precepts of the sponsoring church." The Court also noted that there was no audit to determine whether the school's costs were less than the sums received.

Meed v. Pittenger, 421 U.S. 349 (1975). Pennsylvania had enacted a law in 1972 providing to all nonpublic school children textbooks and auxiliary services such as counseling, testing, remedial help, speech and hearing therapy, and to the schools instructional material such as maps, films, and laboratory equipment. The Court, 5–4, per Justice Stewart, upheld the textbook program. By a vote of 6–3, the Court held the auxiliary services and instructional aids program to be an unconstitutional establishment of religion. The Court emphasized that 75 percent of the nonpublic schools aided were church-related (they were in fact largely Catholic parochial schools). The Court noted that in one year $12 million of aid had been disbursed to these schools through the loan of instructional materials.

The Court at 371–372 asserted that the professionals providing the auxiliary services on the premises of the nonpublic schools would have to be kept under surveillance to prevent impermissible fostering of religion. The Court also found "a serious potential for divisive conflict over the issue of aid to religion." Justices Brennan, Marshall, and Douglas dissented as to the validity of the textbook program, noting that an annual appropriation of $4.6 million had been made for it. Justices Burger, White, and Rehnquist dissented as to the invalidity of the other two programs. Justice Rehnquist at 395: "The Court apparently believes that the Establishment Clause of the First Amendment not only mandates religious neutrality on the part of government but also requires that this Court go further and throw its weight on the side of those who believe that our society as a whole should be a purely secular one." Leo Pfeffer represented the successful taxpayer; William Ball represented one of the losing defendants.

After *Meek v. Pittenger,* Ohio enacted a statute attempting to conform to what the Court had used as criteria. It appropriated $88 million for the first two years to provide nonpublic schools with a variety of aid. More than 96 percent of the schools were religious and more than 92 percent, Catholic. In *Wolman v. Walter,* 433 U.S. 229 (1977), the Court, per Justice Blackmun, upheld as constitutional the provision of textbooks; tests provided by examiners outside the schools; speech, hearing, and psychological diagnostic services; and therapeutic and remedial services provided off the premises, including as possible sites mobile units parked near the schools. The Court invalidated the provision of instructional materials and equipment, and paying for field trips to secular centers of interest. That the statute made the students not the schools the recipients of the instructional material was held to be irrelevant: it supported "the religious role of the schools."

Chief Justice Burger and Justices White and Rehnquist dissented as to the items disallowed. Justice Brennan dissented as to all the items allowed, Justice Marshall as to most, and Justice Stevens as to the textbooks and tests. Justice Powell observed at 262: "Our decisions in this troubling area . . . often must seem arbitrary," but he thought "analytical tidiness" was not to be achieved by "blind absolutism." He would have allowed the field trip funding as indistinguishable from the bus services allowed by *Everson.* He would have permitted instructional materials that went directly to individual students.

Wolman was followed by *Committee for Public Education and Religious Liberty v. Regan,* 444 U.S. 646 (1980). After *Levitt, supra,* New York had amended its statute to reimburse the nonpublic schools only for giving and grading state-prepared examinations and for making state-required reports. PEARL, represented by Leo Pfeffer, challenged this statute, too. The Court, 5–4, per Justice White, upheld the statute, declaring at 654 that "*Wolman v. Walter* controls this case." Justice Blackmun (the author of *Wolman*) and Justices Brennan, Marshall, and Stevens dissented. Justice White for the Court said at 662 that the Court's "course sacrifices clarity and predictability for flexibility," and that would continue to be true until "a single, more encompassing construction of the Establishment Clause" was reached. Dissenting, Justice Blackmun at 664 saw a "defection" from *Wolman* which he could attribute "only to a concern about the continuing and emotional controversy." Justice Stevens at 671 characterized the Court's present course as a "sisyphean task," and exhorted it to return to "the high and impregnable wall."

In 1983 the Court considered a Minnesota statute that permitted all parents to deduct up to between $500 and $700 per child for the actual expenses incurred for tuition, textbooks, and transportation. The Court, 5–4, per Justice Rehnquist, upheld the statute.

Mueller v. Allen
463 U.S. 388 (1983)

. . .

The general nature of our inquiry in this area has been guided, since the decision in *Lemon v. Kurtzman* [XIV, 1], by the "three-part" test laid down in that case:

"First, the statute must have a secular legislative purpose; second, its principal or primary effect must be one that neither advances nor inhibits religion . . .; finally, the statute must not foster 'an excessive government entanglement with religion.' "

Id., at 612–613.

While this principle is well settled, our cases have also emphasized that it provides "no more than [a] helpful signpos[t]" in dealing with Establishment Clause challenges. *Hunt v. McNair* [XIV, 3]. With this caveat in mind, we turn to the specific challenges raised against § 290.09, subd. 22, under the *Lemon* framework.

Little time need be spent on the question of whether the Minnesota tax deduction has a secular purpose. Under our prior decisions, governmental assistance programs have consistently survived this inquiry even when they have run afoul of other aspects of the *Lemon* framework. See, *e.g., Lemon v. Kurtzman, supra; Meek v. Pittenger, supra,* at 363; *Wolman v. Walter, supra,* at 236. This reflects, at least in part, our reluctance to attribute unconstitutional motives to the States, particularly when a plausible secular purpose for the State's program may be discerned from the face of the statute.

A State's decision to defray the cost of educational expenses incurred by parents— regardless of the type of schools their children attend—evidences a purpose that is both secular and understandable. An educated populace is essential to the political and economic health of any community, and a State's efforts to assist parents in meeting the rising cost of educational expenses plainly serves this secular purpose of ensuring that the State's citizenry is well educated. Similarly, Minnesota, like other States, could conclude that there is a strong public interest in assuring the continued financial health of private schools, both sectarian and nonsectarian. By educating a substantial number of students such schools relieve public schools of a correspondingly great burden—to the benefit of all taxpayers. In addition, private schools may serve as a benchmark for public schools, in a manner analogous to the "TVA yardstick" for private power companies. As Justice Powell has remarked:

"Parochial schools, quite apart from their sectarian purpose, have provided an educational alternative for millions of young Americans; they often afford wholesome competition with our public schools; and in some States they relieve substantially the tax burden incident to the operation of public schools. The State has, moreover, a legitimate interest in facilitating education of the highest quality for all children within its boundaries, whatever school their parents have chosen for them." *Wolman v. Walter,* 433 U.S., at 262 (Powell, J., concurring in part, concurring in judgment in part, and dissenting in part).

All these justifications are readily available to support § 290.09, subd. 22, and each is sufficient to satisfy the secular purpose inquiry of *Lemon.*

We turn therefore to the more difficult but related question whether the Minnesota statute has "the primary effect of advancing the sectarian aims of the nonpublic schools." *Committee for Public Education v. Regan,* 444 U.S. 646, 662 (1980); *Lemon v. Kurtzman* [XIV, 1]. In concluding that it does not, we find several features of the Minnesota tax deduction particularly significant. First, an essential feature of Minnesota's arrangement is the fact that § 290.09, subd. 22, is only one among many deductions—such as those for medical expenses, § 290.09, subd. 10, and charitable contributions, § 290.21, subd. 3—available under the Minnesota tax laws.[5] Our decisions consistently have recognized that traditionally "[l]egislatures have especially broad latitude in creating classifications and distinctions in tax statutes," *Regan v. Taxation With Representation of Wash.,* 461 U.S. 540, 547 (1983), in part because the "familiarity with local conditions" enjoyed by legislators especially enables them to "achieve an equitable distribution of the tax burden." *Madden v. Kentucky,* 309 U.S. 83, 88 (1940). Under our prior decisions, the Minnesota Legislature's judgment that a deduction for educational expenses fairly equalizes the tax burden of its citizens and encourages desirable expenditures for educational purposes is entitled to substantial deference.[6]

Other characteristics of § 290.09, subd. 22, argue equally strongly for the provision's constitutionality. Most importantly, the deduction is available for educational expenses incurred by *all* parents, including those whose children attend public schools and those whose children attend nonsectarian private schools or sectarian private schools. Just as in *Widmar v. Vincent* [XIV, 3], where we concluded that the State's provision of a forum neutrally "available to a broad class of nonreligious as well as religious speakers" does not "confer any imprimatur of state approval," *ibid.,* so here: "[t]he provision of benefits to so broad a spectrum of groups is an important index of secular effect."[7] *Ibid.*

In this respect, as well as others, this case is vitally different from the scheme struck down in *Nyquist.* There, public assistance amounting to tuition grants, was provided only to parents of children in *nonpublic* schools. This fact had considerable bearing on our decision striking down the New York statute at issue; we explicitly distinguished

---

[5] Deductions for charitable contributions, allowed by Minnesota law, Minn. Stat. § 290.21, subd. 3 (1982), include contributions to religious institutions, and exemptions from property tax for property used for charitable purposes under Minnesota law include property used for wholly religious purposes, § 272.02. In each case, it may be that religious institutions benefit very substantially from the allowance of such deductions. The Court's holding in *Walz v. Tax Comm'n* [XIII, 3] indicates, however, that this does not require the conclusion that such provisions of a State's tax law violate the Establishment Clause.

[6] Our decision in *Committee for Public Education v. Nyquist* [XIV, 1] is not to the contrary on this point. We expressed considerable doubt there that the "tax benefits" provided by New York law properly could be regarded as parts of a genuine system of tax laws. Plainly, the outright grants to low-income parents did not take the form of ordinary tax benefits. As to the benefits provided to middle-income parents, the Court said:

"The amount of the deduction is unrelated to the amount of money actually expended by any parent on tuition, but is calculated on the basis of a formula contained in the statute. The formula is apparently the product of a legislative attempt to assure that each family would receive a carefully estimated net benefit, and that the tax benefit would be comparable to, and compatible with, the tuition grant for lower income families." *Id.,* at 790 (footnote omitted).

Indeed, the question whether a program having the elements of a "genuine tax deduction" would be constitutionally acceptable was expressly reserved in *Nyquist, supra,* at 790, n. 49. While the economic consequences of the program in *Nyquist* and that in this case may be difficult to distinguish, we have recognized on other occasions that "the form of the [State's assistance to parochial schools must be examined] for the light that it casts on the substance." *Lemon v. Kurtzman* [XIV, 1]. The fact that the Minnesota plan embodies a "genuine tax deduction" is thus of some relevance, especially given the traditional rule of deference accorded legislative classifications in tax statutes.

[7] Likewise, in *Sloan v. Lemon* [XIV, 1], where we held that a Pennsylvania statute violated the First Amendment, we emphasized that "the State [had] singled out a class of its citizens for a special economic benefit." We also observed in *Widmar* that "empirical evidence that religious groups will dominate [the school's] open forum" [XIV, 3] might be relevant to analysis under the Establishment Clause. We address this *infra,* at 400–402.

both *Allen* and *Everson* on the grounds that "[i]n both cases the class of beneficiaries included *all* schoolchildren, those in public as well as those in private schools." 413 U.S., at 782–783, n. 38 (emphasis in original). Moreover, we intimated that "public assistance (*e.g.,* scholarships) made available generally without regard to the sectarian-nonsectarian, or public-nonpublic nature of the institution benefited," *ibid.,* might not offend the Establishment Clause. We think the tax deduction adopted by Minnesota is more similar to this latter type of program than it is to the arrangement struck down in *Nyquist.* Unlike the assistance at issue in *Nyquist,* § 290.09, subd. 22, permits *all* parents—whether their children attend public school or private—to deduct their children's educational expenses. As *Widmar* and our other decisions indicate, a program, like § 290.09, subd. 22, that neutrally provides state assistance to a broad spectrum of citizens is not readily subject to challenge under the Establishment Clause.

We also agree with the Court of Appeals that, by channeling whatever assistance it may provide to parochial schools through individual parents, Minnesota has reduced the Establishment Clause objections to which its action is subject. It is true, of course, that financial assistance provided to parents ultimately has an economic effect comparable to that of aid given directly to the schools attended by their children. It is also true, however, that under Minnesota's arrangement public funds become available only as a result of numerous, private choices of individual parents of school-age children. For these reasons, we recognized in *Nyquist* that the means by which state assistance flows to private schools is of some importance: we said that "the fact that aid is disbursed to parents rather than to . . . schools" is a material consideration in Establishment Clause analysis, albeit "only one among many factors to be considered." 413 U.S., at 781. It is noteworthy that all but one of our recent cases invalidating state aid to parochial schools have involved the direct transmission of assistance from the State to the schools themselves. The exception, of course, was *Nyquist,* which, as discussed previously, is distinguishable from this case on other grounds. Where, as here, aid to parochial schools is available only as a result of decisions of individual parents no "imprimatur of state approval," *Widmar* [XIV, 3] can be deemed to have been conferred on any particular religion, or on religion generally.

We find it useful, in the light of the foregoing characteristics of § 290.09, subd. 22, to compare the attenuated financial benefits flowing to parochial schools from the section to the evils against which the Establishment Clause was designed to protect. These dangers are well described by our statement that " '[w]hat is at stake as a matter of policy [in Establishment Clause cases] is preventing that kind and degree of government involvement in religious life that, as history teaches us, is apt to lead to strife and frequently strain a political system to the breaking point.' " *Nyquist* [XIV, 1] at 796, quoting *Walz v. Tax Comm'n* [XIII, 3] (opinion of Harlan, J.). It is important, however, to "keep these issues in perspective":

> "At this point in the 20th century we are quite far removed from the dangers that prompted the Framers to include the Establishment Clause in the Bill of Rights. See *Walz v. Tax Comm'n* [XIII, 3]. The risk of significant religious or denominational control over our democratic processes—or even of deep political division along religious lines—is remote, and when viewed against the positive contributions of sectarian schools, any such risk seems entirely tolerable in light of the continuing oversight of this Court." *Wolman* [XIV, 1] (Powell, J., concurring in part, concurring in judgment in part, and dissenting in part).

The Establishment Clause of course extends beyond prohibition of a state church or payment of state funds to one or more churches. We do not think, however, that its prohibition extends to the type of tax deduction established by Minnesota. The historic purposes of the Clause simply do not encompass the sort of attenuated financial benefit, ultimately controlled by the private choices of individual parents, that eventually flows to parochial schools from the neutrally available tax benefit at issue in this case.

Petitioners argue that, notwithstanding the facial neutrality of § 290.09, subd. 22, in application the statute primarily benefits religious institutions. Petitioners rely, as they did below, on a statistical analysis of the type of persons claiming the tax deduction. They contend that most parents of public school children incur no tuition expenses, see Minn. Stat. § 120.06 (1982), and that other expenses deductible under § 290.09, subd. 22, are negligible in value; moreover, they claim that 96% of the children in private schools in 1978–1979 attended religiously affiliated institutions. Because of all this, they reason, the bulk of deductions taken under § 290.09, subd. 22, will be claimed by parents of children in sectarian schools. Respondents reply that petitioners have failed to consider the impact of deductions for items such as transportation, summer school tuition, tuition paid by parents whose children attended schools outside the school districts in which they resided, rental or purchase costs for a variety of equipment, and tuition for certain types of instruction not ordinarily provided in public schools.

We need not consider these contentions in detail. We would be loath to adopt a rule grounding the constitutionality of a facially neutral law on annual reports reciting the extent to which various classes of private citizens claimed benefits under the law. Such an approach would scarcely provide the certainty that this field stands in need of, nor can we perceive principled standards by which such statistical evidence might be evaluated. Moreover, the fact that private persons fail in a particular year to claim the tax relief to which they are entitled—under a facially neutral statute—should be of little importance in determining the constitutionality of the statute permitting such relief.

Finally, private educational institutions, and parents paying for their children to attend these schools, make special contributions to the areas in which they operate. "Parochial schools, quite apart from their sectarian purpose, have provided an educational alternative for millions of young Americans; they often afford wholesome competition with our public schools; and in some States they relieve substantially the tax burden incident to the operation of public schools." *Wolman* [XIV, 1] (Powell, J., concurring in part, concurring in judgment in part, and dissenting in part). If parents of children in private schools choose to take especial advantage of the relief provided by § 290.09, subd. 22, it is no doubt due to the fact that they bear a particularly great financial burden in educating their children. More fundamentally, whatever unequal effect may be attributed to the statutory classification can fairly be regarded as a rough return for the benefits, discussed above, provided to the State and all taxpayers by parents sending their children to parochial schools. In the light of all this, we believe it wiser to decline to engage in the type of empirical inquiry into those persons benefited by state law which petitioners urge.

Thus, we hold that the Minnesota tax deduction for educational expenses satisfies the primary effect inquiry of our Establishment Clause cases.

Affirmed.

Justices Brennan, Marshall, Blackmun, and Stevens dissented.

Grand Rapids School District v. Ball
105 S.Ct. 3216 (1985)

Kenneth F. Ripple, Notre Dame, Indiana, for petitioners. Michael W. McConnell, Washington, D.C., for the United States as amicus curiae. A. E. Dick Howard, for respondents.

Justice Brennan delivered the opinion of the Court.

[At issue were two programs offered by the School District of Grand Rapids to pupils in nonpublic schools. The Shared Time Program offered "remedial" and "enrichment" art, mathematics, music, reading, and physical education in the elementary schools.

The teachers were full-time employees of the public schools hired in the usual way. About 10 percent of a nonpublic school student's time would be spent in these courses.

The Community Education Programs were taught in the nonpublic schools at the end of the regular school day and included arts and crafts, drama, and Spanish. The teachers were hired part-time by the School District and were usually full-time teachers at a parochial school. The director of both programs was a public employee who worked out the schedule with the parochial schools. Almost all of the schools benefited were Catholic or Protestant.]

. . .

Given that 40 of the 41 schools in this case are thus "pervasively sectarian," the challenged public-school programs operating in the religious schools may impermissibly advance religion in three different ways. First, the teachers participating in the programs may become involved in intentionally or inadvertently inculcating particular religious tenets or beliefs. Second, the programs may provide a crucial symbolic link between government and religion, thereby enlisting—at least in the eyes of impressionable youngsters—the powers of government to the support of the religious denomination operating the school. Third, the programs may have the effect of directly promoting religion by impermissibly providing a subsidy to the primary religious mission of the institutions affected.

. . .

Our cases have recognized that the Establishment Clause guards against more than direct, state-funded efforts to indoctrinate youngsters in specific religious beliefs. Government promotes religion as effectively when it fosters a close identification of its powers and responsibilities with those of any—or all—religious denominations as when it attempts to inculcate specific religious doctrines. If this identification conveys a message of government endorsement or disapproval of religion, a core purpose of the Establishment Clause is violated. See *Lynch v. Donnelly* [XIII, 3], (O'Connor, J., concurring); cf. *Abington School District v. Schempp,* [XIV, 2] (history teaches that "powerful sects or groups might bring about a fusion of governmental and religious functions or a concert or dependency of one upon the other to the end that official support of the State or Federal Government would be placed behind the tenets of one or of all orthodoxies"). As we stated in *Larkin v. Grendel's Den, Inc.* [XV, 2]: "[T]he mere appearance of a joint exercise of legislative authority by Church and State provides a significant symbolic benefit to religion in the minds of some by reason of the power conferred." See also *Widmar v. Vincent* [*infra,* 3] (finding effect "incidental" and not "primary" because it "does not confer any imprimatur of state approval on religious sects or practices").

It follows that an important concern of the effects test is whether the symbolic union of church and state effected by the challenged governmental action is sufficiently likely to be perceived by adherents of the controlling denominations as an endorsement, and by the nonadherents as a disapproval, of their individual religious choices. The inquiry into this kind of effect must be conducted with particular care when many of the citizens perceiving the governmental message are children in their formative years. Cf. *Tilton v. Richardson* [*infra,* 3]. The symbolism of a union between church and state is most likely to influence children of tender years, whose experience is limited and whose beliefs consequently are the function of environment as much as of free and voluntary choice.

. . .

Petitioners claim that the aid here, like the textbooks in *Allen,* flows primarily to the students, not to the religious schools. Of course, all aid to religious schools ultimately "flows to" the students, and petitioners' argument if accepted would validate all forms of nonideological aid to religious schools, including those explicitly rejected in our prior cases. Yet in *Meek,* we held unconstitutional the loan of instructional materials to religious schools and in *Wolman,* we rejected the fiction that a similar program could be saved by masking it as aid to individual students. *Wolman* [*supra*]. It follows *a fortiori* that the aid here, which includes not only instructional materials but also the provision of instructional services by teachers in the parochial school building, "inescapably [has] the primary effect of providing a direct and substantial advancement of the sectarian enterprise." *Id.,* at 250, 97 S.Ct., at 2606. Where, as here, no meaningful distinction can be made between aid to the student and aid to the school, "the concept of a loan to individuals is a transparent fiction." . . .

Petitioners also argue that this "subsidy" effect is not significant in this case, because the Community Education and Shared Time programs supplemented the curriculum with courses not previously offered in the religious schools and not required by school rule or state regulation. Of course, this fails to distinguish the programs here from those found unconstitutional in *Meek.* See 421 U.S., at 368, 95 S.Ct., at 1765. As in *Meek,* we do not find that this feature of the program is controlling. First, there is no way of knowing whether the religious schools would have offered some or all of these courses if the public school system had not offered them first. The distinction between courses that "supplement" and those that "supplant" the regular curriculum is therefore not nearly as clear as petitioners allege. Second, although the precise courses offered in these programs may have been new to the participating religious schools, their general subject matter—reading, math, etc.—was surely a part of the curriculum in the past, and the concerns of the Establisment Clause may thus be triggered despite the "supplemental" nature of the courses. Cf. *Meek v. Pittenger, supra.* Third, and most important, petitioners' argument would permit the public schools gradually to take over the entire secular curriculum of the religious school, for the latter could surely discontinue existing courses so that they might be replaced a year or two later by a Community Education or Shared Time course with the same content. The average religious school student, for instance, now spends 10 percent of the school day in Shared Time classes. But there is no principled basis on which this Court can impose a limit on the percentage of the religious-school day that can be subsidized by the public school. To let the genie out of the bottle in this case would be to permit ever larger segments of the religious school curriculum to be turned over to the public school system, thus violating the cardinal principle that the State may not in effect become the prime supporter of the religious school system. See *Lemon v. Kurtzman [supra].*

III

[5] We conclude that the challenged programs have the effect of promoting religion in three ways. The state-paid instructors, influenced by the pervasively sectarian nature of the religious schools in which they work, may subtly or overtly indoctrinate the students in particular religious tenets at public expense. The symbolic union of church and state inherent in the provision of secular, state-provided instruction in the religious school buildings threatens to convey a message of state support for religion to students and to the general public. Finally, the programs in effect subsidize the religious functions of the parochial schools by taking over a substantial portion of their responsibility for teaching secular subjects. For these reasons, the conclusion is inescapable that the Community Education and Shared Time programs have the "primary or principal" effect of advancing religion, and therefore violate the dictates of the Establishment Clause of the First Amendment.

Nonpublic schools have played an important role in the development of American education, and we have long recognized that parents and their children have the right to choose between public schools and available sectarian alternatives. As The Chief Justice noted in *Lemon v. Kurtzman, supra,* "nothing we have said can be construed to disparage the role of church-related elementary and secondary schools in our national life. Their contribution has been and is enormous." But the Establishment Clause "rest[s] on the belief that a union of government and religion tends to destroy government and to degrade religion." *Engel v. Vitale* [*infra,* sec. 2]. Therefore, "[t]he Constitution decrees that religion must be a private matter for the individual, the family, and the institutions of private choice, and that while some involvement and entanglement are inevitable, lines must be drawn." *Lemon v. Kurtzman* [*supra*].

It is so ordered.

. . .

Chief Justice Burger concurred as to the Community Education Program but dissented as to the Shared Time Program, as did Justice O'Connor. Justice Rehnquist and Justice White dissented as to both programs.

Aguilar v. Felton
105 S.Ct. 3232 (1985)

Solicitor General Rex E. Lee, Washington, D.C., for appellants. Stanley Geller, New York City, for appellees.

Justice Brennan delivered the opinion of the Court.

. . .

Title I of the Elementary and Secondary Education Act of 1965 [20 U.S.C. § 2071] authorizes the Secretary of Education to distribute financial assistance to local educational institutions to meet the needs of educationally deprived children from low income families. . . .

Since 1966 the City of New York has provided instructional services funded by Title I to parochial school students on the premises of parochial schools. . . . The programs conducted at these schools include remedial reading, reading skills, remedial mathematics, English as a second language and guidance services. These programs are carried out by regular employees of the public schools (teachers, guidance counselors, psychologists, psychiatrists, and social workers) who have volunteered to teach in the parochial schools. . . .

The critical elements of the entanglement proscribed in *Lemon* [*supra* XIV, 1] and *Meek* [*supra* XIV, 1] are thus present in this case. First, as noted above, the aid is provided in a pervasively sectarian environment. Second, because assistance is provided in the form of teachers, ongoing inspection is required to ensure the absence of a religious message. . . .

The administrative cooperation that is required to maintain the educational program at issue here entangles Church and State still another way that infringes interests at the heart of the Establishment Clause. Administrative personnel of the public and parochial school system must work together. . . .

Affirmed.

Justice Powell, concurring.

[After agreeing that there was an "excessive entanglement."]

This risk of entanglement is compounded by the additional risk of political divisiveness stemming from the aid to religion at issue here. . . . In states such as New York that have large and varied sectarian populations, one can be assured that politics will enter into any state decision to aid parochial schools. . . .

The Title I program at issue in this case will also be invalid under the "effects" prong of the test adopted in *Lemon*.

Chief Justice Burger, dissenting.

Under the guise of protecting Americans from the evils of an Established Church such as those of the eighteenth century and earlier times, today's decision will deny countless school children desperately needed remedial teaching services funded under Title I. What is disconcerting about the result reached today is that, in the face of the human cost entailed by this decision, the Court does not even attempt to identify any threat to religious liberty posed by the operation of Title I.

Justice Rehnquist, dissenting.

I dissent for the reason stated in my dissenting opinion in *Wallace v. Jaffree* [XIV, 2].

Justice O'Connor, dissenting.

. . . The abstract theories explaining why on-premises instruction might publicly advance religion dissolve in the face of experience in New York. . . . Indeed, in nineteen years there has never been a single incident in which a Title I instructor "subtly or overtly" attempted to "indoctrinate the students in particular religious tenets at public expense."

Justice White also dissented.

Query. Are *Grand Rapids* and *Aguilar* consistent with *Grove City College v. Bell*, 104 S.Ct. 1211 (1984)? *See* John Garvey, "Another Way of Looking at School Aid," *1985 Supreme Court Review* 61.

NOTE. *Permissible and Impermissible Aid as of 1986.*

Permissible:

Bus transportation to and from school, *Everson*, 1947

Textbooks, *Allen*, 1968

Lunches, *Lemon*, 1971

Diagnostic services, *Wolman*, 1977

Therapy off school grounds, *Wolman*, 1977

Counseling off school grounds, *Wolman*, 1977

Remedial instruction off school grounds, *Wolman*, 1977

Exemption from property tax, *Walz*, 1980

Payments for use and grading of examinations prepared by state, *Regan*, 1980

Tax deduction for tuition, *Mueller*, 1983

Impermissible:

Instructional material to schools, *Lemon*, 1971

Salary supplements, *Earley*, 1971

Tax deductions for nonpublic schools, *Nyquist*, 1973

Tuition reimbursements only for parochial school parents, *Nyquist*, 1973

Payment for examinations prepared by teachers, *Levitt*, 1973

Therapeutic services on premises, *Meek*, 1975

Counseling on premises, *Meek*, 1975

Transportation on school field trips, *Wolman*, 1977

Maps, magazines, tape recorders to children, *Wolman*, 1977

Payment for public school teachers on nonpublic school premises, *Grand Rapids*, 1985

Remedial services on premises, *Aguilar*, 1985

Commentators have echoed the impatience and dissatisfaction expressed by several of the Justices themselves, *e.g.*, Jesse Choper, "The Religion Clauses of the First Amendment: Reconciling the Conflict," 41 *University of Pittsburgh Law Review* 673, 680 (1980): "[A]pplication of the Court's three-prong test has generated ad hoc judgments which are incapable of being reconciled on any principled basis." *Accord*, Note, "The Supreme Court, Effect Inquiry, and Aid to Parochial Education," 37 *Stanford Law Review* 219, 234 (1984).

2. PUBLIC SCHOOLS

The protagonist of the first famous case on religion and the public schools has told her own story of how she came to bring the case. She notes that she was the granddaughter of a Presbyterian elder and was baptized a Lutheran. Her father, a Christian when she was growing up, became an active spokesman for rationalism. As an adult she regarded herself as a humanist. She had inherited the spirit of her mother, who named her for "the first exponent of woman's rights," Vashti, the wife of King Ahasuerus, who lost her position because she refused to obey the king's command to attend a royal drinking party (Esther 1:1–12), see Vashti Cromwell McCollum, *One Woman's Fight* (1951) 9–14.

In 1940, Champaign, Illinois, adopted a plan permitting Roman Catholic, Jewish, and mainline Protestant religious teaching in its schools. The McCollums' son, James Terry, a student in the fourth grade, wanted to attend the Protestant instruction. Vashti McCollum consented but found it to be "indoctrination." She withheld her consent when Jim was in the fifth grade, but the regular teacher told Jim she wanted the class "to be 100%." When he abstained, he was sent, during the religious instruction period, to a small music room and was conspicuous in his isolation, *ibid.* 17–20.

Vashti McCollum took her complaint to the superintendent of schools, a Methodist, who turned a deaf ear. She then consulted a young Unitarian minister who had criticized the religious education plan. He put her in touch with the Chicago Action Council, an offshoot of the Civil Liberties Union. With its help, she brought the case, braving the social difficulties of her stance in a college town in the Midwest Bible Belt and spending $5,000 of her own money on the case. Her husband, an instructor in the Horticultural Department of the University of Illinois, supported her without joining the suit. She received over 6,000 letters praising her or vilifying her, and she became for some "a godless atheist," for others a champion of freedom, *ibid.* 16, 45, 190.

McCollum v. Board of Education
333 U.S. 203 (1948)

Walter F. Dodd and *Edward R. Burke* argued the cause for appellant. *Mr. Dodd* also filed a brief.

John L. Franklin and *Owen Rall* argued the cause and filed a brief for appellees.

Briefs of *amici curiae* urging reversal were filed by *Henry Epstein, Leo Pfeffer* and *Samuel Rothstein* for the Synagogue Council of America et al.; *Herbert A. Wolff* for the American Ethical Union; *E. Hilton Jackson, Challen B. Ellis, W. D. Jamieson* and *Kahl K. Spriggs* for the Joint Conference Committee on Public Relations of several Baptist conventions; *Edward C. Park* for the American Unitarian Association; *Kenneth W. Greenawalt, Leon Despres, Russell Whitman, John D. Miller, William L. Marbury, Thomas H. Eliot, Winthrop Wadleigh, Whitney N. Seymour* and *Gurney Edwards* for the American Civil Liberties Union; and *Homer Cummings* and *William D. Donnelly* for the General Conference of Seventh Day Adventists.

George F. Barrett, Attorney General of Illinois, and *William C. Wines,* Assistant Attorney General, filed a brief as *amici curiae,* urging affirmance.

Charles H. Tuttle filed a brief for the Protestant Council of New York City, as *amicus curiae.*

Justice Black delivered the opinion of the Court.

This case relates to the power of a state to utilize its tax-supported public school system in aid of religious instruction insofar as that power may be restricted by the First and Fourteenth Amendments to the Federal Constitution.

The appellant, Vashti McCollum, began this action for mandamus against the Champaign Board of Education in the Circuit Court of Champaign County, Illinois. Her asserted interest was that of a resident and taxpayer of Champaign and of a parent whose child was then enrolled in the Champaign public schools. Illinois has a compulsory education law which, with exceptions, requires parents to send their children, aged seven to sixteen, to its tax-supported public schools where the children are to remain in attendance during the hours when the schools are regularly in session. Parents who violate this law commit a misdemeanor punishable by fine unless the children attend private or parochial schools which meet educational standards fixed by the State. District boards of education are given general supervisory powers over the use of the public school buildings within the school districts. Ill. Rev. Stat. ch. 122, §§ 123, 301 (1943).

Appellant's petition for mandamus alleged that religious teachers, employed by private religious groups, were permitted to come weekly into the school buildings during the regular hours set apart for secular teaching, and then and there for a period of thirty minutes substitute their religious teaching for the secular education provided under the compulsory education law. The petitioner charged that this joint public-school religious-group program violated the First and Fourteenth Amendments to the United States Constitution. The prayer of her petition was that the Board of Education be ordered to "adopt and enforce rules and regulations prohibiting all instruction in and teaching of religious education in all public schools in Champaign School District Number 71, . . . and in all public school houses and buildings in said district when occupied by public schools." . . .

Although there are disputes between the parties as to various inferences that may or may not properly be drawn from the evidence concerning the religious program, the following facts are shown by the record without dispute. In 1940 interested members of the Jewish, Roman Catholic, and a few of the Protestant faiths formed a voluntary association called the Champaign Council on Religious Education. They obtained permission from the Board of Education to offer classes in religious instruction to public school pupils in grades four to nine inclusive. Classes were made up of pupils whose parents signed printed cards requesting that their children be permitted to attend; they were held weekly, thirty minutes for the lower grades, forty-five minutes for the higher. The council employed the religious teachers at no expense to the school authorities, but the instructors were subject to the approval and supervision of the superintendent of schools. The classes were taught in three separate religious groups by Protestant teachers,[4] Catholic priests, and a Jewish rabbi, although for the past several years there have apparently been no classes instructed in the Jewish religion. Classes were conducted in the regular classrooms of the school building. Students who did not choose to take the religious instruction were not released from public school duties; they were required to leave their classrooms and go to some other place in the school building for pursuit of their secular studies. On the other hand, students who were released from secular study for the religious instructions were required to be present at the religious classes. Reports of their presence or absence were to be made to their secular teachers.[5]

---

[4] There were two teachers of the Protestant faith. One was a Presbyterian and had been a foreign missionary for that church. The second testified as follows: "I am affiliated with the Christian church. I also work in the Methodist Church and I taught at the Presbyterian. I am married to a Lutheran."

[5] The director of the Champaign Council on Religious Education testified: ". . . If any pupil is absent we turn in a slip just like any teacher would to the superintendent's office. The slip is a piece of paper with a number of hours in the school day and a square, and the teacher of the particular room for the particular hour records the absentees. It has their names and the grade and the section to which they belong. It is the same sheet that the geography and history teachers and all the other teachers use, and is furnished by the school. . . ."

The foregoing facts, without reference to others that appear in the record, show the use of tax-supported property for religious instruction and the close cooperation between the school authorities and the religious council in promoting religious education. The operation of the State's compulsory education system thus assists and is integrated with the program of religious instruction carried on by separate religious sects. Pupils compelled by law to go to school for secular education are released in part from their legal duty upon the condition that they attend the religious classes. This is beyond all question a utilization of the tax-established and tax-supported public school system to aid religious groups to spread their faith. And it falls squarely under the ban of the First Amendment (made applicable to the States by the Fourteenth) as we interpreted it in *Everson v. Board of Education* [XIV, 1]. There we said: "Neither a state nor the Federal Government can set up a church. Neither can pass laws which aid one religion, aid all religions, or prefer one religion over another.[6] Neither can force or influence a person to go to or to remain away from church against his will or force him to profess a belief or disbelief in any religion. No person can be punished for entertaining or professing religious beliefs or disbeliefs, for church attendance or non-attendance. No tax in any amount, large or small, can be levied to support any religious activities or institutions, whatever they may be called, or whatever form they may adopt to teach or practice religion.[7] Neither a state nor the Federal Government can, openly or secretly, participate in the affairs of any religious organizations or groups and *vice versa*. In the words of Jefferson, the clause against establishment of religion by law was intended to erect 'a wall of separation between church and State.' " *Id.* at 15–16. The majority in the *Everson* case, and the minority as shown by quotations from the dissenting views in our notes 6 and 7, agreed that the First Amendment's language, properly interpreted, had erected a wall of separation between Church and State. They disagreed as to the facts shown by the record and as to the proper application of the First Amendment's language to those facts.

Recognizing that the Illinois program is barred by the First and Fourteenth Amendments if we adhere to the views expressed both by the majority and the minority in the *Everson* case, counsel for the respondents challenge those views as dicta and urge that we reconsider and repudiate them. They argue that historically the First Amendment was intended to forbid only government preference of one religion over another, not an impartial governmental assistance of all religions. In addition they ask that we distinguish or overrule our holding in the *Everson* case that the Fourteenth Amendment made the "establishment of religion" clause of the First Amendment applicable as a prohibition against the States. After giving full consideration to the arguments presented we are unable to accept either of these contentions.

To hold that a state cannot consistently with the First and Fourteenth Amendments utilize its public school system to aid any or all religious faiths or sects in the dissemination of their doctrines and ideals does not, as counsel urge, manifest a governmental hostility to religion or religious teachings. A manifestation of such hostility would be at war with our national tradition as embodied in the First Amendment's

---

[6] The dissent, agreed to by four judges, said: "The problem then cannot be cast in terms of legal discrimination or its absence. This would be true, even though the state in giving aid should treat all religious instruction alike. . . . Again, it was the furnishing of 'contributions of money for the propagation of opinions which he disbelieves' that the fathers outlawed. That consequence and effect are not removed by multiplying to all-inclusiveness the sects for which support is exacted. The Constitution requires, not comprehensive identification of state with religion, but complete separation." *Everson v. Board of Education* [XIV, 1].

[7] The dissenting judges said: "In view of this history no further proof is needed that the Amendment forbids any appropriation, large or small, from public funds to aid or support any and all religious exercises. . . . Legislatures are free to make, and courts to sustain, appropriations only when it can be found that in fact they do not aid, promote, encourage or sustain religious teaching or observances, be the amount large or small." *Everson v. Board of Education* [XIV, 1].

guaranty of the free exercise of religion. For the First Amendment rests upon the premise that both religion and government can best work to achieve their lofty aims if each is left free from the other within its respective sphere. Or, as we said in the *Everson* case, the First Amendment has erected a wall between Church and State which must be kept high and impregnable.

Here not only are the State's tax-supported public school buildings used for the dissemination of religious doctrines. The State also affords sectarian groups an invaluable aid in that it helps to provide pupils for their religious classes through use of the State's compulsory public school machinery. This is not separation of Church and State.

The cause is reversed and remanded to the State Supreme Court for proceedings not inconsistent with this opinion.

Reversed and remanded.

Justice Frankfurter wrote a separate opinion which Justices Jackson, Rutledge, and Burton joined:

The public school is at once the symbol of our democracy and the most pervasive means for promoting our common destiny. In no activity of the State is it more vital to keep out divisive forces than in its schools, to avoid confusing, not to say fusing, what the Constitution sought to keep strictly apart. . . .

We renew our conviction that "we have staked the very existence of our country on the faith that complete separation between the state and religion is best for the state and best for religion." *Everson v. Board of Education* [XIV, 1]. If nowhere else, in the relation between Church and State, "good fences make good neighbors."

Justice Jackson also wrote a separate opinion, concurring in Justice Frankfurter's opinion and concurring in the result reached by the Court.

. . .

It is idle to pretend that this task is one for which we can find in the Constitution one word to help us as judges to decide where the secular ends and the sectarian begins in education. Nor can we find guidance in any other legal source. It is a matter on which we can find no law but our own prepossessions. If with no surer legal guidance we are to take up and decide every variation of this controversy, raised by persons not subject to penalty or tax but who are dissatisfied with the way schools are dealing with the problem, we are likely to have much business of the sort. And, more importantly, we are likely to make the legal "wall of separation between church and state" as winding as the famous serpentine wall designed by Mr. Jefferson for the University he founded.

Justice Reed dissented.

Zorach v. Clauson
343 U.S. 306 (1952)

Kenneth W. Greenawalt argued the cause for appellants. With him on the brief were *Leo Pfeffer* and *Edwin J. Lukas.*

Wendell P. Brown, Solicitor General, argued the cause for the Commissioner of Education of the State of New York, appellee. With him on the brief were *Nathaniel L. Goldstein,* Attorney General, and *Ruth Kessler Toch* and *John P. Powers,* Assistant Attorneys General.

Michael A. Castaldi argued the cause for the Board of Education of the City of New York, appellee. With him on the brief were *Denis M. Hurley, Seymour B. Quel, Daniel T. Scannell* and *Arthur H. Kahn.*

Charles H. Tuttle argued the cause for the Greater New York Coordinating Committee on Released Time of Jews, Protestants and Roman Catholics, appellee. With him on the brief was *Porter R. Chandler.*

Briefs of *amici curiae* supporting appellees were filed on behalf of the States of California, by *Edmund G. Brown,* Attorney General, *William V. O'Connor,* Chief Deputy Attorney General, and *Howard S. Goldin,* Deputy Attorney General; Indiana, by *J. Emmett McManamon,* Attorney General; Kentucky, by *J. D. Buckman, Jr.,* Attorney General, and *M. B. Holifield,* Assistant Attorney General; Maine, by *Alexander A. LaFleur,* Attorney General; Massachusetts, by *Francis E. Kelly,* Attorney General, *Charles H. Walters,* Assistant Attorney General, and *William F. Marcella;* Oregon, by *George Neuner,* Attorney General, *Robert F. Maguire* and *William E. Dougherty;* Pennsylvania, by *Robert E. Woodside,* Attorney General, and *Harry F. Stambaugh;* and West Virginia, by *William C. Marland,* Attorney General, and *Thomas J. Gillooly, T. D. Kauffelt* and *Eston B. Stephenson,* Assistant Attorneys General.

Justice Douglas delivered the opinion of the Court.

New York City has a program which permits its public schools to release students during the school day so that they may leave the school buildings and school grounds and go to religious centers for religious instruction or devotional exercises. A student is released on written request of his parents. Those not released stay in the classrooms. The churches make weekly reports to the schools, sending a list of children who have been released from public school but who have not reported for religious instruction.

This "released time" program involves neither religious instruction in public school classrooms nor the expenditure of public funds. All costs, including the application blanks, are paid by the religious organizations. The case is therefore unlike *McCollum v. Board of Education,* 333 U.S. 203, which involved a "released time" program from Illinois. In that case the classrooms were turned over to religious instructors. We accordingly held that the program violated the First Amendment which (by reason of the Fourteenth Amendment) prohibits the states from establishing religion or prohibiting its free exercise.

Appellants, who are taxpayers and residents of New York City and whose children attend its public schools, challenge the present law, contending it is in essence not different from the one involved in the *McCollum* case. Their argument, stated elaborately in various ways, reduces itself to this: the weight and influence of the school is put behind a program for religious instruction; public school teachers police it, keeping tab on students who are released; the classroom activities come to a halt while the students who are released for religious instruction are on leave; the school is a crutch on which the churches are leaning for support in their religious training; without the cooperation of the schools this "released time" program, like the one in the *McCollum* case, would be futile and ineffective. The New York Court of Appeals sustained the law against this claim of unconstitutionality. 303 N.Y. 161, 100 N.E. 2d 463. The case is here on appeal. 28 U.S.C. § 1257 (2).

The briefs and arguments are replete with data bearing on the merits of this type of "released time" program. Views *pro* and *con* are expressed, based on practical experience with these programs and with their implications.[5] We do not stop to summarize these

---

[5] See, *e.g.,* Beckes, Weekday Religious Education (National Conference of Christians and Jews, Human Relations Pamphlet No. 6); Butts, American Tradition in Religion and Education, pp. 188, 199; Moehlman, The Wall of Separation between Church and State, pp. 123, 155 ff.; Moehlman, The Church as Educator, pp. 103 ff.; Moral and Spiritual Values in the Public Schools (Educational Policies Commission, 1951); Newman, The Sectarian Invasion of Our Public Schools; Public School Time for Religious Education, 12 Jewish Education 130 (January, 1941); Religious Instruction On School Time, 7 Frontiers of Democracy 72 (1940); Released Time for Religious Education in New York City's Schools (Public Education Association, June 30, 1943); Released Time for Religious Education in New York City's Schools (Public Education Association, June 30, 1945); Released

materials nor to burden the opinion with an analysis of them. For they involve considerations not germane to the narrow constitutional issue presented. They largely concern the wisdom of the system, its efficiency from an educational point of view, and the political considerations which have motivated its adoption or rejection in some communities. Those matters are of no concern here, since our problem reduces itself to whether New York by this system has either prohibited the "free exercise" of religion or has made a law "respecting an establishment of religion" within the meaning of the First Amendment.

It takes obtuse reasoning to inject any issue of the "free exercise" of religion into the present case. No one is forced to go to the religious classroom and no religious exercise or instruction is brought to the classrooms of the public schools. A student need not take religious instruction. He is left to his own desires as to the manner or time of his religious devotions, if any.

There is a suggestion that the system involves the use of coercion to get public school students into religious classrooms. There is no evidence in the record before us that supports that conclusion.[6] The present record indeed tells us that the school authorities are neutral in this regard and do no more than release students whose parents so request. If in fact coercion were used, if it were established that any one or more teachers were using their office to persuade or force students to take the religious instruction, a wholly different case would be presented.[7] Hence we put aside that claim of coercion both as respects the "free exercise" of religion and "an establishment of religion" within the meaning of the First Amendment.

Moreover, apart from that claim of coercion, we do not see how New York by this type of "released time" program has made a law respecting an establishment of religion within the meaning of the First Amendment. There is much talk of the separation of Church and State in the history of the Bill of Rights and in the decisions clustering around the First Amendment. See *Everson v. Board of Education* [XIV, 1]; *McCollum v. Board of Education, supra.* There cannot be the slightest doubt that the First Amendment reflects the philosophy that Church and State should be separated. And so far as interference with the "free exercise" of religion and an "establishment" of religion are concerned, the separation must be complete and unequivocal. The First Amendment within the scope of its coverage permits no exception; the prohibition is absolute. The First Amendment, however, does not say that in every and all respects there shall be a separation of Church and State. Rather, it studiously defines the manner,

---

Time for Religious Education in New York City Schools (Public Education Association, 1949); 2 Stokes, Church and State in the United States, pp. 523–548; The Status Of Religious Education In The Public Schools (National Education Association).

[6] Nor is there any indication that the public schools enforce attendance at religious schools by punishing absentees from the released time programs for truancy.

[7] Appellants contend that they should have been allowed to prove that the system is in fact administered in a coercive manner. The New York Court of Appeals declined to grant a trial on this issue, noting, *inter alia,* that appellants had not properly raised their claim in the manner required by state practice. 303 N.Y. 161, 174, 100 N.E. 2d 463, 469. This independent state ground for decision precludes appellants from raising the issue of maladministration in this proceeding. See *Louisville & Nashville R. Co. v. Woodford,* 234 U.S. 46, 51; *Atlantic Coast Line R. Co. v. Mims,* 242 U.S. 532, 535; *American Surety Co. v. Baldwin,* 287 U.S. 156, 169.

The only allegation in the complaint that bears on the issue is that the operation of the program "has resulted and inevitably results in the exercise of pressure and coercion upon parents and children to secure attendance by the children for religious instruction." But this charge does not even implicate the school authorities. The New York Court of Appeals was therefore generous in labeling it a "conclusory" allegation. 303 N.Y., at 174, 100 N.E. 2d, at 469. Since the allegation did not implicate the school authorities in the use of coercion, there is no basis for holding that the New York Court of Appeals under the guise of local practice defeated a federal right in the manner condemned by *Brown v. Western R. of Alabama,* 338 U.S. 294, and related cases.

the specific ways, in which there shall be no concert or union or dependency one on the other. That is the common sense of the matter. Otherwise the state and religion would be aliens to each other—hostile, suspicious, and even unfriendly. Churches could not be required to pay even property taxes. Municipalities would not be permitted to render police or fire protection to religious groups. Policemen who helped parishioners into their places of worship would violate the Constitution. Prayers in our legislative halls; the appeals to the Almighty in the messages of the Chief Executive; the proclamations making Thanksgiving Day a holiday; "so help me God" in our courtroom oaths—these and all other references to the Almighty that run through our laws, our public rituals, our ceremonies would be flouting the First Amendment. A fastidious atheist or agnostic could even object to the supplication with which the Court opens each session: "God save the United States and this Honorable Court."

We would have to press the concept of separation of Church and State to these extremes to condemn the present law on constitutional grounds. The nullification of this law would have wide and profound effects. A Catholic student applies to his teacher for permission to leave the school during hours on a Holy Day of Obligation to attend a mass. A Jewish student asks his teacher for permission to be excused for Yom Kippur. A Protestant wants the afternoon off for a family baptismal ceremony. In each case the teacher requires parental consent in writing. In each case the teacher, in order to make sure the student is not a truant, goes further and requires a report from the priest, the rabbi, or the minister. The teacher in other words cooperates in a religious program to the extent of making it possible for her students to participate in it. Whether she does it occasionally for a few students, regularly for one, or pursuant to a systematized program designed to further the religious needs of all the students does not alter the character of the act.

We are a religious people whose institutions presuppose a Supreme Being. We guarantee the freedom to worship as one chooses. We make room for as wide a variety of beliefs and creeds as the spiritual needs of man deem necessary. We sponsor an attitude on the part of government that shows no partiality to any one group and that lets each flourish according to the zeal of its adherents and the appeal of its dogma. When the state encourages religious instruction or cooperates with religious authorities by adjusting the schedule of public events to sectarian needs, it follows the best of our traditions. For it then respects the religious nature of our people and accommodates the public service to their spiritual needs. To hold that it may not would be to find in the Constitution a requirement that the government show a callous indifference to religious groups. That would be preferring those who believe in no religion over those who do believe. Government may not finance religious groups nor undertake religious instruction nor blend secular and sectarian education nor use secular institutions to force one or some religion on any person. But we find no constitutional requirement which makes it necessary for government to be hostile to religion and to throw its weight against efforts to widen the effective scope of religious influence. The government must be neutral when it comes to competition between sects. It may not thrust any sect on any person. It may not make a religious observance compulsory. It may not coerce anyone to attend church, to observe a religious holiday, or to take religious instruction. But it can close its doors or suspend its operations as to those who want to repair to their religious sanctuary for worship or instruction. No more than that is undertaken here.

. . .

Affirmed.

Justice Black, dissenting:

. . .

I am aware that our *McCollum* decision on separation of Church and State has been subjected to a most searching examination throughout the country. Probably few opinions from this Court in recent years have attracted more attention or stirred wider debate.

Our insistence on "a wall between Church and State which must be kept high and impregnable" has seemed to some a correct exposition of the philosophy and a true interpretation of the language of the First Amendment to which we should strictly adhere.[1] With equal conviction and sincerity, others have thought the *McCollum* decision fundamentally wrong[2] and have pledged continuous warfare against it.[3] The opinions in the court below and the briefs here reflect these diverse viewpoints. In dissenting today, I mean to do more than give routine approval to our *McCollum* decision. I mean also to reaffirm my faith in the fundamental philosophy expressed in *McCollum* and *Everson v. Board of Education [supra,* XIV, 1]. That reaffirmance can be brief because of the exhaustive opinions in those recent cases.

Difficulty of decision in the hypothetical situations mentioned by the Court, but not now before us, should not confuse the issues in this case. Here the sole question is whether New York can use its compulsory education laws to help religious sects get attendants presumably too unenthusiastic to go unless moved to do so by the pressure of this state machinery. That this is the plan, purpose, design and consequence of the New York program cannot be denied. The state thus makes religious sects beneficiaries of its power to compel children to attend secular schools. Any use of such coercive power by the state to help or hinder some religious sects or to prefer all religious sects over nonbelievers or vice versa is just what I think the First Amendment forbids. In considering whether a state has entered this forbidden field the question is not whether it has entered too far but whether it has entered at all. New York is manipulating its compulsory education laws to help religious sects get pupils. This is not separation but combination of Church and State.

The Court's validation of the New York system rests in part on its statement that Americans are "a religious people whose institutions presuppose a Supreme Being." This was at least as true when the First Amendment was adopted; and it was just as true when eight Justices of this Court invalidated the released time system in *McCollum* on the premise that a state can no more "aid all religions" than it can aid one.[4] It was precisely because Eighteenth Century Americans were a religious people divided into many fighting sects that we were given the constitutional mandate to keep Church and State completely separate. Colonial history had already shown that, here as elsewhere zealous sectarians entrusted with governmental power to further their causes would sometimes torture, maim and kill those they branded "heretics," "atheists" or "agnostics."[5] The First Amendment was therefore to insure that no one powerful sect or combination of sects could use political or governmental power to punish dissenters whom they could not convert to their faith. Now as then, it is only by wholly isolating the state from the religious sphere and compelling it to be completely neutral, that the freedom of each and every denomination and of all nonbelievers can be maintained.

---

[1] See, *e.g.,* Newman, The Sectarian Invasion of Our Public Schools; Moehlman, The Wall of Separation between Church and State; Thayer, The Attack upon the American Secular School, pp. 179–199; Butts, The American Tradition in Religion and Education, pp. 201–208. See also Symposium on Religion and the State, 14 Law & Contemp. Prob. 1–159.

[2] See, *e.g.,* O'Neill, Religion and Education Under the Constitution, pp. 219–253; Parsons, The First Freedom, pp. 158–178; Van Dusen, God in Education. See also Symposium on Religion and the State, *supra.*

[3] See Moehlman, *supra,* n. 1, at p. 42. O'Neill, *supra,* n. 2, at pp. 254–272.

[4] A state policy of aiding "all religions" necessarily requires a governmental decision as to what constitutes "a religion." Thus is created a governmental power to hinder certain religious beliefs by denying their character as such. See, *e.g.,* the Regulations of the New York Commissioner of Education providing that, "The courses in religious observance and education must be maintained and operated by or under the control of *duly constituted* religious bodies." (Emphasis added.) Art. 17, § 154, 1 N.Y. Official Code Comp. 683. This provides precisely the kind of censorship which we have said the Constitution forbids. *Cantwell* v. *Connecticut,* 310 U.S. 296, 305.

[5] Wertenbaker, The Puritan Oligarchy, 213–214.

It is this neutrality the Court abandons today when it treats New York's coercive system as a program which *merely* "encourages religious instruction or cooperates with religious authorities." The abandonment is all the more dangerous to liberty because of the Court's legal exaltation of the orthodox and its derogation of unbelievers.

Under our system of religious freedom, people have gone to their religious sanctuaries not because they feared the law but because they loved their God. The choice of all has been as free as the choice of those who answered the call to worship moved only by the music of the old Sunday morning church bells. The spiritual mind of man has thus been free to believe, disbelieve, or doubt, without repression, great or small, by the heavy hand of government. Statutes authorizing such repression have been stricken. Before today, our judicial opinions have refrained from drawing invidious distinctions between those who believe in no religion and those who do believe. The First Amendment has lost much if the religious follower and the atheist are no longer to be judicially regarded as entitled to equal justice under law.

State help to religion injects political and party prejudices into a holy field. It too often substitutes force for prayer, hate for love, and persecution for persuasion. Government should not be allowed, under cover of the soft euphemism of "co-operation," to steal into the sacred area of religious choice.

. . .

Justice Jackson, dissenting:

As one whose children, as a matter of free choice, have been sent to privately supported Church schools, I may challenge the Court's suggestion that opposition to this plan can only be antireligious, atheistic, or agnostic. My evangelistic brethren confuse an objection to compulsion with an objection to religion. It is possible to hold a faith with enough confidence to believe that what should be rendered to God does not need to be decided and collected by Caesar.

The day that this country ceases to be free for irreligion it will cease to be free for religion—except for the sect that can win political power. The same epithetical jurisprudence used by the Court today to beat down those who oppose pressuring children into some religion can devise as good epithets tomorrow against those who object to pressuring them into a favored religion. And, after all, if we concede to the State power and wisdom to single out "duly constituted religious" bodies as exclusive alternatives for compulsory secular instruction, it would be logical to also uphold the power and wisdom to choose the true faith among those "duly constituted." We start down a rough road when we begin to mix compulsory public education with compulsory godliness.

A number of Justices just short of a majority of the majority that promulgates today's passionate dialectics joined in answering them in *Illinois ex rel. McCollum v. Board of Education* [*supra*]. The distinction attempted between that case and this is trivial, almost to the point of cynicism, magnifying its nonessential details and disparaging compulsion which was the underlying reason for invalidity. A reading of the Court's opinion in that case along with its opinion in this case will show such difference of overtones and undertones as to make clear that the *McCollum* case has passed like a storm in a teacup. The wall which the Court was professing to erect between Church and State has become even more warped and twisted than I expected. Today's judgment will be more interesting to students of psychology and of the judicial processes than to students of constitutional law.

Engel v. Vitale
370 U.S. 421 (1962)

William J. Butler argued the cause for petitioners. With him on the briefs was *Stanley Geller.*

Bertram B. Daiker argued the cause for respondents. With him on the briefs was *Wilford E. Neier.*

Porter R. Chandler argued the cause for intervenors-respondents. With him on the briefs were *Thomas J. Ford* and *Richard E. Nolan.*

Charles A. Brind filed a brief for the Board of Regents of the University of the State of New York, as *amicus curiae,* in opposition to the petition for certiorari.

Briefs of *amici curiae,* urging reversal, were filed by *Herbert A. Wolff, Leo Rosen* and *Nancy Wechsler* for the American Ethical Union; *Louis Caplan, Edwin J. Lukas, Paul Hartman, Theodore Leskes* and *Sol Rabkin* for the American Jewish Committee et al.; and *Leo Pfeffer, Lewis H. Weinstein, Albert Wald, Shad Polier* and *Samuel Lawrence Brennglass* for the Synagogue Council of America et al.

A brief of *amici curiae,* urging affirmance, was filed by *Roger D. Foley,* Attorney General of Nevada, *Robert Pickrell,* Attorney General of Arizona, *Frank Holt,* Attorney General of Arkansas, *Albert L. Coles,* Attorney General of Connecticut, *Richard W. Ervin,* Attorney General of Florida, *Eugene Cook,* Attorney General of Georgia, *Frank Benson,* Attorney General of Idaho, *Edwin K. Steers,* Attorney General of Indiana, *William M. Ferguson,* Attorney General of Kansas, *Jack P.F. Gremillion,* Attorney General of Louisiana, *Thomas B. Finan,* Attorney General of Maryland, *Joe T. Patterson,* Attorney General of Mississippi, *William Maynard,* Attorney General of New Hampshire, *Arthur J. Sills,* Attorney General of New Jersey, *Earl E. Hartley,* Attorney General of New Mexico, *Leslie R. Burgum,* Attorney General of North Dakota, *David Stahl,* Attorney General of Pennsylvania, *J. Joseph Nugent,* Attorney General of Rhode Island, *Daniel R. McLeod,* Attorney General of South Carolina, *A. C. Miller,* Attorney General of South Dakota, *Will Wilson,* Attorney General of Texas, and *C. Donald Robertson,* Attorney General of West Virginia.

Justice Black delivered the opinion of the Court.

The respondent Board of Education of Union Free School District No. 9, New Hyde Park, New York, acting in its official capacity under state law, directed the School District's principal to cause the following prayer to be said aloud by each class in the presence of a teacher at the beginning of each school day:

"Almighty God, we acknowledge our dependence upon Thee, and we beg Thy blessings upon us, our parents, our teachers and our Country."

This daily procedure was adopted on the recommendation of the State Board of Regents, a governmental agency created by the State Constitution to which the New York Legislature has granted broad supervisory, executive, and legislative powers over the State's public school system. These state officials composed the prayer which they recommended and published as a part of their "Statement on Moral and Spiritual Training in the Schools," saying: "We believe that this Statement will be subscribed to by all men and women of good will, and we call upon all of them to aid in giving life to our program." . . .

There can be no doubt that New York's state prayer program officially establishes the religious beliefs embodied in the Regents' prayer. The respondents' argument to the contrary, which is largely based upon the contention that the Regents' prayer is "nondenominational" and the fact that the program, as modified and approved by state courts, does not require all pupils to recite the prayer but permits those who wish to do so to remain silent or be excused from the room, ignores the essential nature of the program's constitutional defects. Neither the fact that the prayer may be denominationally neutral nor the fact that its observance on the part of the students is voluntary can serve to free it from the limitations of the Establishment Clause, as it might from the Free Exercise Clause, of the First Amendment, both of which are operative against the States by virtue of the Fourteenth Amendment. Although these two clauses may in certain instances overlap, they forbid two quite different kinds of governmental encroachment upon religious freedom. The Establishment Clause, unlike the Free Exercise Clause, does not depend upon any showing of direct governmental compulsion and is violated by the enactment of laws which establish an official religion whether those laws operate directly to coerce nonobserving individuals or not. This is not to say, of course, that laws officially prescribing a particular form of religious worship do not involve coercion of such individuals. When the power, prestige and financial support of government is placed behind a particular religious belief, the indirect coercive pressure upon religious minorities to conform to the prevailing officially approved religion is plain. But the purposes underlying the Establishment Clause go much further than that. Its first and most immediate purpose rested on the belief that a union of government and religion tends to destroy government and to degrade religion. The history of governmentally established religion, both in England and in this country, showed that whenever government had allied itself with one particular form of religion, the inevitable result had been that it had incurred the hatred, disrespect and even contempt of those who held contrary beliefs. That same history showed that many people had lost their respect for any religion that had relied upon the support of government to spread its faith. The Establishment Clause thus stands as an expression of principle on the part of the Founders of our Constitution that religion is too personal, too sacred, too holy, to permit its "unhallowed perversion" by a civil magistrate. Another purpose of the Establishment Clause rested upon an awareness of the historical fact that governmentally established religions and religious persecutions go hand in hand. The Founders knew that only a few years after the Book of Common Prayer became the only accepted form of religious services in the established Church of England, an Act of Uniformity was passed to compel all Englishmen to attend those services and to make it a criminal offense to conduct or attend religious gatherings of any other kind.[17]—a law which was consistently flouted by dissenting religious groups in England and which contributed to widespread persecutions of people like John Bunyan who persisted in holding "unlawful [religious] meetings . . . to the great disturbance and distraction of the good subjects of this kingdom. . . ."[18] And they knew that similar persecutions had received the sanction of law in several of the colonies in this country soon after the establishment of official religions in those colonies.[19] It was in large part to get completely away from this sort of systematic religious persecution that the Founders brought into being our Nation, our Constitution, and our Bill of Rights with its prohibition against any governmental establishment of religion. The New York laws officially prescribing the Regents' prayer are inconsistent both with the purposes of the Establishment Clause and with the Establishment Clause itself.

It has been argued that to apply the Constitution in such a way as to prohibit state laws respecting an establishment of religious services in public schools is to indicate a

---

[17] 5 & 6 Edward VI, c. 1, entitled "An Act for the Uniformity of Service and Administration of Sacraments throughout the Realm." This Act was repealed during the reign of Mary but revived upon the accession of Elizabeth. See note 7, *supra.* The reasons which led to the enactment of this statute were set out in its preamble: "Where there hath been a very godly Order set forth by the Authority of Parliament, for Common Prayer and Administration of the Sacraments to be used in the Mother Tongue within the Church of *England,* agreeable to the Word of God and the Primitive Church, very comfortable to all good People desiring to live in Christian Conversation, and most profitable to the Estate of this Realm, upon the which the Mercy, Favour and Blessing of Almighty God is in no wise so readily and plenteously poured as by Common Prayers, due using of the Sacraments, and often preaching of the Gospel, with the Devotion of the Hearers: (1) And yet this notwithstanding, a great Number of People in divers Parts of this Realm, following their own Sensuality, and living either without Knowledge or due Fear of God, do wilfully and damnably before Almighty God abstain and refuse to come to their Parish Churches and other Places where Common Prayer, Administration of the Sacraments, and Preaching of the Word of God, is used upon *Sundays* and other Days ordained to be Holydays."

[18] Bunyan's own account of his trial is set forth in A Relation of the Imprisonment of Mr. John Bunyan, reprinted in Grace Abounding and The Pilgrim's Progress (Brown ed. 1907), at 103–132.

[19] For a vivid account of some of these persecutions, see Wertenbaker, The Puritan Oligarchy (1947).

hostility toward religion or toward prayer. Nothing, of course, could be more wrong. The history of man is inseparable from the history of religion. And perhaps it is not too much to say that since the beginning of that history many people have devoutly believed that "More things are wrought by prayer than this world dreams of." It was doubtless largely due to men who believed this that there grew up a sentiment that caused men to leave the cross-currents of officially established state religions and religious persecution in Europe and come to this country filled with the hope that they could find a place in which they could pray when they pleased to the God of their faith in the language they chose.[20] And there were men of this same faith in the power of prayer who led the fight for adoption of our Constitution and also for our Bill of Rights with the very guarantees of religious freedom that forbid the sort of governmental activity which New York has attempted here. These men knew that the First Amendment, which tried to put an end to governmental control of religion and of prayer, was not written to destroy either. They knew rather that it was written to quiet well-justified fears which nearly all of them felt arising out of an awareness that governments of the past had shackled men's tongues to make them speak only the religious thoughts that government wanted them to speak and to pray only to the God that government wanted them to pray to. It is neither sacrilegious nor antireligious to say that each separate government in this country should stay out of the business of writing or sanctioning official prayers and leave that purely religious function to the people themselves and to those the people choose to look to for religious guidance.[21]

. . .

Reversed and remanded.

Justice Frankfurter took no part in the decision of this case.

Justice White took no part in the consideration or decision of this case.

Justice Douglas, concurring.

---

[20] Perhaps the best example of the sort of men who came to this country for precisely that reason is Roger Williams, the founder of Rhode Island, who has been described as "the truest Christian amongst many who sincerely desired to be Christian." Parrington, Main Currents in American Thought (1930), Vol. 1, at p. 74. Williams, who was one of the earliest exponents of the doctrine of separation of church and state, believed that separation was necessary in order to protect the church from the danger of destruction which he thought inevitably flowed from control by even the best-intentioned civil authorities: "The unknowing zeale of *Constantine* and other Emperours, did more hurt to *Christ Jesus* his Crowne and Kingdome, then the raging fury of the most bloody *Neroes*. In the *persecutions* of the later, *Christians* were sweet and fragrant, like spice pounded and beaten in morters: But those *good* Emperours, persecuting some erroneous persons, *Arrius*, &c. and advancing the professours of some Truths of Christ (for there was no small number of *Truths* lost in those times) and maintaining their *Religion* by the materiall Sword, I say by this meanes *Christianity* was *ecclipsed,* and the Professors of it fell asleep. . . ." Williams, The Bloudy Tenent, of Persecution [*supra*, V, 2]. To Williams, it was no part of the business or competence of a civil magistrate to interfere in religious matters: "[W]hat imprudence and *indiscretion* is it in the most common affaires of Life, to conceive that *Emperours, Kings* and *Rulers* of the earth must not only be qualified with *politicall* and *state abilities* to *make* and *execute* such *Civill Lawes* which may concerne the common *rights, peace* and *safety* (which is worke and businesse, load and burthen enough for the ablest shoulders in the Commonweal) but also furnished with such *Spirituall* and heavenly *abilities* to governe the *Spirituall* and *Christian Commonweale.* . . ." *Id.,* at 366. See also *id.,* at 136–137.

[21] There is of course nothing in the decision reached here that is inconsistent with the fact that school children and others are officially encouraged to express love for our country by reciting historical documents such as the Declaration of Independence which contain references to the Deity or by singing officially espoused anthems which include the composer's professions of faith in a Supreme Being, or with the fact that there are many manifestations in our public life of belief in God. Such patriotic or ceremonial occasions bear no true resemblance to the unquestioned religious exercise that the State of New York has sponsored in this instance.

It is customary in deciding a constitutional question to treat it in its narrowest form. Yet at times the setting of the question gives it a form and content which no abstract treatment could give. The point for decision is whether the Government can constitutionally finance a religious exercise. Our system at the federal and state levels is presently honeycombed with such financing.[1] Nevertheless, I think it is an unconstitutional undertaking whatever form it takes. . . .

Justice Stewart, dissenting:

A local school board in New York has provided that those pupils who wish to do so may join in a brief prayer at the beginning of each school day, acknowledging their dependence upon God and asking His blessing upon them and upon their parents, their teachers, and their country. The Court today decides that in permitting this brief nondenominational prayer the school board has violated the Constitution of the United States. I think this decision is wrong.

The Court does not hold, nor could it, that New York has interfered with the free exercise of anybody's religion. For the state courts have made clear that those who object to reciting the prayer must be entirely free of any compulsion to do so, including any "embarrassments and pressures." Cf. *West Virginia State Board of Education v. Barnette* [XI,2]. But the Court says that in permitting school children to say this simple prayer, the New York authorities have established "an official religion."

With all respect, I think the Court has misapplied a great constitutional principle. I cannot see how an "official religion" is established by letting those who want to say a prayer say it. On the contrary, I think that to deny the wish of these school children to join in reciting this prayer is to deny them the opportunity of sharing in the spiritual heritage of our Nation.

Query. Commenting on *Engle* as "the end of nonsectarianism," that is, of the view that "a common denominator" could unite the denominations, Robert E. Rodes, Jr., offered an alternative approach to "a national consensus." He argued that it could be found in commitment to "freedom" and to "dialogue." By commitment to freedom he meant "a recognition of a purpose in man that cannot be found through the means under the control of organized society," in Abraham Joshua Heschel's words an "openness to transcendence." By "dialogue" Rodes meant "conversation among persons of different beliefs, having for its purpose mutual

---

[1] "There are many 'aids' to religion in this country at all levels of government. To mention but a few at the federal level, one might begin by observing that the very First Congress which wrote the First Amendment provided for chaplains in both Houses and in the armed services. There is compulsory chapel at the service academies, and religious services are held in federal hospitals and prisons. The President issues religious proclamations. The Bible is used for the administration of oaths. N.Y.A. and W.P.A. funds were available to parochial schools during the depression. Veterans receiving money under the 'G.I.' Bill of 1944 could attend denominational schools, to which payments were made directly by the government. During World War II, federal money was contributed to denominational schools for the training of nurses. The benefits of the National School Lunch Act are available to students in private as well as public schools. The Hospital Survey and Construction Act of 1946 specifically made money available to non-public hospitals. The slogan 'In God We Trust' is used by the Treasury Department, and Congress recently added God to the pledge of allegiance. There is Bible-reading in the schools of the District of Columbia, and religious instruction is given in the District's National Training School for Boys. Religious organizations are exempt from the federal income tax and are granted postal privileges. Up to defined limits—15 per cent of the adjusted gross income of individuals and 5 per cent of the net income of corporations—contributions to religious organizations are deductible for federal income tax purposes. There are no limits to the deductibility of gifts and bequests to religious institutions made under the federal gift and estate tax laws. This list of federal 'aids' could easily be expanded, and of course there is a long list in each state." Fellman, The Limits of Freedom (1959), pp. 40–41.

understanding and respect, rather than agreement. To this end, it stresses personal affirmation, and eschews both apologetics and compromise. . . . [Dialogue's] development is largely the work of theologians, perhaps the most influential among them being Martin Buber," Rodes, "The Passing of Nonsectarianism: Some Reflections on the School Prayer Case," 38 *Notre Dame Law* 115, at 133–134 (1963). Rodes recognized that both "freedom" and "dialogue" in his usage were religious, and he contended that the Constitution did not preclude their acceptance. He found their antecedents in what Tocqueville had written of the special place of religion and religious freedom in America. He concluded at 137:

To sum up, the value of freedom and dialogue as the root principles in our national religious consensus lies in their conformity on the one hand to what is deepest and truest in our traditional aspirations as a people, and on the other hand to a recognition of those central mysteries of human existence to which the most important of religious affirmations are addressed.

It would be comforting to be able to derive from this formulation of principles some consequences of practical application to the church-state problems currently facing our schools and our society. But I see these principles less as furnishing a logical basis for solving problems of this kind than as conducing to an atmosphere in which they may be solved. The profoundest consequence of a national religious consensus worked out in terms of freedom and dialogue is that it becomes the concern of every citizen that every other citizen live out his own deepest commitments to the fullest possible extent. It is in the context of heightened spiritual awareness afforded by such a living out that we await the manifestation of divine power whereby freedom may be consummated in salvation, dialogue in unity. And it is in this concern for such a living out that we may hope for a solution to our immediate problems of church and state.

Does Rodes's approach pass constitutional scrutiny?

NOTE. *Grossberg v. Deusebio,* 380 F. Supp. 285 (E.D. Va. 1974). James Grossberg and other graduating high school seniors and their parents sought an injunction against the saying of a short, audible prayer by representatives of the senior class at graduation ceremonies. Attendance at the ceremonies was voluntary; seniors could have their diplomas mailed to them. District Judge Robert Merhige, Jr., refused to grant the injunction, writing that the occasion was

a ceremony geared primarily to the award of honors and diplomas. All other portions of the program are peripheral to this function. . . . I can hardly perceive that the few moments . . . create any significant risk of significant aid to religion. Not every involvement of religion in public life is violative of the Establishment Clause [*ibid.* at 289].

Accord, Wood v. Mt. Lebanon Township School District, 342 F. Supp. 1293 (W.D. Penn. 1972); *Wiest v. Mt. Lebanon School District* 457 Pa. 166, 320 A. 2d 362 (1974), *cert. denied,* 419 U.S. 967 (1974).

NOTE. *Religious Orders in the Public Schools.* State cases before *McCollum* held that the state could prohibit members of religious orders from wearing religious garb while teaching in a public school. The reason given by the New York Court of Appeals was "that the effect of the costume worn by these Sisters of St. Joseph at all times in the presence of their pupils would be to inspire respect, if not sympathy, for the religious denomination to which they so manifestly belong," and so would violate New York's constitutional prohibition against the state aiding any school "wholly or in part" under the control of a religious denomination, *O'Connor v. Hendrick*, 184 N.Y. 421, 77 N.E. 612 (1906). But no prohibition existed against nuns being hired by a public school, and in the absence of state law or policy to the contrary, nuns in religious garb did teach in the public schools, see *Gerhardt v. Heidt*, 66 N.D. 444, 267 N.W. 127 (1936) (Benedictine sisters in dark habits have religious liberty under the North Dakota Constitution to teach in the public schools.)

Post-*McCollum* scrutiny of areas that had relied on Catholic religious orders led to litigation in New Mexico, a state with a tradition of such reliance. In Mora County, Rio Arrida County, San Juan County, San Miguel County, Santa Fe County, and Taos County, New Mexico, a number of public schools had been staffed "for many years" by Sisters of the Most Precious Blood and other Catholic orders. The teachers, who wore religious habits, were employed as public school teachers. School was held in buildings rented from the Catholic archdiocese. The pupils were taught prayers and given religious instruction. Protestant parents complained and, eventually, in the period preceding the litigation, the protesters persuaded the State Board of Education to talk to the archbishop of Santa Fe. He directed that there should be no religious instruction during the school week. The objectors pressed their objections with a suit.

The trial court found that there was "no separation" between the state and the Catholic Church in New Mexico in the schools. The Supreme Court of New Mexico characterized the system as a "Catholic school system supported by public funds." It enjoined further operation of the system, *Zellers v. Huff*, 55 N.M. 501, 236 P.2d 949 (1951). A statute provided, "No teacher shall use any sectarian or denominational books in the schools, or teach sectarian doctrine in the schools; any teacher violating the provision of this section shall be immediately discharged, his certificate to teach school revoked, and be forever barred from receiving any school moneys and employment in the public schools in the state." The court applied the statute to the sisters found to have taught religion.

Compare *Cooper v. Eugene School District No. 48*, 76 Or. App. 146, 708 P.2d 1161 (1985). (Janet Cooper, a public school teacher, wore white clothing and a white turban to show that she had become a Sikh. She explained to her pupils the religious significance of her dress. She refused to abandon the practice at the order of the superintendent of schools, who invoked an Oregon statute that prohibited the wearing of "religious dress" by a teacher on duty. The statute was upheld, but found to be an unconstitutional violation of free exercise to the extent that it required revocation of Cooper's teaching certificate, *review granted*, 300 Ore. 562, 715 P.2d 93 (1986).

NOTE. *The Bible in the Public Schools.* Horace Mann, the apostle of free public education, was an advocate of the use of the Bible in the public schools of Massachusetts. His final report as secretary of the State Board of Education declared:

[O]ur system earnestly inculcates all Christian morals; it founds its morals on the basis of religion; it welcomes the religion of the Bible: and in receiving the Bible, it allows it to do what it is allowed to do in no other system—*to speak for itself* [Mann, *Twelfth Annual Report of the State Board of Education* (1848), in *Life and Works of Horace Mann* (1891) 4, 311–312 (emphasis in original)].

According to Mann, "I suppose there is not, at the present time, a single town in the Commonwealth in whose schools it is not read," *Eleventh Annual Report* (1847), *ibid.* at 4, 177.

Church law forbade Catholics to read Scripture in a translation not approved by ecclesiastical authority. The King James Bible—the Bible normally used in public schools—was an unapproved translation. Besides minor and insubstantial disagreements, the King James version omitted several books of the Old Testament—part of Esther; Tobias; Maccabees—viewed as integral to it by Catholics. But as the Bible was never read in its entirety in the schools, the omitted parts would probably not have been read in any case. The real objection was the sense of believing Catholics that they should not have to use a Protestant text. In Boston in 1859 an eleven-year-old, Thomas Wall, refused to read the Ten Commandments from the King James version and was beaten by his teacher. In an action of battery against the teacher, a Boston court held that the discipline was proper, *Commonwealth v. Cooke*, 7 *University of Pennsylvania Law Review (American Law Register)* 417 (Boston Police Ct. 1859). Outrage over the case led to changes in the membership of the Boston School Committee, but in other Massachusetts communities compulsion was used on Catholics as late as 1865, Robert H. Lord, *A History of the Archdiocese of Boston* (1945) 2, 601–605.

The first appellate case came from Maine where a Catholic girl was expelled from the Ellsworth schools for refusing to read the King James version. Counsel vigorously argued that the legislature had no power to make "a religious test" for admission to school or to prefer Protestants over Catholics. The court declared that "reading the Bible is no more an interference with religious belief, than would reading the mythology of Greece or Rome be regarded as interfering with religious belief or an affirmance of the pagan creeds," *Donahoe v. Richards*, 38 Me. 379, 399 (1854). Responding directly to Bridget Donahoe's "conscientious religious scruples," which forbade her to read the text, the court noted that the Index of Prohibited Books forbade Catholics to read other books and declared, "The right of one sect to interdict or expurgate would place all schools in subordination to the sect interdicting or expurgating," *ibid.* at 407. Counsel had argued why, "in the name of common sense and Christian charity," she should not have been allowed to read from the Catholic translation. Dismissing the action, the court recommended such charity to the school board: "Large masses of foreign population are among us, weak in the midst of our strength." Those entrusted with the duty of educating them should discharge their duty "with magnanimous liberality and Christian kindness." The court cited the Golden Rule, *ibid.* at 413.

Jews as well as Catholics came to complain about Bible reading. In the Jewish case, the whole New Testament was objectionable. The Louisiana Supreme Court, in 1915, finding the practice to violate the Louisiana Constitution, declared the New Testament to be "the foundation and text-book of Christianity, based on the teachings contained therein that Christ is divine. And the lessons therefrom give a preference to Christians, and at the same time make a discrimination against the Jews," *Herold v. Parish Board*, 136 La. 1034, 1049, 68 So. 116, 121 (1915).

Fourteen state courts had upheld the legality of Bible reading, eight state courts had found it to violate state constitutions, Donald E. Boles, *The Bible, Religion and the Public Schools* (1965) 332. In all, thirty-seven states permitted Bible-reading, seventeen by statute. No momentum toward change in state practice was discernible. The earliest decision against state constitutionality had been in Ohio in 1872; the most recent in South Dakota in 1929, *ibid.* at 355. A checkerboard pattern existed and had existed for a long time. Against this background the *Schempp* case was begun in 1959.

Unlike previous challenges, the case was brought in federal court and invoked the First Amendment. The plaintiffs were church-going Unitarians with three children, aged 18, 15, and 12 in Abington schools. The theological doctrine of the Trinity, the divinity of Christ, and God as a vengeful Judge, the Schempps asserted to be in that part of Scripture that was contrary to their belief. The oldest, Ellory, had objected to the regular reading of ten verses of the Bible at the start of each school day, and he had first demonstrated his objections by reading the Koran to himself while the Bible was read aloud. The plaintiffs' expert witness, Solomon Grayzel, a rabbi and editor of the Jewish Publication Society, publisher of the *Holy Scriptures According to the Masoretic Text*, testified that "portions of the New Testament were offensive to Jewish tradition and that, from the standpoint of Jewish faith, the concept of Jesus Christ as the Son of God was 'practically blasphemous' "; also that portions of the New Testament "tended to bring the Jews into ridicule or scorn" and that such passages, unexplained, did psychological harm to Jewish children, *Schempp v. School District,* 177 F. Supp. 398, 401 (E.D. Pa. 1959). Luther A. Weigle, a Lutheran minister and dean emeritus of Yale Divinity School, testified for the defense that the Bible was nonsectarian "within the Christian faiths," and that the Bible was of great moral, literary, and historical value. A three-judge federal court, in an opinion by John Biggs, Jr., Circuit Chief Judge, held the Bible-reading to be unconstitutional, *ibid.* While the case was awaiting decision by the Supreme Court, Pennsylvania amended its statute to make the reading optional for each student. The Supreme Court, on October 24, 1960—an election year—vacated the judgment and remanded the case to be decided in the light of the statutory change, 364 U.S. 298. Again the lower court enjoined the Bible-reading, 201 F. Supp. 815 (1962). As it was appealed, *Engel, supra,* was decided and foreshadowed what the Supreme Court would do here:

District of Abington Township v. Schempp
374 U.S. 203 (1963)

Justice Clark delivered the opinion of the court.

Applying the Establishment Clause principles to the cases at bar we find that the States are requiring the selection and reading at the opening of the school day of verses from the Holy Bible and the recitation of the Lord's Prayer by the students in unison. These exercises are prescribed as part of the curricular activities of students who are required by law to attend school. They are held in the school buildings under the supervision and with the participation of teachers employed in those schools. None of these factors, other than compulsory school attendance, was present in the program upheld in *Zorach v. Clauson.* The trial court in No. 142 had found that such an opening exercise is a religious ceremony and was intended by the State to be so. We agree with the trial court's finding as to the religious character of the exercises. Given that finding, the exercises and the law requiring them are in violation of the Establishment Clause.

There is no such specific finding as to the religious character of the exercises in No. 119, and the State contends (as does the State in No. 142) that the program is an effort to extend its benefits to all public school children without regard to their religious belief. Included within its secular purposes, it says, are the promotion of moral values, the contradiction to the materialistic trends of our times, the perpetuation of our institutions and the teaching of literature. The case came up on demurrer, of course, to a petition which alleged that the uniform practice under the rule had been to read from the King James version of the Bible and that the exercise was sectarian. The short answer, therefore, is that the religious character of the exercise was admitted by the State. But even if its purpose is not strictly religious, it is sought to be accomplished through readings, without comment, from the Bible. Surely the place of the Bible as an instrument of religion cannot be gainsaid, and the State's recognition of the pervading religious character of the ceremony is evident from the rule's specific permission of the alternative use of the Catholic Douay version as well as the recent amendment permitting non-attendance at the exercises. None of these factors is consistent with the contention that the Bible is here used either as an instrument for nonreligious moral inspiration or as a reference for the teaching of secular subjects.

The conclusion follows that in both cases the laws require religious exercises and such exercises are being conducted in direct violation of the rights of the appellees and petitioners.[9] Nor are these required exercises mitigated by the fact that individual students may absent themselves upon parental request, for that fact furnishes no defense to a claim of unconstitutionality under the Establishment Clause. See *Engel v. Vitale, supra,* at 430. Further, it is no defense to urge that the religious practices here may be relatively minor encroachments on the First Amendment. The breach of neutrality that is today a trickling stream may all too soon become a raging torrent and, in the words of Madison, "it is proper to take alarm at the first experiment on our liberties." Memorial and Remonstrance Against Religious Assessments, quoted in *Everson* [VI, 3].

It is insisted that unless these religious exercises are permitted a "religion of secularism" is established in the schools. We agree of course that the State may not establish a "religion of secularism" in the sense of affirmatively opposing or showing hostility to religion, thus "preferring those who believe in no religion over those who do believe." *Zorach v. Clauson, supra,* at 314. We do not agree, however, that this decision in any sense has that effect. In addition, it might well be said that one's education is not complete without a study of comparative religion or the history of religion and its relationship to the advancement of civilization. It certainly may be said that the Bible is worthy of study for its literary and historic qualities. Nothing we have said here indicates that such study of the Bible or of religion, when presented objectively as part of a secular program of education, may not be effected consistently with the First Amendment. But the exercises here do not fall into those categories. They are religious exercises, required by the States in violation of the command of the First Amendment that the Government maintain strict neutrality, neither aiding nor opposing religion.

Finally, we cannot accept that the concept of neutrality, which does not permit a State to require a religious exercise even with the consent of the majority of those affected, collides with the majority's right to free exercise of religion.[10] While the Free Exercise Clause clearly prohibits the use of state action to deny the rights of free exercise to *anyone,* it has never meant that a majority could use the machinery of the State to practice its beliefs. Such a contention was effectively answered by Mr. Justice Jackson for the Court in *West Virginia Board of Education v. Barnette* [XI, 2]:

"The very purpose of a Bill of Rights was to withdraw certain subjects from the vicissitudes of political controversy, to place them beyond the reach of majorities and officials and to establish them as legal principles to be applied by the courts. One's right to . . . freedom of worship . . . and other fundamental rights may not be submitted to vote; they depend on the outcome of no elections."

The place of religion in our society is an exalted one, achieved through a long tradition of reliance on the home, the church and the inviolable citadel of the individual heart

---

[9] It goes without saying that the laws and practices involved here can be challenged only by persons having standing to complain. But the requirements for standing to challenge state action under the Establishment Clause, unlike those relating to the Free Exercise Clause, do not include proof that particular religious freedoms are infringed. *McGowan v. Maryland, supra* [XIII, 2]. The parties here are school children and their parents, who are directly affected by the laws and practices against which their complaints are directed. These interests surely suffice to give the parties standing to complain. See *Engel v. Vitale, supra.* Cf. *McCollum v. Board of Education, supra; Everson v. Board of Education, supra.* Compare *Doremus v. Board of Education,* 342 U.S. 429 (1952), which involved the same substantive issues presented here. The appeal was there dismissed upon the graduation of the school child involved and because of the appellants' failure to establish standing as taxpayers.

[10] We are not of course presented with and therefore do not pass upon a situation such as military service, where the Government regulates the temporal and geographic environment of individuals to a point that, unless it permits voluntary religious services to be conducted with the use of government facilities, military personnel would be unable to engage in the practice of their faiths.

and mind. We have come to recognize through bitter experience that it is not within the power of government to invade that citadel, whether its purpose or effect be to aid or oppose, to advance or retard. In the relationship between man and religion, the State is firmly committed to a position of neutrality. . . .

The judgment in the Pennsylvania case was affirmed. Justices Goldberg and Harlan concurred separately.

Justice Brennan, concurring:

Attendance at the public schools has never been compulsory; parents remain morally and constitutionally free to choose the academic environment in which they wish their children to be educated. The relationship of the Establishment Clause of the First Amendment to the public school system is preeminently that of reserving such a choice to the individual parent, rather than vesting it in the majority of voters of each State or school district. The choice which is thus preserved is between a public secular education with its uniquely democratic values, and some form of private or sectarian education, which offers values of its own. In my judgment the First Amendment forbids the State to inhibit that freedom of choice by diminishing the attractiveness of either alternative—either by restricting the liberty of the private schools to inculcate whatever values they wish, or by jeopardizing the freedom of the public schools from private or sectarian pressures. . . .

It has also been suggested that the "liberty" guaranteed by the Fourteenth Amendment logically cannot absorb the Establishment Clause because that clause is not one of the provisions of the Bill of Rights which in terms protects a "freedom" of the individual. See Corwin, A Constitution of Powers in a Secular State (1951), 113–116. The fallacy in this contention, I think, is that it underestimates the role of the Establishment Clause as a coguarantor, with the Free Exercise Clause, of religious liberty. The Framers did not entrust the liberty of religious beliefs to either clause alone. The Free Exercise Clause "was not to be the full extent of the Amendment's guarantee of freedom from governmental intrusion in matters of faith." *McGowan v. Maryland* [XIII, 2] at 464 (opinion of Frankfurter, J.). . . .

The secular purposes which devotional exercises are said to serve fall into two categories—those which depend upon an immediately religious experience shared by the participating children; and those which appear sufficiently divorced from the religious content of the devotional material that they can be served equally by nonreligious materials. With respect to the first objective, much has been written about the moral and spiritual values of infusing some religious influence or instruction into the public school classroom.[56] To the extent that only *religious* materials will serve this purpose, it seems to me that the purpose as well as the means is so plainly religious that the exercise is necessarily forbidden by the Establishment Clause. The fact that purely secular benefits may eventually result does not seem to me to justify the exercises, for similar indirect nonreligious benefits could no doubt have been claimed for the released time program invalidated in *McCollum.*

The second justification assumes that religious exercises at the start of the school day may directly serve solely secular ends—for example, by fostering harmony and tolerance

---

[56] See, *e.g.*, Henry, The Place of Religion in Public Schools (1950); Martin, Our Public Schools—Christian or Secular (1952); Educational Policies Comm'n of the National Educational Assn., Moral and Spiritual Values in the Public Schools (1951), c. IV; Harner, Religion's Place in General Education (1949). Educators are by no means unanimous however, on this question. See Boles, The Bible, Religion, and the Public Schools (1961), 223–224. Compare George Washington's advice in his Farewell Address:

"And let us with caution indulge the supposition, that morality can be maintained without religion. Whatever may be conceded to the influence of refined education on minds of peculiar structure, reason and experience both forbid us to expect that National morality can prevail in exclusion of religious principle." 35 Writings of George Washington (Fitzpatrick ed. 1940), 229.

among the pupils, enhancing the authority of the teacher, and inspiring better discipline. To the extent that such benefits result not from the content of the readings and recitation, but simply from the holding of such a solemn exercise at the opening assembly or the first class of the day, it would seem that less sensitive materials might equally well serve the same purpose. I have previously suggested that *Torcaso* and the *Sunday Law Cases* forbid the use of religious means to achieve secular ends where nonreligious means will suffice. That principle is readily applied to these cases. It has not been shown that readings from the speeches and messages of great Americans, for example, or from the documents of our heritage of liberty, daily recitation of the Pledge of Allegiance, or even the observance of a moment of reverent silence at the opening of class, may not adequately serve the solely secular purposes of the devotional activities without jeopardizing either the religious liberties of any members of the community or the proper degree of separation between the spheres of religion and government. Such substitutes would, I think, be unsatisfactory or inadequate only to the extent that the present activities do in fact serve religious goals. While I do not question the judgment of experienced educators that the challenged practices may well achieve valuable secular ends, it seems to me that the State acts unconstitutionally if it either sets about to attain even indirectly religious ends by religious means, or if it uses religious means to serve secular ends where secular means would suffice. . . .

It has been suggested that a tentative solution to these problems may lie in the fashioning of a "common core" of theology tolerable to all creeds but preferential to none.[64] But as one commentator has recently observed, "[h]istory is not encouraging to" those who hope to fashion a "common denominator of religion detached from its manifestation in any organized church." Sutherland, Establishment According to *Engel,* 76 Harv. L. Rev. 25, 51 (1962). Thus, the notion of a "common core" litany or supplication offends many deeply devout worshippers who do not find clearly sectarian practices objectionable. Father Gustave Weigel has recently expressed a widely shared view: "The moral code held by each separate religious community can reductively be unified, but the consistent particular believer wants no such reduction." And, as the American Council on Education warned several years ago, "The notion of a common core suggests a watering down of the several faiths to the point where common essentials appear. This might easily lead to a new sect—a public school sect—which would take its place alongside the existing faiths and compete with them." *Engel* is surely authority that nonsectarian religious practices, equally with sectarian exercises, violate the Establishment Clause. Moreover, even if the Establishment Clause were oblivious to nonsectarian religious practices, I think it quite likely that the "common core" approach would be sufficiently objectionable to many groups to be foreclosed by the prohibitions of the Free Exercise Clause. . . .

Justice Stewart, dissenting:

. . .

Since the *Cantwell* prononuncement in 1940, this Court has only twice held invalid state laws on the ground that they were laws "respecting an establishment of religion" in violation of the Fourteenth Amendment. *McCollum v. Board of Education [supra]*;

---

[64] See Abbott, A Common Bible Reader for Public Schools, 56 Religious Education 20 (1961); Note, 22 Albany L. Rev. 156–157 (1958); 2 Stokes, Church and State in the United States (1950), 501–506 (describing the "common denominator" or "three faiths" plan and certain programs of instruction designed to implement the "common core" approach). The attempts to evolve a universal, nondenominational prayer are by no means novel. See, *e.g.,* Madison's letter to Edward Everett, March 19, 1823, commenting upon a "project of a prayer . . . intended to comprehend & conciliate College Students of every [Christian] denomination, by a Form composed wholly of texts & phrases of scripture." 9 Writings of James Madison (Hunt ed. 1910), 126. For a fuller description of this and other attempts to fashion a "common core" or nonsectarian exercise, *see Engel v. Vitale,* 18 Misc. 2d 659, 660–662, 191 N. Y. S. 2d 453, 459–460.

Engel v. Vitale [*supra*]. On the other hand, the Court has upheld against such a challenge laws establishing Sunday as a compulsory day of rest, *McGowan v. Maryland*, [*supra*, XIII, 2] and a law authorizing reimbursement from public funds for the transportation of parochial school pupils. *Everson v. Board of Education* [XIV, 1].

Unlike other First Amendment guarantees, there is an inherent limitation upon the applicability of the Establishment Clause's ban on state support to religion. That limitation was succinctly put in *Everson v. Board of Education* [*supra*]: "State power is no more to be used so as to handicap religions than it is to favor them." And in a later case, this Court recognized that the limitation was one which was itself compelled by the free exercise guarantee. "To hold that a state cannot consistently with the First and Fourteenth Amendments utilize its public school system to aid any or all religious faiths or sects in the dissemination of their doctrines and ideals does not . . . manifest a governmental hostility to religion or religious teachings. A manifestation of such hostility would be at war with our national tradition as embodied in the First Amendment's guaranty of the free exercise of religion."

. . .

Viewed in this light, it seems to me clear that the records in both of the cases before us are wholly inadequate to support an informed or responsible decision. Both cases involve provisions which explicitly permit any student who wishes, to be excused from participation in the exercises. There is no evidence in either case as to whether there would exist any coercion of any kind upon a student who did not want to participate. No evidence at all was adduced in the *Murray* case, because it was decided upon a demurrer. All that we have in that case, therefore, is the conclusory language of a pleading. While such conclusory allegations are acceptable for procedural purposes, I think that the nature of the constitutional problem involved here clearly demands that no decision be made except upon evidence. In the *Schempp* case the record shows no more than a subjective prophecy by a parent of what he thought would happen if a request were made to be excused from participation in the exercises under the amended statute. No such request was ever made, and there is no evidence whatever as to what might or would actually happen, nor of what administrative arrangements the school actually might or could make to free from pressure of any kind those who do not want to participate in the exercises. There were no District Court findings on this issue, since the case under the amended statute was decided exclusively on Establishment Clause grounds. 201 F. Supp. 815.

What our Constitution indispensably protects is the freedom of each of us, be he Jew or Agnostic, Christian or Atheist, Buddhist or Freethinker, to believe or disbelieve, to worship or not worship, to pray or keep silent, according to his own conscience, uncoerced and unrestrained by government. It is conceivable that these school boards, or even all school boards, might eventually find it impossible to administer a system of religious exercises during school hours in such a way as to meet this constitutional standard—in such a way as completely to free from any kind of official coercion those who do not affirmatively want to participate. But I think we must not assume that school boards so lack the qualities of inventiveness and good will as to make impossible the achievement of that goal.

I would remand both cases for further hearings.

NOTE. *The Possibility of Neutrality.*

The urge to ensure that non-belief does not suffer in comparison with belief has often led to practical and theoretical restrictions being placed on religion itself. The classical doctrine of strict separationism rests on an assumption that the state can and must be neutral. But in practice this is impossible. Values are necessary for the functioning of any society, and if they are not consciously adopted and publicly acknowledged they will be smuggled in surreptitiously and often unconsciously. Values are always in real or potential conflict, and the state inevitably favors some values over others [James

Hitchcock, "Church, State and Moral Values: The Limits of American Pluralism," 44 *Law and Contemporary Problems* 3, 21 (1981).

Is Hitchcock right?

"Civil religion" is "that religious dimension, found I think in the life of every people, through which it interprets its historical experience in the light of transcendent reality," Bellah, *The Broken Covenant: American Civil Religion in Time of Trial* (1967) 3. Civil religion invokes the mythology of the nation, that is, not what is untrue but what transfigures reality "so that it provides moral and spiritual meaning," *ibid.* Can the public schools teach civics, government, and history without presenting for acceptance "the civil religion of America"? *See also* Wilson Yates, "Separation of Church and State: Civil Religion and Crossings at the Border," 1 *Hamline Law Review* 67 (1978); Sanford Levinson, " 'The Constitution' in American Civil Religion," 1979 *Supreme Court Review* 123; Michael J. Perry, *The Constitution, the Courts, and Human Rights* (1982) at 98–99: judicial review by the Supreme Court is "the institutionalization of prophecy."

Epperson v. Arkansas
393 U.S. 97 (1968)

Eugene R. Warren argued the cause for appellants. With him on the brief was *Bruce T. Bullion.*

Don Langston, Assistant Attorney General of Arkansas, argued the cause for appellee. With him on the brief was *Joe Purcell,* Attorney General.

Briefs of *amici curiae,* urging reversal, were filed by *Leo Pfeffer, Melvin L. Wulf,* and *Joseph B. Robison* for the American Civil Liberties Union et al., and by *Philip J. Hirschkop* for the National Education Association of the United States et al.

Justice Fortas delivered the opinion of the Court.

I

This appeal challenges the constitutionality of the "anti-evolution" statute which the State of Arkansas adopted in 1928 to prohibit the teaching in its public schools and universities of the theory that man evolved from other species of life. The statute was a product of the upsurge of "fundamentalist" religious fervor of the twenties. The Arkansas statute was an adaptation of the famous Tennessee "monkey law" which that State adopted in 1925. The constitutionality of the Tennessee law was upheld by the Tennessee Supreme Court in the celebrated *Scopes* case in 1927.

The Arkansas law makes it unlawful for a teacher in any state-supported school or university "to teach the theory or doctrine that mankind ascended or descended from a lower order of animals," or "to adopt or use in any such institution a textbook that teaches" this theory. Violation is a misdemeanor and subjects the violator to dismissal from his position.[2]

---

[2] Initiated Act No. 1, Ark. Acts 1929; Ark. Stat. Ann. §§ 80–1627, 80–1628 (1960 Repl. Vol.). The text of the law is as follows:

"§ 80–1627.—Doctrine of ascent or descent of man from lower order of animals prohibited.— It shall be unlawful for any teacher or other instructor in any University, College, Normal, Public School, or other institution of the State, which is supported in whole or in part from public funds derived by State and local taxation to teach the theory or doctrine that mankind ascended or descended from a lower order of animals and also it shall be unlawful for any teacher, textbook commission, or other authority exercising the power to select textbooks for above mentioned educational institutions to adopt or use in any such institution a textbook that teaches the doctrine or theory that mankind descended or ascended from a lower order of animals.

"§ 80–1628.—Teaching doctrine or adopting textbook mentioning doctrine—Penalties—Positions

The present case concerns the teaching of biology in a high school in Little Rock. According to the testimony, until the events here in litigation, the official textbook furnished for the high school biology course did not have a section on the Darwinian Theory. Then, for the academic year 1965–1966, the school administration, on recommendation of the teachers of biology in the school system, adopted and prescribed a textbook which contained a chapter setting forth "the theory about the origin . . . of man from a lower form of animal."

. . .

The State's undoubted right to prescribe the curriculum for its public schools does not carry with it the right to prohibit, on pain of criminal penalty, the teaching of a scientific theory or doctrine where that prohibition is based upon reasons that violate the First Amendment. It is much too late to argue that the State may impose upon the teachers in its schools any conditions that it chooses, however restrictive they may be of constitutional guarantees. *Keyishian* v. *Board of Regents,* 385 U.S. 589, 605–606 (1967).

In the present case, there can be no doubt that Arkansas has sought to prevent its teachers from discussing the theory of evolution because it is contrary to the belief of some that the Book of Genesis must be the exclusive source of doctrine as to the origin of man. No suggestion has been made that Arkansas' law may be justified by considerations of state policy other than the religious views of some of its citizens.[15] It is clear that fundamentalist sectarian conviction was and is the law's reason for existence.[16]

---

to be vacated.—Any teacher or other instructor or textbook commissioner who is found guilty of violation of this act by teaching the theory or doctrine mentioned in section 1 hereof, or by using, or adopting any such textbooks in any such educational institution shall be guilty of a misdemeanor and upon conviction shall be fined not exceeding five hundred dollars; and upon conviction shall vacate the position thus held in any educational institutions of the character above mentioned or any commission of which he may be a member."

[15] Former Dean Leflar of the University of Arkansas School of Law has stated that "the same ideological considerations underlie the anti-evolution enactment" as underlie the typical blasphemy statute. He says that the purpose of these statutes is an "ideological" one which "involves an effort to prevent (by censorship) or punish the presentation of intellectually significant matter which contradicts accepted social, moral or religious ideas." Leflar, Legal Liability for the Exercise of Free Speech, 10 Ark. L. Rev. 155, 158 (1956). See also R. Hofstadter & W. Metzger, The Development of Academic Freedom in the United States 320–366 (1955) *(passim);* H. Beale, A History of Freedom of Teaching in American Schools 202–207 (1941); Emerson & Haber, The *Scopes* Case in Modern Dress, 27 U. Chi. L. Rev. 522 (1960); Waller, The Constitutionality of the Tennessee Anti-Evolution Act, 35 Yale L. J. 191 (1925) *(passim);* ACLU, The Gag on Teaching 7 (2d ed., 1937); J. Scopes & J. Presley, Center of the Storm 45–53 (1967).

[16] The following advertisement is typical of the public appeal which was used in the campaign to secure adoption of the statute:

"THE BIBLE OR ATHEISM, WHICH?

"All atheists favor evolution. If you agree with atheism vote against Act No. 1. If you agree with the Bible vote for Act No. 1. . . . Shall conscientious church members be forced to pay taxes to support teachers to teach evolution which will undermine the faith of their children? The Gazette said Russian Bolshevists laughed at Tennessee. True, and that sort will laugh at Arkansas. Who cares? Vote FOR ACT NO. 1." The Arkansas Gazette, Little Rock, Nov. 4, 1928, p. 12, cols. 4–5.

Letters from the public expressed the fear that teaching of evolution would be "subversive of Christianity," *id.,* Oct. 24, 1928, p. 7, col. 2; see also *id.,* Nov. 4, 1928, p. 19, col. 4; and that it would cause school children "to disrespect the Bible," *id.,* Oct. 27, 1928, p. 15, col. 5. One letter read: "The cosmogony taught by [evolution] runs contrary to that of Moses and Jesus, and as such is nothing, if anything at all, but atheism. . . . Now let the mothers and fathers of our state that are trying to raise their children in the Christian faith arise in their might and vote for this anti-evolution bill that will take it out of our tax supported schools. When they have saved the children, they have saved the state." *Id.,* at cols. 4–5.

Its antecedent, Tennessee's "monkey law," candidly stated its purpose: to make it unlawful "to teach any theory that denies the story of the Divine Creation of man as taught in the Bible, and to teach instead that man has descended from a lower order of animals."[17] Perhaps the sensational publicity attendant upon the *Scopes* trial induced Arkansas to adopt less explicit language.[18] It eliminated Tennessee's reference to "the story of the Divine Creation of man" as taught in the Bible, but there is no doubt that the motivation for the law was the same: to suppress the teaching of a theory which, it was thought, "denied" the divine creation of man.

Arkansas' law cannot be defended as an act of religious neutrality. Arkansas did not seek to excise from the curricula of its schools and universities all discussion of the origin of man. The law's effort was confined to an attempt to blot out a particular theory because of its supposed conflict with the Biblical account, literally read. Plainly, the law is contrary to the mandate of the First, and in violation of the Fourteenth, Amendment to the Constitution.

The judgment of the Supreme Court of Arkansas is

Reversed.

Justice Black, concurring.

I am by no means sure that this case presents a genuinely justiciable case or controversy. Although Arkansas Initiated Act No. 1, the statute alleged to be unconstitutional, was passed by the voters of Arkansas in 1928, we are informed that there has never been even a single attempt by the State to enforce it. And the pallid, unenthusiastic, even apologetic defense of the Act presented by the State in this Court indicates that the State would make no attempt to enforce the law should it remain on the books for the next century. Now, nearly 40 years after the law has slumbered on the books as though dead, a teacher alleging fear that the State might arouse from its lethargy and try to punish her has asked for a declaratory judgment holding the law unconstitutional. She was subsequently joined by a parent who alleged his interest in seeing that his two then school-age sons "be informed of all scientific theories and hypotheses. . . ." But whether this Arkansas teacher is still a teacher, fearful of punishment under the Act, we do not know. It may be, as has been published in the daily press, that she has long since given up her job as a teacher and moved to a distant city, thereby escaping the dangers she had imagined might befall her under this lifeless Arkansas Act. And there is not one iota of concrete evidence to show that the parent-intervenor's sons have not been or will not be taught about evolution. The textbook adopted for use in biology classes in Little Rock includes an entire chapter dealing with evolution. There is no evidence that this chapter is not being freely taught in the schools that use the textbook and no evidence that the intervenor's sons, who were 15 and 17 years old when this suit was brought three years ago, are still in high school or yet to take biology. Unfortunately, however, the State's languid interest in the case has not prompted it to keep this Court informed concerning facts that might easily justify dismissal of this alleged lawsuit as moot or as lacking the qualities of a genuine case or controversy.

Notwithstanding my own doubts as to whether the case presents a justiciable controversy, the Court brushes aside these doubts and leaps headlong into the middle of the very broad problems involved in federal intrusion into state powers to decide what subjects and schoolbooks it may wish to use in teaching state pupils. While I hesitate to enter into the consideration and decision of such sensitive state-federal relationships,

---

[17] Arkansas' law was adopted by popular initiative in 1928, three years after Tennessee's law was enacted and one year after the Tennessee Supreme Court's decision in the *Scopes* case, *supra.*

[18] In its brief, the State says that the Arkansas statute was passed with the holding of the *Scopes* case in mind. Brief for Appellee 1.

I reluctantly acquiesce. But, agreeing to consider this as a genuine case or controversy, I cannot agree to thrust the Federal Government's long arm the least bit further into state school curriculums than decision of this particular case requires.

NOTE. In 1981 Louisiana enacted a "Balanced Treatment Act" requiring that teachers who taught "evolution science" must also teach "creation science." The act was held an unconstitutional establishment of religion by Judge E. Grady Jolly. *Aguillard v. Edwards,* 765 F.2d 1251 (5th Cir. 1985). The statutory scheme, "focusing on the religious *bête noire* of evolution, as it does, demonstrates the religious purpose of the statute. Indeed the Act continues the battle William Jennings Bryan carried to his grave." The Supreme Court noted probable jurisdiction, 106 S.Ct. 1946 (1986). See Hanson, ed., *Science and Creation* (1986).

NOTE. *Malnak v. Yogi,* 592 F. 2d 197 (3rd Cir. 1979). "The Science of Creative Intelligence—Transcendental Meditation" (SCI/TM) was offered as an elective in five high schools using a textbook developed by Maharishi Mahesh Yogi and employing teachers trained by the World Plan Executive Council—United States, an organization promoting the teaching of SCI/TM. Essential to the practice of TM was a mantra personal to each participant. The mantra was obtained by each student in the course by compulsory attendance at a Puja, a ceremony sung in Sanskrit by a Hindu monk who made offerings to the deified Guru Dev. In an action brought by parents of school children and Americans United for Separation of Church and State, the court enjoined the course as an unconstitutional establishment of religion.

Concurring, Judge Arlin M. Adams pointed out the novelty of the case: the defendants argued that the Puja was a secular not a religious ceremony, common in Eastern cultures; they contended that TM was primarily a concentration or relaxation technique without "ultimate significance." Judge Adams observed that under a modern definition of religion, extractable from *Seeger, Welsh,* and *Torcaso, supra,* there had been built an analogy with the traditional religions found in America. A religion laid claim to ultimate truth and to comprehensive truth and typically, though not necessarily, involved clergy, ceremonial observances, organization, and efforts at propagation. He found that SCI/TM "provides answers to questions concerning the nature both of world and man, the underlying sustaining force of the universe, and the way to unlimited happiness"—indeed what its adherents believed to be *"the way."* Consequently, it was sufficiently comprehensive and truth-asserting to be a religion. The trained teachers, organization for propagation, and Puja were sufficiently like the characteristics of older religious groups to confirm the finding that SCI/TM was a nontheistic religion.

Queries. Does not "modern science" lay claim to comprehensive truth about the earth? Are the tentative character of its claims and its abstention from statements as to "ultimate" causes what distinguish it from religion? Or is the difference for those who find their truth only in science one of style more than substance? *See also Note: Marxist Communism as a Religion, supra,* XI, 3.

Stone v. Graham
449 U.S. 39 (1980)

Per Curiam.

A Kentucky statute requires the posting of a copy of the Ten Commandments, purchased with private contributions, on the wall of each public classroom in the State.[1]

---

[1] The statute provides in its entirety:

"(1) It shall be the duty of the superintendent of public instruction, provided sufficient funds are available as provided in subsection (3) of this Section, to ensure that a durable, permanent copy of the Ten Commandments shall be displayed on a wall in each public elementary and

Petitioners, claiming that this statute violates the Establishment and Free Exercise Clauses of the First Amendment, sought an injunction against its enforcement. The state trial court upheld the statute, finding that its "avowed purpose" was "secular and not religious," and that the statute would "neither advance nor inhibit any religion or religious group" nor involve the State excessively in religious matters. App. to Pet. for Cert. 38–39. The Supreme Court of the Commonwealth of Kentucky affirmed by an equally divided court. 599 S. W. 2d 157 (1980). We reverse.

This Court has announced a three-part test for determining whether a challenged state statute is permissible under the Establishment Clause of the United States Constitution:

> "First, the statute must have a secular legislative purpose; second, its principal or primary effect must be one that neither advances nor inhibits religion . . .; finally the statute must not foster 'an excessive government entanglement with religion.' " *Lemon v. Kurtzman* [XIV, 1].

If a statute violates any of these three principles, it must be struck down under the Establishment Clause. We conclude that Kentucky's statute requiring the posting of the Ten Commandments in public school rooms has no secular legislative purpose, and is therefore unconstitutional.

The Commonwealth insists that the statute in question serves a secular legislative purpose, observing that the legislature required the following notation in small print at the bottom of each display of the Ten Commandments: "The secular application of the Ten Commandments is clearly seen in its adoption as the fundamental legal code of Western Civilization and the Common Law of the United States." 1978 Ky. Acts, ch. 436, § 1 (effective June 17, 1978), Ky. Rev. Stat. § 158.178 (1980).

The trial court found the "avowed" purpose of the statute to be secular, even as it labeled the statutory declaration "self-serving." App. to Pet. for Cert. 37. Under this Court's rulings, however, such an "avowed" secular purpose is not sufficient to avoid conflict with the First Amendment. In *Abington School District v. Schempp* [*supra* XIV, 2], this Court held unconstitutional the daily reading of Bible verses and the Lord's Prayer in the public schools, despite the school district's assertion of such secular purposes as "the promotion of moral values, the contradiction to the materialistic trends of our times, the perpetuation of our institutions and the teaching of literature." *Id.,* at 223.

The pre-eminent purpose for posting the Ten Commandments on schoolroom walls is plainly religious in nature. The Ten Commandments are undeniably a sacred text in the Jewish and Christian faiths, and no legislative recitation of a supposed secular purpose can blind us to that fact. The Commandments do not confine themselves to arguably secular matters, such as honoring one's parents, killing or murder, adultery, stealing, false witness, and covetousness. See Exodus 20: 12–17; Deuteronomy 5: 16–21. Rather, the first part of the Commandments concerns the religious duties of believers: worshipping the Lord God alone, avoiding idolatry, not using the Lord's name in vain, and observing the Sabbath Day. See Exodus 20: 1–11; Deuteronomy 5: 6–15.

This is not a case in which the Ten Commandments are integrated into the school curriculum, where the Bible may constitutionally be used in an appropriate study of

---

secondary school classroom in the Commonwealth. The copy shall be sixteen (16) inches wide by twenty (20) inches high.

"(2) In small print below the last commandment shall appear a notation concerning the purpose of the display, as follows: 'The secular application of the Ten Commandments is clearly seen in its adoption as the fundamental legal code of Western Civilization and the Common Law of the United States.'

"(3) The copies required by this Act shall be purchased with funds made available through voluntary contributions made to the state treasurer for the purposes of this Act." 1978 Ky. Acts, ch. 436, § 1 (effective June 17, 1978), Ky. Rev. Stat. § 158.178 (1980).

history, civilization, ethics, comparative religion, or the like. *Abington School District v. Schempp, supra,* at 225. Posting of religious texts on the wall serves no such educational function. If the posted copies of the Ten Commandments are to have any effect at all, it will be to induce the schoolchildren to read, meditate upon, perhaps to venerate and obey, the Commandments. However desirable this might be as a matter of private devotion, it is not a permissible state objective under the Establishment Clause.

It does not matter that the posted copies of the Ten Commandments are financed by voluntary private contributions, for the mere posting of the copies under the auspices of the legislature provides the "official support of the State . . . Government" that the Establishment Clause prohibits. 374 U.S., at 222; see *Engel v. Vitale* [*supra* XIV, 2]. Nor is it significant that the Bible verses involved in this case are merely posted on the wall, rather than read aloud as in *Schempp* and *Engel,* for "it is no defense to urge that the religious practices here may be relatively minor encroachments on the First Amendment." *Abington School District v. Schempp, supra,* at 225. We conclude that Ky. Rev. Stat. § 158.178 (1980) violates the first part of the *Lemon v. Kurtzman* test, and thus the Establishment Clause of the Constitution.

The petition for a writ of certiorari is granted, and the judgment below is reversed.

It is so ordered.

The Chief Justice and Justice Blackmun dissent. They would grant certiorari and give this case plenary consideration.

Justice Stewart dissents from this summary reversal of the courts of Kentucky, which, so far as appears, applied wholly correct constitutional criteria in reaching their decisions.

Justice Rehnquist, dissenting.

With no support beyond its own *ipse dixit,* the Court concludes that the Kentucky statute involved in this case "has *no* secular legislative purpose," *ante,* at 41 (emphasis supplied), and that "[t]he pre-eminent purpose for posting the Ten Commandments on schoolroom walls is plainly religious in nature," *ibid.* This even though, as the trial court found, "[t]he General Assembly thought the statute had a secular legislative purpose and specifically said so." App. to Pet. for Cert. 37. The Court's summary rejection of a secular purpose articulated by the legislature and confirmed by the state court is without precedent in Establishment Clause jurisprudence.

Wallace v. Jaffree
105 S.Ct. 2479 (1985)

John S. Baker, Jr. for appellants. Paul M. Bator, Cambridge, Mass., for United States as amicus curiae. Ronnie L. Williams, Mobile, Alabama, for appellees.

Justice Stevens delivered the opinion of the Court.

[An Alabama Law enacted in 1978 authorized a one-minute period of silence in all public schools "for meditation." An amendment enacted in 1981 authorized a period of silence "for meditation or voluntary prayer." An amendment enacted in 1982 authorized teachers to lead "willing students" in a prescribed prayer to "Almighty God . . . the Creator and Supreme Judge of the world."

The 1978 statute was held constitutional by the District Court. No appeal was taken. As to the 1981 and 1982 amendments, the District Court, in a sharp display of disrespect for the Supreme Court, held that the Supreme Court decisions on the establishment clause were "wrong" and that Alabama had the power to establish a state religion if it chose. The Fifth Circuit reversed and the Supreme Court affirmed as to the 1982 statute with its prescribed prayer. The question left for decision was whether the 1981 statute authorizing "meditation or voluntary prayer" was an establishment of religion.

The plaintiff was Ishmael Jaffree who filed the complaint on behalf of his children, two in the second grade, one in kindergarten. Jaffree stated that his children were exposed to ostracism for not participating in prayers led by the teachers and that the teachers refused to stop leading the prayers.]

. . .

In applying the purpose test, it is appropriate to ask "whether government's actual purpose is to endorse or disapprove of religion." In this case, the answer to that question is dispositive. For the record not only provides us with an unambiguous affirmative answer, but it also reveals that the enactment of § 16-1-20.1 was not motivated by any clearly secular purpose—indeed, the statute had *no* secular purpose. . . .

The sponsor of the bill that became § 16-1-20.1, Senator Donald Holmes, inserted into the legislative record—apparently without dissent—a statement indicating that the legislation was an "effort to return voluntary prayer" to the public schools. Later Senator Holmes confirmed this purpose before the District Court. In response to the question whether he had any purpose for the legislation other than returning voluntary prayer to public schools, he stated, "No, I did not have no other purpose in mind." The State did not present evidence of *any* secular purpose.

The unrebutted evidence of legislative intent contained in the legislative record and in the testimony of the sponsor of § 16-1-20.1 is confirmed by a consideration of the relationship between this statute and the two other measures that were considered in this case. The District Court found that the 1981 statute and its 1982 sequel had a common, nonsecular purpose. The wholly religious character of the later enactment is plainly evident from its text. When the differences between § 16-1-20.1 and its 1978 predecessor, § 16-1-20, are examined, it is equally clear that the 1981 statute has the same wholly religious character.

There are only three textual differences between § 16-1-20.1 and § 16-1-20: (1) the earlier statute applies only to grades one through six, whereas § 16-1-20.1 applies to all grades; (2) the earlier statute uses the word "shall" whereas § 16-1-20.1 uses the word "may"; (3) the earlier statute refers only to "meditation" whereas § 16-1-20.1 refers to "meditation or voluntary prayer." The first difference is of no relevance in this litigation because the minor appellees were in kindergarten or second grade during the 1981–1982 academic year. The second difference would also have no impact on this litigation because the mandatory language of § 16-1-20 continued to apply to grades one through six. Thus, the only significant textual difference is the addition of the words "or voluntary prayer."

The legislative intent to return prayer to the public schools is, of course, quite different from merely protecting every student's right to engage in voluntary prayer during an appropriate moment of silence during the school day. The 1978 statute already protected that right, containing nothing that prevented any student from engaging in voluntary prayer during a silent minute of meditation. Appellants have not identified any secular purpose that was not fully served by § 16-1-20 before the enactment of § 16-1-20.1. Thus, only two conclusions are consistent with the text of § 16-1-20.1: (1) the statute was enacted to convey a message of State endorsement and promotion of prayer; or (2) the statute was enacted for no purpose. No one suggests that the statute was nothing but a meaningless or irrational act.

[8] We must, therefore, conclude that the Alabama Legislature intended to change existing law and that it was motivated by the same purpose that the Governor's Answer to the Second Amended Complaint expressly admitted; that the statement inserted in the legislative history revealed; and that Senator Holmes' testimony frankly described. The Legislature enacted § 16-1-20.1 despite the existence of § 16-1-20 for the sole purpose of expressing the State's endorsement of prayer activities for one minute at the beginning of each school day. The addition of "or voluntary prayer" indicates that the State intended to characterize prayer as a favored practice. Such an

endorsement is not consistent with the established principle that the Government must pursue a course of complete neutrality toward religion.

The importance of that principle does not permit us to treat this as an inconsequential case involving nothing more than a few words of symbolic speech on behalf of the political majority. For whenever the State itself speaks on a religious subject, one of the questions that we must ask is "whether the Government intends to convey a message of endorsement or disapproval of religion." The well-supported concurrent findings of the District Court and the Court of Appeals—that § 16-1-20.1 was intended to convey a message of State-approval of prayer activities in the public schools—make it unnecessary, and indeed inappropriate, to evaluate the practical significance of the addition of the words "or voluntary prayer" to the statute. Keeping in mind, as we must, "both the fundamental place held by the Establishment Clause in our constitutional scheme and the myriad, subtle ways in which Establishment Clause values can be eroded," we conclude that § 16-1-20.1 violates the First Amendment.

The judgment of the Court of Appeals is affirmed.

It is so ordered.

Justice Powell concurred in order "to respond to criticism of the three-pronged *Lemon* test" which he found "useful." Justice O'Connor concurred, proposing "a refinement of the *Lemon* test," to the effect that the establishment clause was violated "when the government makes adherence to religion relevant to a person's standing in the community." The government, she wrote, must not convey a message that religion or a particular religious belief is favored or preferred. After noting that twenty-five states permitted students to observe a moment of silence, she added that "moment of silence laws in many states should pass Establishment Clause scrutiny because they do not favor the child who chooses to pray during a moment of silence over the child who chooses to meditate or reflect."

Chief Justice Burger dissented.

Some who trouble to read the opinions in this case will find it ironic—perhaps even bizarre—that on the very day we heard arguments in this case, the Court's session opened with an invocation for Divine protection. Across the park a few hundred yards away, the House of Representatives and the Senate regularly open each session with a prayer. These legislative prayers are not just one minute in duration, but are extended, thoughtful invocations and prayers for Divine guidance. They are given, as they have been since 1789, by clergy appointed as official Chaplains and paid from the Treasury of the United States. Congress has also provided chapels in the Capitol, at public expense, where Members and others may pause for prayer, meditation—or a moment of silence.

Inevitably some wag is bound to say that the Court's holding today reflects a belief that the historic practice of the Congress and this Court is justified because members of the Judiciary and Congress are more in need of Divine guidance than are schoolchildren. Still others will say that all this controversy is "much ado about nothing," since no power on earth—including this Court and Congress—can stop any teacher from opening the school day with a moment of silence for pupils to meditate, to plan their day—or to pray if they voluntarily elect to do so.

Justice White dissented, supporting "a basic reconsideration of our precedents."

. . .

Justice Rehnquist, dissenting.

Thirty-eight years ago this Court, in *Everson v. Board of Education* [*supra* XIV, 1] summarized its exegesis of Establishment Clause doctrine thus:

"In the words of Jefferson, the clause against establishment of religion by law was intended to erect 'a wall of separation between church and State.' *Reynolds v. United States*" [*supra,* IX].

This language from *Reynolds,* a case involving the Free Exercise Clause of the First Amendment rather than the Establishment Clause, quoted from Thomas Jefferson's letter to the Danbury Baptist Association the phrase "I contemplate with sovereign reverence that act of the whole American people which declared that their legislature should 'make no law respecting an establishment of religion, or prohibiting the free exercise thereof,' thus building a wall of separation between church and State" [VII, 1].

It is impossible to build sound constitutional doctrine upon a mistaken understanding of constitutional history, but unfortunately the Establishment Clause has been expressly freighted with Jefferson's misleading metaphor for nearly forty years. Thomas Jefferson was of course in France at the time the constitutional amendments known as the Bill of Rights were passed by Congress and ratified by the states. His letter to the Danbury Baptist Association was a short note of courtesy, written fourteen years after the amendments were passed by Congress. He would seem to any detached observer as a less than ideal source of contemporary history as to the meaning of the Religion Clauses of the First Amendment.

Jefferson's fellow Virginian James Madison, with whom he was joined in the battle for the enactment of the Virginia Statute of Religious Liberty of 1786, did play as large a part as anyone in the drafting of the Bill of Rights. He had two advantages over Jefferson in this regard: he was present in the United States, and he was a leading member of the First Congress. But when we turn to the record of the proceedings in the First Congress leading up to the adoption of the Establishment Clause of the Constitution, including Madison's significant contributions thereto, we see a far different picture of its purpose than the highly simplified "wall of separation between church and State."

. . .

The repetition of this error in the Court's opinion in *Illinois ex rel. McCollum v. Board of Education,* and, *inter alia, Engel v. Vitale,* does not make it any sounder historically. Finally, in *Abington School District v. Schempp,* the Court made the truly remarkable statement that "the views of Madison and Jefferson, preceded by Roger Williams came to be incorporated not only in the Federal Constitution but likewise in those of most of our States" (footnote omitted). On the basis of what evidence we have, this statement is demonstrably incorrect as a matter of history. And its repetition in varying forms in succeeding opinions of the Court can give it no more authority than it possesses as a matter of fact; *stare decisis* may bind courts as to matters of law, but it cannot bind them as to matters of history.

. . .

The true meaning of the Establishment Clause can only be seen in its history. . . . As drafters of our Bill of Rights, the Framers inscribed the principles that control today. Any deviation from their intentions frustrates the permanence of that Charter and will only lead to the type of unprincipled decisionmaking that has plagued our Establishment Clause cases since *Everson.*

The Framers intended the Establishment Clause to prohibit the designation of any church as a "national" one. The Clause was also designed to stop the Federal Government from asserting a preference for one religious denomination or sect over others. Given the "incorporation" of the Establishment Clause as against the States via the Fourteenth Amendment in *Everson,* States are prohibited as well from establishing a religion or discriminating between sects. As its history abundantly shows, however, nothing in the Establishment Clause requires government to be strictly neutral between religion and irreligion, nor does that Clause prohibit Congress or the States from pursuing legitimate secular ends through nondiscriminatory sectarian means.

The Court strikes down the Alabama statute in No. 83–812, *Wallace v. Jaffree,* because the State wished to "endorse prayer as a favored practice." *Ante,* at 2492. It would come as much of a shock to those who drafted the Bill of Rights as it will to a large number of thoughtful Americans today to learn that the Constitution, as construed by the majority, prohibits the Alabama Legislature from "endorsing" prayer. George Washington himself, at the request of the very Congress which passed the Bill of Rights, proclaimed a day of "public thanksgiving and prayer, to be observed by acknowledging with grateful hearts the many and signal favors of Almighty God." History must judge whether it was the father of his country in 1789, or a majority of the Court today, which has strayed from the meaning of the Establishment Clause.

The State surely has a secular interest in regulating the manner in which public schools are conducted. Nothing in the Establishment Clause of the First Amendment, properly understood, prohibits any such generalized "endorsement" of prayer. I would therefore reverse the judgment of the Court of Appeals in *Wallace v. Jaffree.*

Queries. In commenting on Justice Rehnquist's dissent, Robert Cord has written that "the Supreme Court has used its American 'history'—and little else—to justify its present Establishment Clause requirements. That fact alone makes an historical analysis germane, if not crucial, to any re-examination of present Supreme Court policy." Robert Cord, "Church-State Separation: Restoring the 'No Preference' Doctrine of the First Amendment," *Harvard Journal of Law and Public Policy* (1986) 129, 131, n. 10. Do you agree? Cf. the "non-interpretist approach" of Michael L. Perry in *The Constitution, The Courts and Human Rights* 98–99 (the function of the Court is prophetic). See also Leonard W. Levy, *The Establishment Clause* (1986).

"One striking fact about both the *Jaffree* and *Thornton* [*supra*, XI, 4] decisions is the irrelevance of the *Lemon* test." Michael W. McConnell, "Accommodation of Religion," *1985 Supreme Court Review* 58. Do you agree? "The opinions in *Jaffree* and *Thornton*, despite their surface appearance, present no obstacles to the development of a principled doctrine of the accommodation of religion, under which the purposes of the Free Exercise and Establishment Clauses are harmonized," *ibid.* at 59. Do you agree?

NOTE. *Congressional Compromise.* President Ronald Reagan recommended to Congress the enactment of a constitutional amendment permitting voluntary group prayer in the public schools, Message to Congress, 18 *Weekly Compilation of Presidential Documents* 664 (May 17, 1982). The measure did not get out of committee. A 1983 bill, the Religious Speech Protection Act, was eventually replaced by the Equal Access Act, which provided protection not only for religious speech but for all forms of speech by voluntary student groups. The bill drew support from evangelicals, from some civil rights groups, and from organizations often suspicious of religion in the schools such as the Baptist Joint Committee on Public Affairs and the National Council of Churches. Signed into law by President Reagan on August 11, 1984, it reads as follows:

20 U.S.C. § 4071. Denial of equal access prohibited

(a) Restriction of limited open forum on basis of religious, political, philosophical, or other speech content prohibited

It shall be unlawful for any public secondary school which receives Federal financial assistance and which has a limited open forum to deny equal access or a fair opportunity to, or discriminate against, any students who wish to conduct a meeting within that limited open forum on the basis of the religious, political, philosophical, or other content of the speech at such meetings.

(b) "Limited open forum" defined

A public secondary school has a limited open forum whenever such school grants an offering to or opportunity for one or more noncurriculum related student groups to meet on school premises during noninstructional time.

(c) Fair opportunity criteria

Schools shall be deemed to offer a fair opportunity to students who wish to conduct a meeting within its limited open forum if such school uniformly provides that—

(1) the meeting is voluntary and student-initiated;

(2) there is no sponsorship of the meeting by the school, the government, or its agents or employees;

(3) employees or agents of the school or government are present at religious meetings only in a nonparticipatory capacity;

(4) the meeting does not materially and substantially interfere with the orderly conduct of educational activities within the school; and

(5) nonschool persons may not direct, conduct, control, or regularly attend activities of student groups.

(d) Federal or State authority nonexistent with respect to certain rights

Nothing in this subchapter shall be construed to authorize the United States or any State or political subdivision thereof—

(1) to influence the form or content of any prayer or other religious activity;

(2) to require any person to participate in prayer or other religious activity;

(3) to expend public funds beyond the incidental cost of providing the space for student-initiated meetings;

(4) to compel any school agent or employee to attend a school meeting if the content of the speech at the meeting is contrary to the beliefs of the agent or employee;

(5) to sanction meetings that are otherwise unlawful;

(6) to limit the rights of groups of students which are not of a specified numerical size; or

(7) to abridge the constitutional rights of any person.

(e) Unaffected Federal financial assistance to schools

Notwithstanding the availability of any other remedy under the Constitution or the laws of the United States, nothing in this subchapter shall be construed to authorize the United States to deny or withhold Federal financial assistance to any school.

(f) Authority of schools with respect to order-and-discipline, well-being, and voluntary-presence concerns

Nothing in this subchapter shall be construed to limit the authority of the school, its agents or employees, to maintain order and discipline on school premises, to protect the well-being of students and faculty, and to assure that attendance of students at meetings is voluntary.

§ 4072. Definitions

As used in this subchapter—

(1) The term "secondary school" means a public school which provides secondary education as determined by State law.

(2) The term "sponsorship" includes the act of promoting, leading, or participating in a meeting. The assignment of a teacher, administrator, or other school employee to a meeting for custodial purposes does not constitute sponsorship of the meeting.

(3) The term "meeting" includes those activities of student groups which are permitted under a school's limited open forum and are not directly related to the school curriculum.

(4) The term "noninstructional time" means time set aside by the school before actual classroom instruction begins or after actual classroom instruction ends.

The Equal Access Act relied on the rationale of *Widmar, infra*, XIV, 3, that public universities could not constitutionally bar religious activities from campus. Before the bill became law, four federal courts of appeals had found *Widmar* inapplicable to high schools and had held it an unconstitutional establishment of religion for a school to permit voluntary group prayer meetings, *e.g., Bender v. Williamsport*, 741 F.2d 538 (3rd Cir., 1984), *vacated* 106 S.Ct. 1326 (1986). The Anti-Defamation League of B'nai B'rith, which had opposed the legislation, used these cases to argue that the Equal Access Act was itself an unconstitutional establishment, enacted solely to promote prayer, entangling the public school in the supervision and arrangement of religious meetings, symbolically giving state support to religion, and in general violating the principle established by *McCollum, supra* this section, see Anti-Defamation League, *Religion and the Public Schools* (1984) 9–15.

3. HIGHER EDUCATION

Just as age has been a criterion in free exercise cases (*e.g., Prince, supra* XI, 1), so it has been in the area of education. Colleges and universities have been approached differently from schools.

Subsidy

Tilton v. Richardson
403 U.S. 672 (1971)

Leo Pfeffer argued the cause for appellants. With him on the briefs were *Peter L. Costas, Paul W. Orth,* and *Jerry Wagner.*

Daniel M. Friedman argued the cause for appellees Richardson et al. On the brief were *Solicitor General Griswold, Assistant Attorney General Ruckelshaus, Robert V. Zener,* and *Donald L. Horowitz. F. Michael Ahern,* Assistant Attorney General of Connecticut, argued the cause for appellee Peterson. With him on the brief was *Robert K. Killian,* Attorney General. *Edward Bennett Williams* argued the cause for appellee colleges and universities. With him on the brief were *Jeremiah C. Collins, Howard T. Owens, Lawrence W. Iannotti,* and *Bruce Lewellyn.*

Briefs of *amici curiae* urging reversal were filed by *Franklin C. Salisbury* for Protestants and Other Americans United for Separation of Church and State, and by *Peter L. Costas* and *Paul W. Orth* for the Connecticut State Conference of Branches of the NAACP et al.

Briefs of *amici curiae* urging affirmance were filed by *Wilber G. Katz* and *John Holt Myers* for the American Council on Education et al., and by *Nathan Lewin* for the National Jewish Commission on Law and Public Affairs.

Chief Justice Burger announced the judgment of the Court and an opinion in which Justice Harlan, Justice Stewart, and Justice Blackmun join.

[After quoting the purpose of the Act of Congress in question to assure colleges for American youth] This expresses a legitimate secular objective entirely appropriate for governmental action.

The simplistic argument that every form of financial aid to church-sponsored activity violates the Religion Clauses was rejected long ago in *Bradfield v. Roberts* [X, 2]. . . .
The Act itself was carefully drafted to ensure that the federal subsidized facilities would

be devoted to the secular and not the religious functions of the recipient institutions. . . . Finally, this record fully supports the findings of the District Court that none of the four church-related institutions in this case has violated the statutory restrictions. . . .

[After stating that two of the buildings involved were libraries where no classes were conducted; that one was a language laboratory; that one was a science building; and that one was a music, drama, and arts building], there was no evidence that religion seeps into the use of any of these facilities. . . . Although appellants introduced several institutional documents that stated certain religious restrictions on what could be taught, other evidence showed that these restrictions were not in fact enforced and that the schools were characterized by an atmosphere of academic freedom rather than religious indoctrination. [The Court went on to reject the appellant's use of a "hypothetical composite" profile of a "typical sectarian" institution. The four colleges in this case were all Catholic: Albertus Magnus, Annhurst, Fairfield, and Sacred Heart University.

The Court went on to consider a provision of the statute that provided that after twenty years the restriction on the buildings would expire and the colleges would be free to use them as they chose. A library, for example, could be turned into a chapel.] To this extent, the Act therefore trespasses on the Religion Clauses.

[Finally, the Court considered whether there were "excessive entanglements" and distinguished the colleges from parochial schools.]

. . .

There is substance to the contention that college students are less impressionable and less susceptible to religious indoctrination. Common observation would seem to support that view, and Congress may well have entertained it. The skepticism of the college student is not an inconsiderable barrier to any attempt or tendency to subvert the congressional objectives and limitations. Furthermore, by their very nature, college and postgraduate courses tend to limit the opportunities for sectarian influence by virtue of their own internal disciplines. Many church-related colleges and universities are characterized by a high degree of academic freedom and seek to evoke free and critical responses from their students.

The record here would not support a conclusion that any of these four institutions departed from this general pattern. All four schools are governed by Catholic religious organizations, and the faculties and student bodies at each are predominantly Catholic. Nevertheless, the evidence shows that non-Catholics were admitted as students and given faculty appointments. Not one of these four institutions requires its students to attend religious services. Although all four schools require their students to take theology courses, the parties stipulated that these courses are taught according to the academic requirements of the subject matter and the teacher's concept of professional standards. . . .

The entanglement between church and state is also lessened here by the nonideological character of the aid that the Government provides. Our cases from *Everson* to *Allen* have permitted church-related schools to receive government aid in the form of secular, neutral, or non-ideological services, facilities, or materials that are supplied to all students regardless of the affiliation of the school that they attend. In *Lemon* and *DiCenso,* however, the state programs subsidized teachers, either directly or indirectly. Since teachers are not necessarily religiously neutral, greater governmental surveillance would be required to guarantee that state salary aid would not in fact subsidize religious instruction. There we found the resulting entanglement excessive. Here, on the other hand, the Government provides facilities that are themselves religiously neutral. The risks of Government aid to religion and the corresponding need for surveillance are therefore reduced.

Finally, government entanglements with religion are reduced by the circumstance that, unlike the direct and continuing payments under the Pennsylvania program, and all the incidents of regulation and surveillance, the Government aid here is a one-time, single-purpose construction grant. There are no continuing financial relationships or dependencies, no annual audits, and no government analysis of an institution's expenditures on secular as distinguished from religious activities. Inspection as to use is a minimal contact.

No one of these three factors standing alone is necessarily controlling; cumulatively all of them shape a narrow and limited relationship with government which involves fewer and less significant contacts than the two state schemes before us in *Lemon* and *DiCenso*. The relationship therefore has less potential for realizing the substantive evils against which the Religion Clauses were intended to protect.

We think that cumulatively these three factors also substantially lessen the potential for divisive religious fragmentation in the political arena. This conclusion is admittedly difficult to document, but neither have appellants pointed to any continuing religious aggravation on this matter in the political processes. Possibly this can be explained by the character and diversity of the recipient colleges and universities and the absence of any intimate continuing relationship or dependency between government and religiously affiliated institutions. The potential for divisiveness inherent in the essentially local problems of primary and secondary schools is significantly less with respect to a college or university whose student constituency is not local but diverse and widely dispersed.

V

Finally, we must consider whether the implementation of the Act inhibits the free exercise of religion in violation of the First Amendment. Appellants claim that the Free Exercise Clause is violated because they are compelled to pay taxes, the proceeds of which in part finance grants under the Act. Appellants, however, are unable to identify any coercion directed at the practice or exercise of their religious beliefs. *Board of Education v. Allen* [*supra* XIV, 1]. Their share of the cost of the grants under the Act is not fundamentally distinguishable from the impact of the tax exemption sustained in *Walz* or the provision of textbooks upheld in *Allen*.

We conclude that the Act does not violate the Religion Clauses of the First Amendment except that part of § 754(b)(2) providing a 20-year limitation on the religious use restrictions contained in § 751(a)(2). We remand to the District Court with directions to enter a judgment consistent with this opinion.

Vacated and remanded.

Justices Douglas, Black, and Marshall concurred in part and dissented in part.

NOTE. *The Tilt of* Tilton. *Hunt v. McNair*, 413 U.S. 734 (1973). South Carolina authorized the issue of revenue bonds to assist institutions of higher learning to construct buildings except those to be used for worship or sectarian instruction. A taxpayer challenged the issue of the bonds for the benefit of the Baptist College at Charleston, a college whose trustees were elected by the South Carolina Baptist Convention. The Supreme Court, 6–3, per Justice Powell, upheld the statute, finding it to pass the three-part *Lemon* test. The plaintiff had produced little evidence as to the Baptist College's actual curriculum; the usual opponents of state aid to religion did not enter the case. Justices Brennan, Douglas, and Marshall dissented, contending at 755 that, by borrowing, the college turned over to the state "a comprehensive and continuing surveillance" of its "educational, religious and fiscal affairs."

Roemer v. Board of Public Works of Maryland, 426 U.S. 736 (1976). Maryland enacted an annual grant program for any private institution of higher learning in the state except ones awarding only theological degrees; none of the money received could be used "for sectarian purposes." The grants were supervised by the Maryland Council for Higher Education, which required the recipient colleges to segregate the grants and to certify that they had not been used for sectarian purposes. In the first year of the program, seventeen institutions, five of them church-related, received grants. Four taxpayers sued to prevent the grants being made to four Catholic colleges. The Court, 5–4, per Justice Blackmun, upheld the program.

Applying *Lemon, supra,* XIV, 1, Justice Blackmun found that the program had a secular purpose, the support of private higher education; that the primary effect was not to advance religion because the encouragement of spiritual development at the four colleges was "only one secondary objective" of each college; that the review of the Maryland Council for High Education was not excessive entanglement; and that because other private institutions were also subsidized the danger of political divisiveness was not great. The Court brushed aside the facts that the colleges had required theology courses, that a number of teachers opened their classes with prayer, and that some members of the college faculties were members of religious orders.

Justices White and Rehnquist concurred, agreeing that the purpose of the legislators was secular and labeling the entanglement test as superfluous. Justices Brennan, Marshall, Stewart, and Stevens dissented. Justice Stevens at 775 referred "to the pernicious tendency of a state subsidy to tempt religious schools to compromise their religious mission without wholly abandoning it." Protestants and Other Americans United and the ACLU were among the original planitiffs, but were dismissed for lack of standing, 387 F. Supp. 1282, 1284 n. 1 (D. Md. 1974); Leo Pfeffer filed an *amicus* brief for PEARL.

Query. Is Justice Stevens's concern a legitimate concern for an official of the government to take into account?

Access

Widmar v. Vincent
454 U.S. 263 (1981)

Ted D. Ayres argued the cause for petitioners. With him on the brief was *Jackson A. Wright.*

James M. Smart, Jr., argued the cause for respondents. With him on the brief was *Michael K. Whitehead.*

Justice Powell delivered the opinion of the court.

This case presents the question whether a state university, which makes its facilities generally available for the activities of registered student groups, may close its facilities to a registered student group desiring to use the facilities for religious worship and religious discussion.

I

It is the stated policy of the University of Missouri at Kansas City to encourage the activities of student organizations. The University officially recognizes over 100 student groups. It routinely provides University facilities for the meetings of registered organizations. Students pay an activity fee of $41 per semester (1978–1979) to help defray the costs to the University.

From 1973 until 1977 a registered religious group named Cornerstone regularly sought and received permission to conduct its meetings in University facilities. In 1977, however, the University informed the group that it could no longer meet in University buildings. The exclusion was based on a regulation, adopted by the Board of Curators in 1972, that prohibits the use of University buildings or grounds "for purposes of religious worship or religious teaching."

Eleven University students, all members of Cornerstone, brought suit to challenge the regulation in the Federal District Court for the Western District of Missouri. They alleged that the University's discrimination against religious activity and discussion violated their rights to free exercise of religion, equal protection, and freedom of speech under the First and Fourteenth Amendments to the Constitution of the United States.

Upon cross-motions for summary judgment, the District Court upheld the challenged regulation. *Chess* v. *Widmar,* 480 F. Supp. 907 (1979). It found the regulation not only justified, but required, by the Establishment Clause of the Federal Constitution. *Id.,* at 916. Under *Tilton v. Richardson [supra],* the court reasoned, the State could not provide facilities for religious use without giving prohibited support to an institution of religion. 480 F. Supp., at 915–916. The District Court rejected the argument that the University could not discriminate against religious speech on the basis of its content. It found religious speech entitled to less protection than other types of expression. *Id.,* at 918.

The Court of Appeals for the Eighth Circuit reversed. *Chess* v. *Widmar,* 635 F.2d 1310 (1980). Rejecting the analysis of the District Court, it viewed the University regulation as a content-based discrimination against religious speech, for which it could find no compelling justification. *Id.,* at 1315–1320. The court held that the Establishment Clause does not bar a policy of equal access, in which facilities are open to groups and speakers of all kinds. *Id.,* at 1317. According to the Court of Appeals, the "primary effect" of such a policy would not be to advance religion, but rather to further the neutral purpose of developing students' " 'social and cultural awareness as well as [their] intellectual curiosity.' " *Ibid.* (quoting from the University bulletin's description of the student activities program, reprinted in *id.,* at 1312, n. 1).

We granted certiorari. 450 U.S. 909. We now affirm.

II

Through its policy of accommodating their meetings, the University has created a forum generally open for use by student groups. Having done so, the University has assumed an obligation to justify its discriminations and exclusions under applicable constitutional norms.[5] The Constitution forbids a State to enforce certain exclusions from a forum generally open to the public, even if it was not required to create the forum in the first place. See, *e.g., Madison Joint School District v. Wisconsin Employment Relations Comm'n,* 429 U.S. 167, 175, and n. 8 (1976) (although a State may conduct business in private session, "[w]here the State has opened a forum for direct citizen

---

[5] This Court has recognized that the campus of a public university, at least for its students, possesses many of the characteristics of a public forum. See generally *Police Dept. of Chicago v. Mosley,* 408 U.S. 92 (1972); *Cox v. Louisiana,* 379 U.S. 536 (1965). "The college classroom with its surrounding environs is peculiarly 'the marketplace of ideas.' " *Healy v. James,* 408 U.S. 169, 180 (1972). Moreover, the capacity of a group or individual "to participate in the intellectual give and take of campus debate . . . [would be] limited by denial of access to the customary media for communicating with the administration, faculty members, and other students." *Id.,* at 181–182. We therefore have held that students enjoy First Amendment rights of speech and association on the campus, and that the "denial [to particular groups] of use of campus facilities for meetings and other appropriate purposes" must be subjected to the level of scrutiny appropriate to any form of prior restraint. *Id.,* at 181, 184.

At the same time, however, our cases have recognized that First Amendment rights must be analyzed "in light of the special characteristics of the school environment." *Tinker v. Des Moines Independent School District,* 393 U.S. 503, 506 (1969). We continue to adhere to that view. A university differs in significant respects from public forums such as streets or parks or even municipal theaters. A university's mission is education, and decisions of this Court have never denied a university's authority to impose reasonable regulations compatible with that mission upon the use of its campus and facilities. We have not held, for example, that a campus must make all of its facilities equally available to students and non-students alike, or that a university must grant free access to all of its grounds or buildings.

involvement," exclusions bear a heavy burden of justification); *Southeastern Promotions, Ltd.* v. *Conrad,* 420 U.S. 546, 555–559 (1975) (because municipal theater was a public forum, city could not exclude a production without satisfying constitutional safeguards applicable to prior restraints).

The University's institutional mission, which it describes as providing a *"secular education"* to its students, Brief for Petitioners 44, does not exempt its actions from constitutional scrutiny. With respect to persons entitled to be there, our cases leave no doubt that the First Amendment rights of speech and association extend to the campuses of state universities. See, *e.g., Healy* v. *James,* 408 U.S. 169, 180 (1972); *Tinker* v. *Des Moines Independent School District,* 393 U.S. 503, 506 (1969); *Shelton* v. *Tucker,* 364 U.S. 479, 487 (1960).

Here UMKC has discriminated against student groups and speakers based on their desire to use a generally open forum to engage in religious worship and discussion. These are forms of speech and association protected by the First Amendment. See, *e.g., Heffron* v. *International Society for Krishna Consciousness, Inc.* [*supra,* XI, I] (1981); *Niemotko* v. *Maryland,* 340 U.S. 268 (1951); *Saia* v. *New York,* 334 U.S. 558 (1948).[6] In order to justify discriminatory exclusion from a public forum based on the religious content of a group's intended speech, the University must therefore satisfy the standard of review appropriate to content-based exclusions. It must show that its regulation is necessary to serve a compelling state interest and that it is narrowly drawn to achieve that end. See *Carey* v. *Brown,* 447 U.S. 455, 461, 464–465 (1980).

III

In this case the University claims a compelling interest in maintaining strict separation of church and State. It derives this interest from the "Establishment Clauses" of both the Federal and Missouri Constitutions.

---

[6] The dissent argues that "religious worship" is not speech generally protected by the "free speech" guarantee of the First Amendment and the "equal protection" guarantee of the Fourteenth Amendment. If "religious worship" were protected "speech," the dissent reasons, "the Religion Clauses would be emptied of any independent meaning in circumstances in which religious practice took the form of speech." *Post,* at 284. This is a novel argument. The dissent does not deny that speech *about* religion is speech entitled to the general protections of the First Amendment. See *post,* at 283–284, and n. 2,286. It does not argue that descriptions of religious experiences fail to qualify as "speech." Nor does it repudiate last Term's decision in *Heffron* v. *International Society for Krishna Consciousness, Inc.,* which assumed that religious appeals to nonbelievers constituted protected "speech." Rather, the dissent seems to attempt a distinction between the kinds of religious speech explicitly protected by our cases and a new class of religious "speech act[s]," *post,* at 285, constituting "worship." There are at least three difficulties with this distinction.

First, the dissent fails to establish that the distinction has intelligible content. There is no indication when "singing hymns, reading scripture, and teaching biblical principles," *post,* at 283, cease to be "singing, teaching, and reading"—all apparently forms of "speech," despite their religious subject matter—and become unprotected "worship."

Second, even if the distinction drew an arguably principled line, it is highly doubtful that it would lie within the judicial competence to administer. Cf. *Fowler* v. *Rhode Island,* [XIII, 1]. Merely to draw the distinction would require the university—and ultimately the courts—to inquire into the significance of words and practices to different religious faiths, and in varying circumstances by the same faith. Such inquiries would tend inevitably to entangle the State with religion in a manner forbidden by our cases. E.g., *Walz* v. *Tax Comm'n,* [*supra,* XIII, 3].

Finally, the dissent fails to establish the *relevance* of the distinction on which it seeks to rely. The dissent apparently wishes to preserve the vitality of the Establishment Clause. See *post,* at 284–285. But it gives no reason why the Establishment Clause, or any other provision of the Constitution, would require different treatment for religious speech designed to win religious converts, see *Heffron, supra,* than for religious worship by persons already converted. It is far from clear that the State gives greater support in the latter case than in the former.

A

The University first argues that it cannot offer its facilities to religious groups and speakers on the terms available to other groups without violating the Establishment Clause of the Constitution of the United States. We agree that the interest of the University in complying with its constitutional obligations may be characterized as compelling. It does not follow, however, that an "equal access" policy would be incompatible with this Court's Establishment Clause cases. Those cases hold that a policy will not offend the Establishment Clause if it can pass a three-pronged test: "First, the [governmental policy] must have a secular legislative purpose; second, its principal or primary effect must be one that neither advances nor inhibits religion . . .; finally, the [policy] must not foster 'an excessive government entanglement with religion.'" *Lemon v. Kurtzman* [XIV, 1]. See *Committee for Public Education v. Regan* [XIV, 2]; *Roemer v. Maryland Public Works Bd.* [*supra*].

In this case two prongs of the test are clearly met. Both the District Court and the Court of Appeals held that an open-forum policy, including nondiscrimination against religious speech would have a secular purpose and would avoid entanglement with religion. But the District Court concluded, and the University argues here, that allowing religious groups to share the limited public forum would have the "primary effect" of advancing religion.

The University's argument misconceives the nature of this case. The question is not whether the creation of a religious forum would violate the Establishment Clause. The University has opened its facilities for use by student groups, and the question is whether it can now exclude groups because of the content of their speech. See *Healy v. James,* 408 U.S. 169 (1972). In this context we are unpersuaded that the primary effect of the public forum, open to all forms of discourse, would be to advance religion.

We are not oblivious to the range of an open forum's likely effects. It is possible—perhaps even foreseeable—that religious groups will benefit from access to University facilities. But this Court has explained that a religious organization's enjoyment of merely "incidental" benefits does not violate the prohibition against the "primary advancement" of religion. *Committee for Public Education v. Nyquist* [*supra* XIV, 1]; see, *e.g., Roemer v. Maryland Public Works Bd.* [*supra*]; *Hunt v. McNair* [*supra*]; *McGowan v. Maryland* [XIII, 2].

We are satisfied that any religious benefits of an open forum at UMKC would be "incidental" within the meaning of our cases. Two factors are especially relevant.

First, an open forum in a public university does not confer any imprimatur of state approval on religious sects or practices. As the Court of Appeals quite aptly stated, such a policy "would no more commit the University . . . to religious goals" than it is "now committed to the goals of the Students for a Democratic Society, the Young Socialist Alliance," or any other group eligible to use its facilities. 635 F. 2d, at 1317.[14]

Second, the forum is available to a broad class of nonreligious as well as religious speakers; there are over 100 recognized student groups at UMKC. The provision of benefits to so broad a spectrum of groups is an important index of secular effect. See,

---

[14] University students are, of course, young adults. They are less impressionable than younger students and should be able to appreciate that the University's policy is one of neutrality toward religion. See *Tilton v. Richardson* [XIV, 3]. The University argues that the Cornerstone students themselves admitted in affidavits that "[s]tudents know that if something is on campus, then it is a student organization, and they are more likely to feel comfortable attending a meeting." Affidavit of Florian Frederick Chess, App. 18, 19. In light of the large number of groups meeting on campus, however, we doubt students could draw any reasonable inference of University support from the mere fact of a campus meeting place. The University's student handbook already notes that the University's name will not "be identified in any way with the aims, policies, programs, products, or opinions of any organization or its members." 1980–1981 UMKC Student Handbook 25.

e.g., Wolman v. Walter [XIV, 1]; *Committee for Public Education v. Nyquist* [XIV, 1]. If the Establishment Clause barred the extension of general benefits to religious groups, "a church could not be protected by the police and fire departments, or have its public sidewalk kept in repair." *Roemer v. Maryland Public Works Bd., supra,* at 747 (plurality opinion); quoted in *Committee for Public Education v. Regan* [*supra* XIV, 1]. At least in the absence of empirical evidence that religious groups will dominate UMKC's open forum, we agree with the Court of Appeals that the advancement of religion would not be the forum's "primary effect."

B

Arguing that the State of Missouri has gone further than the Federal Constitution in proscribing indirect state support for religion, the University claims a compelling interest in complying with the applicable provisions of the Missouri constitution.

The Missouri courts have not ruled whether a general policy of accommodating student groups, applied equally to those wishing to gather to engage in religious and nonreligious speech, would offend the State Constitution. We need not, however, determine how the Missouri courts would decide this issue. It is also unnecessary for us to decide whether, under the Supremacy Clause, a state interest, derived from its own constitution, could ever outweigh free speech interests protected by the First Amendment. We limit our holding to the case before us.

On one hand, respondents' First Amendment rights are entitled to special constitutional solicitude. Our cases have required the most exacting scrutiny in cases in which a State undertakes to regulate speech on the basis of its content. See, *e.g., Carey v. Brown,* 447 U.S. 455 (1980); *Police Dept. of Chicago v. Mosley,* 408 U.S. 92 (1972). On the other hand, the state interest asserted here—in achieving greater separation of church and State than is already ensured under the Establishment Clause of the Federal constitution— is limited by the Free Exercise Clause and in this case by the Free Speech Clause as well. In this constitutional context, we are unable to recognize the State's interest as sufficiently "compelling" to justify content-based discrimination against respondents' religious speech.

IV

Our holding in this case in no way undermines the capacity of the University to establish reasonable time, place, and manner regulations. Nor do we question the right of the University to make academic judgments as to how best to allocate scarce resources or "to determine for itself on academic grounds who may teach, what may be taught, how it shall be taught, and who may be admitted to study." *Sweezy v. New Hampshire,* 354 U.S. 234, 263 (1957) (Frankfurter, J., concurring in result); see *University of California Regents v. Bakke,* 438 U.S. 265, 312–313 (1978) (opinion of Powell, J., announcing the judgment of the Court). Finally, we affirm the continuing validity of cases, *e.g., Healy v. James,* 408 U.S., at 188–189, that recognize a university's right to exclude even First Amendment activities that violate reasonable campus rules or substantially interfere with the opportunity of other students to obtain an education.

The basis for our decision is narrow. Having created a forum generally open to student groups, the University seeks to enforce a content-based exclusion of religious speech. Its exclusionary policy violates the fundamental principle that a state regulation of speech should be content-neutral, and the University is unable to justify this violation under applicable constitutional standards.

For this reason, the decision of the Court of Appeals is

Affirmed.

Justice Stevens concurred in the judgment.

Justice White, dissenting:

[After referring to *Stone v. Graham* (XIV, 2) *Abington School District v. Schempp* (XIV, 2), *Engel v. Vitale* (XIV, 2), and *Torcaso v. Watkins* (XI, 1)] If the majority were right that no distinction may be drawn between verbal acts of worship and other verbal acts, all of these cases would have to be reconsidered. Although I agree that the line may be difficult to draw in many cases, surely the majority cannot seriously suggest that no line may ever be drawn. If that were the case, the majority would have to uphold the University's right to offer a class entitled "Sunday Mass." Under the majority's view such a class would be—as a matter of constitutional principle—indistinguishable from a class entitled "The History of the Catholic Church."

Exemption

Bob Jones University v. United States
461 U.S. 574 (1983)

William G. McNairy argued the cause for petitioner in No. 81–1. With him on the briefs were *Claude C. Pierce, Edward C. Winslow,* and *John H. Small. William Bentley Ball* argued the cause for petitioner in No. 81–3. With him on the briefs were *Philip J. Murren* and *Richard E. Connell.*

Assistant Attorney General Reynolds argued the cause for the United States in both cases. With him on the briefs were *Acting Solicitor General Wallace* and *Deputy Assistant Attorney General Cooper.*

William T. Coleman, Jr., pro se, by invitation of the Court, 456 U.S. 922, argued the cause as *amicus curiae* urging affirmance. With him on the brief were *Richard C. Warmer, Donald T. Bliss, John W. Stamper, Ira M. Feinberg,* and *Eric Schnapper.*

Chief Justice Burger delivered the opinion of the Court.

We granted certiorari to decide whether petitioners, nonprofit private schools that prescribe and enforce racially discriminatory admissions standards on the basis of religious doctrine, qualify as tax-exempt organizations under § 501(c)(3) of the Internal Revenue Code of 1954.

I

A

Until 1970, the Internal Revenue Service granted tax-exempt status to private schools, without regard to their racial admissions policies, under § 501(c)(3) of the Internal Revenue Code, 26 U.S.C. § 501(c)(3), and granted charitable deductions for contributions to such schools under § 170 of the Code, 26 U.S.C. § 170.

On January 12, 1970, a three-judge District Court for the District of Columbia issued a preliminary injunction prohibiting the IRS from according tax-exempt status to private schools in Mississippi that discriminated as to admissions on the basis of race. *Green v. Kennedy,* 309 F. Supp. 1127, appeal dism'd *sub nom. Cannon v. Green,* 398 U.S. 956 (1970). Thereafter, in July 1970, the IRS concluded that it could "no longer legally justify allowing tax-exempt status [under § 501(c)(3)] to private schools which practice racial discrimination." IRS News Release, July 7, 1970, reprinted in App. in No. 81–3, p. A235. At the same time, the IRS announced that it could not "treat gifts to such schools as charitable deductions for income tax purposes [under § 170]." *Ibid.* By letter dated November 30, 1970, the IRS formally notified private schools, including those involved in this litigation, of this change in policy, "applicable to all private schools in the United States at all levels of education." See *id.,* at A232.

On June 30, 1971, the three-judge District Court issued its opinion on the merits of the Mississippi challenge. *Green v. Connally,* 330 F. Supp. 1150, summarily aff'd *sub nom. Coit v. Green,* 404 U.S. 997 (1971). That court approved the IRS's amended construction of the Tax Code. The court also held that racially discriminatory private schools were not entitled to exemption under § 501(c)(3) and that donors were not entitled to deductions for contributions to such schools under § 170. The court permanently enjoined the Commissioner of Internal Revenue from approving tax-exempt status for any school in Mississippi that did not publicly maintain a policy of nondiscrimination.

The revised policy on discrimination was formalized in Revenue Ruling 71–447, 1971–2 Cum. Bull. 230:

"Both the courts and the Internal Revenue Service have long recognized that the statutory requirement of being 'organized and operated exclusively for religious, charitable, . . . or educational purposes' was intended to express the basic common law concept [of 'charity']. . . . All charitable trusts, educational or otherwise, are subject to the requirement that the purpose of the trust may not be illegal or contrary to public policy."

Based on the "national policy to discourage racial discrimination in education," the IRS ruled that "a [private] school not having a racially nondiscriminatory policy as to students is not 'charitable' within the common law concepts reflected in sections 170 and 501(c)(3) of the Code." *Id.,* at 231.

The application of the IRS construction of these provisions to petitioners, two private schools with racially discriminatory admissions policies, is now before us.

B

No. 81–3, Bob Jones University v. United States

Bob Jones University is a nonprofit corporation located in Greenville, S.C. Its purpose is "to conduct an institution of learning . . ., giving special emphasis to the Christian religion and the ethics revealed in the Holy Scriptures." Certificate of Incorporation, Bob Jones University, Inc., of Greenville, S.C., reprinted in App. in No. 81–3, p. A119. The corporation operates a school with an enrollment of approximately 5,000 students, from kindergarten through college and graduate school. Bob Jones University is not affiliated with any religious denomination, but is dedicated to the teaching and propagation of its fundamentalist Christian religious beliefs. It is both a religious and educational institution. Its teachers are required to be devout Christians, and all courses at the University are taught according to the Bible. Entering students are screened as to their religious beliefs, and their public and private conduct is strictly regulated by standards promulgated by University authorities.

The sponsors of the University genuinely believe that the Bible forbids interracial dating and marriage. To effectuate these views, Negroes were completely excluded until 1971. From 1971 to May 1975, the University accepted no applications from unmarried Negroes but did accept applications from Negroes married within their race.

Following the decision of the United States Court of Appeals for the Fourth Circuit in *McCrary v. Runyon,* 515 F. 2d 1082 (1975), aff'd, 427 U.S. 160 (1976), prohibiting racial exclusion from private schools, the University revised its policy. Since May 29, 1975, the University has permitted unmarried Negroes to enroll; but a disciplinary rule prohibits interracial dating and marriage. That rule reads:

"There is to be no interracial dating.

"1. Students who are partners in an interracial marriage will be expelled.

"2. Students who are members of or affiliated with any group or organization which holds as one of its goals or advocates interracial marriage will be expelled.

"3. Students who date outside of their own race will be expelled.

"4. Students who espouse, promote, or encourage others to violate the University's dating rules and regulations will be expelled." App. in No. 81–3, p. A197.

The University continues to deny admission to applicants engaged in an interracial marriage or known to advocate interracial marriage or dating. *Id.,* at A277.

Until 1970, the IRS extended tax-exempt status to Bob Jones University under § 501(c)(3). By the letter of November 30, 1970, that followed the injunction issued in *Green v. Kennedy,* 309 F. Supp. 1127 (DC 1970), the IRS formally notified the University of the change in IRS policy, and announced its intention to challenge the tax-exempt status of private schools practicing racial discrimination in their admissions policies.

After failing to obtain an assurance of tax exemption through administrative means, the University instituted an action in 1971 seeking to enjoin the IRS from revoking the school's tax-exempt status. That suit culminated in *Bob Jones University v. Simon,* 416 U.S. 725 (1974), in which this Court held that the Anti-Injunction Act of the Internal Revenue Code, 26 U.S.C. § 7421(a), prohibited the University from obtaining judicial review by way of injunctive action before the assessment or collection of any tax.

Thereafter, on April 16, 1975, the IRS notified the University of the proposed revocation of its tax-exempt status. On January 19, 1976, the IRS officially revoked the University's tax-exempt status, effective as of December 1, 1970, the day after the University was formally notified of the change in IRS policy. The University subsequently filed returns under the Federal Unemployment Tax Act for the period from December 1, 1970, to December 31, 1975, and paid a tax totalling $21 on one employee for the calendar year of 1975. After its request for a refund was denied, the University instituted the present action, seeking to recover the $21 it had paid to the IRS. The Government counterclaimed for unpaid federal unemployment taxes for the taxable years 1971 through 1975, in the amount of $489,675.59, plus interest.

The United States District Court for the District of South Carolina held that revocation of the University's tax-exempt status exceeded the delegated powers of the IRS, was improper under the IRS rulings and procedures, and violated the University's rights under the Religion Clauses of the First Amendment. 468 F. Supp. 890, 907 (1978). The court accordingly ordered the IRS to pay the University the $21 refund it claimed and rejected the IRS's counterclaim.

The Court of Appeals for the Fourth Circuit, in a divided opinion, reversed. 639 F. 2d 147 (1980). Citing *Green v. Connally,* 330 F. Supp. 1150 (DC 1971), with approval, the Court of Appeals concluded that § 501(c)(3) must be read against the background of charitable trust law. To be eligible for an exemption under that section, an institution must be "charitable" in the common-law sense, and therefore must not be contrary to public policy. In the court's view, Bob Jones University did not meet this requirement, since its "racial policies violated the clearly defined public policy, rooted in our Constitution, condemning racial discrimination and, more specifically, the government policy against subsidizing racial discrimination in education, public or private." 639 F. 2d, at 151. The court held that the IRS acted within its statutory authority in revoking the University's tax-exempt status. Finally, the Court of Appeals rejected petitioner's arguments that the revocation of the tax exemption violated the Free Exercise and Establishment Clauses of the First Amendment. The case was remanded to the District Court with instructions to dismiss the University's claim for a refund and to reinstate the IRS's counterclaim.

II

A

. . .

When the Government grants exemptions or allows deductions all taxpayers are affected; the very fact of the exemption or deduction for the donor means that other taxpayers can be said to be indirect and vicarious "donors." Charitable exemptions are justified on the basis that the exempt entity confers a public benefit—a benefit which the society or the community may not itself choose or be able to provide, or which supplements and advances the work of public institutions already supported by tax revenues. History buttresses logic to make clear that, to warrant exemption under § 501(c)(3), an institution must fall within a category specified in that section and must demonstrably serve and be in harmony with the public interest. The institution's purpose must not be so at odds with the common community conscience as to undermine any public benefit that might otherwise be conferred.

B

We are bound to approach these questions with full awareness that determinations of public benefit and public policy are sensitive matters with serious implications for the institutions affected; a declaration that a given institution is not "charitable" should be made only where there can be no doubt that the activity involved is contrary to a fundamental public policy. But there can no longer be any doubt that racial discrimination in education violates deeply and widely accepted views of elementary justice. Prior to 1954, public education in many places still was conducted under the pall of *Plessy v. Ferguson,* 163 U.S. 537 (1896); racial segregation in primary and secondary education prevailed in many parts of the country. See, *e.g.,* Segregation and the Fourteenth Amendment in the States (B. Reams & P. Wilson eds. 1975). This Court's decision in *Brown v. Board of Education,* 347 U.S. 483 (1954), signalled an end to that era. Over the past quarter of a century, every pronouncement of this Court and myriad Acts of Congress and Executive Orders attest a firm national policy to prohibit racial segregation and discrimination in public education.

  . . .

The governmental interest at stake here is compelling. As discussed in Part II-B, *supra,* the Government has a fundamental, overriding interest in eradicating racial discrimination in education—discrimination that prevailed, with official approval, for the first 165 years of this Nation's constitutional history. That governmental interest substantially outweighs whatever burden denial of tax benefits places on petitioners' exercise of their religious beliefs. The interests asserted by petitioners cannot be accommodated with that compelling governmental interest, see *United States v. Lee, supra,* at 259–260; and no "less restrictive means," see *Thomas v. Review Board of Indiana Employment Security Div., supra,* at 718, are available to achieve the governmental interest.

  . . . *Affirmed.*

Justice Powell wrote separately, concurring in part and concurring in the judgment.

Justice Rehnquist dissented.

Query. The amicus brief on behalf of the Mennonites put forward these considerations:

There is in our consciousness a strong sense of an often torturous history, in which our predecessors passed through periods of extreme hardship and suffering, a history that includes the records of many martyrs who suffered for those tenets that still constitute our confession of faith. A notable feature of our church history is that of a church in a migratory status, migrating from one place, or nation, to another in search of religious consideration or toleration, a defenseless people looking for a place to be. This has left within us an extremely high regard for religious liberty. We consider the religious liberty that this nation concedes as possibly its greatest virtue. . . . The tremendous stress that we have faced and face when we find ourselves in conflict between the will of secular government and what we understand as the will of God constitutes one of the most difficult aspects of our religious experience.

Our faith and understanding of scripture enjoin respect and obedience to the secular governments under which we live. We recognize them as institutions established by

God for order in society. For that reason alone, without the added distress of punitive action for failure to do so, we always exercise ourselves to be completely law abiding. Our religious beliefs, however, are very deeply held. When these beliefs collide with the demands of society, our highest allegiance must be toward God, and we must say with men of God of the past, 'We must obey God rather than men,' and *these are the crisis from which we would be spared* [*Brief Amicus Curaie in Support of Petition for Writ of Certiorari on Behalf of Church of God in Christ, Mennonite* 1–4].

Does the Court adequately respond to the Mennonites' concerns?

For a particularly penetrating criticism of *Bob Jones University* as "a case that gives too much to the statist determinations of the normative world," see Robert M. Cover, "The Supreme Court 1982 Term—Foreword: *Nomos* and Narrative," 97 *Harvard Law Review* 4, 66 (1983).

Query. If an institution's purpose must not be seriously "at odds with the common community conscience" and cannot "be contrary to public policy," what is the status of a college expelling students who have an abortion? Would the status of the college change if the Equal Rights Amendment was adopted? After adoption of the ERA, what would be the tax-exempt status of a church refusing to ordain women?

NOTE. Compare *Oral Roberts University v. American Bar Association*, 8 *Legal Aff. MAN*, 205 (N.D. Ill. 1981). Like a number of states, Oklahoma prescribed as a condition for admission to the bar that the applicant have attended a school accredited by the American Bar Association. The ABA in 1981 refused to approve the accreditation of the law school of Oral Roberts University, which required applicants to the law school to sign a statement of Christian religious belief. The university sued, alleging that its free exercise of religion was being infringed. The court found that the ABA was engaged in state action and that its action was an unconstitutional infringement. Within the month the ABA revised its policy, Leonard J. Nelson III, "Religious Discrimination, Christian Mission, and Legal Education: The Implications of the Oral Roberts University Accreditation Controversy," 15 *Cumberland Law Review* 663, 679–680 (1985). See also Cassou and Curran "Secular Orthodoxy and Sacred Freedoms: Accreditation of Church-Related Law Schools," 11 *Journal of College and University Law* 293–322 (1984) pointing to hostility in the Association of American Law Schools (AALS) toward religious schools and speculating on the vulnerability of the AALS to antitrust suits.

Individual Assistance

NOTE. *Witters v. Washington Department of Services for the Blind*, 106 S.Ct. 748 (1986). Larry Witters applied for aid to the Washington Commission for the Blind, a state agency authorized to help the visually handicapped in obtaining education. Witters was a student at Inland Empire School of the Bible, a Christian college in Spokane. The commission denied him assistance on the ground that the Washington Constitution, Art. 1, sec. 11, provided that no public money should "be applied to any religious worship, exercise, or instruction." The Washington Supreme court upheld the commission, on the grounds of the First Amendment and *Lemon v. Kurtzman* [*supra*, XIV, 1]. The United States Supreme Court reversed, remanding the case for the Washington court to apply its own constitution. Justice Marshall writing for the Court found no violations of the First Amendment or *Lemon*. He wrote at 752: "Any aid provided under Washington's program that ultimately flows to religious institutions does so only as a result of the genuinely independent and private choices of aid recipients." Remarkably, in a case involving aid to religion, all the Justices agreed in the result, although reaching it by diverse routes.

One cannot say that the case is one of the blind leading the blind, but it would be difficult to believe that Witters's handicap did not make even the staunchest defender of the wall hesitate to hold help for him illegal.

NOTE. *The Importance of a Written Constitution.* Does the present state of affairs in America result primarily from the First Amendment and its interpretation by the Supreme Court or does it flow from other general social considerations? Consider the following from a book review by myself of St. John A. Robillard, *Religion and the Law* (1984) in 33 *American Journal of Comparative Law* 765 (1985):

Six areas exist in which religion is special and privileged by both British and American law: (1) taxation, both as to income tax and property tax, so that large financial benefits are governmentally bestowed on religious bodies; (2) charitable status, so that religion has the favored position of a public charity; (3) clerical status, so that, for example, clerics do not fall under the National Labor Relations Act in this country, and the Sex Discrimination Act in Britain has two exemptions relating to the ministry; (4) the celebration of Sunday, so that in both nations this Christian holy day is set aside as the usual day of rest even though a hodgepodge of exceptions make the day far from a Puritan sabbath in either country; (5) marriage, so that bigamy is a crime in Britain and in every state despite the number of Moslems in England and the general relaxation of laws on sex in both countries; (6) priestly services in state institutions, so that in both countries the armed forces and prisons have chaplains representing the major denominations. The different constitutional systems of the two countries have not resulted in substantially different results in these significant matters.

Three areas exist where there are some differences:

(1) The Church of England, still the established church of the land, has courts which can compel testimony and hold persons in contempt; decisions of these courts are part of the general law of England. The church's bishops are appointed by the Prime Minister although convention dictates that the government select from the church's nominees. Parliament is still able to control the church's liturgy and Prayer Book. In practice, the benefits the church receives are not large, and the government's normal deference to ecclesiastical preferences results in equally limited government interference. No comparable relationship exists in the United States.

(2) By the Education Act 1944, religious education is undertaken by English state schools according to "the agreed syllabus" for a given local area. The agreed syllabus is drawn up by such religious groups as the local education authorities choose to invite to write it; the invited groups must then agree unanimously, a provision that no doubt assures a certain blandness if not tepidity. Communism and humanism may form part of the content of the syllabus; Christianity is always a major part. A teacher may be dismissed for teaching contrary to the syllabus; in *Watson v. Hertfordshire County Council* (1977, unreported) a fundamentalist was discharged for teaching Genesis literally when the syllabus stipulated that it was symbolic.

In fact, an agreed syllabus is closely followed by only 17% of the schools; over half even ignore the statutory requirement that religious education be provided to all their pupils. Local option seems to have become *laissez-faire*. In the same way the Education Act 1944 requires that every day every school begin with "collective worship on the part of the pupils" in a way not distinctive of any particular religious denomination. In practice, as Robilliard reports, there is no uniformity as to what "collective worship" means, and worship varies from hymn singing to "happenings". The evidence also suggests no very general compliance with the requirement that the service occur daily.

At a formal level, the American scene is very different. The Supreme Court has meticulously purified the public schools of the Bible, the Ten Commandments, and prayer, Christian or nondenominational. One may, however, wonder if the practical results—since the Bible may still be studied in American schools as literature—are so different from a British "agreed syllabus"; and whether an American high school assembly, with the religious words of our national anthem still sung, is a different species of collective worship than a "happening" in a British state school. Statutory as well as constitutional law on public education is different in the two countries. Much more empirical information is needed before one can be certain of the true differences in practice.

(3) The Supreme Court has gone very far in interpreting the draft laws to recognize conscientious objection to war; in England the recognition of conscientious objection in 1916 and again in 1939 was left to special tribunals whose decisions could not be reviewed by the regular courts. On the face of it at least, the British C.O. has had to proceed on a much more ad hoc basis than his American counterpart. On the other hand, the American decisions are post-World War II, and British tribunals might behave similarly if a British draft law were now in force. Any difference is in the decisions of two different eras.

On other issues of conscience, there is some variation. Robilliard, basing himself on dicta in the Court of Appeal, believes that in Britain there is a right to suicide. But there is only a qualified right to refuse to perform an abortion, and conscientious objection to abortion is a bar to a doctor's advancement in gynecology. A Briton has a right to kill himself but no unqualified right to refrain from killing others. In America there is no generally recognized right to suicide, and there is a right, generally acknowledged by statutes, to refrain from committing an abortion. The difference appears to arise not from constitutional considerations but political realities: the right-to-life movement is far stronger in the United States than in Britain.

The chief difference produced by the different constitutional systems of the two countries appears to be the status of the Church of England, whose anomalous and not very significant privileges are owed to history. Robilliard speaks wistfully of "the absence of any clear landmark for the [British] courts, such as a Bill of Rights," but the Bill of Rights in America has led to blurrier and blurrier lines. Words in a constitution cannot create clarity. Nor is logic much help. It is over a century since Holmes observed that logic was not the life of the law, but the expectation that logic will rule dies hard. What the courts, the legislature, and the citizenry are doing in the field of religion is balancing values—values of faith, of tolerance, of tradition, of charity, etc. The balance is far more affected by economic structures, political movements, historical survivals, and the cultural level of the countries than by specific constitutional or statutory prescriptions.

FIFTEEN

Political Participation

1. THE RIGHTS OF CHURCHES

Kedroff v. St. Nicholas Cathedral, supra, XII, 3, invalidated a statute because it prohibited "the free exercise of an ecclesiastical right, the Church's choice of its hierarchy." Mark De Wolfe Howe, then the leading academic authority on the law and churches, celebrated this sentence as recognizing "the liberty of the group as something different from the individual liberties of its members," Howe, "Foreword: Political Theory and the Nature of Liberty, The Supreme Court, 1952 Term," 67 *Harvard Law Review* 91 at 93 (1953). Howe saw the Court as acknowledging "a corporate liberty" for churches which political theorists such as John Neville Figgis had long ago claimed as their due.

A large number of cases had, of course, recognized the religious rights of individuals because they were exercised on behalf of a group and as a group activity. For example, *Cantwell v. Connecticut, supra,* XI, 1, the first of these cases, identified Cantwell's sidewalk proselytizing as religious because he was a Jehovah's Witness. But it was his right to free exercise, not the Jehovah's Witnesses' as a body, that was vindicated. In this line of cases, *Wisconsin v. Yoder, supra,* XI, 5, is the most striking. The defendants prevailed because their way of life was part of a church's way of life. Again, however, it was the individual believers' rights that were asserted and upheld.

In *Larson v. Valente,* 456 U.S. 228 (1982), a Minnesota statute required all charitable organizations to register with the state and to report their receipts and costs of management and fundraising. The statute excepted "a religious society" that received more than half of its contributions from its members. The Holy Spirit Association for the Unification of World Christianity (Unification Church) and four followers of the church sought a declaration that the statute abridged their free exercise of religion. The state defended the statute on the ground that members of a religious organization would exercise sufficient control over a religious organization's activities when they contributed over half of the funds; the state did not have to exercise close supervision.

The Supreme Court, speaking through Justice Brennan, found the state's rationale implausible. The Court took notice of the legislative discussion that indicated that the sponsors of the law did not want to reach a Catholic archdiocese and did want to reach the Unification Church. The Court held at 254 that the 50 percent rule "effects the *selective* legislative imposition of burdens and advantages upon particular denominations." The Court held at 255 that by achieving an "official denominational preference" the statute violated the establishment clause. Justices Rehnquist, White, O'Connor, and Chief Justice Burger dissented on the ripeness of the case for constitutional adjudication; Justices Rehnquist and White dissented on the merits. Still left to be litigated was the basic question whether the Unification Church was a religious organization. Implicitly, however, the majority opinion recognized a corporate right in a church to protest denominational preferences by a state.

Coupled with *Kedroff*, *Larson* affords a basis for contending that churches as well as individuals are protected by the religion clauses.

2. EXERCISE OF GOVERNMENTAL POWER BY CHURCHES AND CHURCHMEN

In *Larkin v. Grendel's Den, Inc.*, 459 U.S. 116 (1982), a Massachusetts law gave churches a discretionary power to veto liquor licenses within 500 feet of a church. Grendel's Den, a restaurant in Harvard Square, applied for a liquor license. The Holy Cross Armenian Catholic Church, ten feet away, objected; the license was denied. Grendel's Den sued the licensing boards. Represented by Laurence Tribe, a leading constitutional law professor at Harvard Law School, the restaurant raised the issue that the statute was an establishment of religion. The Supreme Court, 8–1, per Chief Justice Burger, held that the statute had the primary and principal effect of advancing religion for two reasons: (1) the churches had the power to use their veto in a way that was not "religiously neutral"; (2) "the mere appearance of a joint exercise of legislative authority by Church and State provides a significant symbolic benefit to religion in the minds of some." Moreover, the Court said at 126–127, the statute entangled the churches with the government: "The Framers did not set up a system of government in which important, discretionary governmental powers would be delegated to or shared with religious institutions." Justice Rehnquist dissented, noting that the state could absolutely ban liquor licenses within a given distance of a church and finding the Massachusetts statute "sensible."

See also State v. Celmer, 80 N.J. 405, 404 A.2d 1 (1979), *cert. denied*, 444 U.S. 951 (1979). The defendant was convicted of drunk driving in Ocean Grove municipal court. He challenged the state statutes that incorporated "The Ocean Grove Camp Meeting Association of the United Methodist Church" and gave this association power to construct and maintain public highways and to "preserve order" in Ocean Grove. The municipal court had been established by the Association, ten out of twenty-six of whose trustees had to be Methodist ministers. The court found it to be "first and foremost a religious organization" and concluded: "Such a fusion of secular and ecclesiastical power not only violates both the letter and the spirit of the First Amendment, it also runs afoul of the 'establishment clause' of our own State constitution, see N.J. Const. (1947) Art I, ¶ 4."

In *Oregon v. City of Rajneeshpuram*, 598 F.Supp. 1208 (D. Ore. 1984), the state moved to void the incorporation of the City of Rajneeshpuram, alleging:

The primary purpose for establishing the City of Rajneeshpuram was to advance the religion of Rajneeshism. The City was founded to fulfill a religious vision. The City was designed and functions as a spiritual mecca for followers of the Bhagwan worldwide. It serves as a monument to and the residence of the Bhagwan, and as a gathering place for followers at institutions of religious training and at three annual religious festivals [*ibid.* at 1211].

The state contended that to pay public monies or provide public services to the City of Rajneeshpuram would violate the constitutions of Oregon and the United States. The defendants replied that the benefits to their religion were incidental, like police and fire services; and that to deny them the right to run the City of Rajneeshpuram would be to deny them the free exercise of their religion.

On the defendants' motion to dismiss, accepting the state's claims as true, Judge Helen J. Frye ruled at 1216:

the potential injury to the anti-establishment principle of the first amendment by the existence and operation of the City of Rajneeshpuram clearly outweighs the potential harm to the defendants' free exercise of religious rights. To deny defendants the right to operate a city is the only means of achieving a compelling state and federal interest— that of avoiding an establishment of religion.

McDaniel v. Paty
435 U.S. 618 (1978)

Frederic S. Le Clercq argued the cause and filed a brief for appellant.

Kenneth R. Herrell, Assistant Attorney General of Tennessee, argued the cause for appellees. With him on the brief for appellees Hassler et al. were *Brooks McLemore,* Attorney General, and *C. Hayes Cooney,* Chief Deputy Attorney General. *Philip C. Lawerence* filed a brief for appellee Paty.

Chief Justice Burger announced the judgment of the Court and delivered an opinion in which Justice Powell, Justice Rehnquist, and Justice Stevens joined.

The question presented by this appeal is whether a Tennessee statute barring "Minister[s] of the Gospel, or priest[s] of any denomination whatever" from serving as delegates to the State's limited constitutional convention deprived appellant McDaniel, an ordained minister, of the right to the free exercise of religion guaranteed by the First Amendment and made applicable to the States by the Fourteenth Amendment. The First Amendment forbids all laws "prohibiting the free exercise" of religion.

I

In its first Constitution, in 1796, Tennessee disqualified ministers from serving as legislators. That disqualifying provision has continued unchanged since its adoption; it is now Art. 9, § 1, of the State Constitution. The state legislature applied this provision to candidates for delegate to the State's 1977 limited constitutional convention when it enacted ch. 848, § 4, of 1976 Tenn. Pub. Acts: "Any citizen of the state who can qualify for membership in the House of Representatives of the General Assembly may become a candidate for delegate to the convention. . . ."

McDaniel, an ordained minister of a Baptist Church in Chattanooga, Tenn., filed as a candidate for delegate to the constitutional convention. An opposing candidate, appellee Selma Cash Paty, sued in the Chancery Court for a declaratory judgment that McDaniel was disqualified from serving as a delegate and for a judgment striking his name from the ballot. Chancellor Franks of the Chancery Court held that § 4 of ch. 848 violated the First and Fourteenth Amendments to the Federal Constitution and declared McDaniel eligible for the office of delegate. Accordingly, McDaniel's name remained on the ballot and in the ensuing election he was elected by a vote almost equal to that of three opposing candidates.

After the election, the Tennessee Supreme Court reversed the Chancery Court, holding that the disqualification of clergy imposed no burden upon "religious belief" and restricted "religious action . . . [only] in the lawmaking process of government—where religious action is absolutely prohibited by the establishment clause. . . ." 547 S. W. 2d 897, 903 (1977). The state interests in preventing the establishment of religion and in avoiding the divisiveness and tendency to channel political activity along religious lines, resulting from clergy participation in political affairs, were deemed by that court sufficiently weighty to justify the disqualification, notwithstanding the guarantee of the Free Exercise Clause.

We noted probable jurisdiction. 432 U. S. 905 (1977).

II

A

The disqualification of ministers from legislative office was a practice carried from England by seven of the original States; later six new States similarly excluded clergymen from some political offices. 1 A. Stokes, Church and State in the United States 622 (1950) (hereafter Stokes). In England the practice of excluding clergy from the House of Commons was justified on a variety of grounds: to prevent dual officeholding, that is, membership by a minister in both Parliament and Convocation; to insure that the priest or deacon devoted himself to his "sacred calling" rather than to "such mundane activities as were appropriate to a member of the House of Commons"; and to prevent ministers, who after 1533 were subject to the Crown's powers over the benefices of the clergy, from using membership in Commons to diminish its independence by increasing the influence of the King and the nobility. *In re MacManaway,* [1951] A.C. 161, 164, 170–171.

The purpose of the several States in providing for disqualification was primarily to assure the success of a new political experiment, the separation of church and state. Stokes 622. Prior to 1776, most of the 13 Colonies had some form of an established, or government-sponsored, church. *Id.,* at 364–446. Even after ratification of the First Amendment, which prohibited the Federal Government from following such a course, some States continued pro-establishment provisions. See *id.,* at 408, 418–427, 444. Massachusetts, the last State to accept disestablishment, did so in 1833. *Id.,* at 426–427.

In light of this history and a widespread awareness during that period of undue and often dominant clerical influence in public and political affairs here, in England, and on the Continent, it is not surprising that strong views were held by some that one way to assure disestablishment was to keep clergymen out of public office. Indeed, some of the foremost political philosophers and statesmen of that period held such views regarding the clergy. Earlier, John Locke argued for confining the authority of the English clergy "within the bounds of the church, nor can it in any manner be extended to civil affairs; because the church itself is a thing absolutely separate and distinct from the commonwealth." 5 Works of John Locke 21 (C. Baldwin ed. 1824). Thomas Jefferson initially advocated such a position in his 1783 draft of a constitution for Virginia.[4] James Madison, however, disagreed and vigorously urged the position which in our view accurately reflects the spirit and purpose of the Religion Clauses of the First Amendment. Madison's response to Jefferson's position was:

---

[4] 6 Papers of Thomas Jefferson 297 (J. Boyd ed. 1952). Jefferson later concluded that experience demonstrated there was no need to exclude clergy from elected office. In a letter to Jeremiah Moor in 1800, he stated: "[I]n the same scheme of a constitution [for Virginia which I prepared in 1783, I observe] an abridgment of the right of being elected, which after 17 years more of experience & reflection, I do not approve. It is the incapacitation of a clergyman from being elected. The clergy, by getting themselves established by law, & ingrafted into the machine of government, have been a very formidable engine against the civil and religious rights of man. They are still so in many countries & even in some of these United States. Even in 1783 we doubted the stability of our recent measures for reducing them to the footing of other useful callings. It now appears that our means were effectual. The clergy here seem to have relinquished all pretensions to privilege, and to stand on a footing with lawyers, physicians &c. They ought therefore to possess the same rights." 9 Works of Jefferson 143 (P. Ford ed. 1905).

"Does not The exclusion of Ministers of the Gospel as such violate a fundamental principle of liberty by punishing a religious profession with the privation of a civil right? does it [not] violate another article of the plan itself which exempts religion from the cognizance of Civil power? does it not violate justice by at once taking away a right and prohibiting a compensation for it? does it not in fine violate impartiality by shutting the door [against] the Ministers of one Religion and leaving it open for those of every other." 5 Writings of James Madison 288 (G. Hunt ed. 1904).

Madison was not the only articulate opponent of clergy disqualification. When proposals were made earlier to prevent clergymen from holding public office, John Witherspoon, a Presbyterian minister, president of Princeton University, and the only clergyman to sign the Declaration of Independence, made a cogent protest and, with tongue in cheek, offered an amendment to a provision much like that challenged here:

" 'No clergyman, of any denomination, shall be capable of being elected a member of the Senate or House of Representatives, because (here insert the grounds of offensive disqualification, which I have not been able to discover) Provided always, and it is the true intent and meaning of this part of the constitution, that if at any time he shall be completely deprived of the clerical character by those by whom he was invested with it, as by deposition for cursing and swearing, drunkenness or uncleanness, he shall then be fully restored to all the privileges of a free citizen; his offense [of being a clergyman] shall no more be remembered against him; but he may be chosen either to the Senate or House of Representatives, and shall be treated with all the respect due to his *brethren,* the other members of Assembly,' " Stokes 624–625.

As the value of the disestablishment experiment was perceived, 11 of the 13 States disqualifying the clergy from some types of public office gradually abandoned that limitation. New York, for example, took that step in 1846 after delegates to the State's constitutional convention argued that the exclusion of clergymen from the legislature was an "odious distinction." 2 C. Lincoln, The Constitutional History of New York 111–112 (1906). Only Maryland and Tennessee continued their clergy-disqualification provisions into this century and, in 1974, a District Court held Maryland's provision violative of the First and Fourteenth Amendments' guarantees of the free exercise of religion. *Kirkley v. Maryland,* 381 F. Supp. 327. Today Tennessee remains the only State excluding ministers from certain public offices.

The essence of this aspect of our national history is that in all but a few States the selection or rejection of clergymen for public office soon came to be viewed as something safely left to the good sense and desires of the people.

B

This brief review of the history of clergy-disqualification provisions also amply demonstrates, however, that, at least during the early segment of our national life, those provisions enjoyed the support of responsible American statesmen and were accepted as having a rational basis. Against this background we do not lightly invalidate a statute enacted pursuant to a provision of a state constitution which has been sustained by its highest court. The challenged provision came to the Tennessee Supreme Court clothed with the presumption of validity to which that court was bound to give deference.

However, the right to the free exercise of religion unquestionably encompasses the right to preach, proselyte, and perform other similar religious functions, or, in other words, to be a minister of the type McDaniel was found to be. *Murdock v. Pennsylvania,* [XI, 1]; *Cantwell v. Connecticut* [XI, 1]. Tennessee also acknowledges the right of its adult citizens generally to seek and hold office as legislators or delegates to the state constitutional convention. Tenn. Const. Art. 2, §§ 9, 25, 26; Tenn. Code Ann. §§ 8–1801, 8–1803 (Supp. 1977). Yet under the clergy-disqualification provision, McDaniel cannot exercise both rights simultaneously because the State has conditioned the exercise of one on the surrender of the other. Or, in James Madison's words, the State is "punishing a religious profession with the privation of a civil right." 5 Writings of James Madison, *supra,* at 288. In so doing, Tennessee has encroached upon McDaniel's right to the free exercise of religion. "[T]o condition the availability of benefits [including access to the ballot] upon this appellant's willingness to violate a cardinal principle of [his] religious faith [by surrendering his religiously impelled ministry] effectively penalizes the free exercise of [his] constitutional liberties." *Sherbert v. Verner* [XI, 4].

If the Tennessee disqualification provision were viewed as depriving the clergy of a civil right soley because of their religious beliefs, our inquiry would be at an end. The Free Exercise Clause categorically prohibits government from regulating, prohibiting, or rewarding religious beliefs as such. *Id.,* at 402; *Cantwell v. Connecticut, supra,* at 304. In *Torcaso v. Watkins,* [XII, 2], the Court reviewed the Maryland constitutional requirement that all holders of "any office of profit or trust in this State" declare their belief in the existence of God. In striking down the Maryland requirement, the Court did not evaluate the interests assertedly justifying it but rather held that it violated freedom of religious belief.

In our view, however, *Torcaso* does not govern. By its terms, the Tennessee disqualification operates against McDaniel because of his *status* as a "minister" or "priest." The meaning of those words is, of course, a question of state law.[5] And although the question has not been examined extensively in state-law sources, such authority as is available indicates that ministerial status is defined in terms of conduct and activity rather than in terms of belief.[6] Because the Tennessee disqualification is directed primarily at status, acts, and conduct it is unlike the requirement in *Torcaso,* which focused on *belief.* Hence, the Free Exercise Clause's absolute prohibition of infringements on the "freedom to believe" is inapposite here.

This does not mean, of course, that the disqualification escapes judicial scrutiny or that McDaniel's activity does not enjoy significant First Amendment protection. The Court recently declared in *Wisconsin v. Yoder,* [XI, 5]:

> "The essence of all that has been said and written on the subject is that only those interests of the highest order and those not otherwise served can overbalance legitimate claims to the free exercise of religion."

Tennessee asserts that its interest in preventing the establishment of a state religion is consistent with the Establishment Clause and thus of the highest order. The constitutional history of the several States reveals that generally the interest in preventing establishment prompted the adoption of clergy disqualification provisions, see Stokes 622; Tennessee does not appear to be an exception to this pattern. Cf. *post,* at 636 n.9 (Brennan, J., concurring in judgment). There is no occasion to inquire whether promoting such an interest is a permissible legislative goal, however, see *post,* at 636–642, for Tennessee has failed to demonstrate that its views of the dangers of clergy participation in the political process have not lost whatever validity they may once have enjoyed. The essence of the rationale underlying the Tennessee restriction on ministers is that

---

[5] In this case, the Tennessee Supreme Court concluded that the disqualification of McDaniel did not interfere with his religious *belief.* 547 S. W. 2d 897, 903, 904, 907 (1977). But whether the ministerial status, as defined by state law, implicates the "freedom to act" or the absolute "freedom to believe," *Cantwell v. Connecticut* [XI, 1], must be resolved under the Free Exercise Clause. Thus, although we consider the Tennessee court's resolution of that issue, we are not bound by it.

[6] The Tennessee constitutional provision embodying the disqualification inferentially defines the ministerial profession in terms of its "duties," which include the "care of souls." Tenn. Const., Art. 9, § 1. In this case, the Tennessee Supreme Court stated that the disqualification reaches those filling a "leadership role in religion," and those "dedicated to the full time *promotion* of the religious objectives of a particular religious sect." 547 S. W. 2d, at 903 (emphasis added). The Tennessee court, in defining "priest," also referred to the dictionary definition as "one who *performs* sacrificial, ritualistic, mediatorial, interpretative, or ministerial functions. . . ." *Id.,* at 908 (quoting Webster's Third New International Dictionary 1799–1800 (1971)) (emphasis added).

if elected to public office they will necessarily exercise their powers and influence to promote the interests of one sect or thwart the interests of another, thus pitting one against the others, contrary to the anti-establishment principle with its command of neutrality. See *Walz v. Tax Comm'n* [XIII, 3]. However widely that view may have been held in the 18th century by many, including enlightened statesmen of that day, the American experience provides no persuasive support for the fear that clergymen in public office will be less careful of anti-establishment interests or less faithful to their oaths of civil office than their unordained counterparts.

We hold that § 4 of ch. 848 violates McDaniel's First Amendment right to the free exercise of his religion made applicable to the States by the Fourteenth Amendment. Accordingly, the judgment of the Tennessee Supreme Court is reversed, and the case is remanded to that court for further proceedings not inconsistent with this opinion.

Reversed and remanded.

Justice Blackmun took no part in the consideration of this case.

Justice Brennan, joined by Justice Marshall, concurring:

. . .

That public debate of religious ideas, like any other, may arouse emotion, may incite, may foment religious divisiveness and strife does not rob it of constitutional protection. *Cantwell v. Connecticut,* [XI, 1]; cf. *Terminiello v. Chicago,* 337 U.S. 1, 4–5 (1949). The mere fact that a purpose of the Establishment Clause is to reduce or eliminate religious divisiveness or strife, does not place religious discussion, association, or political participation in a status less preferred than rights of discussion, association, and political participation generally. "Adherents of particular faiths and individual churches frequently take strong positions on public issues including . . . vigorous advocacy of legal or constitutional positions. Of course, churches as much as secular bodies and private citizens have that right." *Walz v. Tax Comm'n* [XI, 1.]

The State's goal of preventing sectarian bickering and strife may not be accomplished by regulating religious speech and political association. The Establishment Clause does not license government to treat religion and those who teach or practice it, simply by virtue of their status as such, as subversive of American ideals and therefore subject to unique disabilities. Cf. *Wieman v. Updegraff,* 344 U.S. 183 (1952). Government may not inquire into the religious beliefs and motivations of officeholders—it may not remove them from office merely for making public statements regarding religion, or question whether their legislative actions stem from religious conviction. Cf. *Bond v. Floyd,* 385 U.S. 116 (1966).

In short, government may not as a goal promote "safe thinking" with respect to religion and fence out from political participation those, such as ministers, whom it regards as overinvolved in religion. Religionists no less than members of any other group enjoy the full measure of protection afforded speech, association, and political activity generally. The Establishment Clause, properly understood, is a shield against any attempt by government to inhibit religion as it has done here; *Abington School Dist. v. Schempp* [XIV, 2]. It may not be used as a sword to justify repression of religion or its adherents from any aspect of public life.

3. THE CIVIL RIGHTS MOVEMENT

The first meeting of what became the Southern Christian Leadership Conference (SCLC) was held at the call of four black ministers and one layman. They invited black churchmen and other black leaders to meet at the Ebenezer Baptist Church in Atlanta. The meeting, held in January 1957, developed working papers on busing, economic survival, and social protest against the discriminatory treatment of blacks. The papers stated: "We must recognize in this new period that *direct action is our most potent political weapon.* . . . The campaign is based on the most stable social institution in Negro culture—the church," Aldon D. Morris, *The Origins of the Civil Rights Movement* (1984), 83–85 (emphasis in original).

The SCLC was the force that developed the infrastructure of the civil rights movement. It provided moral, material, and organizational support to local protesters, otherwise isolated and at a disadvantage with the white power structure. It produced among local communities "the mental attitudes conducive to protest." It led to large numbers of people wanting "freedom," *ibid.* 77, 95–97. The "most magnificent accomplishment" of the SCLC was "the creation of a disciplined mass movement of Southern blacks," Bayard Ruskin, *Strategies for Freedom* (1976) 80.

No political movement in America succeeds alone. The SCLC was joined by the older National Association for the Advancement of Colored People and the newer Congress of Racial Equality, both organizations with Baptist Church support, Morris 120–138. The Student Nonviolent Coordinating Committee was founded in 1960 with help from SCLC, *ibid.* at 219–220. The American Friends Service Committee, the Fellowship for Reconciliation, and the Alabama Christian Movement for Human Rights all played supporting roles. The SCLC was central.

The SCLC had the following church connections:

1. Twenty-one of its original twenty-five officers were ordained ministers, *ibid.* at 80–87.
2. Its president, Martin Luther King, Jr., was a Baptist minister.
3. Its members (it had no individual members) were chiefly churches or church-related organizations, *ibid.* at 91.
4. Its characteristic form of meeting was a rally modeled on a church revival, featuring a charismatic minister, usually the Reverend King, *ibid.* at 91–92, 97.
5. Its imagery was religious—for example, Moses was put forward as an exemplar. The present state of subservience was seen as "Egypt," *ibid.* at 98.
6. Financing came largely from the churches, chiefly from "black church-oriented mass meetings outside the South." In King's words:

> Most of my speaking is in the interest of raising funds for this conference. One of the methods that I have used in the past few months is that of selecting cities across the country and asking the ministerial groups to come together and sponsor a city-wide meeting at which time I speak, and funds are raised through the churches and other organizations for the work of the Southern Christian Leadership Conference [King to Rev. Wilber B. Miller, September 4, 1959, *ibid.* at 118].

7. It transferred the emphasis of the preaching of black churches on acceptance of one's lot in this world to an emphasis on religion as having social significance. In doing so it used the traditional power of religious teachers to affect cultural consciousness. "The mass-based black church played the leading role in interpreting reality and providing moral standards for blacks," *ibid.* at 96.

For these reasons, the SCLC could be described by the Reverend Joseph Lowery, one of its founders, as "the black church coming alive," *ibid.* at 88.

The means adopted by this religious organization were political. Its strategy focused on franchising voters, with the aim of doubling the black vote in the South. To this end, the SCLC launched "The Crusade for Citizenship" in 1958, a movement to register blacks to vote, *ibid.* at 101–109. The kind of resistance that this movement could expect to meet is captured by the following letter to the Reverend George Lee, a leader in an earlier local voting registration drive in Humphreys County, Mississippi (shortly after receiving the letter, he was murdered):

Preacher, instead of preaching the Gospel, what you say you are called to do, you are preaching to Negroes here in Humphreys County to register and vote. You had better do what you claim that you were called to do, preach the Gospel [*ibid.* at 105].

A climactic moment in the drive for civil rights was the confrontation planned by the SCLC in Birmingham in 1963. The local head, the Reverend Fred Shuttlesworth, has described Birmingham as launching "a systematic, wholehearted battle against segregation which would set the pace for the nation." The confrontation succeeded because of the cohesion produced by "music, religious oratory, prayers, and shared symbols," *ibid.* at 251. By this date the SCLC had a budget of $1 million and a highly organized staff. The Birmingham demonstrators were carefully coordinated, with the 16th Street Baptist Church as headquarters; this church and three other Baptist churches provided the leadership with a starting constituency "of close to 5000," *ibid.* at 262. Martin Luther King, Jr., stayed out of jail by not participating in any street demonstration until Good Friday. He then chose this day to defy an injunction, and he was arrested.

Addressing his "fellow clergymen" on April 16, 1963, he wrote from Birmingham City jail:

. . . Just as the apostle Paul left his village of Tarsus and carried the gospel of Jesus Christ to the far corners of the Greco-Roman world, so I am compelled to carry the gospel of freedom beyond my home town. . . .

One may well ask how can you advocate breaking some laws and obeying others? . . . I would agree with St. Augustine that "an unjust law is no law at all." . . . To put it in the terms of St. Augustine, an unjust law is a human law that is not rooted in eternal law and natural law. . . .

Was not Jesus Christ an extremist for love? . . . Was not Amos an extremist for justice? . . . Was not Paul an extremist for the Christian gospel? . . . Was not Martin Luther an extremist? . . . And John Bunyan? . . . And Abraham Lincoln? . . . And Thomas Jefferson? . . .

There was a time when the church was very powerful. . . . In those days the church was not merely a thermometer that recorded the ideas and principles of popular opinion; it was a thermostat that transformed the mores of society. . . . The Christians pressed on, in the conviction that they were a "colony of heaven," called to obey God rather than man. . . . By their effort and example they brought an end to such ancient evils as infanticide and gladiatorial contests. . . . I hope the church as a whole will meet the challenge of this decisive hour. Martin Luther King, *Letter from Birmingham Jail* (Stamford, Ct.: Overbrook Press, 1968).

Nearly a million copies of this letter were distributed before King was bailed from jail, Morris 266.

Following Birmingham, 758 demonstrations occurred in 186 cities across the South; 14,733 persons were arrested. A year later, the national government passed the Civil Rights Act of 1964, *ibid.* at 274. As effectively as the northern ministers of 1850, the black ministers of the Southern Christian Leadership Conference had intervened in American government.

Compare the following statement by a Methodist pastor who is the executive director of the Christian Legal Society:

The practical consequence of this assertion that Christ is Lord of all is that the evangelical Christian community will resist the attempt to constrain its activities to what the secularist defines as "religion." Politics, art, science and philosophy are all part of the arena of activity by the believing community. The criticism of religious groups on the right based on their involvement in politics is particularly ill conceived. One may indeed debate their choice of issues or even the side they take on some, but no one emerging from the biblical tradition dare challenge their assertion that as believers they feel compelled to speak to the moral character and the political life of the nation. [Lynn Buzzard, "The Evangelical Rediscovery of Law and Politics," 1 *Journal of Law and Religion* 187, 199 (1983)].

Compare the following by a leading Catholic writer:

The aspiration to a fully human life requires a social agenda. Respect for people of other, or no, religious beliefs should not stop a Christian from formulating his social principles on the basis of a Christian understanding of human destiny and affairs. Indeed, such an understanding gives the firmest possible support to that very respect. That respect in turn gives a solid foundation not only to traditional educational and charitable endeavors, but also to continuing efforts to eliminate race discrimination, to provide the poor with decent homes and enough to eat, to secure to the worker both the psychological and the economic fruits of his labor, to promote a radical redistribution of income and resources, to resist unjust war, or to establish the right of the unborn to live. These are all matters on which Christians can make common cause with other people, but I believe that a Christian must base his own support for them on his own commitments [Robert E. Rodes, Jr., "Pluralist Christendom and the Christian Civil Magistrate," 9 *Communio* 321, 329 (1982)].

Compare the following by a rabbi who is director of the Religious Action Center of the Union of American Hebrew Congregations and a lawyer:

When the religious lobby *is* successful, and uniquely successful, it is only on those issues where there is an overwhelming consensus in the religious community on the substance and the priority of a particular issue. When this happens, the religious community can play an influential role in defining the public's moral perception of the particular issue in keeping with our traditional values and goals. Since millions of Americans look to religious leaders for such guidance, these leaders can often have a significant, occasionally determinative, impact on the political decision-making process. Key examples of this in American history include the outlawing of dueling, the anti-slavery movement, the temperance movement, the industrial reforms of the progressive era, the recognition of the labor movement, the generation of public and Congressional support for the United Nations, the civil rights movement, and the anti-Vietnam War movement. In recent years, the religious community has played a crucial role in the development of international food relief policy resulting from the 1974–1975 world hunger crisis and in originating and lobbying for the human rights provisos to the foreign aid bills in 1978.

When one analyzes the fundamental postulates and axioms which underlie the political vision of mainstream religious groups, it is clear that they are virtually indistinguishable from the postulates and axioms which underlie modern political liberalism. There is, however, one profound difference which I think is important to point out. Political liberalism presumes virtually complete freedom of the individual, or as John Stuart Mill's famous dictum asserts, you may do your own thing so long as you do not infringe on the freedom or rights of others. But the *Halakhah,* and most religious traditions today, categorically reject this idea. *Halakhah* has embodied the recognition that issues of law and morality involve not only the relationship of person-to-person but also the relationship of person-to-God [David Saperstein, "Jewish Perspectives on the Role of Religion in the Political Process," 1 *Journal of Law and Religion* 220 (1983)].

Consider the following by James M. Dunn, executive director of the Baptist Joint Committee on Public Affairs:

Where does one draw the line between mixing politics–religion and merging church–state? It is a popular question, often asked simply to shut off debate. The challenge works as a cutoff valve because there is no simple, easy, short answer.

The question implies a neat worldview in which everything is black or white, good or bad. This either-or mentality is not the exclusive disease of religious and political fundamentalists. In fact, a dualism infects American life. It insists upon every issue being divided from top to bottom by a vertical line with a right side and a wrong side.

Instead of this vertical line, a horizontal line with opposing views, differing ways of looking at things, or balancing consideration at either end is probably a more useful model. In many of the polarities, paradoxes, contradictions, or competing goods that complicate the church–state debate, one draws the line and then travels it, or draws the line and discovers that traveling the line is fraught with creative tension [Dunn, "The Christian as Political Activist," 81 *Liberty* 18 (July-August, 1986)].

4. MOVEMENTS FOR AND AGAINST ABORTION

Since the first century the Christian Church had regarded abortion as a serious sin. The Reformation produced no division on this point. At the beginning of the 1960s the churches, Protestant and Catholic, asserted the sanctity of life and rejected abortion for invading it, Noonan, *A Private Choice: Abortion in America in the Seventies* (1979) 59-61. When predominantly professional and secular organizations—the American Civil Liberties Union; the American Medical Association; Planned Parenthood of America—began to ask for changes in the abortion laws, a division occurred in the religious ranks. Some theological casuists found occasions on which abortion, although a grave act, could be justified by its preservation of other values. Some religious bodies objected to making abortion a matter of civil law.

The General Assembly of the Unitarian-Universalists in 1963 characterized existing statutes as "an affront to human life and dignity" and called for legalizing abortion for any "compelling reason, physical, psychological, mental, spiritual, or economic," Lawrence Lader, *Abortion* (1967) 100. In California nearly 1,300 Protestant ministers and Jewish rabbis called for change, *ibid.* at 147. Joseph Fletcher, an Episcopal priest and professor of Christian ethics at Episcopal Theological School, became a leader for reform and a director of the Association for the Study of Abortion, a spearhead of change, *ibid.* at 148. In 1971, the Eighth General Synod of the United Church of Christ called for legalization. In 1972 the General Conference of the United Methodist Church called for removal of "abortion from the criminal code," Noonan 61.

Ever since the "birth control" movement had taken shape in the United States under the leadership of Margaret Higgins Sanger, its most vocal and persistent opponent had been the Catholic Church. Despite the opposition of the church, the movement had succeeded. Contraception had become widely accepted in the United States. American public policy supported contraception. The federal government paid for "family planning programs." Within the Catholic Church itself a strong strain of opinion argued for the moral acceptability of contraception.

When the abortion battle opened, it was entirely natural for the old birth controllers to see it as a replay of the battle over contraception. Their nemesis, the Catholic Church, appeared again to them as the principal foe. The scenario was clear. They would attack the Roman menace. Secular, Protestant, and Jewish opinion would rally to them. The Church's own ranks would divide. After a struggle, abortion would be triumphantly established as national policy.

Roe v. Wade, 410 U.S. 113 (1973), held the abortion laws to be an unconstitutional denial of liberty. The Court did not mention a First Amendment basis for its decision. But one commentator defended the decision on the ground that the existing abortion laws had been kept in place by the pressure of religious groups: "Whenever the views of organized religious groups have come to play a pervasive role in an entire subject's legislative consideration for reasons intrinsic to the subject matter as then understood," the legislature cannot act without favoring a particular religious doctrine and thereby 'establishing' a religion," Laurence Tribe, "Foreword to the Supreme Court—1972 Term: Toward a Model of Roles in the Due Process of Life and Law," 87 *Harvard Law Review* 20 (1973) at 23.

In the political sphere, the leaders of the movement to restrict abortion by law were often Protestants. The president of the largest anti-abortion group, the National Right to Life Committee, Mildred Jefferson, was a Methodist. The president of Americans United for Life was George Huntston Williams, Hollis Professor of Divinity at Harvard Divinity School and an ordained Unitarian minister. The president of American Citizens Concerned for Life, Marjory Mecklenburg, was a Methodist. In the Congress, early sponsors of a Human Life Amendment included Senator Mark Hatfield, a Baptist, and Senator Harold Hughes, an ordained Methodist minister, Noonan 61. Near the end of the 1970s the most powerful and politically effective opposition to legalized abortion came from evangelical and fundamentalist Protestants; the Moral Majority put forward their position. The Church of Jesus Christ of Latter-Day Saints was an effective opponent in the states where the Mormons were numerous. Nevertheless, in the eyes of the proponents of the abortion liberty, the *bête noire* was still the Catholic Church.

In 1976 an amendment introduced to a appropriations act by Congressman Henry Hyde sharply restricted the federal funding of abortion. Immediately after the act's passage, Planned Parenthood of New York City sought a preliminary injunction against the secretary of health, education, and welfare observing the limitations of the Hyde Amendment. Judge John Dooling, a federal district judge in Brooklyn, granted the injunction, making it applicable to the secretary's actions throughout the country, *McRae v. Mathews*, 421 F. Supp. 533 (E.D.N.Y. 1976). The case then went to trial.

Among the contentions of the plaintiff were (1) that the Hyde Amendment was an establishment of Catholic doctrine because it reflected Catholic religious teaching; and (2) that it was a denial of the free exercise of religion by those who believed that religious duty required them to secure an abortion. Judge Dooling, himself a Catholic, gave the plaintiffs wide latitude in introducing evidence to prove these points, including evidence on the religious habits of Congressman Hyde. Over three years after the preliminary injunction had been granted, Judge Dooling gave his decision, making the injunction permanent. He summarized the Catholic involvement in abortion politics as follows [*McRae v. Califano*, 491 F.Supp. 630 (E.D.N.Y. 1980)]:

1. Testimony before the Subcommittee on Constitutional Amendments of the Senate Committee on the Judiciary in support of a constitutional amendment to protect the unborn child— Testimony on March 7, 1974, by the cardinal archbishops of Boston, Chicago, Los Angeles, and Philadelphia.

2. Promulgation on November 20, 1975, by the National Conference of Catholic Bishops of a "Pastoral Plan for Prolife Activities" recommending an educational effort; a pastoral effort, addressed to the specific needs of women with problems related to pregnancy and

abortion; and a public policy effort to insure "effective legal protection for the right to life."

3. Evidence showing that the Diocese of Fargo, North Dakota, had attempted to carry out this plan by instruction from the bishop to the clergy.

4. Evidence that many Catholic newspapers and magazines gave "a great deal of attention" to the Catholic position on abortion and solicited support for the enactment of constitutional and statutory provisions on abortion.

5. Evidence that in the Archdiocese of Los Angeles the Feast of the Holy Innocents (December 28th) had been made the occasion in each year from 1971 to 1978 for a candlelit procession followed by the celebration of a Mass of Atonement.

6. Evidence that in 1976–1977 the New York Right to Life Committee had received $116,000 from "Respect Life" contributions solicited outside churches after mass.

7. Evidence that the Minnesota Right to Life organizations were stated beneficiaries of the annual Catholic appeal collection of the Archdiocese of St. Paul.

8. Evidence that Mary Peek, a candidate for the House of Representatives in Minnesota, "experienced an erosion of support" after criticism of her position on abortion and that she lost the election by 116 votes. Peek did not believe that there was any institutional coercion of Catholics but that the social disapprobation of abortion within the Catholic community, resulting from the hierarchically created atmosphere of disapproval, must to some extent carry through to the voting booth.

9. Evidence that in 1972–1974 Minnesota Citizens Concerned for Life was particularly active in the Minnesota legislature and that it received support from Catholic parishioners, although it was nondenominational "and practically interdenominational."

10. Evidence that a lobbyist for the National Committee for a Human Life Amendment, "the lobbying arm" of the National Conference of Catholic Bishops, kept in close touch with the Senate and House conferees on the abortion funding bill in 1977.

Judge Dooling then said:

Religious motivation and allegiance to religiously perceived principle on the part of many legislators, on both sides of the issue, are easy and necessary inferences from the record and the legislative history. That does not signify that only religious motivation can explain the pro-life position nor does it signify that secular reasoning could not readily arrive at the pro-life principle. What finally influenced the votes of the decisive number of legislators cannot be said with any confidence to be religious motivation or religious conviction or will to make effective a religiously perceived principle of conduct or the influence of institutional religion and religious pleading or fear of reprisal from religiously oriented voters. What can be said is that an organized effort of institutional religion to influence the vote on the enactments in question on religious grounds was made, that it cannot be said that the effort did not influence a decisive number of votes through a combination of religious belief and principle on the part of some with a fear of political reprisal on the part of others, and that the narrow votes in both houses are open to the inference that in one or the other way the religious factor was decisive of the issue for enough legislators to affect the outcome of the voting. On the specific effect of Roman Catholic institutional intervention Representative Hyde said in his April 22, 1978, St. Louis speech:

"It would be amusing (if it weren't so threatening) that the current crusade of the American Civil Liberties Union is to prove in Federal Court that the pro-life movement in America is a religious plot—specifically a Catholic plot—and hence a violation of the First Amendment. I should like to point out that while several Catholic voices— many Catholic voices—are heard in Congress on behalf of innocent pre-natal life—

the leading Senatorial pro-life spokesmen are mostly non-Catholic. I speak of Senator Jesse Helms of North Carolina, Senator Dick Schweiker of Pennsylvania.

"The most prominent Catholics in the Senate—the senior senator from Massachusetts and the junior senator from New York—do not support our effort to stop the abortion tidal wave. The same sad truth applies to the celebrated Catholic governors of California and New York. In the House we have a Jesuit Priest Congressman who wears his Roman collar while casting votes to continue the use of taxpayers' money to pay for medicaid abortions. To my knowledge, he remains in good standing with his religious superiors. In a nearby state, one Catholic college invited a Senator who was a leader of the pro-abortion forces in Congress to address its graduating class last June. The point of all this I suggest, is that the outrage of abortion isn't all that disturbing to some influential Catholics. That is what Jacques Maritain calls 'kneeling to the world.'

"There is one nun based in Chicago who travels the country attacking me for opposing abortion. Occasionally, the newspapers give her coverage which I suggest ought to embarrass every Catholic."

When Representative Hyde voted in 1976 to override President Ford's veto of the 1976 enactment despite his agreement with the veto on the appropriations aspect of the bill (which exceeded the President's budget by $4 billion), he said (123 Cong.Rec. H11855):

"I am, nevertheless, voting to override the President's veto because within this legislation is a provision forbidding the use of Federal funds to pay for abortions. In starkest terms, the potential exists of saving some 300,000 lives which otherwise might be destroyed with the use of taxpayers' funds. The saving of these lives far outweighs the economic considerations involved in this legislation."

. . .

Yet it would not be difficult to point to considerable pro-life argument that counted on the evident facts that the fetus begins in a union of living human cells and is from nearly the first moment a potential human being, and that its dependent existence, is, for all its dependence, separate life of human quality; and to pro-life argument that the "right to life"—the affirmation that only great reasons can justify frustrating the natural growth into being of rational human life—is separately significant, and that the reasons advanced for funding abortion are for the most part empty. Others argued that federal neutrality would be represented by not subsidizing abortion, that the right to choose abortion did not imply a right to have an abortion paid for from public funds. Others argued that if there was a public duty it was a duty to provide alternatives to abortion, and so to relieve poor women of the need to resort to the always tragic recourse of abortion.

The repeated use during the debates of "human life" terminology extended at times to referring to the immortal soul of the fetus, to invoking Herod's "slaughter of the innocent," and to emphasizing that the fetus is "defenseless," is "innocent." Much of this language is seen in the Roman Catholic literature already referred to, and it implies humanity in the fetus—for only rational beings can be "innocent" in moral terms. The language and references are specifically religious, but, again, much other argument was in the debates that was free of religious reference, whether or not the debaters were motivated by their religious convictions. Other parts of the debates are very insistent that the issue was a moral issue, and that the members had to, or ought to, vote their consciences. The pro-choice debaters, in their reference to the pro-life members' positions, frequently emphasized their respect for the pro-life members' views and, in so doing, manifested an evidently informed belief that the pro-life views were essentially religious. More broadly, the pro-life members at times portrayed abortion as one element of the moral decay that they saw about them in this country and against which they sought to rouse the Congress.

The charge that the pro-life members were seeking to impose their "morality" or their religious views on the Congress, and on poor women, and the counter-charge that the pro-choice members were preparing to require taxpayers to whom abortion was morally abhorrent to subsidize it with their taxes, resulted in frequent avowals by members of their religious affiliations; indeed, members did not hesitate to instance in aid of their arguments their own religious upbringing, their conduct of their own families, and their legal and medical professional experience with abortion. The positions of the various churches on abortion were referred to more than once. The pro-choice members argued that the abortion decision was a matter of individual conscience. And there was a recognition that in the minds of some members their religious beliefs did not really leave them a free vote.

The debates were often bitterly controversial, even inflamed; the members returned to the debate again and again with expressed reluctance but with unabated resolution. The members recognized that the debates were often emotion-charged, and much of the argument, even read in the black and white of the Congressional Record, is deeply felt, personal in tone, and consciously moralistic—because the speaker sees no escape from the moral issue or from its importance. The members were plainly aware, were made aware, of the pressures exerted upon them by their sense of their constituencies' views on the issue and of the religious setting in which the views were entertained and expressed.

The intense lobbying on both sides of the issue is reflected in the debates and made clear in the record. The members were fully aware of it, and the not infrequent references to the picketing, the March for Life, and the letters from the constituencies indicate general consciousness that the issue was one that had gained wide popular attention and recognition that their votes would be reported to their constituencies. While the overall impression is that the pro-life lobbying effort was better centralized and more strongly presented than the pro-choice lobbying, the pro-choice lobbying was effectively present and skillful. Remarkably, the issue cut across party lines, so that the lobbying effort had to be more personal than organizational in its address. To an extent the essentially non-partisan cast that the issue assumed seems to have cost the pro-choice advocates a substantial part of the Democratic support that might normally have been expected on a DHEW issue affecting medicaid. Representative Flood's 1976 change from opposition to support of the Hyde amendment is illustrative. See Annex pages 744, 750 and 764.

No measure of the effect of the lobbying is possible. The unanswered question is whether there would have been any abortion legislation if the pro-life group had not used the expedient of presenting the issue as a "rider" on the appropriation bill for 1976. The inference from the fact that the funding restriction has survived only as a rider for four successive years is that the expedient itself is responsible for the fund restrictions, and not any congressional consensus on abortion, or any fruition of effective lobbying effort. It is evident enough that the amendments are legislation on an appropriation bill, and that, although each side has charged the other with hostage taking, the reality has been that the pro-life forces have held the appropriation bills hostage until the amendments were passed. Yet that would not have been possible unless in one of the two bodies there was a consensus for abortion legislation. In a sense the amendments are enactments of the House of Representatives to which the Senate has acceded, with such amendments as it could negotiate, rather than risk the appropriation bills. . . .

As pointed out earlier, right to life language has found its way into a number of statutes, and, in the case of the pregnancy amendment to Title VII (Equal Employment Opportunities), 42 U.S.C. § 2000e(k), occasioned exchanges as bitter as many of those that occurred during the Hyde amendment debates. In addition to the other enactments referred to above, Public Law 95–444 of October 10, 1978, 92 Stat. 1067, added to the section enumerating the duties and functions of the Civil Rights Commission the provision:

"(f) Nothing in this or any other Act shall be construed as authorizing the Commission, its Advisory Committees, or any person under its supervision or control to appraise, or to study and collect information about, laws and policies of the Federal Government, or any other governmental authority in the United States, with respect to abortion."

The Commission had issued a report in 1975 on *The Constitutional Aspects of the Right to Limit Childbearing* which argued against legislation aimed at narrowing the effect of *Roe v. Wade.*

E

What ultimately emerges from the facts found in parts XII through XIV is that the major religions whose views were presented all regard abortion as presenting religiously framed questions of moral right, moral duty and conscience, that they are in disagreement on the appropriate rules of conduct but in agreement that abortion is a morally grave undertaking in any circumstances, and that their sharpest disagreement concerns the role of civil government.

Judge Dooling held that the Hyde Amendment did not violate the establishment clause but that it did violate other parts of the Bill of Rights:

A woman's conscientious decision, in consultation with her physician, to terminate her pregnancy because that is medically necessary to her health, is an exercise of the most fundamental of rights, nearly allied to her right to be, surely part of the liberty protected by the Fifth Amendment, doubly protected when the liberty is exercised in conformity with religious belief and teaching protected by the First Amendment. To deny necessary medical assistance for the lawful and medically necessary procedure of abortion is to violate the pregnant woman's First and Fifth Amendment rights. The irreconcilable conflict of deeply and widely held views on this issue of individual conscience excludes any legislative intervention except that which protects each individual's freedom of conscientious decision and conscientious nonparticipation.

Judgment must be for plaintiffs.

Judge Dooling's injunction was vacated and his decision reversed:

Harris v. McRae
448 U.S. 297 (1980)

Solicitor General McCree argued the cause for appellant. With him on the briefs were *Assistant Attorney General Daniel* and *Eloise E. Davies. Victor G. Rosenblum, Dennis J. Horan, John D. Gorby, Carl Anderson, Patrick A. Trueman, A. Lawrence Washburn, Jr.,* and *Gerald E. Bodell* filed briefs for Buckley et al., appellees under this Court's Rule 10(4), in support of appellant.

Rhonda Copelon argued the cause for appellees McRae et al. With her on the briefs were *Nancy Stearns, Sylvia Law, Ellen K. Sawyer, Janet Benshoof, Judith Levin, Harriet Pilpel,* and *Eve Paul.*

Briefs of amici curiae urging reversal were filed by *John T. Noonan, Jr.,* and *William B. Ball* for Representative Jim Wright et al.; and by *Wilfred R. Caron* and *Patrick F. Geary* for the United States Catholic Conference.

Briefs of *amici curiae* urging affirmance were filed by *Robert Abrams,* Attorney General, *Shirley Adelson Siegel,* Solicitor General, and *Peter Bienstock, Arnold D. Fleischer,* and *Barbara E. Levy,* Assistant Attorneys General, for the State of New York et al., joined by *Rufus L. Edmisten,* Attorney General of North Carolina, *William F. O'Connell,* Special Deputy Attorney General, and *Steven Mansfield Shaber,* Associate Attorney General, and *James A. Redden,* Attorney General of Oregon; by *Leo Pfeffer* for the American Ethical Union et al.; by *Barbara Ellen Handschu* for the Association of Legal Aid Attorneys of the City of New York—District 65—U.A.W. et al.; and by *Phyllis N. Segal* and *Judith I. Avner* for the National Organization for Women et al.

Briefs of *amici curiae* were filed by *Nadine Taub* for the Bergen-Passaic Health Systems Agency et al.; by *James G. Kolb* for the Coalition for Human Justice; by *Sanford Jay Rosen* for the National Council of Churches of Christ in the U.S.A.; and by *Sanford Jay Rosen* for the United Presbyterian Church in the U.S.A.

Justice Stewart delivered the opinion of the Court.

. . .

The appellees also argue that the Hyde Amendment contravenes rights secured by the Religion Clauses of the First Amendment. It is the appellees' view that the Hyde Amendment violates the Establishment Clause because it incorporates into law the doctrines of the Roman Catholic Church concerning the sinfulness of abortion and the time at which life commences. Moreover, insofar as a woman's decision to seek a medically necessary abortion may be a product of her religious beliefs under certain Protestant and Jewish tenets, the appellees assert that the funding limitations of the Hyde Amendment impinge on the freedom of religion guaranteed by the Free Exercise Clause.

1

It is well settled that "a legislative enactment does not contravene the Establishment Clause if it has a secular legislative purpose, if its principal or primary effect neither advances nor inhibits religion, and if it does not foster an excessive governmental entanglement with religion." *Committee for Public Education* v. *Regan* [XIV, 1]. Applying this standard, the District Court properly concluded that the Hyde Amendment does not run afoul of the Establishment Clause. Although neither a State nor the Federal Government can constitutionally "pass laws which aid one religion, aid all religions, or prefer one religion over another," *Everson* v. *Board of Education* [XIV, 1], it does not follow that a statute violates the Establishment Clause because it "happens to coincide or harmonize with the tenets of some or all religions." *McGowan* v. *Maryland* [XIII, 2]. That the Judaeo-Christian religions oppose stealing does not mean that a State or the Federal Government may not, consistent with the Establishment Clause, enact laws prohibiting larceny. *Ibid.* The Hyde Amendment, as the District Court noted, is as much a reflection of "traditionalist" values towards abortion, as it is an embodiment of the views of any particular religion. 491 F. Supp., at 741. See also *Roe* v. *Wade,* 410 U.S., at 138–141. In sum, we are convinced that the fact that the funding restrictions in the Hyde Amendment may coincide with the religious tenets of the Roman Catholic Church does not, without more, contravene the Establishment Clause.

2

We need not address the merits of the appellees' arguments concerning the Free Exercise Clause, because the appellees lack standing to raise a free exercise challenge to the Hyde Amendment. The named appellees fall into three categories: (1) the indigent pregnant women who sued on behalf of other women similarly situated, (2) the two officers of the Women's Division, and (3) the Women's Division itself. The named appellees in the first category lack standing to challenge the Hyde Amendment on free exercise grounds because none alleged, much less proved, that she sought an abortion under compulsion of religious belief. See *McGowan* v. *Maryland, supra,* at 429. Although the named appellees in the second category did provide a detailed description of their religious beliefs, they failed to allege either that they are or expect to be pregnant or that they are eligible to receive Medicaid. These named appellees, therefore, lack the personal stake in the controversy needed to confer standing to raise such a challenge to the Hyde Amendment. See *Warth* v. *Seldin,* 422 U.S. 490, 498–499.

Finally, although the Women's Division alleged that its membership includes "pregnant Medicaid eligible women who, as a matter of religious practice and in accordance with their conscientious beliefs, would choose but are precluded or discouraged from obtaining abortions reimbursed by Medicaid because of the Hyde Amendment," the Women's Division does not satisfy the standing requirements for an organization to assert the rights of its membership. One of those requirements is that "neither the claim asserted nor the relief requested requires the participation of individual members in the lawsuit." *Hunt* v. *Washington Apple Advertising Comm'n,* 432 U.S. 333, 343. Since "it is necessary in a free exercise case for one to show the coercive effect of the enactment as it operates against him in the practice of his religion," *Abington School Dist.* v. *Schempp* [XIV, 2], the claim asserted here is one that ordinarily requires individual participation. In the present case, the Women's Division concedes that "the permissibility, advisability and/or necessity of abortion according to circumstance is a matter about which there is diversity of view within . . . our membership, and is a determination which must be ultimately and absolutely entrusted to the conscience of the individual before God." It is thus clear that the participation of individual members of the Women's Division is essential to a proper understanding and resolution of their free exercise claims. Accordingly, we conclude that the Women's Division, along with the other named appellees, lack standing to challenge the Hyde Amendment under the Free Exercise Clause.

Justices Brennan, Marshall, Blackmun, and Stevens dissented but did not focus on the religious issues.

Standing (II). In *Valley Forge Christian College v. Americans United for Separation of Church and State,* 454 U.S. 464 (1982), the Department of Health, Education, and Welfare gave a surplus army hospital, appraised at $577,500, to Northeast Bible College. A "public benefit" allowance made by the department made the transfer gratuitous. The college—now known as Valley Forge Christian College—operated under the direction of the Assemblies of God. Its purpose was to train persons "for Christian service as either ministers or laymen." All its faculty had to have been "baptized in the Holy Spirit and be living consistent Christian lives; all members of the administration had to be affiliated with the Assemblies of God," *ibid.* at 468–469. Americans United (the former Protestants and Others United) sued to have the conveyance nullified on the ground that the gift had breached the establishment clause. Americans United described itself as a nonprofit organization composed of 90,000 members who were taxpayers. The Third Circuit granted Americans United and four of its employees standing to sue not as taxpayers but as citizens, claiming "injury in fact" to "their shared individuated right to a government that 'shall make no law respecting the establishment of religion,'" 619 F. 2d 252, 261 (1980). The Supreme Court, per Justice Rehnquist, reversed. "The federal courts," Justice Rehnquist wrote at 487, "were simply not constituted as ombudsmen of the general welfare." Justice Brennan, joined by Justices Marshall and Blackmun, dissented:

. . .

More fundamentally, no clear division can be drawn in this context between actions of the Legislative Branch and those of the Executive Branch. To be sure, the First Amendment is phrased as a restriction on Congress' legislative authority; this is only natural since the Constitution assigns the authority to legislate and appropriate only to the Congress. But it is difficult to conceive of an expenditure for which the last governmental actor, either implementing directly the legislative will, or acting within the scope of legislatively delegated authority, is not an Executive Branch official. The First Amendment binds the Government as a whole, regardless of which branch is at work in a particular instance.

The Court's second purported distinction between this case and *Flast* [XIV, 1] is equally unavailing. The majority finds it "decisive" that the Federal Property and Administrative Services Act of 1949 "was an evident exercise of Congress' power under the Property Clause, Art. IV, § 3, cl. 2," *ante,* at 480, while the Government action in *Flast* was taken under Art. I, § 8. The Court relies on *United States* v. *Richardson,* 418 U.S. 166 (1974), and *Schlesinger* v. *Reservists Committee to Stop the War,* 418 U.S. 208 (1974), to support the distinction between the two Clauses, noting that those cases involved alleged deviations from the requirements of Art. I, § 9, cl. 7, and Art. I, § 6, cl. 2, respectively. The standing defect in each case was *not,* however, the failure to allege a violation of the Spending Clause; rather, the taxpayers in those cases had not complained of the distribution of Government largesse, and thus failed to meet the essential requirement of taxpayer standing recognized in *Doremus.*

It can make no constitutional difference in the case before us whether the donation to the petitioner here was in the form of a cash grant to build a facility. . . .

Justice Stevens also dissented.

Valley Forge was followed in *Allen v. Wright,* 468 U.S. 737 (1984), a class action by black parents who maintained that the Internal Revenue Service unconstitutionally permitted racially discriminatory private schools to be tax-exempt. The Court found that the "denigration" suffered by the plaintiffs was not an actionable injury. Do *Valley Forge* and *Allen* bear on *Abortion Rights Mobilization v. Regan, infra,* this section?

A group of twenty organizations headed by Americans United for Separation of Church and State sued to protest the establishment on January 10, 1984, of diplomatic relations between the United States and the Holy See. The case was dismissed on May 8, 1985, for lack of standing, *Americans United for Separation of Church and State v. Reagan,* 607 F.Supp. 747 (E.D. Pa. 1985), *aff'd,* 786 F.2d 194 (3rd Cir. 1986).

Under Internal Revenue Code sec. 501(c)(3) a religious organization is exempt from federal income tax if it does not participate in any political campaigns on behalf of candidates for public office. Is the limitation on political activity constitutional?

Under current regulations, the prohibitions of 501(c)(3) extend to both direct and indirect participation or intervention in a political campaign, on behalf of or in opposition to any candidate [26 C.F.R. § 1.501(c)-1(c)(3)(iii) (1985)]. Such activity includes, but is not limited to, the publication or distribution of written or printed statements or the making of oral statements on behalf of or in opposition to a candidate. Revenue rulings issued by the IRS strictly limit the role of religious organizations in voter education projects designed to inform the electorate of the views of candidates on issues of importance to members of the faith, *see* Revenue Ruling 78–248, 1978–1 C.B. 154; Revenue Ruling 80–282, 1980–2 C.B. 178.

The IRS has determined that it is permissible for an exempt organization to publish voter guides stating the position of incumbents on a wide range of issues, or to distribute questionnaires to candidates on such issues, Revenue Ruling 78–248, 1978–1 C.B. 154. The IRS has stated, however, that voter guides or questionnaires are impermissible if they "evidence a bias on certain issues," or concentrate on a "narrow range of issues," even if not expressly stating support or opposition for any candidate.

Query. How would the IRS rules apply to the Baptist churches that supported the civil rights movement in the 1960s? To the churches that gave a forum for Jesse Jackson in the 1984 presidential campaign?

Abortion Rights Mobilization, Inc. v. Regan
544 F.Supp. 471 (S.D. N.Y. 1982)

Judge Robert L. Carter:

. . .

Plaintiffs seek a declaration from the court that the political activities of the Roman Catholic Church and the inaction by the Secretary and the Commissioner violate the Constitution and the Code. In addition, plaintiffs request an order requiring the government defendants to take all actions necessary to enforce the Constitution and the Code, including revocation of the church defendants' § 501(c)(3) status, collection of all taxes due, and notification to church contributors that they may not deduct such contributions.
Jurisdiction is founded on 28 U.S.C. §§ 1331, 1340, 1361.

Defendants challenge plaintiffs' standing to bring an action concerning the tax status of third parties. Plaintiffs respond by asserting three bases for their right to proceed: establishment clause standing, voter standing, and equal protection standing.

A. *Article III Requirements*

[1] The Supreme Court recently has had occasion to examine and clarify the rules for standing in federal courts. . . .
[2] 1. *Establishment Clause Standing.* The existence of Article III injury "often turns on the nature and source of the claim asserted." *Warth v. Seldin, supra,* 422 U.S. at 500, 95 S.Ct. at 2205. The injury in fact requirement can be satisfied by a wide range of harms, including economic, aesthetic, environmental, or spiritual damage. *See, e.g., Gladstone, Realtors v. Village of Bellwood,* 441 U.S. 91, 111–12, 99 S.Ct. 1601, 1613–1614, 60 L.Ed.2d 66 (1979) (denial of right to interracial association); *Duke Power Co. v. Carolina Env. Study Group, supra,* 438 U.S. at 73–74, 98 S.Ct. at 2629–2630 (environmental and aesthetic consequences of pollution); *United States v. Students Challenging Regulatory Agency Procedures (SCRAP),* 412 U.S. 669, 686, 93 S.Ct. 2405, 2415, 37 L.Ed.2d 254 (1973) (enjoyment of natural resources); *School Dist. of Abington Township, Pa. v. Schempp* [XIV, 2] (spiritual values). There is no invariant meaning to the term "palpable injury"; the Constitution or a statute can create an interest that exists only in the legal regime, and damage to such an interest may fulfill the injury in fact requirement. *See Valley Forge* [*supra*] (Brennan, J., dissenting); *Joint Anti-Fascist Refugee Comm. v. McGrath,* 341 U.S. 123, 152, 71 S.Ct. 624, 638, 95 L.Ed. 817 (1951) (Frankfurter, J., concurring).

Although the Supreme Court has recognized that violation of a person's "spiritual stake in the First Amendment values" of separation of church and state may inflict sufficient harm to satisfy the injury in fact test, *see Data Processing Service Organizations v. Camp,* 397 U.S. 150, 154, 90 S.Ct. 827, 830, 25 L.Ed.2d 184 (1970), *citing School Dist. of Abington Township, Pa. v. Schempp,* [*supra*], it has cautioned that offense to one's sense of fidelity to separatist principles is an insufficient injury to bring suit for an alleged establishment clause violation. *See Valley Forge* [*supra*]; *Doremus v. Bd. of Education* [XIV, 2]. Would-be plaintiffs must show that they are "directly affected by the laws and practices against which their complaints are directed." *School Dist. of Abington Township, Pa. v. Schempp.* . . .

The individual plaintiffs' concern about the establishment clause violations perpetrated by the defendants does not rise above the whistleblowing that the Supreme Court held, in *Valley Forge,* does not satisfy the injury requirement. Plaintiffs attempt to articulate injury in fact by linking the offending activity with their involvement in the abortion rights controversy. They describe the government action of which they complain as a subsidy to opponents of abortion that impacts on plaintiffs' particularized interest to preserve reproductive choice. Plaintiffs argue, in effect, that because they object to an establishment violation occurring in a particular arena of public controversy in which they are involved, they have suffered a discrete and palpable injury not experienced by the *Valley Forge* plaintiff. Plaintiffs' characterization of their injury shares the defect that caused the demise of the *Valley Forge* complaint. In both cases, plaintiffs described an interest that brought them to court, but they did not articulate an injury that they had suffered. . . .

The clergy plaintiffs and the Women's Center for Reproductive Health ("Women's Center") have disclosed, in their affidavits, compelling and personalized injuries flowing from the tacit government endorsement of the Roman Catholic Church position on abortion that are sufficient to confer standing on them to complain of the alleged establishment clause violations. The clergy plaintiffs have devoted their lives to religious communities and beliefs that are denigrated by government favoritism to a different theology. They provide spiritual leadership to and care for the spiritual needs of their congregations. As part of these duties, they must counsel those in their care in accordance with religious laws that command consideration of abortion as the morally required response to pregnancy. The Women's Center provides guidance to women in decision-making on issues pertaining to family life, including childbearing. It was founded by Reverend Lutz along with others to put the principles of the Presbyterian Church into effect. As with the clergy plaintiffs, the Women's Center's religiously inspired mission is denigrated by government endorsement of a theology contrary to its guiding principles.

Tacit government endorsement of the Roman Catholic Church view of abortion hampers and frustrates these plaintiffs' ministries. The government need not silence these plaintiffs to cause discrete spiritual injury because official approval of an orthodoxy antithetical to their spiritual mission diminishes their position in the community, encumbers their calling in life, and obstructs their ability to communicate effectively their religious message. The spiritual values protected by the establishment clause can be injured without direct coercion against individuals, *see Engle v. Vitale* [XIV, 2] (indirect coercive pressure to conform to officially approved doctrine), even if plaintiffs have not alleged that particular religious freedoms have been infringed, *School Dist. of Abington Township, Pa. v. Schempp, supra.* It is sufficient to establish injury in fact that plaintiffs can show, as the clergy plaintiffs have, that the challenged action adversely affects them in their daily lives. *See id.*

These plaintiffs also clearly satisfy the second and third aspects of the Article III standing test—causation and redressability. Their injury flows directly from the federal defendants' allowing the church defendants the privilege of retaining § 501(c)(3) status while electioneering and denying this privilege to other religious organizations. The granting of a uniquely favored tax status to one religious entity is an unequivocal statement of preference that gilds the image of that religion and tarnishes all others. A decree ordering the termination of this illegal practice and restoring all sects to equal footing will redress this injury. Accordingly, the clergy plaintiffs and the Women's Center meet the Article III requirements for standing to raise claims under the establishment clause.

[3] 2. *Voter standing.* In *Baker v. Carr,* 369 U.S. 186, 82 S.Ct. 691, 7 L.Ed.2d 663 (1962), the Supreme Court conferred "voter standing" on a group of Tennessee citizens challenging that state's apportionment scheme as "effecting a gross disproportion of representation to voting population." *Id.* at 207, 82 S.Ct. at 704. The plaintiffs asserted that the classification disfavored the voters in some counties by "placing them in a position of unjustifiable inequality *vis-a-vis*" voters in other counties. *Id.* These allegations stated sufficient injury to satisfy the Article III standing requirements. . . .

Grounded in the equal protection safeguards of the fifth, rather than the fourteenth, amendment, plaintiffs' claims seem barely distinguishable from those involved in *Baker.* Both cases center on allegations that some arbitrary government action diluted the strength of voters in one group at the expense of those in another. Plaintiffs' injury is no less real because they claim discrimination based on issues rather than geography, nor is it relevant that the impact of allegedly harmful government conduct is felt during the battle over choosing representatives rather than in the number of representatives technically available to the aggrieved voters. The bottom line is that plaintiffs have alleged government action which has improperly biased the political process against the discrete group to which they belong.

The court dismissed the complaint as it related to the United States Catholic Conference (USCC) and the National Conference of Catholic Bishops (NCCB) on the ground that their enjoyment of the exemption did not violate the First Amendment; the government remained as a defendant. The plaintiffs subpoenaed all USCC and NCCB papers relating to the Pastoral Plan for Pro-Life Activities; all documents reflecting any contact with any candidate for any public office in the United States; and all documents reflecting financial support or involvement of the USCC, the NCCB, any archdiocese, diocese, parish church, or any church personnel with twelve pro-life organizations, Brief of the USCC and NCCB, amici curiae, *Abortion Rights Mobilization, Inc. v. Baker*, Second Circuit, 1985. Would a court order requiring production of such documents constitute excessive entanglement of the government with religion? Note *NAACP v. Alabama*, 357 U.S. 449 (1958), holding that state-compelled disclosure of the membership list of the National Association for the Advancement of Colored People was an unconstitutional infringement of the right of association.

Subsequently Judge Carter imposed a fine of $50,000 per day on the USCC and the NCCB for refusing to respond to subpoenas for documents sought by the plaintiffs in the case, *Abortion Rights Mobilization, Inc. v. Baker* (S.D.N.Y. 1986) (slip opinion). The Second Circuit stayed Judge Carter's order.

SIXTEEN

Sexual Morals

1. POLYGAMY

NOTE. A group of Mormons, disassociated from the main church and sometimes referred to as "Fundamentalists," practiced plural marriage in the twentieth century. Their publication *Truth* taught, "Plural marriage is one of the laws of heaven that has been restored." See *United States v. Barlow*, 56 F.Supp. 795 (D. Utah 1944), *appeal dismissed* 323 U.S. 805 (1944). They claimed to act on the basis of "the divinity of the Doctrine and the Covenants of the Church of Jesus Christ of Latter Day Saints (exclusive of the Manifesto)." See *State v. Barlow*, 107 Utah 292, 153 P.2d 647 (1944), *appeal dismissed, Barlow v. Utah* 324 U.S. 829 (1945). They were "strenuously opposed" by the Church of Jesus Christ of Latter Day Saints. Note, "Interstate Immorality: the Mann Act and the Supreme Court," 56 *Yale L.J.* 718, 721 (1947).

Truth was indicted as obscene literature, but the indictment was quashed, *United States v. Barlow, supra.* The State of Utah convicted several persons under a state statute of being guilty of "unlawful cohabitation with more than one person of the opposite sex," *State v. Barlow, supra.* Among the defendants convicted in this case was Heber Kimball Cleveland, who became a defendant in the following federal case.

Cleveland v. United States
329 U.S. 14 (1946)

Claude T. Barnes argued the cause for petitioners. With him on the brief were *Ed. D. Hatch* and *O. A. Tangren.*

Assistant Solicitor General Judson argued the cause for the United States on the original argument, and *Robert M. Hitchcock* on the reargument. With *Mr. Judson* on the brief were *W. Marvin Smith, Robert S. Erdahl* and *Beatrice Rosenberg.*

Justice Douglas delivered the opinion of the Court.

Petitioners are members of a Mormon sect, known as Fundamentalists. They not only believe in polygamy; unlike other Mormons, they practice it. Each of petitioners, except Stubbs, has, in addition to his lawful wife, one or more plural wives. Each transported at least one plural wife across state lines, either for the purpose of cohabiting with her, or for the purpose of aiding another member of the cult in such a project. They were convicted of violating the Mann Act (36 Stat. 825, 18 U.S.C. § 398) on a trial to the court, a jury having been waived. 56 F.Supp. 890. The judgments of conviction were affirmed on appeal. 146 F.2d 730. The cases are here on petitions for certiorari which we granted in view of the asserted conflict between the decision below and *Mortensen v. United States,* 322 U.S. 369.

The Act makes an offense the transportation in interstate commerce of "any woman or girl for the purpose of prostitution or debauchery, or for any other immoral purpose." The decision turns on the meaning of the latter phrase, "for any other immoral purpose."

United States v. Bitty, 208 U.S. 393, involved a prosecution under a federal statute making it a crime to import an alien woman "for the purpose of prostitution or for any other immoral purpose." The act was construed to cover a case where a man imported an alien woman so that she should live with him as his concubine. Two years later the Mann Act was passed. Because of the similarity of the language used in the two acts, the *Bitty* case became a forceful precedent for the construction of the Mann Act. Thus one who transported a woman in interstate commerce so that she should become his mistress or concubine was held to have transported her for an "immoral purpose" within the meaning of the Mann Act. *Caminetti v. United States*, 242 U.S. 470.

It is argued that the *Caminetti* decision gave too wide a sweep to the Act; that the Act was designed to cover only the white slave business and related vices; that it was not designed to cover voluntary actions bereft of sex commercialism; and that in any event it should not be construed to embrace polygamy which is a form of marriage and, unlike prostitution or debauchery or the concubinage involved in the *Caminetti* case, has as its object parenthood and the creation and maintenance of family life. In support of that interpretation an exhaustive legislative history is submitted which, it is said, gives no indication that the Act was aimed at polygamous practices.

While *Mortensen v. United States, supra*, p. 377, rightly indicated that the Act was aimed "primarily" at the use of interstate commerce for the conduct of the white slave business, we find no indication that a profit motive is a *sine qua non* to its application. Prostitution, to be sure, normally suggests sexual relations for hire. But debauchery has no such implied limitation. In common understanding the indulgence which that term suggests may be motivated solely by lust. And so we start with words which by their natural import embrace more than commercialized sex. What follows is "any other immoral purpose." Under the *ejusdem generis* rule of construction the general words are confined to the class and may not be used to enlarge it. But we could not give the words a faithful interpretation if we confined them more narrowly than the class of which they are a part.

That was the view taken by the Court in the *Bitty* and *Caminetti* cases. We do not stop to reexamine the *Caminetti* case to determine whether the Act was properly applied to the facts there presented. But we adhere to its holding, which has been in force for almost thirty years, that the Act, while primarily aimed at the use of interstate commerce for the purposes of commercialized sex, is not restricted to that end.

We conclude, moreover, that polygamous practices are not excluded from the Act. They have long been outlawed in our society. As stated in *Reynolds v. United States* [*supra*, IX].

"Polygamy has always been odious among the northern and western nations of Europe, and, until the establishment of the Mormon Church, was almost exclusively a feature of the life of Asiatic and of African people. At common law, the second marriage was always void (2 Kent, Com. 79), and from the earliest history of England polygamy has been treated as an offence against society."

As subsequently stated in *Mormon Church v. United States*, "The organization of a community for the spread and practice of polygamy is, in a measure, a return to barbarism. It is contrary to the spirit of Christianity and of the civilization which Christianity has produced in the Western world." And see *Davis v. Beason*. Polygamy is a practice with far more pervasive influences in society than the casual, isolated transgressions involved in the *Caminetti* case. The establishment or maintenance of polygamous households is a notorious example of promiscuity. The permanent advertisement of their existence is an example of the sharp repercussions which they have in the community. We could conclude that Congress excluded these practices from the

Act only if it were clear that the Act is confined to commercialized sexual vice. Since we cannot say it is, we see no way by which the present transgressions can be excluded. These polygamous practices have long been branded as immoral in the law. Though they have different ramifications, they are in the same genus as the other immoral practices covered by the Act.

. . .

It is also urged that the requisite criminal intent was lacking since petitioners were motivated by a religious belief. That defense claims too much. If upheld, it would place beyond the law any act done under claim of religious sanction. But it has long been held that the fact that polygamy is supported by a religious creed affords no defense in a prosecution for bigamy. *Reynolds v. United States, supra.* Whether an act is immoral within the meaning of the statute is not to be determined by the accused's concepts of morality. Congress has provided the standard. The offense is complete if the accused intended to perform, and did in fact perform, the act which the statute condemns, viz., the transportation of a woman for the purpose of making her his plural wife or cohabiting with her as such.

We have considered the remaining objections raised and find them without merit.

Affirmed.

Justices Black and Jackson think the cases should be reversed. They are of the opinion that affirmance requires extension of the rule announced in the *Caminetti* case and that the correctness of that rule is so dubious that it should at least be restricted to its particular facts. Justice Rutledge concurs in the result.

Justice Murphy, dissenting.

. . .

It is not my purpose to defend the practice of polygamy or to claim that it is morally the equivalent of monogamy. But it is essential to understand what it is, as well as what it is not. Only in that way can we intelligently decide whether it falls within the same genus as prostitution or debauchery.

There are four fundamental forms of marriage: (1) monogamy; (2) polygyny, or one man with several wives; (3) polyandry, or one woman with several husbands; and (4) group marriage. The term "polygamy" covers both polygyny and polyandry. Thus we are dealing here with polygyny, one of the basic forms of marriage. Historically, its use has far exceeded that of any other form. It was quite common among ancient civilizations and was referred to many times by the writers of the Old Testament; even today it is to be found frequently among certain pagan and non-Christian peoples of the world. We must recognize, then, that polygyny, like other forms of marriage, is basically a cultural institution rooted deeply in the religious beliefs and social mores of those societies in which it appears. It is equally true that the beliefs and mores of the dominant culture of the contemporary world condemn the practice as immoral and substitute monogamy in its place. To those beliefs and mores I subscribe, but that does not alter the fact that polygyny is a form of marriage built upon a set of social and moral principles. It must be recognized and treated as such.

The Court states that polygamy is "a notorious example of promiscuity." The important fact, however, is that, despite the differences that may exist between polygamy and monogamy, such differences do not place polygamy in the same category as prostitution or debauchery. When we use those terms we are speaking of acts of an entirely different nature, having no relation whatever to the various forms of marriage. It takes no elaboration here to point out that marriage, even when it occurs in a form of which we disapprove, is not to be compared with prostitution or debauchery or other immoralities of that character.

The Court's failure to recognize this vital distinction and its insistence that polygyny is "in the same genus" as prostitution and debauchery do violence to the anthropological factors involved. Even etymologically, the words "polygyny" and "polygamy" are quite distinct from "prostitution," "debauchery" and words of that ilk. There is thus no basis in fact for including polygyny within the phrase "any other immoral purpose" as used in this statute.

2. MARRIAGE

Loving v. Virginia
388 U.S. 1 (1967)

Bernard S. Cohen and *Philip J. Hirschkop* argued the cause and filed a brief for appellants. *Mr. Hirschkop* argued *pro hac vice,* by special leave of Court.

 R. D. McIlwaine III, Assistant Attorney General of Virginia, argued the cause for appellee. With him on the brief were *Robert Y. Button,* Attorney General, and *Kenneth C. Patty,* Assistant Attorney General.

 William M. Marutani, by special leave of Court, argued the cause for the Japanese American Citizens League, as *amicus curiae,* urging reversal.

 Briefs of *amici curiae,* urging reversal, were filed by *William M. Lewers* and *William B. Ball* for the National Catholic Conference for Interracial Justice et al.; by *Robert L. Carter* and *Andrew D. Weinberger* for the National Association for the Advancement of Colored People, and by *Jack Greenberg, James M. Nabrit III* and *Michael Meltsner* for the N. A. A. C. P. Legal Defense & Educational Fund, Inc.

 T. W. Bruton, Attorney General, and *Ralph Moody,* Deputy Attorney General, filed a brief for the State of North Carolina, as *amicus curiae,* urging affirmance.

Chief Justice Warren delivered the opinion of the Court.

This case presents a constitutional question never addressed by this Court: whether a statutory scheme adopted by the State of Virginia to prevent marriages between persons solely on the basis of racial classifications violates the Equal Protection and Due Process Clauses of the Fourteenth Amendment. For reasons which seem to us to reflect the central meaning of those constitutional commands, we conclude that these statutes cannot stand consistently with the Fourteenth Amendment.

In June 1958, two residents of Virginia, Mildred Jeter, a Negro woman, and Richard Loving, a white man, were married in the District of Columbia pursuant to its laws. Shortly after their marriage, the Lovings returned to Virginia and established their marital abode in Caroline County. At the October Term, 1958, of the Circuit Court of Caroline County, a grand jury issued an indictment charging the Lovings with violating Virginia's ban on interracial marriages. On January 6, 1959, the Lovings pleaded guilty to the charge and were sentenced to one year in jail; however, the trial judge suspended the sentence for a period of 25 years on the condition that the Lovings leave the State and not return to Virginia together for 25 years. He stated in an opinion that:

 "Almighty God created the races white, black, yellow, malay and red, and he placed them on separate continents. And but for the interference with his arrangement there would be no cause for such marriages. The fact that he separated the races shows that he did not intend for the races to mix."

. . .

There is patently no legitimate overriding purpose independent of invidious racial discrimination which justifies this classification. The fact that Virginia prohibits only interracial marriages involving white persons demonstrates that the racial classifications must stand on their own justification, as measures designed to maintain White Supremacy. We have consistently denied the constitutionality of measures which restrict the rights of citizens on account of race. There can be no doubt that restricting the freedom to marry solely because of racial classifications violates the central meaning of the Equal Protection Clause.

These statutes also deprive the Lovings of liberty without due process of law in violation of the Due Process Clause of the Fourteenth Amendment. The freedom to marry has long been recognized as one of the vital personal rights essential to the orderly pursuit of happiness by free men.

Marriage is one of the "basic civil rights of man," fundamental to our very existence and survival. *Skinner v. Oklahoma,* 316 U.S. 535, 541 (1942). See also *Maynard v. Hill,* 125 U.S. 190 (1888). To deny this fundamental freedom on so unsupportable a basis as the racial classifications embodied in these statutes, classifications so directly subversive of the principle of equality at the heart of the Fourteenth Amendment, is surely to deprive all the State's citizens of liberty without due process of law. The Fourteenth Amendment requires that the freedom of choice to marry not be restricted by invidious racial discriminations. Under our Constitution, the freedom to marry, or not marry, a person of another race resides with the individual and cannot be infringed by the State.

These convictions must be reversed.

It is so ordered.

Justice Stewart concurred in the judgment.

NOTE. *The End of Marriage?* Holding a Massachusetts statute barring the distribution of contraceptives to single persons to be an unconstitutional invasion of privacy, Justice Brennan for the Court wrote that the rights of access "must be the same for the married and the unmarried alike," *Eisenstadt v. Baird,* 405 U.S. 438 (1972) at 453. In a passage that seemed to go out of its way to challenge the religious metaphor of Genesis 2:24 that man and wife are one flesh, Justice Brennan added that "the marital couple is not an independent entity with a mind and heart of its own . . .," *ibid.* at 453.

Reviewing *Eisenstadt* and other decisions of the Supreme Court obliterating on constitutional grounds the difference between marriage and nonmarriage, I raised the question whether the legal status of marriage had rested on "covert religious assumptions," making for a consensus now shattered, Noonan, "The Family and the Supreme Court," 23 *Catholic University Law Review* 255 at 268 (1973). This article concluded at 274:

The Gingerbread Man, you may remember, was an exceptionally well-made work of human artifice. After outrunning many dangers he was taken on the tail of an old fox. The fox moved him from his tail to his back, from his back to his nose, and then threw him, topsy-turvey, in the air and on his descent began to eat him.

"I'm a quarter gone," cried the Gingerbread Man. Then, "I'm half gone," he cried. Then, "I'm three-quarters gone." And then there was silence.

If marriage had a tongue like the Gingerbread Man, what would it cry out now?

3. SODOMY

As early as 1964, a sentence of twenty to thirty years' imprisonment for a homosexual act of oral copulation was challenged as cruel and unusual punishment, unconstitutional under the Eighth Amendment. A federal court rejected the challenge although releasing the prisoner for lack of effective counsel at his trial. *Perkins v. State of North Carolina,* 234 F.Supp. 333 (W.D.N.C. 1964). After *Eisenstadt v. Baird,* 405 U.S. 438 (1972), it was argued, "If the right of privacy extends to the sexual conduct of unmarried heterosexuals, it's hard to see why it would not also apply to the private sexual conduct of homosexuals." Note, "The Constitutionality of Laws Forbidding Private Homosexual Conduct," 72 *Mich. L. Rev.* 1613,

1619 (1974). But a privacy right to homosexual conduct was rejected. *Doe v. Commonwealth's Attorney for Richmond*, 425 U.S. 901 (1976), *summarily affirming* 403 F.Supp. 1199 (E.D. Va 1975); cf. *Dronenburg v. Zech*, 741 F.2d 1388 (D.C. 1984) (per Bork, J.) (Navy's policy of mandatory discharge for homosexual conduct not unconstitutional).

Bowers v. Hardwick
54 U.S.L.W. 4919 (1986)

Michael E. Hobbs, Georgia Senior Assistant Attorney General (Michael J. Bowers, Ga. Atty. Gen., Marion O. Gordon, Ga. First Asst. Atty. Gen., and Daryl A. Robinson, Ga. Sr. Asst. Atty. Gen., with him on the brief) for petitioner; Laurence H. Tribe (Kathleen M. Sullivan, Brian Koukoutchos, and Kathleen L. Wilde with him on the brief) for respondents.

Justice White delivered the opinion of the Court.

In August 1982, respondent was charged with violating the Georgia statute criminalizing sodomy by committing that act with another adult male in the bedroom of respondent's home. After a preliminary hearing, the District Attorney decided not to present the matter to the grand jury unless further evidence developed.

Respondent then brought suit in the Federal District Court, challenging the constitutionality of the statute insofar as it criminalized consensual sodomy. He asserted that he was a practicing homosexual, that the Georgia sodomy statute, as administered by the defendants, placed him in imminent danger of arrest, and that the statute for several reasons violates the Federal Constitution.

. . .

This case does not require a judgment on whether laws against sodomy between consenting adults in general, or between homosexuals in particular, are wise or desirable. It raises no question about the right or propriety of state legislative decisions to repeal their laws that criminalize homosexual sodomy, or of state court decisions invalidating those laws on state constitutional grounds. The issue presented is whether the Federal Constitution confers a fundamental right upon homosexuals to engage in sodomy and hence invalidates the laws of the many States that still make such conduct illegal and have done so for a very long time. The case also calls for some judgment about the limits of the Court's role in carrying out its constitutional mandate.

We first register our disagreement with the Court of Appeals and with respondent that the Court's prior cases have construed the Constitution to confer a right of privacy that extends to homosexual sodomy and for all intents and purposes have decided this case. The reach of this line of cases was sketched in *Carey v. Population Services International*, 431 U.S. 678, 685 (1977). *Pierce v. Society of Sisters* [X, 7], and *Meyer v. Nebraska*, 262 U.S. 390 (1923), were described as dealing with child rearing and education; *Prince v. Massachusetts* [XI, 1], with family relationships; *Skinner v. Oklahoma ex rel. Williamson*, 316 U.S. 535 (1942), with procreation; *Loving v. Virginia* [*supra*], with marriage; *Griswold v. Connecticut, supra*, and *Eisenstadt v. Baird, supra*, with contraception; and *Roe v. Wade*, 410 U.S. 113 (1973), with abortion. The latter three cases were interpreted as construing the Due Process Clause of the Fourteenth Amendment to confer a fundamental individual right to decide whether or not to beget or bear a child. *Carey v. Population Services International, supra*, at 688–689.

Accepting the decisions in these cases and the above description of them, we think it evident that none of the rights announced in those cases bears any resemblance to the claimed constitutional right of homosexuals to engage in acts of sodomy that is asserted in this case. No connection between family, marriage, or procreation on the one hand and homosexual activity on the other has been demonstrated, either by the Court of Appeals or by respondent. Moreover, any claim that these cases nevertheless stand for the proposition that any kind of private sexual conduct between consenting adults is constitutionally insulated from state proscription is unsupportable. Indeed, the Court's opinion in *Carey* twice asserted that the privacy right, which the *Griswold* line of cases found to be one of the protections provided by the Due Process Clause, did not reach so far. 431 U.S., at 688, n. 5, 694, n. 17.

Precedent aside, however, respondent would have us announce, as the Court of Appeals did, a fundamental right to engage in homosexual sodomy. This we are quite unwilling to do. It is true that despite the language of the Due Process Clauses of the Fifth and Fourteenth Amendments, which appears to focus only on the processes by which life, liberty, or property is taken, the cases are legion in which those Clauses have been interpreted to have substantive content, subsuming rights that to a great extent are immune from federal or state regulation or proscription. Among such cases are those recognizing rights that have little or no textual support in the constitutional language. *Meyer, Prince,* and *Pierce* fall in this category, as do the privacy cases from *Griswold* to *Carey.*

Striving to assure itself and the public that announcing rights not readily identifiable in the Constitution's text involves much more than the imposition of the Justices' own choice of values on the States and the Federal Government, the Court has sought to identify the nature of the rights qualifying for heightened judicial protection. In *Palko v. Connecticut,* 302 U.S. 319, 325, 326 (1937), it was said that this category includes those fundamental liberties that are "implicit in the concept of ordered liberty," such that "neither liberty nor justice would exist if [they] were sacrificed." A different description of fundamental liberties appeared in *Moore v. East Cleveland,* 431 U.S. 494, 503 (1977) (opinion of Powell, J.), where they are characterized as those liberties that are "deeply rooted in this Nation's history and tradition." *Id.,* at 503 (Powell, J.). See also *Griswold v. Connecticut,* 381 U.S., at 506.

It is obvious to us that neither of these formulations would extend a fundamental right to homosexuals to engage in acts of consensual sodomy. Proscriptions against that conduct have ancient roots. See generally, Survey on the Constitutional Right to Privacy in the Context of Homosexual Activity, 40 Miami U.L. Rev. 521, 525 (1986). Sodomy was a criminal offense at common law and was forbidden by the laws of the original thirteen States when they ratified the Bill of Rights.[5] In 1868, when the Fourteenth

---

[5] Criminal sodomy laws in effect in 1791:

Connecticut: Public Statute Laws of the State of Connecticut, 1808, Title LXVI, Ch. 1, § 2 (rev. 1672).

Delaware: 1 Laws of the State of Delaware, 1797, ch. 22, § 5 (passed 1719).

Georgia had no criminal sodomy statute until 1816, but sodomy was a crime at common law, and the General Assembly adopted the Common Law of England as the law of Georgia in 1784. The First Laws of the State of Georgia, pt. 1 (1981).

Maryland had no criminal sodomy statute in 1791. Maryland's Declaration of Rights, passed in 1776, however, stated that "the inhabitants of Maryland are entitled to the common law of England," and sodomy was a crime at common law. 4 Sources and Documents of United States Constitutions 372 (W. Swindler ed. 1975).

Massachusetts: Acts and Laws passed by the General Court of Massachusetts, ch. 14, Act of March 3, 1785.

New Hampshire passed its first sodomy statute in 1718. Acts and Laws of New Hampshire 1680–1726, p. 141 (1978).

Sodomy was a crime at common law in New Jersey at the time of the ratification of the Bill of Rights. The State enacted its first criminal sodomy law five years later. Acts of the Twentieth General Assembly, March 18, 1796, Ch. DC, § 7, p. 93.

New York: Laws of New York, ch. 21, p. 391 (passed 1787).

At the time of ratification of the Bill of Rights, North Carolina had adopted the English statute of Henry VIII outlawing sodomy. See Collection of the Statutes of the Parliament of England in Force in the State of North Carolina 314 (1792).

Pennsylvania: Laws of the Fourteenth General Assembly of the Commonwealth of Pennsylvania,

Amendment was ratified, all but 5 of the 37 States in the Union had criminal sodomy laws.[6] In fact, until 1961, all 50 States outlawed sodomy, and today, 24 States and the District of Columbia continue to provide criminal penalties for sodomy performed in private and between consenting adults. Survey, Miami U.L. Rev., *supra,* at 524, n. 9. Against this background, to claim that a right to engage in such conduct is "deeply rooted in this Nation's history and tradition" or "implicit in the concept of ordered liberty" is, at best, facetious.

Nor are we inclined to take a more expansive view of our authority to discover new fundamental rights embedded in the Due Process Clause. The Court is most vulnerable and comes nearest to illegitimacy when it deals with judge-made constitutional law

---

ch. CLIV, § 2, p. 293 (passed 1790).

Rhode Island passed its first sodomy law in 1662. The Earliest Acts and Laws of the Colony of Rhode Island and Providence Plantations 1647–1719 142 (1977).

South Carolina: Public Laws of the State of South Carolina, p. 49 (1790).

At the time of the ratification of the Bill of Rights, Virginia had no specific statute outlawing sodomy, but had adopted the English common law. 9 Hening's Laws of Virginia, ch. 5, § 6, p. 127 (1821) (passed 1776).

[6] Criminal sodomy statutes in effect in 1868:

Alabama: Ala. Code, § 3604 (1867).

Arizona (Terr.): Howell Code, ch. 10, § 48 (1865).

Arkansas: Ark. Stat., ch 51, Art. IV, § 5 (1858).

California: 1 Cal. Gen. Laws, ch. 99, § 48 (1865).

Colorado (Terr.): Colo. Rev. Stat., ch. 22, §§ 45, 46 (1868).

Connecticut: Conn. Gen. Stat., Tit. 122, ch. 7, § 124 (1866).

Delaware: Del. Code Ann., Tit. 20, ch. 131, § 7 (1852).

Florida: Acts and Resolutions, ch. 8, § 17 (1868).

Georgia: Ga. Code §§ 4286, 4287, 4290 (1867).

Kingdom of Hawaii: Hawaii Penal Code, ch. 13, § 11 (1868).

Illinois: Ill. Rev. Stat., div. 5, §§ 49, 50 (1845).

Kansas: Kan. (Terr.) Stat., ch. 53, § 7 (1855).

Kentucky: 1 Ky. Rev. Stat., ch. 28, Art. IV, § 11 (1860).

Louisiana: La. Rev. Stat., Crimes and Offences, § 5 (1856).

Maine: Me. Rev. Stat., tit. XII, ch. 160, § 4 (1847).

Maryland: 1 Md. Code, Art. 30, § 201 (1860).

Massachusetts: Mass. Gen. Laws, ch. 165, § 18 (1860).

Michigan: Mich. Rev. Stat., Tit. 30, ch. 158, § 16 (1846).

Minnesota: Minn. Stat., ch. 96, § 13 (1859).

Mississippi: Miss. Rev. Code, ch. 64, Art. 238, § LII, art. 238 (1857).

Missouri: 1 Mo. Rev. Stat., ch. 50, Art. VIII, § 7 (1856).

Montana (Terr.): Mont. Laws, Criminal Practice Acts, ch. IV, § 44 (1864).

Nebraska (Terr.): Neb. Rev. Stat., Crim. Code, ch. 4, § 47 (1866).

Nevada (Terr.): Nev. Comp. Laws, ch. 28 § 45 (1862).

New Hampshire: N. H. Rev. Laws, Act. of June 19, 1812, § 5 (1815).

New Jersey: N. J. Rev. Stat., Tit. 8, ch. 1, § 9 (1847).

New York: 3 N. Y. Rev. Stat., pt. 4, ch. 1, tit. 5, art. 3, § 20 (1858).

North Carolina: N. C. Rev. Code, ch. 34, § 6 (1854).

Oregon: Laws of Ore., Crimes—Against Morality, etc., ch. 7, § 655 (1874).

Pennsylvania: Act of March 31, 1860, § 32, Pub. Law 392, in 1 Digest of Statute Law of Pa. 1700–1903 1011 (Purdon 1905).

Rhode Island: R. I. Gen. Stat., ch. 232, § 12 (1872).

South Carolina: Act of 1712, in 2 Stat. at Large of S. C. 1682–1716, p. 493 (1837).

Tennessee: Tenn. Code, ch. 8, Art. 1, § 4843 (1858).

Texas: Tex. Rev. Stat., Penal Code, tit. 10, ch. 5, Art. 342 (1887) (passed 1860).

Vermont: Laws of the State of Vermont (1779).

Virginia: Va. Code, ch. 149, § 12 (1868).

West Virginia: W. Va. Code, ch. 149, § 12 (1860).

Wisconsin (Terr.): Wis. Stat., § 14 (1839).

having little or no cognizable roots in the language or design of the Constitution. That this is so was painfully demonstrated by the face-off between the Executive and the Court in the 1930's, which resulted in the repudiation of much of the substantive gloss that the Court had placed on the Due Process Clause of the Fifth and Fourteenth Amendments. There should be, therefore, great resistance to expand the substantive reach of those Clauses, particularly if it requires redefining the category of rights deemed to be fundamental. Otherwise, the Judiciary necessarily takes to itself further authority to govern the country without express constitutional authority. The claimed right pressed on us today falls far short of overcoming this resistance.

Respondent, however, asserts that the result should be different where the homosexual conduct occurs in the privacy of the home. He relies on *Stanley v. Georgia,* 394 U.S. 557 (1969), where the Court held that the First Amendment prevents conviction for possessing and reading obscene material in the privacy of his home: "If the First Amendment means anything, it means that a State has no business telling a man, sitting alone in his house, what books he may read or what films he may watch." *Id.,* at 565.

Stanley did protect conduct that would not have been protected outside the home, and it partially prevented the enforcement of state obscenity laws; but the decision was firmly grounded in the First Amendment. The right pressed upon us here has no similar support in the text of the Constitution, and it does not qualify for recognition under the prevailing principles for construing the Fourteenth Amendment. Its limits are also difficult to discern. Plainly enough, otherwise illegal conduct is not always immunized whenever it occurs in the home. Victimless crimes, such as the possession and use of illegal drugs do not escape the law where they are committed at home. *Stanley* itself recognized that its holding offered no protection for the possession in the home of drugs, firearms, or stolen goods. *Id.,* at 568, n. 11. And if respondent's submission is limited to the voluntary sexual conduct between consenting adults, it would be difficult, except by fiat, to limit the claimed right to homosexual conduct while leaving exposed to prosecution adultery, incest, and other sexual crimes even though they are committed in the home. We are unwilling to start down that road.

Even if the conduct at issue here is not a fundamental right, respondent asserts that there must be a rational basis for the law and that there is none in this case other than the presumed belief of a majority of the electorate in Georgia that homosexual sodomy is immoral and unacceptable. This is said to be an inadequate rationale to support the law. The law, however, is constantly based on notions of morality, and if all laws representing essentially moral choices are to be invalidated under the Due Process Clause, the courts will be very busy indeed. Even respondent makes no such claim, but insists that majority sentiments about the morality of homosexuality should be declared inadequate. We do not agree, and are unpersuaded that the sodomy laws of some 25 States should be invalidated on this basis.

Accordingly, the judgment of the Court of Appeals is

Reversed.

Chief Justice Burger, concurring.

I join the Court's opinion, but I write separately to underscore my view that in constitutional terms there is no such thing as a fundamental right to commit homosexual sodomy.

As the Court notes, *ante* at 5, the proscriptions against sodomy have very "ancient roots." Decisions of individuals relating to homosexual conduct have been subject to state intervention throughout the history of Western Civilization. Condemnation of those practices is firmly rooted in Judeao-Christian moral and ethical standards. Homosexual sodomy was a capital crime under Roman law. See Code Theod. 9.7.6; Code Just. 9.9.31. See also D. Bailey, Homosexuality in the Western Christian Tradition 70–81 (1975). During the English Reformation when powers of the ecclesiastical courts were transferred to the King's Courts, the first English statute criminalizing sodomy was passed. 25 Hen. VIII, c. 6. Blackstone described "the infamous crime against nature" as an offense of "deeper malignity" than rape, an heinous act "the very mention of which is a disgrace to human nature," and "a crime not fit to be named." Blackstone's Commentaries *215. The common law of England, including its prohibition of sodomy, became the received law of Georgia and the other Colonies. In 1816 the Georgia Legislature passed the statute at issue here, and that statute has been continuously in force in one form or another since that time. To hold that the act of homosexual sodomy is somehow protected as a fundamental right would be to cast aside millennia of moral teaching.

This is essentially not a question of personal "preferences" but rather one of the legislative authority of the State. I find nothing in the Constitution depriving a State of the power to enact the statute challenged here.

Justice Powell concurred.

Justice Blackmun, with whom Justice Brennan, Justice Marshall, and Justice Stevens join, dissenting.

. . .

We protect those rights not because they contribute, in some direct and material way, to the general public welfare, but because they form so central a part of an individual's life. "[T]he concept of privacy embodies the 'moral fact that a person belongs to himself and not others nor to society as a whole.' " *Thornburgh v. American Coll. of Obst. & Gyn.,*——U. S., at——, n. 5 (Stevens, J., concurring) (slip op. 6, n. 5), quoting Fried, Correspondence, 6 Phil. & Pub. Affairs 288–289 (1977). And so we protect the decision whether to marry precisely because marriage "is an association that promotes a way of life, not causes; a harmony in living, not political faiths; a bilateral loyalty, not commercial or social projects." *Griswold v. Connecticut,* 381 U.S., at 486. We protect the decision whether to have a child because parenthood alters so dramatically an individual's self-definition, not because of demographic considerations or the Bible's command to be fruitful and multiply. Cf. *Thornburgh v. American Coll. of Obst. & Gyn., supra,* at——, n.6. (Stevens, J., concurring) (slip op. 6, n. 6). And we protect the family because it contributes so powerfully to the happiness of individuals, not because of a preference for stereotypical households. Cf. *Moore v. East Cleveland,* 431 U.S., at 500–506 (plurality opinion). The Court recognized in *Roberts,* 468 U.S., at 619, that the "ability independently to define one's identity that is central to any concept of liberty" cannot truly be exercised in a vacuum; we all depend on the "emotional enrichment of close ties with others." *Ibid.*

Only the most willful blindness could obscure the fact that sexual intimacy is "a sensitive, key relationship of human existence, central to family life, community welfare, and the development of the human personality," *Paris Adult Theatre I v. Slayton,* 413 U.S. 49, 63 (1973); see also *Carey v. Population Services International,* 431 U.S. 678, 685 (1977). The fact that individuals define themselves in a significant way through their intimate sexual relationships with others suggests, in a Nation as diverse as ours, that there may be many "right" ways of conducting those relationships, and that much of the richness of a relationship will come from the freedom an individual has to *choose* the form and nature of these intensely personal bonds. See Karst, The Freedom of Intimate Association, 89 Yale L.J. 624, 637 (1980); cf. *Eisenstadt v. Baird,* 405 U.S. 438, 453 (1972); *Roe v. Wade,* 410 U.S., at 153.

. . .

The core of petitioner's defense of § 16–6–2, however, is that respondent and others who engage in the conduct prohibited by § 16–6–2 interfere with Georgia's exercise of the " 'right of the Nation and of the States to maintain a decent society,' " *Paris Adult Theater I v. Slaton,* 413 U.S., at 59–60, quoting *Jacobellis v. Ohio,* 378 U.S. 184, 199 (1964) (Warren, C.J., dissenting). Essentially, petitioner argues, and the Court agrees, that the fact that the acts described in § 16–6–2 "for hundreds of years, if not thousands, have been uniformly condemned as immoral" is a sufficient reason to permit a State to ban them today. . . .

I cannot agree that either the length of time a majority has held its convictions or the passions with which it defends them can withdraw legislation from this Court's scrutiny. See, *e.g., Roe v. Wade,* 410 U.S. 113 (1973); *Loving v. Virginia* [*supra*]; *Brown v. Board of Education,* 347 U.S. 483 (1954).[5] As Justice Jackson wrote so eloquently for the Court in *West Virginia Board of Education v. Barnette* [XI, 2], "we apply the limitations of the Constitution with no fear that freedom to be intellectually and spiritually diverse or even contrary will disintegrate the social organization. . . . [F]reedom to differ is not limited to things that do not matter much. That would be a mere shadow of freedom. The test of its substance is the right to differ as to things that touch the heart of the existing order." See also Karst, 89 Yale L.J., at 627. It is precisely because the issue raised by this case touches the heart of what makes individuals what they are that we should be especially sensitive to the rights of those whose choices upset the majority.

The assertion that "traditional Judeo-Christian values proscribe" the conduct involved, Brief for Petitioner 20, cannot provide an adequate justification for § 16-6-2. That certain, but by no means all, religious groups condemn the behavior at issue gives the State no license to impose their judgments on the entire citizenry. The legitimacy of secular legislation depends instead on whether the State can advance some justification for its law beyond its conformity to religious doctrine. See, *e.g., McGowan v. Maryland* [XIII, 2]; *Stone v. Graham* [XIV, 2]. Thus, far from buttressing his case, petitioner's invocation of Leviticus, Romans, St. Thomas Aquinas, and sodomy's heretical status during the Middle Ages undermines his suggestion that §16-6-2 represents a legitimate use of secular coercive power.[6] A State can no more punish private behavior because of religious intolerance than it can punish such behavior because of racial animus. "The Constitution cannot control such prejudices, but neither can it tolerate them. Private

---

[5] The parallel between *Loving* and this case is almost uncanny. There, too, the State relied on a religious justification for its law. Compare 388 U.S., at 3 (quoting trial court's statement that "Almighty God created the races white, black, yellow, malay and red, and he placed them on separate continents. . . . The fact that he separated the races shows that he did not intend for the races to mix"), with Brief for Petitioner 20-21 (relying on the Old and New Testaments and the writings of St. Thomas Aquinas to show that "traditional Judeo-Christian values proscribe such conduct"). There, too, defenders of the challenged statute relied heavily on the fact that when the Fourteenth Amendment was ratified, most of the States had similar prohibitions. Compare Brief for Appellee in *Loving v. Virginia,* O. T. 1966, No. 395, pp. 28-29, with *ante,* at 5-7 and n. 6. There, too, at the time the case came before the Court, many of the States still had criminal statutes concerning the conduct at issue. Compare 388 U.S., at 6, n. 5 (noting that 16 States still outlawed interracial marriage), with *ante,* 6-7 (noting that 24 States and the District of Columbia have sodomy statutes). Yet the Court held, not only that the invidious racism of Virginia's law violated the Equal Protection Clause, see 388 U.S., at 7-12, but also that the law deprived the Lovings of due process by denying them the "freedom of choice to marry" that had "long been recognized as one of the vital personal rights essential to the orderly pursuit of happiness by free men." *Id.,* at 12.

[6] The theological nature of the origin of Anglo-American antisodomy statutes is patent. It was not until 1533 that sodomy was made a secular offense in England. 25 Hen. VIII, cap. 6. Until that time, the offense was, in Sir James Stephen's words, "merely ecclesiastical." 2 J. Stephen, A History of the Criminal Law of England 430 (1883). Pollock and Maitland similarly observed that "[t]he crime against nature. . . . was so closely connected with heresy that the vulgar had but one name for both." 2 F. Pollock & F. Maitland, The History of English Law 554 (1895). The transfer of jurisdiction over prosecutions for sodomy to the secular courts seems primarily due to the alteration of ecclesiastical jurisdiction attendant on England's break with the Roman Catholic Church, rather than to any new understanding of the sovereign's interest in preventing or punishing the behavior involved. Cf. E. Coke, The Third Part of the Institutes of the Laws of England, ch. 10 (4th ed. 1797).

biases may be outside the reach of the law, but the law cannot, directly or indirectly give them effect." *Palmore v. Sidoti,* 466 U.S. 429, 433 (1984). No matter how uncomfortable a certain group may make the majority of this Court, we have held that "[m]ere public intolerance or animosity cannot constitutionally justify the deprivation of a person's physical liberty." *O'Connor v. Donaldson,* 422 U.S. 563, 575 (1975). See also *City of Cleburne v. Cleburne Living Center,*——U.S.——(1985); *U. S. Dept. of Agriculture v. Moreno,* 413 U.S. 528, 534 (1973).

Epilogue

No War of Religion has been fought on the American continent. No person has been put to death in America on account of religion. Religion has not disappeared or declined but has flourished in multiple forms in this country. That the first two achievements are great goods will be disputed by no one. Their greatness can be appreciated only by consideration of the history of our ancestors. That the third achievement is a great good will be doubted by no one who is a believer or is able to empathize with a believer. These great goods are owed to biblical religion, European experience, and the Constitution of the United States.

Amish, Baptists, Black Muslims, Catholics, Christian Scientists, Episcopalians, Evangelicals, Hopi, Jehovah's Witnesses, Jews, Lutherans, Mennonites, Methodists, Mormons, Native Americans, Navahos, Presbyterians, Rumanian Orthodox, Russian Orthodox, Scientologists, Serbian Orthodox, Unification Church members—to list only the principal religious litigants—have found in the framework afforded by the Constitution a way of living with governmental power not always satisfying to their demands but always accommodating enough not to destroy them or even to choke their development. The most successful litigants—the Jehovah's Witnesses—have been the most persistent. Like the unjust judge of the gospel parable (Luke 18:2-5), the Supreme Court ultimately appears to yield to importunity—not because it is unjust but because it is responsive to advocacy. The Supreme Court is responsive to advocacy because the Constitution is open to argument, interpretation, and reinterpretation.

"Contemporary constitutional law just does not know how to handle problems of religion," writes a keen observer in the summer of 1986.[1] Few who attempt to analyze and bring order to the cases set out in Part III will challenge this judgment. Two comments must be added. First, "contemporary constitutional law" is a phrase that personifies doctrine; the concept of doctrine is substituted for persons. It is persons who make the law. The failures, such as they are, are the failures of justices, collectively and individually, of the Supreme Court: hence the interest in the religion and other relevant characteristics of the justices. Second, the failures—the arbitrariness, omissions, and incoherences—occur within the broad peaceful boundaries set by our constitutional scheme. They do not subvert the sound structure.

Within that structure, not only has religious belief flourished; religious animosity has withered. The consensus on the goods of religious peace and religious liberty is unchallenged. Each of the main religious groups in America can claim an ancestor whose voice and actions were crucial in forming the consensus—Isaiah, asserting the basic claim that governmental power is subject to religious criticism; Thomas Becket, dying for the freedom of the Church; Roger Williams, defending religious freedom as a corollary to religious principle. Believers and unbelievers alike have patron prophets in James Madison and Thomas Jefferson, the most significant of the Founding Fathers. To a cynic, Isaiah was a self-righteous fool, Becket a meddlesome priest, Williams a dreamer in the wilderness, Madison and Jefferson politicians who knew how to count a majority. To a believer, these men have been illuminated by a light greater than that of human making; and their vision, to which millions have responded, has made possible a nation under law and under God.

Note

1. Mark Tushnet, "The Constitution of Religion," *Connecticut Law Review*, 18(1986):702.

Bibliography

Abbreviations

CSEL   *Corpus scriptorum ecclesiasticorum latinorum* (Vienna: C. Geroldi, 1866–   ).
PG   J. P. Migne, *Patrologiae cursus completus. Series graeca* (Paris: Migne, 1857–1866).
PL   J. P. Migne, *Patrologiae cursus completus. Series latina* (Paris: Migne, 1844–1880).
RS   Rolls Series or *Rerum britanicarum medii aevi scriptores* (London: Longmans, 1858–1896).

Adams, John. *Diary and Autobiography of John Adams,* ed. L. H. Butterfield, Leonard C. Faber, and Wendell D. Garrett (Cambridge, Mass.: Belknap Press of Harvard University Press, 1961).

Alexander of Hales. "De conscientia." In Odon Lottin, *Psychologie et morale aux XIIe et XIIIe siècles* (1945).

American Law Institute. *Restatement of Torts, Second* (St. Paul, Minn.: American Law Institute Publishers, 1977).

Ames, Fisher. *Works,* ed. W. B. Allen (Indianapolis: Library Classics, 1983).

Aniteau, Chester J., Arthur T. Downey, and Edward C. Roberts. *Freedom from Federal Establishment* (Milwaukee, Wisc.: Bruce Publishing Co., 1964).

Anti-Defamation League of B'nai B'rith. *ADL Law Report: Litigation Docket: 1986* (New York, 1986).

———. *Religion and the Public Schools* (New York, 1984).

Aquinas, Thomas. *Scriptum super quatuor libros in sententiarun Magister Petri Lombardi* (Parma, 1852–1873).

———. *Summa theologiae* (Rome: Leonine ed., 1903).

Archives of Maryland: Proceedings and Acts of the General Assembly of Maryland, Jan. 1637/ 1638–Sept. 1664, ed. William Hand Browne (Baltimore: Maryland Historical Society, 1883).

Aristotle, *Nichomachean Ethics,* tr. D. P. Chase (New York: E. P. Dutton, 1930).

Arrington, Leonard J. *Brigham Young: American Moses* (New York: Alfred A. Knopf, 1985).

——— and Davis Bitton. *The Mormon Experience: A History of the Latter Day Saints* (New York: Alfred A. Knopf, 1979).

Augustine. *Letters, CSEL* 44.

———. *De Civitate Dei contra paganos (The City of God), CSEL* 40.

Backus, Isaac. *A History of New England with particular reference to the denomination of Christians called Baptists* (Newton, 1871; New York: Arno Press reprint, 1969).

Baker, Liva. *Felix Frankfurter* (New York: Coward-McCann, 1969).

Ball, Milner S. *Lying Down Together: Law, Metaphor and Theology* (Madison: University of Wisconsin Press, 1985).

Ball, William B. "Building a Landmark Case." In *Compulsory Education and the Amish,* ed. Albert N. Keim (Boston: Beacon Press, 1975).

Bau, Ignatius. *This Ground Is Holy: Church Sanctuary and Central American Refugees* (New York: Paulist Press, 1985).

Beckford, James A. *The Trumpet of Prophecy: A Sociological Study of Jehovah's Witnesses* (Oxford: Basil Blackwell, 1975).

Beecher, Lyman. *Autobiography*, ed. Barbara M. Cross (Cambridge, Mass.: Belknap Press of Harvard University Press, 1961).

Bellah, Robert N. *The Broken Covenant: American Civil Religion in Time of Trial* (New York: Seabury Press, 1967).

Bender, Harold S. "A Brief Biography of Menno Simons," *The Complete Writings of Menno Simons* (Scottdale, Pa.: Mennonite Publishing House, 1956).

Biographical Dictionary of the Federal Judiciary, comp. Harold Chase, Samuel Krislov, Keith Boyum, and Jerry N. Clark (Detroit: Gale Research Co., 1976).

Black, Hugo, Jr. *My Father: A Remembrance* (New York: Random House, 1975).

Blanshard, Paul. *American Freedom and Catholic Power* (Boston: Beacon Press, 1949).

Boles, Donald E. *The Bible, Religion, and the Public Schools* (Ames: Iowa State University Press, 1965).

Book of Doctrines and Covenants. Reorganized Church of Jesus Christ of Latter Day Saints (Independence, Mo.: Herald Publishing House, 1970).

Bracton, Henri de. *Bracton's Notebook*, ed. F. W. Maitland (London: B. Quaritch, 1895).

―――. *The Laws and Customs of England*, ed. Samuel Thorne (Cambridge, Mass.: Belknap Press of Harvard University Press, 1968).

Bradley, Joseph Philo. *Miscellaneous Writings*, ed. Charles Bradley (Newark, N.J.: L. J. Hardman, 1902).

Brückner, Aleksander. "The Polish Reformation in the Sixteenth Century." In *Polish Civilization*, ed. Mieczyslaw Giergielwic (New York: New York University Press, 1979).

Buchbinder, Reinhard. *Bibelzitate, Bibelanspielungen, Bibelparodien, theologische Vergleiche und Analogien bei Marx und Engels* (Berlin: E. Schmidt, 1976).

Buckley, Thomas E., S.J. *Church and State in Revolutionary Virginia 1776-1787* (Charlottesville: University Press of Virginia, 1977).

Bushman, Richard L. *Joseph Smith and the Beginnings of Mormonism* (Chicago: University of Illinois Press, 1984).

Buzzard, Lynn. "The Evangelical Rediscovery of Law and Politics." *Journal of Law and Religion* 1 (1983).

Carmichael, Calum. *Law & Narrative in the Bible* (Ithaca, N.Y.: Cornell University Press, 1985).

Cassou, April Kestell and Robert Curran. "Secular Orthodoxy and Sacred Freedoms: Accreditation and Church-Related Schools." *Journal of College and University Law* (1984).

Cheney, Christopher R. *Pope Innocent III and England* (Stuttgart: A. Hierseman, 1976).

―――― and F. W. Powicke. *Councils and Synods with Other Documents Relating to the English Church* (Oxford: Clarendon Press, 1964).

Cherrington, Ernest. *History of the Anti-Saloon League* (Westerville, Ohio: 1913).

Choper, Jesse H. "The Religion Clauses of the First Amendment: Reconciling the Conflict." *University of Pittsburgh Law Review* 41 (1980):673-701.

Clark, Norman H. *Deliver Us from Evil: An Interpretation of American Prohibition* (New York: W. W. Norton, 1976).

Comment. "State v. Faith Baptist Church: State Regulation of Religious Education." *Creighton Law Review* 15 (1981).

Conciliorum oecumenicorum decreta, ed. Giuseppe Alberigo (1973).

Cord, Robert. "Church-State Separation: Restoring the 'No Preference' Doctrine of the First Amendment." *Harvard Journal of Law and Public Policy* 9 (1986).

Cover, Robert M. "The Supreme Court 1982 Term-Foreword: Nomos and Narrative." *Harvard Law Review* 97 (1983):4-79.

Curry, Thomas J. *The First Freedoms: Church and State in America to the Passage of the First Amendment* (New York: Oxford University Press, 1986).

Cushing, John D. "Notes on Disestablishment in Massachusetts, 1780–1833." *William and Mary Quarterly* (1969).

Cyprian. *De lapsis (The Lapsed), PL* 4.

Dewey, John. "S. 2499, Its Antidemocratic Implications." *The Nation's Schools* 39 (March 1947).

Doncoeur, P. and Y. Lanners. *La Réhabilitation de Jeanne La Purcelle. L'enquête ordonnée par Charles VII en 1450 et le codicille de Guillaume Bouille* (Paris: Librairie d'Argences, 1956).

Douglas, William O. *Go East, Young Man* (New York: Random House, 1974).

Dresser, Amos. "The Narrative of Amos Dresser." In *Slavery Attacked: The Abolitionist Crusade,* ed. John L. Thomas. (Englewood Cliffs, N.J.: Prentice-Hall, 1965).

Dunn, James M. "The Christian as Political Activist." *Liberty* 81 (July–August 1986).

Eckenrode, H. J. *Separation of Church and State in Virginia* (New York: Da Capo Press Reprint, 1971).

Elliot, Jonathan. *The Debates in the Several State Conventions on the Adoption of the Federal Constitution* (Philadelphia: J. B. Lippincott, 1836).

Ellis, George D. (comp.). *Platforms of the Two Great Political Parties* (Washington, D.C.: Government Printing Office, 1928).

Elton, G. R. *Reform and Reformation: England, 1509–1558* (Cambridge, Mass.: Harvard University Press, 1978).

Eusebius. *Ecclesiastical History* (Cambridge: At the University Press, 1898).

———. *The Life of Constantine, PL* 8.

Fairman, Charles. "Does the Fourteenth Amendment Incorporate the Bill of Rights?" *Stanford Law Review* 2 (1949):5–173.

Fehrenbacher, Don E. *The Dred Scott Case: Its Significance in American Law and Politics* (New York: Oxford University Press, 1978).

Fitzmyer, Joseph A. "A Life of Paul" and "The Letter to the Romans." In *The Jerome Biblical Commentary,* ed. Raymond E. Brown, Joseph A. Fitzmyer, and Roland E. Murphy (Englewood Cliffs, N.J.: Prentice-Hall, 1968).

Foliot, Gilbert. *Foliot to Thomas* (1166), *RS* 67.

Foxe, John. *Acts and Monuments of these latter and perilous days* (London: George Seeley, 1870).

Freund, Paul A. "Public Aid to Parochial Schools." *Harvard Law Review* 82 (1980):1680–1692.

"Fundamentalists Leave Jail, But Nebraska Church Schools Are Still in Trouble." *Christianity Today* (July 13, 1984).

Furniss, Norman F. *The Mormon Conflict, 1850–1859* (New Haven, Conn.: Yale University Press, 1960).

Gal, Allon. *Brandeis of Boston* (Cambridge, Mass.: Harvard University Press, 1980).

Garvey, John. "Another Way of Looking at School Aid." *Supreme Court Review* (1985) 61–92.

Giannella, Donald A. "*Lemon* and *Tilton:* The Bitter and the Sweet of Church–State Entanglement." *Supreme Court Review* (1971) 147–200.

Given, James B. *Society and Homicide in Thirteenth Century England* (Stanford, Calif.: Stanford University Press, 1977).

Goodel, William. "Slavery Tested by Its Own Code." *Quarterly Anti-Slavery Magazine* (1836).

Gratian. *Concordia discordantium canonum (Harmony of Unharmonious Canons),* ed. Emil Friedberg (Leipzig: B. Tauchnitz, 1879).

Green, Beriah. "Letter to a Minister of the Gospel." *Quarterly Anti-Slavery Magazine* (1836).

Gregory IX. *Decretales,* ed. Emil Friedberg (Leipzig: B. Tauchnitz, 1881).

Grosseteste, Robert. *Letters, RS* 25.

Gunther, Gerald. *Constitutional Law: Cases and Materials* (Mineola, N.Y.: Foundation Press, 1975).

Hastings, Hugh. *Ecclesiastical Records of the State of New York* (Albany, N.Y.: James B. Lyon, 1901).

Heiser, Francis. "The Law Versus the Conscientious Objector." *University of Chicago Law Review* 20 (1953):441–460.

Hill, John Edward Christopher. *Change and Continuity in Seventeenth Century England* (London: Weidenfeld & Nicolson, 1974).

Hirsch, Samson Raphael. *Hirsch Siddur: The Order of Prayers for the Whole Year* (Eng. trans., Jerusalem, 1969).

Hitchcock, James. "Church, State and Moral Values: The Limits of American Pluralism." *Law & Contemporary Problems* 44 (1981):13–23.

Holmes, O. W., Jr. *Holmes–Laski Letters,* ed. Mark DeWolfe Howe (Cambridge, Mass.: Harvard University Press, 1953).

Holt, James C. *Magna Carta* (Cambridge: At the University Press, 1965).

Hostetler, John A. *Amish Society,* 3rd ed. (Baltimore: Johns Hopkins University Press, 1980).

———. "The Cultural Context of the Wisconsin Case." In *Compulsory Education and the Amish: The Right Not to Be Modern,* ed. Albert N. Keim (Boston: Beacon Press, 1975).

How to Settle the Texas Question (Boston: E. Wright, 1845).

Howard, J. Woodford. *Mr. Justice Murphy: A Political Biography* (Princeton, N.J.: Princeton University Press, 1968).

Howe, Mark DeWolfe. "Foreword: Political Theory and the Nature of Liberty, The Supreme Court, 1952 Term." *Harvard Law Review* 67 (1953):91–95.

———. *The Garden and the Wilderness: Religion and Government in American Constitutional History* (Chicago: University of Chicago Press, 1965).

"In Nebraska, the War Between Church and State Rages On." *Christianity Today* (February 17, 1984).

Innocent III, *Gesta Innocenti III, PL* 216.

———. *De miseria humanae conditionis (The Misery of the Human Condition),* ed. Michele Maccarrone (Lucca: Thesaurus Mundi 1955).

———. *Selected Letters of Pope Innocent III Concerning England, 1198–1216,* ed. Christopher R. Cheney and W. H. Semple (New York: T. Nelson, 1953).

"Is the Nebraska School Trouble Finally Over?" *Christianity Today* (July 13, 1984).

Isaac, Rhys. " 'The Rage of Malice of the Old Serpent Devil': The Dissenters and the Making and Remaking of the Virginia Statute for Religious Freedom" (Cambridge: At the University Press, forthcoming).

Israel, Fred L. "Wiley Rutledge." In *The Justices of the United States Supreme Court 1789–1969,* ed. Leon Friedman and Fred L. Israel (New York: Chelsea House, 1969).

Jefferson, Thomas. *Autobiography, Writings,* ed. Albert E. Bergh (Washington, D.C.: Jefferson Memorial Association, 1907).

———. *Jefferson's Reports* in *Virginia Reports Annotated* (1903).

———. *Notes on Virginia, Works,* ed. Paul L. Ford (New York: C. P. Putnam's Sons, 1892).

———. *Papers,* ed. Julian P. Boyd (Princeton, N.J.: Princeton University Press, 1950).

Jerome Biblical Commentary, ed. Raymond E. Brown, Joseph A. Fitzmyer, and Roland E. Murphy (Englewood Cliffs, N.J.: Prentice-Hall, 1962).

John of Salisbury. *The Letters of John of Salisbury,* ed. W. J. Millor and C. N. L. Brooke (Oxford: Clarendon Press, 1979).

———. *Policraticus,* ed. C. I. Webb (Oxford: Clarendon Press, 1909).

Johnson, Samuel. *Dictionary* (London: W. Strahan, 1755).

Kauper, Paul G. and Steven C. Ellis. "Religious Corporations and the Law." *Michigan Law Review* 71 (1973):1499–1574.

Keim, Albert N. "From Erlanbach to New Glarus." In *Compulsory Education and the Amish: The Right Not to Be Modern,* ed. Albert N. Keim (Boston: Beacon Press, 1975).

Kent, James. *Commentaries on American Law* (New York: The Author, 1844).

King, Martin Luther. *Letter from Birmingham Jail* (Stamford, Conn.: Overbrook Press, 1968).

Klein, Isaac. *A Guide to Jewish Religious Practice* (New York: Jewish Theological Seminary of America, 1979).

Klibansky, Raymond. "Preface to John Locke." *Epistola de Tolerantia* (Oxford: Clarendon Press, 1968).

Knauer, Peter. "The Hermeneutic Function of the Principle of Double Effect." *Natural Law Forum* 12 (1967):132–162.

Knowles, David. *Thomas Becket* (Stanford, Calif.: Stanford University Press, 1971).

Lactantius. *De mortibus persecutorum (The Deaths of the Persecutors), PL* 7.

Lader, Lawrence. *Abortion* (Boston: Beacon Press, 1967).

Lake, Beverly. "Freedom to Worship Curiously." *Florida University Law Review* 1 (1948):203–241.

Laplatte, C. "Cauchon," *Dictionnaire d'histoire et de géographie écclesiastiques* (Paris: Letouzey et Ané, 1953), vol. 12.

Latimer, Hugh. *Selected Sermons of Hugh Latimer,* ed. Allan G. Chester (Cranburynswick, N.Y.: Folger Books, 1978).

Lecler, Joseph. *Toleration and the Reformation,* trans. T. L. Weslow (New York: Association Press, 1960).

Leo XIII. *Arcanum,* February 10, 1880, *Acta Sanctae Sedis* 12:385–402.

Levinson, Sanford. " 'The Constitution' in American Civil Religion." *Supreme Court Review* (1979) 123–151.

Levy, Leonard W. *Blasphemy in Massachusetts* (New York: Da Capo Press, 1973).

———. *The Religion Clauses* (New York: Macmillan, 1986).

Lieber, Francis. *Contributions to Political Science, Miscellaneous Writings,* vol. 2 (Philadelphia: J. B. Lippincott, 1881).

———. *Manual of Political Ethics* (Boston: C. C. Brown and J. Little, 1839).

———. *On Civil Liberty and Self Government* (Philadelphia: J. B. Lippincott, 1859).

Lincoln, Abraham. *Collected Works,* ed. Roy P. Basler (New Brunswick, N.J.: Rutgers University Press, 1953).

Loades, D. M. *The Oxford Martyrs* (London: Batsford, 1970).

Locke, John. *Epistola de Tolerantia (Letter on Toleration),* ed. Raymond Klibansky (Oxford: Clarendon Press, 1968).

———. *The Second Treatise of Government,* ed. J. W. Gough (Oxford: Basil Blackwell, 1966).

Lord, Robert H., John E. Sexton, and Edward T. Harrington. *History of the Archdiocese of Boston* (Boston: Pilot Publishing Co., 1945).

MacMaster, R. K., S. L. Holste, and R. F. Ulle. *Conscience in Crisis: Mennonite and Other Peace Churches in America, 1739–1789* (Scottdale, Pa.: Herald Press, 1979).

Madison, James. (Posthumously Published Essay). *Harper's* (March 1914).

———. *Papers,* ed. William T. Hutchinson and William M. E. Rachal (Chicago: University of Chicago Press, 1962).

———. *Record of the Federal Convention of 1787,* ed. Max Farrand (New Haven, Conn.: Yale University Press, 1911).

————. Alexander Hamilton, and John Jay. *The Federalist Papers* (Baltimore: Johns Hopkins University Press, 1960).

Mann, Horace. *Eleventh Annual Report of the State Board of Education* [in Massachusetts] (1847). In *Life and Works of Horace Mann* Boston: Lee & Shepard, 1891).

————. *Twelfth Annual Report of the State Board of Education* [in Massachusetts] (1848). In *Life and Works of Horace Mann* (Boston: Lee & Shepard, 1891).

Mansfield, John H. "Conscientious Objection–1964 Term." In *Religion and Public Order,* ed. Donald A. Giannella (Chicago: University of Chicago Press, 1965).

Manwaring, David R. *Render unto Caesar: The Flag-Salute Controversy* (Chicago: University of Chicago Press, 1962).

Marcus, Jacob R. *The Colonial American Jew, 1492–1776* (Detroit: Wayne State University Press, 1970).

Mason, Alpheus Thomas. *Harlan Fiske Stone: Pillar of the Law* (New York: Viking, 1956).

Massie, Robert K. *Peter the Great* (New York: Alfred A. Knopf, 1980).

McCollum, Vashti Cromwell. *One Woman's Fight* (Garden City, N.Y.: Doubleday, 1951).

McConnell, Michael W. "Accommodation of Religion." *Supreme Court Review* (1985) 1–60.

McLoughlin, William G. *New England Dissent 1630–1833* (Cambridge, Mass.: Harvard University Press, 1971).

Melton, J. Gordon (ed.). *Encyclopedia of American Religion* (Wilmington, N.C.: McGrath Publishing, 1978).

Menno [Simons], "Een klare beantwoordinge over eene schrift Gelii Fabri." In *The Complete Writings of Menno Simons,* ed. John Christian Wenger (Scottdale, Pa.: Herald Press, 1966).

Messages and Papers of the Presidents 1789–1897, ed. James D. Richardson (Washington, D.C.: Government Printing Office, 1896).

Meyer, Jacob C. *Church and State in Massachusetts from 1740 to 1833* (Cleveland, Ohio: Western Reserve University Press, 1930).

Miller, Perry. *Nature's Nation* (Cambridge, Mass.: Harvard University Press, 1967).

————. *Roger Williams* (Indianapolis: Bobbs-Merrill, 1953).

Miller, William Lee. *The First Liberty: Religion and the American Republic* (New York: Alfred A. Knopf, 1986).

More, Thomas. *Correspondence of Sir Thomas More,* ed. Elizabeth Frances Rogers (Princeton, N.J.: Princeton University Press, 1947).

————. *Utopia,* ed. Robert M. Adams (New York: W. W. Norton, 1976).

Morgan, Edmund S. *The Puritan Dilemma* (Boston: Little, Brown, 1958).

Morison, Samuel Eliot. "The Struggle over the Adoption of the Constitution of Massachusetts, 1780." Massachusetts Historical Society, *Proceedings* 50 (1916–1917).

————. "The Great Rebellion in Harvard College and the Resignation of President Kirkland." Colonial Society of America *Transactions* (1920).

Morris, Aldon D. *The Origins of the Civil Rights Movement* (New York: Free Press, 1984).

Murray, John Courtney. "Governmental Repression of Heresy." *Proceedings of the Catholic Theological Society of America* (1948).

————. "War and Conscience." In *A Conflict of Loyalties: The Case for Selective Conscientious Objection,* ed. James Finn (New York: Pegasus, 1968).

Noonan, John T., Jr. *A Private Choice: Abortion in America in the Seventies* (New York: Free Press, 1979).

————. *Bribes* (New York: Macmillan, 1985).

————. "The Family and the Supreme Court." *Catholic University Law Review* 23 (1973):255.

————. "Book Review of Robillard." *American Journal of Comparative Law* 33 (1985).

Note. "The Establishment Clause and Religion in Child Custody Disputes: Factoring Religion into the Best Interest Equation." *Michigan Law Review* 82 (1984):1702–1738.

Note. "The Supreme Court, Effect Inquiry, and Aid to Parochial Education." *Stanford Law Review* 37 (1984):219–251.

O'Dea, Thomas. *The Mormons* (Chicago: University of Chicago Press, 1957).

Paludan, Phillip S. *A Covenant with Death* (Urbana: University of Illinois Press, 1975).

Parker, Theodore. *The Slave Power*, ed. James K. Hosner. (Boston: American Unitarian Association; reprint, New York: Arno Press, 1969).

———. *Works* (Boston: American Unitarian Association, 1907–1913).

Penton, M. James. *Apocalypse Delayed* (Toronto: University of Toronto Press, 1985).

Pepys, Samuel. *Diary*, ed. Robert Latham and William Matthews (Berkeley: University of California Press, 1970).

Perry, Michael J. *The Constitution, the Courts, and Human Rights* (New Haven, Conn.: Yale University Press, 1982).

Pfeffer, Leo. "Amici in Church-State Litigation." *Law & Contemporary Problems* 44 (1981):83–110.

Phelps, Amos A. *Lectures on Slavery and Its Remedy* (Boston: New England Anti-Slavery Society, 1834; republished St. Clair Shores, Mich.: Scholarly Press, 1970).

Pospielovsky, Dimitry. *The Russian Church under the Soviet Regime, 1917–1982* (Crestwood, N.Y.: St. Vladimir's Seminary Press, 1984).

Potter, Ralph. "Conscientious Objection to Particular Wars." In *Religion and the Public Order*, ed. Donald Giannella. (Ithaca, N.Y.: Cornell University Press, 1968).

Prucha, Francis P. *The Churches and the Indian Schools 1888–1912* (Lincoln: University of Nebraska Press, 1979).

Pusey, Merlo. *Charles Evans Hughes* (New York: Macmillan, 1951).

Religious Law Reporter (Oak Park, Ill.: Christian Legal Society, 1981–   ).

Richardson, Herbert (ed.). *Constitutional Issues in the Case of Rev. Moon* (New York: Edwin Mellen Press, 1984).

Rhodes, James Ford. *History of the United States* (New York: Macmillan, 1910).

Rodes, Robert E., Jr. *Lay Authority and Reformation in the English Church* (Notre Dame, Ind.: University of Notre Dame Press, 1982).

———. "Pluralist Christendom and the Christian Civil Magistrate." *Communio* 9 (1982):321–338.

———. "The Passing of Nonsectarianism: Some Reflections on the School Prayer Case." *Notre Dame Lawyer* 38 (1963):115–137.

Rohr, John A. *Prophets Without Honor, Public Policy and the Selective Conscientious Objector* (Nashville, Tenn.: Abingdon Press, 1971).

Rowe, H. Edward. *The Day They Padlocked the Church* (Shreveport, La.: Huntington House, 1983).

Ruskin, Bayard. *Strategies for Freedom* (New York: Columbia University Press, 1976).

Sandburg, Carl. *Abraham Lincoln* (New York: Harcourt, Brace, 1939).

Saperstein, David. "Jewish Perspectives on the Role of Religion in the Political Process." *Journal of Law and Religion* 1 (1983):220.

Scarisbrick, J. J. *Henry VIII* (Berkeley: University of California Press, 1968).

Schumpeter, Joseph. *Capitalism, Socialism, and Democracy* (New York: Harper & Row, 1950).

Second Vatican Council. *Acta Synodalia* (Rome: Vatican Polyglot Press, 1978).

Shugrue, Richard E. "An Approach to Mutual Respect: The Christian School Controversy." *Creighton Law Review* 18 (1984–85):219–257.

Sibley, Mulford Q. and Philip E. Jacob. *Conscription of Conscience: The American State and the Conscientious Objector, 1940–1947* (Ithaca, N.Y.: Cornell University Press, 1952).

Sinclair, Andrew. *Prohibition: The Era of Excess* (Boston: Little, Brown, 1962).

Smith, Michael E. "The Special Place of Religion in the Constitution." *Supreme Court Review* (1983):105–118.

Sorauf, Frank J. *The Wall of Separation* (Princeton, N.J.: Princeton University Press, 1976).

Spinoza, Baruch. *The Political Works*, ed. A. G. Wernham (Oxford: Clarendon Press, 1958).

Stokes, Anson Phelps. *Church and State in the United States* (New York: Harper, 1950).

Stoll, Joseph. "Who Shall Educate Our Children?" In *Compulsory Education and the Amish: The Right Not to Be Modern*, ed. Albert N. Keim (Boston: Beacon Press, 1975).

Stroup, Herbert Hewitt. *The Jehovah's Witnesses* (New York: Columbia University Press, 1945).

Swaney, Charles Baumer. *Episcopal Methodism and Slavery* (New York: Negro University Press, 1962; reprint of 1926 edition).

Synan, Edward A. *The Popes and the Jews in the Middle Ages* (New York: Macmillan, 1965).

Thayer, Eli. *A History of the Kansas Crusade: Its Friends and Its Foes* (New York: Harper & Brothers, 1889).

Theodosian Code, tr. Clyde Pharr (Princeton, N.J.: Princeton University Press, 1952).

Thompson, Robert Ellis. *A History of the Presbyterian Churches in the United States* (New York: Christian Literature Co., 1895).

Thorpe, Francis Newton (ed.). *Federal and State Constitutions* (Washington, D.C.: Government Printing Office, 1909).

Tocqueville, Alexis de. *Democracy in America*, tr. Henry Reeves (Boston: J. Allyn, 1875).

———. *Oeuvres et correspondance inéditees* (Paris, 1861).

Trevelyan, George Macaulay. *England under the Stuarts* (London: Methuen & Co., 1904; 6th ed., New York: Putnam, 1914).

Tribe, Laurence H. "Foreword: Toward a Model of Roles in the Due Process of Life and Law." *Harvard Law Review* 87 (1973):1–54.

Trimble, Bruce R. *Chief Justice Waite* (Princeton, N.J.: Princeton University Press, 1938).

Tucker, Robert C. *Philosophy and Myth in Karl Marx* (Cambridge, Mass.: Harvard University Press, 1972).

Vawter, Bruce. "The Gospel According to John." In *The Jerome Biblical Commentary*, ed. Raymond E. Brown, Joseph A. Fitzmyer, and Roland E. Murphy (Englewood Cliffs, N.J.: Prentice-Hall, 1962).

Vrga, Djuro J. and Frank J. Fahey. *Changes and Socio-Religious Conflict in an Ethnic Minority Group: The Serbian Orthodox Church in America* (San Francisco: R and E Research Associates, 1975).

Warren, W. L. *King John* (Berkeley: University of California Press, 1978).

Weld, Thomas Dwight. *The Bible Against Slavery* (New York: American Anti-Slavery Society, 1838).

Welles, Gideon. *Diary of Gideon Welles* (Boston: Houghton, Mifflin & Co., 1911).

Williams, George H. *Wilderness and Paradise in Christian Thought* (New York: Harper, 1962).

Williams, Roger. *The Complete Writings of Roger Williams*, ed. Perry Miller (New York: Russell & Russell, 1963).

———. *Letters of Roger Williams*, ed. John Russell Bartlett (Providence: Printed for Narragansett Club, 1874).

———. *The Bloudy Tenent, of Persecution, for cause of Conscience, discussed, in A Conference between Truth and Peace* (1644).

Winthrop, John. *Papers* (Boston: Massachusetts Historical Society, 1931).

Wolfson, Harry. *The Philosophy of Spinoza* (New York: Schocken Books, 1969).

Yates, Wilson. "Separation of Church and State: Civil Religion and Crossings at the Border." *Hamline Law Review* 1 (1978):67–105.

Zahn, Gordon C. *In Solitary Witness: The Life and Death of Franz Jägerstätter* (New York: Holt, Rinehart & Winston, 1964).

INDEXES

Index of Cases

(Page numbers of opinions extensively quoted are italicized)

General Index